Recommended by **Teachers**
Trusted by **Toppers**

All in One®

HISTORY
Class 12

EVERYTHING YOU NEED TO SCORE

- Simplified Theory
- NCERT, Diksha & Other Imp. Ques.
- CBQs; MCQs, A-R, Source Based
- Board Questions Upto 2025
- Sample Question Papers

CBSE Exams 2026

Recommended by **Teachers**
Trusted by **Toppers**

All in One®

HISTORY
Class 12

EVERYTHING YOU NEED TO SCORE
- Simplified Theory
- NCERT, Diksha & Other Imp. Ques.
- CBQs; MCQs, A-R, Source Based
- Board Questions Upto 2025
- Sample Question Papers

CBSE Exams 2026

Author
Vagisha Mehta

arihant
SUCCESS AND NOTHING LESS

arihant
SUCCESS AND NOTHING LESS

ARIHANT PRAKASHAN

(School Division Series)

卐 ADMINISTRATIVE & PRODUCTION OFFICES

Regd. Office

'Ramchhaya' 4577/15, Agarwal Road, Darya Ganj, New Delhi -110002
Tele: 011- 47630600, 43518550; Fax: 011- 23280316

卐 *Head Office*

Kalindi, TP Nagar, Meerut (UP) - 250002, Tel: 0121-7156203, 7156204

卐 SALES & SUPPORT OFFICES

Agra, Ahmedabad, Bengaluru, Bareilly, Chennai, Delhi, Guwahati, Hyderabad, Jaipur, Jhansi, Kolkata, Lucknow, Nagpur & Pune.

PO No : TXT-XX-XXXXXXX-X-XX

Published By Arihant Publications (India) Ltd.

For further information about the books published by Arihant, log on to www.arihantbooks.com or e-mail at info@arihantbooks.com

Follow us on

卐 PRICE ₹ 425.00

PRODUCTION TEAM

Publishing Managers	*Cover Designer*	*Inner Designer*
Mahendra Singh Rawat & Keshav Mohan	Salman Shaikh	Ankit Tyagi
Project Head	*Page Layouting*	*Proof Reader*
Shivam Gupta	Sundar Bisht	Priya

Index *cum* Study Planner

PART I Themes in Indian History

		Studied	Revised	Exam ready
1. Bricks, Beads and Bones	**1-32**			
Beginnings	2	☐	☐	☐
Mohenjodaro: A Planned Urban Centre of Harappan Civilisation	3	☐	☐	☐
Art and Crafts Production	4	☐	☐	☐
Social and Economic Differences in Harappan Civilisation	6	☐	☐	☐
End of the Harappan Civilisation	7	☐	☐	☐
Ancient Authority of Harappan Civilisation	9	☐	☐	☐
Mind Map	10	☐	☐	☐
NCERT Folder	11-15	☐	☐	☐
Exam Pattern Questions	16-31	☐	☐	☐
Self Assessment Test	32	☐	☐	☐
2. Kings, Farmers and Towns	**33-63**			
The Earliest States	33	☐	☐	☐
An Early Empire: Mauryan Empire	35	☐	☐	☐
A Changing Countryside	37	☐	☐	☐
Towns and Trade	39	☐	☐	☐
Deciphering Inscriptions	40	☐	☐	☐
The Limitations of Inscriptional Evidence	41	☐	☐	☐
Mind Map	42	☐	☐	☐
NCERT Folder	43-47	☐	☐	☐
Exam Pattern Questions	48-62	☐	☐	☐
Self Assessment Test	63	☐	☐	☐
3. Kinship, Caste and Class	**64-93**			
The Critical Edition of Mahabharata	64	☐	☐	☐
Kinship and Marriage: Rules and Practices	65	☐	☐	☐
Social Differences: Within and Beyond the Framework of Caste	67	☐	☐	☐
Control over Resources and Status	69	☐	☐	☐
A Dynamic Text: Mahabharata	71	☐	☐	☐
Mind Map	73	☐	☐	☐
NCERT Folder	74-78	☐	☐	☐
Exam Pattern Questions	79-92	☐	☐	☐
Self Assessment Test	93	☐	☐	☐
4. Thinkers, Beliefs and Buildings	**94-122**			
Thinkers, Beliefs and Traditions	94	☐	☐	☐
The Buddha and the Quest for Enlightenment	96	☐	☐	☐
Building and Architecture	98	☐	☐	☐
New Religious Traditions	100	☐	☐	☐
Mind Map	103	☐	☐	☐
NCERT Folder	104-107	☐	☐	☐
Exam Pattern Questions	108-121	☐	☐	☐
Self Assessment Test	122	☐	☐	☐

PART II Themes in Indian History

		Studied	Revised	Exam ready
5. Through the Eyes of Travellers	**123-155**			
Al-Biruni	123	☐	☐	☐
Ibn-Battuta	125	☐	☐	☐
Francois Bernier	129	☐	☐	☐
Women: Slaves, Sati and Labourers	132	☐	☐	☐
Mind Map	134	☐	☐	☐
NCERT Folder	135-138	☐	☐	☐
Exam Pattern Questions	138-154	☐	☐	☐
Self Assessment Test	155	☐	☐	☐
6. Bhakti-Sufi Traditions	**156-187**			
Development of Religious Beliefs and Practices	156	☐	☐	☐
Early Traditions of Bhakti	158	☐	☐	☐
Islamic Traditions	160	☐	☐	☐
The Growth of Sufism	162	☐	☐	☐
Poet-Saints of Devotional Paths	165	☐	☐	☐
Reconstructing Histories of Religious Traditions	167	☐	☐	☐
Mind Map	169	☐	☐	☐
NCERT Folder	170-173	☐	☐	☐
Exam Pattern Questions	173-186	☐	☐	☐
Self Assessment Test	187	☐	☐	☐
7. An Imperial Capital : Vijayanagara	**188-218**			
Vijayanagara	188	☐	☐	☐
Rayas, Nayakas and Sultans	189	☐	☐	☐
Vijayanagara: The Capital and its Surroundings	191	☐	☐	☐
The Sacred Centre of Vijayanagara	194	☐	☐	☐
Plotting Palaces, Temples and Bazaars	196	☐	☐	☐
Mind Map	198	☐	☐	☐
NCERT Folder	199-202	☐	☐	☐
Exam Pattern Questions	203-217	☐	☐	☐
Self Assessment Test	218	☐	☐	☐
8. Peasants, Zamindars and the State	**219-251**			
Peasants and Agricultural Production	219	☐	☐	☐
The Village Community	222	☐	☐	☐
Women in Agrarian Society	224	☐	☐	☐
Land Revenue System	227	☐	☐	☐
The Ain-i Akbari of Abu'l Fazl Allami	228	☐	☐	☐
Mind Map	231	☐	☐	☐
NCERT Folder	232-235	☐	☐	☐
Exam Pattern Questions	236-250	☐	☐	☐
Self Assessment Test	251	☐	☐	☐

PART III Themes in Indian History

		Studied	Revised	Exam ready
9. Colonialism and the Countryside	**252-278**			
Bengal and the Zamindars	252	☐	☐	☐
Rural Areas of Bengal	255	☐	☐	☐
A Revolt in the Countryside: The Bombay Deccan	257	☐	☐	☐
The Deccan Riots Commission	260	☐	☐	☐
Mind Map	261	☐	☐	☐
NCERT Folder	262-264	☐	☐	☐
Exam Pattern Questions	265-277	☐	☐	☐
Self Assessment Test	278	☐	☐	☐
10. Rebels and the Raj	**279-308**			
Emergence of Revolt of 1857	279	☐	☐	☐
Pattern of the Rebellion	280	☐	☐	☐
Awadh in Revolt	282	☐	☐	☐
Images of the Revolt	285	☐	☐	☐
Mind Map	287	☐	☐	☐
NCERT Folder	288-291	☐	☐	☐
Exam Pattern Questions	292-307	☐	☐	☐
Self Assessment Test	308	☐	☐	☐
11. Mahatma Gandhi and the Nationalist Movement	**309-337**			
The Making of a Nation	309	☐	☐	☐
Non-Cooperation: A Mass Movement	310	☐	☐	☐
The Salt Satyagraha: A Case Study	312	☐	☐	☐
Quit India Movement	315	☐	☐	☐
Sources about Gandhiji	316	☐	☐	☐
Mind Map	318	☐	☐	☐
NCERT Folder	319-321	☐	☐	☐
Exam Pattern Questions	322-336	☐	☐	☐
Self Assessment Test	337	☐	☐	☐
12. Framing the Constitution	**338-363**			
Constitution of India	338	☐	☐	☐
The Vision of the Constitution	340	☐	☐	☐
Defining Rights	341	☐	☐	☐
The Language of the Nation	343	☐	☐	☐
Mind Map	346	☐	☐	☐
NCERT Folder	347-349	☐	☐	☐
Exam Pattern Questions	349-362	☐	☐	☐
Self Assessment Test	363	☐	☐	☐
Project Work	**367-383**			
Sample Question Papers (1-5)	**384-419**			
CBSE Solved Paper 2025	**420-432**			

One Book- Endless Features

to Help you Succeed

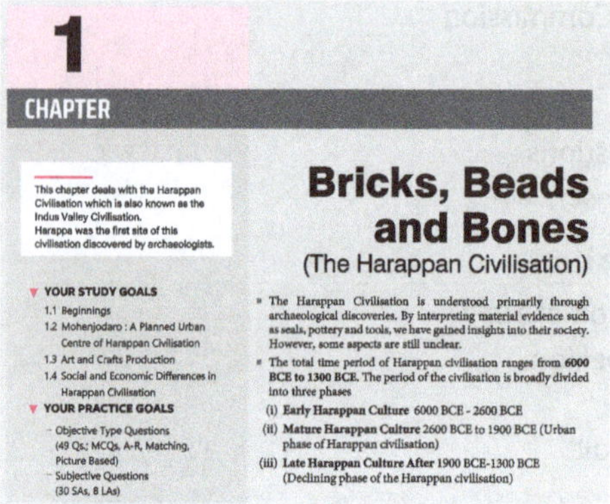

1

CHAPTER

This chapter deals with the Harappan Civilisation which is also known as the Indus Valley Civilisation.
Harappa was the first site of this civilisation discovered by archaeologists.

▼ YOUR STUDY GOALS

1.1 Beginnings
1.2 Mohenjodaro : A Planned Urban Centre of Harappan Civilisation
1.3 Art and Crafts Production
1.4 Social and Economic Differences in Harappan Civilisation

▼ YOUR PRACTICE GOALS

- Objective Type Questions (49 Qs.; MCQs, A-R, Matching, Picture Based)
- Subjective Questions (30 SAs, 8 LAs)

Bricks, Beads and Bones

(The Harappan Civilisation)

- The Harappan Civilisation is understood primarily through archaeological discoveries. By interpreting material evidence such as seals, pottery and tools, we have gained insights into their society. However, some aspects are still unclear.
- The total time period of Harappan civilisation ranges from **6000 BCE to 1300 BCE.** The period of the civilisation is broadly divided into three phases
  (i) **Early Harappan Culture** 6000 BCE - 2600 BCE
  (ii) **Mature Harappan Culture** 2600 BCE to 1900 BCE (Urban phase of Harappan civilisation)
  (iii) **Late Harappan Culture After** 1900 BCE-1300 BCE (Declining phase of the Harappan civilisation)

Complete Theory

Each chapter has Complete, Easy to Understand and Simplified theory covering latest syllabus and NCERT Textbook.

Quick Test

To make students understand the chapter in a smooth part-by-part manner, Quick Tests have been given in each chapter. These help students to assess the understanding of related concepts at regular interval.

Quick Test 1

1. What is the time period of the Early Harappan Culture?
2. Where have terracotta models of the plough had been found?
3. For what purpose was the Great Bath used?
4. What type of bricks were used for the settlements?
5. Mention the purpose of the courtyard in the residential buildings at Mohenjodaro?

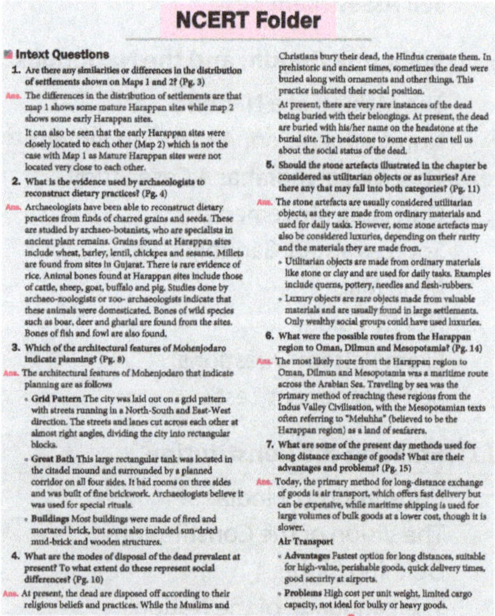

NCERT Folder

Intext Questions

1. **Are there any similarities or differences in the distribution of settlements shown on Maps 1 and 2? (Pg. 3)**

Ans. The differences in the distribution of settlements are that map 1 shows some mature Harappan sites while map 2 shows some early Harappan sites.

It can also be seen that the early Harappan sites were closely located to each other (Map 2) which is not the case with Map 1 as Mature Harappan sites were not located very close to each other.

2. **What is the evidence used by archaeologists to reconstruct dietary practices? (Pg. 4)**

Ans. Archaeologists have been able to reconstruct dietary practices from finds of charred grains and seeds. These are studied by archaeo-botanists, who are specialists in ancient plant remains. Grains found at Harappan sites include wheat, barley, lentil, chickpea and sesame. Millets are found from sites in Gujarat. There is rare evidence of rice. Animal bones found at Harappan sites include those of cattle, sheep, goat, buffalo and pig. Studies done by archaeo-zoologists or zoo- archaeologists indicate that these animals were domesticated. Bones of wild species such as boar, deer and gharial are found from the sites. Bones of fish and fowl are also found.

3. **Which of the architectural features of Mohenjodaro indicate planning? (Pg. 8)**

Ans. The architectural features of Mohenjodaro that indicate planning are as follows

- **Grid Pattern** The city was laid out on a grid pattern with streets running in a North-South and East-West direction. The streets and lanes cut across each other at almost right angles, dividing the city into rectangular blocks.
- **Great Bath** This large rectangular tank was located in the citadel mound and surrounded by a planned corridor on all four sides. It had rooms on three sides and was built of fine brickwork. Archaeologists believe it was used for special rituals.
- **Buildings** Most buildings were made of fired and mortared brick, but some also included sun-dried mud-brick and wooden structures.

4. **What are the modes of disposal of the dead prevalent at present? To what extent do these represent social differences? (Pg. 10)**

Ans. At present, the dead are disposed off according to their religious beliefs and practices. While the Muslims and Christians bury their dead, the Hindus cremate them. In prehistoric and ancient times, sometimes the dead were buried along with ornaments and other things. This practice indicated their social position.

At present, there are very rare instances of the dead being buried with their belongings. At present, the dead are buried with his/her name on the headstone at the burial site. The headstone to some extent can tell us about the social status of the dead.

5. **Should the stone artefacts illustrated in the chapter be considered as utilitarian objects or as luxuries? Are there any that may fall into both categories? (Pg. 11)**

Ans. The stone artefacts are usually considered utilitarian objects, as they are made from ordinary materials and used for daily tasks. However, some stone artefacts may also be considered luxuries, depending on their rarity and the materials they are made from.

- Utilitarian objects are made from ordinary materials like stone or clay and are used for daily tasks. Examples include querns, pottery, needles and flesh-rubbers.
- Luxury objects are rare objects made from valuable materials and are usually found in large settlements. Only wealthy social groups could have used luxuries.

6. **What were the possible routes from the Harappan region to Oman, Dilmun and Mesopotamia? (Pg. 14)**

Ans. The most likely route from the Harappan region to Oman, Dilmun and Mesopotamia was a maritime route across the Arabian Sea. Traveling by sea was the primary method of reaching these regions from the Indus Valley Civilisation, with the Mesopotamian texts often referring to "Meluhha" (believed to be the Harappan region) as a land of seafarers.

7. **What are some of the present day methods used for long distance exchange of goods? What are their advantages and problems? (Pg. 15)**

Ans. Today, the primary method for long-distance exchange of goods is air transport, which offers fast delivery but can be expensive, while maritime shipping is used for large volumes of bulk goods at a lower cost, though it is slower.

Air Transport

- **Advantages** Fastest option for long distances, suitable for high-value, perishable goods, quick delivery times, good security at airports.
- **Problems** High cost per unit weight, limited cargo capacity, not ideal for bulky or heavy goods.

NCERT Folder

Complete explanations of all the questions of NCERT Exercises.

One Book- Endless Features

to Help you Succeed

Exam Pattern Questions

This section has all types of questions; Objective Type Questions, SA, LA, Source & Map Based Questions.

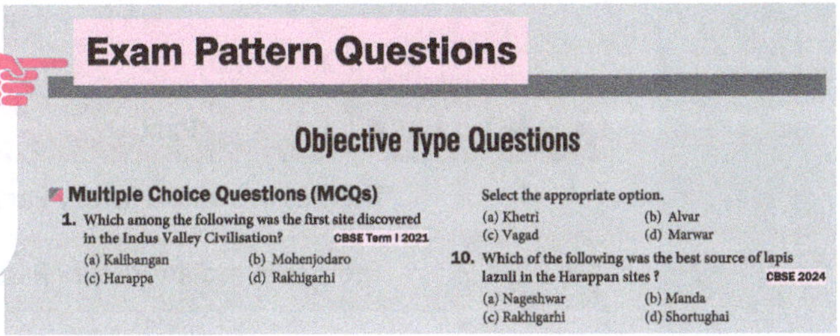
Exam Pattern Questions

Objective Type Questions

Multiple Choice Questions (MCQs)

1. Which among the following was the first site discovered in the Indus Valley Civilisation? CBSE Term I 2021
(a) Kalibangan (b) Mohenjodaro
(c) Harappa (d) Rakhigarhi

Select the appropriate option.
(a) Khetri (b) Alvar
(c) Vagad (d) Marwar

10. Which of the following was the best source of lapis lazuli in the Harappan sites? CBSE 2024
(a) Nageshwar (b) Manda
(c) Rakhigarhi (d) Shortughai

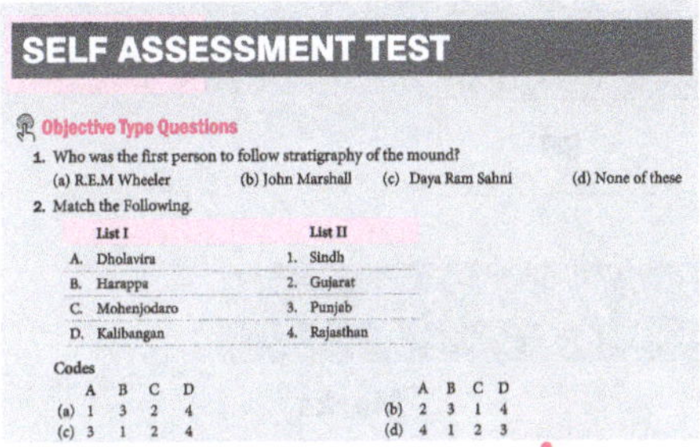
SELF ASSESSMENT TEST

Objective Type Questions

1. Who was the first person to follow stratigraphy of the mound?
(a) R.E.M Wheeler (b) John Marshall (c) Daya Ram Sahni (d) None of these

2. Match the Following.

List I	List II
A. Dholavira	1. Sindh
B. Harappa	2. Gujarat
C. Mohenjodaro	3. Punjab
D. Kalibangan	4. Rajasthan

Codes

	A	B	C	D		A	B	C	D
(a)	1	3	2	4	(b)	2	3	1	4
(c)	3	1	2	4	(d)	4	1	2	3

Self Assessment Test

Complete Test of chapter in Exam format.

Mind Map

A quick revision visual tool for the complete chapter.

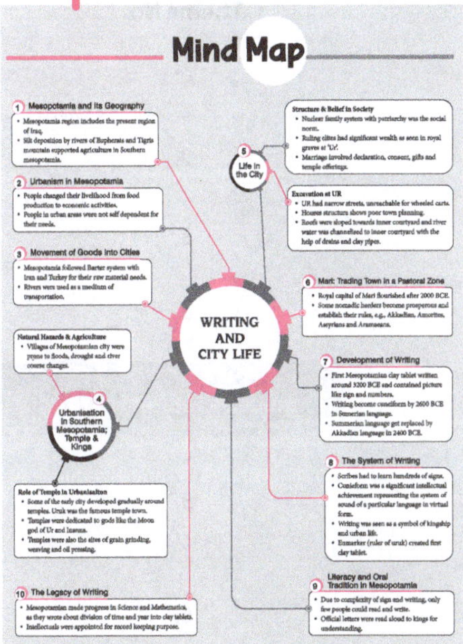

Sample Question Papers

To make students practice of examination in real sense, there are 5 Sample Question Papers at the end. All these Sample Question Papers are exactly prepared on the latest syllabus & pattern of examination.

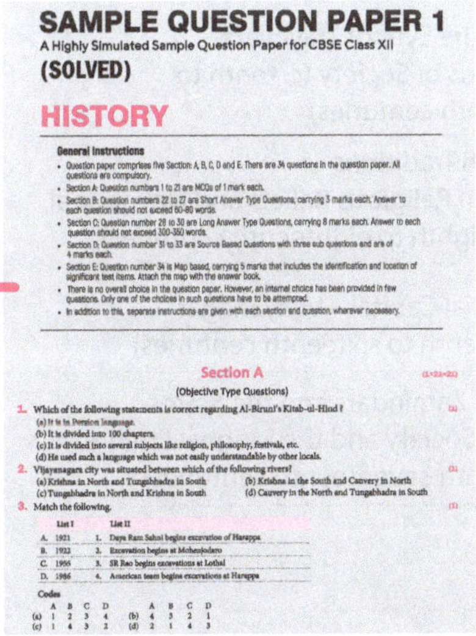
SAMPLE QUESTION PAPER 1

A Highly Simulated Sample Question Paper for CBSE Class XII

(SOLVED)

HISTORY

General Instructions

Section A

(Objective Type Questions)

1. Which of the following statements is correct regarding Al-Biruni's Kitab-ul-Hind?

2. Vijayanagara city was situated between which of the following rivers?

3. Match the following.

Latest Course Structure

S. NO.	Part	Marks
1.	Themes in Indian History Part--I	25
2.	Themes in Indian History Part--II	25
3.	Themes in Indian History Part--III	25
4.	Map	05
	Total	**80**

Themes in Indian History	Part-I	25 Marks
Theme No.	**Theme Title**	**Marks**
1.	Bricks, Beads and Bones The Harappa Civilisation	25
2.	Kings, Farmers and Towns Early States and Economies (c.600 BCE-600 CE)	
3.	Kinship, Caste and Class Early Societies (c. 600 BCE-600 CE)	
4.	Thinkers, Beliefs and Buildings Cultural Developments (c. 600 BCE-600 CE)	

Themes in Indian History	Part-II	25 Marks
5.	Through the Eyes of Travellers Perceptions of Society (c. tenth to seventeenth centuries)	25
6.	Bhakti-Sufi Traditions Changes in Religious Beliefs and Devotional Texts (c. eighth to eighteenth centuries)	
7.	An Imperial Capital – Vijayanagar (c. fourteenth to sixteenth centuries)	
8.	Peasants, Zamindars and the States Agrarian Society and the Mughal Empire (c. sixteenth-seventeenth centuries)	

Themes in Indian History	Part-III	25 Marks
Theme No.	**Theme Title**	**Marks**
9.	Colonialism and The Countryside Exploring Official Archives	
10.	Rebels and Raj 1857 Revolt and its Representations	
11.	Mahatma Gandhi and the National Movement Civil Disobedience and Beyond	25
12.	Framing of the Constitution The Beginning of a New Era	
	Including Map work of the Related Themes	05
	Theory Total	80
	Project Work	20
	Total	**100**

1. **BRICKS, BEADS AND BONES**

   The Harappan Civilisation

   Learning outcomes with specific competencies

   - Investigate, explore and interpret the early urban centres and social institutions.
   - State and deduce the multi-lateral aspects of Harappan civilisation to understand the first civilisation of the world.
   - Investigate and interpret historical and contemporary sources and viewpoints of ASI and historians on Harappa.

2. **KINGS, FARMERS AND TOWNS: Early States and Economies (c.600 BCE-600 CE)**

   Learning outcomes with specific competencies

   - Critically evaluate and interpret major trends in the political and economic history of the subcontinent.
   - Decode inscriptional evidence.
   - Analyse inscriptional evidences and the ways in which these have shaped the understanding of political and economic processes.

3. **KINSHIP, CASTE AND CLASS, Early Societies (c. 600 BCE-600 CE)**

   Learning outcomes with specific competencies

   - Examine, analyse the issues of social history.
   - Analyse social norms in order to understand the perspectives of society given in the scriptures of ancient India.
   - Examine the varied dimensions explored by historians in order to understand dynamic approach of Mahabharata.

4. THINKERS, BELIEFS AND BUILDINGS
Cultural Developments (c. 600 BCE-600 CE)

Learning outcomes with specific competencies

- Infer and compare the major religious developments in early India.
- Elucidate the rich religious sculpture and infer the stories hidden in it.
- Create a picture album of the Buddhist Sculpture

5. THROUGH THE EYES OF TRAVELLERS
Perceptions of Society (c. tenth to seventeenth centuries)

Learning outcomes with specific competencies

- Understand salient features of social histories described by the travellers and apply the learning in real life.
- Elucidating the accounts of foreign travellers in order to understand the social political and economic life during the tenure of different rulers in the medieval period.

6. BHAKTI-SUFI TRADITIONS
Changes in Religious Beliefs and Devotional Texts (c. eighth to eighteenth centuries)

Learning outcomes with specific competencies

- Understand the religious developments.
- Summarise the philosophies of different Bhakti and Sufi saints to understand the religious developments during medieval period.
- Comprehend the religious movement in order to establish unity, peace harmony and brotherhood in society.

7. AN IMPERIAL CAPITAL: VIJAYANAGARA
(c. fourteenth to sixteenth centuries

Learning outcomes with specific competencies

- Students will be able to Classify the distinctive architectural contributions of the Vijayanagar empire to comprehend the richness of mingled cultures of deccan India.
- Analyse accounts of foreign traveller's on Vijayanagar in order to interpret political, social and cultural life of the city.
- Assess and appreciate the city planning, water management system, administration of the rulers.

8. PEASANTS, ZAMINDARS AND THE STATE
Agrarian Society and the Mughal Empire
(c. sixteenth-seventeenth centuries)

Learning outcomes with specific competencies

- Comprehend the facets of agrarian developments in order to understand the relationship between the state and the agriculture during Mughal period.
- Compare and contrast the agrarian changes occurred during sixteenth and seventeenth centuries.
- Make a table and bring out the differences in the agrarian sector.

9. COLONIALISM AND THE COUNTRYSIDE
Exploring Official Archives

Learning outcomes with specific competencies

- Evaluate the revenue systems introduced by the British to understand the economic aspects of colonisation in India.
- Analyse the colonial official records& reports to understand the divergent interest of British and Indians.
- Find solution to be taken to protect the peasants and artisans in this century.

10. REBELS AND THE RAJ: 1857 Revolt and its Representations

Learning outcomes with specific competencies

- Examine the events of 1857.
- Correlate the Planning and coordination of the rebels of 1857 to infer its domains and nature.
- Examine the momentum of the revolt to understand its spread.
- Analyse how revolt created vision of unity amongst Indians.
- Interpret visual images to understand the emotions portrayed by the nationalist and British.

11. MAHATMA GANDHI AND THE NATIONALIST MOVEMENT Civil Disobedience and Beyond

Learning outcomes with specific competencies

- Understand the nationalist movement in chronological order.
- Correlate the significant elements of the nationalist movement and the nature of ideas, individuals, and institutions under the Gandhian leadership.
- Debate on the significant contributions of Gandhi to understand his mass appeal for nationalism.
- Explore the ways of interpreting historical source such as newspapers, biographies and autobiographies diaries, letters

12. FRAMING THE CONSTITUTION The Beginning of a New Era

Learning outcomes with specific competencies

- Highlight the role of Constituent Assembly to understand functionaries in framing the constitution of India.
- Analyse how debates and discussions around important issues in the Constituent Assembly shaped our Constitution

List of Maps

S. No.	Page No.	Part-I Maps
1.	2	**Mature Harappan Sites**: Harappa, Banawali, Kalibangan, Balakot, Rakhigarhi, Dholavira, Nageshwar, Lothal, Mohenjodaro, Chanhudaro, Kotdiji.
2.	3	**Mahajanapada and Cities**: Vajji, Magadha, Kosala, Kuru, Panchala, Gandhara, Avanti, Rajgir, Ujjain, Taxila, Varanasi.
3.	33	**Distribution of Ashokan Inscriptions**: • Pillar inscriptions - Sanchi, Topra, Meerut Pillar and Kaushambi. • Kingdom of Cholas, Cheras and Pandyas.
4.	43	**Important Kingdoms and Towns**: • Kushanas, Shakas, Satavahanas, Vakatakas,Guptas • Cities/towns: Mathura, Kannauj, Puhar, Braghukachchha, Shravasti, Rajgir, Vaishali, Varanasi,Vidisha
5.	95	**Major Buddhist Sites**: Nagarjunakonda, Sanchi, Amaravati, Lumbini, Bharhut, Bodh Gaya, Ajanta
S. No.	**Page No.**	**Part-II Maps**
6.	174	Bidar, Golconda, Bijapur, Vijayanagara, Chandragiri, Kanchipuram, Mysore, Thanjavur, Kolar, Tirunelveli
7.	214	**Territories under Babur, Akbar and Aurangzeb**: • Delhi, Agra, Panipat, Amber, Ajmer, Lahore, Goa.
S. No.	**Page No.**	**Part-III Maps**
8.	287	**Territories/cities under British Control in1857**: Punjab, Sindh, Bombay, Madras, Berar, Bengal, Bihar, Odisha, Surat, Calcutta, Patna, Allahabad
9.	260	**Main centres of the Revolt of 1857**: Delhi, Meerut, Jhansi, Lucknow, Kanpur, Azamgarh, Calcutta, Benaras, Gwalior, Jabalpur, Agra, Awadh
10.		**Important centres of the National Movement**: Champaran, Kheda, Ahmedabad, Benaras, Amritsar, Chauri Chaura, Lahore, Bardoli, Dandi, Bombay (Quit India Resolution), Karachi

Question Paper Design - Class XII

Book	MCQ		SA		LA		Source Based		Map	Total	
	No or Ques	MM	No or Ques	MM	No or Ques	MM	No or Ques	MM		Theory	Internat
Part I	7	1	2	3	1	8	1	4		25	
Part II	7	1	2	3	1	8	1	4		25	
Part III	7	1	2	3	1	8	1	4		25	
Map									05	05	
Project											20
Total	7×3=21				6×3=18		3×8=24		1×5=5	100 Marks	

1 CHAPTER

Bricks, Beads and Bones

(The Harappan Civilisation)

This chapter deals with the Harappan Civilisation which is also known as the Indus Valley Civilisation.
Harappa was the first site of this civilisation discovered by archaeologists.

YOUR STUDY GOALS

1.1 Beginnings
1.2 Mohenjodaro : A Planned Urban Centre of Harappan Civilisation
1.3 Art and Crafts Production
1.4 Social and Economic Differences in Harappan Civilisation
1.5 End of the Harappan Civilisation
1.6 Problems of Piecing Together the Past
1.7 Ancient Authority of Harappan Civilisation

YOUR PRACTICE GOALS

- Objective Type Questions (49 Qs.; MCQs, A-R, Matching, Picture Based)
- Subjective Questions (30 SAs, 8 LAs)
- Source Based Questions (3 Qs)
- Map Based Questions (3 Qs)

- The Harappan Civilisation is understood primarily through archaeological discoveries. By interpreting material evidence such as seals, pottery and tools, we have gained insights into their society. However, some aspects are still unclear.
- The total time period of Harappan civilisation ranges from **6000 BCE to 1300 BCE**. The period of the civilisation is broadly divided into three phases
  (i) **Early Harappan Culture** 6000 BCE - 2600 BCE
  (ii) **Mature Harappan Culture** 2600 BCE to 1900 BCE (Urban phase of Harappan civilisation)
  (iii) **Late Harappan Culture After** 1900 BCE-1300 BCE (Declining phase of the Harappan civilisation)
- Harappan pottery, bricks (baked and unbaked), seals[1], weights, beads, copper and bronze articles, have been found from the regions of **Afghanistan, Baluchistan, Sind** and **Punjab** provinces of **Pakistan.**
- Evidence of Harappan civilisation is also found in India in the regions of Jammu and Kashmir, Punjab, Haryana, Rajasthan, Uttar Pradesh, Gujarat and Maharashtra.

1 Seal An official design or mark on a document, an envelope, etc to show that it has not been opened.

1.1 Beginnings

- Before the mature Harappan period, there were several archaeological cultures[2] in the region.
- Evidence of pottery, agriculture, pastoralism and crafts related to these cultures has been found.
- The settlements were small in size and had no large buildings.

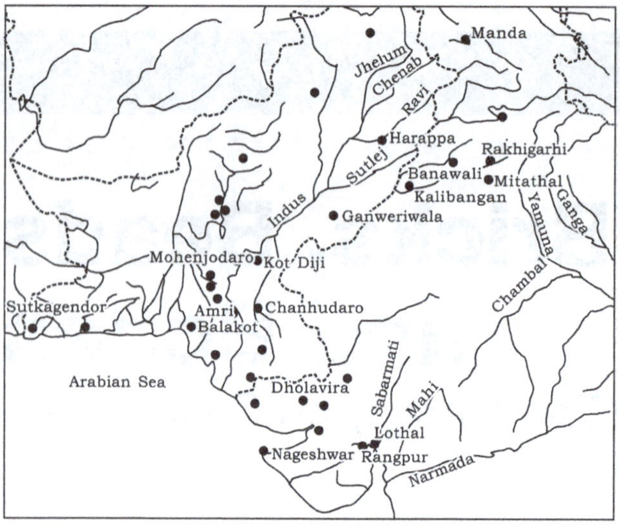

▲ *Mature Harappan sites*

- The recent archaeological evidence indicates the Harappan culture emerged from early farming communities around 7000 BCE.

Subsistence Strategies in Harappan Civilisation

- There were many subsistence (means of livelihood) strategies in Harappan civilisation, out of which agriculture and pastoralism were most significant. These are discussed below

Agriculture

- Agriculture was the main occupation of the Harappans. The Harappans ate wide range of plant and animal products.
- Grains like wheat, barley, lentil, chickpea and sesame are found from Harappan sites.
- Millets are found from sites in Gujarat. There is rare evidence of rice.

Agricultural Technologies

- Terracotta sculptors of the **bull** and their representation on the seals indicate that bull was known to Harappans and **oxen** were used for ploughing the field.
- Terracotta models of the plough have been found from **Cholistan** and **Banawali** (Haryana) sites.

▲ *A Terracotta Bull*

- Evidence of a ploughed field was found at **Kalibangan** (Rajasthan).
- This field had rows going in two different directions, crossing each other. This shows that two types of crop were grown together on the same field.
- Most Harappan sites are located in semi-arid lands. So, to enhance agricultural produce , they needed irrigation facilities.
- Traces of canals have been found at the Harappan site of Shortughai in Afghanistan.
- Water drawn from wells was used for irrigation.
- Water reservoirs found in Dholavira (Gujarat) may have been used to store water for agriculture.

Pastoralism and Hunting

- Animal bones of cattle, sheep, goat, buffalo and pig were found at Harappan sites , which indicate that these animals were domesticated.
- Bones of deer and gharial are also found. It is not clear whether the Harappans hunted these animals themselves or obtained meat from other hunting communities.
- Bones of fish and fowl were also found.

---

2 **Culture** A term used for a specific group of objects, distinct in style found specifically within a geographical area and period of time.

1.2 Mohenjodaro : A Planned Urban Centre of Harappan Civilisation

- Mohenjodaro was one of the largest cities of the ancient Harappan Civilisation. However, Harappa was the first site to be discovered. Mohenjodaro was divided into two parts
  (i) Citadel (smaller but higher settlement)
  (ii) The Lower Town (larger but lower settlement)

Citadel

- It was built on mud brick platforms. The walls of the citadel separated it from the Lower Town.
- There were many variations in the settlements of the Citadel. For example, the entire settlement of Dholavira and Lothal (Gujarat) was fortified and sections within the town were also separated by walls.
- There were no walls around the citadel in Lothal, but it was built at a height. The citadel was probably used for special public purposes. These included the warehouse and the **Great Bath**.

Great Bath

- The Great Bath was a large rectangular tank in a courtyard surrounded by corridors on all four sides.
- There were two flights of steps on the North and the South to reach the tank.
- The tank was made watertight by laying bricks on the edge and using the plaster of gypsum.
- Rooms were made on three sides of the tank, with one room having a large well.
- Water from the tank flowed into a huge drain.
- In the North side, there was a smaller building having eight bathrooms, four on each side of its corridor.
- From each bathroom, drains were coming out and these were connected to a drain that ran along the corridor.
- According to scholars, the great bath was used for a **special ritual bath**.

Lower Town

- The Lower Town was also walled and had buildings built on platforms.
- Bricks used for settlements were sun-dried or baked. They had a standardised ratio, with the length four times the height and the breadth twice the height.
- Archaeologists believe that it was probably the city where most of the people lived and worked.
- The roads and streets in the Lower Town were laid out in a grid pattern, intersecting at right angles.
- The streets and drains were first laid out and then houses were built on the same pattern.
- If domestic waste water had to flow into the street drains, then every house needed to have at least one wall along a street.

Domestic Architecture

- The Lower Town at Mohenjodaro provides examples of residential buildings. Most of the residential buildings were centered on a courtyard with rooms on all sides.
- The courtyard was probably the centre of activities such as cooking and weaving.
- There were no windows in the walls along the ground level. The main entrance does not give a direct view of the interior or the courtyard.

- Every house had its own bathroom with drains connected through the walls to the street drains.
- Some houses have remains of staircases to reach a second storey or the roof.
- Many houses had wells in those rooms, where outsiders could easily use them. Total number of wells in Mohenjodaro was about 700.

▲ *A drain in Mohenjodaro*

Drainage System

- Every house was connected to the street drains. The drains were made of mortar, lime and gypsum.
- They were covered with big bricks which could be lifted easily to clean the drains.
- For sewage from the houses, pits were provided at either side of the street.
- Very long drainage channels were provided at intervals with sumps for cleaning.
- In smaller settlements such as Lothal, the houses were built of mud bricks and drains were made of burnt bricks.

Quick Test 1

1. What is the time period of the Early Harappan Culture?
2. Where have terracotta models of the plough had been found?
3. For what purpose was the Great Bath used?
4. What type of bricks were used for the settlements?
5. Mention the purpose of the courtyard in the residential buildings at Mohenjodaro?

1.3 Art and Crafts Production

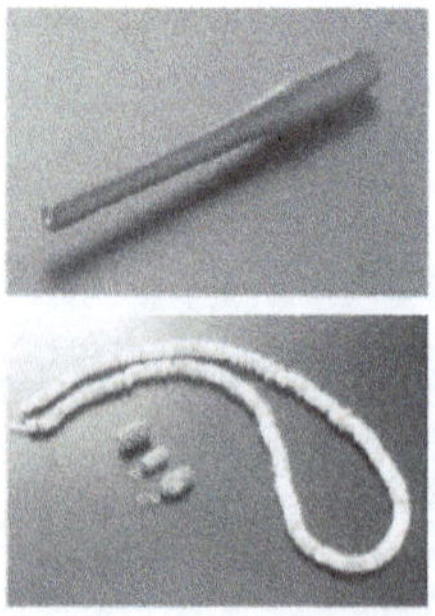

▲ *A Tool and Beads*

- **Chanhudaro** is a small town which was famous for craft production like bead-making, shell-cutting, metal-working, seal-making and weight-making.
- The materials used in making the beads were carnelian (beautiful red colour), jasper, crystal, quartz, copper, bronze, gold, shell, faience and terracotta.
- The beads were made of different shapes and forms like disc-shaped, cylindrical, spherical, barrel-shaped and segmented.
- Special drills were found at Chanhudaro, Lothal and Dholavira.
- The cities like Balakot and Nageshwar were specialised centres for making shell objects like bangles, a large long handled spoon with a cup-shaped bowl (ladle) and inlay.

Centres for Procuring Materials

▲ *A Terracotta Cart*

- Some materials for craft production such as clay were locally available and some materials like stone, timber and metal were transported from outside the alluvial plain.
- Terracotta toy models of bullock carts have been found. This suggests that the bullock cart was one of the important means of land transport at that time. Riverine and coastal routes were also probably used.

For procuring raw materials, expeditions were sent to other areas.

- They obtained different materials from different cities which were as follows

Material	Cities
Shell	Nageshwar, Balakot
Blue stone (Lapis Lazuli)	Shortughai (Afghanistan)
Carnelian (a glossy stone)	Bharuch in Gujarat
Steatite	South Rajasthan and North Gujarat
Metal	Rajasthan
Copper	Khetri (Rajasthan). Archaeologists named the Khetri area as Ganeshwar-Jodhpura Culture
Gold	South India

Evidence of Harappan Contacts with Distant Lands

- Traces of nickel have been found after chemical analyses of both the Omani copper and Harappan artefacts.
- A large Harappan jar coated with a thick layer of black clay has been found at Omani sites. It is possible that the Harappans exchanged the contents of these vessels for Omani copper.
- Some text shows that copper came from a region called **Magan**. Mesopotamian sites also show evidence of nickel traces.

▲ *A Cylinder Seal*

- Mesopotamia texts mention contact with regions named Dilmun (Island of Bahrain), Magan and Meluhha. Mesopotamian texts refer to Meluhha as a land of seafarers.
- Depictions of ship and boats on seals have been found.

Seals, Script and Weights

Seals and Sealings

- Seals and Sealings were used to facilitate long-distance communication.
- When a bag of goods was sent from one place to another, the mouth was tied with a rope. On the knot, some wet clay was affixed on which one or more seals were pressed, leaving an impression.
- If the bag reached with its sealing intact, it meant that it had not been opened. The sealing established the identity of the sender.
- The seal is made of a stone called **steatite**[3]. The seals also contain animal **motifs**[4] (shapes) and signs from a script.
- A cylinder seal found in Mesopotamia has a humped bull motif, which can be derived from the Indus region.

▲ *A Harappan Seal*

- The round **Persian Gulf** seal found in Bahrain sometimes carries the Harappan pattern of seal.

Script

- Harappan seals usually have written information, probably having the name and title of the owner.
- Harappan script was very difficult to understand. Scholars have suggested that the motif (generally an animal) conveyed a meaning to those people who could not read.

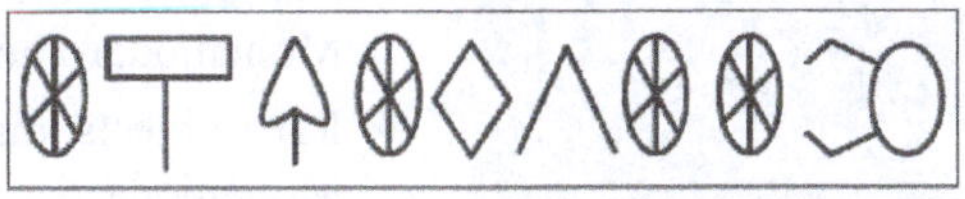
▲ *Letters on an Ancient Signboard*

3 **Steatite** The mineral talc in consolidated form.
4 **Motif** A symbol used by the Harappans on seals.

- Most inscriptions were short and the longest contained about **26 signs**. The script was written from **right to left**.
- Writing has been found on seals, copper tools, rims of jars, bone rods, copper and terracotta tablets and jewellery, bone rods and an ancient signboard.
- The script was not alphabetical and had many signs, somewhere between 375 and 400. The Harappan scripts remain undeciphered (not understood) by historians even today.

Weights

- Exchanges were regulated by a precise system of weights, usually made of a **cubical stone** called chert.
- The lower denominations of weights were binary i.e., 1, 2, 4, 8, 16, 32, etc., while the higher denominations followed the **decimal system** (160, 200, 320, 640).
- The smaller weights were probably used for weighing jewellery and beads.
- Metal scale-pans have also been found.
- The local "**Dilmun**" weights followed the Harappan standard.

1.4 Social and Economic Differences in Harappan Civilisation

- Archaeologists find out about social or economic differences amongst people living within a particular culture by using strategies such as studying burials and artefacts.

Burials

- The dead were generally laid in pits. There were differences in the way burial pits were built.
- In some cases, the empty spaces were lined with bricks.
- Some graves contain pottery and ornaments which indicates that these could be used in the afterlife.
- Jewellery has been found in burials of both men and women.
- An ornament consisting of three shell rings, a jasper (a kind of semi-precious stone) bead and many microbeads were found near the skull of a male.
- The dead were also buried with copper mirrors. However, the Harappans did not believe in burying precious things with the dead.

Artefacts

- Artefacts are broadly classified as **utilitarian** and **luxuries**.
- Utilitarian artefacts include objects of daily use made easily with ordinary materials such as stone or clay. For example, querns, pottery, needles, flesh-rubbers (body scrubbers), etc.
- Luxury artefacts include rare objects or objects made from costly, non-local materials or with complex technologies.
- **Little pots of faience**[5] were probably considered precious because they were difficult to make.
- Miniature pots of faience, perhaps used as perfume bottles, are mostly found in Mohenjodaro and Harappa.
- Rare objects made of valuable materials are generally found in large settlements like Mohenjodaro and Harappa.
- Gold was rare and all the gold jewellery found at Harappan sites was recovered from **hoards**[6].

▲ *A faience pot*

5 **Little pots of faience** A material made of ground sand or silica mixed with colour and a gum and then fired.

6 **Hoards** An archaeological term for a collection of valuable objects or artefacts.

Quick Test 2

1. What materials were used to construct the drains?
2. How is Meluhha described in Mesopotamian texts?
3. What material is the seal primarily made from?
4. Which local weights followed the Harappan standard?
5. Where are rare objects mostly concentrated in the Harappan civilisation?

1.5 End of the Harappan Civilisation

By 1800 BCE most of the Mature Harappan sites in regions such as **Cholistan** had been abandoned (completely left). There was also an expansion of population into new settlements in Gujarat, Haryana and Western Uttar Pradesh.

Transformation of Material Culture

- After 1900 BCE, transformation of material culture took place. There is disappearance of the distinctive artefacts such as weights, seals and special beads. Writing, long-distance trade and craft specialisation also disappeared.
- House construction techniques started becoming worse and large public structures were no longer made.
- Overall, artefacts and settlements indicate a rural lifestyle which is known as **Late Harappan** or **successor cultures.**
- The reasons for the end of Harappan civilisation include climatic change, deforestation, excessive floods, the shifting and/or drying up of rivers and overuse of the landscape.

Discovering the Harappan Civilisation

The Harappan civilisation was discovered by the efforts of many archaeologists. They used their own methods to find out information about the Harappan civilisation.

Some of them are discussed below

Alexander Cunningham

- Cunningham was the first **Director-General of the ASI** and is often regarded as the father of Indian Archaeology.
- He began archaeological excavations in the mid-nineteenth century.
- He used the accounts left by **Chinese Buddhist pilgrims,** who had visited the sub-continent between the fourth and seventh centuries CE to locate early settlements.
- He also collected, documented and translated inscriptions found during his surveys.
- He tried to place a Harappan seal into the time period he knew. He and many others believed that Indian history began with the first cities in the Ganga valley. Because of this, he missed the significance of Harappa.

Daya Ram Sahni and Rakhal Das Banerji

- Daya Ram Sahni discovered seals at Harappa in the early decades of the twentieth century.
- Rakhal Das Banerji found similar seals as discovered by Daya Ram Sahni at Mohenjodaro. It suggested that these sites were part of a single archaeological culture.

John Marshall

- Based on the findings by previous archaeologists, John Marshall, Director-General of the ASI, announced the discovery of a new civilisation in the Indus Valley in 1924.

- He excavated the sites horizontally, even layers across the mound, without paying attention to the different stratigraphy[7] of the site.
- His period as the Director-General of the ASI marked a major change in Indian archaeology. He was the first professional archaeologist to work in India.
- He used his experience of working in Greece and Crete (Greek island) in finding information about the Harappan civilisation.

R.E.M. Wheeler

- He was the Director-General of the ASI in **1944**.
- According to him, it was necessary to follow the stratigraphy of the mound rather than dig mechanically along uniform horizontal lines.

1.6 Problems of Piecing Together the Past

- Material evidence allows better reconstruction of Harappan life. This material could be pottery, tools, ornaments, household objects, etc.
- Organic materials such as cloth, leather, wood and reeds generally decompose, especially in tropical regions. The objects which survive include stone, burnt clay (or terracotta), metal, etc.

Classifying Finds

- Archaeological finds were classified in terms of **material**, such as stone, clay, metal, bone, ivory, etc. The other way to classify is in terms of **function**.
- Sometimes, archaeologists also depend on **indirect evidence**. For example, traces of cotton have been found at some Harappan sites, but we must look at other sources, like sculptures, to learn more about clothing.

Problems of Interpretation

- The problems of interpreting archaeology can be seen clearly in efforts to understand religious practices.
- Early archaeologists thought that certain unusual or unfamiliar objects may have had a religious significance. These included

▲ *A proto shiva seal*

  - Terracotta figurines of women wearing lots of jewellery and head-dresses, were considered mother goddesses.
  - Rare stone statuary of men are often found in a posture. It is shown seated with one hand on the knee. For example, priest king.
  - Certain structures, like the **Great Bath** and fire altars at Kalibangan and Lothal, had religious importance.
  - Seals with plant motifs are thought to indicate nature worship.
  - Some seals depict a one-horned animal, called the "unicorn" which seems to be mythical.
  - In some seals, a figure shown seated cross-legged in a yogic posture which is surrounded by animals has been regarded as proto-Shiva[8].
  - Conical stone objects have been classified as lingas[9].
  - The earliest religious text, **the Rigveda** (compiled c. 1500-1000 BCE) mentions a God named Rudra, which was a name used for Shiva in later Puranic traditions.

7 Stratigraphy It refers to the study of historical layers.
8 Proto-Shiva One of the earliest depictions of the Hindu God Shiva.
9 Lingas The polished stones which were often worshipped as symbols of the God Shiva.

1.7 Ancient Authority of Harappan Civilisation

There was similarity in Harappan artefacts like pottery, seals, weights, and bricks across the whole civilisation. This indicates that complex decisions were taken and implemented in Harappan society.

Palaces and kings

- A large building found at Mohenjodaro was named as a palace by archaeologists but no impressive finds were associated with it.
- A stone statue was recognised and continues to be known as the **priest-king**. This is because archaeologists were familiar with Mesopotamian history and its "priest-kings". That is why, they think it is similar to the ones they have found in the Indus region.
- According to some archaeologists, Harappan society had no rulers and everybody enjoyed equal status. Some others suggest that there were separate rulers for different cities like Mohenjodaro and Harappa.
- Some people believe there was only one state because of the similarities in artefacts, the presence of planned settlements, the uniform sizes of bricks and the location of settlements near raw materials.
- According to some historians, Harappans practiced some sort of democratic system.

▲ *A Priest-King*

Conclusion

After decades of archaeological work, we have a good understanding of the Harappan economy, functioning of the civilisation and social differences. However, many things are yet to be properly understood.

Quick Test 3

1. What term is used to describe the rural way of life that emerged after the decline of the Harappan Civilisation?
2. Who is often regarded as the father of Indian archaeology?
3. What excavation method did John Marshall used during his work?
4. Which major deity is associated with the name Rudra in the Rigveda?
5. Which feature indicates that Harappan settlements were planned?

TIMELINE

Major Periods in Early Indian Archaeology	
2 million BP (Before Present)	Lower Palaeolithic
80,000	Middle Palaeolithic
35,000	Upper Palaeolithic
12,000	Mesolithic
10,000	Neolithic (early agriculturists and pastoralists)
6,000	Chalcolithic (first use of copper)
2600 BCE	Harappan civilisation
1000 BCE	Early iron, megalithic burials
600 BCE-400 CE	Early Historic
Major Developments in Harappan Archaeology	
1875	Report of Alexander Cunningham on Harappan Seal
1921	Daya Ram Sahni begins excavations at Harappa
1922	Excavations begin at Mohenjodaro
1946	R.E.M. Wheeler excavates at Harappa
1955	S.R. Rao begins excavations at Lothal
1960	B.B. Lal and B.K. Thapar begin excavations at Kalibangan
1974	M.R. Mughal begins explorations in Bahawalpur
1980	A team of German and Italian archaeologists begins surface explorations at Mohenjodaro
1986	American team begins excavations at Harappa
1990	R.S. Bisht begins excavations at Dholavira
1997	Amrendra Nath started excavations at Rakhigarhi
2013	Vasant Shinde begins archaeogenetic research at Rakhigarhi.

Mind Map

BRICKS, BEADS AND BONES

1 Beginnings

Harappan culture emerged from early farming communities around 700 BCE.

2 Subsistence Strategies

Agriculture Technologies

- Terracotta plough models were found at Cholistan and Banawali (Haryana).
- A plough field at Kalibangan (Rajasthan) had furrows at right angles, suggesting mixed cropping.
- Archaeologists believed that Harappans used oxen for ploughing and tools made from stone or metal for harvesting.

3 Mohenjodaro: A Planned Urban Centre

Laying Out Drains

- Streets were laid out in a grid pattern.
- Houses were built along streets with drains.

Domestic Architecture

Houses were built around a central courtyard, which served as main area for activities like cooking and weaving.

The Citadel

- It was a large rectangular tank surrounded by a corridor on all four sides.
- It has structures for public and ritual purposes.

4 Finding Out about Craft Production

Identifying Centres of Production

- Archaeologists usually look for raw materials like stone, shells, copper ore, etc.

5 Centres for Procuring Materials

Materials from the Subcontinent and Beyond

- Harappans established settlements near sources of valuable materials.
- Harappan artefacts found in distant regions suggest trade connections.

6 Seals, Script & Weights

Weights

Harappan exchanges were regulated by a precise system of weights, made from chert and cubical in shape

Seals and Sealings

Used to facilitate long distant communication.

An Enigmatic Script

- Harappan seals often have a line of writing, possibly indicating the name and title of owner.
- Most inscriptions are short, the longest containing about 26 signs.

7 Tracking Social Differences

Burials

- At burials in Harappan sites, the dead were generally laid in pits.
- Harappan people did not believe in burying precious things with dead.

Artefacts

Artefacts are classified as utilitarian (daily use items like querns, pottery, needles, etc) or luxuries (rare, costly items made with complex techniques).

8 The End of Civilisation

Decline of the Harappan Civilisation due to environment and disunity.

9 Problems of Piecing Together the Past

Classifying finds

Archaeologists have to decide the purpose of the artefact found such as whether it is a tool or ornament, or something meant for ritual use.

Problems of Interpretation Many reconstructions of Harappan religion are made on assumptions that later traditions are similar to earlier traditions.

Limited Evidence

Organic materials decompose, only durable items survived.

NCERT Folder

Intext Questions

1. Are there any similarities or differences in the distribution of settlements shown on Maps 1 and 2? (Pg. 3)

Ans. The differences in the distribution of settlements are that map 1 shows some mature Harappan sites while map 2 shows some early Harappan sites.

It can also be seen that the early Harappan sites were closely located to each other (Map 2) which is not the case with Map 1 as Mature Harappan sites were not located very close to each other.

2. What is the evidence used by archaeologists to reconstruct dietary practices? (Pg. 4)

Ans. Archaeologists have been able to reconstruct dietary practices from finds of charred grains and seeds. These are studied by archaeo-botanists, who are specialists in ancient plant remains. Grains found at Harappan sites include wheat, barley, lentil, chickpea and sesame. Millets are found from sites in Gujarat. There is rare evidence of rice. Animal bones found at Harappan sites include those of cattle, sheep, goat, buffalo and pig. Studies done by archaeo-zoologists or zoo- archaeologists indicate that these animals were domesticated. Bones of wild species such as boar, deer and gharial are found from the sites. Bones of fish and fowl are also found.

3. Which of the architectural features of Mohenjodaro indicate planning? (Pg. 8)

Ans. The architectural features of Mohenjodaro that indicate planning are as follows

- **Grid Pattern** The city was laid out on a grid pattern with streets running in a North-South and East-West direction. The streets and lanes cut across each other at almost right angles, dividing the city into rectangular blocks.
- **Great Bath** This large rectangular tank was located in the citadel mound and surrounded by a planned corridor on all four sides. It had rooms on three sides and was built of fine brickwork. Archaeologists believe it was used for special rituals.
- **Buildings** Most buildings were made of fired and mortared brick, but some also included sun-dried mud-brick and wooden structures.

4. What are the modes of disposal of the dead prevalent at present? To what extent do these represent social differences? (Pg. 10)

Ans. At present, the dead are disposed off according to their religious beliefs and practices. While the Muslims and Christians bury their dead, the Hindus cremate them. In prehistoric and ancient times, sometimes the dead were buried along with ornaments and other things. This practice indicated their social position.

At present, there are very rare instances of the dead being buried with their belongings. At present, the dead are buried with his/her name on the headstone at the burial site. The headstone to some extent can tell us about the social status of the dead.

5. Should the stone artefacts illustrated in the chapter be considered as utilitarian objects or as luxuries? Are there any that may fall into both categories? (Pg. 11)

Ans. The stone artefacts are usually considered utilitarian objects, as they are made from ordinary materials and used for daily tasks. However, some stone artefacts may also be considered luxuries, depending on their rarity and the materials they are made from.

- Utilitarian objects are made from ordinary materials like stone or clay and are used for daily tasks. Examples include querns, pottery, needles and flesh-rubbers.
- Luxury objects are rare objects made from valuable materials and are usually found in large settlements. Only wealthy social groups could have used luxuries.

6. What were the possible routes from the Harappan region to Oman, Dilmun and Mesopotamia? (Pg. 14)

Ans. The most likely route from the Harappan region to Oman, Dilmun and Mesopotamia was a maritime route across the Arabian Sea. Traveling by sea was the primary method of reaching these regions from the Indus Valley Civilisation, with the Mesopotamian texts often referring to "Meluhha" (believed to be the Harappan region) as a land of seafarers.

7. What are some of the present day methods used for long distance exchange of goods? What are their advantages and problems? (Pg. 15)

Ans. Today, the primary method for long-distance exchange of goods is air transport, which offers fast delivery but can be expensive, while maritime shipping is used for large volumes of bulk goods at a lower cost, though it is slower.

Air Transport

- **Advantages** Fastest option for long distances, suitable for high-value, perishable goods, quick delivery times, good security at airports.
- **Problems** High cost per unit weight, limited cargo capacity, not ideal for bulky or heavy goods.

Maritime Shipping

- **Advantages** Most cost-effective for large volumes of bulk goods, suitable for heavy and large items, global reach.
- **Problems** Relatively slow delivery times, potential for delays due to weather conditions, customs clearance complexities.

8. Could everybody in Harappan society have been equal? (Pg. 16)

Ans. No, it does not appear that everyone in the Harappan society was equal. It is because archaeologists have used strategies to find out if social differences existed in society. The dead were buried in pits. Differences in the way of making burial pits was probably an indication of social differences existing in society.

9. What are the similarities and differences between Maps 1, 2 and 4? (Pg. 17)

Ans. Maps 1, 2 and 4 depict the different aspects of the ancient civilisation process where Map 1 shows the different settlement patterns, Map 2 displays the distribution of the inscription of Ashoka and Map 4 shows the trade networks and cultural interaction processes with a geographic focus.

10. Which of the themes in this chapter would have interested Cunningham? Which are the issues that have been of interest since 1947? (Pg. 21)

Ans. Cunningham was primarily interested in the archaeology of the Early Historic period (around sixth century BCE to fourth century CE) and later. He used records from Chinese Buddhist pilgrims who travelled in the subcontinent from the fourth to the seventh centuries CE to locate early settlements. A site like Harappa did not attract his attention since it wasn't known as an Early Historic city and wasn't mentioned in the accounts of these Chinese pilgrims. Therefore, although Harappan artifacts were found and some even reached Cunningham, he didn't recognise how old these were.

Issues of interest since 1947 were

- Understanding the social hierarchy within Harappan society.
- Investigating the nature and extent of trade connections both within the region and with other civilisations.
- Analysing factors that led to the decline of the Harappan civilisation.
- Examining burial methods to gain insights into cultural and social practices.
- Studying differences in pottery styles to learn more about daily life and cultural diversity.
- Interpreting tools, seals and other artifacts to understand Harappan society and economy.

10. What are the aspects of Harappan economy that have been reconstructed from archaeological evidence? (Pg. 24)

Ans. The aspects of Harappan economy that have been reconstructed from archaeological evidence are as follows

- **Trade and Commerce** The Harappans were engaged in long-distance trade with regions like Mesopotamia, Central Asia and the Persian Gulf. Archaeological findings of seals, weights and pottery also suggest a sophisticated trade network. The presence of dockyards at sites like Lothal indicates maritime trade.
- **Agriculture** The Harappans practiced advanced agricultural techniques as indicated by the presence of well-planned drainage systems and reservoirs. Wheat, barley, peas and sesame were some of the crops cultivated by the Harappans.
- **Crafts and Industries** The Harappans were skilled in crafts like pottery, metal working and bead-making. They produced goods such as jewellery, seals, tools and pottery for trade and local consumption.
- **Urban Planning and Infrastructure** The well-planned cities of the Harappan civilisation, with grid-like streets and standardised brick sizes, indicate centralised planning. The presence of granaries and public baths suggests a sophisticated urban infrastructure.
- **Social Organisation and Economy** The presence of a standardised weight system and seals for trade indicates a centralised authority overseeing economic activities.

Answer in 100-150 words

1. List the items of food available to people in Harappan cities. Identify the groups who would have provided these.

Ans. The items of food available to people in Harappan cities and the groups who would have provided these are as follows

Food available to people	Groups who provide these food items
Food items from plants	Food gatherers
Flesh and Fish	Hunter groups
Grains like wheat barley, lentil, chickpea, sesame and millets	Argricultural groups

2. How do archaeologists trace socio- economic differences in Harappan society? What are the differences that they notice?

***Or* Explain the strategies used by the archaeologists to understand socio-economic differences among the Harappans.**

Ans. Archaeologists have traced socio-economic differences among the Harappans through two types of evidences. These were

Evidence of Burials These have been significant evidence to establish social differences within Harappan society. The dead were generally laid in pits. There were differences in the way the burial pit was made. In some cases, the hollowed out spaces were lined with bricks. However, whether these variations were an indication of social differences or not, it is not yet established. Pottery, ornaments and jewellery have been found in some burials of both men and women. But the Harappans did not believe in burying precious things with the dead.

Evidence of Artefacts Two types of artefacts have been found, i.e. 'luxuries' and 'utilitarian'. Luxuries artefacts were made from costly and rare, non-local material with complicated technology, e.g. little faience pots.

Utilitarian objects included objects of daily use made of stone or clay, e.g. querns, pottery, needles, flesh-rubbers (body scrubbers), etc. As far as distribution of such artefacts is concerned, the rare objects made of valuable materials were generally concentrated in large settlements like Mohenjodaro and Harappa and are rarely found in smaller settlements.

Thus, the findings of the above artefacts prove that there were social and economic differences in Harappan culture.

3. Would you agree that the drainage system in Harappan cities indicates town planning? Give reasons for your answer.

***Or* Explain briefly the distinctive features of Harappan drainage system.**

***Or* Describe briefly the drainage system of Harappan cities.**

***Or* Mention two features of drainage system of the Harappan cities.**

***Or* 'One of the most distinctive features of the Harappan cities was the carefully planned drainage system.' Elaborate.**

Ans. Yes, I agree that the drainage system in Harappan cities indicates town planning.

This can be justified through the following features

- At the plan of the Lower Town, roads and streets were laid out along an approximate 'grid' pattern, intersecting at right angles.
- Every house had one wall alongside the street having its drain connected to the street drain to remove domestic waste water. It seems that streets with drains were laid out first and then houses built along them.
- Every house was connected to the street drains. The main channels were made of bricks set in mortar (plaster) and were covered with loose bricks that could be removed for cleaning. Sometimes limestone was used for the covers.
- In Harappa, house drains first emptied into a sump or cesspit into which solid matter settled while waste water flowed out into the street drains.
- Drainage systems were also found in smaller settlement and were not unique to the larger cities. For instance, at Lothal while houses were built of mud bricks, drains were made of burnt bricks.

Therefore, we can say that Harappan cities had a carefully planned drainage system.

4. List the materials used to make beads in the Harappan civilisation. Describe the process by which any one kind of bead was made.

Ans. A large variety of materials were used for making beads in the Harappan civilisation which included

It included

- Carnelian
- Jasper
- Bronze
- Gold
- Shell
- Faience
- Terracotta
- Burnt clay

The shapes of beads were of different types i.e. disc-shaped, cylindrical, spherical, barrel-shaped and segmented. They were also decorated.

Process of Making Beads

The process of making beads differed according to the materials used. Beads had a variety of shapes, but not geometric shapes as ones made from stones.

The process used for making beads was as follows

- Cutting steatite and filling the cuts with red paste. Beads of steatite were easily made, because it was a very soft stone.
- The red colour of carnelian was obtained by firing the yellowish raw material and beads at various stages.
- Grinding, polishing and drilling completed the process. Special kinds of tools were used in drilling the beads.

5. Look at the figure below and describe what you see? How is the body placed? What are the objects placed near it? Are there any artefacts on the body? Do these indicate the sex of the skeleton?

Ans. The figure shows the body buried in the North-South direction in a pit.

At burial in Harappan sites, the dead were generally laid in pits.

Pottery, ornaments, jewellery were placed near the dead bodies. It suggests that they had a belief, these could be used in the afterlife. In this figure, we can see some utensils are lying near the dead body. These utensils are a jug, pitcher, some plates, etc.

The artefacts like bangles and on the body are jewellery used by Harappan women. Thus, we can say that this is a skeleton of a woman.

Write a short essay (about 500 words) on the following

6. Describe some of the distinctive features of Mohenjodaro.

Or **Describe the distinctive features of domestic architecture of Mohenjodaro.**

Ans. The most unique feature of the Harappan Civilisation was the development of urban centres. Mohenjodaro is the most well-known site of Harappan Civilisation.

The features of Mohenjodaro were as follows

Citadel It was smaller but higher than the Lower Town. It was walled and was physically separated from the Lower Town. Here, the buildings were constructed with mud brick platforms. Here, we find some structures that were probably used for special public purposes. These included the warehouse and the Great Bath. The Great Bath was a large rectangular tank in a courtyard surrounded by a corridors on all four sides.

The Great Bath was made watertight by setting bricks on their edges and using the plaster of gypsum. On three sides of it there were rooms, in one of which was a large well. Water from the tank flowed into a huge drain.

The Lower Town The Lower Town was also walled. Several buildings were built on platforms, which served as foundations. All building activity within the city was restricted to a fixed area on the platforms. It had been built meticulously by mobilising labour on a very large scale.

Drainage System Mohenjodaro had a carefully planned drainage system. The roads and the streets were laid out along an approximate 'grid' pattern, intersecting at right angles. It seems that streets with drains were laid out first and then houses built along them. Every house had its own bathroom paved with bricks, with drains connected through a wall to the street drain.

Usage of Standard Bricks The quality of sun-dried bricks or baked bricks also prove the concept of planning. All the bricks were of a standard ratio. The length and width was four times and twice the height of the bricks respectively. Such bricks were used in all the settlements of the Harappan Civilisation.

7. List the raw materials required for craft production in the Harappan civilisation and discuss how these might have been obtained.

Or **Describe briefly how the centres of craft production are identified.**

Ans. In order to identify the centres of craft production, archaeologists usually look for the raw materials, like stone modules, whole shells, copper ore, unfinished objects and waste materials. Waste products also indicate craft work.

They obtained different materials from different cities which were as follows

- Shell from Nageshwar, Dalakot
- Blue stone (Lapis Lazuli) from (Shortughai, Afghanistan)
- Carnelian (a glossy stone) from Bharuch in Gujarat
- Steatite from South Rajasthan and North Gujarat
- Metal from Rajasthan
- Copper from Khetri (Rajasthan). Archaeologists named the Khetri area as Ganeshwar-Jodhpura culture.
- Gold from South India

8. Discuss how archaeologists reconstruct the past.

Ans. To reconstruct Harappan life, archaeologists were not only dependent on Harappan script, they used material evidence too. The material evidence could be pottery, tools, ornaments etc. But organic materials such as cloth, leather and wood generally decompose. Archaeologists classified the finds in terms of materials and by function.

The materials were stone, clay, metal, bone, ivory etc. But functions were more difficult to determine. For instance, sometimes it was difficult to decide whether the artefact was a tool or an ornament.

To reconstruct religious practices was also a problematic issue for archaeologists. Most archaeologists thought that certain objects which seemed unusual or unfamiliar have had a religious significance. These include terracotta figurines of women which were heavily jewelled with head-dresses. These are regarded as Mother Goddesses.

Structures like the Great Bath and fire altars have had ritual significance. Plant motifs are thought to indicate nature worship.

A one-horned animal called the Unicorn, depicted on seals seem to be mythical. *Linga* is a polished stone that is worshipped as a symbol of Shiva. A figure surrounded by animals has been regarded as proto-Shiva.

9. Discuss the functions that may have been performed by rulers in Harappan society.

Ans. Some archaeologists have given their opinions about the functions that may have been performed by rulers in Harappan society.

These were as follows

- Evidences show that complex decisions were taken and implemented in Harappan society. Extraordinary uniformity of Harappan artefacts as evident in pottery, seals, weights and bricks show the complex decisions.
- Plans and layouts of the city were prepared under the guidance and supervision of the rulers. Big buildings, palaces, forts, tanks, wells, canals and granaries were also constructed.
- Cleanliness was the responsibility of the ruler. Road lanes and drains were also constructed.
- The rulers also looked after the welfare of the economy. They used to inspire the farmers to increase agricultural production. They also motivated the craftsmen to promote different handicrafts. External and internal trade were both promoted by the ruler. The ruler used to issue common acceptable coins or seals, weights and measurements.

10. On Map 1, use a pencil to circle sites where evidence of agriculture has been recovered. Mark an '×' against sites where there is evidence of craft production and 'R' against sites where raw materials were found.

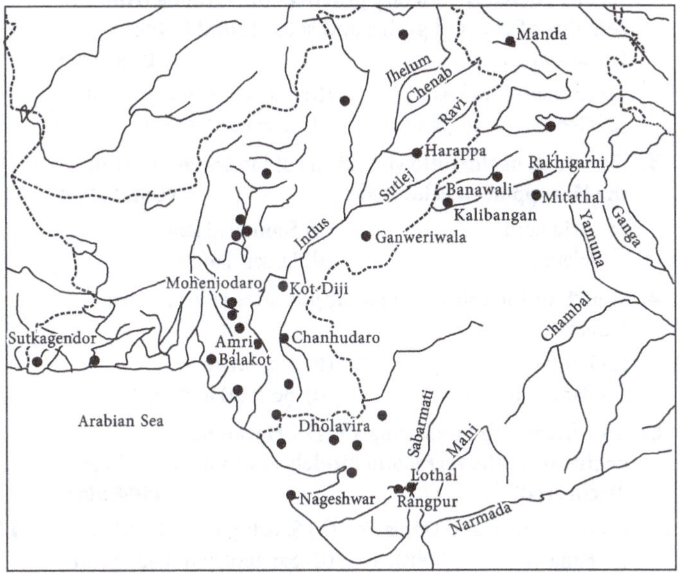

Ans. Evidence of agriculture has been recovered at Harappa, Banawali, Mohenjodaro, Kalibangan and Dholavira. Evidence of craft production has been found at Chanhudaro, Nageshwar and Balakot. Raw materials were found at Nageshwar, Balakot and Khetri (Rajasthan).

Exam Pattern Questions

Objective Type Questions

Multiple Choice Questions (MCQs)

1. Which among the following was the first site discovered in the Indus Valley Civilisation? CBSE Term I 2021

(a) Kalibangan (b) Mohenjodaro
(c) Harappa (d) Rakhigarhi

2. Which group of scholars among the following reconstructed the dietary practices of Harappa from the remains of charred grains and seeds found in the Harappan sites? Delhi 2020

(a) Archeo-Zoologists (b) Archeo-Ethnographists
(c) Geo-Archeologists (d) Archeo-Botanists

3. On which of the following kinds of land were most of the Harappan sites located ? CBSE 2024 C

(a) Arid land (b) Semi-arid land
(c) Wetland (d) Desert land

4. Which of the following Harappan sites is located in Gujarat?

(a) Lothal (b) Dholavira
(c) Banawali (d) Both (a) and (b)

5. In which of the following sites of Harappan civilization, the terracotta models of plough have been discovered? CBSE 2025

(a) Kalibangan and Dholavira (b) Shortughai and Lothal
(c) Banawali and Cholistan (d) Sanghol and Rakhigarhi

6. Where was a public bath and a warehouse found in the Indus Valley during excavation?

(a) Mohenjodaro (b) Rangpur
(c) Kalibangan (d) Ropar

7. Who among the following is often known as the 'Father of Indian Archaeology'? CBSE Term I 2021

(a) Daya Ram Sahni (b) Alexander Cunningham
(c) Rakhal Das Banerji (d) R.E.M. Wheeler

8. Which one of the following regions of Harappa was called as 'Ganeshwar Jodhpur Culture'? CBSE 2023

(a) Nageshwar (b) Khetri
(c) Amri (d) Chanhudaro

9. Strategy used by Harappans for procuring raw materials may have been to send expeditions to areas such as the .... region of Rajasthan (for copper) and South India (for gold). CBSE SQP Term I 2021

Select the appropriate option.

(a) Khetri (b) Alvar
(c) Vagad (d) Marwar

10. Which of the following was the best source of lapis lazuli in the Harappan sites ? CBSE 2024

(a) Nageshwar (b) Manda
(c) Rakhigarhi (d) Shortughai

11. Which one of the following regions was called as 'Magan' during Harappan period? CBSE Term I 2021

(a) Meluhha (b) Bahrain
(c) Oman (d) Dilmun

12. Who among the following was an ex-army official and worked as Director-General of Archaeological Survey of India (ASI)? CBSE 2024

(a) John Marshal
(b) Alexander Cunningham
(c) R.D. Bannerjee
(d) REM Wheeler

13. Who among the following is the author of the book 'The Story of Indian Archaeology' ? CBSE 2024

(a) John Marshall (b) Daya Ram Sahni
(c) S.N. Roy (d) REM Wheeler

14. Who among the following was the first Director General of Archaeological Survey of India (A.S.I.)? CBSE 2024

(a) S.N. Roy (b) John Marshall
(c) Daya Ram Sahni (d) Alexander Cunningham

15. What is unique about Nageshwar and Balakot sites of the Harappan culture?

(a) They are both near the coast.
(b) Now they are in Pakistan.
(c) Both were specialised centres for making metal tools.
(d) All of the above

16. Which one of the following is the correct statement regarding Harappan culture? CBSE 2024

(a) Most of the Harappan sites were located in semi-arid lands.
(b) Irrigation was probably not required for agriculture at the Harappan sites.
(c) No trace of canals have been found at the Harappan sites.
(d) The iron tipped ploughshare was used at the Harappan sites.

17. **Which of the following statement(s) related to the drainage system of Harappan Civilisation are true?**

(a) Drains were built of bricks with the help of lime and gypsum.

(b) The one defect of drainage system was that in some places drains run near wells.

(c) Both (a) and (b)

(d) None of the above

18. **In the domestic architecture of Harappa, there were no windows in the walls along the ground level. Identify the possible cause mentioned by the archaeologists from the following options.** **CBSE SQP Term I 2021**

(a) It was a custom

(b) To maintain privacy

(c) No concern of ventilation

(d) Part of unplanned process

19. **Which of the following is correct regarding Harappan script?** **CBSE 2025**

(a) This script was alphabetical

(b) It was written from left to right

(c) This script has not been deciphered so far

(d) This script has a few signs or symbols

20. **Why is the Harappan script called enigmatic? Choose the correct reason from the following options.**

(a) It resembles the Hieroglyphic script of Egypt.

(b) It had too many symbols, between 600 and 1000 in number.

(c) It was written from left to right.

(d) Its writing remains undeciphered to date.

21. **Which one of the following is not the limitation of inscriptional evidence in the study of archaeology ?**

(a) Letters are very faintly engraved

(b) Inscriptions might be damaged

(c) Many inscriptions have not been deciphered

(d) All inscriptions were in Sanskrit language

22. **Which of the following is true about Harappan religion?**

(a) Nature worship was in vogue.

(b) Female deities were not dominant.

(c) No cult of Mother Goddess was found.

(d) Temple structures were unearthed.

23. **Which of the following statements is not correct about the subsistence strategy of Harappa ?** **CBSE 2024**

(a) Terracotta sculpture of oxen indicates ploughing.

(b) Two sets of furrows at right angles indicate two cropping patterns.

(c) Traces of canals have been found at Shortughai, Afghanistan.

(d) Deep water reservoirs have been found in Sindh for irrigation.

24. **Consider the following statements regarding Harappan Civilisation.**

(i) The Harappans ate plants and animal products.

(ii) Evidence of a ploughed field was found at Banawali.

(iii) Chanhudaro is a small town which was famous for crafts production.

(iv) Bones of deer and gharial are also found.

Which of the above statements are correct?

(a) (i) and (ii) (b) (ii) and (iii)

(c) (i), (iii) and (iv) (d) All of these

25. **Consider the following statements regarding the Harappan Culture and choose the correct option.**

(i) The most unique feature was the development of urban centres.

(ii) The settlements were divided into two sections i.e. the Citadel and the Lower Town.

(iii) Drainage system was ordinary and unplanned.

(iv) Roads were not laid out along a grid pattern.

Options

(a) Only (i) is correct

(b) Only (i) and (ii) are correct

(c) Only (ii) and (iii) are correct

(d) Only (iii) and (iv) are correct

26. **Which one of the following pairs is correctly matched?**

(a) Banawali–Gujarat (b) Harappa–Baluchistan (Pakistan)

(c) Kalibangan–Gujarat (d) Lothal–Gujarat

27. **Which one of the following pairs is correctly matched?**

(a) Banawali – Rajasthan

(b) Kalibangan – Haryana

(c) Shortughai – Afghanistan

(d) Cholistan – Gujarat

28. **Which one of the following pairs is incorrectly matched?**

(a) Citadel – Built on higher ground

(b) House Drains – Directly connected to street drains

(c) Lower Town – Some buildings were built on platforms

(d) Great Bath – Located in a courtyard surrounded by a corridor

29. **Which one of the following pairs is correctly matched?**

(a) Shells – South India

(b) Carnelian – Bharuch

(c) Gold – Afghanistan

(d) Lapis Lazuli – Nageshwar and Balakot

30. **Arrange the location of the following sites of the Harappan civilisation in correct sequence from East to West.**

(i) Banawali (ii) Dholavira

(iii) Kalibangan (iv) Mohenjodaro

Codes

(a) (i), (ii), (iii), (iv) (b) (i), (iii), (ii), (iv)

(c) (ii), (i), (iii), (iv) (d) (iv), (i), (ii), (iii)

31. **Arrange the following events in correct chronological sequence from the earliest to the latest.**
(i) R.E.M. Wheeler recognised that it was necessary to follow the stratigraphy of the mound.
(ii) Daya Ram Sahni discovered seals at Harappa.
(iii) Harappan artefacts reached Alexander Cunningham but he failed to understand their significance.
(iv) Rakhal Das Banerji found seals at Mohenjodaro.

Codes
(a) (iv), (iii), (ii), (i) (b) (ii), (iv), (i), (iii)
(c) (iii), (iv), (ii), (i) (d) (iii), (ii), (iv), (i)

32. **Identify the part of the settlement from the following information given below.**
(i) It was smaller but higher part of the settlement.
(ii) It was walled.
(iii) It was used for special public purposes.
(iv) It included warehouse and Great Bath.

Options
(a) Large house (b) Lower town
(c) Drain system (d) Citadel

33. **Identify the Director-General of the ASI with the help of the following information.**
(i) He began archaeological excavations in the mid-nineteenth century.
(ii) His main interest was in the archaeology of the early Historic and later periods.

Options
(a) Alexander Cunningham (b) Daya Ram Sahni
(c) Rakhal Das Banerji (d) John Marshall

34. **Identify the Harappan site with the help of the following information.**
(i) It is a tiny settlement as compared to Mohenjodaro.
(ii) It is almost exclusively devoted to craft production.

Options
(a) Lothal (b) Dholavira
(c) Chanhudaro (d) Rakhigarhi

35. **Complete the following with the correct option regarding the raw material for craft production with their respective sites.**
Carnelian: Gujarat, :: Steatite: ....
(a) Haryana (b) Oman
(c) Punjab (d) Rajasthan

36. **Fill in the blank with the appropriate option out of those given below** CBSE 2024 C
Scholars have estimated that the total number of wells in Mohenjodaro was about ....
(a) 600 (b) 500 (c) 400 (d) 700

37. **Fill in the blank with the appropriate word from the given options** CBSE 2024
The Harappan site of...... is located in present day Rajasthan.
(a) Rakhigarhi (b) Lothal (c) Kalibangan (d) Manda

Assertion-Reason

38. **Assertion** (A) The Harappans ate a wide range of plant and animal products, including fish.
Reason (R) Animal bones found at Harappan sites include those of cattle, sheep, goat, buffalo and pig.

Codes
(a) Both A and R are true and R is the correct explanation of A
(b) Both A and R are true, but R is not the correct explanation of A
(c) A is true, but R is false
(d) A is false, but R is true

39. **Assertion** (A) Streets with drains were laid out first and then houses built along them.
Reason (R) Harappan cities had a carefully planned drainage system.

Codes
(a) Both A and R are true and R is the correct explanation of A
(b) Both A and R are true, but R is not the correct explanation of A
(c) A is true, but R is false
(d) A is false, but R is true

40. **Assertion** (A) Recovering artefacts is merely the initial step in the archaeological process. SQP 2024
Reason (R) Archaeologists employ various methods such as classification based on material and function, analysis of contextual clues, and reliance on indirect evidence to understand the significance and purpose of artefacts.

Codes
(a) Both A and R are true and R is the correct explanation of A
(b) Both A and R are true, but R is not the correct explanation of A
(c) A is true, but R is false
(d) A is false, but R is true

41. **Assertion** (A) The Harappan culture is named after the first site where this culture was discovered.
Reason (R) Alexander Cunningham announced the discovery of this culture to the world in 1924.

Codes
(a) Both A and R are true and R is the correct explanation of A
(b) Both A and R are true, but R is not the correct explanation of A
(c) A is true, but R is false
(d) A is false, but R is true

42. Assertion (A) The Harappan cities carried on a considerable trade in stone, metals, shells, etc in the Indian sub-continent.

Reason (R) Each of the cities used to provided all the necessary raw materials for the commodities produced there.

Codes

(a) Both A and R are true and R is the correct explanation of A
(b) Both A and R are true, but R is not the correct explanation of A
(c) A is true, but R is false
(d) A is false, but R is true

Match the Following

43.

List I (Harappan Site)	List II (Famous for)
A. Lothal	1. Specialised centres for making shell objects
B. Kalibangan	2. Near sources of carnelian
C. Dholavira	3. Evidence of ploughed field found
D. Nageshwar	4. Water reservoirs found

Codes **CBSE SQP 2022**

	A	B	C	D		A	B	C	D
(a)	2	3	4	1	(b)	1	4	3	2
(c)	3	2	4	1	(d)	4	1	2	3

44.

List I	List II
A. S.N. Roy	1. Discovered seals at Mohenjodaro similar as Harappa
B. Rakhal Das Banerji	2. Used the accounts left by Chinese pilgrims
C. Alexander Cunningham	3. Author of 'The Story of Indian Archaeology'
D. GF Dales	4. Author of 'The Mythical Massacre at Mohenjodaro'

Codes **CBSE Term I 2021**

	A	B	C	D		A	B	C	D
(a)	3	1	2	4	(b)	1	3	4	2
(c)	2	4	1	3	(d)	4	2	3	1

45.

List I	List II
A. Daya Ram Sahni	1. Authored 'Mohenjo daro and the Indus Civilisation'
B. Rakhal Das Banerji	2. Began excavations at Harappa in 1921
C. John Marshall	3. Found seals at Mohenjo daro
D. R.E.M. Wheeler	4. Authored 'Ancient India'

Codes **CBSE SQP 2022**

	A	B	C	D		A	B	C	D
(a)	3	1	2	4	(b)	3	4	1	2
(c)	1	2	3	4	(d)	2	3	1	4

46.

List I (Harappan Site)	List II (Present Region)
A. Manda	1. Gujarat
B. Rakhigarhi	2. Rajasthan
C. Nageshwar	3. Haryana
D. Kalibangan	4. Jammu

Codes **CBSE SQP 2022**

	A	B	C	D		A	B	C	D
(a)	3	1	2	4	(b)	1	2	4	3
(c)	2	4	3	1	(d)	4	3	1	2

Picture Based Questions

47. The statue of Priest King was made from

(a) stone (b) gold (c) copper (d) carnelian

48. Identify the image shown below.

(a) Terracotta bull art (b) Seal from Harappa
(c) Proto Shiva Seal (d) Seal from Mohenjodaro

49. Identify the image given below.

(a) Mother Goddess (b) Divine Lady
(c) Jewelled Woman (d) Queen of the Earth

Answers

1. (c) Harappa
2. (d) Archeo-Botanists
3. (b) Semi-arid land
4. (d) Both (a) and (b)
5. (c) Banawali and Cholistan
6. (a) Mohenjodaro
7. (b) Alexander Cunningham
8. (b) Khetri
9. (a) Khetri
10. (d) Shortughai
11. (c) Oman
12. (d) R.E.M. Wheeler
13. (c) S.N. Roy
14. (d) Alexander Cunningham
15. (a) They are both near the coast
16. (a) Most of the Harappan sites were located in semi-arid lands.
17. (a) Drains were built of bricks with the help of lime and gypsum.
18. (b) To maintain privacy
19. (c) This script has not been deciphered so far
20. (d) Its writing remains undeciphered to date.
21. (d) All inscriptions were in Sanskrit language
22. (a) Nature worship was in vogue.
23. (d) Deep water reservoirs have been found in Sindh for irrigation.
24. (c) (i), (iii) and (iv)
25. (b) Only (i) and (ii) are correct
26. (d) Lothal–Gujarat
27. (c) Shortughai : Afghanistan
28. (c) Lower Town – Some buildings were built on platforms
29. (b) Carnelian – Bharuch
30. (b) (i), (iii), (ii), (iv)
31. (d) (iii), (ii), (iv), (i)
32. (d) Citadel
33. (a) Alexander Cunningham
34. (c) Chanhudaro
35. (d) Rajasthan
36. (d) 700
37. (c) Kalibangan
38. (b) Both A and R are true, but R is not the correct explanation of A
39. (a) Both A and R are true and R is the correct explanation of A
40. (a) Both A and R are true and R is the correct explanation of A
41. (c) A is true, but R is false
42. (c) A is true, but R is false
43. (a)
44. (a)
45. (d)
46. (d)
47. (a)
48. (b)
49. (a)

Subjective Questions

Short Answer Type Questions

1. How have historians provided new insight into the subsistence strategies of the Harappan culture?

Or **Write the subsistence strategies adopted by Harappans.** **CBSE Diksha**

Ans. According to historians, the subsistence strategies of the Harappan culture is discussed below

- The Harappans ate a wide range of plant and animal products including fish and meat, wheat, maize, millets, pulses, etc.
- Cattle, sheep, goat, buffalo and pig were domesticated by the Harappans for their sustenance.
- Archaeological evidences suggested that oxen were used for ploughing and two different crops were grown together.

2. In the present day, cities undergo some form of planning before they are created. Explain why historians compared Mohenjodaro to present-day cities in terms of planning.

Ans. Historians compared Mohenjodaro to present-day cities in terms of planning due to the following reasons

- Building activities within the city were restricted to a fixed area, proving that there was prior planning.
- The bricks which were used had fixed and standardised dimensions.
- The extensive drainage system arranged in grids, ran under the residential areas.

3. **'Mohenjodaro was a planned urban centre'. Support the statement with suitable statements.** CBSE 2023

Or **"The most unique feature of the Harappan civilisation was the development of urban centres". Explain.** CBSE 2024

Ans. Mohenjodaro was a planned urban centre due to its following features

- **Citadel** It was smaller but higher than the lower town. It was walled and was physically separated from the Lower Town. Here, the buildings were constructed with mud brick platforms. Here, we find some structures that were probably used for special public purposes. These included the warehouse and the Great Bath.
- **Drainage System** Mohenjodaro had a carefully planned drainage system. The roads and the streets were laid out along an approximate 'grid' pattern, intersecting at right angles. It seems that streets with drains were laid out first and then houses built along them. Every house had its own bathroom paved with bricks, with drains connected through a wall to the street drain.
- **Usage of Standard Bricks** The quality of sun-dried bricks or baked bricks also prove the concept of planning. All the bricks were of a standard ratio.

4. **Mention any three features of Harappan cities.**

Ans. The three features of Harappan cities were

(i) They were well planned. The cities were divided into two sections which are one smaller and higher, i.e. the citadel and other much larger but lower, i.e. the Lower town.

(ii) One of the most distinctive features of Harappan cities was the carefully planned drainage system. If we look at the plan of the lower town, the roads and streets were laid out along an approximate 'grid' pattern, intersecting at right angles.

(iii) At burials in Harappan areas, the dead were generally laid in pits. Some graves contained pottery and ornament which indicated the belief that these materials could be used in the afterlife.

5. **Explain the methods of irrigation used by the Harappans at different sites.** CBSE 2024

Ans. The methods of irrigation used by the Harappans at different sites are as follows

- **Canals** One of the most significant methods of irrigation used by the Harappans was through canals. Archaeological evidence from the Harappan site of Shortughai in Afghanistan shows traces of canals, which likely served to bring water from rivers to agricultural fields. However, such canal systems have not been found at other prominent Harappan sites, such as those in Punjab or Sind, which suggests that irrigation methods may have varied regionally.
- **Wells for Irrigation** Another common method of irrigation likely used by the Harappans was drawing water from wells. Evidence suggests that wells were widely used at Harappan sites to access groundwater. Water from these wells could have been used to irrigate fields, particularly in areas where canals were not available or were less practical.
- **Water Reservoirs** At the Harappan site of Dholavira in Gujarat, evidence of sophisticated water reservoirs have been found. These reservoirs were likely used to collect and store water, especially during the monsoon season, when there was an excess of rain.

6. **"The most distinctive feature of Harappan cities was the carefully planned drainage system". Explain the statement.** CBSE 2024

Or **Why is the Harappan drainage system considered a planned and complete drainage system ? Explain.** CBSE 2024

Ans. The most distinctive feature of Harappan cities was the carefully planned drainage system as it highlights the advanced urban planning of the Harappan Civilisation. The Harappan cities were laid out in a grid pattern, with streets intersecting at right angles. This kind of systematic planning allowed for efficient management of infrastructure, including water and drainage systems. Streets were lined with drains designed to carry wastewater away from the residential and public areas. The drains were often covered with bricks and were placed along the streets, providing a method for the controlled disposal of domestic and street waste.

7. **Analyse the layout of Harappan cities to identify features that promoted cleanliness and public health.** CBSE SQP 2024

Ans. The Harappan civilisation, which flourished in the Indus Valley between 2500 and 1900 BCE, is well-known for its advanced urban planning and emphasis on cleanliness and health.

The features that promoted cleanliness and public health are as follows

- The main drains were made of bricks and covered with loose bricks that could be removed for cleaning.
- Harappan cities had an advanced network of brick-lined drains running through the streets. These drains were covered with stone or bricks to keep waste out and let water flow easily.
- Drains from houses emptied into a pit, which connected to the main street drains, helping carry wastewater away from homes.

8. Explain how did archaeologists identify the centres of craft production of the Harappan age. CBSE 2024

Ans. To identify the centers of craft production of the Harappan age, archaeologists typically look for key indicators such as raw materials, tools, unfinished objects, and waste material. These elements are discussed below

- Archaeologists often find raw materials such as stone nodules, whole shells, or copper ore at certain locations. The presence of these materials in large quantities indicates that the site was used for crafting.
- Tools used in the crafting process, such as chisels, grinding stones, or drills, are found in areas of production. These tools are specifically designed for working with materials like stone, shell, or metal.
- Unfinished or semi-finished objects, such as beads, pottery, or figurines, are often found in production areas. These items were in the process of being shaped or worked on but were not yet complete. The presence of these unfinished products indicates a dedicated place for crafting.
- Waste material is one of the most important indicators of craft production. For instance, when materials like shell or stone are cut to make objects, the leftover pieces, or waste, are discarded in the same area. These waste fragments, whether small or large, provide evidence of production activities.

9. Explain the three exclusive features of craft production in Chanhudaro.

Ans. Chanhudaro was a tiny settlement as compared to Mohenjodaro. This area was exclusively devoted to craft production. Its features are

(i) The main craft productions included bead-making, shell-cutting, metal-working, seal-making and weight-making.

(ii) Here, a variety of materials were used to make beads, such as stones like carnelian, jasper, crystal, quartz, steatite; metals like copper, bronze and gold. Moreover shell, faience and terracotta or burnt clay were used.

(iii) Some beads were made of two or more stones. These were cemented together and some were made of stones with beautiful gold caps. The shapes were of different types.

10. 'The archaeological evidence shows that the Harappan civilisation had a flourishing, vibrant craft production.' Discuss the two ways in which the people of the Harappan civilisation procured raw materials for this enterprise. Give examples of archaeological and textual evidence to show that overseas trade was also practiced in aid of this enterprise.

Ans. The two ways in which the people of the Harappan civilisation procured raw materials for this enterprise are as follows

- They established settlements in areas where the raw materials were easily accessible like Nageshwar and Balakot where shells are easily available.
- They sent expeditions to areas where they could find raw materials such as Khetri in Rajasthan for copper and gold in South India.
- Recent archaeological evidence shows that Oman copper was used in artefacts made in Harappan region.
- Other evidences that support long-distance communication include weights, seals, dice and beads.
- Mesopotamian texts mention contact with regions named Dilmun (probably the island of Bahrain), Magan and Meluhha, possibly the Harappan region.
- Oman, Bahrain and Mesopotamia were reached through maritime communication.

11. (a) **Explain the strategies adopted by Harappans to procure raw material for their craft production.**

(b) **Explain how archaeologists have been able to reconstruct dietary practices of the Harappans.**

Ans. (a) The strategies adopted by Harappans to procure raw materials for craft production were

- They established settlements in resource-rich areas like Nageshwar, Balakot and Shortughai, allowing direct access to local materials.
- Additionally, they likely organised expeditions to distant regions such as the khetri region of Rajasthan for copper and South India for gold. These expeditions involved skilled craftsmen and traders who negotiated with local communities to acquire the necessary resources, ensuring a steady supply for craft production.

(b) Archaeologists have been able to reconstruct dietary practices of the Harappan society from finds of charred grains and seeds. Grains found at Harappan sites include wheat, barley, lentil, chickpea, sesame and rice. Millets are found from sites in Gujarat. Animal bones found at Harappan sites include those of cattle, sheep, goat, buffalo and pig. Studies done by archaeo-zoologists or zoo- archaeologists indicate that these animals were domesticated.

12. How were Harappan seals and sealings used to facilitate long distance communication? What did the sealings convey?

Or **Seals and sealings facilitated long distance communication. Elaborate.** CBSE Diksha

Ans. Harappan seals and sealings were used to facilitate long distance communication. The mouth of the bag of goods was tied up with rope and on the knot was affixed some wet clay on which one or more seals were pressed, leaving an impression. This sealing conveyed that if the bag reached with its sealing intact, then it had been reached safely and it also conveyed the true identity of the sender of the goods.

13. **Why do archaeologists and historians find Harappan script enigmatic? Explain the reasons.**

Or **Why Harappan script is considered enigmatic?** CBSE Diksha

Or **Why is the Harappan script called an enigmatic script? Explain.** CBSE 2024

Ans. Archaeologists and historians found Harappan script enigmatic. The reasons behind it were

- Harappan seals usually had a line of writing, containing the name and title of the owner, sometimes the motif conveyed a meaning to those who could not read.
- The script was non-alphabetical, it had many signs, somewhere between 375 and 400. It was written from right to left.
- Most inscriptions were short, the longest contained about 26 signs but sometimes it contained wider space, sometimes shorter, it had no consistency. Till today, the script remains undeciphered.

14. **Examine the challenges historians face in deciphering the Harappan script.** CBSE SQP 2024

Ans. Historians face significant challenges in deciphering the Harappan script as

- The inscriptions are short, with the longest having about 26 signs.
- The script is not alphabetical but syllabic, making it harder to decode.
- There are between 375 and 400 signs. It was written from right to left, as seen in some seals with wider spacing on the right and cramped signs on the left.
- The lack of bilingual inscriptions and limited context makes it even harder to understand.

15. **Archaeologists have found a copper mirror and a few beaded ornaments in a burial chamber in Harappa. Along with these, they have also found shards of faience pots scattered around. What can these artefacts tell us about the person who was buried? Justify your answer.**

Ans. These artefacts can tell us about the following things

- Copper mirrors and beaded ornaments would have been precious items during the Harappan civilisations, so if they are being buried with the person, it is possible that the person might have been rich or important.
- Faience was considered a luxury item as it was difficult to make and so finding it in the burial would indicate that the person was rich.

16. **How do we know that the Harappan civilisation had trade contacts with Oman?**

Ans. Evidence of trade contacts between the Harappan civilisation and Oman comes from several archaeological findings such as

- Chemical analyses show that copper from Oman and Harappan artefacts both contain traces of nickel, indicating a shared source.
- Large Harappan jars with thick black clay coatings, discovered at Omani sites, likely transported liquids, suggesting they carried goods for trade.
- Mesopotamian texts from the third millennium BCE mention a place called "Magan", thought to be Oman, as a copper source, supporting the trade connection.
- Other Harappan artefacts, like seals, weights, dice and beads, found in Mesopotamian areas, further point to extensive trade with Oman and beyond.

17. **Describe the opinions of the archaeologists over the central authority of the Harappan Civilisation.**

Or **"The archaeological records provide no immediate answer to the Harappan central authority." Analyse different views given on the same.** Competency Based Que

Ans. The opinions of some of the archaeologists about the central authority of Harappan Civilisation are as follows

- Some archaeologists believe that Harappan society had no rulers and that everybody enjoyed equal status.
- According to other scholars, there was no single ruler but several. Mohenjodaro had a separate ruler and Harappans had another. In the same way, other regions had different rulers.
- Some scholars also argued that there was a single state given the similarity in artefacts, the evidence for planned settlements, the standardised ratio of brick size and the establishments near source of raw material.

18. **"There are indications of complex decisions being taken and implemented in the Harappan society." Substantiate the statement with suitable arguments.** CBSE 2024 C

Ans. Historians suggest that there are indications of complex decisions being taken and implemented in Harappan society. The extraordinary uniformity of Harappan artefacts is found in pottery, seals, weights and bricks. The settlements were strategically set up in specific locations for various reasons. Labour was mobilised for making bricks and also for the construction of massive walls, platform, etc to develop the urban civilisation.

According to some archaeologists, there were no rulers in Harappan society. Some suggests that Mohenjodaro and Harappa had different rulers. Some argue that there was a single state which is evident from the similarity of artefacts, the planned settlement, the standardised ratio of brick size and the establishments of settlements near sources of raw material.

19. Present four pieces of evidences that support the theory that the Harappan civilisation was ruled by a single state.

Ans. Four pieces of evidences that support the theory that the Harappan civilisation was ruled by a single state are as follows

(i) The extraordinary uniformity of Harappan artefacts is evident in pottery, seals and weights.

(ii) Bricks were of a uniform ratio throughout the region, from Jammu to Gujarat.

(iii) Settlements were established near sources of raw materials in strategic places.

(iv) Huge amounts of labour was mobilised for making bricks and for the construction of massive walls and platforms. This could have been done only with a large unifying element like a single state.

20. How does the disappearance of writing, seals, distinctive beads and the standardised weight system after 1900 BCE reflect the changes in society and economy?

Ans The disappearance of writing, seals, distinctive beads, and the standardised weight system after 1900 BCE marks a significant shift in the Harappan society and economy. These elements were key to the functioning of the complex urban system, which relied on organised trade, administration, and craftsmanship. The loss of writing and seals suggests a breakdown in communication and record-keeping, while the disappearance of specialised trade goods, like beads and seals, indicates a collapse in long-distance trade networks.

The shift from a standardised weight system to local measures points to decentralisation and the decline of a unified economic system. These changes reflect a move towards a simpler, more rural economy and a shift in social structures as the urban centres declined and eventually disappeared.

21. Write any three views on the decline of the Harappan Civilisation.

***Or* What are the possible causes of end of Harappan Civlisation?** CBSE Diksha

Ans. The three views about the decline of the Harappan Civilisation are

(i) The decline was due to natural climate such as floods, earthquakes, droughts or epidemics.

(ii) Another view suggests that Aryans were responsible for the decline of the Harappan Civilisation.

(iii) The change of the course of river indus transformed it into a tract of sand and affected the soil's fertility.

22. Who was Cunningham? Mention any one account used by him to locate the early settlements of Harappan Civilisation.

Ans. Cunningham was the first Director General of the Archaeological Survey of India who began archaeological excavations in the mid-nineteenth century.

To date the early settlements of Harappan Civilisation, he mostly used the accounts left by Chinese Buddhist pilgrims who had visited the subcontinent between the fourth and seventh centuries CE. He also collected, documented and translated inscriptions found during his surveys. When he excavated sites, he tended to recover artefacts that he thought had cultural value.

23. 'John Marshall's time as Director-General of the ASI marked a major change in Indian archaeology.' Critically analyse this statement. Competency Based Que

Ans. 'John Marshall's time as Director-General of the ASI marked a major change in Indian archaeology due to the following reasons

- John Marshall's experience of working in Greece and Crete helped him with the excavation exercise in India.
- He was equally keen to look for patterns of everyday life as he was with the spectacular finds.
- All the artefacts recovered from the same unit were grouped together, even if they were found at different stratigraphic layers. As a result, valuable information about the context of these finds was irretrievably lost.
- Marshall tended to excavate along regular horizontal units, measured uniformly throughout the mound, ignoring the stratigraphy of the site.

24. Who was John Marshall? How did he mark a change in Indian archaeology?

Ans. John Marshall was a famous archaeologist who was the Director-General of the Archaeological Survey of India in 1924 when site of Harappa was excavated.

He marked a change in Indian archaeology by announcing the discovery of the Indus Valley Civilisation. Thus, he brought forth 3000-year-old discoveries of civilisations. He was the first professional archaeologist to work in India.

He brought his experience of working in Greece and Crete to the field. More importantly, though like Cunningham he too was interested in spectacular finds, he was equally keen to look for patterns of everyday life.

25. Who was R.E.M. Wheeler? Mention any one of his contributions in the field of archaeology?

Ans. R.E.M. Wheeler was an archaeologist who was the Director General of the Archaeological Survey of India in 1944.

He contributed in the field of archaeology by rectifying the excavations done by John Marshall, so as to follow stratigraphy of the mound of excavate. He classified objects according to the layer of soil where it was found. He brought military precision to the practice of archaeology. Driven by a sense of adventure, he relentlessly excavated Harappa inspite of the hot and humid weather. He also tried to correlate archaeological findings of the Harappan Civilisation with the Rigveda.

26. "Over the decades, new issues have assumed importance in the archaeology of Harappa." Give two evidences to justify the statement.

Ans. It is true that over the decades, new issues have assumed importance in the archaeology of Harappa.

Two evidences to justify the statement are

(i) Some archaeologists are keen to obtain a cultural sequence.

(ii) Few of them try to understand the logic behind the location of specific sites.

There has also been growing international interest in Harappan archaeology. They are using modern scientific techniques including surface explorations to recover traces of clay, stone metal and plant and animal remains.

27. 'The problems of archaeological interpretation are perhaps most evident in attempts to reconstruct religious practices of the Harappan civilisation.' Explain this statement with examples wherever necessary.

Ans. The above statement can be explained by

- Early archaeologists thought that certain objects which seemed unusual or unfamiliar may have had a religious significance. Examples- Terracotta Figurines of Women, and stone statuary of men such as 'Priest king'
- Some attempts of reconstruction of religious practices and beliefs have been made by examining seals. Other seals with plant motifs are thought to indicate nature worship. Examples- seals with 'unicorn', 'yogic' surrounded with plants and animals.
- Many times reconstruction of Harappan religion are made on the the assumption that later traditions provide parallels with earlier ones.

28. Explain the problems of interpretations in context of "proto Shiva seals and how does the depiction of a figure in a 'Yogic' posture related to later Hindu deities.

Ans. The problems of interpretations in context of proto Shiva seals are as follows

- The earliest religious text, the Rigveda, mentions a god named Rudra, which is a name used for Shiva in later Puranic traditions.
- However, unlike Shiva, Rudra in the Rigveda is neither depicted as Pashupati, nor as a yogi.
- In other words, this depiction does not match the description of Rudra in the Rigveda.

The depiction of a figure in a "yogic" posture on Harappan seals is often interpreted as an early representation of "proto Shiva", suggesting a connection to later Hindu deities, particularly Shiva, who is associated with meditation and ascetic practices.

29. Explain the different approaches used for the classification of found objects by archaeologists, with examples from the Harappan ruins.

Ans. The different approaches used for the classification of found objects by archaeologists are as follows

- Archaeologists classify the finds on two principles. One is based on the material they are made of and the other is based on their functions.
- Based on the materials they are made of like stone, clay, metal, bone, etc.
- Based on the functions that these artefacts most likely served. One way of doing this was to estimate this by its resemblance to its present-day things. Another way of finding function by investigating the context it was found in.
- Sometimes the archaeologists have to depend on indirect evidence. Example, to find out what Harappans wore; they had to depend on indirect evidence including depictions in sculptures.

30. "Many reconstructions of Harappan religion are made on assumptions and archaeological interpretation." Substantiate the statement. Competency Based Que

Ans. Many reconstructions of Harappan religion are made on the assumption and archaeological interpretations. This statement can be justified by the following assumptions made to reconstruct Harappan religion.

- Archaeologists thought that certain objects which seemed unusual or unfamiliar may have had a religious significance. These included terracotta figurines of women, heavily jewelled with elaborate head dresses. These were regarded as mother Goddesses.

- Rare stone statuary of men seated with one hand on the knee was regarded as 'Priest king'. Other structures found in Harappan Civilisation, like the Great Bath and fire altars found at Kalibangan and Lothal also were taken as significant for ritual practices.
- Mythical creatures like unicorn, figure seated cross-legged in yogic posture of proto-Shiva were all examples of Hindu religion.

Long Answer Type Questions

1. How did architectural features of Mohenjodaro indicate planning? Support the statement with examples.

Ans. The architectural features of Mohenjodaro clearly indicate a high level of planning and organisation, reflecting a well-thought-out approach to urban design in the following ways

- Mohenjodaro was divided into two distinct sections the Citadel and the Lower Town. The Citadel was elevated and walled, serving as a fortified area, while the Lower Town was much larger and also walled. This physical separation suggests a deliberate plan to organise different functions of the city, with a higher, possibly more important or religious, zone separated from the lower, residential and commercial areas.
- The city's grid-like street pattern further demonstrates planning. Roads and streets intersected at right angles, creating a neat grid pattern that would have made navigation easier and more systematic. This design was not random but was laid out with street drains running along them, indicating foresight in urban sanitation.
- Each house was connected to the street drains, a remarkable feature indicating a planned approach to waste management. The drains themselves were made of brick and mortar, with removable covers for cleaning, highlighting the city's attention to hygiene and infrastructure maintenance.
- Another example is the use of platforms for building houses. In the Lower Town, residential buildings were constructed on raised platforms, which required significant labour to prepare. This suggests that the city planners ensured that houses were built on stable ground, minimizing the risk of flooding or structural damage. The materials used for construction were also standardised, with bricks of a specific size and ratio, which was consistent across the Harappan settlements.

2. Explain how burials help in understanding the social and economic differences amongst the people in Harappan Civilisation. CBSE 2024

Ans. Burials in Harappan sites provide valuable insights into the social and economic differences amongst the people of the Harappan civilisation in the following ways

- In Harappan burial sites, the dead were generally placed in pits, but there were variations in how these pits were constructed. Some graves were lined with bricks, which could indicate a more elaborate burial for individuals of higher status.
- Items found in some graves provide clues about social and economic differences. Pottery and ornaments, often placed in graves, suggest that the Harappans believed these objects were useful in the afterlife. Jewellry, including beads and other items, has been found in the graves of both men and women, showing that certain personal belongings were important in death. However, these items were not found in all graves, meaning not everyone had access to such luxury goods.
- The discovery of items like shell rings, semi-precious stones, and beads near the skull of a man in Harappa suggests that men were also buried with important personal items. This may mean that social differences in Harappan Civilisation were based on factors like wealth or status, rather than just gender.

3. What are the aspects of Harappan economy that have been reconstructed from archaeological evidence?

Ans. The aspects of Harappan economy that have been reconstructed from the archaeological evidence are

Agriculture It has been found that agriculture was one of the most important sources of food.

Evidences such as charred grains have been found in the Harappan civilisation. The seeds like wheat, barley, lentil, chickpea and sesame were cultivated in the Harappa whereas millets were found in Gujarat. The evidence of rice cultivation was not there.

Evidence of agriculture was easy to find out, but there is difficulty in finding out agricultural practices. From the finds of terracotta sculpture, it has been assumed that the oxen were used for ploughing the land. Moreover, terracotta models of plough also have been found at the sites in Cholistan and at Banawali. The field had two sets of furrows at right angles to each other. Irrigation was also known to the Harappans. Traces of canals and wells also have been found at the Harappan site of Shortughai in Afghanistan. Besides these finds, several water reservoirs also have been traced which may have been used for the irrigation of agriculture.

Animal Domestication From the finds of bones of animals such as sheep, goat, cow, oxen, buffalo, etc, it has been assumed that the domestication of animals was also done there.

Procurement of Crafts Prevalence of artefacts such as pottery sculptures, bead making, seal and sealings was also found. Besides these, weaving, building construction, jewellery-making were also done there.

Trade The Harappans had long distance communication which is evident from the finds of seals and sealings of Harappans in the distant sites of Mesopotamia.

Certain metals such as bronze, copper and gold in Harappa which were procured in different sites were traded with the other distant civilisations developed in Oman. Archaeologists think that there were communication between Oman, Bahrain or Mesopotamia with the Harappan Civilisation.

4. What are the evidences found by the archaeologists which show that the Harappans had contacts with distant lands? Does it show that the contacts proved to have good trade relations with each other? **CBSE Diksha**

Ans. The archaeologists found many evidences which show that the Harappans had contacts with distant lands. The important evidences are

- Archaeological finds suggest that copper was probably brought from Oman, on the South-Eastern tip of the Arabian Peninsula. Moreover, chemical analysis proved traces of nickel both in Omani copper and Harappan artefacts. This suggests a common origin of both. A large Harappan jar coated with a thick layer of black clay was found at Omani sites. It is possible that the Harappans exchanged the contents of these vessels for Omani copper.
- Mesopotamian texts of third millennium BCE referred that copper came from a region called Magan. Historians thought that probably it was another name of Oman. Mesopotamian texts also mentioned contact with regions named Dilmun (probably the island of Bahrain), Magan and Meluhha, possibly the Harappan region. Meluhha was a land of seafarers. Many products of Meluhha were mentioned. These were carnelian, lapis lazuli, copper, gold and varieties of wood.
- Other archaeological finds suggest of long distance contacts which include Harappan seals, weights, dice and beads. All these evidences suggest that Harappan civilisation was connected with Oman, Bahrain or Mesopotamia by sea. Depictions of ships and boats on seals indicate the trade relations between different countries.
- A cylinder seal found in Mesopotamia has humped bull motif which can be derived from the Indus region. The round 'Persian Gulf' seal found in Bahrain sometimes carries Harappan motifs. Local 'Dilmun' weights followed the Harappan standard.

All these evidences show that Harappan Civilisation had good trade relations with other regions.

5. What factors in your opinion are responsible for the collapse of a mature Harappan Civilisation by 1800 BCE?

Or **"There is evidence that by 1800 BCE most of the Harappan sites had been abandoned". Substantiate the statement in the context of causes and evidences.**

CBSE 2024 C

Ans. There is strong evidence that by 1800 BCE, most of the mature Harappan sites in regions like Cholistan had been abandoned. Simultaneously, there was a growth of settlements in Gujarat, Haryana and Western Uttar Pradesh. At that time, distinctive artefacts of civilisation like weights, seals, special beads, writing, long-distance trade and craft specialisation disappeared. House construction technique deteriorated and large public structures were not produced.

A variety of explanations were given by scholars to explain the causes of decline of mature Harappan Civilisation. These causes are

(i) Climatic change
(ii) Deforestation
(iii) Excessive floods
(iv) Shifting and drying up of rivers
(v) Overuse of the landscape

Some of these reasons may be holding true for certain settlements, but they do not account for the collapse of the entire civilisation. No single reason was responsible for the decline of this civilisation.

The civilisation might be destroyed by invaders which was proved by the bulk of bones found. It indicated a slaughter. But the skeletons found did not belong to the same period according to George Dales.

Thus, it was not concluded in favour of a dramatic collapse, rather it was believed that the end of Harappan culture was a gradual process.

6. Describe the contribution of John Marshall, Director-General of the ASI to Indian archaeology.

Ans. John Marshall was the Director-General of the ASI. In 1924, on the basis of discoveries of seals by Daya Ram Sahni and Rakhal Das Banerji, he announced the discovery of a new civilisation in the Indus valley to the world. Similar seals were also found in the excavation of archaeological sites of Mesopotamia. In this way, not only new civilisation came to limelight but we also came to know that this civilisation was contemporary to Mesopotamia.

Sir John Marshall's as the Director-General of ASI was actually a term of major change in Indian archaeology. He was the first professional archaeologist who worked in India. He brought with himself his experience of Greece and Crete. Like Cunningham, he was also interested in spectacular findings. But he was equally interested in looking for patterns of daily life.

John Marshall tended to excavate along regular horizontal units, measured uniformly throughout the mound. He ignored the stratigraphy of the site and this was the biggest drawback in his excavation process. It means all the artefacts, found from the same unit, were grouped together, even if they were found at different stratigraphic layers. As a result, valuable information found about the civilisation was lost forever.

7. Explain the role of various archaeologists in the discovery of Harappa. CBSE 2024

Ans. The role of various archaeologists in the discovery of Harappa is discussed below

Alexander Cunningham

- Cunningham, in the mid-19th century, was the first Director-General of the Archaeological Survey of India (ASI). His primary focus was on the archaeology of the Early Historic period (around the 6th century BCE to the 4th century CE). He relied heavily on written texts and inscriptions, especially those left by Chinese Buddhist pilgrims who visited India between the 4th and 7th centuries CE, to locate ancient settlements.
- Cunningham also documented and translated inscriptions during his surveys. However, his interest was primarily in the early historic cities, and he did not focus on ancient civilisations like Harappa.

Daya Ram Sahni

- In the early 20th century, Daya Ram Sahni played a crucial role in the excavation of Harappa. During his work at the Harappa site, he discovered seals in the lower layers of the excavation, which were much older than those from the Early Historic period.
- These discoveries began to show that Harappa was not just another ancient settlement but was part of a distinct and much older civilisation.

Rakhal Das Banerji

- Rakhal Das Banerji made significant contributions by discovering similar seals at Mohenjodaro in the early 1920s. His findings were crucial in linking Harappa and Mohenjodaro as part of the same civilisation.
- Banerji's work helped establish the idea that these sites were part of one unified culture, which led to more exploration and excavations in the Indus Valley.

John Marshall

- In 1924, John Marshall, the Director-General of the ASI, played a pivotal role in the global recognition of the Indus Valley Civilisation. Based on the findings of Sahni and Banerji, Marshall announced the discovery of a new civilisation in the Indus Valley.
- Marshall's work was instrumental in connecting the Harappan Civilisation with other contemporary civilisations, particularly Mesopotamia, as similar seals were found there.

R.E.M. Wheeler

- R.E.M. Wheeler took over as Director-General of the ASI in 1944, and he introduced important changes to the methods of excavation. Unlike Marshall, who had focused on uniform horizontal excavations, Wheeler emphasised the importance of following the stratigraphy of the mound.
- As an ex-army brigadier, Wheeler also brought military precision to archaeological practice.

8. 'Early Harappan archaeologists thought that certain objects which seem unusual and unfamiliar may have had a religious significance'. Substantiate. Competency Based Que

Ans. Archaeological interpretation to reconstruct religious practices of Harappan civilisation was not easy. The important facts to reconstruct the religious beliefs of the Harappan period as follows

- Archaeologists thought that certain objects which seemed unusual or unfamiliar may have had a religious significance. These included terracotta figurines of women, heavily jewelled with elaborate head dresses. These were regarded as mother goddesses.
- Rare stone statuary of man seated with one hand on the knee was regarded as 'priest king'. Other structures found in Harappan Civilisation, like the Great Bath and fire altars found at Kalibangan and Lothal also were taken as significant for ritual practices.
- Attempts were made to reconstruct religious beliefs and practices by examining different seals.

- Mythical creatures like unicorn, figure seated with cross- legged in yogic posture, sometimes surrounded by animals, regarded as 'proto-Shiva' were all examples of Hindu religion. Conical stone objects were classified as 'lingas'.

Many reconstructions of Harappan religion are made on the assumption that later traditions provide similarity with earlier ones. It follows from the rule that archaeologists try to know the facts by following the process of 'known to the unknown.' Thus, reconstructing religious practices was not easy for the archaeologists.

Source Based Questions

Read the sources given below and answer the following questions.

1. Processing of food required grinding equipment as well as vessels for mixing, blending and cooking. These were made of stone, metal and terracotta. This is an excerpt from one of the earliest reports on excavations at Mohenjodaro, the best-known Harappan site

Saddle querns are found in considerable numbers and they seem to have been the only means in use for grinding cereals.

As a rule, they were roughly made of hard, gritty, igneous rock or sandstone and mostly show signs of hard usage. As their bases are usually convex, they must have been set in the Earth or in mud to prevent their rocking. Two main types have been found: those on which another smaller stone was pushed or rolled to and fro and others with which a second stone was used as a pounder, eventually making a large cavity in the other stone.

Querns of the former type were probably used solely for grain; the second type possibly only for pounding herbs and spices for making curries. In fact, stones of this latter type are dubbed "curry stones" by our workmen and our cook asked for the loan of one from the museum for use in the kitchen.

From Ernest Mackay, Further Excavations at Mohenjodaro, 1937.

(i) Which type of querns have been found in Mohenjodaro? Describe the surface of grinding equipment.

(ii) Write any two characteristics of saddle querns.

(iii) What are two kinds of saddle?

Ans. (i) Saddle querns have been found in Mohenjodaro. The surface of grinding equipment was rough. It was made of hard rock or sandstone.

(ii) Two characteristics of saddle querns are as follows

(a) They were found in considerable numbers.

(b) They were made of hard, gritty igneous rocks or sandstone.

(iii) Two kinds of saddle are as follows

(a) These saddles were used to grind grain and cereals and were also called grinding saddles.

(b) In another type of saddle, a second stone was used as a pounder. These saddles were used to grind herbs and spices.

2. About the drains, Mackay noted: "It is certainly the most complete ancient system as yet discovered." Every house was connected to the street drains. The main channels were made of bricks set in mortar and were covered with loose bricks that could be removed for cleaning. In some cases, limestone was used for the covers.

House drains first emptied into a sump or cesspit into which solid matter settled while waste water flowed out into the street drains. Very long drainage channels were provided at intervals with sumps for cleaning.

It is a wonder of archaeology that "little heaps of material, mostly sand, have frequently been found lying alongside drainage channels, which shows ... that the debris was not always carted away when the drain was cleared."

From Ernest Mackay, Early Indus Civilisation, 1948.

Drainage systems were not unique to the larger cities, but were found in smaller settlements as well. At Lothal for example, while houses were built of mud bricks, drains were made of burnt bricks. **CBSE 2025**

(i) Analyse the possible reason behind the uniformity in the drainage systems across the Harappan cities.

(ii) Analyse the implications of finding little heaps of material, mostly sand, alongside drainage channels.

(iii) Assess the impact of Harappan drainage system.

Ans. (i) The uniform drainage systems suggest centralised planning, standardised construction methods, and efficient urban governance across Harappan cities.

(ii) The presence of sand heaps indicates regular drain maintenance but also suggests inefficiency in debris disposal after cleaning.

(iii) The Harappan drainage system showcased advanced urban planning, ensuring efficient waste disposal and sanitation. It minimized waterlogging, reduced health hazards, and improved living conditions. The well-structured drains, cesspits, and sumps highlight their engineering skills and focus on hygiene, setting a precedent for future civilizations in urban infrastructure and public health.

3. Deadman Lane is a narrow alley, varying from 3 to 6 feet in width ... At the point where the lane turns Westward, part of a skull and the bones of the thorax and upper arm of an adult were discovered, all in very friable condition, at a depth of 4 ft 2 in.

The body lay on its back diagonally across the lane. Fifteen inches to the West were a few fragments of a tiny skull. It is to these remains that the lane owes its name.

From John Marshall, Mohenjodaro and the Indus Civilisation, 1931.

Sixteen skeletons of people with the ornaments that they were wearing when they died were found from the same part of Mohenjodaro in 1925.

Much later, in 1947, R.E.M. Wheeler, then Director-General of the ASI, tried to correlate this archaeological evidence with that of the Rigveda, the earliest known text in the sub-continent. He wrote: The Rigveda mentions pur, meaning rampart, fort or stronghold.

Indra, the Aryan war-god is called puramdara, the fort-destroyer. Where are – or were – these citadels?

It has in the past been supposed that they were mythical ... The recent excavation of Harappa may be thought to have changed the picture. Here we have a highly evolved civilisation of essentially non-Aryan type, now known to have employed massive fortifications ... What destroyed this firmly settled civilisation? Climatic, economic or political deterioration may have weakened it, but its ultimate extinction is more likely to have been completed by deliberate and large-scale destruction. It may be no mere chance that at a late period of Mohenjodaro men, women, and children, appear to have been massacred there. On circumstantial evidence, Indra stands accused.

FROM R.E.M. WHEELER, "Harappa 1946", Ancient India, 1947.

In the 1960s, the evidence of a massacre in Mohenjodaro was questioned by an archaeologist named George Dales. He demonstrated that the skeletons found at the site did not belong to the same period. Whereas a couple of them definitely seem to indicate a slaughter, ... the bulk of the bones were found in contexts suggesting burials of the sloppiest and most irreverent nature. There is no destruction level covering the latest period of the city, no sign of extensive burning, no bodies of warriors clad in armour and surrounded by the weapons of war. The citadel, the only fortified part of the city, yielded no evidence of a final defence.

From Gf Dales, "The Mythical Massacre at Mohenjodaro", Expedition, 1964.

As you can see, a careful re-examination of the data can sometimes lead to a reversal of earlier interpretations.

(i) Why is the lane called deadman Lane? How did John Marshall tend to excavate?

(ii) Why are earlier interpretations sometimes reversed?

(iii) According to R.E.M. Wheeler, what were the reasons for the destruction of Harappan culture?

Ans. (i) It is called deadman lane because in the narrow street a part of the skull, the bones of the thorax and upper arm of an adult were discovered.

John Marshall tended to excavate along regular horizontal units, measured uniformly throughout the mound, ignoring the stratigraphy of the site.

(ii) It is because many new facts came into the limelight observed by new scholars, archaeologists, who discovered new sites of the same phase related to this civilisation.

(iii) According to R.E.M. Wheeler, Harappan social and economic culture changed due to climatic changes. This might have brought deliberate and large-scale destruction. Another reason was that there might be a large scale massacre of men, women and children.

Map Based Questions

1. **On the given political outline map of India, locate and label the followings with appropriate symbols.**

(i) **Rakhigarhi-Indus Valley Site** **CBSE SQP 2022**

(ii) **Name of two mature Harappan sites**

(iii) **(a) Chanhudaro** (b) **Kot Diji**

(iv) **Kalibangan** **CBSE 2025** (v) **Lothal**

Or **On the given political outline map of India, locate and label the following with appropriate symbols**

(i) Dholavira - A Harappan site **CBSE 2024**

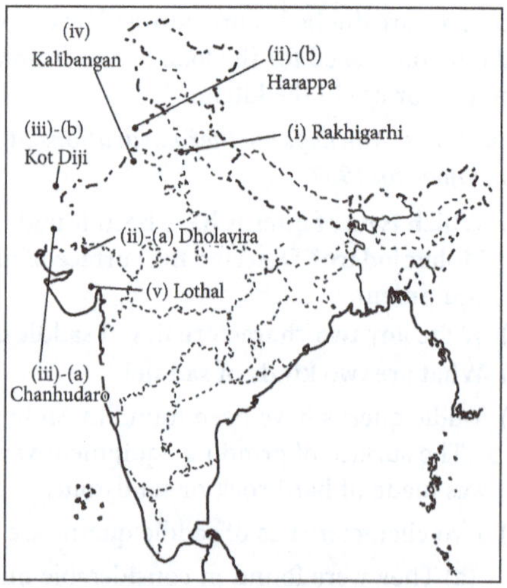

2. Point out the following on the given map.
(i) Nageshwar (ii) Banawali
(iii) Balakot (iv) Mohenjodaro

Or On the given political outline map of India, locate and label the following with appropriate symbols.
Banawali, a Harappan site. **CBSE 2024**

Ans.

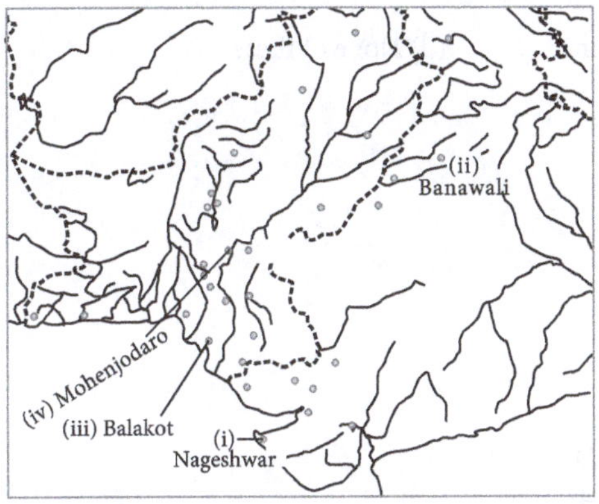

3. On the political outline map of India, three places have been marked as A, B and C, which are related to matured Harappan sites. Identify them and write their correct names on the lines drawn near them.

Or On the given political outline map of India, locate and label the following with appropriate symbols.
– Kalibangan, Mature Harappan site
CBSE SQP 2024, 2024 C

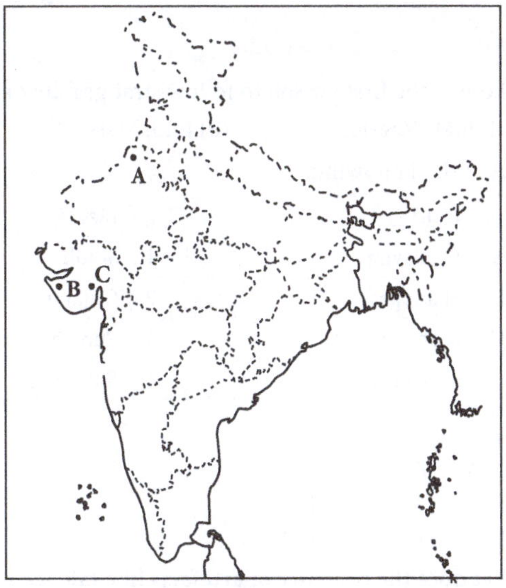

Ans. (a) Kalibangan (b) Nageshwar (c) Lothal

SELF ASSESSMENT TEST

Objective Type Questions

1. Who was the first person to follow stratigraphy of the mound?

   (a) R.E.M Wheeler (b) John Marshall (c) Daya Ram Sahni (d) None of these

2. Match the Following.

List I	List II
A. Dholavira	1. Sindh
B. Harappa	2. Gujarat
C. Mohenjodaro	3. Punjab
D. Kalibangan	4. Rajasthan

Codes

	A	B	C	D		A	B	C	D
(a)	1	3	2	4	(b)	2	3	1	4
(c)	3	1	2	4	(d)	4	1	2	3

3. **What does the presence of artefacts like faience pots in large settlements suggest about Harappan society?**

   (a) All settlements had equal wealth.
   (b) Large settlements likely had more luxury goods than smaller ones.
   (c) Small settlements had the same artefacts.
   (d) Harappan society didn't value luxury items.

4. **What unique structure on the Citadel in Mohenjodaro is believed to have been used for ritual purposes?**

   (a) The Great Bath (b) The Central Hall
   (c) The Royal Palace (d) The Lower Well

Short Answer Type Questions

5. Examine why is Indus Valley Civilisation called the Harappan culture.
6. Elaborate the evidences used by archaeologists to reconstruct dietary practices of the Harappans.
7. Describe any two changes that were observed after 1900 BC in Harappan Civilisation.
8. Should stone artefacts be considered as utilitarian objects or as luxuries? Why?
9. What do the seals with plant motifs suggest about Harappan religious beliefs? Explain.

Long Answer Type Questions

10. "It is certainly the most complete ancient system as yet discovered," said Mackay. Justify the statement.
11. Explain the different ways in which Harappans procured materials for craft production.
12. Miniature pots of faience, perhaps used as perfume bottles, are found mostly in Mohenjodaro and Harappa. Elaborate.
13. Examine the significance of the uniformity of Harappan artefacts.
14. Discuss the factors that contributed to the abandonment of mature Harappan sites around 1800 BCE. How did these changes affect Harappan culture and settlements?

2

CHAPTER

This chapter deals with the establishment of Mahajanapadas and Mauryan empire. Mahajanapadas were 16 in number with Magadha being the most important. After the Mahajanapada period, Mauryan empire became the first pan India empire under the reign of Asoka.

YOUR STUDY GOALS

2.1 The Earliest States
2.2 An Early Empire : Mauryan Empire
2.3 New Notions of Kingship
2.4 A Changing Countryside
2.5 Towns and Trade
2.6 Deciphering Inscriptions
2.7 Limitations of Inscriptional Evidence

YOUR PRACTICE GOALS

- Objective Type Questions (57 Qs ; MCQs, A-R, Matching, Picture Based)
- Subjective Questions (15 SAs, 7 LAs)
- Source Based Questions (7 Qs)
- Map Based Questions (4 Qs)

Kings, Farmers and Towns

(Early States and Economies)

After the end of Harappan civilisation, many changes happened in India over a period of 1500 years such as

- **Composition of the *Rigveda*** and development of agricultural settlements in North India, the Deccan Plateau and parts of Karnataka.
- **Emergence of pastoral communities** in the Deccan and Southern regions.
- New burial practices, including elaborate stone structures called megaliths in Central and South India from the first millennium BCE.

Historians study inscriptions, texts, coins and visual materials of 600 BCE-600 CE to understand these developments.

2.1 The Earliest States

The Sixteen *Mahajanapadas*

- The sixth century BCE marked the development of early cities, coinage and the growing use of iron. Diverse systems of thought, including **Buddhism** and **Jainism** also began to grow.
- **Sixteen states** known as *mahajanapadas* were mentioned in early Buddhist and Jaina texts. Each *mahajanapada* had a capital city.
- **Vajji, Magadha, Koshala, Kuru, Panchala, Gandhara** and **Avanti** were the most important *mahajanapadas*. Most *mahajanapadas* were ruled by kings.

- Some *mahajanapadas* known as *ganas* or *sanghas* were **oligarchies**[1]. Both Mahavira and the Buddha belonged to *ganas*.
- From the sixth century BCE onwards, Brahmanas composed Sanskrit texts known as **Dharmasutras**.
- **Dharmasutras** contained norms for rulers, who were ideally expected to be Kshatriyas. Rulers were advised to collect taxes and tributes from cultivators, traders and artisans.
- Some states acquired armies and maintained regular bureaucracies. Others were dependent on **militia**[2].

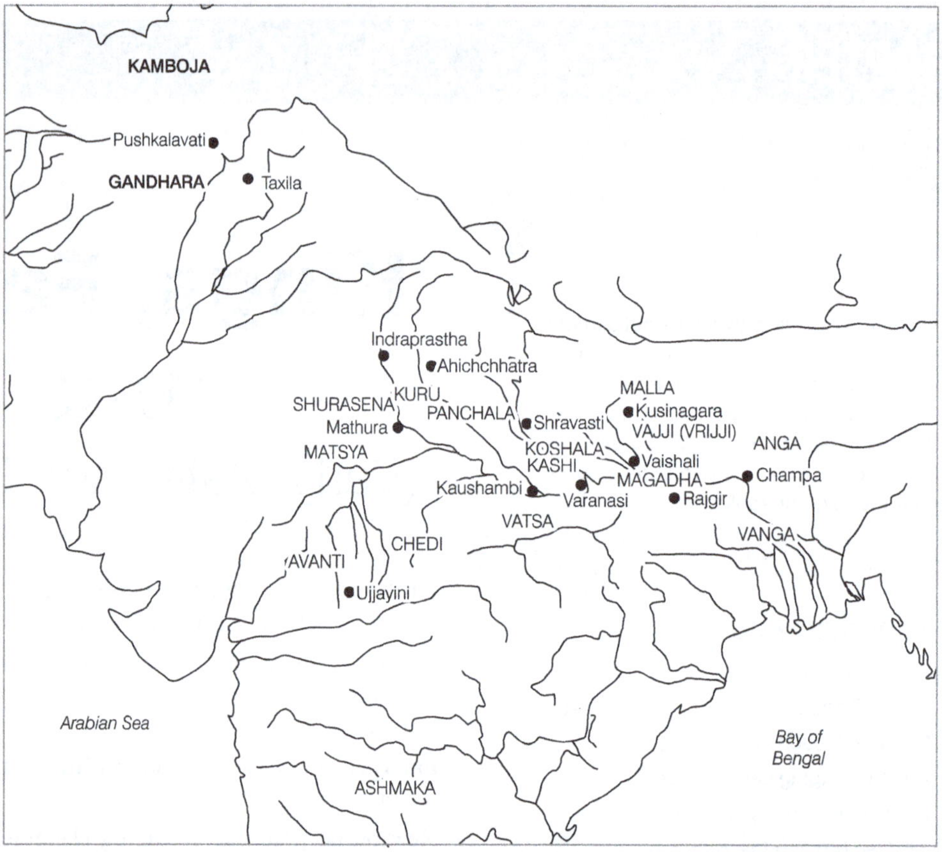

▲ *Early States and their Capitals*

Magadha: The First *Mahajanapada*

- Magadha (in present-day Bihar) was the most powerful *mahajanapada* because of its productive agriculture and accessible iron mines.
- Elephants were an important component of the army, that were found in forests in the region.
- The **River Ganga** and its tributaries provided cheap and convenient means of communication.
- Kings like **Bimbisara, Ajatasattu** and **Mahapadma Nanda** played an important role in implementing policies of Magadha.
- Initial capital of Magadha was **Rajagaha** (the Prakrit name for present-day **Rajgir** in Bihar). Later, it was shifted to **Pataliputra** (present-day Patna) in the 4th century BCE as it was situated on main routes of communication along the Ganga.

1 **Oligarchies** A form of government where power was shared by a number of men, collectively known as *rajas*.
2 **Militia** It did not have professional soldiers but worked as an army.

2.2 An Early Empire : Mauryan Empire

Chandragupta Maurya was the founder of the Mauryan Empire (c. 321 BCE). His empire extended as far as North-West upto Afghanistan and Baluchistan.

Finding out about the Mauryas

Historians have used a variety of sources to reconstruct the history of the Mauryan Empire. These include

- Archaeological findings, especially sculpture.
- Accounts of **Magasthenes**, a Greek ambassador in the court of Chandragupta Maurya.
- Kautilya's *Arthashastra* which contains details of administrative and military organisation of the Mauryan Empire.
- Later Buddhist, Jaina, Puranic and Sanskrit literary works.
- Inscriptions of Asoka on rocks and pillars.

Asoka

- Asoka was the grandson of Chandragupta Maurya. He conquered Kalinga (present-day coastal Odisha). Asoka tried to hold his empire together by promoting *dhamma*.
- According to Asoka, *dhamma* would ensure the well-being of people. Principles of his dhamma were
    - Respect towards elders
    - Generosity towards Brahmanas
    - Treating slaves and servants kindly
    - Respect for all religions and traditions.
    - Appointment of ***dhamma mahamatta***[3].

Inscriptions of Asoka (Piyadassi)

- **James Prinsep** deciphered the **Kharosthi** and **Brahmi scripts** to know about the major dynasties that had ruled the subcontinent.
- He found that most of the earliest inscriptions and coins mentioned a king as **Piyadassi**, meaning **'pleasant to behold'**. There were a few inscriptions which also referred to the king as **Asoka**.
- Most inscriptions were in Prakrit language (a language used by ordinary people), while inscriptions found in the North-West were in Aramaic and Greek.
- Most Prakrit inscriptions were written in the Brahmi Script, while some in North-West were written in Kharosthi Script.
- The Aramaic and Greek scripts were used for inscriptions in Afghanistan.

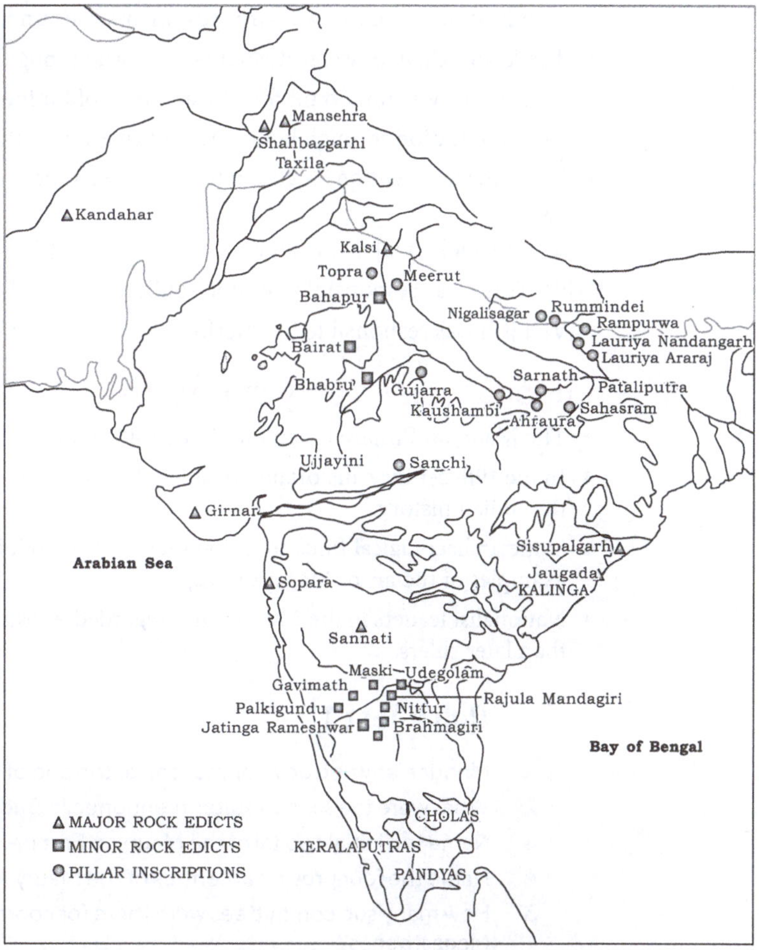

▲ *Distribution of Asokan Inscriptions*

3 *Dhamma mahamatta* Special officers to spread the message of *dhamma*.

- Asoka refers to himself as ***devanampiya*** (beloved of the gods) in the inscriptions.
- Asokan inscriptions reflect the pain of the ruler as well as a change in his attitude towards warfare after the Kalinga war. It shows that many people were deported, killed and died during the Kalinga war.

Inscriptions

- Inscriptions are writings engraved on **hard surfaces** such as stone, metal or pottery.
- They usually records the achievements, activities or ideas of those who commissioned them.
- They also include the military achievements of kings, or donations made by women and men to religious institutions.
- Inscriptions are virtually permanent records. Some inscriptions carry dates while others are dated on the basis of *palaeography*[4] or styles of writing.
- Names of rulers such as **Ajatasattu** and **Asoka** were known from Prakrit texts and inscriptions.
- **Pali, Tamil** and **Sanskrit** languages were also used to write inscriptions and texts.

Administration of Mauryan Empire

- The five major political centres of Mauryan Empire were the capital Pataliputra and the provincial centres of Taxila, Ujjayini, Tosali and Suvarnagiri.
- Administrative control was strongest in areas around the capital and the provincial centres.
- Taxila and Ujjayini were situated on important long distance trade routes.
- Suvarnagiri was important for utilising the gold mines of Karnataka.
- Communication through both land and riverine routes was important for the empire.
- Megasthenes mentions a committee with six subcommittees for military coordination activity. These were

(i) One looked after the navy
(ii) Second managed transport and provisions
(iii) Third was responsible for foot-soldiers
(iv) Fourth was responsible for horses
(v) Fifth was responsible for chariots
(vi) Sixth was responsible for elephants

Importance of Mauryan Empire

- The Mauryan Empire lasted for about **150 years**.
- In the 19th century, historians considered the emergence of the Mauryan Empire as a major landmark in the Indian history.
- Some archaeological finds from the Mauryan period, including stone sculptures, were considered to be examples of the art of Mauryan Empire.
- Nationalist leaders in the 20th century regarded Asoka as inspiring as he was more powerful and humble than later rulers.

Quick Test 1

1. Mention any one development after the end of Harappan Civilisation.
2. What were the sixteen states mentioned in Buddhist and Jaina texts ?
3. Name the initial capital of the Mauryan Empire.
4. Name the four provincial centres of the Mauryan Empire.
5. How many sub committees were there for coordinating military activity according to Megasthenes?

---

4 *Palaeography* Study of ancient and historical handwriting.

2.3 New Notions of Kingship

Chiefs and Kings in the South

- The new kingdoms of Cholas, Cheras and Pandyas emerged in Tamilakam[5].
- Kings like the **Satavahanas** who ruled over parts of Western and Central India, and the Shakas of Central Asia, got revenues from long distance trade.
- The social origins of these rulers were uncertain, but on acquiring power, the Satavahanas tried to claim social status in various ways.

Chiefs and Chiefdoms

- A chief is a powerful man whose position may or may not be hereditary. He derives support from his kinfolk.
- A chief may perform special rituals, leadership in warfare and resolve disputes. He receives gifts from his subordinates (unlike kings who usually collect taxes) and often distributes these amongst his supporters.
- Generally, there are no regular armies and officials in chiefdoms. Ancient Tamil Sangam epics consist of poems depicting chiefs and chiefdoms. For example, ***Silappadikaram*** depicts the forest visit of Pandya Chief Senguttuvan.

Divine Kings

- From first century BCE to first century CE, Kushanas ruled over a vast kingdom from Central Asia to North-West India. Their ideas of kingship were found in coins and sculpture.
- Kushanas used many ways of claiming high status to identify them as a variety of deities.
- Very large statues of Kushana rulers have been found in a shrine at Mat near Mathura. Similar statues were also found in a shrine in Afghanistan.
- Many Kushana rulers adopted the title ***devaputra*** or ***Son of God***. By the fourth century CE, evidence of larger states, including the Gupta Empire had been found. Many of these depended on *samantas*[6].
- Historians reconstructed information about Gupta rulers from literature, coins, inscriptions and *prashastis*. The ***Prayaga Prashasti*** known as Allahabad Pillar inscription was composed in Sanskrit by **Harishena**.
- Harishena was the court poet of Samudragupta who is regarded as the greatest among the Gupta rulers.

▲ *Kushana Coins*

2.4 A Changing Countryside

Kings and Peasants

- The relationship between a king and his subjects, especially the rural population, was not friendly. Rulers demanded high taxes which was criticised by the peasants.
- To meet growing demand for taxes, peasants used different ways to increase production which were discussed in the ***Jatakas*** and ***Panchatantra*** tales. The *Jatakas* were written in Pali around the middle of the first millennium CE.

---

5 Tamilakam The name of the ancient Tamil country which included parts of present-day Andhra Pradesh and Kerala.

6 Samantas Men who maintained themselves through local resources including control over land.

Strategies for Increasing Production

- **Ploughing agriculture** became prevalent from 6th century BCE. It was used in fertile alluvial river valleys such as in the Ganga and the Kaveri.
- **Increase in paddy production** in some parts of the Ganga valley with the introduction of transplantation.
- **Restriction of iron ploughshare** to certain parts such as areas of Punjab and Rajasthan which were semi-arid till the twentieth century.
- **Hoe agriculture** was practiced by the people living in hilly areas.
- **Use of irrigation** mainly through wells and tanks.

Differences in Rural Society

- The rise in production resulted in unequal benefits for the people. There was a growing difference amongst landless agricultural labourers, small peasants and large landholders.
- The term ***gahapati*** was often used in Pali texts to designate the small peasants and larger landholders.
- The large landholders and village headsman exercised control over other cultivators.
- The early Tamil literature (the Sangam texts) mentions different categories of people living in villages i.e. landowners or *vellalar*, ploughmen or *uzhavar* and slaves or *adimai*.
- The differences were based on unequal access to land, labour and some new technologies.

Gahapati

- A ***gahapati*** was the owner, master or head of a household. He exercised control over the women, children, slaves and workers who shared a common residence.
- He was also the owner of the resources i.e. land, animals and other things that belonged to the household.
- Sometimes the term ***gahapati*** was used as a mark of status for men belonging to the urban elite, including wealthy merchants.

Land Grants and New Rural Elites

- Grants of land was started from the early centuries of the Common Era. They provide information about the relationship between cultivators and the state.
- Land granted to a Brahamana was called ***agrahara.*** Evidence of this was found on Sanskrit inscriptions on stone and copper plates.
- The records suggest that grants were given to religious institutions or to Brahmanas only.
- Sanskrit legal texts did not allow women to have independent access to resources such as land. But Prabhavati Gupta, daughter of Chandragupta II, had access to land.
- Some historians suggest that land grants were made to extend agriculture to new areas. Others suggest that they indicated weakening of political power.

Quick Test 2

1 What title was adopted by Kushana rulers?
2 Which Tamil epic depicts the forest visit of Senguttuvan?
3 Who composed *Prayaga Prashasti*?
4 What was used to turn the alluvial soil in areas which had high rainfall?
5 Prabhavati was the daughter of which ruler?

2.5 Towns and Trade

New Cities

- From the sixth century BCE, urban centres emerged in several parts of the subcontinent. Many of these were the capitals of *mahajanapadas*.
- Major towns of *mahajanapadas* were located along the routes of communication.
- Some towns such as Pataliputra were located on riverine routes. Others such as Ujjayini, were located along land routes and Puhar was located near the coast.
- Cities like Mathura were vibrant hubs of commercial, cultural and political activity.
- The Magadhan rulers during fifth century BCE, shifted their capital from Rajgaha to Pataliputra. Pataliputra was earlier known as Pataligrama. By the fourth century BCE, it became the capital of the Mauryan Empire. It grew into one of the largest cities in Asia, but later it declined.
- The Chinese pilgrim **Xuan Zang**, visited Magadha in the seventh century CE. He noted the ruins and small population of Magadha.

Urban Populations : Elites and Craftpersons

- Kings and ruling elites lived in fortified cities. Different artefacts found from these cities include fine pottery bowls and dishes with a glossy finish, (known as Northern Black Polished Ware) ornaments, tools, weapons, vessels, figurines etc, made of gold, silver, copper, bronze, ivory, glass, shell and terracotta.
- By the second century BCE, short **votive inscriptions**[7] were found in many cities.
- Weavers, scribes, carpenters, potters, goldsmiths, blacksmiths, officials, religious teachers, merchants and kings lived in the cities.
- Organisations of craft producers and merchants were known as **guilds** or ***shrenis***. These guilds collected raw materials, regulated production and sold the finished product in the market.
- Craftspersons used various iron tools to meet the demand of urban elites.

Trade in the Subcontinent

- From the sixth century BCE, land and river routes spread across the subcontinent and extended in various directions, both overland and overseas. Those who crossed these routes included
  - Peddlers who probably travelled on foot.
  - Merchants who travelled with caravans of bullock carts and pack-animals.
  - Seafarers whose journey were risky but highly profitable.
- Some successful merchants were known as ***masattuvan*** in Tamil and ***setthis*** and ***sattavahas*** in Prakrit.
- Goods such as salt, grain, cloth, metal ores and finished products, stone, timber, medicinal plants, etc. were carried from one place to another. Spices such as pepper were in high demand in the Roman Empire.
- Textiles and medicinal plants were also transported across the Arabian Sea to the Mediterranean Sea.
- In Kodumanal (Tamil Nadu), there is a evidence of **bead**-making industry. The local traders brought the stones mentioned in the ***Periplus***[8] of the ***Erythraean***[9] Sea from such sites to the coastal ports.

---

7 **Votive inscriptions** Inscriptions which contain records of gifts given to religious institutions.

8 ***Periplus*** Greek word which means sailing around.

9 ***Erythraean*** Greek name for the Red Sea.

Coins and Kings

▲ *A Gupta coin*

▲ *A punch-marked coin*

▲ *A Yaudheya coin*

- Silver and copper punch-marked coins (6th century BCE onwards) were used during this period. **Numismatists**[10] have studied these coins to find possible commercial networks.
- The first coins having the names and images of rulers were issued by the Indo-Greeks.
- The kushanas issued the first gold coins in the first century CE. These were almost similar in weight with those issued by contemporary Roman emperors and Parthian rulers of Iran.
- Collection of Roman coins have been found from archaeological sites in South India.
- Copper coins were also issued by tribal republics such as that of the Yaudheyas of Punjab and Haryana (c. first century CE).
- Some of the most beautiful gold coins were issued by the Gupta rulers which helped in long-distance transactions.

Economic Crisis

- Punched-marked coins got their named because symbols were punched onto their metal surface using punchies.
- From c. sixth century CE onwards, the quantity of gold coins decreased.
- According to some historians, long-distance trade declined due to the collapse of the Western Roman Empire. It affected the prosperity of the states, communities and regions.
- Some historians suggest that new towns and trade networks developed around this time. According to them, few coins were found of this period, but they were continued to be mentioned in inscriptions and other records.

2.6 Deciphering Inscriptions

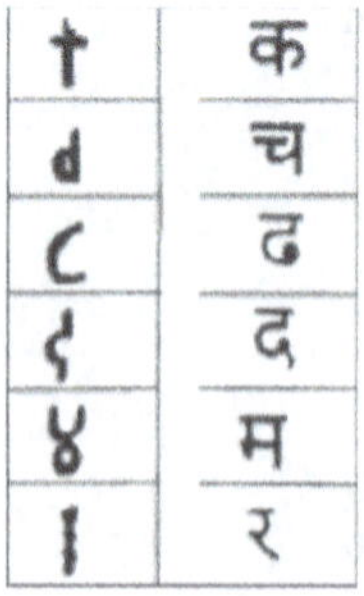
▲ *Asokan Brahmi with Devanagari equivalents*

Deciphering Brahmi

- Most scripts used to write modern Indian languages are derived from **Brahmi script**. This script was used in most Asokan inscriptions.
- From the late eighteenth century, European scholars, with the help of Indian *pandits*, studied several manuscripts in Bengali and Devanagari, and compared their letters with older samples.
- Scholars who studied early inscriptions sometimes assumed that these were in Sanskrit language, but the earliest inscriptions were written in Prakrit language.
- James Prinsep deciphered Asokan Brahmi in 1838.

Deciphering Kharosthi

- Kharosthi is used in the inscriptions of North-West.
- Coins of Indo-Greek kings who ruled over the area (c. second-first centuries BCE) contained the names of kings in Greek and Kharosthi scripts.
- European scholars could read the Kharosthi script by comparing the letters. The language used in Kharosthi script was Prakrit.

10 **Numismatist** A person who collects or studies coins and medals.

2.6 The Limitations of Inscriptional Evidence

- **Technical Limitations** Letters were lightly engraved, making them difficult to be read.
- **Damaged or Missing Letters** Such letters make the work of epigraphists more difficult.
- **Lack of Clarity** It is not always easy to be sure about the exact meaning of the words used in the inscriptions, some of which may be specific to a particular place or time.
- **Undeciphered Inscriptions** Not all the inscriptions have been deciphered, published and translated. Many inscriptions were destroyed and only a few are available.
- **Non-relevance of Inscriptions** Inscriptions were composed in praise of kings and patrons. Many important things were not recorded in the inscriptions, e.g. routine agricultural practice and the life of the common man.

Conclusion

Epigraphy alone does not give complete information about political and economic history.

Scholars in the late nineteenth and early twentieth centuries were primarily interested in the histories of kings. Recently, the focus has been growing on exploring histories of various social groups. This shift is likely to result in new examinations of existing sources and the development of innovative approaches.

Quick Test 3

1 Name one vibrant hub of commercial, cultural and political activity.
2 What type of inscriptions were found in several cities by the second century BCE?
3 Who was the first to issue coins bearing the names and images of rulers?
4 Which script is the foundation for most modern Indian languages?
5 Name the language identified by James Prinsep as the language of Kharosthi inscriptions.

TIMELINE

Major Political and Economic Developments

c.600-500 BCE	Paddy transplantation; urbanisation in the Ganga valley; *mahajanapadas*; punch-marked coins
c. 500-400 BCE	Rulers of Magadha consolidate power
c. 327-325 BCE	Invasion of Alexander of Macedon
c. 321 BCE	Accession of Chandragupta Maurya
c. 272/268-231 BCE	Reign of Asoka
c. 185 BCE	End of the Mauryan Empire
c. 200-100 BCE	Indo-Greek rule in the North-West; Cholas, Cheras and Pandyas in South India; Satavahanas in the Deccan
c. 100 BCE-200 CE	Shaka (peoples from Central Asia) rulers in the North-West; Roman trade; gold coinage
c. 78 CE	Accession of Kanishka
c.100-200 CE	Earliest inscriptional evidence of land grants by Satavahana and Shaka rulers
c. 320 CE	Beginning of Gupta rule
c. 335-375 CE	Samudragupta
c. 375-415 CE	Chandragupta II; Vakatakas in the Deccan
c. 500-600 CE	Rise of the Chalukyas in Karnataka and of the Pallavas in Tamil Nadu
c. 606-647 CE	Harshavardhana king of Kanauj; Chinese pilgrim Xuan Zang comes in search of Buddhist texts
c. 712	Arabs conquer Sind

Major Advances in Epigraphy

1784	Founding of the Asiatic Society (Bengal)
1810s	Colin Mackenzie collects over 8,000 inscriptions in Sanskrit and Dravidian languages
1838	Decipherment of Asokan Brahmi by James Prinsep
1877	Alexander Cunningham publishes a set of Asokan inscriptions
1886	First issue of *Epigraphia Carnatica*, a journal of South Indian inscriptions
1888	First issue of *Epigraphia Indica*
1965-66	D.C. Sircar publishes Indian *Epigraphy* and Indian *Epigraphical Glossary*

Mind Map

KINGS, FARMERS AND TOWNS

1 The Earliest Empire

Sixteen Mahajanapadas
- Mahajanapadas included monarchies and oligarchic sanghas with rajas.
- Magdha empire became the most powerful mahajanapada between the 6th and 4th century.

2 Prinsep and Piyadassi

Deciphering Ancient Scripts
- James Prinsep deciphered Brahmi and Kharosthi scripts in 1830's.
- Inscriptions mentioned kings like Ashoka as Piyadassi.

3 An Early Empire

Finding Out about the Mauryas
Mauryan history sources include sculptures, texts and inscriptions.

Administering the Empire
- The capital Pataliputra and provincial centres of Taxila, Ujjayini, Tosali and Suvarnagiri were the main political centres of empire.
- Army and trade routes ensured administration across diverse region.

4 New Notions of Kingships

Chiefs and Kings in the South
- Cholas, Cheras and Pandyas formed stable kingdoms in Tamilakam.
- Chiefs led rituals, warware, resolved disputes and received gifts.

Divine Kings
- Kushanas claimed god like status, using titles and colossal statues.
- Gupta rulers relied on Samantas for land and military support.

5 A Changing Countryside

Strategies for Increasing Production
- Plough agriculture increased productivity in fertile, high rainfall areas.
- Irrigation system like wells and tanks increased agricultural yields.

Land Grants and New Rural Elites
- Land grants were often given to religious institutions and Brahmanas.
- Land grants aimed to expand agriculture or strengthen political control.

6 Towns and Trade

Urban Populations: Elites and Craftpersons
- Kings and elites lived in fortified cities.
- Craftpersons made ornaments, tools and figurines from various materials.

Trade in the Subcontinent and Beyond
- Land and river routes connected subcontinent to distant regions.
- Rulers controlled trade routes, offering protection for a price.

Coins and Kings
Coins, like punch-marked and gold coins, facilitated long distant trade.

7 Back to Basics: How are Inscriptions Deciphered?

How Kharosthi was Read?
Scholars compared Greek and Kharosthi scripts together.

Historical Evidence from Inscriptions
- Ashoka's inscriptions used titles to identify the ruler.
- Epigraphists analyse content, style and language of inscriptions.
- King's order were inscribed on rocks near cities or important routes of communication.

8 The Limitations of Inscriptional Evidence

- Epigraphy has limitations due to damaged inscriptions and unclear meanings.
- Inscriptions often focus on grand events, missing daily life details.

NCERT Folder

Intext Questions

1. What are the different explanations offered by early writers and present-day historians for the growth of Magadhan power? (Pg. 31)

Ans. The different explanations offered by early writers and present-day historians for the growth of Magadhan power are as follows

- Magadha was located in the Gangetic basin, where the soil was very fertile and yielded good agricultural produce.
- Land was fertile which yielded a good harvest. Land revenue was high which provided huge income for the kingdom.
- The thick forests supplied timber and elephants. Timber was used in the construction of houses while elephants were used in the army.
- It had large deposits of copper and iron ore. The iron was used to make weapons and agriculture implements.

2. Read the excerpts from Megasthenes and the *Arthashastra* (Sources 1 and 2). To what extent do you think these texts are useful in reconstructing a history of Mauryan administration? (Pg. 34)

Ans. As a Greek ambassador, Megasthenes provides valuable insight into the Mauryan Empire. It also gives us a detailed view of the political, social and economic structure of the whole empire. On the other hand, the *Arthashastra* was written by Chanakya. The book gives us an overview of the taxation, law enforcement, diplomacy and military strategy of the Mauryan Empire. The *Arthashastra* lays down minute details of administrative and military organisation of the Mauryan Empire.

3. Why do you think kings claimed divine status? (Pg. 37)

Ans. The kings claimed divine status as it could help them to legitimize a ruler's power and authority. By suggesting that they were chosen by the gods, kings could present themselves as being above the common people and therefore deserving of respect and obedience.

4. Find out whether plough agriculture, irrigation and transplantation are prevalent in your state. If not, are there any alternative systems in use? (Pg. 41)

Ans. Yes, plough agriculture, irrigation and transplantation are prevalent in our state. These methods are integral to regional agricultural practices and are commonly employed in subsistence farming. In addition to these traditional methods, some alternative systems are also in use that focus on sustainability and soil health.

5. What are the transactions involved in trade? Which of these transactions are apparent from the sources mentioned? Are there any that are not evident from the sources? (Pg. 45)

Ans. Trade transactions includes various processes, such as purchasing, selling, transporting, storing, distributing and negotiating. From the available sources, several aspects of trade transactions can be observed as follows

- **Purchasing and Selling** Merchant records and travel accounts often document individual transactions, such as sales agreements and purchase details.
- **Transporting** Archaeological evidence, such as the remnants of trade routes or transport artefacts, sheds light on the logistics of moving goods.
- **Storage and Distribution** Findings like storage facilities and distribution networks can be inferred from archaeological excavations and historical texts.

However, there are some aspects of trade transactions that may not be fully evident from these sources. For example

- **Negotiation** Detailed accounts of negotiation processes are less commonly recorded and are often inferred from the context of trade agreements rather than clearly describing it.
- **Day-to-Day Operations** Routine aspects of trade operations, such as the daily activities of traders or the specifics of market interactions, might be underrepresented in historical records.

6. Look at map below and discuss the location of Asokan inscriptions. Do you notice any patterns? (Pg. 48)

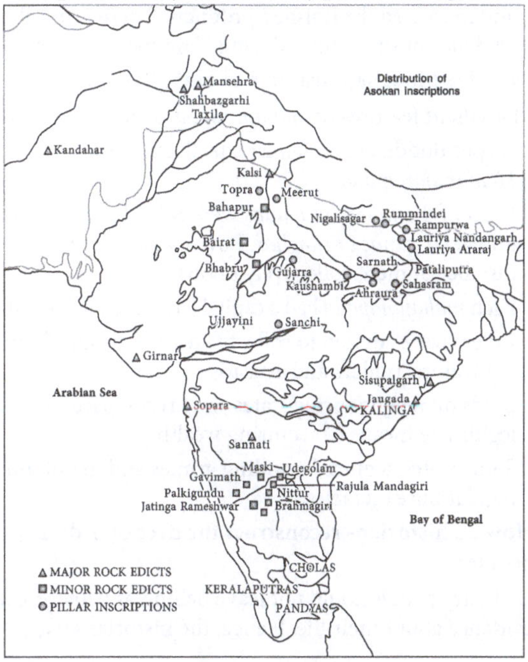

Ans. Yes, there are patterns in the location of Asokan inscriptions on the map. The inscriptions have been found in so many places and they are located on the trade routes majorly. The minor rock edicts are found in the Asoka territory including the Hindu Kush region.

Answer in 100-150 Words

1. Discuss the evidence of craft production in early historic cities. In what ways is this different from the evidence of Harappan cities?

Ans. Evidences of Craft Production in Early Historic Cities

Archaeologists have found many artefacts from different sites in early historic cities, so it is clear that craft production flourished in early historic cities. These evidences were

- A wide range of artefacts have been recovered from the historic cities which include five pottery bowls and dishes with glossy finish known as Northern Black Polished Ware. It shows that they were used by rich people.
- Ornaments, tools, weapons, vessels, figurines made of a wide range of materials such as gold, silver, copper, bronze, ivory, glass, shell and terracotta were also found.
- Inscriptions were also found which tells us about people who lived in towns with different occupations.

Differences between the Evidences of Early Historic Cities and Harappan Cities

- The artefacts and crafts made of iron were unknown during the bronze age of Harappan civilisation, but they were known during the period of early historic cities.
- In Historic cities, there were guilds or *shrenis* who probably procured raw materials, regulated production and marketed the finished products. There is hardly any evidence of such guilds during Harappan Civilisation.

2. Describe the salient features of *mahajanapadas*.

Ans. The salient features of *mahajanapadas* were as follows

- As per Buddhist and Jaina texts, there were 16 *mahajanapadas*.
- Most of the *mahajanapadas* were ruled by kings, some known as *ganas or sanghas*. Power was shared by number of men, collectively known as *rajas*.
- Each *mahajanapada* had a capital city which was fortified.
- Rulers were advised to collect taxes and tribute from cultivators, traders and artisans.
- Raids on neighbouring states were recognised as a legitimate means of acquiring wealth.
- Some states acquired standing armies and maintained regular bureaucracies.

3. How do historians reconstruct the lives of ordinary people?

Ans. Ordinary people could not leave behind any historical evidence about their life. Hence, the historians use a variety of sources to reconstruct the lives of the common people during ancient times.

These sources were

- Remains of houses and pottery gives us an idea of the lives of common men.
- Some scriptures talk about the relation between the monarch and the subjects. They tell us about taxes on the common men.
- Changing tools of craftsmen and farmers talk about the lifestyle of the people.
- Historians also depend upon folklore (*Jatakas* and *Panchatantras*) to reconstruct the lives of the people during ancient times.

Different types of foodgrains and animal bones found during excavation, gives us information about dietary practices of people.

4. Compare and contrast the list of things given to the Pandyan chief (Source 3) with those produced in the village of Danguna (Source 8). Do you notice any similarity or difference?

Ans. The gifts given by Pandyan Chief to Pandyan King include ivory, fragrant wood, fans made of the hair of deer, honey, sandalwood, red ochre, antimony, turmeric, cardamom, pepper, coconuts, mangoes, medicinal plants, fruits, onions, sugarcane, flowers, areca nut, bananas, baby tigers, lions, elephants, monkeys, bear, deer, fox, peacocks, musk cat, wild cocks, speaking parrots, etc.

On the other hand, the village of Danguna produced grass, animal hides, charcoal, fermanting liquors, salt, *khadira* trees, flowers and milk.

Similarity and Difference

The only similarity between the two was flowers.

The difference was that for the people of Danguna, the products were mostly cultivated or produced, while the gifts given to the Pandya Chief were purely the products of the forest.

5. List some of the problems faced by epigraphists.

Ans. Some of the important problems faced by epigraphists while deciphering inscriptions are as follows

- **Technical Limitations** Sometimes letters are very lightly engraved and thus making it difficult to be read.
- **Damaged or Missing Letters** Sometimes important letters are damaged or missing in the inscription. It makes the work of epigraphists more difficult.
- **Lack of Clarity** It is not always easy to be sure about the exact meaning of the words used in the inscriptions, some of which may be specific to a particular place or time. So, scholars are constantly debating on alternative ways to read inscriptions.

- **Undeciphered Inscriptions** Thousands of inscriptions have been discovered, but not all have been deciphered, published and translated. Many inscriptions were destroyed and only a fraction is available with us.
- **Non-relevance of Inscriptions** Inscriptions were composed in praise of kings and patrons. Not everything that is economically or politically important was recorded in the inscriptions, e.g. routine agricultural practice and the joys and sorrows of the common man were not mentioned in the inscriptions.

Write a short Essay (About 500 words) on the following

6. Discuss the main features of Mauryan administration. Which of these elements are evident in the Asokan inscriptions that you have studied?

Ans. The main features of Mauryan administration were as follows

- There were five major political centres in the empire i.e. the capital Pataliputra and the provincial centres of Taxila, Ujjayini, Tosali and Suvarnagiri, that are all mentioned in Asokan inscriptions.
- Due to vastness of the empire, administrative system of this empire was not uniform. It is likely that administrative control was strongest in areas around the capital and the provincial centres.
- Both Taxila and Ujjayini were situated on important long-distance trade routes, while Suvarnagiri (literally, the golden mountain) was possibly important for tapping the gold mines of Karnataka.
- Strong network of roads and communications were established.
- Committee and subcommittees were formed to run the administration and safety of boundaries. Megasthenes has mentioned that there were one committee with six subcommittees. These were

(i) first looked after the navy
(ii) The second managed transport and provisions
(iii) The third was responsible for foot-soldiers
(iv) The fourth was responsibile for horses
(v) The fifth was responsibile for chariots
(vi) The sixth was responsibile for elephants

- The activities of the second subcommittee were many, such as arranging for bullock carts to carry equipment and recruiting servants and artisans to look after the soldiers.

Asokan inscriptions mention all the elements of the administrative system of the Mauryan Empire. Thus, the features of the administration are evident in the inscriptions of the Asokan age.

7. This is a statement made by one of the best-known epigraphists of the twentieth century, DC Sircar : "There is no aspect of life, culture and activities of the Indians that is not reflected in inscriptions." Discuss.

Ans. This statement is correct as inscriptions are helpful in reflecting the aspect of life, culture and activities of the Indians in the following ways

- The ancient kings erected the inscriptions within the borders of their states. This help us to find out boundaries of kingdoms and their expansions.
- From inscriptions we also come to know about the names of various kings. For instance, titles like *devanampiya* and Piyadassi refers to Asoka.
- Inscriptions also helps us to understand about historical events. In one inscription we get the information about Kalinga War fought by Asoka. Apart from this, we also get to know about major life events of Samudragupta from Allahabad *Prashasti*.
- We also come to know about the conduct of kings through inscriptions. Asoka's *dhamma* policy can be understood through inscription wherein he talked about respect towards elders, generosity towards Brahmanas, treating slaves and servants kindly, etc.
- Through inscriptions, we also get information about land systems and administration. Some of these inscriptions were probably given as a record of the transaction to those who received the land.
- The inscription also gives us an idea about rural populations including Brahmanas and peasants.
- Through inscriptions we come to know about the languages used during that period. These languages include Sanskrit, Pali, Prakrit, Tamil, etc.

8. Discuss the notions of kingship that developed in the post-Mauryan period.

Ans. In the post-Mauryan age, the idea of kingship got associated with the divine theory of state. Now, the monarchs began to talk about divine sanction to rule the people. Kushana rulers propagated the idea of the divine rule. They ruled from Central Asia to Western India. The concept of kingship based on the dynasties is discussed below

- **Kushana Kings** Kushana kings called themselves *devaputra* which means a divine status. They built large statues of themselves in temples.
- **Gupta Rulers** Another development of kingship is found during the Gupta dynasty. It was a period of large-sized states. Such states were dependent on *samantas* who sometimes became powerful enough to usurp the power of kings also.

Literature, coins and inscriptions help us in creating a history of those days. Very often poets would describe monarchs often to praise them and also give insight into their history and kingship. A good example is of Harishena who praised Samudragupta.

9. To what extent were agricultural practices transformed in the period under consideration?

Ans. Agricultural practices were transformed from sixth century BCE onwards because of the increasing burden of taxes imposed by the state. The kings demanded a lot of taxes from the subjects. In order to fulfil this demand for more taxes, the farmers started finding new means to increase the production of their crops. These new means were

Shift Towards Plough Agriculture Agricultural practices were significantly transformed by the shift to plough agriculture which spread in fertile alluvial river valleys such as those of the Ganga and the Kaveri.

Use of Iron-Tipped Ploughshare In the areas of high rainfall, the use of iron-tipped ploughshare turned the alluvial soil into highly fertile ground.

Use of Paddy Transplantation Paddy transplantation technique was used in which seeds were first broadcast and then the saplings were transplanted in waterlogged fields. This ensured a higher ratio of survival of saplings and higher yields. It dramatically increased the production of the paddy crop. However, this process requires a large amount of manual labour.

Use of Irrigation to Increase Productivity Irrigation was another strategy to increase agricultural production.

The irrigation was mostly done through wells and tanks, but sometimes canals were used. Communities as well as individuals organised the construction of irrigation works. The process of construction of irrigation facilities was often recorded on inscriptions by the kings.

The use of such technologies led to an increase in agricultural production which ultimately led to a growing inequality amongst people engaged in agriculture.

The large landholders and village headmen emerged as powerful figures who exercised control over smaller cultivators and agricultural labourers. Thus, there was a remarkable change in the field of agriculture during this period.

10. Compare Map 1 and 2 and list the *mahajanapadas* that might have been included in the Mauryan Empire. Are any Asokan inscriptions found in these areas?

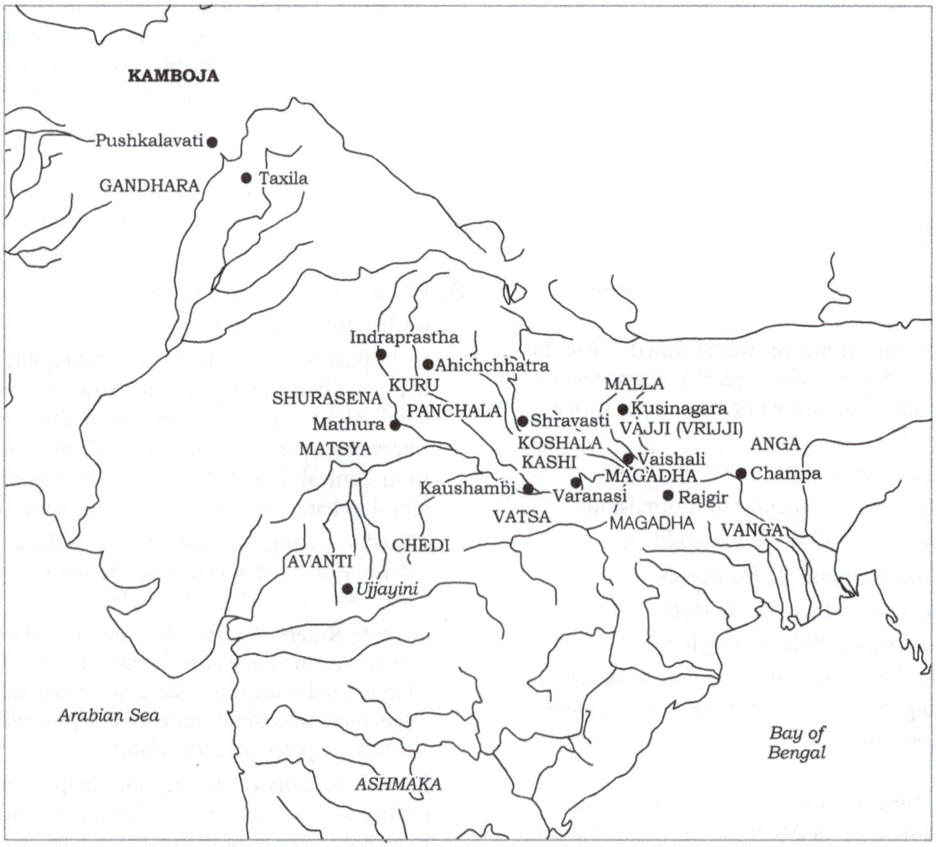

Map 1

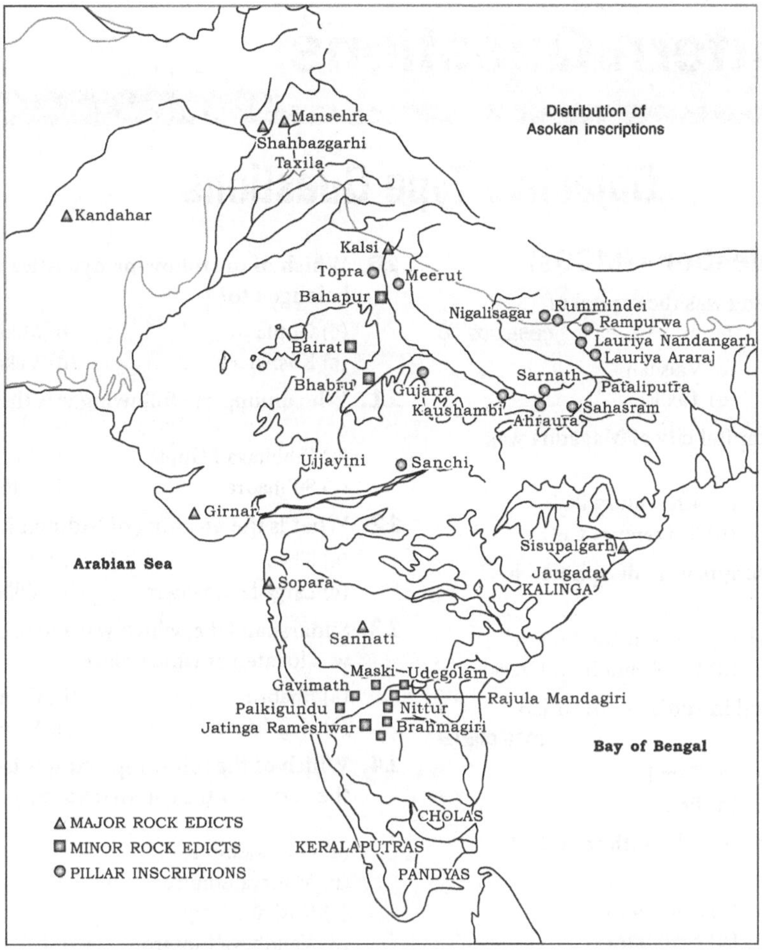

Map 2

Ans. All the *mahajanapadas* have been included in the Mauryan Empire.
Yes, Asokan inscriptions have been found in these areas. These areas are Ashmaka (Sannati), Magadha (Sarnath), Kuru (Meerut) and Gandhara (Kandahar).

Exam Pattern Questions

Objective Type Questions

Multiple Choice Questions (MCQs)

1. Which one of the following was the capital of Magadha? **CBSE 2024 C**

(a) Rajagaha (b) Vaishali
(c) Ujjain (d) Taxila

2. During the ………, the capital city of Magadha was shifted to Pataliputra.

(a) 5th century BCE (b) 4th century BCE
(c) 2nd century BCE (d) 3rd century CE

3. Which of the following scripts were deciphered by James Prinsep?

(a) Bengali and Devanagari (b) Sanskrit and Prakrit
(c) Brahmi and Kharosthi (d) Greek and Indo-Greek

4. Earliest inscriptions found in India are in which language? **CBSE Diksha**

(a) Pali (b) Tamil
(c) Sanskrit (d) Prakrit

5. Who among the following was the author of the book '*Arthashastra*'?

(a) *Bimbisara* (b) *Ajatshattu*
(c) Chanakya (d) *Bindusara*

6. Who among the following was a Greek Ambassador to the court of Chandragupta Maurya ? **CBSE Term I 2021**

(a) Kautilya (b) Fa-Xian
(c) Megasthenes (d) Harisena

7. Which one of the following is not a sub-committee formed by Mauryans for coordinating military activity, as mentioned by Megasthenes? **CBSE Diksha**

(a) Sub-committee for navy
(b) Sub-committee for horses
(c) Sub-committee for elephants
(d) Sub-committee for cannons

8. Which one of the following was not the provincial centre of Mauryan Empire? **CBSE Diksha**

(a) Taxila (b) Sopara
(c) Ujjayini (d) Suvarnagiri

9. In which of the following language has 'Allahabad Pillar Inscription' been composed? **CBSE Term I 2021**

(a) Prakrit (b) Hindi
(c) Sanskrit (d) Brahmi

10. Which of the following dynasties queen Prabhavati belonged to? **CBSE 2023**

(a) Gupta (b) Maurya
(c) Kushana (d) Vakataka

11. Who among the following was the Vakataka queen ? **CBSE 2024 C**

(a) Prabhavati Gupta (b) Gautami
(c) Subhadra (d) Dithya

12. What is the meaning of 'Adimai'? **CBSE Diksha**

(a) Slave (b) Ploughmen
(c) Large landowners (d) Village headman

13. Sudarshan lake, which was repaired by Rudradaman, was located at which place? **CBSE Diksha**

(a) Bhabru (b) Girnar
(c) Kaushambi (d) Kandahar

14. Which of the following empires issued gold coins for the very first time in first century CE? **CBSE SQP Term I 2021**

(a) Gupta Empire
(b) Maurya Empire
(c) Kushana Empire
(d) Yaudheya Empire

15. Which traveller when visited Pataliputra in seventh century CE, found it in ruins? **CBSE Diksha**

(a) Fa Xian (b) Xuan Zang
(c) Megasthenes (d) Strabo

16. What is the meaning of the title *devanampiya* adopted by Asoka?

(a) Pleasant to be hold
(b) Beloved of the Gods
(c) Both (a) and (b)
(d) Neither (a) nor (b)

17. Select the correct statement.

(a) Mahavira and Buddha did not belong to *ganas.*
(b) Megasthenes deciphered Kharosthi and Brahmi scripts.
(c) Early Tamil Sangam texts contain poems.
(d) Chandragupta Maurya conquered Kalinga.

18. What does the word Janapada means? **CBSE Diksha**

(a) An urban settlement of people.
(b) Capital cities which were often fortified.
(c) The land where a Jana, a people, clan or tribe settles.
(d) None above these

19. **Which of the following statements is true with reference to Mahajanapadas?** **CBSE Diksha**

(a) They were 18 in number
(b) They had capital city, which were often fortified
(c) There were monarchies only
(d) They were located in the Deccan Plateau

20. **Which one of the following is not the factor for being Magadha the most powerful mahajanapada in 600 BCE ?** **CBSE Diksha**

(a) Fine quality of beads found in forests of Magadha .
(b) Accessibility to iron-ore mines.
(c) Ganga and its tributaries for cheap and convenient communication.
(d) Ambitious kings.

21. **Which of the following statements regarding 'Gahapati' is not correct?** **CBSE Term I 2021**

(a) A gahapati was the owner or head of the household.
(b) The term is often used in Pali texts to designate large landholders.
(c) He was not the owner of resources such as land and minerals.
(d) 'Gahapati' was used as a marker of status for men belonging to urban elite.

22. **The *manusmriti* was compiled ....**

(a) Under Satavahanas rulers
(b) between second century CE and sixth century CE
(c) between second century BCE and second century CE
(d) None of the above

23. **What are Votive inscriptions?** **CBSE Diksha**

(a) A record gifts made to religious institutions.
(b) A record gifts made to officials by king.
(c) A land grant to a Brahman.
(d) A land grant to samantas.

24. **Prabhavati Gupta is best known for which of the following roles?** **CBSE 2025**

(a) Wife of Ashoka and Promoter of Buddhist Sangha
(b) Queen of Mauryan Empire and Promoter of Buddhism
(c) Wife of Samudragupta and Poet of the Gupta Era
(d) Daughter of Chandragupta-II and Wife of Vakataka King

25. **Which of the following options are correct regarding Magadha ?** **CBSE 2024**

I. Magadha was the most powerful Mahajanapada.
II. Rajgaha was the capital of Magadha.
III. Magadha was in a semi-arid area.
IV. Magadha was rich in natural resources.

Options

(a) I, II and IV are correct (b) I, II and III are correct
(c) I, III and IV are correct (d) II, III and IV are correct

26. **Read the following statements about the Mauryan Empire.** **CBSE 2024**

I. The growth of Magadha culminated in the emergence of the Mauryan Empire.
II. Chandragupta Maurya founded the Mauryan Empire.
III. Kautilya was the successor of Chandragupta Maurya.
IV. Asoka was the son of Chandragupta Maurya.

Which of the above statements are correct ?

(a) I and III (b) I and II
(c) III and IV (d) II and III

27. **Consider the following statements about Prabhavati Gupta and choose the correct option.** **CBSE 2024**

(i) She was the daughter of Chandragupta Maurya.
(ii) She was married to a Vakataka ruler.
(iii) She had independent access to resources.
(iv) She gave land grants to people.

Options

(a) (i), (ii) and (iii) (b) (ii), (iii) and (iv)
(c) (i), (iii) and (iv) (d) (i), (ii) and (iv)

28. **Arrange the pillar inscriptions of Asoka in the following locations in correct sequence from East to West**

(i) Kaushambi (ii) Meerut
(iii) Sahasaram (iv) Sarnath

Codes

(a) (ii), (i), (iv), (iii) (b) (iii), (i), (iv), (ii)
(c) (iii), (iv), (i), (ii) (d) (iii), (ii), (iv), (i)

29. **Arrange the following events in correct chronological sequence from the earliest to the latest.**

(i) Arabs conquer Sind
(ii) Beginning of Gupta rule
(iii) End of Mauryan Empire
(iv) Alexander's invasion

Codes

(a) (i), (ii), (iv), (iii) (b) (ii), (iii), (i), (iv)
(c) (iii), (iv), (ii), (i) (d) (iv), (iii), (ii), (i)

30. **Arrange the following in chronological order and choose the correct option from the following.**

(i) Rule of Ashoka
(ii) Invasion of Alexander
(iii) Beginning of Gupta dynasty
(iv) Rise of Chalukyas in Karnataka

Codes

(a) (i), (iii), (ii), (iv) (b) (iv), (ii), (i), (iii)
(c) (ii), (i), (iii), (iv) (d) (iii), (iv), (ii), (i)

31. Which one of the following pairs is incorrectly matched?

(a) Magadha – Most powerful *mahajanapada* between 6th and 4th century BCE
(b) Panchala – A *mahajanapada*
(c) Rajgir – Capital city of a *mahajanapada*
(d) Vaishali – A *mahajanapada*

32. Arrange the following events in a chronological order and choose the correct option. **CBSE 2024**

I. Beginning of Gupta rule
II. End of Mauryan Empire
III. Rise of Pallavas in Tamil Nadu
IV. Rise of Harshavardhana as a king of Kannauj

Options

(a) I, III, II and IV (b) II, I, III and IV
(c) III, IV, I and II (d) IV, I, II and III

33. Arrange the following in chronological order and choose the correct option. **CBSE 2024**

I. Rule of Asoka
II. Rule of Mahapadma Nanda
III. Rule of Harshavardhana
IV. Rule of Samudragupta

Options

(a) I, III, IV, II (b) II, I, IV, III
(c) III, II, I, IV (d) IV, III, I, II

34. Which one of the following pairs is correctly matched?

(a) Chandragupta – Grandson of Asoka
(b) Kautilya – Also known as Brahmana
(c) Principles of *dhamma* – Simple and almost universally applicable
(d) A principal of *dhamma* – Respect for your own religion

35. Which of the following is correctly matched location with its properties?

(a) Ujjayini – Centre of commercial, cultural and political activity
(b) Puhar – On a land trade route
(c) Pataliputra – On a riverine trade route
(d) Mathura – On a sea trade route

36. Identify the name of the person from the information given below.

(i) He was one of the most famous ruler known from Buddha texts.
(ii) He was the first ruler who inscribed his messages to his subjects and officials on stone surfaces-natural rocks as well as polished pillars.

Options

(a) Kautilya (b) Bindusara
(c) Chandragupta Maurya (d) Asoka

37. Identify the ruler of ancient India with the help of the given information and choose the correct option.

(i) He got the title of Devanampiya.
(ii) He distributed a portion of Buddha's relics for stupas.
(iii) He was the first ruler who inscribed messages on rocks and pillars. **CBSE 2024**

Options

(a) Samudragupta (b) Harshavardhana
(c) Rudradaman (d) Asoka

38. Study the following statements carefully. **CBSE Term I 2021**

(i) An officer in the mint of East India Company.
(ii) He deciphered Asokan Bramhi in 1838.

Identify this person from the given options.

(a) Peter Mundy
(b) James Prinsep
(c) Marco Polo
(d) Ernest Mackay

39. Identify the name of the historian from the following information.

(i) He deciphered Brahmi and Kharosthi, two scripts used in the earliest inscriptions and coins.
(ii) His findings gave a new direction to investigations into early Indian political history.

Options

(a) Henry Prinsep
(b) James Prinsep
(c) Alexander Cunningham
(d) Charles Edward

40. Identify the ruler of the ancient India with the help of following information. **CBSE SQP 2024**

(i) He was a prominent Shaka ruler.
(ii) He rebuilt Sudarshana Lake in the second century CE.
(iii) He showcased his engagement with Sanskritic traditions.

Options

(a) Vikramaditya II (b) Bhaskaravarman
(c) Bimbisara (d) Rudradaman

41. Identify the ancient dynasty with the help of the following information. **CBSE 2024**

(i) They issued spectacular gold coins.
(ii) Their history can be reconstructed through Prashastis.
(iii) Harisena was the court poet of one of its rulers.

Options

(a) Chola dynasty (b) Satavahana dynasty
(c) Kushana dynasty (d) Gupta dynasty

42. **Complete the following with the correct option regarding books and their respective languages.**

***Jatakas* : Pali :: *Silappadikaram*: ....**

(a) Sanskrit (b) Tamil (c) Kharosthi (d) Sharada

Assertion-Reason

43. **Assertion** (A) In inscriptions Asoka refers to himself as Devanampiya.

Reason (R) It means son of soil.

Codes

(a) Both A and R are true and R is the correct explanation of A
(b) Both A and R are true, but R is not the correct explanation of A
(c) A is true, but R is false
(d) A is false, but R is true

44. **Assertion** (A) Chandragupta Maurya was the founder of Mauryan Empire.

Reason (R) The growth of Magadha culminated in the emergence of Mauryan Empire.

Codes

(a) Both A and R are true and R is the correct explanation of A
(b) Both A and R are true, but R is not the correct explanation of A
(c) A is true, but R is false
(d) A is false, but R is true

45. **Assertion** (A) Asoka inscribed his messages to his subjects and officials on stone surfaces.

Reason (R) He wanted to proclaim what religion should be followed by all.

Codes

(a) Both A and R are true and R is the correct explanation of A
(b) Both A and R are true, but R is not the correct explanation of A
(c) A is true, but R is false
(d) A is false, but R is true

46. **Assertion** (A) Very large size statues of Kushana rulers have been found from many places.

Reason (R) The Kushana rulers considered themselves as son of God.

Codes

(a) Both A and R are true and R is the correct explanation of A
(b) Both A and R are true, but R is not the correct explanation of A
(c) A is true, but R is false
(d) A is false, but R is true

47. **Assertion** (A) Historians use a variety of sources to understand developments over the ages.

Reason (R) These sources include inscription, texts, coins, sculptures and other visual materials.

Codes

(a) Both A and R are true and R is the correct explanation of A
(b) Both A and R are true, but R is not the correct explanation of A
(c) A is true, but R is false
(d) A is false, but R is true

48. **Assertion** (A) There are limits to what epigraphy can reveal.

Reason(R) Routine agricultural practices and the joys and sorrows of daily existence find no mention in inscriptions. **CBSE Diksha**

Codes

(a) Both A and R are true and R is the correct explanation of A
(b) Both A and R are true but R is not the correct explanation of A
(c) A is true, but R is false
(d) A is false, but R is true

Match the Following

49.

List I		List II	
A.	Mahapadma Nanda	1.	Kushana dynasty
B.	Kanishka	2.	Magadha
C.	Samudragupta	3.	Maurya dynasty
D.	Asoka	4.	Gupta dynasty

Codes

	A	B	C	D		A	B	C	D
(a)	1	2	3	4	(b)	3	1	2	4
(c)	4	3	1	2	(d)	2	1	4	3

50.

List I (Ancient Mahajanpadas)		List II (Present Region)	
A.	Magadh	1.	Qandhar (Eastern Afghanistan)
B.	Avanti	2.	Ayodhya (Uttar Pradesh)
C.	Gandhara	3.	Patna (Bihar)
D.	Koshala	4.	Ujjain (Madhya Pradesh)

Codes

	A	B	C	D		A	B	C	D
(a)	3	2	1	4	(b)	4	2	1	3
(c)	3	4	1	2	(d)	2	1	3	4

51.

	List I (Advances in epigraphy)		List II (Approximate dates)
A.	First issue of Epigraphia Carnatica	1.	1784
B.	First issue of Epigraphia Indica	2.	1838
C.	Founding of the Asiatic Society (Bengal)	3.	1886
D.	Decipherment of Brahmi by Prinsep	4.	1888

Codes

	A	B	C	D		A	B	C	D
(a)	3	1	4	2	(b)	2	4	3	1
(c)	4	3	1	2	(d)	3	4	1	2

Picture Based Questions

52. Identify the given image from the following options.

(a) Lion capital (b) Sculpture of Kushanas
(c) Sanchi Sculpture (d) Prayaga Prashasti

53. Identify the given image from the following options. **CBSE SQP 2022**

(a) Sculpture of a Gupta king
(b) Sculpture of a Maurya king
(c) Sculpture of a Kushana king
(d) Sculpture of a Chola king

54. Study this figure of Asokan Inscription'.

The first person to decipher, the 'Asokan Inscription' was

(a) James Prinsep
(b) Alexander Cunningham
(c) Colin Mackenzie
(d) R.E.M. Wheeler

55. Script mentioned in image is found in Ashokan inscription. Identify the name of the script

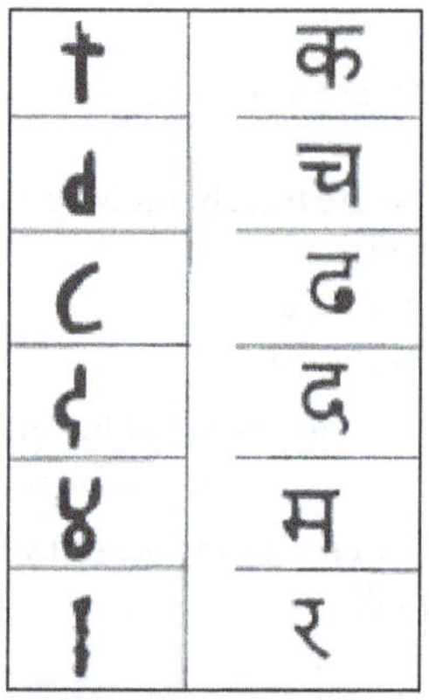

(a) Brahmi Script (b) Kharoshti Script
(c) Roman Script (d) Indus Script

56. Identify the given image from the following options.

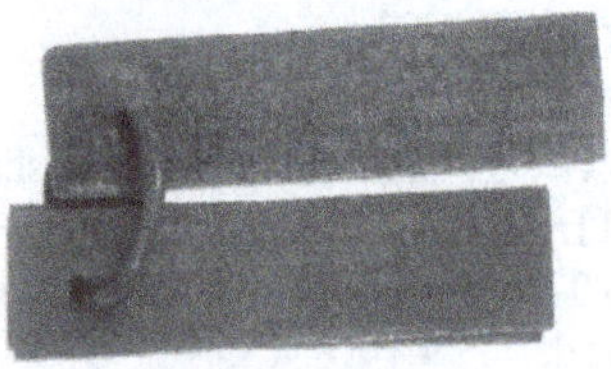

(a) Inscription from Karnataka
(b) Manuscript from Pataliputra
(c) Kushana copperplate
(d) Asokan inscription

Answers

1. (a) Rajagaha
2. (b) 4th century BCE
3. (c) Brahmi and Kharosthi
4. (d) Prakrit
5. (c) Chanakya
6. (c) Megasthenes
7. (d) Sub-committee for cannons
8. (b) Sopara
9. (c) Sanskrit
10. (a) Gupta
11. (a) Prabhavati Gupta
12. (a) Slave
13. (b) Girnar
14. (c) Kushana Empire
15. (b) Xuan Zang
16. (c) Both (a) and (b)
17. (c) Early Tamil Sangam texts contain poems.
18. (c) The land where a Jana, a people, clan or tribe settles.
19. (b) They had capital city, which were often fortified.
20. (a) Fine quality of beads found in forests of Magadha.
21. (c) He was not the owner of resources such as land and minerals.
22. (c) between second century BCE and second century CE
23. (a) A record gifts made to religious institutions.
24. (d) Daughter of Chandragupta-II and Wife of Vakataka King
25. (b) I, II and III are correct
26. (b) I and II
27. (b) (ii), (iii) and (iv)
28. (c) (iii), (iv), (i), (ii)
29. (d) (iv), (iii), (ii), (i)
30. (c) (ii), (i), (iii), (iv)
31. (b) II, I, III and IV
32. (b) II, I, IV, III
33. (d) Vaishali – A *mahajanapada*
34. (c) Principles of *dhamma* –Simple and almost universally applicable
35. (c) Pataliputra –On a riverine trade route
36. (d) Asoka
37. (d) Asoka
38. (b) James Prinsep
39. ((b) James Prinsep
40. (d) Rudradaman
41. (d) Gupta dynasty
42. (b) Tamil
43. (c) A is true, but R is false
44. (b) Both A and R are true, but R is not the correct explanation of A
45. (c) A is true, but R is false
46. (a) Both A and R are true and R is the correct explanation of A
47. (b) Both A and R are true, but R is not the correct explanation of A
48. (a) Both A and R are true and R is the correct explanation of A
49. (d)
50. (c)
51. (d)
52. (a) Lion Capital
53. (c) Sculpture of a Kushana king
54. (a) James Prinsep
55. (a) Brahmi Script
56. (a) Inscription from Karnataka

Subjective Questions

Short Answer Type Questions

1. Describe any three features of the Mahajanapadas.
Compartment 2024

Ans. The three features of the Mahajanapadas are as follows

- Most Mahajanapadas were ruled by kings, but some were republics (called "ganas" or "sanghas"), where power was shared among a group of men, often referred to as rajas. These oligarchies were notable for their collective governance, where decisions were made collectively rather than by a single ruler.
- Each Mahajanapada had a capital city, often fortified for protection. These fortified cities were important centers for administration, trade and defense. They required significant resources to maintain, especially when armies and bureaucracies started to emerge within these states.
- The Mahajanapadas were increasingly reliant on resources to sustain their fortified cities, armies, and growing bureaucracies. Land and other resources were often controlled by the ruling elite.

  In some ganas, like Vajji, the rajas likely controlled resources collectively, which helped maintain the power structures of these oligarchies.

2. "The 6th century BCE was a period of emergence of early states, empires and diverse thoughts in the early Indian history." Justify the statement.

Ans The 6th century BCE was an important period in early Indian history for the emergence of states, empires and diverse thoughts due to the following reasons

- This period saw the rise of states and empires from chiefdoms to *mahajanapadas*. Smaller tribal societies called 'janapadas' merged into larger, more organised states known as '*mahajanapadas*'. Examples include Magadha, Kosala and Kuru.
- This period also saw the developing of diverse thoughts which challenged traditional order.
- New ideas emerged, questioning the dominance of the vedas and the rigid caste system.
- Birth of new Philosophies, this period saw the rise of Jainism and Buddhism, with Mahavira and Gautama Buddha offering alternative spiritual paths.

3. "Magadha was the most powerful *mahajanapada*." Examine the statement. CBSE SQP 2022

Or Write any three reasons for Magadha becoming most powerful *mahajanapada* of its time. CBSE Diksha

Or Describe any three causes of the growth of Magadha as a powerful Mahajanapada. CBSE 2024 C

Ans. Magadha (in present-day Bihar) was the most powerful among the sixteen *mahajanapadas* in the following ways

- Magadha was a region where agriculture was especially productive.
- Also, the river Ganga and its tributaries provided a means of cheap and convenient communication.
- Besides, the iron mines were easily accessible. It provided resources for tools and weapons.
- Ambitious kings like Bimbisara, Ajatasattu and Mahapadma Nanda have played an important role in implementing policies of Magadha.
- Elephants, which were an important component of the army, were found in forests in the region.
- The capital was shifted from Rajagaha to Pataliputra, on the routes of communication along the Ganga.

4. State any three sources used by historians to reconstruct the history of Mauryan Empire.

Or What type of sources have been used to reconstruct the history of the Mauryan Empire? CBSE Diksha

Or Analyse the various sources to know about the Mauryan Empire. CBSE 2024

Or "Historians have used a variety of sources to reconstruct the history of the Mauryan Empire". Explain the statement with examples. CBSE 2024, CBSE 2025

Ans. Historians have used a variety of sources to reconstruct the history of Mauryan Empire. These were

- Things found in archaeological excavation, specially sculpture are regarded as an important source.
- Contemporary works like writings of Megasthenes, Arthashastra by Chanakya are important sources regarding that period. They give us an idea about Mauryan administration.
- The Mauryas were also mentioned in later Buddhist, Jaina, Puranic and Sanskrit literature.
- Inscriptions found in different places gives us the idea of political boundary of the empire.

5. What does Megasthenes tell about the administration of Mauryan Empire?

Ans. Megasthenes was a Greek historian who came to India in the 4th century BC as an ambassador of Seleucus Nictor. He lived in the court of Chandragupta Maurya for about five years (302-298 BC). He has written an account of India and also that of Chandragupta's reign. Megasthenes has written in detail about Chandragupta Maurya's administration as well as Indian society in the Mauryan Period.

Megasthenes mentioned a committee with six subcommittees for military coordination activity. These were as follows

- One looked after the navy.
- Second managed transport and provisions.
- Third was responsible for foot-soldiers.
- Fourth was responsible for horses.
- Fifth was responsible for chariots.
- Sixth was responsible for elephants.

6. Classify the primary and secondary sources that helped the historians in understanding the Mauryan Empire. Competency Based Ques

Ans. Primary sources

- The inscriptions of Asoka on rocks and pillars.
- Contemporary works, such as the account of Megasthenes (a Greek ambassador to the court of Chandragupta Maurya), which survives in fragments.
- The *Arthashastra*, parts of which were probably composed by Kautilya or Chanakya, traditionally believed to be the minister of Chandragupta Maurya.
- Archaeological finds, especially sculpture.

Secondary sources

- The Mauryas are mentioned in later Buddhist, Jaina and Puranic literature, as well as in Sanskrit literary works.

7. "Ashokan inscriptions are the most significant sources to understand the administration of Ashoka". Explain the statement. CBSE 2025

Ans. Ashokan inscriptions are the most significant sources for understanding Ashoka's administration as they provide direct evidence of his governance, policies, and principles. These inscriptions, written in Prakrit, Greek, and Aramaic, highlight his commitment to Dhamma, welfare measures, judicial reforms, and efficient communication across the empire.

They also reflect his efforts in spreading Buddhist values and maintaining a just rule. The edicts, placed across the empire, reveal Ashoka's administrative control, moral governance, and the role of officials, making them crucial for historical analysis.

Mention any two pieces of evidence which referred to Asoka as the most popular ruler of the 6th century BCE.

8. Explain why the communication along both land and riverine routes was vital for the existence of the empire during the Mauryan period.

Ans. During the Mauryan period, communication along both land and riverine routes was vital for the existence of the empire because

- The Mauryan empire was a very vast empire. Thus, for political control, military activity and people's movement, both land and riverine routes were required.
- Communication through both roadways and waterways was necessary for trade and commerce and also for the exchange of ideas and knowledge etc.

9. 'Once the kings and chiefs attained power, they attempted to claim social status in a variety of ways.' State two ways in which the new kings who emerged between 1st century BCE to 1st century CE try to achieve this. Competency Based Que

Ans. Ways by which kings attempted to achieve social status are as follows

- **By building colossal statues of the rulers** Colossal statues of Kushana rulers have been found installed in a shrine at Mat near Mathura (Uttar Pradesh). Similar statues have been found in a shrine in Afghanistan as well. Some historians says that this indicates that the Kushanas considered themselves like God.
- By adopting titles like '*devaputra*' that signify god-like characteristics. This was inspired by Chinese rulers who called themselves sons of heaven.
- By commissioning *prashastis* to poets in praise of kings. For example, the Prayaga *Prashasti* composed in Sanskrit by Harishena, the court poet of Samudragupta.

10. Describe the economic and social conditions of the people living in rural areas from 600 BCE to 600 CE.

Ans. The economic and social conditions of the people living in rural areas from 600 BCE to 600 CE can be described as follows

Economic Conditions The iron-tipped ploughshare was used to turn the alluvial soil in areas which had high rainfall. Moreover, in some parts of the Ganga valley, production of paddy was dramatically increased by the introduction of transplantation.

Social Conditions The relations between the landlords and the farmers were not good, as landlords imposed huge taxes on farmers or common people. To pay these taxes, farmers tried to increase the agricultural production. According to Sanskrit legal texts, women were not given independent access to resources like land. But the women from royal family like Prabhavati Gupta, daughter of Chandragupta II had access to land.

11. How is the relationship between cultivators and the monarchy perceived by historians on the basis of land grants? State any three points. Competency Based Que

Ans. The relationship between cultivators and the monarchy was perceived by historians on the basis of land grants in the following ways

(i) Some feel that land grants were part of a strategy adopted by ruling lineages to extend agriculture to new areas.

(ii) Others suggest that land grants were indicative of weakening political power, as kings were losing control over their samantas, they tried to win allies by making grants of land.

(iii) As kings were losing power over the area, they gave more land grants to exert their power over an area.

12. Discuss the trade in the subcontinent during 6th century BCE.

Ans. From the 6th century BCE, land and river routes criss-crossed the subcontinent and extended in various directions over land into Central Asia and overseas. Those who transversed these routes included

Peddlers They probably travelled on foot.

Merchants They travelled with caravans of bullock carts and pack-animals.

Seafarers Their journey were risky but highly profitable.

A wide range of goods were carried from one place to another. These were salt, grain, cloth, metal ores and finished products, stone, timber, medicinal plants, etc. Pepper was in high demand in the Roman Empire. Textiles and medicinal plants were transported across the Arabian sea to the Mediterranean Sea.

13. **Based on gold coins unearthed in India, write insights about trade in the early common era. What are two possible reasons for the drop in coin usage after the sixth century?** **Competency Based Que**

Ans. Gold coins discovered in India from the early Common Era provide insights into the extensive trade connections of ancient India, especially with the Roman Empire. These coins, particularly from the Kushana and later Gupta empires, highlight the high value and volume of trade. Precious goods like spices, textiles, and precious stones were likely exchanged, marking India as a major player in global trade networks.

The decline in coinage usage after the sixth century could be due to several factors.

- The fall of the Western Roman Empire may have disrupted trade, leading to reduced demand for coins.
- Economic shifts within India, possibly moving towards barter systems and localised trade, may have decreased the need for a large-scale coin economy.

14. **What is the role played by coins in the decipherment of Kharosthi script?**

Ans. The coins played an important role in the decipherment of Kharosthi script were

- The coins of Indo-Greek kings who ruled over the North-Western part of the subcontinent in the second century were analysed by the epigraphists.
- The Indo-Greek coins contain the names of kings written in Greek and Kharosthi scripts. The Kharosthi script was compared with the Greek one. The European scholars who could read Greek compared it with Kharosthi. There were a few similarities between Kharoshti and Greek scripts e.g. letter 'a' was used in both scripts for writing names such as 'Apollodotus'.
- James Prinsep identified the language of Kharosthi as Prakrit. After that, it became possible to read longer inscriptions easily.

15. **Critically examine the limitations of the inscriptional evidences in understanding political and economic history of India.**

Or **Write any three limitations of inscriptional evidence.** **CBSE Diksha**

Ans. The limitations of inscriptional evidences in understanding the political and economic history of India are as follows

(i) Several thousand inscriptions were discovered, but not all of them were deciphered or translated.

(ii) The context of the inscriptions describes the perspective of the person who commissioned it. For instance, routine agricultural practices, the joys and sorrows of common people were not mentioned in these inscriptions.

(iii) From the mid-20th century, historians became more interested in political and economic changes in society. This led to fresh investigations of old sources. Here, inscriptions had their own limitations to interpret political and economical history of India.

Long Answer Type Questions

1. **How do historians come to known about Maurya period? Explain the administrative structure of Mauryan Empire.** **CBSE 2023**

Or **Explain the main features of the Mauryan administration.**

Or **Explain any four sources to reconstruct the history of Mauryas. Examine the system of Mauryan administration.**

Or **What types of sources have been used to reconstruct the history of Mauryan Empire? Explain with suitable examples.**

Ans. Here are four key sources for reconstructing the history of the Mauryas

(i) **Ashokan Inscriptions** Emperor Ashoka's inscriptions on rocks and pillars across the empire reveal governance practices, administrative policies, and the promotion of dhamma, or moral values.

(ii) **Literary Texts** The Arthashastra, linked to Kautilya (Chanakya), provides insight into Mauryan political strategies, economic policies and administrative systems. Buddhist and Jaina texts also provide reference of Mauryan rulers, reflecting the period's religious influence.

(iii) **Foreign Accounts** Megasthenes, a Greek ambassador at Chandragupta Maurya's court, documented aspects of Mauryan society, governance and economic life, offering a valuable external viewpoint.

(iv) **Archaeological Finds** Sculptures, monuments, and other material remains provide evidence of the Mauryan Empire's architectural style, artistic achievements, and the extent of its economic prosperity.

Key features of the Mauryan administration include

(i) **Centralised Governance** The Mauryan Empire was highly centralised, with Pataliputra as the capital and other major administrative centers in Taxila, Ujjayini, Tosali, and Suvarnagiri, which helped maintain control across vast territories.

(ii) **Bureaucratic System** The Mauryan administration had a complex bureaucracy with officials overseeing various functions, including revenue collection, trade regulation, and military coordination. Megasthenes noted that the empire was divided into committees handling different aspects of governance.

(iii) **Provincial Administration** The empire was divided into provinces, each managed by a governor who represented the central authority. Provincial centers played vital roles in local governance and maintaining law and order.

(iv) **Military Organisation** The Mauryans maintained a large standing army, with departments managing infantry, cavalry, elephants, and chariots, ensuring robust defense and territorial expansion.

(v) **Promotion of Dhamma** Ashoka appointed dhamma officers to promote social and moral values, fostering harmony among diverse populations.

2. 'Communication from the central capital to the capitals of provinces was vital for the existence of the Mauryan Empire.' Why were provincial capitals important to the Mauryan Empire? How was communication between the central capital and provinces accomplished?
Competency Based Que

Ans. The provincial capitals were important to the Mauryan Empire because

- Historians argue that the Mauryan Empire was too diverse to rule effectively from the central capital alone. Thus provincial capitals have been established to give more importance to the administration of the empire.
- These provincial capitals were chosen so as to be useful for the administration. Some were situated on important long-distance trade routes, and others were located near important natural resources.

Communication between the central capital and provinces was accomplished in the following ways

- Communication between capital and the provinces happened along both land and riverine routes.
- Journeys from the centre to the provinces took a long time. So provisions and protection had to be provided for the journey.
- The army was an important means for ensuring the protection of people undertaking the journey from the capital to the provinces.

3. Describe briefly the sources used for reconstructing the history of the Gupta rulers.

Ans. The Gupta rulers established a vast empire in the 4th century which was reconstructed from various sources. These sources are explained in the following ways

Inscriptions These are writings engraved on hard surfaces like stones, metals etc.

These are generally composed in praise of kings in particular, and patrons in general by the poets. For example, Allahabad Pillar Inscription or *Prayaga Prashasti* was composed in Sanskrit by Harishena, the court poet of Samudragupta in praise of him.

Coins These are also an important source of reconstructing the history of Gupta rulers, as they include elements like scripts, images and the context in which they are found. Some of the most spectacular gold coins were issued by the Gupta rulers. These coins facilitated long distance transactions from which the expansion of trade and commerce was known.

Literature Historians attempted to draw factual information from the compositions of *Prashastis*. These were written in praise of kings and patrons. Thus, historians have to constantly assess the statements made in inscriptions to judge whether they are true, or exaggerations.

Prashastis They contribute prominently in reconstructing the history of the Gupta rulers, e.g. Prayaga *Prashasti* was composed in Sanskrit for Samudragupta.

4. Explain the system of land grants and trade from 600 BCE to 600 CE.

Ans. Land Grants

From the early centuries, grants of land were recorded in inscriptions. Some inscriptions were recorded on copper plates. The records that have survived give us the following information

- Land grants were given to religious institutions or to Brahmanas. The Brahmanas were usually exempted from paying land revenue and other dues to the king. The Brahmanas were often given the right to collect these dues from the local people.
- Women were not supposed to have independent access to resources like land. But aristocratic women like Prabhavati Gupta, daughter of Chandragupta II, had access to land. All the people in rural areas had to obey the new lord of the village and pay him all the taxes.
- Some historians claim that land grants were indicative of weakening political power, as kings were losing control over their *samantas*. Sometimes kings tried to win allies by making grants of land.
- Land grants provide some insight into the relationship between cultivators and the state.

System of Trade

The system of trade from 600 BCE to 600 CE can be explained in the following ways

- Land and river routes criss-crossed the subcontinent and extended in different directions from the 6th century BCE. The rulers tried to control these routes by offering protection for a price.
- These different routes were transversed by the peddlers who travelled on foot. But the merchants travelled with caravans of bullock carts and pack-animals.

- There were seafarers. Their journey were risky but highly profitable.
- Successful merchants, designated as *masattuvan* in Tamil and *setthis* and *satavahanas* in Prakrit, were very rich.
- A wide range of goods were carried from one place to another. These were salt, grain, cloth, metal ores and finished products, stone, timber, medicinal plants, spices and pepper and textiles. All these were transported across the Arabian Sea to the Mediterranean Sea.

5. Explain the agricultural practices followed by the cultivators to increase productivity from c. 600 BCE to 600 CE.

Ans. Between c. 600 BCE and 600 CE, Indian agricultural practices evolved significantly, especially in the fertile river valleys. Key developments in agriculture practices included

- **Iron Tools** Iron-tipped ploughshares enabled cultivators to work on nutrient-rich alluvial soils, expanding arable land, especially in the Ganga valley, where iron resources were accessible.
- **Paddy Transplantation** In the Ganga valley, farmers adopted the technique of paddy transplantation. Instead of direct seeding, saplings were first grown and then transplanted into waterlogged fields. This labour-intensive method increased crop yields due to a higher sapling survival rate and better control over spacing.
- **Irrigation Systems** In semi-arid regions, where water was less reliable, communities and influential individuals, including kings, constructed wells, tanks and canals. These irrigation systems provided a stable water supply during dry seasons, encouraging farming in previously challenging areas.
- **Agricultural Surplus and Urban Growth** Enhanced agricultural productivity led to a significant surplus, which supported the growth of towns and urban centers. The surplus allowed for more non-agricultural professions, fueling trade networks and encouraging economic diversity.
- **Regional Variation in Techniques** The adoption of these techniques varied across regions. In semi-arid and hilly areas, hoe-based agriculture persisted due to the unsuitability of the terrain for ploughs.

However, these advancements in agriculture were not uniformly applied across all regions. For instance, in semi-arid and hilly areas, hoe-based agriculture persisted due to the challenges of using ploughs. Overall, these innovations in agricultural techniques significantly contributed to the economic foundation of early historic Indian societies.

6. What do you mean by numismatics? How has the study of coins helped numismatists to reconstruct possible commercial networks? **CBSE Diksha**

Ans. Numismatics is the study of coins, including visual elements such as scripts and images, metallurgical analysis and the contexts in which they have been found.

The study of coins has helped numismatists to reconstruct possible commercial networks in the following ways

Introduction of Coinage for Trade Facilitation To some extent, exchanges were facilitated by the introduction of coinage. A wide range of goods were carried from one place to another like salt, grain, cloth, metal ores and finished products, stone, timber, medicinal plants, etc. These certainly required some kind of currency for exchange.

Hence, these led to the development of coinage across trading cultures.

Excavation of Punch-marked Coins across the Subcontinent Punch-marked coins made of silver and copper (16th century BCE onwards) were amongst the earliest to be minted and used. These have been recovered from excavations at a number of sites throughout the subcontinent. Numismatists have studied these and other coins to reconstruct possible commercial networks.

Kings, Merchants and Bankers as Issuing Authority Attempts were made to identify the symbols on punch-marked coins with specific ruling dynasties, including the Mauryas. It is also likely that merchants, bankers and people living in towns issued some of these coins.

Similarity of Kushana Coins with those of Greeks and Parthians The first gold coins were issued in 1st century CE by the Kushanas. These were virtually identical in weight with those issued by contemporary Roman emperors and the Parthian rulers of Iran. These coins have been found from several sites in North India and Central Asia.

Close Connections with the Roman Empire The widespread use of gold coins indicates the enormous value of the transactions that were taking place. Besides, hoards of Roman coins have been found from archaeological sites in South India. It is obvious that networks of trade were not confined within political boundaries. South India was not a part of the Roman Empire, but there were close connections through trade.

7. **"Although inscriptions provide strong evidence for reconstructing history yet there are few limitations to these evidences." Justify the statement.** Competency Based Que

Ans. Although inscriptions provide valuable evidence for reconstructing history yet there are few limitations to these evidences because

- Firstly, technical constraints such as lightly engraved letters, damages and missing parts make reconstructions uncertain.
- Secondly, the ambiguity of certain words and their contextual meanings can pose challenges in interpretation, potentially altering the intended message.
- Thirdly, despite the existence of several thousand inscriptions, only few have been deciphered, published and translated, limiting the scope of available historical records.
- Additionally, inscriptions often focus on politically and economically significant matters, ignoring daily activities, which are crucial for a comprehensive understanding of society. Historians and epigraphists must critically evaluate inscriptional statements to distinguish between truth, and exaggeration.

Thus, while inscriptions offer strong evidence, these limitations underscore the need for cautious interpretation and complementation with other historical sources for a more better understanding of the past.

Source Based Questions

Read the sources given below and answer the following questions.

1. Inscriptions CBSE SQP 2024

Inscriptions are writings engraved on hard surfaces such as stone, metal, or pottery. They usually record the achievements, activities, or ideas of those who commissioned them and include the exploits of kings, or donations made by women and men to religious institutions. Inscriptions are virtually permanent records, some of which carry dates.

Others are dated on the basis of palaeography or styles of writing, with a fair amount of precision. For instance, in c. 250 BCE the letter "a" was written like this (By c. 500 CE, it was written like this) The earliest inscriptions were in Prakrit, a name for languages used by ordinary people. Names of rulers such as Ajatasattu and Asoka, known from Prakrit texts and inscriptions, have been spelt in their Prakrit forms in this chapter. You will also find terms in languages such as Pali, Tamil and Sanskrit, which too were used to write inscriptions and texts. It is possible that people spoke in other languages as well, even though these were not used for writing.

(i) **What role does palaeography play in determining the age of inscriptions?**

Ans. Palaeography helps scholars determine the age of inscriptions by analysing the styles of writing used, allowing them to assign approximate dates based on changes in script over time.

(ii) **How do inscriptions contribute to our understanding of ancient societies and cultures?**

Ans. Inscriptions offer insights into ancient societies by documenting achievements, activities and beliefs. They reveal historical events, social structures, cultural practices, and linguistic evolution, enriching our understanding of past civilisations.

(iii) **What insights can be gained from studying the languages used in inscriptions across different regions and time periods?**

Ans. The insights that can be gained from studying the languages used in inscriptions across different regions and time periods are as follows

- **Cultural Exchange** Analysing inscription languages reveals interactions between different regions, highlighting how cultural and intellectual exchanges shaped societies over time.
- **Linguistic Evolution** Studying language changes in inscriptions shows how scripts and linguistic practices evolved, offering insights into historical developments and shifts in communication across periods and regions.

2. The Sudarshana (beautiful) lake in Gujarat

The Sudarshana lake was an artificial reservoir. We know about it from a rock inscription (second century CE) in Sanskrit, composed to record the achievements of the Shaka ruler Rudradaman.

The inscription mentions that the lake, with embankments and water channels, was built by a local governor during the rule of the Mauryas. However, a terrible storm broke the embankments and water gushed out of the lake. Rudradaman, who was then ruling in the area, claimed to have got the lake repaired using his own resources, without imposing any tax on his subjects.

Another inscription on the same rock (c. fifth century) mentions how one of the rulers of the Gupta dynasty got the lake repaired once again.

(i) **How do we get to know about the Sudarshana lake?**

(ii) **Why did this lake require repair?**

(iii) **Explain why did rulers make arrangements for irrigation.**

Ans. (i) We get to know about the Sudarshana lake from a rock inscription (c. second century CE) in Sanskrit, composed to record the achievements of the Shaka ruler, Rudradaman.

(ii) The Sudarshana lake required repair because a terrible storm broke the embankments of the lake and water flowed out of the lake.

(iii) Rulers made arrangements for irrigation that included the repair of lakes because irrigation was crucial for the advancement of agriculture and food security. Irrigation was adopted to increase the agricultural production through the provision of lakes, wells, tanks and canals.

3. The Importance of Boundaries

The *Manusmriti* is one of the best-known legal texts of early India, written in Sanskrit and complied between c. second century BCE and second century CE. This is what the text advises the king to do

Seeing that in the world controversies constantly arise due to the ignorance of boundaries, he should have concealed boundary markers buried—stones, bones, cow's hair, chaff, ashes, potsherds, dried cow dung, bricks, coal, pebbles and sand. He should also have other similar substances that would not decay in the soil buried as hidden markers at the intersection of boundaries.

(i) Why did the controversies of boundaries arise?

(ii) Suggest the ways to solve the boundary problems.

(iii) Explain with an example any such problem being faced by India today.

Ans. (i) The ignorance of kings regarding demarcation of boundaries of their lands led to controversies.

(ii) Marking the boundaries by concealed markers such as stones, bones, cow's hair, chaff, ashes, potsherds, dried cow dung, bricks, coal, pebbles and sand can be done. These substances do not decay in the soil and will act as markers at the intersection of boundaries.

(iii) India faces such problems in the villages where the land records are poorly maintained and various stakeholders try to claim their ownership of the same disputed land. Controversy regarding the ownership of agricultural land is very common in India.

4. Life in a Small Village

The *Harshacharita* is a biography of Harshavardhana, the ruler of Kanauj (see Map 3), composed in Sanskrit by his court poet, Banabhatta (c. seventh century CE). This is an excerpt from the text, an extremely rare representation of life in a settlement on the outskirts of a forest in the Vindhyas.

The outskirts being for the most part of forest, many parcels of rice-land, threshing ground and arable land were being apportioned by small farmers ... it was mainly spade culture ... owing to the difficulty of ploughing the sparsely scattered fields covered with grass, with their few clear spaces, their black soil stiff as black iron ... There were people moving along with bundles of bark ... countless sacks of plucked flowers, ... loads of flax and hemp bundles, quantities of honey, peacocks' tail feathers, wreaths of wax, logs and grass. Village wives hastened en route for neighbouring villages, all intent on thoughts of sale and bearing on their heads baskets filled with various gathered forest fruits.

(i) Comment on *Harshacharita*.

(ii) How was the outskirts of a forest in the Vindhyas ?

(iii) What was the activity of village women?

Ans. (i) The *Harshacharita* is a biography of Harshavardhana. He was the ruler of Kanauj. The biography was composed in Sanskrit by Banabhatta, court poet of Harshavardhana.

(ii) The outskirts of a forest included, many parcels of rice-land, threshing ground and arable land cultivated by small farmers. It was mainly spade culture. It was difficult to plough the sparsely scattered fields covered with grass.

(iii) Village women went to neighbouring villages with the thoughts of sale and bearing on their heads baskets filled with various gathered forest fruits.

5. Prabhavati Gupta and the Village of Danguna

This is what Prabhavati Gupta states in her inscription. Prabhavati Gupta commands the *gramakutumbinas* (householders / peasants living in the village), Brahmanas and others living in the village of Danguna ...

"Be it known to you that on the twelfth (lunar day) of the bright (fortnight) of Karttika, we have, in order to increase our religious merit donated this village with the pouring out of water, to the Acharya (teacher) Chanalasvamin ... You should obey all (his) commands ... ...

We confer on (him) the following exemptions typical of an *agrahara* ...... (this village is) not to be entered by soldiers and policeman; (it is) exempt from (the obligation to provide) grass, (animal) hides as seats, and charcoal (to touring royal officers); exempt from (the royal prerogative of) purchasing fermenting liquors and digging (salt); exempt from (the right to) mines and *khadira* trees, exempt from (the obligation to supply) flowers and milk; (it is donated) together with (to right to) hidden treasures and deposits (and) together with major and minor taxes ...... "

This charter has been written in the thirteenth (regional) year. (It has been) engraved by Chakradasa.

(i) **What was the condition of women in that era?**

(ii) **How did the inscription give us an idea about the rural population?**

(iii) **Examine the importance of the charter issued by Prabhavati Gupta.**

Ans. (i) Women during that era were not supposed to have independent access to resources such as land. But the inscription shows that Prabhavati Gupta had the authority to access the land.

(ii) Through the inscription we come to know about the rural population which included Brahmanas and peasants, as well as others who were expected to provide a range of produce to the king or his representatives.

(iii) The importance of the charter issued by Prabhavati Gupta indicated her supreme authority. Even though she was a woman, she had an access to resources which was not allowed for women during that era.

6. The orders of the king **CBSE 2024**

Thus speaks king Devanampiya Piyadassi

In the past, there were no arrangements for disposing affairs, nor for receiving regular reports. But I have made the following (arrangement). *Pativedakas* should report to me about the affairs of the people at all times, anywhere, whether I am eating, in the inner apartment, in the bedroom, in the cow pen, being carried (possibly in a palanquin), or in the garden. And I will dispose off the affairs of the people everywhere.

(i) **Who was referred to as Devanampiya Piyadassi ?**

Ans. The ruler, Asoka was referred to as Devanampiya Piyadassi.

(ii) **How did Devanampiya's approach differ from past arrangements regarding the handling of affairs ?**

Ans. Devanampiya's approach to handling affairs was a significant departure from past arrangements. Devanampiya introduced a highly structured and continuous system of oversight. Unlike previous times, Devanampiya established a system where *Pativedakas* (officials or messengers) were required to report to him about the affairs of the people at all times and from any location.

(iii) **In what way did Devanampiya receive reports and disposed off the affairs of the people ?**

Ans. Devanampiya received reports and disposed of the affairs of the people in a highly organised and continuous manner, which was a departure from past practices. In contrast to earlier systems where governance might have been confined to a palace or certain locations, Devanampiya emphasised that he would dispose of the affairs of the people everywhere. This meant that decision-making and problem-solving were not limited to formal settings but occurred continuously, even in the most informal or personal situations.

7. The Anguish of the King

When the king Devanampiya Piyadassi had been ruling for eight years, the (country of the) Kalingas (present-day coastal Odisha) was conquered by him. One hundred and fifty thousand men were deported, a hundred thousand were killed, and many more died.

After that, now that (the country of) the Kalingas has been taken, Devanampiya (is devoted), to an intense study of *Dhamma*, to the love of *Dhamma* and to instructing (the people) in *Dhamma*. This is the repentance of Devanampiya on account of his conquest of the (country of the) Kalingas. For this considered very painful and deplorable by Devanampiya that, while one is conquering an unconquered (country) slaughter, death and deportation of people (take place) there.

(i) **Who was called 'Devanampiya Piyadassi'? Give his brief description.**

(ii) **Mention the importance and limitation of inscriptions.**

(iii) **Explain the effects of the war of Kalinga on Asoka. Why did the king repent after the war of Kalinga?**

Ans. (i) Emperor Asoka was called 'Devanampiya Piyadassi'. Asoka was the most important ruler of the Mauryan dynasty. He captured Kalinga and later regreted on it and established the notion of *Dhamma*.

(ii) **Importance of Inscriptions** provide valuable information about those who commissioned them. They tell us about social and political conditions of that time when they were inscribed.

Limitations of Inscriptions is that they do not project the opinion of common people.

(iii) After the war of Kalinga, Asoka devoted himself to intense study of *dhamma* and started instructing the people about the message of *dhamma*.

The king regreted after the war of Kalinga because it was very painful for him as the war led to slaughter, death and deportation of thousands of people.

Map Based Questions

1. On the given outline map of India, locate and label the following.

(i) Avanti (ii) Magadha (iii) Vajji
(iv) Kosala (v) Gandhara (vi) Kuru
(viii) Shravasti

Ans.

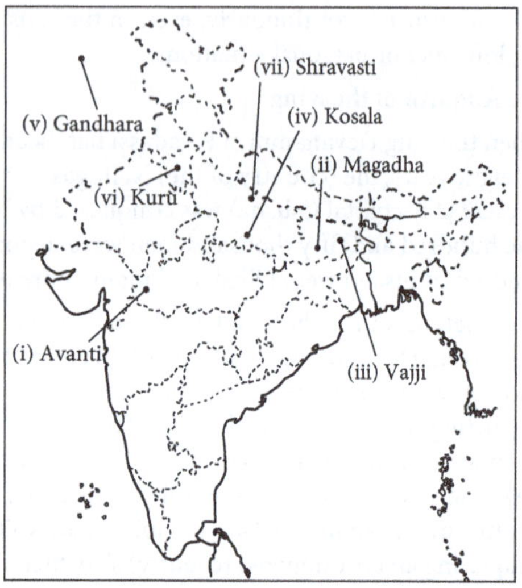

2. On the given political map of India, locate and label the following.

(i) Rajgir (ii) Ujjain (iii) Panchala
(iv) Varanasi (v) Taxila

Or On the given political outline map of India, locate and label the following with appropriate symbols. **CBSE 2024**

(i) Ujjain (ii) Mahajanpada

Ans.

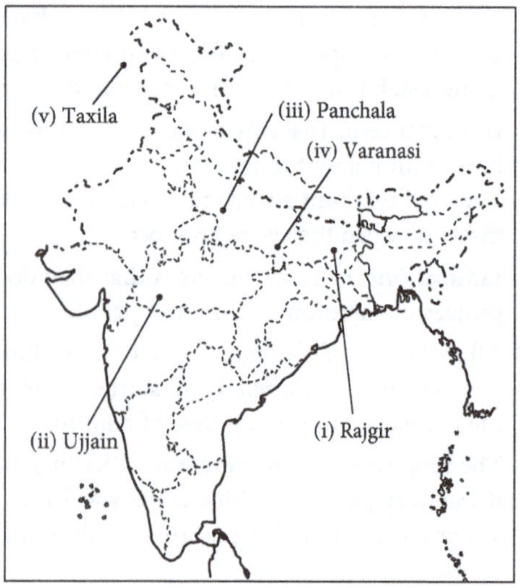

3. Locate the important kingdoms and towns from where Asokan inscriptions have been found. Also locate Vidisha and Vaishali as important cities/towns.

Ans.

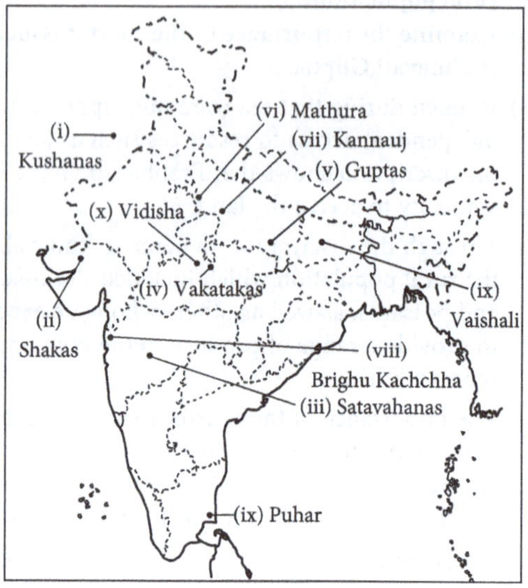

4. Locate the places from where pillar inscriptions of Asoka have been found and the kingdom of Cholas, Cheras and Pandayas.

Or On the given political outline map of India, locate and label the following with appropriate symbols.

(i) Kaushambi
(ii) Ashokan inscription **CBSE 2024 C**

Ans.

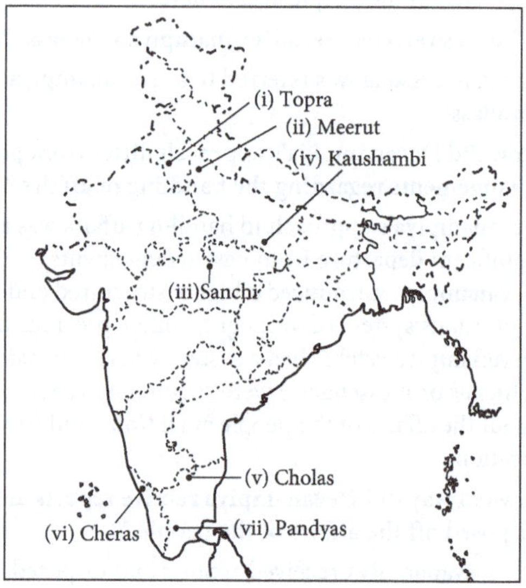

SELF ASSESSMENT TEST

Objective Type Questions

1. Who was the founder of Mauryan Dynasty?
   (a) Chandragupta Maurya (b) Kumargupta
   (c) Asoka (d) Skandgupta
2. What was one of the main contributions of James Prinsep in the 1830s to Indian history?
   (a) Establishing the Mauryan Empire
   (b) Deciphering the Brahmi and Kharosthi scripts
   (c) Writing the Arthashastra
   (d) Constructing the Sudarshana lake
3. Which of the following mahajanapadas was known for its powerful army and was the first to emerge as a dominant state in early Indian history?
   (a) Kosala (b) Magadha
   (c) Avanti (d) Vajji
4. Match the Following.

List I		List II	
A.	Asoka's inscription in Afghanistan	1.	Tamil
B.	Harshacharita	2.	Prakrit
C.	Asoka's inscription in Kalinga	3.	Greek
D.	*Silappadikaram*	4.	Sanskrit

Codes

	A	B	C	D		A	B	C	D
(a)	1	2	3	4	(b)	2	3	4	1
(c)	3	4	2	1	(d)	2	1	4	3

Short Answer Type Questions

5. Describe in brief about the Allahabad Pillar inscription.
6. Discuss the impact of Indo-Greek and Kushana coinage on trade and economy.
7. "Buddhist sangha is an important part of Buddhism." Explain its function in brief.
8. Punch-marked coins were the first coins issued in India. Explain its importance.
9. Mention two titles adopted by Asoka. What does this title show us about the policies of Akbar?

Long Answer Type Questions

10. Army was important for the protection of the empire. Discuss.
11. "Communication along both land and riverine routes was vital for the existence of the Mauryan Empire." Justify the statement.
12. Describe how inscriptions are helpful for historians to write the history of Gupta period.
13. Write about the coins and kings of Mauryan Empire.

3

CHAPTER

This chapter deals with the system of Kinship, Caste and Class in ancient India. Various sources like Dharmasutras, Dharmashastras and the Mahabharata help us to understand about the beliefs, practices and social codes in ancient India.

Kinship, Caste and Class
(Early Societies)

▼ **YOUR STUDY GOALS**

3.1 The Critical Edition of Mahabharata
3.2 Kinship and Marriage : Rules and Practices
3.3 Social Differences : Within and Beyond the Framework of Caste
3.4 Control over Resources and Status
3.5 A Social Contract
3.6 A Dynamic Text : Mahabharata

▼ **YOUR PRACTICE GOALS**

- Objective Type Questions (48 Qs ; MCQs, A-R, Matching, Picture Based)
- Subjective Questions (20 SAs, 6 LAs)
- Source Based Questions (8 Qs)

From the period between c. 600 BCE and 600 CE, there were many changes in the economic and political life such as

- Expansion of farming into forested areas, which changed the lives of people living in those forests.
- Formation of social groups by skilled craftsmen.
- Increased social differences due to the unequal distribution of wealth.
- Textual traditions (written records) are studied by historians to understand the changes in history. Some texts contain rules for social behaviour, others comment on different social situations and practices.
- For example, the *Mahabharata* has over **100,000 verses** and was composed over a period of about 1000 years (c. 500 BCE onwards). The text also has sections which contain norms of behaviour for various social groups.

3.1 The Critical Edition of the Mahabharata

- The making of the critical edition of the *Mahabharata* began in **1919** by **V.S. Sukthankar** and his team. The project took 47 years to complete.
- The team collected **Sanskrit manuscripts** written in a variety of scripts.

- **Verses** from each manuscript were compared and the most common text was selected. These verses were published in several volumes which includes over 13,000 pages.
- There were several common elements in the Sanskrit versions of *Mahabharata*. Many regional variations were also found in the ways in which the text was spread over the centuries. These variations were recorded in footnotes and appendices to the main text. More than half of the 13,000 pages focus on these variations.
- Early historians in the 19th and 20th centuries often assumed these texts to represent actual practices. Later, scholars began exploring Pali, Prakrit and Tamil traditions and found that Sanskrit texts were considered authoritative. However, ideas in Sanskrit texts were also questioned and sometimes rejected.

3.2 Kinship and Marriage: Rules and Practices

Finding out about Families

- Families are usually parts of larger networks of people which are referred to as *'kinfolk'*.
- In Sanskrit texts, the term "*kula*" refers to families, "*jnati*" denotes a larger network of kinfolk and "*vamsha*" is used for family lineage.
- Familial ties are regarded as "natural" and based on blood. However, they are defined in different ways. For example, some societies regard cousins as being blood relations, whereas others do not.

The Ideal of Patriliny

- In patriliny, family relationships are traced through the father's side. On the other hand, in matriliny, they are traced through the mother's side.
- Under patriliny, sons could claim the resources (including the throne in the case of kings) of their fathers after their death.
- Mahabharata points at the beginning of changes in **kinship**[1] relations. It is a story of a fight over land and power between the Kauravas and the Pandavas, who were cousins. They belonged to a single ruling family, Kurus.
- The conflict between the Kauravas and the Pandavas led to a battle, in which the Pandavas won. After the war, patrilineal succession was declared.
- Patriliny was practiced even before the composition of the *Mahabharata*, but its central story focussed on the importance of this idea.
- From the sixth century BCE onwards, the patriliny system was followed by most ruling dynasties. However, there were variations such as
  - If there were no sons, brothers succeeded one another.
  - Sometimes other kinsmen claimed the throne.
  - In rare cases, women like **Prabhavati Gupta** exercised power.

Rules of Marriage

Sons were considered important for continuing the family line. However, daughters were seen differently as

- They had no claims to the resources of the household.
- It was desired that women were married into families outside the kin. This system was called exogamy.
- The lives of young girls and women belonging to high status families were regulated to ensure that they were married at the "right" time and to the "right" person.
- *Kanyadana* or the gift of a daughter in marriage became an important religious duty of the father.

1 **Kinship** Persons of the same family.

Changes in Social Life

- With the emergence of new towns, social life became more complex as people met and shared their ideas in the urban background which led to a criticism of earlier beliefs and practices.
- The Brahmanas laid down codes of social behaviour which were compiled in Sanskrit texts known as the **Dharmasutras** and **Dharmashastras**. The most important of such works, the ***Manusmriti***[2], was compiled between c. 200 BCE and 200 CE.

Eight forms of Marriage

- The Dharmasutras and Dharmashastras recognised eight forms of marriage.
- The first four were considered "good" while the remaining were not accepted. These were practised by those who did not accept Brahmanical norms.
- The first, fourth, fifth and sixth forms of marriage from Manusmriti are

First The daughter is married to a learned man chosen by her father. The daughter wears fine clothes and is adorned with jewels.

Fourth The father honours the bridegroom and gives his blessing to the couple.

Fifth A marriage where the groom gives his wealth to the bride and her family according to his own will.

Sixth A marriage between a woman and her lover, based on mutual desire.

The Gotra of Women

- From c.1000 BCE onwards, people (especially Brahmanas) were classified in terms of *gotras*.
- Each gotra was named after a **Vedic seer**. All those who belonged to the same gotra were regarded as his descendants.
- There were two important rules about *gotra*
  (i) Women were expected to give up their father's *gotra* and adopt the *gotra* of their husband on marriage.
  (ii) Members of the same *gotra* could not marry.
- These rules were commonly followed as the names of men and women were sometimes derived from *gotra* names. These names are available for **Satavahanas** who ruled over parts of Western India and the Deccan (c. second century BCE-second century CE).
- Some of the Satavahana rulers were polygynous.
- The women who married Satavahana rulers derived their names from *gotras* such as Gotama and Vasistha, their father's *gotras*. They did not adopt their husband's *gotra* as required by the Brahmanical rules.
- Some women belonged to the same *gotra* which was against the ideal of exogamy recommended in the Brahmanical texts.
- **Endogamy**[3] was exemplified as alternative practice to the ideal of exogamy. It was practiced amongst many South Indian communities ensuring a close-knit community.

---

2 Manusmriti One of the important Dharmashastras.

3 Endogamy Marriage within the unit, such as a caste or a group living in the same locality.

Satavahana Kings

The names of several generations of Satavahana rulers, recovered from inscriptions are as follows

- Raja Gotami-puta Siri-Satakani
- Raja Vasithi-puta (sami) Siri-Pulumayi
- Raja Gotami-puta sami-Siri-Yana-Satakani
- Raja Madhari-puta svami-Sakasena
- Raja Vasathi-puta Chatarapana-Satakani
- Raja Hariti-puta Vinhukada Chutukulanamda-Satakamni
- Raja Gotami-puta Siri-Vijaya-Satakani

▲ *A Satavahana Ruler and his wife*

Practice of Polyandry in Marriage

- In *Mahabharata*, Draupadi's marriage with the Pandavas is an example of **polyandry**[4].
- Contemporary historians believe that polyandry might have been common among the ruling elites.
- Others suggest that there may have been a shortage of women during wars which led to polyandry.
- It is also suggested that polyandry gradually lost popularity amongest the Brahmanas, who reworked and developed the text through the centuries.

Importance of Mothers

Satavahana rulers were identified through **metronymics** (names derived from that of the mother). However, succession to the throne was generally patrilineal.

Quick Test 1

1. Which scholar started preparing the critical edition of the Mahabharata?
2. Mention any one variation in practice in the patriliny system.
3. The Dharmashastras and Dharmasutras recognised how many types of marriages?
4. From which sources have historians traced family ties and marriages of the Satavahanas?
5. What was the benefit of endogamy?

3.3 Social Differences: Within and Beyond the Framework of Caste

- Caste refers to a set of order of social categories in rank.
- According to the ideal order in the Dharmasutras and Dharmashastras, Brahmanas ranked first and Shudras and untouchables were at the very bottom.
- Positions within the order were determined by birth.

The Right Occupation

The Dharmasutras and Dharmashastras also contained rules about the ideal occupations of the four categories or varnas. These were

- Brahmanas were responsible for studying and teaching the Vedas, performing sacrifices and exchanging gifts.

4 **Polyandry** Practice of women having several husbands.

- Kshatriyas were responsible for warfare, protection of people, administering justice, study of Vedas and performance of sacrifices.
- Vaishyas were expected to perform agriculture, pastoralism and trade.
- Shudras only had to serve the three higher varnas.

The strategies followed by the Brahmanas to enforce these norms were

- Asserting that the varna order was created by God.
- Advising kings to ensure that these norms were followed within their kingdoms.
- Attempting to convince people that their status was determined by birth.

To justify their claims, Brahmanas quoted a verse from *Rigveda* known as *Purush Sukta*. It described the sacrifice of Purusha, the primeval or earliest man.

Non- Kshatriya Kings

▲ *Silver coin depicting a Shaka ruler*

According to the Shastras, only Kshatriyas could be kings. However, many non-Kshatriya kings also ruled such as

- According to the later Buddhist texts, the Mauryas were Kshatriyas. However, the Brahmanical texts described them as being of low origin.
- The Shungas and Kanvas, the immediate successors of the Mauryas, were Brahmanas.
- Rulers such as the Shakas from Central Asia, were regarded as ***mlechchhas***[5].
- **Rudradaman**, the best-known Shaka ruler, rebuilt **Sudarshana Lake**. This suggests that powerful mlechchhas knew about Sanskritic traditions.
- The best-known Satavahana ruler, Gotami-puta Siri-Satakani, claimed to be both a unique Brahmana (*eka bamhana*) and a destroyer of the pride of Kshatriyas.

The integration within the caste system was complex as

- The Satavahanas claimed to be Brahmanas, whereas according to the Brahmanas, only Kshatriyas could be the kings.
- Even though Satavahanas followed the four fold *varna* order, they entered into marriage alliances with people excluded from the system. For example, Gotami-puta Siri-Satakani married the kin of Rudradaman.
- They also practised endogamy instead of the exogamous system which was recommended in the Brahmanical texts.

Jatis and Social Mobility

- According to Brahmanical theory, *jati*, like *varna*, was based on birth.
- The number of varnas was fixed at four, however there was no limit on the number of *jatis*.
- People living in forests such as the **nishadas**[6] – or goldsmith or *suvarnakara*, were classified as a *jati* by the Brahmanical authorities as they did not easily fit into the fourfold *varna* system.
- Jatis sharing a common occupation were sometimes organised into **shrenis**[7] or **guilds**.

5 Mlechchas They were regarded as Barbarians or outsiders by the Brahmanas in ancient India.
6 Nishadas A hunting community.
7 Shrenis Guilds or unions or associations of craftsmen and traders in ancient India.

Mandasor Stone Inscription (Madhya Pradesh)

It records the history of a guild of silk weavers who originally lived in Lata (Gujarat) but migrated to *Dashapura*. It contains the following information about guilds or shrenis

- The membership was based on a shared **craft specialisation**, but some members also practiced other occupations.
- The members collectively **invested their wealth** which they earned through their craft. It was used to construct a great temple in honour of the Sun god.
- They undertook the **difficult journey** along with their children and kinfolk, to know about the greatness of the local king, or to settle in his kingdom.

Communities without Varna System

- Some groups were not influenced by Brahmanical ideas. In Sanskrit texts, they are often described as uncivilised, or forest-dwellers. For example, **Ekalavya** belonged to the ***Nishada*** community.
- Groups such as nomadic pastoralists could not easily fit within the category of settled agriculturists.
- Those who spoke non-Sanskritic languages were referred to as *Mlechchas*.
- The Brahmanas classified some people as untouchable and being outside the system. Those who considered themselves pure, avoided taking food from the untouchables.
- Those who disposed of the dead bodies and dead animals were called ***chandalas***. They were placed at the very bottom of the order.
- The *Manusmriti* laid down the following rules and duties of the *chandalas*
  - They had to live outside the village, use waste utensils and wear clothes of the dead and ornaments of iron.
  - They could not walk around in villages and cities at night.
  - They had to dispose of the bodies of those who had no relatives and serve as executioners.

A Mendicant Seeking Alms

Chinese Travellers about Untouchables

- Chinese Buddhist monk **Fa Xian** (c. fifth century CE) wrote that untouchables had to make a sound by clapping in the streets so that people could avoid seeing them.
- Chinese pilgrim, **Xuan Zang** (c. seventeenth century CE) observed that executioners and scavengers were forced to live outside the city.

3.4 Control over Resources and Status

Slaves, landless agricultural labourers, hunters, fisherfolk, pastoralists, peasants, village headmen, craftspersons, merchants and kings emerged as social participants in different parts of the subcontinent. Their social positions were often shaped by their access to economic resources.

Gendered Access to Property

Issues of ownership are mentioned in the Dharmasutras and Dharmashastras. There were different rights for different genders according to the *Manusmriti* as

- The paternal estate was to be divided equally amongst sons after the death of the parents, with a special share for the eldest son. Women could not claim a share of these resources.

- Women were allowed to keep the gifts they got in their marriage as ***stridhana***. This could be inherited by their children and the husband did not have any claim on it.
- Women could not keep family property, or even their own valuables, without the husband's permission.

Epigraphic[8] and textual evidence show that upper-class women could have access to resources. However, land, cattle and money were generally controlled by men.

Varna and Access to Property

- According to the Brahmanical texts, *varna* played an important role in regulating access to wealth.
- Servitude[9] was the only occupation for the Shudras, while many occupations were given for the first three varnas.
- Kings are shown as being wealthy. Priests are generally shown rich, but they can also be depicted poor.
- The Buddhists recognised differences in society, but did not regard these as natural or inflexible. They also rejected the claims to status on the basis of birth.

Sharing wealth

- There were other ways to assign status beyond wealth. For example, men who helped people in need were respected, while those who stored wealth for themselves were not liked. These values were respected in the ancient **Tamilakam**.
- Around 2,000 years ago, there were several chiefdoms. The chiefs supported bards and poets who sang in their praise.
- The **Tamil Sangam** literature described the socio-economic relationships and the differences in society. It also showed that owners of the resources were also expected to share them.

3.5 A Social Contract

- The Buddhists developed a different understanding of social inequalities and of the institutions required to regulate social conflict.
- A myth in the ***Sutta Pitaka*** suggested that originally, humans and plants were not fully developed. All beings lived peacefully and took only necessary things from nature for each meal.
- The institution of kingship was based on human choice, with taxes as a form of payment for services provided by the king.
- Sutta Pitaka also recognises human agency in creating and establishing economic and social relations. If human beings created the system, they could also change it in future.

Quick Test 2

1. According to the Dharmashastras and Dharmasutras, the Vaishyas were expected to engage in which profession?
2. Who were the immediate successors of the Mauryas?
3. Which Satavahana ruler claimed to be a destroyer of the pride of the Kshatriyas?
4. The guild membership was based on which factor?
5. What were women allowed to retain according to the Manusmriti?

8 Epigraphic Written records on hard surfaces.
9 Servitude The condition of being forced to obey another person.

3.6 A Dynamic Text: Mahabharata

The growth of the *Mahabharata* continued even after the Sanskrit version as

- Many versions were written in different languages through continuous interactions.
- The central story of the epic was often retold in different ways.
- Its episodes were presented in sculpture and painting.
- They also provided themes for performing plays, dance and other kinds of narrations.

Handling the Text by Historians

The elements considered by historians while analysing the *Mahabharata* were

- Search for the languages in which the texts were written such as Prakrit, Pali or Tamil, that were used by ordinary people, or Sanskrit, which was spoken only by priests and elites.
- Studying the types of text wheather it was a mantra for rituals or a story that people could have read or heard.
- Finding about authors whose views and ideas shaped the text. The authors keep the interests of their audience in mind while composing their work.
- Possible date and place of the composition or compilation of the texts.

Language and Content

- The *Mahabharata* was written in **Sanskrit**, but there are versions in other languages also.
- The Sanskrit used in the *Mahabharata* is easier than that of the Vedas, or of the *prashastis*.
- The contents of the *Mahabharata* is divided into the following categories
  - **Narrative** Sections that contain stories.
  - **Didactic**[10] Sections that contain prescriptions about social norms.

Author(s) and Dates

- The original story of the *Mahabharata* was composed by charioteer-bards known as **sutas**[11].
- Brahmanas began writing the story from the fifth century BCE. Between c. 200 and 400 CE, large sections having instructions similar to the *Manusmriti* were added.
- The text finally had about 100,000 verses. This composition is traditionally known to be written by a sage named Vyasa.

The Search for Convergence

- In 1951-52, the archaeologist **B.B. Lal** excavated a village named Hastinapura in Meerut (Uttar Pradesh).
- The site is located in the Upper Ganga doab, where the Kuru kingdom was situated. This suggests that it may have been the capital of the Kurus.
- Lal found evidence of **five occupational levels**, of which he described the second and third levels.
- Second occupational level (c. twelfth-seventh centuries BCE) : The walls of mud and mud-bricks were found. Some houses were made of bamboo walls.
- Third occupational level (c. sixth-third centuries BCE) : Houses were built of mud and burnt bricks. Soakage jars and brick drains were used for draining out refuse water. Terracotta ring-wells were also found.

▲ *A wall excavated at Hastinapura*

---

10 **Didactic** Designed to teach people something, especially a moral lesson.

11 **Sutas** They generally accompanied Kshatriya warriors to the battlefield and composed poems celebrating their victories and other achievements.

Quick Test 3

1 Mention any one element which is considered by the historians while analysing texts such as *Mahabharata*.
2 The content of the *Mahabharata* is divided into which categories?
3 What was the role of the Sutas in *Mahabharata*?
4 Which archaeologist excavated a site at Hastinapur?
5 What do the excavated levels at Hastinapur indicate?

TIMELINE

Major Textual Traditions

500 BCE	*Ashtadhyayi* of Panini, a work on Sanskrit grammar
500-200 BCE	Major Dharmasutras (in Sanskrit)
500-100 BCE	Early Buddhist texts including the *Tripitaka* (in Pali)
500 BCE-400 CE	*Ramayana* and *Mahabharata* (in Sanskrit)
200 BCE-200 CE	*Manusmriti* (in Sanskrit); composition and compilation of Tamil Sangam literature
100 CE	*Charaka* and *Sushruta Samhitas*, works on medicine (in Sanskrit)
200 CE onwards	Compilation of the *Puranas* (in Sanskrit)
300 CE	*Natyashastra* of Bharata, a work on dramaturgy (in Sanskrit)
300-600 CE	Other Dharmashastras (in Sanskrit).
400-500 CE	Sanskrit plays including the works of Kalidasa; works on astronomy and mathematics by Aryabhata and Varahamihira (in Sanskrit); compilation of Jaina works (in Prakrit)

Major Landmarks in the Study of the *Mahabharata*

1919-66	Preparation and publication of the Critical Edition of the *Mahabharata*
1973	J.A.B. Van Buitenen begins English translation of the Critical Edition; remains incomplete after his death in 1978

Mind Map

KINGSHIP, CASTE AND CLASS

1 The Critical Edition of the Mahabharata

Local ideas often questioned and reshaped dominant Sanskrit traditions.

2 Kinship and Marriage: Many Rules and Varied Practices

The Idea of Patriliny
Mahabharata highlights changes in kinship through patrilineal succession.

Finding out about Families
- Families differ in size, relationships and shared activities.
- Kingship ties vary across societies and cultural definitions.

Rules of Marriage
- Manusmriti and Dharmashastras outlined detailed social norms and marriages.
- Eight marriage forms existed; only four aligned with Brahmanical norms.

3 Social Differences: Within and Beyond the Framework of Caste

The Right Occupation
- Dharmasutras defined ideal occupations for the four varnas.
- Kings were advised to enforce varna norms in society.

Non-Kshatriya Kings
Kingship was open to anyone with support and resources.

Jatis and Social Mobility
- Jati system classified groups outside the four field varna structure.
- Mandasor inscriptions shows guilds migration unity and contributions.

4 Control over Resources and Birth

Gendered Access to Property
- Manusmriti restricted women's rights to inherit family property.
- Womens were allowed to retain the gifts of marriage as stridhanas.

Varna and Access to Property
- Shudras were limited to servitude; wealth favoured higher varnas.
- Kings and priests were depicted as wealthy in texts.
- Buddhists rejected rigid varna-based status and birth claims.

5 Explaining Social Differences: A Social Contact

- Buddhists viewed kingship as a human choice, not divine.
- Human greed led to social inequality and need for kings.

6 A Dynamic Text: Mahabharta

- Mahabharata grew through versions in different languages over centuries.
- The epic inspired sculpture, painting and various performing arts.

7 Handling the Texts by Historians

Language and Content
- Mahabharta has a simpler language than the vedas making it more widely understood.
- Text divided into narrative stories and instructive social prescriptions.

Authors and Dates
- Original story likely composed by charioteer-bards known as Sutas.
- Brahmanas began writing the epic from the 5th century BCE

NCERT Folder

Intext Questions

1. How are children named today? Are these ways of naming similar to or different from those described in this section? (Pg. 60)

Ans. Today, children are named according to their family traditions and cultural practices. They often have meaningful names, and the connection of their names with their gotra is not always necessary. In ancient India, gotra was an important factor in naming. Sometimes, names were derived from gotras. The names of women who married Satavahana rulers were derived from their fathers' gotras. Satavahana rulers were identified by their mothers' names, such as Gotami-puta Siri-Satakani.

2. Which of the sources mentioned in this section suggest that people followed the occupations laid down by Brahmanas? Which sources suggest other possibilities? (Pg. 67)

Ans. The Brahmans laid down the rules about the ideal "occupations" of the four varnas in sources like Dharmasutras and Dharmashastras. However, there were people who could not fit into varna system, such as forest dwellers, pastoralists, etc . Whenever Brahmans encountered new groups or wanted to assign a name to occupational categories fourfold varna system, they classified them as a *jati*. *Jatis* which shared a common occupation or profession were sometimes organised into shrenis or guilds.

From Mandasor inscription, we get information about a guild of silk weavers who settled in Mandasor. As per Brahmanical texts, trading was the profession of Vaishyas. But, Mrichhakatika written by a Shudraka described his hero Charudutta as both a brahmana and merchant.

3. How do social relationships operate in present-day societies? Are there any similarities or differences with patterns of the past? (Pg. 71)

Ans. Social relationships are crucial in contemporary society, just as they were in the past, though the ways they operate have evolved significantly. Technological advances have transformed how these relationships are made and maintained.

In the past, social relationships were primarily built through face-to-face interactions within close-knit communities. People relied on direct, personal contact and established relationships through family, local networks, and communal activities.

Social relationships in present-day societies are influenced by a variety of factors, including culture class and technology. With the help of technology, the extent of social relationships is broad. People belonging to far-off lands can connect with each other.

In many ways, social relationships are similar to the patterns of the past. But there are some differences also.

Similarities between present-day social relationships and past social relationships are

- **Importance of family** The family still plays an important role in social relationships like the past.
- **Importance of kinship** Many social relationships at present are based on kinship from the past. There are also marriages between cousins, which helps to ensure a close-knit community.

Differences between present-day social relationships and past social relationships are

- **Decline in importance of gotra** Unlike the past, gotra is not important for social relationships today.
- **Broader social relationship** In the past, the scope of social relationships was limited. They generally made relationships within their communities. But today, with the help of technology, people can make social relationships despite belonging to distant lands.

4. Read the excerpts from the *Mahabharata* included in this chapter once more. For each of these, discuss whether they could have been literally true. What do these excerpts tell us about those who composed the text? What do they tell us about those who must have read or heard the epic? (Pg. 77)

Ans. The excerpts from the *Mahabharata* offer rich insights into the nature of ancient storytelling and the values of the society that composed and engaged with the text. Many of these passages contain elements that are highly exaggerated, suggesting that they were not intended to be taken literally. For example, the account of the battle between Bhima and Duryodhana, which reportedly lasted for ten days and nights, is likely an exaggeration. Such dramatic depictions are more symbolic than factual, representing broader themes of moral and cosmic struggle, such as the battle between good and evil or the quest for righteousness.

These narratives reveal much about the storytellers and composers of the *Mahabharata*. They were skilled in crafting elaborate and symbolic stories that conveyed deeper truths and moral lessons rather than strictly historical accounts. For the readers or listeners of the epic, these stories were not just entertainment but also a means of connecting with cultural and spiritual values.

Answer in 100-150 words

1. Explain why patriliny may have been particularly important among elite families.

Ans. Patriliny is the system through which descent from father to son and grandson is traced. The principle of patriliny would have been essential for the elite families for the following reasons

Continuity of Dynasty As per the Dharmashastras, it was an established belief that the son carried forward the dynasty. That was the main reason that the families wished for sons and not for daughters.

Inheritance In royal families, the acquisition of the throne was included in the inheritance. After the death of a king, his eldest son was supposed to inherit the throne. After the death of the parents, the property was to be equally divided among all the sons. In fact, parents avoided disputes in the family after their death.

Most of the royal families followed patriliny since 600 B.C. But sometimes this system had exceptions also. The brother of the king ascended the throne in case the former had no son. Relatives also claimed inheritance of the throne. In some special cases, women also ascended the throne, like Prabhavati Gupta.

2. Discuss whether kings in early states were invariably Kshatriyas.

Ans. Kings in early states were not invariably Kshatriyas. Many important ruling lineages had different origins. Mauryas were considered Kshatriyas by many people but some Brahmanical texts described Mauryas as of low origin.

The Shungas and Kanvas, who were immediate successors of the Mauryas, were Brahmanas.

There were other rulers like Shakas who came from Central Asia. But the Brahmanas considered them as *mlechchhas*, barbarians and outsiders. However, Rudradaman, the best known Shaka ruler, was a powerful ruler.

Similarly, Gautami-puta Siri-Satakani, the best known ruler of the Satavahana dynasty, became a destroyer of the pride of Kshatriyas.

Thus, we see that the Satavahanas claimed to be Brahmanas, whereas the Brahmanas were of the opinion that the king should be a Kshatriya.

3. Compare and contrast the *dharma* or norms mentioned in the stories of Drona, Hidimba and Matanga.

Ans. Drona

Drona was a Brahmana. As per the Dharmashastras, it was the duty of the Brahmana to impart education. It was considered as a religious activity of the Brahmanas. Drona was also following that system. He taught archery to the princes of the Kuru Dynasty.

In those days, people of low caste were not entitled to get education. Keeping this view in mind, Drona refused imparting education to Ekalavya. But in the course of time, Ekalavya learnt archery and acquired great skill, attributing his skill to Drona. But Drona demanded the right thumb of Ekalavya as his teaching fee. This was against religious norms.

In fact, Drona did this just to ensure that no one could be a better archer than Arjuna in the field of archery.

Hidimba

Hidimba was a female demon (Rakshashi) and all Rakshasas were man eaters. One day her brother ordered her to capture the Pandavas so he could eat them. However, Hidimba did not obey him. Instead she tell she is in love with Bhima and married him. They had a son named Ghatotkacha who was a Rakshsha. In this way Hidimba did not follow the traditional ways of Rakshasa.

Matanga

Matanga was the Bodhisattava who was born in the family of a *chandala*. But he married Dittha Mangalika who was the daughter of a merchant. A son was born to them named Mandavya Kumara. In the course of time, he learnt three Vedas. He used to offer food to sixteen hundred Brahmanas every day. But when his father appeared before him dressed in rags with a clay alms bowl in his hand, he refused to offer food to him. A donor is considered generous but Mandavya failed to follow the norms of religion and generosity.

4. In what ways was the Buddhist theory of a social contract different from the Brahmanical view of society derived from the *Purusha Sukta*?

Ans. The *Purusha Sukta* of the *Rigveda* says that the four *varnas* emerged because of the sacrifice of Purusha, the primeval (ancient) man. The four *varnas* were Brahmanas, Kshatriyas, Vaishyas and Shudras. These varnas had different occupations

- The Brahmanas had the supreme position in society. They were also considered as teachers.
- Kshatriyas were considered as warriors. They also ran the administration.
- The Vaishyas were the masters of trade.
- The Shudras were at the lowest strata. Their duty was to serve the above three *varnas*.
- Under the Brahmanical system, birth was the only criteria to judge the status and prestige in society.

But the Buddhist theory of a social contract was different. As per the Buddhist concept, there was inequality in society. But they also opined that this inequality was neither natural nor permanent. They did not favour the idea of birth being the criteria of social status.

5. The following is an excerpt from the *Mahabharata*, in which Yudhisthira, the eldest Pandava, speaks to Sanjaya, a messenger.

Sanjaya, convey my respectful greetings to all the Brahmanas, and the chief priest of the house of Dhritarashtra. I bow respectfully to teacher Drona...... I hold the feet of our preceptor Kripa...... (and) the chief of the Kurus, the great Bhishma.
I bow respectfully to the old king (Dhritarashtra). I greet and ask after the health of his son Duryodhana and his younger brother .... Also greet all the young Kuru warriors who are our brothers, sons and grandsons.... Greet above all him, who is to us like father and mother, the wise Vidura (born of a slave woman)..... I bow to the elderly ladies who are known as our mothers.

To those who are our wives you say this, "I hope, they are well-protected".... Our daughters-in-law born of good families and mothers of children, greet on my behalf.

Embrace for me those who are our daughters...... The beautiful, fragrant, well-dressed courtesans of ours you should also greet. Greet the slave women and their children, greet the aged, the maimed (and) the helpless....

Try and identify the criteria used to make this list in terms of age, gender, kinship ties. Are there any other criteria? For each category, explain why they are placed in a particular position in the list.

Ans. Yes, there were other factors too which were considered to prepare the list. These were

- The Brahmanas, the *purohits* and the *gurus* were bestowed the highest honours. They all were widely respected.
- Fraternal kings were also given respect as they were considered like parents.
- People who were of equal age or younger were placed at the third rank. In the next order, the young Kuru warriors were respected.
- Women also received their due place. Mothers, wives, daughters-in-law, daughters, courtesans and slave women came in this order.
- Orphans and handicapped had also been taken care of. Yudhisthira also greeted them.

Write a short Essay (about 500 words) on the following

6. This is what a famous historian of Indian literature, Maurice Winternitz, wrote about *Mahabharata*: "Just because the *Mahabharata* represents more of an entire literature... and contains so much and so many kinds of things ...... (it) gives us an insight into the most profound depths of the soul of the Indian folk." Discuss.

Ans. According to Maurice Winternitz, *Mahabharata* is not only a production of poetry, but is an entire literature.

Mahabharata is considered one of the important epic of ancient India. It gives us a vivid description of almost all aspects of contemporary life.

The Aryan influence had expanded throughout the country by the time of the *Mahabharata*. The war between the Kauravas and the Pandavas was a war between *dharma* and *adharma* or between justice and the injustice.

The Pandavas represent *dharma* and justice, whereas Kauravas are the representatives of *adharma* and injustice.

That is why Shri Krishna extends his support to the Pandavas. The victory of Pandavas in the war is the victory of *dharma* over *adharma*. The Indian masses have been encouraged to follow the path of *dharma*.
When we assess an excerpt between Sanjay, a messenger, and Yudhishthira, the eldest Pandava, and the way in which Gandhari advised her son Duryodhana, we find Indian civility and politeness in its ideal form in the *Mahabharata*. It relates Indian society and culture to the basic values of human life.

The *Mahabharata* is also important from the historical point of view. It furnishes significant information regarding the social and cultural conditions of some period of the later Vedic period. The epic had a deep impact on Indian life from political, social, cultural, moral and spiritual points of view.

Thus, Maurice Winternitz writes "just because the *Mahabharata* represent more of an entire literature and contains, so much and so many kinds of things, it gives us an insight into the most profound depths of the soul of the Indian folk".

7. Discuss whether the *Mahabharata* could have been the work of a single author.

Ans. As per tradition, the Mahabharata was written by Lord Ganesha dictated by Vyasa. However, modern historians say that the text was neither authored in a specific period nor it was the work of a single author.

The *Mahabharata* was composed over a period of about 1000 year between 500 BCE and 400 CE. The original story of the *Mahabharata* was composed by charioteer bards popularly called as *sutas*.

Brahmanas began to unite their story from the 500 BCE. During this period, the chiefdoms of the Kurus and Panchals were becoming kingdoms step by step.

The new kings wanted their history to be recorded and preserved in a more systematic way. It is also possible that the upheals that often accompanied the establishment of these states, when old social values were often replaced by new norms, are reflected in some parts of the story.

Historians classified the contents of the text into two broad heads, i.e. narrative and didactic. The didactic sections contain prescriptions about social norms based on stories.

The narrative sections contain stories often having a social message. After analysing both the classifications, historians suggest that *Mahabharata* was not the work of a single author.

The historians suggest that the composition of the *Mahabharata* remained in process for a long time. Another phase of its composition began between c. 200 BCE and 200 CE. It is assumed that large didactic sections resembling the Manusmriti were added to the epic during the period c. 200-400 CE. It was because of these additions that it grew into a large text containing 1,00,000 verses.

8. How important were gender differences in early societies? Give reasons for your answer.

Ans. **Gender inequality**

Gender differences in early societies were important. Women had a respectable place in society but their status was inferior as compared to men.

While sons were important for the continuity of the patrilineage, daughters were viewed rather differently within this framework. They had no claims to the resources of the household. At the same time, marrying them into families outside the kin was considered desirable.

Patriliny

According to *Mahabharata's* central story, the idea of patriliny was valuable. Under patriliny, sons could claim the resources (throne in case of kings) of their fathers after his death.

From c. Sixth century BCE onwards, this system was followed by most ruling dynasties. But there were variations in practice. These were

- If there were no sons, brothers succeeded one another.
- Sometimes other kinsmen claimed the throne.
- In very exceptional circumstances, women exercised power, like Prabhavati Gupta.

Patriliny was not unique to ruling families because it already existed prior to the *Mahabharata* war. It is evident in mantras in ritual texts such as the Rigveda. It is possible that these attitudes were shared by wealthy men and those who claimed high status, including Brahmanas.

Women's Right to Property

Women had no such right to claim property. It was ensured that young girls and women should be married at the right time and to the right person. This gave rise to the belief that *kanyadana*, or the gift of a daughter in marriage, was an important religious duty of the father.

The parental estate was to be divided equally among sons after the death of the parents, with a special share for the eldest. Women could not claim a share of these resources.

Concept of Stridhana

Women were allowed to retain the gifts they received on the occasion of their marriage as *stridhana*. This could be inherited by their children, without the husband having any claim on it. Women were considered as the property of their husbands.

9. Discuss the evidence that suggests that Brahmanical prescriptions about kinship and marriage were not universally followed.

Ans. It is true, that Brahmanical prescriptions about kinship and marriage were not universally followed. Families are usually parts of larger networks of people. The term *'Kinfolk'* is used for these networks of relatives. In Sanskrit texts, *kula* word is used to designate families, *jati* is used for a larger network of families and the term *vamsha* is used for lineage defined as relatives.

Familial ties are regarded as 'natural' and based on blood. For instance, some societies regard cousins as being blood relations, whereas others do not.

The idea of patriliny existed prior to the composition of the epic *Mahabharata*. The story of kinship relations describes a feud over land and power between two groups of cousins, the Kauravas and the Pandavas.

They belonged to a single ruling family of the Kurus, a lineage dominating one of the *janapadas*. Under patriliny, sons could claim the resources (the one in case of kings) of their fathers after his death. Patriliny is evident in mantras in ritual texts such as the Rigveda.

The rules of marriage for women were different. These were as follows

- Women had no claims to the resources of the household but they could marry into families outside the kin. This system is called exogamy.
- Young girls and women got married at the 'right' time and to the 'right' man.

- Sons were important for the continuity of the patrilineage.
- Daughters had not claims to the resources of the household.
- Marrying daughters into families outside the kin was considered desirable. This was known as exogamy.
- Girls and women who belonged to high status were ensured that they would get married at right time and to right person.
- Kanyadana, or the gift of daughter in marriage, was an important religious duty of the father.

The Dharmasutras and Dharmashastras recognised as many as eight forms of marriage. Out of these, first four were considered as 'good' while the remaining were condemned. These condemned forms were only practised by those who did not accept Brahmanical norms, Endogamy was also practiced by Satvahana rulers which was prohibited by Brahmins.

10. Compare the map in this chapter with Map 1 in Chapter 2. List the *Mahajanapadas* and cities located near the Kuru-Panchala lands.

Ans. The *Mahajanapadas* located near the Kuru-Panchala lands were Shurasena, Matsya, Koshala and Kashi.

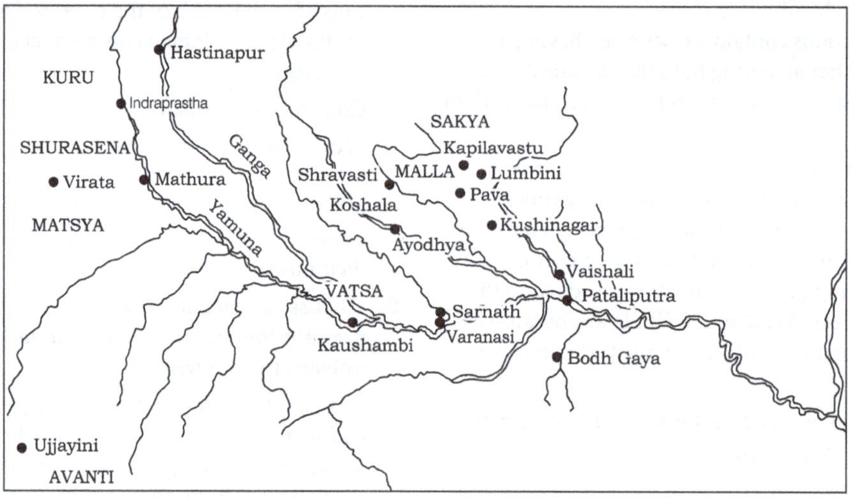

The cities located near the Kuru-Panchala lands were Mathura, Shravasti and Ayodhya.

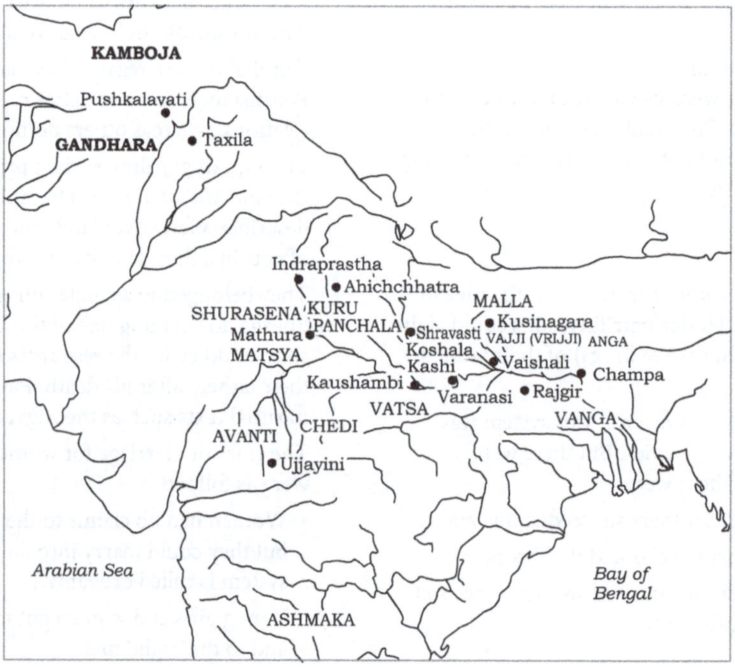

Exam Pattern Questions

Objective Type Questions

Multiple Choice Questions (MCQs)

1. Who among the following initiated the task of preparing the critical edition of Mahabharata ? **CBSE 2024**

(a) D.N. Jha (a) Irawati Karve
(c) V.S. Sukthankar (d) Ram Karan Sharma

2. The critical edition of the *Mahabharata* was completed in the year ....

(a) 1919 (b) 1925
(c) 1927 (d) 1966

3. The .... is one of the most colossal epics of the subcontinent which has in its present form. **CBSE Diksha**

(a) *Rigveda* (b) *Ramayana*
(c) *Mahabharata* (d) *Ashtadhyayi*

4. The term used for names derived from the name of the mother or female ancestor is called ....

(a) matriliny (b) matrimonial
(c) metronymic (d) matrilineal

5. In which of the following types of marriages does a man keep several wives? **CBSE Term I 2021**

(a) Endogamy (b) Exogamy
(c) Polygyny (d) Polyandry

6. In the case of the Satavahanas, succession to the throne was ....

(a) matrilineal (b) patrilineal
(c) Both (a) and (b) (d) Neither (a) nor (b)

7. The term *vamsha* is used for ....

(a) families (b) lineage
(c) descent (d) caste

8. The Shungas and Kanvas, the immediate successors of the Mauryas, were ....

(a) Brahmanas (b) Kshatriyas
(c) of 'low' origin (d) *mlechchhas*

9. Who among the following was the best-known ruler of the Satavahana dynasty? **CBSE SQP Term I 2021**

(a) Yagnasri Satakani (b) Simuka Satakani
(c) Gotami-puta Siri-Satakani (d) Vashisthaputra Satakani

10. According to *Manusmriti*, which among the following is not one of the means for men to acquire wealth?

(a) Inheritance (b) As a token of affection
(c) Conquest (d) Investment

11. According to Brahmanical texts, 'servitude' was the occupation of **CBSE Diksha**

(a) Brahmana (b) Kshatriya
(c) Vaishya (d) Shudra

12. Buddhist text *'Majjhima Nikaya'* is written in which language? **CBSE Diksha**

(a) Prakrit (b) Sanskrit
(c) Pali (d) Tamil

13. The composition of the *Mahabharata* has been traditionally attributed to a Rishi. Identify his name from the following options. **CBSE SQP Term I 2021**

(a) Rishi Kanada (b) Rishi Kapila
(c) Rishi Agastya (d) Rishi Vyasa

14. Who has written the short story "Kunti O Nishadi" based on *Mahabharata*? **CBSE Diksha**

(a) J.A.B Van Buitenen (b) B.B Lal
(c) V.S. Suthankar (d) Mahashweta Devi

15. Panini's book 'Ashtadhyayi' is based on which of the following themes ? **CBSE 2024**

(a) Puranas
(b) Grammar
(c) Mathematics
(d) Medicine (Ayurveda)

16. Sushruta's book 'Sushruta Samhita' is based on which of the following themes ? **CBSE 2024**

(a) Grammar (b) Medicine (Ayurveda)
(c) Astronomy (d) Mathematics

17. Which of the following is true regarding '*Rigveda*' ? **CBSE Term I 2021**

(a) *Rigveda* was compiled between 2500 BCE and 2000 CE.
(b) *Rigveda* consists of hymns in praise of deities like Agni, Indra and Soma.
(c) Hymns of *Rigveda* were not chanted when sacrifices were performed.
(d) *Rigveda* is a part of Upanishads.

18. Which one of the following statements is the correct explanation of 'Endogamy'? **CBSE SQP 2022**

(a) Marriage outside a kin group.
(b) Marriage within a kin group.
(c) A woman having several husbands.
(d) A man having several wives.

19. **According to the *gotra* rules followed by Brahamanas in ancient India** CBSE Diksha

(a) Two people of the same *gotra* could not marry.
(b) Two people of the same *gotra* could marry.
(c) Men were expected to give up their *gotra* after marriage.
(d) Men were expected to take up their wife's *gotra* after marriage.

20. **Which of the following statements is correct?**

(a) Brahmanas were supposed to study and teach the vedas.
(b) Kshatriyas were expected to engage in agriculture.
(c) Vaishyas were to engage in warfare.
(d) Shudras were engaged in any work which they liked.

21. **Which of the following statements regarding ancient Brahmanical ideas of Chaturvarna is incorrect?** CBSE Term I 2021

(a) Ancient Brahmanical ideas were not universally followed.
(b) Nomadic pastoralists did not follow these ideas.
(c) The *Nishadas*, followed these ideas.
(d) Subsistence hunters and gatherers did not follow these ideas.

22. **Which of the following statements is incorrect?** CBSE Diksha

(a) *Mahabharata* is a static text.
(b) Marriage of Draupadi with the Pandavas is central to the narrative of *Mahabharata.*
(c) Sanskrit used in *Mahabharata* is far simpler than that of the Vedas.
(d) Sections of *Mahabharata* are both didactic and narrative.

23. **According to Manusmriti, the paternal estate was to be divided** CBSE Diksha

(a) Equally amongst sons after the death of the parents.
(b) Equally amongst daughters after the death of the parents.
(c) To be given to a trust.
(d) Equally among the servants after the death of the parents.

24. **Consider the following statements and choose the correct answer.**

(i) The original version of the *Mahabharata* is in Sanskrit.
(ii) According to the shastras, only kshatriyas could be kings.
(iii) During the *Mahabharata* age, *gotras* were considered very important by the higher *varnas* of Hindu society.
(iv) The *Mahabharata* contains vivid descriptions of battles, forests, palaces and settlements.

Codes

(a) (i) and (ii)
(b) (ii) and (iii)
(c) (i), (iii) and (iv)
(d) All of these

25. **Which of the following strategies was adopted to enforce the norms of *Varna* order in the ancient period ?**

Choose the correct option CBSE Term I 2021

(i) It was asserted that *Varna* order was of divine origin.
(ii) The kings were advised to ensure the implementation of these norms.
(iii) People were made to follow norms.
(iv) *Varna* order was not determined by birth.

Options

(a) Only (i) and (ii) are correct
(b) Only (ii) and (iii) are correct
(c) Only (iii) and (iv) are correct
(d) Only (i) and (iii) are correct

26. **Arrange the location of the following cities of the Kuru-Panchala region and neighbouring areas in correct sequence from East to West**

(i) Ayodhya
(ii) Hastinapura
(iii) Indraprastha
(iv) Kushinagara

Codes

(a) (i), (ii), (iii), (iv)
(b) (i), (iii), (ii), (iv)
(c) (ii), (i), (iii), (iv)
(d) (iv), (i), (ii), (iii)

27. **Arrange the following major textual traditions written or compiled in the Sanskrit language in correct chronological sequence from the earliest to the latest**

(i) *Ramayana* and *Mahabharata*
(ii) *Manusmriti*
(iii) Major Dharmasutras
(iv) *Puranas*

Codes

(a) (iv), (iii), (ii), (i)
(b) (ii), (iv), (i), (iii)
(c) (iii), (i), (ii), (iv)
(d) (iii), (ii), (iv), (i)

28. **Which of the following pairs is correctly matched ?** CBSE 2024

(a) Endogamy - Marriage outside the unit
(b) Exogamy - Man having several wives
(c) Polygyny - Marriage inside the unit
(d) Polyandry - Woman having several husbands

29. **Which one of the following pairs is correctly matched?**

(a) Vaishya – Study the Vedas
(b) Shudra – Engage in agriculture
(c) Kshatriya – Give and receive gifts
(d) Brahmana – Exchanging gifts

30. **Which one of the following pairs is incorrectly matched?**

(a) Critical edition of the *Mahabharata* – VS Sukthankar
(b) The Bhagavad Gita – Advice offered by Lord Krishna to Arjun
(c) *Purusha Sukta* in the *Rigveda* – Created by Brahmanas
(d) *Manusmriti* – Laid down the duties of *Chandalas*

31. **Which one of the following pairs is correctly matched?**

(a) *Ashtadhyayi* of Panini - 500 BCE

(b) *Charaka and Sushruta Samhita* - 400-500 CE

(c) *Natyashastra* of Bharata - 100 CE

(d) *Puranas* (in Sanskrit) - 400 BCE onwards

32. **Identify the character of Mahabhrata with the help of following information.** **CBSE 2024**

(i) He was the son of Bheema.

(ii) He belonged to Rakshasa clan from maternal side.

(a) Duryodhan (b) Abhimanyu

(c) Ghatotkatch (d) Bheeshama

33. **Study the following statements carefully** **CBSE Term I 2021**

(i) A favourite student of Dronacharya.

(ii) Blessed by Dronacharya to be unrivalled among his pupils.

Identify this character of *Mahabharata* from the following

(a) Arjuna (b) Yudhisthira

(c) Eklavya (d) Duryodhana

34. **Identify the social category of people from the information given below.**

(i) Their task was to handle corpses and dead animals.

(ii) They were placed at the very bottom of the hierarchy.

(iii) They had to live outside the village, use discarded utensils and wear clothes of the dead and ornaments of iron.

(iv) They could not walk about in villages and cities at night.

Options

(a) Nishadas (b) *Chandalas*

(c) Kshatriyas (d) *Mlechchas*

35. **Identify the name of the following text from the information given below.**

(i) The Sanskrit used in this text is far simpler than that of the Vedas, or of the Prashastis.

(ii) The original story of the text was probably composed by charioteer-bards known as sutas.

(iii) This text included over 1,00,000 verses with depictions of a wide range of social categories and situation.

(iv) The text also contains sections laying down norms of behaviour for various social groups.

Options

(a) *Ramayana* (b) *Rigveda*

(c) *Mahabharata* (d) Silappadikaram

36. **Complete the following with the correct option regarding person and their respective caste.**

Drona: Brahmana :: Eklavya: ....

(a) *Nishada* (b) *Mlechchas*

(c) *Chandala* (d) Shudra

37. **Complete the following with the correct option regarding books and their respective authors.**

Vyas: *Mahabharata* :: Shudraka: ....

(a) *Manusmriti* (b) Puranaruru

(c) *Majjhima Nikaya* (d) *Mrichchhakatika*

Assertion-Reason

38. **Assertion** (A) Historians often use textual traditions to understand changes in economic and political life.

Reason (R) These texts lay down norms of social behaviour or describe and comment on social situations and practices.

Codes

(a) Both A and R are true and R is the correct explanation of A

(b) Both A and R are true, but R is not the correct explanation of A

(c) A is true, but R is false

(d) A is false, but R is true

39. **Assertion** (A) The practice of endogamy meant that marrying daughters into families outside the kin was considered desirable.

Reason (R) Daughters had no claims to the resources of the household.

Codes

(a) Both A and R are true and R is the correct explanation of A

(b) Both A and R are true, but R is not the correct explanation of A

(c) A is true, but R is false

(d) A is false, but R is true

40. **Assertion** (A) The *Manusmriti* is considered the most important of the Dharmasutras and Dharmashastras.

Reason (R) It lays down codes of social behaviour in great detail.

Codes

(a) Both A and R are true and R is the correct explanation of A

(b) Both A and R are true, but R is not the correct explanation of A

(c) A is true, but R is false

(d) A is false, but R is true

Match the Following

41.

List I (Form of Marriage)		List II (Meaning)
A.	Endogamy	1. Practice in which one man has several wives.
B	Exogamy	2. Marriage within the same family unit living in the same locality.
C.	Polyandry	3. Practice in which one woman has several husbands.
D.	Polygyny	4. Marriage outside the family unit.

Codes

	A	B	C	D		A	B	C	D
(a)	3	1	4	2	(b)	2	4	3	1
(c)	2	1	3	4	(d)	3	4	1	2

42.

List I		List II
A.	*Gotra*	1. Lineage
B.	*Vanik*	2. Common descendants of Vedic seer
C.	Polygyny	3. Practice of a man having several wives
D.	*Vamsha*	4. Merchants

Codes

	A	B	C	D		A	B	C	D
(a)	2	4	3	1	(b)	4	2	1	3
(c)	2	3	1	4	(d)	1	4	2	3

43.

List I		List II
A.	Brahmanas	1. Administer Justice
B.	Kshatriya	2. Study and teach the veda
C.	Vaishya	3. Agriculture
D.	Shudra	4. Serve the higher three vernas

Codes

	A	B	C	D		A	B	C	D
(a)	1	2	3	4	(b)	2	1	4	3
(c)	2	1	3	4	(d)	3	1	4	2

44.

List I		List II
A.	Duryodhana	1. Son of Hidimba
B.	Gandhari	2. Eldest son of Dhritrashtra
C.	Kunti	3. Mother of Pandavas
D.	Ghatotkacha	4. Mother of Duryodhana

Codes

	A	B	C	D		A	B	C	D
(a)	4	3	2	1	(b)	2	1	4	3
(c)	2	1	3	4	(d)	2	4	3	1

Picture Based Questions

45. Identify the following picture.

(a) A scene from *Mahabharata*
(b) A scene from Manusmriti
(c) A scene from Arthashastra
(d) A scene from *Rigveda*

46. The Satavahana ruled from which of the following regions of India?

(a) Andhra Pradesh and Maharashtra
(b) Bengal and Assam
(c) Rajasthan and Gujarat
(d Tamil Nadu and Kerala

47. Identify the following picture.

(a) A Kshatriya ruler
(b) A Satavahana ruler
(c) A Pandava
(d) A Shaka ruler

48. This image of the Lord Krishna advises Arjuna on the battlefield is based on the

(a) didatic section of *Mahabharata*, the Bhagavad Gita.
(b) narrative section of *Mahabharata*, the *Adi Parvan*.
(c) narrative section of the *Matanga Jataka*.
(d) didactic section of the ancient law book, the *Manusmriti*.

Answers

1. (c) V.S. Sukthankar
2. (d) 1966
3. (c) Mahabharata
4. (c) metronymic
5. (c) Polygyny
6. (b) patrilineal
7. (b) lineage
8. (a) Brahmanas
9. (c) Gotami-puta Siri-Satakarni
10. (b) As a token of affection
11. (d) Shudra
12. (c) Pali
13. (d) Rishi Vyasa
14. (d) Mahashweta Devi
15. (b) Grammar
16. (b) Medicine (Ayurveda)
17. (b) *Rigveda* consists of hymns in praise of deities like Agni, Indra and Soma.
18. (b) Marriage within a kin group.
19. (a) Two people of the same *gotra* could not marry.
20. (a) Brahmanas were supposed to study and teach the vedas.
21. (c) The *Nishadas*, followed these ideas.
22. (a) *Mahabharata* is a static text.
23. (a) Equally amongst sons after the death of the parents.
24. (d) All of these
25. (a) Only (i) and (ii) are correct
26. (d) (iv), (i), (ii), (iii)
27. (c) (iii), (i), (ii), (iv)
28. (d) Polyandry - Woman having several husbands
29. (d) Brahmana –Exchanging gifts
30. (c) Purusha Sukta in the Rigveda –Created by Brahmanas
31. (a) Ashtadhyayi of Panini – 500 BCE
32. (c) Ghatotkatch
33. (a) Arjuna
34. (b) Chandalas
35. (c) Mahabharata
36. (a) *Nishada*
37. (d) *Mrichchhakatika*
38. (a) Both A and R are true and R is the correct explanation of A
39. (d) A is false, but R is true
40. (a) Both A and R are true and R is the correct explanation of A
41. (b)
42. (a)
43. (c)
44. (d)
45. (a) A scene from *Mahabharata*
46. (a) Andhra Pradesh and Maharashtra
47. (d) A Shaka ruler
48. (a) didatic section of *Mahabharata*, the Bhagavad Gita.

Subjective Questions

Short Answer Type Questions

1. Write the main inferences which can be taken from the critical edition of *Mahabharata*. **CBSE Diksha**

Ans. The main inferences which can be taken from the critical edition of *Mahabharata* are as follows

- There were several common elements in the Sanskrit versions of the story, evident in manuscripts found all over the subcontinent, from Kashmir and Nepal in the North to Kerala and Tamil Nadu in the South.
- Enormous regional variations were also evident in the ways in which the text had been transmitted over the centuries. These variations were documented in footnotes and appendices to the main text. Taken together, more than half the 13,000 pages are devoted to these variations.

2. Describe the various stages through which a critical edition of *Mahabharata* was compiled in the 20th century. **CBSE Diksha**

Or **Analyse the role of scholars in the task of preparing the critical edition of the Mahabharata.** **CBSE 2024**

Ans. The various stages through which a critical edition of *Mahabharata* was compiled in the 20th century were as follows

- The compilation of *Mahabharata* started in 1919 under the leadership of a noted scholar, V.S. Sukthankar. The team consisted of dozens of scholars.

- They collected Sanskrit manuscripts of the text, written in a variety of scripts, from different parts of the country.
- They compared verses from each manuscript. The verses that appeared common to most versions were selected and published in several volumes, running into over 13,000 pages. The project took 47 years to complete.

3. With the emergence of new towns, social life became more complex. Examine the statement. **Competency Based Que**

Ans. The statement 'With the emergence of new towns, social life became more complex' can be examined through the following points

- **Change in beliefs** With the emergence of new towns, people of different places came in contact with each other. They discussed their ideas in an urban background, which led to a criticism of earlier beliefs and practices such as *kanyadana* and exogamy.
- **Codes of social behaviour** Brahmanas responded to changes in beliefs and practices by laying down codes of social behaviour in great detail.
- **Diversity** Despite strict social codes, the social relations were more complicated. Even Dharmasutras and Dharmashastras recognised eight forms of marriage, of which four were condemned. It shows that people did not strictly follow social codes.

4. Why did Gandhari make an appeal to Duryodhana not to fight against the Pandavas?

Ans. Gandhari appealed to Duryodhana not to fight against the Pandavas and instead he should make peace with the Pandavas. By doing so he would honour his father and mother, as well as, his all well-wishers.

According to Gandhari, every wisemen always tries to control his senses, specially the ruler or the person who acts as guards of their kingdoms. She further appealed her son to give up greed and anger because these two evils drag a man away from his profits.

She further appealed that if a king defeat greed and anger, he can become the great conquerer of the whole earth.

5. "The Dharmasutras and Dharmashastras also contained rules about the ideal occupations of the four categories of *varnas*." Critically examine the statement. **Competency Based Que**

Ans. The Dharmasutras and Dharmashastras contained rules about the ideal occupations of four categories of *varnas*. These categories are as follows

(i) Brahmanas were supposed to study and teach the Vedas, perform sacrifices and get sacrifices performed and give and receive gifts.

(ii) Kshatriyas were to engage in warfare, protect people and administer justice, study the Vedas, get sacrifices performed and make gifts.

(iii) Vaishyas were assigned to study the Vedas, get sacrifices performed and make gifts as the Kshatriyas and in addition were expected to engage in agriculture, pastoralism and trade.

(iv) Shudras were assigned only one occupation i.e. of serving the three higher *varnas*.

6. Write a brief note on non-Kshatriyas kings.

Or **"In the ancient India, the kinship was not only with Kshatriyas but also with Non-Kshatriyas". Explain the statement with examples.** **CBSE 2024**

Ans. Non-Kshatriya kings ruled during early societies, while according to the Shastras only Kshatriyas could be kings. An inscription in Sanskrit describes how Rudradaman, the best known Shaka ruler, rebuilt Sudarshana lake. This suggests that Shaka rulers were familiar with Sanskritic traditions.

Gotami-puta Siri-Satakani claimed to be both a unique Brahmana and a destroyer of the pride of Kshatriyas. He also claimed that there was no inter-marriage amongst members of the four *varnas*. At the same time, he entered into a marriage alliance with the kin of Rudradaman.

The Satavahanas claimed to be Brahmanas whereas, according to the Brahmanas, kings ought to have been Kshatriyas. They practised endogamy instead of the exogamous system recommended in Brahmanical texts.

7. Give some examples of Non-Kshatriya rulers and kingdoms between c. 600 BCE- 600 CE. **CBSE Diksha**

Ans. Some examples of Non-Kshatriya rulers and kingdoms between c. 600 BCE- 600 CE were as follows

- Brahmanical texts described Mauryas as being of "low" origin. The Shungas and Kanvas, the immediate successors of the Mauryas, were Brahmanas.
- The Shakas who came from Central Asia, were regarded as mlechchhas, barbarians or outsiders by the Brahmanas.
- The Satavahanan rulers were Brahmanas and Gotami-puta Siri-Satakani, claimed to be both a unique Brahmana and a destroyer of the pride of Kshatriyas. He also claimed to have ensured that there was no intermarriage amongst members of the four *varnas*.

8. Integration within the framework of caste was often a complicated process. Discuss with an example. **Competency Based Que**

Ans. Integration within the framework of caste was often a complicated process as

- The Satavahanas claimed to be Brahmanas, whereas according to the Brahmanas, kings ought to have been Kshatriyas.
- They claimed to uphold the fourfold *varna* order, but entered into marriage alliances with people who were supposed to be excluded from the system.

- They also practised endogamy instead of the exogamous system recommended in the Brahmanical texts.

For example, the best-known ruler of the Satavahana dynasty, Gotami-puta Siri-Satakani, claimed to be both a unique Brahmana (eka bamhana) and a destroyer of the pride of Kshatriyas. He also claimed to have ensured that there was no intermarriage amongst members of the four *varnas*. At the same time, he entered into a marriage alliance with the kin of Rudradaman.

9. The Mandasor inscription provides insights into the nature of guilds or shrenis. Comment.

Competency Based Que

Ans. The stone inscription found in Mandasor (Madhya Pradesh) was made in the fifth century CE. It records the history of a guild of silk weavers who originally lived in Lata (Gujarat). The guilds migrated to Mandasor, then known as Dashapura.

The Mandasor inscription provides the following insights into the nature of guilds or shrenis.

- Although membership was based on a shared craft specialisation, some members adopted other occupations.
- It also indicates that the members shared more than a common profession.
- The guilds collectively decided to invest their wealth, earned through their craft, to construct a splendid temple in honour of the sun god.

10. "In the ancient Indian subcontinent there were populations beyond the influence of Brahminical idea of four Varnas". Explain this statement with examples.

CBSE 2024

Ans. The above statement highlights the existence of populations in ancient India who were not influenced by the Brahmanical system of the four varnas. Examples of such populations include

- **Forest-dwellers** They relied on hunting and gathering as their primary means of subsistence, rather than agriculture, which was central to the Brahmanical system. One example is the Nishadas, a group to which the character Ekalavya from the Mahabharata is believed to have belonged.
- **Nomadic Pastoralists** These were communities that moved from place to place with their livestock. Since their lifestyle did not fit into the Brahmanical agricultural model, they were often viewed with suspicion.
- **Mlechcha** These were people who spoke non-Sanskritic languages, often considered outsiders by Brahmanical society. The term "mlechchha" was used to describe those who did not follow the Vedic traditions, and they were often looked down upon as barbaric or foreign.

11. How did Brahmanas develop a sharper social divisions? Give two examples.

Ans. Brahmanas developed a sharper social divisions by suggesting the ideal occupations of the four *varnas* in society. For example

(i) They classified certain social categories as untouchables.

(ii) Those who considered themselves as pure avoided taking food from those designated as untouchables.

(iii) Some activities like handling corpses and dead animals were regarded polluting. Those who performed these activities were called chandalas.

12. Describe the position of the untouchables in ancient society.

Ans. In the ancient society, the position of untouchables was very miserable. Their position was as follows

- They were kept at the lowest place in the society.
- They had to live outside the village.
- They used discarded utensils.
- They wore clothes worn out by the dead at the time of their death.
- They were not permitted to walk in villages and cities at night.
- They served as executioners and had to dispose of the bodies of those who had no relatives.

13. Describe how, according to *Manusmriti*, paternal estate was to be divided after the death of the parents with special reference to the rights of women.

Ans. According to the *Manusmriti*, after the death of the parents, the paternal estate was to be divided equally amongst sons, with a special share for the eldest son. Women had no right to claim the share of the property.

Further, the scripture suggested that women were allowed to retain the gifts they received on the occasion of their marriage as *stridhana*. This could be inherited by their children, but the husband could not claim it. Further, this scripture warned women against hoarding family property, or even their own valuables without the permission of the husband.

14. State whether gender differences were really important in the early societies from c. 600 BCE to 600 CE.

Ans. Yes, the gender differences were really important in the early societies. Societies were generally patrilineal. But matrilineal family was also present. Sons were considered important for the continuity of the family and had share in paternal estate. But women could not claim a share of these resources.

Women were allowed to retain the gifts they received on the marriage ceremony. They were also warned not to hoard family property without husband's permission. In other words, gender differences between men and women were sharpened due to unethical and biased rules.

15. Describe Buddhist view of social inequalities.

Ans. The Buddhists developed an alternative understanding of social inequalities and of the institutions required to regulate social conflict. In a text *Sutta Pitaka*, they suggested that originally human beings did not have fully evolved bodily forms and the world of plants was also not fully developed. All beings lived in a calm and peaceful environment.

It suggests that the institution of kingship was based on human choice, with taxes as a form of payment for services rendered by the king.

It also clears that human agency was important in clearing and institutionalising economic and social relations. If human beings were responsible for the creation of the system, they could also change it in future.

16. "Historians find it particularly a difficult task to understand a text as complex as the *Mahabharata*." Justify this statement. **Competency Based Que**

Ans. Historians find it particularly a difficult task to understand a text as complex as the *Mahabharata* because

- Historians have to consider several elements when they analyse text to examine the language of the text.
- The historians have to find out about the authors whose perspectives and ideas have shaped the text, as well as the intended audience. The authors have to keep in mind the interests of their audience while composing their work.
- They also have to ascertain the possible date of the composition or compilation of the texts as well as the place where they may has been composed.

17. Explain the language and content of the *Mahabharata*. **CBSE Diksha**

Ans. The language and content of the *Mahabharata* are discussed below

- **Language** *Mahabharata* was written in Sanskrit (although there are versions in other languages as well). However, the Sanskrit used in the *Mahabharata* is far simpler than that of the Vedas, or of the Prashastis.
- **Content** Historians usually classify the contents of the present text of the Mahabharata under two broad categories narrative and instructive.

  The division of the text into narrative and instructive is not strict. The instructive sections include stories. Similarly, narrative often contains a social message.

  Generally, historians agree that the instructive portions were probably added later. The *Mahabharata* is described as an *itihasa* (history) within early Sanskrit tradition. It is not clear whether events described in the text are historical or not. Some historians think that the narrative preserves the memory of an actual conflict between cousins, whereas others point out a lack of supportive evidence of the battle.

18. What were the findings of excavations done by archaeologist B.B. Lal at a village named Hastinapura in Meerut (Uttar Pradesh)? **CBSE Diksha**

Ans. In 1951-52, the archaeologist B.B. Lal excavated at a village named Hastinapura in Meerut (Uttar Pradesh).

The findings of excavations were as follows

- Lal found evidence of five occupational levels, of which the details of second and third occupational levels have been recorded.
- **Second occupational level (c. twelfth-seventh centuries BCE)** The walls of mud and mud-bricks were found. Some houses were made of bamboo walls.
- **Third occupational level (c. sixth-third centuries BCE)** Houses of this level were built of mud-brick as well as burnt bricks. Soakage jars and brick drains were used for draining out refuse water, while terracotta ring- wells may have been used both as wells and drainage pits.

19. *Mahabharata* is a dynamic text. Justify. **CBSE 2024, CBSE Diksha**

Or **"There are various elements on which historians have analysed Mahabharata and called it a dynamic text". Explain with example.** **CBSE 2024**

Ans. The *Mahabharata* is considered a dynamic text as

- The growth of the *Mahabharata* did not stop with the Sanskrit version. Over the centuries, versions of the epic were written in a variety of languages through an ongoing process of dialogue between peoples, communities and those who wrote the texts.
- Several stories that originated in specific regions or circulated amongst certain people found their way into the epic.
- The central story of the epic was often told in different ways and depicted in sculpture and painting. It also inspired themes for a wide range of performing arts – plays, dance and other kinds of narrations.

20. How does the Mahabharata show the multicultural nature of ancient Indian society? Explain with examples. **SQP 2024**

Ans. The Mahabharata shows the multicultural nature of ancient Indian society in the following ways

- **Incorporation of Diverse Elements** The Mahabharata includes stories and traditions from different Indian regions, like the tale of Hidimba, a tribal character.

- **Social Practices** It depicts different social practices, such as polyandry and exogamy, reflecting the diverse social norms of ancient India and its acceptance of various marriage and ritual customs.
- **Cultural Exchange** The epic shows interactions between different social classes-Brahmanas, Kshatriyas, Vaishyas, and Shudras-and outside cultures like the mlechchas, highlighting the exchange and coexistence in ancient Indian society.

Long Answer Type Questions

1. Describe the elements considered by historians to analyse *Mahabharata*. State the efforts of V.S. Sukthankar and his team for the preparation of the critical edition of *Mahabharata*.

Ans. Historians considered several elements when they analysed the *Mahabharata*. These were

- They examine whether texts were written in Prakrit, Pali or Tamil language that were probably used by ordinary people, or in Sanskrit, a language meant almost exclusively for priests and elites.
- They considered the kinds of texts, *viz*, whether it was mantras or stories read by the people.
- They tried to find out about the authors whose perspectives and ideas shaped the text, the intended audience for whom authors wrote the text.
- They tried and ascertained the possible data and place where it was composed. After that they tried to find out the historical significance of the text.

V.S. Sukthankar, an Indian scholar of Sanskrit literature initiated the task of preparing critical edition of *Mahabharata*. The Sanskrit manuscripts of the texts were collected which were written in a variety of scripts, from different parts of the country. The project began in 1919 with a team of comprising many scholars.

The team worked in the following ways

- The team worked out a method of comparing verses from each manuscripts and finally selected the verses that appeared common to most versions and published the verses.
- The project comprised of several volumes, totaling over 13,000 pages.
- The scholars observed the enormous regional variations of the text over the centuries. These variations were documented in footnotes and appendices to the main text. More than half of the 13,000 pages of the text consists of these variations.

2. Describe the familial ties and rules of marriage as per the Brahmanical prescription during c. 600 BCE - 600 CE.

Or **Describe the familial relationship observed during *Mahabharata* era.** CBSE SQP 2022

Or **"Historians have studied many rules and varied practices of familial ties during the Mahabharata period." Explain the statement with examples.** CBSE 2024

Or **Theme were specific features of the familial relationship during the Mahabharata Period." Explain the statement with examples.** CBSE 2025

Ans. The familial relationship observed during *Mahabharata* era can be described as below

- **About families** Families are usually parts of larger networks of people. The term kinfolk is used for these networks of relatives. Familial ties are regarded as 'natural' and based on blood. People belonging to the same family share food, resources, work and live together and perform rituals together.
- **Rules about Patriliny** Patriliny means tracing descent from father to son, grandson and so on. *Mahabharata* is a story of kinship relations which describes a conflict over land and power between two groups of cousins, the Kauravas and the Pandavas. According to *Mahabharata*, the idea of patriliny was valuable. From the 6th century BCE onwards, patriliny system was followed by most ruling dynasties. But there were variations in practice. If there were no sons, brothers succeeded one another. Sometimes other kinsmen claimed the throne. In very exceptional circumstances, women exercised the power, like Prabhavati Gupta.
- **Rules of marriage** The rules of marriage for women were different. Women had no claims to the resources of the household but they could marry into families outside the kin. This system is called exogamy. Young girls and women got married at the 'right' time and to the 'right' man. Sons were important for the continuity of the family line.
- **Forms of marriage** The Dharmasutras and Dharmashastras recognised eight forms of marriage. Out of these, first four were considered as 'good' while the remaining were condemned. These condemned forms were only practiced by those who did not accept Brahmanical norms.
- **Changes in social life** Social life of people became more complex with the emergence of new towns. To deal with this, Brahmanas responded by laying down codes of social behaviour.
- ***Gotra* system** From c 1000 BCE onwards, people (especially Brahmanas) were classified in terms of *gotras*. Two rules about *gotra* were important, women were expected to give up their father's *gotra* and adopt the *gotra* of their husband on marriage. Members of the same *gotra* could not marry among themselves.

- **Practice of polyandry** Polyandry is the practice of a woman having several husbands. In *Mahabharata*, Draupadi's marriage with the Pandavas is an instance of polyandry.
- **Importance of mothers** Satavahana rulers were identified through metronymics (names derived from that of the mother). But the succession to the throne was generally patrilineal.

3. "The *Mahabharata* is a good source to study the kinfolk values of ancient times." Justify the statement with suitable arguments. **Competency Based Que**

Ans. The *Mahabharata* is a good source to study the kinfolk values of ancient times. This statement can be justified in the following ways

- Families are usually parts of the larger networks of people defined as kinfolk. While familial ties are often regarded as 'natural' and based on blood, they are defined in many different ways. Some societies regard cousins as being blood relations, some others do not. The *Mahabharata* was a story of kinship relations. It described a fight over land and power between two groups of cousins, *viz*, the Kauravas and the Pandavas. Both of the groups had different set of ideas which shaped their actions and led to changes in their attitude towards life.
- *Mahabharata* puts strong focus on the idea of patriliny, i.e. tracing descent from father to son, grandson and so on. Under patriliny, sons could claim the resources including the throne in the case their father died. In *Mahabharata*, both the Kauravas and the Pandavas believed that they were the real successors to the throne.
- Draupadi's marriage with the five Pandavas was the most challenging episode in the *Mahabharata*. It indicated polyandry among the elite during that period.
- It is clear that literature gives us an idea about the perception of the writer, but sometimes it contains conflicting ideas. Thus, epic such as *Mahabharata* do not always depict the real picture of society.

4. What are the rules of *gotra* as given in Brahmanical practice? Give some examples to show that these rules were not always followed.

Ans. Brahmanical practice from 1000 BCE onwards classified people in terms of *gotra*. Each *gotra* was named after a Vedic seer. All those who belonged to the same *gotra* were regarded as the descendants of the particular Vedic seer. Two rules about *gotra* were particularly important. These were

(i) Women were expected to give up their father's *gotra* and adopt their husband's *gotra* on marriage.

(ii) Members of the same *gotra* could not marry with each other.

However, these rules were not always followed. Many women who married Satavahana rulers retained their father's names instead of adopting names derived from their husband's *gotra*.

For instance, there were Satavahana rulers who were recognised by their mother's name, such as Gotami-puta Siri-Satakani, Vasithi-puta (Sami) Siri-Pulumayi etc. This meant that these women did not adopt their husband's *gotra* name and rejected the Brahmanical rules.

Moreover, some of these women belonged to the same *gotra* i.e., the *gotras* of their father and husband were the same. This was against the rules of exogamy (marriage outside the unit), recommended by Brahmanical scriptures.

5. Discuss several theories regarding the author of the *Mahabharata*.

Ans. There are several theories regarding the author of the *Mahabharata*. These are as follows

- **Composition by charioteer-bards** The original story was probably composed by charioteer-bards known as sutas who generally accompanied Kshatriya warriors to the battlefield and composed poems in celebration of their victories and other achievements. These compositions were circulated orally.
- **Transition to written form** Fifth century BCE onwards, Brahmanas took over the story and started to commit it to writing. This transition coincided with the rise of chiefdoms such as those of the Kurus and Panchalas into kingdoms. The story of the epic is based on these chiefdoms.
- **Reflection of social upheaval** It might be that the new kings wanted their history to be recorded and preserved more systematically. With the establishment of new kingdoms, new norms replaced old social values. It is possible that some parts of the story reflect these changes.
- **Growing worship of Vishnu** This phase in the composition of the text was between c. 200 BCE and 200 CE. This was the period when the worship of Vishnu was growing in importance and Krishna, one of the important figures of the epic, was coming to be identified with Vishnu.
- Addition of didactic sections- between c. 200 and 400 CE, large didactic sections resembling the Manusmriti were added. With these additions, a text which originally began with less than 10,000 verses grew to about 100,000 verses. This enormous composition is traditionally attributed to a sage named Vyasa.

6. "The political power or kingship was rarely dependent on birth as Kshatriyas but also open to anyone who could muster support and resources." Explain the statement with the examples from sixth century BCE onwards. **CBSE 2025**

Ans. The statement that political power or kingship was rarely dependent on birth as Kshatriyas but was also open to anyone who could muster support and resources is evident from various ruling lineages from the sixth century BCE onwards. While the Shastras stated that only Kshatriyas could be kings, historical evidence suggests that rulers emerged from different social backgrounds, often challenging this traditional notion.

One of the most debated examples is the Maurya dynasty. While later Buddhist texts suggested that the Mauryas were Kshatriyas, Brahmanical texts described them as being of "low" origin. Despite this, the Mauryas established a vast empire, proving that political power was not strictly limited to Kshatriyas.

The Shungas and Kanvas, who succeeded the Mauryas, were Brahmanas, further demonstrating that kingship was not exclusive to the Kshatriya varna. These rulers gained power based on their resources and political influence rather than hereditary claims.

Another significant example is the Shakas, who came from Central Asia and were considered mlechchhas (barbarians or outsiders) by the Brahmanas. However, their rulers, such as Rudradaman (2nd century CE), played an essential role in governance. An inscription in Sanskrit praises Rudradaman for rebuilding the Sudarshana lake, showing that even non-Kshatriya rulers contributed to public welfare and were familiar with Sanskritic traditions.

Similarly, the Satavahana dynasty presents a complex case. The most well-known ruler, Gotami-puta Siri-Satakani, claimed to be both a unique Brahmana (eka bamhana) and a destroyer of the pride of Kshatriyas. This contradiction highlights that rulers could assert their authority based on their strength and achievements rather than their birth. Additionally, while the Satavahanas claimed to uphold the varna order, they also entered into marriage alliances with non-Kshatriyas, further proving that kingship was not strictly hereditary.

Source Based Questions

Read the sources given below and answer the following questions.

1. Why Kinfolk Quarrelled

This is an excerpt from the *Adi Parvan* (literally, the first section) of the Sanskrit *Mahabharata*, describing why conflicts arose amongst the Kauravas and Pandavas.

The Kauravas were the sons of Dhritarashtra, and the Pandavas were their cousins. Since Dhritarashtra was blind, his younger brother Pandu ascended the throne of Hastinapura. However, after the premature death of Pandu, Dhritarashtra became king, as the royal princes were still very young. As the princes grew up together, the citizens of Hastinapura began to express their preference for the Pandavas, for they were more capable and virtuous than the Kauravas. This made Duryodhana, the eldest of the Kauravas, jealous. He approached his father and said, "You yourself did not receive the throne, although it fell to you, because of your defect. If the Pandava receives the patrimony from Pandu, his son will surely inherit it in turn, and so will his son, and his. We ourselves with our sons shall be excluded from the royal succession and become of slight regard in the eyes of the world, lord of the earth!"

Passages such as these may not have been literally true, but they give us an idea about what those who wrote the text thought. Sometimes, as in this case, they contain conflicting ideas.

(i) Why did Pandu become the King of Hastinapura?

(ii) How did Dhritrashtra become King of Hastinapura despite being blind?

(iii) What do we know from the given passage about the time of the *Mahabharata*?

Ans. (i) Pandu became the King of Hastinapura because his elder brother Dhritrashtra was blind.

(ii) After the death of Pandu, the royal princes were still very young. So, Dhritrashtra became the King of Hastinapura despite being blind.

(iii) We come to know from the given passage that during *Mahabharata* time, patriliny was important. Under patriliny, the son could inherit the father's resources after the death of his father.

2. 'Proper' Social Roles

Here is a story from the *Adi Parvan* of the *Mahabharata*.

Once Drona, a Brahmana who taught archery to the Kuru princes, was approached by Ekalavya, a forest-dwelling *nishada* (a hunting community).

When Drona, who knew the *dharma*, refused to have him as his pupil, Ekalavya returned to the forest, prepared an image of Drona out of clay and treating it as his teacher, began to practise on his own. In due course, he acquired great skill in archery. One day, the Kuru princes went hunting and their dog, wandering in the woods, came upon Ekalavya. When the dog smelt the dark *Nishada* wrapped in black deer skin, his body caked with dirt, it began to bark. Annoyed, Ekalavya shot seven arrows into its mouth. When the dog returned to the Pandavas, they were amazed at this superb display of archery.

They tracked down Ekalavya, who introduced himself as a pupil of Drona. Drona had once told his favourite student Arjuna, that he would be unrivalled amongst his pupils. Arjuna now reminded Drona about this. Drona approached Ekalavya, who immediately acknowledged and honoured him as his teacher.

When Drona demanded his right thumb as his fee, Ekalavya, unhesitatingly cut it off and offered it. But thereafter, when he shot with his remaining fingers, he was no longer as fast as he had been before. Thus, Drona kept his word no one was better than Arjuna.

(i) Why did Drona refuse to accept Ekalavya as his pupil?

(ii) How did Ekalavya acquire the supreme skill of archery?

(iii) After giving his thumb to Drone, did Ekalavya repent? Give your opinion.

Ans. (i) Drona promised to Arjuna that no one would beat him in archery. In order to fulfil his promise, he refused to accept Ekalavya as his pupil.

(ii) Ekalavya acquire the supreme skill of archery by practising on his own in front of Drona's image made of clay, prepared by himself.

(iii) No, Ekalavya did not repent. Ekalavya honoured Drona as his teacher. He obeyed his word and fulfilled his teacher's wish of having his right thumb. In this way, he had proved himself a sincere and faithful student.

3. What the silk weavers did

Here is an excerpt from the inscription, which is in Sanskrit.

Some are intensely attached to music (so) pleasing to the ear; others, being proud of (the authorship of) a hundred excellent biographies, are conversant with wonderful tales; (others), filled with humility, are absorbed in excellent religious discourses; ... some excel in their own religious rites; likewise by others, who were self-possessed, the science of (Vedic) astronomy was mastered. **CBSE 2024**

(i) How was love for music expressed in the inscription ?

(ii) How did individuals demonstrate their mastery in the science of Vedic astronomy ?

(iii) In what ways did the various talents mentioned in the inscription contribute to the overall fabric of society ?

Ans. (i) In the inscription, love for music is expressed by mentioning people who are deeply attached to music "pleasing to the ear", highlighting music as a cherished and important part of life, alongside other cultural and intellectual pursuits.

(ii) Individuals demonstrated their mastery in Vedic astronomy by being self-possessed, indicating a deep understanding and skill in the subject, likely applied in religious or ritual contexts.

(iii) The talents mentioned in the inscription contributed to society by enriching culture, preserving knowledge, promoting spiritual growth, ensuring proper religious practices, and supporting practical needs.

4. A Tiger-Like Husband

This is a summary of a story from the *Adi Parvan* of the *Mahabharata*.

The Pandavas had fled into the forest. They were tired and fell asleep; only Bhima, the second Pandava, renowned for his powers, was keeping watch. A man-eating rakshasa caught the scent of the Pandavas and sent his sister Hidimba to capture them. She fell in love with Bhima, transformed herself into a lovely maiden and proposed to him. He refused. Meanwhile, the *rakshasa* arrived and challenged Bhima to a wrestling match. Bhima accepted the challenge and killed him. The others woke up hearing the noise. Hidimba introduced herself and declared her love for Bhima.

She told Kunti, "I have forsaken my friends, my dharma and my kin; and good lady, chosen your tiger-like son for my man...whether you think me a fool or your devoted servant, let me join you, great lady, with your son as my husband." Ultimately, Yudhisthira agreed to the marriage on one condition that they would spend the day together, but that Bhima would return every night.

The couple roamed all over the world during the day. In due course, Hidimba gave birth to a *rakshasa* boy named Ghatotkacha. Then, the mother and son left the Pandavas. Ghatotkacha promised to return to the Pandavas whenever they needed him.

Some historians suggest that the term *rakshasa* is used to describe people whose practices differed from those laid down in Brahmanical texts. **CBSE 2023**

(i) How was Hidimba's culture different from Pandavas?

(ii) Why did Kunti approve Hidimba's plea for Bhima?

(iii) How did the incident prove Kunti's far sightedness ?

Or **(i) Who was Hidimba? Why was she sent to Pandavas and what did she do? Explain.**

(ii) How did Hidimba plead with Kunti for her love?

(iii) On what conditions did Bhima agree for marriage with Hidimba?

Ans. (i) The Hidimba culture was different from the Pandavas in terms of their beliefs, customs, rituals and many other social practices, as well as their geographical and historical contexts.

(ii) Kunti approved Hidimba's plea for Bhima because she recognised Hidimba sincerity and devotion towards Bhima and believed that Bhima would be happy with Hidimba.

(iii) Kunti's approval of Hidimba's plea for Bhima demonstrated her far-sightedness as a mother and a leader. She recognised that Bhima's happiness and well-being were more important than traditional societal expectations and that her support for Hidimba would strengthen the Pandavas' ties with the local community and benefit them in the long run.

Or (i) Hidimba was the sister of a man-eating *rakshasa*. She was sent by her brother to capture the Pandavas. Later, she fell in love with Bhima and married him with some conditions.

(ii) Hidimba pleaded with Kunti in order to declare her love for Bhima. She told Kunti that she had left her family, friends and *dharma* for the sake of Bhima and requested Kunti for the approval to her marriage with Bhima.

(iii) Bhima agreed for marriage with Hidimba on the condition that they would spend the day together, but Bhima would return every night.

5. Draupadi's Questions

Draupadi is supposed to have asked Yudhisthira whether he had lost himself before staking her. Two contrary opinions were expressed in response to his question. Once, that even if Yudhisthira had lost himself earlier, his wife remained under his control, so he could stake her. Two, that an unfree man (as Yudhisthira was when he had lost himself) could not stake another person. The matter remained unresolved; ultimately, Dhritarashtra restored to the Pandavas and Draupadi their personal freedom.

(i) **How did Draupadi's questions unsettle everyone in the assembly?**

(ii) **What was the implication of her questions?**

(iii) **What makes Draupadi's question admirable?**

Or (i) **What was Draupadi's question to the Assembly?**

(ii) **How did Draupadi's questions in the Assembly redefine the notions of societal norms?**

(iii) **"Draupadi's character represented various virtues". Explain any two.**

Ans. (i) Draupadi's questions unsettled everyone in the assembly because she asked the questions that women during those times were not supposed to ask. She asked whether Yudhisthira had the right to stake her although he had lost himself earlier and a lost person could not stake another person.

(ii) The implication of her questions was that whether a wife could be treated as property of husband and whether she enjoyed her own freedom and identity.

(iii) Draupadi's question is admirable because she had questioned the male dominated system prevailing during those times. She had also questioned the unlimited control exercised by men over their wives, which in turn made the wives as the properties of their husbands. Her question raised the justification about personal freedom and dignity of women.

Or (i) Draupadi's question to the assembly was whether Yudhisthira had lost himself before staking her. She wanted to know if it was legitimate for Yudhisthira to stake her in the game, given that he had already lost himself in the game of dice.

(ii) Draupadi's question in the assembly redefine societal norms in many ways. It questioned the patriarchal idea that women were possessions controlled by their husbands. The debate also highlighted the importance of personal autonomy showing that individual's rights and dignity should be respected.

(iii) Draupadi's character represented the following virtues

- **Courage** She boldly questioned whether Yudhisthira had the right to stake her, showing her strength to stand up for herself in a patriarchal society.
- **Dignity and self-respect** She upheld her honour by challenging the morality of her treatment, demanding justice and focusing on the importance of personal freedom.

6. How could Men and Women acquire Wealth?

For men, the *Manusmriti* declares, there are seven means of acquiring wealth inheritance, finding, purchase, conquest, investment, work and acceptance of gifts from good people.

For women, there are six means of acquiring wealth what was given in front of the fire (marriage) or the bridal procession or as a token of affection and what she got from her brother, mother or father.

She could also acquire wealth through any subsequent gift and whatever her 'affec-tionate' husband might give her.

(i) **Explain the means how men could acquire wealth, according to *Manusmriti*? Do you agree with such division of acquiring wealth or not? Give one reason.**

(ii) **Explain the means of acquiring wealth by women.**

(iii) **Explain the results of having different ways of acquiring wealth by men and women.**

Ans. (i) According to *Manusmriti*, men could acquire wealth by inheritance, finding, purchase, conquest, investment, work and acceptance of gifts from good people etc.

No, I do not agree with such a division of acquiring wealth as it is gender biased, which leads to inequality in society.

(ii) Women could acquire wealth by what was given in front of the fire (marriage) or the bridal procession or as a token of affection and what they got from their brother, mother or father and also as a gift from her husband.

(iii) The following are the results of having different ways of acquiring wealth by men and women
- The gender based access to property leads to a low economic and social position of women.
- The dependency of women for wealth remained on the goodwill of the men in the family.

7. The Wealthy Shudra

This story based on a Buddhist text in Pali known as the *Majjhima Nikaya*, is part of a dialogue between a king named Avantiputta and a disciple of the Buddha named Kach- chana. While it may not be literally true, it reveals Buddhist attitudes towards *varna*.

Avantiputta asked Kachchana what he thought about Brahmanas who held that they were the best caste and that all other castes were low; that Brahmanas were a fair caste while all other castes were dark; that only Brahmanas were pure, not non-Brahmanas; that Brahmanas were sons of Brahma, born of his mouth, born of Brahma, formed by Brahma, heirs to Brahma.

Kachchana replied "What if a Shudra were wealthy....would another Shudra,.,,..or a "Kshatriya or a Brahmana or a Vaishya... speak politely to him?" Avantiputta replied that if a Shudra had wealth or corn or gold or silver, he could have as his obedient servant another Shudra to get-up earlier than he, go to rest later, to carry out his orders, to speak politely; or he could even have a Kshatriya or a Brahmana or a Vaishya as his obedient servant.

Kachchana asked "This being so, are not these four *varnas* exactly the same?" Avantiputta conceded that there was no difference amongst the *varnas* on this count.

(i) What did Avantiputta want to know from Kachchana about Brahmanas?

(ii) What was Kachchana's reply? Explain.

(iii) If a Shudra had wealth, would Brahmanas and others speak to him politely? Give reasons.

Ans. (i) Avantiputta wanted to know from Kachchana his thought about Brahmanas, whether the Brahmanas were the best caste having fair skin while other castes were dark; whether they were sons of Brahma or born of Brahma's mouth.

(ii) Kachchana replied that if a Shudra were wealthy then he could have another Shudra or Kshatriya or a Brahmana as his servant.

(iii) Yes, if a Shudra had wealth, Brahmanas and others would speak to him politely because he had the power of wealth.

8. Draupadi's Marriage

Drupada, the king of Panchala, organised a competition where the challenge was to string a bow and hit a target; the winner would be chosen to marry his daughter Draupadi. Arjuna was victorious and was garlanded by Draupadi.

The Pandavas returned with her to their mother Kunti, who, even before she saw them, asked them to share whatever they had got. She realised her mistake when she saw Draupadi, but her command could not be violated. After much deliberation, Yudhisthira decided that Draupadi would be their common wife.

When Drupada was told about this, he protested. However, the Seer Vyasa arrived and told him that the Pandavas were in reality incarnations of Indra, whose wife had been reborn as Draupadi and they were thus destined for each other.

Vyasa added that in another instance a young woman had prayed to Shiva for a husband, and in her enthusiasm, had prayed five times instead of once. This woman was now reborn as Draupadi and Shiva had fulfilled her prayers. Convinced by these stories, Drupada consented to the marriage.

(i) How does this story reveal that mother was considered as the highest guru?

(ii) Why did Kunti not save Draupadi from the dire situation?

(iii) Why did Drupada and Seer Vyasa agree to Draupadi's strange marriage with five men?

Ans. (i) After marriage of Arjuna with Draupadi, the Pandavas returned with her to their mother Kunti. Before seeing Draupadi, Kunti asked them to share whatever they had got. Kunti's command could not be violated. So, the Pandavas married Draupadi and she became their common wife. This story reveals that mother was considered as the highest guru by the Pandavas.

(ii) Kunti did not save Draupadi from the dire situation because she had given command to her son to share whatever they had got. The command of Kunti could not be violated. As a result, Draupdi became common wife of the Pandavas.

(iii) The seer Vyasa told Drupada that the Pandavas were in reality an incarnation of Indra, whose wife has been reborn as Draupadi. So, they were destined for each other. Further, Vyasa said that, according to another version, a young woman had prayed to Shiva for a husband five times. Shiva fulfilled her wish and the woman was reborn as Draupadi. Hearing this, Draupada agreed to Draupadi's strange marriage with five men.

SELF ASSESSMENT TEST

Objective Type Questions

1. Which among these were ruling Hastinapura during the *Mahabharata*?
   (a) The Shakas
   (b) The Satavahanas
   (c) The Kurus
   (d) The Mauryas
2. Choose the correct statement regarding *chandalas*.
   (a) They were allowed to live inside villages.
   (b) They could easily roam in the villages in daytime and at night.
   (c) They had to dispose off the bodies of those who had no relatives and serve as executioners.
   (d) Chinese pilgrim Xuan Zang observed and mentioned that *Chandalas* lived respectful lives.
3. Who were termed as *Nishads*? Choose the correct option.
   (a) People engaged in making gold ornaments.
   (b) People engaged in warfare.
   (c) People living in forests.
   (d) People engaged in trade.
4. Match the Following.

	List I		List II
A.	*Rigveda*	1.	Rules governing four *varnas*
B.	*Mahabharata*	2.	Purusha Sukta
C.	Dharmasutras	3.	Buddhist Text
D.	Matanga Jataka	4.	War between Kauravas and Pandavas

Codes

	A	B	C	D		A	B	C	D
(a)	4	1	3	2	(b)	1	3	4	2
(c)	3	4	1	2	(d)	2	4	1	3

Short Answer Type Questions

5. Why should historians work carefully to find out the historical evidences from literary texts?
6. Describe how the kinship relations changed with reference to *Mahabharata*.
7. There were populations whose social practices were not influenced by Brahmanical ideas. Comment.
8. Critically examine the duties as laid down in *Manusmriti* for the *Chandalas*.
9. Describe the caste mechanism of ancient Indian society.

Long Answer Type Questions

10. Explain rules and practices related with kinship in ancient India from 600 BCE to 600 CE.
11. Write in brief the events related to Ekalavya and Dronacharya.
12. Critically discuss the opinion of the different historians about *Mahabharata* as a historical source.
13. "The epic *Mahabharata* is analysed and classified at different levels by the historians on the basis of its content." Assess the statement by analysing the various aspects of the epic.

4

CHAPTER

This chapter deals with major religions present during the 6th century BC. Buddhism and Jainism emerged as new popular religions at that time, which spread throughout the world.

YOUR STUDY GOALS

4.1 Thinkers, Beliefs and Traditions
4.2 Beyond Worldly Pleasures : The Message of Mahavira
4.3 The Buddha and the Quest for Enlightenment
4.4 Buildings and Architecture
4.5 New Religious Traditions

YOUR PRACTICE GOALS

- Objective Type Questions (45 Qs ; MCQs, A-R, Matching, Picture Based)
- Subjective Questions (18 SAs, 6 LAs)
- Source Based Questions (7 Qs)
- Map Based Questions (2 Qs)

Thinkers, Beliefs and Buildings

(Cultural Development)

- Historians use various sources like Buddhist, Jaina and Brahmanical texts to reconstruct the exciting world of ideas and beliefs that existed in ancient times.
- Archeological evidences like monuments and inscriptions are also used to know about the period of that time. One such example is Sanchi **Stupa**[1].

4.1 Thinkers, Beliefs and Traditions

The mid-first millennium BCE has been the turning point in world history as

- It saw the rise of thinkers such as **Zarathustra** (Iran), **Kong Zi** (China), **Socrates, Plato** and **Aristotle** (Greece), and **Mahavira** and **Gautam Buddha** (India).
- New cities and kingdoms started to develop around this time.
- There were changes in social and economic conditions in the Ganga valley.

The Tradition of Sacrifice

- The early Vedic tradition was recorded in the ***Rigveda*** which was compiled around 1500 to 1000 BCE.
- *Rigveda* contains hymns in praise of deities, such as **Agni, Indra** and **Soma**. Many hymns were chanted during sacrifices, where people prayed for cattle, children, good health and long life.

1. **Stupa** A dome-shaped structure erected as a Buddhist shrine.

- Initially, sacrifices were performed collectively but from 1000 BCE-500 BCE onwards, they were performed by the heads of households for the well-being of the domestic unit.
- Sacrifices such as ***rajasuya*** and ***ashvamedha*** were performed by chiefs and kings who depended on Brahmana priests to conduct the rituals.
- According to Upanishads from the c. sixth century BCE onwards, people were curious about the meaning of life, the possibility of life after death and rebirth.
- Chhandogya Upanishad, was composed in the sixth century BCE in Sanskrit. It has two verses - the nature of the self and the true sacrifice which were composed in Vedic Sanskrit. They were taught orally to men belonging to priestly families.

Debates and Discussions

- Buddhist texts give ideas of lively discussions and debates. These texts have **64 sects** (schools of thoughts).
- Debates took place in ***kutagarashala***[2] or in groves where travelling **mendicants**[3] stay.
- The support for any sect could grow and reduce over time. If a philosopher succeeded in convincing any of his rivals, the followers of the latter also became his disciples.
- Philosophers like **Mahavira** and **Buddha**, questioned the authority of the Vedas and focused on individual agency. They suggested that men and women could overcome the problems of life and attain liberation.
- These ideas were different from Brahmanical ideas in which a person's position was decided by his or her birth in a specific caste.

4.2 Beyond Worldly Pleasures: The Message of Mahavira

- The basic philosophy of the Jainas was already known in North India even before the birth of **Vardhamana Mahavira** in the sixth century BCE.
- According to Jaina tradition, there were **23** ***tirthankaras***[4] before Mahavira.
- The teachings of Mahavira were recorded by his disciples in the form of stories, which could appeal to ordinary people.
- ***Uttaradhyayana Sutta***, a Prakrit text described how a queen, Kamalavati tried to convince her husband to renounce the world.

The Jaina monks and nuns took five vows

(i) To abstain from killing
(ii) To abstain from stealing
(iii) To abstain from lying
(iv) To observe self-restraint
(v) To refrain from having property (the state of refraining from marriage).

Important Messages of Jainism

- The entire world is animated; even rocks , stones and water have life.
- Non-injury to living beings, especially to humans, animals, plants and insects is central to Jaina philosophy.
- The **principle of ahimsa** emphasised within Jainism has influenced Indian thinking as a whole.
- The cycle of birth and rebirth is shaped through ***karma***.
- **Self discipline** and **penance** are important to free oneself from *karma*.

---

2 *Kutagarashala* A hut with a pointed roof.
3 Mendicant A member of a religious group, who lives by asking money to unknown people.
4 *Tirthankaras* A term used in Jainism for a person who has crossed over the river of life and suffering.

▲ *A page from a fourteenth-century Jaina Manuscript*

The Spread of Jainism

- Jainism gradually spread to many parts of India. Jaina scholars created many literature in Prakrit, Sanskrit and Tamil languages.
- Some of the earliest stone sculptures associated with religion were made by devotees of the Jaina *tirthankaras*.

Quick Test 1

1. Rigveda was compiled around which period of ancient history?
2. Mention the names of deities who were worshipped during Rigveda period.
3. Chhandogya Upanishad was compiled in which language?
4. Who is considered as the founder of Jainism?
5. According to Jaina tradition how many tirthankaras were present before Mahavira.

4.3 The Buddha and the Quest for Enlightenment

One of the most influential teachers of Buddhism was the Buddha. Over time, his message spread across the countries like China, Korea and Japan, Sri Lanka, Myanmar, Thailand and Indonesia.

The Buddha

- **Hagiographies**[5] give details of Buddha's life. The childhood name of Budhha was **Siddhartha**. He was the son of a chief of the **Sakya clan.**
- Siddharatha grew up inside the palace which kept him away from the harsh realities of life.
- One day, on a journey to the city, Siddhartha saw an old man, a sick man, and a corpse (dead body). He realised that the decay and destruction of the human body is inevitable (unavoidable).
- He also saw a homeless saint who found peace by overcoming the problems of old age, diseases and death. Influenced by the saint, Siddhartha left the palace to adopt the similar path.
- In search of his own truth, he explored different ways including **bodily mortification**[6] which led him to a situation of near death.
- He meditated for several days and finally got enlightenment after which he came to be known as **Buddha** or the **Enlightened One.**
- For the rest of his life, Buddha taught *dhamma* or the path of righteous living.

Teachings of Buddha

The Buddha's teachings have been reconstructed from stories, mainly found in the *Sutta Pitaka*. Stories suggest that the Buddha convinced people through reason and persuasion. His teachings were as follows

- The world is **transient** (*anicca*) and constantly changing.
- It is also **soulless** (*anatta*) as there is nothing permanent or eternal in it.
- **Sorrow** (*dukkha*) is a fundamental part of human existence.
- By following a balanced path between severe **penance** (self-punishment) and self-indulgence, humans can rise above these worldly problems.
- In early Buddhism, the existence of God was irrelevant.
- The Buddha regarded the social world as the creation of humans rather than of divine origin. Therefore, he advised kings and *gahapatis* to be humane and ethical.

5 **Hagiographies** The writing and critical study of the saints.
6 **Bodily mortification** Practice of self-denial to control bodily desires, often by causing self-pain or discomfort

- Buddha emphasised **personal responsibility** and **righteous action** as the means to escape from the cycle of rebirth.This was important to achieve self-realisation and *nibbana*[7] and end the suffering for those who renounce worldly attachments.

Followers of the Buddha

- Buddha founded a *sangha*, an organisation of monks who also became teachers of *dhamma.*
- These monks lived in a very simple way with minimum needs. They were known as ***bhikkhus***.
- Initially, only men were allowed into the *sangha*, but later women were also admitted.
- According to Buddhist texts, **Ananda**, one of the Buddha's dearest disciples, persuaded him to allow women into the *sangha.*
- The Buddha's foster mother, **Mahapajapati Gotami** was the first woman to be appointed as a *bhikkhuni.*
- Many women in the *sangha* became teachers of *dhamma* and later ***theris***, or respected women who had attained liberation.
- The Buddha's followers came from many social groups such as kings, wealthy men and ***gahapatis*** and also ordinary people like workers, slaves and craftspeople.
- After entering the *sangha*, all were regarded as equal on becoming *bhikkhus* and *bhikkhunis.*
- The internal functioning of the *sangha* was based on the traditions of *ganas* and *sanghas*, where decisions were made by discussions. If that failed, decisions were taken by a vote on the subject.
- Buddhism grew rapidly both during the lifetime of the Buddha and after his death, as it appealed to many people who were dissatisfied with existing religious practices.
- The main ideas which attracted men and women to Buddhist teachings were
  - The importance of conduct and values rather than the claims of superiority based on birth.
  - The emphasis placed on ***metta*** (fellow feeling) and ***karuna*** (compassion), especially towards the younger and weaker.

Buddhist Literature

- The Buddha taught orally through discussion and debate. People attended these lessons and discussed them.
- None of the Buddha's speeches were written down during his lifetime.
- After Buddha's death (c. fifth-fourth century BCE), his teachings were compiled by his disciples at a **council of elders** or senior monks at Vesali (in present-day Bihar).
- These compilations were known as *Tipitaka*[8]. They were first transmitted orally and then written and classified according to length and subject matter. It includes the ***Sutta Pitaka, Vinaya Pitaka*** and ***Abhidhamma Pitaka.***
  - *Sutta Pitaka* includes the Buddha's teachings.
  - *Vinaya Pitaka* included rules and regulations for those who joined the sangha.
  - *Abhidhamma Pitaka* dealt with philosophical matters.
- Each *pitaka* comprised a number of individual texts. **Commentaries**[9] were written later on these texts by Buddhist scholars.
- Texts such as the ***Dipavamsa*** (the chronicle of the island) and ***Mahavamsa*** (the great chronicle) contained regional histories of Buddhism.
- Buddhist texts were preserved in manuscripts in different parts of Asia.
- Modern translations have been prepared from Pali, Sanskrit, Chinese and Tibetan texts.

---

7 **Nibbana** It means extinguishing of the ego and desire.
8 **Tipitaka** A collection of ancient Buddhist sacred scriptures.
9 **Commentaries** A book or article that explains or discusses a topic.

The Therigatha

- It is a unique Buddhist text which is a part of the ***Sutta Pitaka***. It is a collection of verses composed by *bhikkhunis*.
- It provides information about women's social and spiritual experiences.

Quick Test 2

1. How did the Buddha get enlightenment?
2. Who persuaded Buddha to allow women into the sangha?
3. How were decisions made in the Buddhist Sangha?
4. Name the three pitakas.
5. What does *Sutta Pitaka* include?

4.4 Buildings and Architecture

- Buddhist ideas and practices emerged through discussions with other traditions, including the Brahmanas, Jainas and several others.
- Some ideas and practices are identified by the historical buildings and sculptures. Among all, **Sanchi** and **Amaravati stupas** are the best examples to represent these traditions.
- From earliest times, certain places such as sites with special trees or unique rocks were regarded as sacred. Small shrines attached to these sites were sometimes described as ***chaityas***[10].
- Buddhist literature mentions several *chaityas*. It also describes places associated with Buddha's life as follows

Place	Event of Buddha's life
Lumbini	Buddha's birth
Bodh Gaya	Attainment of enlightenment
Sarnath	Buddha's first sermon
Kusinagara	Attainment of *nibbana*

About 200 years after the time of the Buddha, Asoka constructed a pillar at Lumbini to mark his visit to the place.

Stupas

- Stupas were built to keep relics of Buddha such as his bodily remains or things related to him.
- According to the Buddhist text, ***Ashokavadana***, Asoka distributed portions of Buddhist relics to every important town for the construction of stupas over them.
- The stupas came to be worshipped as an emblem of both the Buddha and Buddhism.
- By the second century BCE, many stupas were built like *Bharhut*, *Sanchi* and *Sarnath*.

Building of Stupas

- The stupas were built with the help of donations by kings such as Satavahanas.
- Donations were also given by business organisations. For example association of ivory workers contributed financially to the construction of one of the gateways at Sanchi.
- ***Bhikkhus*** and ***bhikkhunis*** also contributed towards building these monuments.

10 *Chaityas* It refers to a shrine, temple or prayer hall.

The Structure of the Stupa

- The stupa originated as a **simple semi-circular mound of Earth**, later called the ***anda***.
- Above *anda*, there lies a balcony-like structure known as *harmika*. It represented the place where the Gods live.
- A mast[11] called the *yashti*, arised from the *harmika* which was often surmounted by a *chhatri* or umbrella.
- Around the mound was a railing which separated the sacred space from the secular world.
- The early stupas at Sanchi and Bharhut were plain except for the stone railings. The railings resembled a bamboo or wooden fence and the richly carved gateways were installed at the four important points.

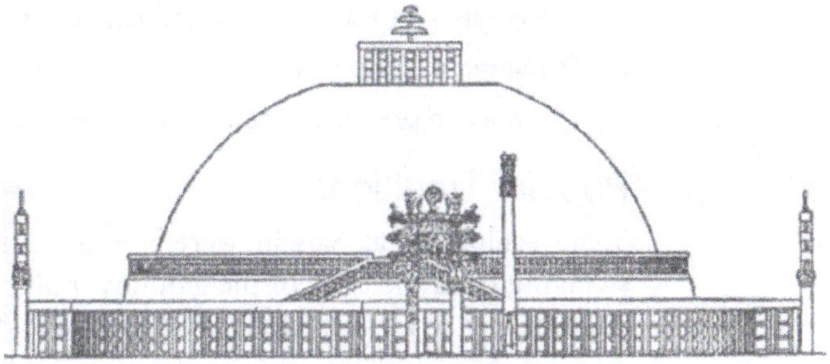

▲ *An Elevation of the Great Stupa*

- Later, the mound of the stupas came to be carved with niches (hollow space in a wall) and sculptures. For example, Amaravati and Shah-ji-ki Dheri in Peshawar (Pakistan).

Amaravati

- A British official, Colin Mackenzie found several pieces of sculpture at Amaravati. He made detailed drawings of them but they were never published.
- In 1854, Walter Elliot, the commissioner of Guntur (Andhra Pradesh) also visited Amaravati and collected several sculpture panels and took them away to Madras.
- He also discovered the remains of the Western gateway and concluded that the structure at Amaravati was one of the largest and most greatest Buddhist stupas ever built.
- By the 1850s, some of the slabs from Amaravati were taken to different places like the Asiatic Society of Bengal (Calcutta), to the India Office in (Madras) and even to London. An archaeologist named H.H. Cole opposed this but did not succeed in convincing the authorities.

Sanchi Stupa

- Sanchi is one of the most important Buddhist centres. The greatest ancient buildings in Bhopal are at Sanchi Kanakhera which were examined by Alexander Cunningham.
- When Sanchi was discovered in **1818**, three of its four gateways were still standing. The fourth gateway was lying on the place where it had fallen and the mound was in good condition.
- The rulers of Bhopal, **Shahjehan Begum** and her successor **Sultan Jehan Begum** provided money for its preservation.
- Sultan Jehan financed the construction of the museum and the guest house where **John** Marshall lived and wrote his works on Sanchi.

Sculpture

- The sculptures were removed from stupas and transported to Europe. This was because people who considered such sculptures to be beautiful and valuable, wanted to keep them for themselves.
- Initially, the sculpture at Sanchi seemed to depict a rural scene. However, art historians identified it as a scene from the ***Vessantara Jataka***[12].

▲ *The Eastern Gateway, Sanchi*

---

11 Mast A central pole that rises from the dome of a stupa.

12 Vessantara Jataka It is a story about a generous prince who gave away everything to a Brahmana, and went to live in the forest with his wife and children.

Symbols of Worship

Many early sculptors represented the presence of Buddha through symbols as follows

- The empty seat was meant to indicate the **meditation of the Buddha.**
- The stupa was meant to represent the ***mahaparinibbana.***
- The wheel represented the first **sermon of the Buddha at Sarnath.**

Popular Traditions

Some sculptures at Sanchi were not inspired by Buddhist ideas. For example, beautiful women swinging from the edge of the gateway, holding onto a tree. This is called ***shalabhanjika*** in Sanskrit and was seen as an auspicious symbol used to decorate the stupa.

▲ *An Elephant at Sanchi*

▲ *A Serpent at Sanchi*

- Some of the best animal representations at Sanchi include elephants, horses, monkeys and cattle. The *Jatakas* contain several animal stories depicted at Sanchi and animals often symbolise human traits. For instance, elephants represent strength and wisdom.
- Another motif shows a woman surrounded by lotuses and elephants. It seems to be sprinkling water for an *a*bhisheka or consecration. Some historians identify her as **Maya**, Buddha's mother, while others see her as **Gajalakshmi**, the goddess of good fortune associated with elephants.
- For historian ***James Fergusson***, Sanchi was a centre of **tree** and serpent worship.

Paintings from the Past

- Other visual means of communication, including paintings, were also used in the past. The best paintings are found on the walls of caves. The most famous are found in **Ajanta (Maharashtra).**
- The Ajanta paintings depict stories from the *Jatakas* such as courtly life, processions, men and women at work and festivals.
- The artists used shading to give a three-dimensional quality. Some paintings appear to be natural.

Quick Test 3

1. Name two places having stupas by the second century BCE?
2. Where did later stupas begin to include carved niches and sculptures?
3. Mention the animals which are depicted in the sculptures at Sanchi.
4. What did James Fergusson consider Sanchi to be a center of?
5. Where are some of the best-preserved paintings found?

4.5 New Religious Traditions

The Development of Mahayana Buddhism

- By the first century CE, there were changes in Buddhist ideas and practices.
- Early teachings focused on self-effort for ***nibbana***. They also regarded the Buddha as a human being who got *nibbana* through his own efforts. However, the idea of a saviour started to emerge. It suggested that Buddha would ensure salvation.

- The concept of the **Bodhisatta** also developed who were seen as concerned beings who collected merit by helping others. Worship of images of the Buddha and Bodhisattas became important to this tradition, known as ***Mahayana***.
- Supporters of **Mahayana** regarded other Buddhists as followers of Hinayana or the older tradition.
- Followers of the Hinayana described themselves as ***theravadins*** who followed the path of old, respected teachers, the ***theras*** (old teachers).

The Growth of Puranic Hinduism

- Hinduism included Vaishnavism and Shaivism.
- In Vishnuism, Vishnu was worshipped as the main deity and in Shaivism, Shiva was the chief god.
- The bond between the devotee and the god was of love and devotion or bhakti.
- In Vaishnavism, cults[13] developed around the various avatars or incarnations of the deity.
- In Vaishnavism, the deity is believed to have ten avatars, to rescue the world from evil forces. Some of these forms were represented in sculptures, along with other deities. Shiva was symbolised by the ***linga***.
- Stories behind the sculptures are contained in the **Puranas**, compiled by Brahmanas (middle of the first millennium CE).
- Puranas were written in simple Sanskrit and were meant for everyone, including women and Shudras, who did not have access to Vedic learning.
- The content in the Puranas evolved through interaction amongst people travelling from place to place sharing ideas and beliefs.

▲ *The Varaha or boar avatar of Vishnu*

Building Temples

- The early temple was a small square room, called the ***garbhagriha***. It had a single doorway for the worshipper to enter. Gradually, a tall structure, ***shikhara***, was built over the central shrine.
- Some temples were built out of huge rocks, as artificial caves.
- Some of the earliest caves were built in the third century BCE on the orders of Asoka for those belonging to the Ajivika sect. For example, Kailashnatha Temple in Ellora (Maharashtra) is carved out of a single piece of rock.
- Later temples had assembly halls, huge walls, gateways and arrangements for supplying water.

Indian Sculptures

- The early scholars found early Indian sculpture inferior to the works of Greek artists.
- The images of the Buddha and Bodhisattas which they discovered, were based on Greek models. These were found in the North-West, in cities such as Taxila and Peshawar, where Indo-Greek rulers had established kingdoms in the second century BCE.
- These images were considered to be the best examples of early Indian art.
- To understand sculptures, historians depend upon text records. While it is an efficient strategy to compare Indian images with Greek statues, but it is not always easy to use. For example, a famous sculpture in **Mahabalipuram** (Tamil Nadu).

---

13 Cults A type of unusual religion or religious group.

Sculpture at Mahabalipuram

▲ A Sculpture in Mahabalipuram

Art historians studied the Puranas to identify this sculpture. They had different views as

- Some historians feel that this represents the descent of the river Ganga from heaven. The natural split in the centre of the rock surface might represent the river. The story itself is narrated in the Puranas and the epics.
- Other historians feel that it represents a story from the *Mahabharata* in which Arjuna does penance[14] on the river bank to acquire arms.

Quick Test 4

1. Name the new way of thinking in Buddhism by the first century CE.
2. What was the focus of early Buddhist teachings?
3. In which language were the Puranas generally written?
4. How did the content in the Puranas evolve?
5. Which temple is an example of being carved from a single piece of rock?

TIMELINE

Major Religious Developments

c. 1500-1000 BCE	Early Vedic traditions
c. 1000-500 BCE	Later Vedic traditions
c. sixth century BCE	Early Upanishads; Jainism, Buddhism
c. third century BCE	First stupas
c. second century BCE onwards	Development of Mahayana Buddhism, Vaishnavism, Shaivism and goddess cults
c. third century CE	Earliest temples

Landmarks in the Discovery and Preservation of Early Monuments and Sculpture

Nineteenth Century

1814	Founding of the Indian Museum, Calcutta
1834	Publication of Essay on *the Architecture of the Hindus*, by Ram Raja; Cunningham explores the stupa at Sarnath
1835 -1842	James Fergusson surveys major archaeological sites
1851	Establishment of the Government Museum, Madras
1854	Alexander Cunningham publishes *Bhilsa Topes*, one of the earliest works on Sanchi
1878	Rajendra Lala Mitra publishes *Buddha Gaya*: *The Heritage* of *Sakya Muni*
1880	H.H. Cole appointed Curator of Ancient Monuments
1888	Passing of the Treasure Trove Act, giving the government the right to acquire all objects of archaeological interest

Twentieth Century

1914	John Marshall and Alfred Foucher publish *The Monuments of Sanchi*
1923	John Marshall publishes the *Conservation Manual*
1955	Prime Minister Jawaharlal Nehru lays the foundation stone of the National Museum, New Delhi
1989	Sanchi declared a World Heritage Site

14 Penance A punishment given to self when a person apologises for a mistake

Mind Map

THINKERS, BELIEFS AND BUILDINGS

1 The Background: Sacrifices and Debates

The Sacrificial Tradition
- In early sacrifices, people prayed for cattle, sons, health and life.
- Sacrifices such as *rajasuya* and *ashvamedha* were performed by chiefs and kings.

Debate and Discussions
- Buddhist text mentions 64 sects engaging in debates.
- Debates occured in *kutagarashalas* or groves during travels.

2 Beyond Worldly Pleasures: The Message of Mahavira

Teaching and Philosophy of Jainism
- Jainism teaches non-injury (ahimsa) to all living beings.
- Jaina monks/nuns follow five vows, including truth and non-violence.

3 The Buddha and the Quest for Enlightenment

The life and Teachings of Buddha
- His life details are reconstructed from texts and hagiographies.
- Buddha's teachings spread widely across Asia and beyond.
- Buddha emphasised reason over supernatural displays for teaching.

4 Stupas

- Stupas evolved from simple mounds to complex structures with harmika.
- Early stupas were plain, later adorned with carvings and sculptures.
- Stupas were built to enshrine Buddha's relics and sacred objects.
- Donations for stupa came from kings, guilds and individuals.

5 A Glimpse of Sanchi

- Preservation of Sanchi stupa was supported by Bhopal rulers.
- Sanchi reveals early Buddhist history through texts and artefacts.
- Art historians use texts to interpret sculpture's meanings.

6 Sculpture

Symbols of Worship
Tree, seat and wheel symbolise Buddha's meditation and teachings.

Stories in Stone
Sculpture at Sanchi represents with Vessantara Jataka story.

Popular Traditions
- Ajanta paintings illustrate Jataka tales, festivals and courtly life.
- Serpent motifs derive from popular, non-textual traditions and beliefs.

7 New Religious Traditions

Building Temples
- Early temples had a small garbhagriha to house deity images.
- Temples evolved with shikhara, assembly halls and grand walls.

The Development of Mahayana Buddhism
Mahayana became a 'great vehicle' compared to the old tradition described as Hinayana or the 'lesser vehicle'

The Growth of Puranic Hinduism
Interaction among priest, merchants and people shaped religious traditions.

NCERT Folder

Intext Questions

1. Compare what Shahjehan Begum described with what you see in the figure below. What similarities and differences do you notice? (Pg.84)

Ans. On comparison of Shahjehan Begum's description of the "great mound" with the above image, we can see significant similarities in the overall structure being a large, elevated mound with a staircase leading to the top, indicating a stupa-like architecture.

However, key differences can be seen in the details mentioned by Begum, like the presence of a "stone railing" and "small chambers" around the base, which are not clearly visible in the image.

2. What are the problems in reconstructing histories of ideas and beliefs when texts are not available or have not survived? (Pg. 87)

Ans. When texts have not survived, reconstructing histories of ideas and beliefs poses significant challenges, including scope for bias in interpretation of remaining evidence, difficulty in verifying information, incomplete understanding of diverse viewpoints and the risk of projecting modern ideas onto the past.

3. Is ahimsa relevant in the twenty-first century? (Pg. 89)

Ans. Yes, ahimsa is relevant in the twenty-first century. The principle of non-violence has been an integral part of Indian traditional values for a long time. It has been emphasised by Buddhism, Jainism in ancient history and Gandhi in modern times. Ahimsa stresses the principle of not causing physical harm to anyone.

In today's time, where conflicts, violence and issues like climate change are prevalent, the teachings of ahimsa play an important role. It encourages individuals and communities to seek peaceful resolutions to disputes, promote tolerance and embrace empathy.

4. Compare the Buddha's advice to Sigala with Asoka's advice to his subjects (Chapter 2). Do you notice any similarities and differences? (Pg. 92)

Ans. The Buddha's advice to Sigala and Asoka's advice to his subjects differ in the following ways

- The Buddha's advice to Sigala was about how to behave in various relationships, such as with parents, teachers and employees. Asoka's advice to his subjects was about *Dhamma*, which covered topics such as tolerance, ethics and morals.
- The Buddha taught his principles directly to his followers, while Asoka communicated with his subjects through edicts.

However, there are also some similarities between the Buddha's advice and Asoka's *Dhamma* such as

- Both the Buddha and Asoka's *Dhamma* focussed on the importance of following noble paths, discipline and simple living.
- Both the Buddha and Asoka's *Dhamma* promoted respect for elders and love for all.

5. Why do you think a *dasi* like Punna wanted to join the *sangha*? (Pg. 94)

Ans. A *dasi* like *Punna* may have wanted to join the *sangha* for the following reasons

- To renounce worldly pleasures.
- The *sangha* provided an opportunity to study Buddhist literature and philosophy with other monks.
- The *sangha* had a democratic environment where decisions were made by consensus.

6. What are the similarities and differences between the plan of the Great Stupa, Sanchi and its photo given below? (Pg. 97)

Ans. Both have the main structural similarities of a hemispherical dome on a square base, a circular path around the base, and a decorative railing (vedika) with ornate gateways (toranas) at the important directions.

However, the key difference is in the level of detail. The photograph shows a more elaborately decorated stupa, likely representing later additions and renovations with intricate carvings and sculptures compared to the simpler plan view of the Great Stupa in which focus is on the basic architectural layout.

7. Give your reasons why Sanchi survived. (Pg. 99)

Ans. The Sanchi Stupa survived because of a number of factors such as

- The rulers of Bhopal, Shahjehan Begum and Sultan Jehan Begum, provided money for the preservation of the site.
- Nineteenth-century Europeans were interested in the stupa, but were satisfied with plaster-cast copies and the original stupa remained at the site.
- When the stupa was discovered in 1818, scholars were already aware of the value of such findings and the importance of preserving them where they were found.
- The stupa escaped the attention of builders, railway contractors, and those looking to take its parts to European museums.

Answer in 100-150 words

1 Were the ideas of the Upanishadic thinkers different from those of the fatalists and materialists? Give reasons for your answer.

Ans The ideas of fatalists and materialists were not very different from those of Upanishadic thinkers. This can be elaborated in following ways

- **Central Philosophical Concepts** The Upanishads are collection of texts that contain some of the central philosophical concepts of Hinduism, which are also shared with Buddhism and Jainism. The concepts of Brahmana (ultimate reality) and Atman (soul, self) are central ideas in all the Upanishads. These are also accepted as central ideas in Jainism and Buddhism.
- **Ahimsa as a Universal Value** Ahimsa is equally given importance by Jaina text, Buddhist texts and Upanishads. All Hindus believe in *Ahimsa Parmo Dharma* (i.e. *Ahimsa* is supreme religion).
- **Theory of Karma** Upanishads believed in the theory of *karma*. It means that one should perform his *karma* or action without caring for its result. Fatalists also believed that one should be carefree because everything is determined.
- **Composition of Human Body** Fatalists and materialists both believed that human being is made-up of elements namely the Earth, the water, the air, the sky and the fire. These elements pass into space of incarnation.

2. Summarise the central teachings of Jainism.

Ans Following are the important teachings of Jainism

Life All Over the World The entire world is animated. It is believed that even the stones, rocks and water have life.

Not to Harm Any Living Being No living being should be given any injury. The basic philosophy of Jainism is not to harm or cause injury to human beings, animals, plants and insects. The principle of *ahimsa* is emphasised within Jainism.

Practice of Asceticism and Penance The cycle of birth and re-birth is shaped through *karma*. If one is to escape from this cycle of *karma*, one must practice asceticism (self-discipline) and penance (self-punishment). It is possible if one renounces the world. So, one has to live in monastery to attain salvations.

Five Vows Jain monks and nuns took five vows as not to kill, not to steal, not to tell a lie, not to possess property, and to observe celibacy (self-discipline).

3. Discuss the role of the begums of Bhopal in preserving the stupa at Sanchi.

Ans The begums of Bhopal helped in preserving the stupa at Sanchi in the following ways

- Both Sultan Jehan Begum and Shahjehan Begum provided money for the preservation of the ancient site.
- Shahjahan Begum funded the museum that was built there as well as the guesthouse where John Marshall wrote the text on stupa. She funded the publication of the volumes.
- They have preserved the stupa from the railway contractors and builders.

4. Read this short inscription and answer:

In the year 33 of the *maharaja* Huvishka (a Kushana ruler) in the first month of the hot season on the eighth day, a Bodhisatta was set up at Madhuvanaka by the *bhikkhuni* Dhanavati, the sister's daughter of the *bhikkhuni* Buddhamita, who knows the *Tipitaka*, the female pupil of the *bhikkhu* Bala, who knows the *Tipitaka*, together with her father and mother.

(i) How did Dhanavati date her inscription?

(ii) Why do you think she installed an image of Bodhisatta?

(iii) Who were the relatives she mentioned?

(iv) What Buddhist text did she know?

(v) From whom did she learn this text?

Ans (i) Dhanavati dated her inscription by referencing the reign of the Kushana ruler Maharaja Huvishka. She specified that it was the 33rd year of Huvishka's rule, further detailing the time as the 'first month of the hot season' and the 'eighth day'.

(ii) She installed an image of Bodhisatta at Madhuvanaka. To express her deep faith in Buddhism and to prove herself a real *bhikkhuni*.

(iii) Dhanavati mentioned her maternal aunt Buddhamita, her teacher or guru *Bhikkhu* Bala and her own parents.

(iv) Dhanavati knew *Tipitaka*.

(v) She learnt this text from Buddhamita, the pupil of *Bhikkhu* Bala.

5. Why do you think women and men joined the *sangha*?

Ans During ancient times, men and women probably joined *sanghas* due to the following reasons

- **Avoiding Worldly Pleasures** They wanted to remain away from worldly pleasures.
- **Simple and Disciplined Life** The life in *sanghas* was simple and disciplined. They could deeply study the Buddhist philosophy by staying in the *sanghas*.
- **Teachers of Dhamma** Many people entered the *sanghas* to become teachers of *dhamma*. They went on to become *theris* or respected women who had attained liberation.
- **Equality among the Followers of Sanghas** All were considered equal in *sanghas*. There were kings, wealthy men and *gahapatis*. There were also the humble folk such as the workers, the slaves and the craftsmen. Nobody could retain earlier social identity after becoming a *bhikkhu* or *bhikkhunis*.
- **Democratic set up of *Sanghas*** The internal functioning of the *sangha* was democratic. It emphasised consensus through discussions. If there was no consensus, decision was taken on the basis of votes.

Write a short Essay (about 500 words) on the following

6. To what extent does knowledge of Buddhist literature help in understanding the sculpture at Sanchi.

Ans Buddhist literature, the *Tipitakas, Jataka* stories based on the life of Gautama Buddha helped art historians to understand the sculpture at Sanchi in the following ways

Symbols Buddhist literature helped in understanding the symbols on the sculptures. Many early sculptures did not show the Buddha in human form, but they showed his presence through different symbols. These symbols were the empty seat that was meant to indicate the meditation of the Buddha, the stupa was meant to represent the *mahaparinibbana*, the wheel stood for the first sermon of the Buddha, tree stood for an event in the life of the Buddha, etc.

Popular Traditions Some other sculpture at Sanchi, e.g. beautiful women swinging from the edge of the gateway holding only a tree were not directly inspired by the Buddhist literature, rather they were derived from other Sanskrit texts.

***Jataka* Stories** The finest depiction of animals like elephants, horses, monkeys and cattle found in Sanchi most probably derived from the stories of *Jatakas*. Elephants was to signify strength and wisdom. Maya was the mother of Buddha or a popular goddess, all related with the stories of *Jatakas*.

7. The pictures 1 and 2 given below are two scenes from Sanchi. Describe what you see in each of them, focusing on the architecture, plants and animals, and the activities. Identify which one shows a rural scene and which an urban scene, giving reasons for your answer.

Picture 1

Picture 2

Ans Picture 1 is a part of the North pillar at Sanchi. Rural scenes are depicted in these pictures. Trees, plants, animals have been shown in the pictures. Animals like buffalo and deer have been depicted. Several heads of animals and some men with arches and bows have been depicted.

Picture 2 shows royal figures of Gods with attendants. Urban scenes are depicted in the figure. The panels represent heavenly scenes. The panel is carved and could be the work of ivory carvers. The pillars are supported with the animals seated back to back, e.g. elephants, horses and lions.

8. Discuss the development in sculpture and architecture associated with the rise of Vaishnavism and Shaivism.

Ans Vaishnavism was a form of Hinduism within which Vishnu was worshipped as the principle deity. Shaivism was a tradition within which Shiva was regarded as the chief God. These were forms that the deity was believed to have whenever the world was threatened by disorder and destruction because of the dominance of evil forces.

In Shaivism, there was growing emphasis on the worship of a chosen deity. In such worship, the bond between the devotee and the God was visualised as one of love and devotion, or *bhakti*. Some dieties were represented in sculpture. Shiva was symbolised by the *linga*, although he was occasionally represented in human form too.

The tradition of Vaishnavism and Shaivism also impacted the tradition of architecture and sculpture. The early temple was a small square room, called the *garbhagriha*, with a single doorway for the worshipper to enter and offer worship to the image. Gradually, a tall structure, known as the *Shikhara*, was built over the central shrine. Temple walls were often decorated with sculpture.

The tradition of building artificial caves was old. By eighth century AD, entire temple came to be carved out of a single rock, e.g. Kailashnatha temple and Ellora.

To understand the meanings of sculptures, historians have to be familiar with the stories behind them. Many of them are contained in the Puranas, compiled by Brahmanas. They were in Sanskrit verse.

9 Discuss how and why stupas were built. CBSE Diksha

Ans **Reasons of Building Stupas**

- Stupas originated as pre-Buddhist structures that evolved to show the essence of Buddhist tradition, serving as sacred mounds for enshrining relics, especially those of the Buddha. The idea of storing relics in stupas transformed these mounds into symbols of the Buddha himself and objects of worship, as described in the Asokavadana, which mentions Emperor Asoka distributing Buddha's relics and establishing stupas across major cities.
- Stupas were built not only to honour the Buddha's physical remains but to offer a place for meditation and devotion to the followers. They represented the Buddhist philosophy. Through rituals, such as circumambulating the stupa, devotees symbolically aligned themselves with the Buddha's enlightened path.

Structure of Stupas

- Building stupas was a community effort involving donations from various societal segments. Inscriptions on stupa pillars and railings reveal contributions from kings, guilds, individuals, and even Buddhist monks and nuns.
- Kings like the Satavahanas funded parts of these projects, as did guilds like the ivory workers who financed a gateway at Sanchi. Contributions were detailed by name, origin, and often by family affiliations, highlighting the broad, collective devotion to the Buddhist cause.
- Initially, stupas were simple, semicircular mounds of Earth (anda), which later became architecturally complex. The structure typically included a raised platform with a harmika (a railing symbolising the heavens) and a central mast (yashti) crowned with an umbrella (chhatri), marking the sacred space.
- Surrounding railings enclosed the stupa, distinguishing it from the secular world. Entrances at the four cardinal directions guided visitors to circumambulate clockwise, an act of reverence.
- Stupa mounds were decorated with elaborate carvings and statues, reflecting regional artistic influences. For example, Sanchi's gateways were richly carved, illustrating Jataka tales and scenes from Buddha's life. These visual elements not only attracted worshippers but also educated them about Buddhist teachings through symbolic art.

Preservation of Stupas

The preservation of stupas, like those at Sanchi, owes much to supportive figures and institutions. Unlike the stupa at Amaravati, whose sculptures were scattered due to colonial-era explorations, Sanchi benefitted from conservation efforts by local rulers and later the Archaeological Survey of India, which protected it as a national heritage site.

Stupas serve as a testament to the communal spirit, spiritual dedication, and architectural skill of ancient Indian societies, showing a lasting importance of the Buddha's teachings and Buddhist philosophy.

10 On an outline world map, mark the areas to which Buddhism spread. Trace the land and sea routes from the subcontinent to these routes.

Ans

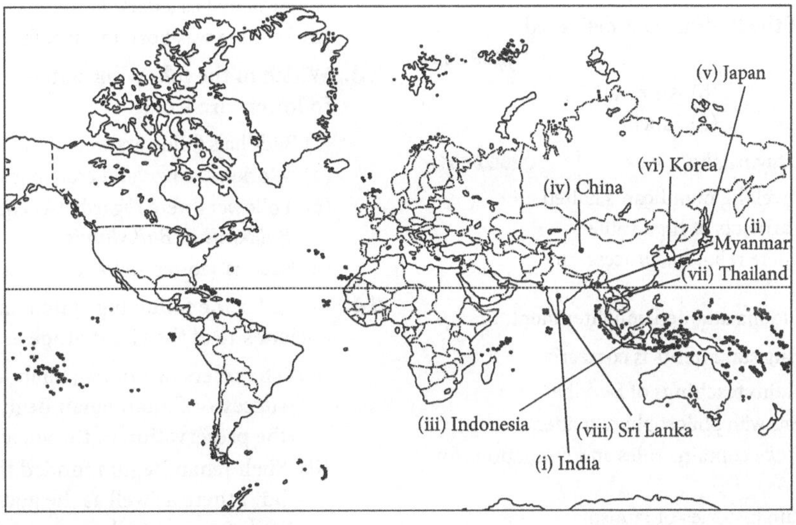

The second part of question is for self attempt.

Exam Pattern Questions

Objective Type Questions

Multiple Choice Questions (MCQs)

1. The famous archaeologist John Marshall dedicated his important volumes on Sanchi to which ruler of Bhopal? CBSE Diksha

(a) Gulbadan Begum (b) Sultan Jehan Begum
(c) Shah jehan Begum (d) Nur Jahan

2. Who was the favourite disciple of Buddha? CBSE Diksha

(a) Gajalakshmi (b) Maya
(c) Gotami (d) Ananda

3. At which of the following places Buddha attained enlightenment?

(a) Sarnath (b) Bodh Gaya
(c) Lumbini (d) Kusinagara

4. Which of the following is the oldest stupa in India and was commissioned by the Mauryan King Asoka? CBSE SQP Term I 2021

(a) Shanti Stupa
(b) Amaravati Stupa
(c) Sanchi Stupa
(d) Nagarjuna Konda Stupa

5. Which one of the following options indicate the sculpture of '*Shalabhanjika* Motif' in the Sanchi Stupa?

(a) *Mahaparinibbana*
(b) Strength and wisdom
(c) Auspicious symbol
(d) Devotion towards Goddess

6. The first Sermon of the Buddha was delivered at .... CBSE 2024

(a) Bodh Gaya (b) Amravati
(c) Sarnath (d) Sanchi

7. In ancient India, *kutagarashala* was CBSE Diksha

(a) A place where travelling mendicants halted.
(b) A place housing artifacts of high value
(c) An open place where religious processions took place.
(d) A place where Buddha attained enlightenment.

8. Which of the following statements is correct?

(a) *Sutta Pitaka* contains teachings of Buddha.
(b) *Vinaya Pitaka* deals with philosophical matters.
(c) *Abhidhamma Pitaka* contains rules and regulations for Sangha.
(d) *Dipavamsa* contain histories of Jainism.

9. Which of these is not one of the Five Vows taken by monastic jains? CBSE Diksha

(a) Follow the life of Mahavira
(b) To abstain from killing
(c) To observe celibacy
(d) To abstain from possessing property

10. Which one of the following aspects describes the meaning of '*Tirthankaras*' in Jainism? CBSE SQP Term I 2021

(a) Supreme being who is the incarnation of God
(b) Those who guide men and women across the river of existence
(c) Those who follow the path of Vedanta asceticism
(d) Those who know the ultimate truth and dharma

11. Which of the following statements is incorrect about Jainism? CBSE Term I 2021

(a) The entire world is animated.
(b) The cycle of birth and rebirth is shaped through donation.
(c) Asceticism and penance are required to free oneself from the cycle of Karma.
(d) Monastic existence is a necessary condition of salvation.

12. Which of the following statement is incorrect?

(a) The childhood name of Buddha was Siddhartha
(b) *Sutta Pitaka* is a collection of verses.
(c) Mahapajapati Gotami was the first woman to be ordained as a *bhikkhuni*.
(d) Buddha was born in Sarnath.

13. Which of the following statements regarding Buddha's followers are true? CBSE Term I 2021

(a) Buddha's followers were kings and *gahapatis* only.
(b) Workers, slaves and craftspersons worked in *sanghas*.
(c) Followers were regarded as equal on becoming *Bhikkhus* or *Bhikkhunis*.
(d) Buddha's foster mother, Gotami, never adopted Buddhism.

14. Consider the following statements regarding the ancient site of the Great Stupa at Sanchi. CBSE Diksha

(i) The rulers of Bhopal, Shah Jehan Begum and her successor Sultan Jehan Begum, provided money for the preservation of the ancient site.
(ii) Shah Jehan Begum funded the museum that was built there as well as the guest house where he lived and wrote the volumes on Sanchi.

(iii) One of the most important Buddhist centres, the discovery of Sanchi has vastly transformed our understanding of early Buddhism.

Which of the above statements is/are correct?

(a) Only (i) (b) (ii) and (iii)
(c) (i) and (iii) (d) All of these

15. Consider the following statements regarding Buddhist philosophy and choose the correct option.

(i) *Anicca* means the world is transient.
(ii) *Anatta* means the world is soulless.
(iii) The world is full of sorrows.

Options

(a) (i) and (ii) (b) Only (iii)
(c) (ii) and (iii) (d) All of these

16. Which among the following are Buddha's teachings? **CBSE Term I 2021**

(i) The world is transient and constantly changing.
(ii) The world is soulless as there is nothing eternal.
(iii) Sorrows are not intrinsic to human existence.
(iv) Death is inevitable.

Choose the correct option

(a) Only (i), (ii) and (iii) (b) Only (ii), (iii) and (iv)
(c) Only (i), (iii) and (iv) (d) Only (i), (ii) and (iv)

17. Study the following statements regarding Buddhism carefully.

(i) Buddhism grew rapidly, both during the lifetime and after the death of Buddha.
(ii) Buddhism did not give much importance to conduct and values.
(iii) Buddhism appealed to many people who were dissatisfied with the existing religious practices.
(iv) Buddhism laid much stress on superiority based on birth.

Which of the above statements are correct?

(a) (i) and (ii) (b) (ii) and (iv)
(c) (i) and (iii) (d) (iii) and (iv)

18. Read the following statements regarding the followers of the Buddha and choose the correct option **CBSE 2024 C**

(i) Mahapajapati Gotami was the first woman to be ordained as a Bhikkhuni.
(ii) Many women who entered the Sangha became the teachers of Dhamma.
(iii) The Buddha's followers came from many social groups, including kings and slaves.
(iv) Once within the Sangha, all were regarded as Dhamma Mahamatya.

Options

(a) (i) and (ii) (b) (i) and (iii)
(c) (i), (ii) and (iv) (d) (i), (ii) and (iii)

19. Consider the following statements regarding the motif of *shalabhanjika* and choose the correct option.

(i) This was regarded as an auspicious symbol.
(ii) This was a woman whose touch caused the trees to flower.
(iii) It was a symbol of strength and wisdom.
(iv) It was a symbol of renunciation. **CBSE Term I 2021**

Codes

(a) Only (i) and (ii) are correct
(b) Only (ii) and (iii) are correct
(c) Only (iii) and (iv) are correct
(d) All are correct

20. Consider the following statements regarding Jainism and choose the correct option **CBSE 2025**

I. The cycle of birth and rebirth is shaped through Karma.
II. There is a need to renounce the world.
III. Worldly existence is a necessary condition for attaining salvation.
IV. Principle of Ahimsa is important.

Options

(a) I, II and III (b) II, III and IV
(c) I, II and IV (d) I, III and IV

21. Consider the following statements regarding Buddhism and choose the correct option. **CBSE SQP 2024**

(i) The concept of Bodhisattva is central to Hinayana sect of Buddhism.
(ii) Bodhisattva is a compassionate one on his way to enlightenment.
(iii) Bodhisattva achieve nibbana for personal salvation.

Codes

(a) (ii) and (iii) (b) (ii) and (iii)
(c) (i) and (ii) (d) (i) and (iii)

22. Which of the following pairs is correctly matched? **CBSE 2023**

First Millennium Thinker		Country they Belonged
(a) Zarathustra	–	Iran
(b) Kungzi	–	Japan
(c) Socrates	–	Rome
(d) Mahavira	–	Sri Lanka

23. Identify the name of the writing from the information given below.

- It is a biography of a saint or religious leader.
- It often praise the saint's achievements and may not always be literally accurate.
- These writing tell us about the beliefs of the followers of that particular tradition.

(a) Hagiography (b) Documentary
(c) Bibliography (d) Autobiography

24. **Identify the name of the person from the information given below.**

- He was the commissioner of Guntur (Andhra Pradesh) and Visited Amaravati in 1854.
- He also discovered the remains of Western Gateway.
- He came to the conclusion that the structure at Amaravati was one of the largest and most significant stupas ever built.
- He collected several sculptural panels and took them away to Madras.

(a) H.H. Cole
(b) Walter Elliot
(c) James Fergusson
(d) John Marshall

25. **Identify the term which is the correct term for the given statement.**

"Those who were the supporters of materialism"

(a) Tirthankaras
(b) Rajasuya
(c) Ashvamedha
(d) Ajivikas

26. **Identify the term which defines the given below statement and give the correct answer.**

"The stupa originated as a sample semi-circular mound of Earth".

(a) *Marmik*
(b) *Anda*
(c) *Amalka*
(d) *Pradakshinapath*

27. **Chhandogya Upanishad : Sanskrit :: *Uttaradhyayana Sutta*: ....**

(a) Pali (b) Prakrit
(c) Tamil (d) Urdu

28. **"Be lamps unto yourselves as all of you must work out your own liberation."**
Identify the essence of the words of Buddha from the options given below. CBSE SQP 2022

(a) One should connect to inner being.
(b) One should live life of brahmacharya.
(c) One should focus and express feelings.
(d) One should spread religion everywhere.

29. **Complete the following with the correct option regarding the Buddhist texts and their respective contents. *Sutta Pitaka*: Buddha's teachings :: *Abhidhamma Pitaka*: ....**

(a) Philosophical matters
(b) Rules and regulations
(c) Criticism of Brahamanical authority
(d) Praise of Kshatriya kings

Assertion-Reason

30. **Assertion** (A) The sixth century BCE is often regarded as a major turning point in early Indian history.
Reason (R) This was an era associated with early states, cities, use of iron, development of coinage and growth of Buddhism and Jainism. CBSE 2024

Codes

(a) Both A and R are true and R is the correct explanation of A
(b) Both A and R are true, but R is not the correct explanation of A
(c) A is true, but R is false
(d) A is false, but R is true

31. **Assertion** (A) The principle of ahimsa, emphasised within Jainism.
Reason (R) Cycle of birth is shaped through karma but rebirth is not.

Codes

(a) Both A and R are true and R is the correct explanation of A
(b) Both A and R are true, but R is not the correct explanation of A
(c) A is true, but R is false
(d) A is false, but R is true

32. Two statements have been given below as Assertion (A) and Reason R). Read the statements and choose the appropriate answer : CBSE 2025

Assertion (A) Buddhism grew rapidly both during the lifetime and after the death of Buddha. (D) (B) Sanghol and Rakhigarhi Shortughai and Lothal.
Reason (R): Many people were dissatisfied with existing religious practices and confused by the rapid social changes taking place around them.

Codes

(a) Both A and R are true and R is the correct reasoning of A
(b) Both A and R are true but R is not the correct reasoning of A
(c) A is true, R is untrue
(d) A is untrue, R is true

33. **Assertion** (A) In the eighth century, the Kailashnatha temple was carved out of a mountain. CBSE 2024
Reason (R) King Asoka had given the directive to create artificial caves by cutting into the mountains to resemble temples.

Codes

(a) Both A and R are true and R is the correct explanation of A
(b) Both A and R are true, but R is not the correct explanation of A
(c) A is true, but R is false
(d) A is false, but R is true

Match the Following

34.

List I (Sculpture of Sanchi)		List II (Symbolism)	
A.	Empty Seat	1.	Symbol of good fortune
B.	Wheel	2.	Auspicious symbol
C.	Shalabhanjika	3.	First sermon of Buddha
D.	Gajalakshmi	4.	Mahaparinibbana

Codes

	A	B	C	D		A	B	C	D
(a)	2	1	3	4	(b)	1	2	4	3
(c)	4	3	2	1	(d)	3	4	1	2

35.

List I		List II	
A.	It means greater wheel	1.	Vaishnavism
B.	It means lesser wheel	2.	*Hinayana*
C.	It is a religious town near Bhopal	3.	*Mahayana*
D.	It is a form of Hinduism	4.	Sanchi

Codes

	A	B	C	D		A	B	C	D
(a)	1	3	4	2	(b)	3	2	4	1
(c)	3	2	1	4	(d)	4	1	3	2

36.

List I		List II	
A.	Chaitya	1.	Contains relics of Buddha
B.	Vihara	2.	Prayer hall for the Buddhist monks
C.	Sangha	3.	Dwelling place of Buddhist monks
D.	Stupa	4.	Organisation of monks

Codes

	A	B	C	D		A	B	C	D
(a)	1	2	4	3	(b)	1	3	4	2
(c)	2	3	4	1	(d)	3	4	2	1

37.

List I		List II	
A.	Descent of river Ganga	1.	Ellora
B.	Kailashnatha Temple	2.	Deogarh
C.	Vishnu reclining on the serpent Sheshnag	3.	Aihole
D.	Vishnu rescuing the Earth goddess	4.	Mahabalipuram

Codes

	A	B	C	D		A	B	C	D
(a)	1	2	3	4	(b)	4	1	3	2
(c)	4	1	2	3	(d)	2	4	1	3

Picture Based Questions

38. **Identify the following picture from the given options.** **CBSE 2024**

(a) Sultan Jahan Begum (b) Shah Jehan Begum
(c) Jahanara Begum (d) Ruksar Begum

39. **Identify the picture given below.**

(a) Tirthankara from Mathura
(b) Englightenment of Buddha
(c) Gajalakshmi
(d) A Kshatriya king

40. **Identify which of the following options refers to the Gateway of Sanchi stupa given below.**

(a) Eastern gateway (b) Western gateway
(c) Northern gateway (d) Southern gateway

41. The following picture shows the structure of a temple carved out of single piece of rock. Identify this temple correctly from the given options : **CBSE 2025**

(a) Deogarh Temple
(b) Kailashnatha Temple
(c) Mahabalipuram Temple
(d) Brihideshwara Temple

42. Identify the school of art with the help of the given image of Buddha. **CBSE 2024**

(a) Gandhara School of Art
(b) Mathura School of Art
(c) Sarnath School of Art
(d) Amravati School of Art

43. Identify the structural feature marked 'A' of Sanchi Stupa and choose the correct option from the following: **CBSE 2024**

(a) Harmika
(b) Yashti
(c) Chhatri
(d) Anda

44. Identify which of the following options refers to the ancient cave painting given below? **CBSE SQP 2024**

(a) Ajanta Cave Paintings
(b) Bagh Cave Paintings
(c) Sittanavasal Cave Paintings
(d) Ellora Cave Paintings

Answers

1. (b) Sultan Jehan Begum
2. (d) Ananda
3. (b) Bodh Gaya
4. (c) Sanchi Stupa
5. (c) Auspicious symbol
6. (c) Sarnath
7. (a) A place where travelling mendicants halted.
8. (a) *Sutta Pitaka* contains teachings of Buddha.
9. (a) Follow the life of Mahavira
10. (b) Those who guide men and women across the river of existence
11. (b) The cycle of birth and rebirth is shaped through donation.
12. (d) Buddha was born in Sarnath.
13. (c) Followers were regarded as equal on becoming *Bhikkhus* or *Bhikkhunis*.
14. (d) All of these
15. (d) All of these
16. (d) Only (i), (ii) and (iv)
17. (c) (i) and (iii)
18. (d) (i), (ii) and (iii)
19. (a) Only (i) and (ii) are correct
20. (c) (i), (ii) and (iv)
21. (c) (i) and (ii)
22. (a) Zarathustra – Iran
23. (a) Hagiography
24. (b) Walter Elliot
25. (d) Ajivikas
26. (b) *Anda*
27. (b) Prakrit

28. (a) One should connect to inner being.
29. (a) Philosophical matters
30. (a) Both A and R are true and R is the correct explanation of A
31. (c) A is true, but R is false
32. (a) Both A and R are true and R is the correct reasoning of A
33. (c) A is true, but R is false
34. (c) 35. (b)
36. (c)
37. (c)
38. (b) Shah Jehan Begum
39. (a) Tirthankara from Mathura
40. (a) Eastern Gateway
41. (b) Kailashnatha Temple
42. (b) Mathura School of Art
43. (d) Anda
44. (a) Ajanta cave paintings.

Subjective Questions

Short Answer Type Questions

1. 'Shahjahan Begum worked extensively for the protection of Sanchi Stupa.' Explain the statement. CBSE 2025

Ans. Shahjehan Begum played a crucial role in protecting the Sanchi Stupa. She provided funds for its preservation, ensuring the site remained intact. When European powers wanted to take the eastern gateway, she helped prevent its removal. She and her successor, Sultan Jehan Begum, supported archaeological efforts, including funding a museum and guesthouse for John Marshall. Her contributions enabled the site's restoration and survival, protecting it from railway contractors and builders. Her efforts ensured that Sanchi remains a key monument reflecting early Buddhism's rich history.

2. "The mid-first millennium BCE is often regarded as a major turning point in the world history." Justify. Competency Based Que

"The mid-first milleunium BCE is considered as a significant turnning point in the course of world History". Justify the statement. CBSE 2025

Ans The mid-first millennium BCE is often regarded as a major turning point in the world history because of the following reasons

Emergence of Thinkers It saw the emergence of thinkers such as Zarathustra in Iran, Kong Zi in China, Socrates, Plato and Aristotle in Greece and Mahavira and Gautam Buddha among others in India.

Understanding of the Mysteries of Existence Thinkers tried to understand the problems of existence and the relationship between human beings and the cosmic order.

Development of New Kingdoms and Cities It was the time when new kingdoms and cities were developed.

Change in Social and Economic Life Social and economic life was changing in a variety of ways, e.g. in the Ganga valley growth of town, new crafts and trade took place.

New Agricultural Technology There was an extension of agriculture due to occupation of new lands, application of new techniques and use of iron tools.

3. "Support for any particular sect could grow and shrink over time." Justify the statement. Competency Based Que

Ans. The support for any particular sect could grow and shrink over time as

- The Buddhist texts mention 64 sects or schools of thought which gives an idea of lively discussions and debates.
- Teachers travelled from place to place, and tried to convince people about the importance of their philosophy. Debates took place in the *kutagarashala*.
- If a philosopher convinced one of his rivals, the followers of the latter also became his disciples.

4. Why did new religious sects emerged during sixth century?

Ans New religious sects emerged during the sixth century BCE due to the following reasons

Social Evil The society was divided into four *varnas*. The Shudras were badly treated by upper three *varnas*. Many social and religious restrictions were put on them. They wanted to get rid of these restrictions and adopt another religion, which could give them right place in the society.

Complexity in Vedic Religion Earlier, Vedic religion was very easy to practice, but with the passage of time many rituals came in it which made it complex. So people wanted a new religion in which there will be no place for useless traditions.

Language Sanskrit was the main language at that time. Many vedic texts were composed in it. People could not read and write it. So, they wanted to have common language which could be easily understood.

5. **"According to Jaina teachings, the birth and rebirth is shaped through Karma". Explain the statement.** CBSE 2024

Ans. According to Jaina teachings, the cycle of birth and rebirth is shaped by karma, which is the result of one's actions, thoughts, and words. Karma attaches to the soul, affecting future lives. Jainism teaches that all living beings, including humans, animals, plants, and even rocks, have life, and non-violence (ahimsa) is a key principle. Harmful actions add negative karma, while compassionate actions reduce it. To escape the cycle of karma and achieve liberation (moksha), Jainism emphasises asceticism, penance, and giving up worldly desires.

6. **What is the similarity between Mahavira's teachings and Mahatma Gandhi's philosophy? How is Mahavira's teaching different?**

Ans. The similarity between Mahavira's teachings and Mahatma Gandhi's philosophy is that both believed in ahimsa or non-violence.

Mahavira's teaching is different from the teachings of Mahatma Gandhi as

- Mahavira believed that there is life in all objects of the world, even non- living things like stones, rocks and water have life.
- Ahimsa towards living things like animals, plants, and insects was also given importance.

7. **Write about early life of Buddha.**

Ans. The childhood name of Buddha was Siddhartha. He was the son of a chief of the Sakya clan. He grew up inside the palace far from the harsh realities of life. One day, Buddha convinced his charioteer to take him into the city. Buddha was deeply suffered when he saw an old man, sick man and a corpse.

Then, he realised that the decay and destruction of the human body was bound to happen . He also saw a homeless mendicant, who found peace overcoming sufferings of old age, disease and death. Buddha was influenced by the mendicant and left the palace to adopt the same path in search of his own truth.

8. **Describe the main teachings of Buddhism.** CBSE 2023

Or **Write down the eternal truth of Buddhism.**

Or **Explain briefly the teachings of Buddha.**

Or **Describe the teachings of Buddhism.** Compartment 2024

Ans The teachings of Buddhism are as follows

- The world is transient and constantly changing. It is also soulless as there is nothing permanent or eternal in it.
- Sorrow is a fundamental part of human life.
- By following the path of moderation between (self-punishment) and self-indulgence, human beings can rise above these worldly pleasures.
- He advised kings and *gahapatis* to be humane and ethical. Buddha regarded the social world as the creation of humans rather than of divine origin.
- He emphasised individual agency and righteous action as the means to escape from the cycle of rebirth and attain self-realisation and *nibbana* which literally means the extinguishing of ego and desire.

9. **Explain the internal functioning of the Buddhist *sanghas*.** CBSE Diksha

Ans. The internal functioning of the *sangha* was based on the traditions of *ganas* and *sanghas*. Within the *sanghas*, everyone was given equal status as they had to leave their earlier social identities on becoming *bhikkhus* and *bhikkhunis*. Agreement in the *sangha* was arrived at through discussions. All decisions were taken with the majority opinion or by a vote on the subject.

10. **Write any four causes for the popularity of Buddhism.**

Ans. Four causes for the popularity of Buddhism are

(i) Buddhism was a simple religion. People did not find its teachings difficult to follow. Thus, the people began to prefer Buddhism over Hinduism.

(ii) Buddha preached his message in the local language of the people which was easy to understand.

(iii) Buddhism did not believe in elaborating ceremonies into which Hinduism had sunk. These ceremonies were very complicated and costly.

(iv) Many kings had adopted Buddhism and set personal examples for the subjects to follow the religion.

11. **Describe the impact of Buddhism on Indian society.**

Ans. Impact of Buddhism on Indian society is as follows

- Caste system began to decline. People came closer to each other.
- The morale of the people was raised due to equal statues.
- People began to adopt the principle of non-violence. As a result, peace was established in the society.
- Buddhism played a significant role in the state-policy decision making. Influenced by Buddhism, Asoka gave up war and devoted his life for the public welfare.

12. **Describe briefly the early stupas at Sanchi and Bharhut.**

Or **Explain the main features of the stupa at Sanchi.** CBSE 2024

Ans. The early stupas at Sanchi and Bharhut were built in the second century BCE. The main features of these stupas were as follows

- These were plain except for the stone railings, which resembled a bamboo or wooden fence. The gateways of these stupas were richly carved and installed at the four cardinal points.

- Worshippers entered through the Eastern gateway and walked around the mound in a clockwise direction, keeping the mound on the right, imitating the sun's course through the sky.
- Later, the mound of the stupas made to be elaborately carved with niches and sculptures, like Amaravati and Shah-ji-ki-Dheri in Peshawar.

13. Critically examine why Sanchi survived while Amaravati did not?

Ans The stupa at Amaravati was one of the largest and the most significant among the Buddhist stupas. The stupa at Sanchi survived while Amaravati did not because of the following reasons

- The stupa at Amaravati was discovered sometime earlier than the one at Sanchi. By the 1850s many of the slabs from Amaravati were taken to different places like Asiatic Society of Bengal, India Office at Madras, and to London.
- The scholars were not aware of the significance of preserving the archaeological remains of the site where they were originally found.
- The Sanchi stupa was discovered in the year 1818. At that time, three of its four gateways were still standing, the fourth was lying on the spot and the mound was in good condition. But the Amaravati, became an insignificant little mound and lost its former glory.

14. "Art historians had to acquire familiarity with Hagiographies of Buddha in order to understand Buddhist sculpture." Explain the statement in context of Sanchi Stupa. **CBSE 2025**

Ans. Art historians study hagiographies of the Buddha to understand Buddhist sculptures, including those at Sanchi Stupa. These hagiographies, though not always historically accurate, depict key events like the Buddha's renunciation and enlightenment. Since early Buddhist art, including Sanchi's carvings, often used symbols (like an empty throne or footprints) instead of direct depictions, familiarity with these texts helps historians interpret the scenes.

The carvings at Sanchi reflect stories from the Buddha's life, and understanding hagiographies allows historians to connect these symbols with Buddhist teachings.

15. Explain about the two major sects of Hinduism.

Ans. Hinduism include Vaishnavism and Shaivism.

Vaishnavism was a form of Hinduism within which Vishnu was worshipped as the principal deity of Hinduism. In Vaishnavism, cults developed around the various avatars or incarnations of the deity.

Shaivism was a tradition within which Shiva was regarded as the chief God. Shiva was symbolised by the *linga*. All such representations depicted a complex set of ideas about the deities and their attributes through symbols.

16. Analyse the notion of saviour in Vaishnavism.

Ans. In the case of Vaishnavism, cults developed around the various avatars or incarnations of the deity. Ten avatars were recognised within the tradition. These were forms that the deity was believed to have assumed in order to save the world whenever it was threatened by disorder and destruction because of the dominance of evil forces. It is likely that different avatars were popular in different parts of the country.

17. How the European scholars grappled with unfamiliar images of Buddha and Bodhisattas based on Greek models? **CBSE Diksha**

Ans. The European scholars were very excited when they discovered images of the Buddha and Bodhisattas that were evidently based on Greek models. These images were mostly found in the North-West, in cities such as Taxila and Peshawar, where Indo-Greek rulers had established kingdoms in the second century BCE. As these images were closest to the Greek statues these scholars were familiar with, they were considered to be the best examples of early Indian art.

18. "Many rituals, religious beliefs and practices were not recorded in a permanent visible form as monuments or sculptures or even paintings." Critically examine the statement. **Competency Based Que**

Ans. Many rituals, religious beliefs and practices were not recorded in a permanent visible form as monuments, sculptures or even paintings.

There are many communities and people, who may not have known to keep records for their rituals, religious beliefs and practices. However, they may have had vibrant traditions of religious activities and their own philosophical ideas. This is due to the following reasons

- Generally, people want to record those things which are clearly visible.
- People do not feel urgency to record their daily practices about religion and philosophy.

Long Answer Type Questions

1. How did the philosophical and religious developments during the first millennium BCE in India influence the socio-political aspects? Explain with examples. **CBSE SQP 2024**

Ans. The philosophical and religious developments during the first millennium BCE in India influence the socio-political aspects in the following ways

- **Influential Thinkers** During this era, notable thinkers like Mahavira and Gautama Buddha emerged in India, alongside contemporaries such as Zarathustra in Iran, Kong Zi (Confucius) in China, and Socrates, Plato, and

Aristotle in Greece. Their philosophical questions focused on basic issues like existence, ethics, and human nature, helping to create new ways of understanding the world and society.

- **Cosmic Order and Human Relationship** Philosophical discussions explored the connection between humans and the Universe. Thinkers like the Buddha and Mahavira studied karma and dharma, looking at how actions affect one's fate. This influenced society's values, promoting ethical behaviour and spiritual growth.
- **Development of Kingdoms and Cities** The rise of new kingdoms and urban centers, particularly in the Ganga valley, led to significant socio-economic changes. As cities grew and economies developed, religious practices shifted from Vedic sacrificial rituals to more personal and socially relevant ones, reflecting the changes in urban life.
- **Societal Contemplations** The social and economic changes led philosophers and religious leaders to think about these changes. The move from group sacrifices to personal rituals showed a focus on individual responsibility and spiritual needs. Early Vedic traditions, as seen in the Rigveda, involved hymns praising gods like Agni, Indra, and Soma. These rituals were meant to bring blessings like health, wealth, and children, highlighting the communal aspect of early religious practices.
- **Elaborate Rituals** The Rajasuya and Ashvamedha were important rituals held by chiefs and kings, showing how religion helped legitimise political power. Brahmana priests played a key role in these ceremonies, emphasising the strong connection between religion and politics.

2. "Among the best preserved monuments of the 600 BCE to 600 CE is the Stupa at Sanchi." Justify the statement with suitable arguments in the context of its sculptural features and conservation policy taken up in the nineteenth century. Competency Based Que

Ans "Among the best preserved monuments of the 600 BCE to 600 CE is the stupa at Sanchi." The sculptural features of the Sanchi stupa are as follows

- Many symbols like empty seat, wheel, tree were used to indicate the different teachings of Buddhism in Sanchi stupa. For instance, the empty seat was meant to represent the mahaparinibbana. The wheel represents Buddha's first sermon.
- Other sculptures at Sanchi were perhaps not directly inspired the by the Buddhist ideas. These figures included beautiful women swinging from the edge of the gateway holding into a tree, like *Shalabhanjika* was a woman whose touch caused trees to flower and bear fruit.
- There are other images in Sanchi Stupa. Depiction of animals like elephants, horses, monkeys and cattle were also found. Animals were used as a symbols of human attributes, e.g. elephants were depicted to signify strength and wisdom.
    - There is a motif in Sanchi Stupa of a woman surrounded by lotuses and elephants, which seems to be sprinkling water on her as if performing an *abhisheka* or consecration. It has been identified by some historians as Maya, the mother of Buddha while others identify her with a popular Goddess Gajalakshmi (Goddess of good fortune).

The conservation policy regarding Sanchi Stupa in nineteenth century was

- The rulers of Bhopal, Shah Jehan Begum and her successor Sultan Jahan Begum provided money for the preservation of the ancient site of stupa at Sanchi.
- Sultan Jehan funded the museum, guesthouse at Sanchi where John Marshall lived and wrote books on Sanchi Stupa. She also funded the publication of the volumes of Marshall's book.
  Marshall dedicated this book on Sanchi to Sultan Jehan. The rulers of Bhopal protected the Sanchi stupa from railway contractors, builders and European collectors who took relics for museums.

3. How did *Sutta Pitaka* reconstruct the philosophy of Buddhism? Mention about Buddhist Tipitaka. CBSE Diksha

Ans. The Buddha's teachings have been reconstructed from stories found mainly in the *Sutta Pitaka*. Some stories describe his miraculous powers and other stories suggest that the Buddha tried to convince people through reason and persuasion, rather than through display of supernatural power. Sometimes through stories, the teachings of the Buddha were narrated to transform social relations.

The Buddha emphasised individual agency and righteous action

According to Buddhist philosophy, the world is transient and constantly changing. The world is soulless as there is nothing permanent or eternal in it.

Within this transient world, sorrow is intrinsic to human existence. It is by following the path of moderation between severe penance and self-indulgence, the human beings can rise above these worldly troubles.

The Buddha regarded the social world as the creation of human rather than of divine origin. Therefore, he advised kings and *gahapatis* to be humane and ethical.

Buddhist Tipitaka

Tipitaka literally means three baskets to hold different types of texts. It included *Vinaya Pitaka*, *Sutta Pitaka* and *Abhidhamma Pitaka*. Each *pitaka* comprised a number of texts.

The main features of Tipitaka are

- The *Vinaya Pitaka* included rules and regulations for those who joined the *sangha* or monastic order.
- The *Sutta Pitaka* included the teachings of the Buddha.
- The *Abhidhamma Pitaka* dealt with philosophical matters.

4. "Buddhism grew rapidly both during the lifetime of the Buddha and after his death." Justify the statement with suitable arguments. Competency Based Que

Or **Explain why Buddhism grew rapidly during the time of Buddha.** CBSE 2024

Ans. Buddhism grew rapidly both during the lifetime of the Buddha and after his death. This statement can be justified through the following arguments

- The Buddha preached his message in the common language of the people. His teachings were very simple and could be understood easily.
- The Buddha regarded the social order as the creation of humans rather than of divine origin. He advised kings and *gahapatis* to be humane and ethical.
- He opposed caste system. Thus people of all caste groups became his followers.
- Buddhist monks spread message very quickly to different corners of India and abroad.
- The Buddha emphasised individual agency and righteous action as to escape from the cycle of rebirth and attain self-realisation and *nibbana*. It oppossed ritual and custom practised by other religion. The simple path of Buddhism attracted many people across India.
- Buddhism was patronised by many contemporary kings like Asoka and Harsha.

5. How did the construction of stupas contribute to the spread of Buddhist teachings? Explain with examples. CBSE SQP 2024

Ans. The construction of stupas contributed to the spread of Buddhist teachings in the following ways

- **Sacred Sites** Stupas were built at sacred sites linked to the Buddha's life or relics. For example, the stupa at Bodh Gaya marks where the Buddha gained enlightenment, while the one at Sarnath marks where he gave his first sermon. These sites became important for Buddhist worship and pilgrimage.
- **Artistic Depictions** Stupas often had detailed carvings and inscriptions showing scenes from the Buddha's life and teachings. These artworks helped convey Buddhist teachings, especially to those who couldn't read.
- **Jataka Tales** Many stupas had carvings or inscriptions of Jataka tales, which are stories about the Buddha's past lives. These stories taught moral lessons and showed virtues like compassion and wisdom. For example, the Vessantara Jataka tells about the Buddha's past life as a prince who gave up everything to help others, highlighting generosity and selflessness.
- **Cultural Integration** The use of local artistic styles in stupa decorations helped blend Buddhism with regional cultures, making its teachings more relatable and accessible to different people.
- **Educational Role** Stupas used visual depictions of important events and teachings as educational tools. This was especially important in areas with low literacy, helping to spread and explain Buddhist teachings to a wider audience.
- **Communal Engagement** Building and maintaining stupas often involved local communities, creating a sense of shared participation in Buddhist practices. This helped spread Buddhism and strengthen Buddhist institutions in various regions.

6. Explain the structure of the Sanchi Stupa and hindu temples. CBSE Diksha

Ans. The Sanchi Stupa was built in the second century BCE and regarded as one of the important stupas in India. It was discovered in 1818. The structural features of the Sanchi Stupa are

- The stupa originated as a simple semi-circular mound of Earth, later called *anda*. Above the *anda* was the *harmika*, a balcony-like structure that represented the abode of the gods.
- There was a mast called the yashti, arising from the *harmika* and it was surmounted by a *chhatri* or umbrella. Around the mound, there was a railing, separating the sacred space from the world.
- There were stone railings and the gateways, which were richly carved and installed at the four cardinal points.

The Hindu temple structure evolved as a reflection of religious ideas and cultural developments. Structural features of temples are as follows

- **Garbhagriha** (Sanctum Sanctorum) This is the innermost and most sacred area of a Hindu temple, where the main deity's idol is placed. Worshippers enter this space to offer prayers, as it represents the deity's dwelling.

- **Shikhara** (Tower or Spire) Built above the garbhagriha, the shikhara rises high, symbolising a link between the earthly and divine realms. It reflects a mountain shape, signifying the cosmic links that connects heaven and Earth.
- **Mandapa** (Pillared Hall) Adjacent to the sanctum, the mandapa serves as an assembly hall for devotees. It is used for various rituals, gatherings, and chanting sessions.
- **Pradakshina Patha** (Circumambulatory Path) A pathway around the garbhagriha, allowing worshippers to walk around the deity in a clockwise direction.This act of circumambulation is an essential part of Hindu worship, symbolising reverence and dedication.
- **Gopuram** (Gateway) It is common in South Indian temples. The gopuram is a monumental gateway tower at the temple's entrance. Often decorated with sculptures of deities, mythological scenes, and motifs, it signifies a grand entrance into the sacred space.

These architectural elements together symbolise various aspects of Hindu cosmology and religious beliefs, merging art and spirituality.

Source Based Questions

Read the sources given below and answer the following questions.

1. Sanchi in the Nineteenth Century

The most wonderful ancient buildings in the state of Bhopal are at Sanchi Kanakhera, a small village under the brow of a hill some 20 miles North-East of Bhopal which we visited yesterday. We inspected the stone sculptures and statues of the Buddha and an ancient gateway…. The ruins appear to be the object of great interest to European gentlemen. Major Alexander Cunningham… stayed several weeks in this neighbourhood, and examined these ruins most carefully. He took drawings of the place, deciphered the inscription and bored shafts down these domes. The results of his investigations were described by him in an English work.

From Shahjahan Begum. Nawab of Bhopal (ruled 1868-1901), Taj-ul Iqbal Tarikh Bhopal (A History of Bhopal), translated by H.D. Barstow, 1876. **CBSE SQP 2022**

(i) Why was Sanchi an interest to Alexander Cunningham?

(ii) How was Sanchi related with the Buddhism?

(iii) How did Shah Jahan Begum conserve Sanchi Stupa?

Ans. (i) Alexander Cunningham excavated Sanchi, where he discovered Buddha's relics from the stupa as he was supposed to prepare illustrated reports on the stupa.

(ii) The monument of Sanchi is related with Buddhism as it is one of the oldest Buddhist monuments that contains the relics of Buddha. The domed shape of the stupa represent Buddha seated in meditation. The monuments comprises a series of Buddhist monuments starting from the Mauryan Empire period to the Gupta Empire period.

(iii) Shah Jahan Begum provided money for the preservation of the Sanchi Stupa. She funded the museum that was built there as well as the guest house where John Marshall lived. She also funded the volumes that John Marshall wrote on Sanchi.

2. A Prayer to Agni

Here are two verses from the *Rigveda* invoking Agni, the god of fire, often identified with the sacrificial fire, into which offerings were made so as to reach the other deities: Bring, O strong one, this sacrifice of ours to the Gods, O wise one, as a liberal giver.

Bestow on us, O priest, abundant food. Agni obtain by sacrificing, mighty wealth for us.

Procure, O Agni, forever to him who prays to you (the gift of) nourishment, the wonderful cow. May a son be ours, offspring that continues our line … Verses such as these were composed in a special kind of Sanskrit, known as Vedic Sanskrit. They were taught orally to men belonging to priestly families.

(i) What is the source of this verse? Who has been invoked in it?

(ii) When was *Rigveda* compiled?

(iii) What were the objectives of the sacrificial traditions prevailing during vedic age?

Ans. (i) The source of this verse is *Rigveda*, the oldest veda among the four Vedas. It has been invoked to Agni God.

(ii) *Rigveda* was compiled between 1500-1000 BCE, according to vedic tradition. In Rigveda, hymns are composed in praise of vedic Gods i.e., Agni, Indra and Soma.

(iii) The objectives of the sacrificial traditions prevailing during vedic age were to procure abundant food, wealth, cattle, sons, good health, long life, etc.

3. Verses from the Upanishads

Here are two verses from the *Chhandogya* Upanishad, a text composed in Sanskrit c. sixth century BCE:

The nature of the self

This self of mine within the heart, is smaller than paddy or barley or mustard or millet or the kernel of a seed of millet. This self of mine within the heart is greater than the earth, greater than the intermediate space, greater than heaven, greater than these worlds.

The true sacrifice

This one (the wind) that blows, this is surely a sacrifice … While moving, it sanctifies all this; therefore it is indeed a sacrifice.

(i) When were the above given verses composed? What is the source of these verses?

(ii) What ideology is given in the Upanishads?

(iii) Write any three objectives, why Yajanas were performed.

Ans (i) The above given verses in excerpt were composed in sixth century BCE. The source of these verses is Chhandogya Upanishad.

(ii) The ideology of Upanishads is based on works on which his rebirth depends. Man always wanted to know the ultimate reality.

(iii) Yajanas were performed

(a) To gain victory in the war.

(b) To have a son.

(c) To stay fit for long age.

4. Fatalists and Materialists

Here is an excerpt from the *Sutta Pitaka*, describing a conversation between king Ajatasattu, the ruler of Magadha, and the Buddha:

On one occasion King Ajatasatru visited the Buddha and described what another teacher, named Makkhali Gosala, had told him:

"Though the wise should hope, by this virtue … by this penance I will gain karma … and the fool should by the same means hope to gradually rid himself of his karma, neither of them can do it. Pleasure and pain, measured out as it were, cannot be altered in the course of *samsara* (transmigration).

It can neither be lessened or increased … just as a ball of string will when thrown unwind to its full length, so fool and wise alike will take their course and make an end of sorrow."

And this is what a philosopher named Ajita Kesakambalin taught:

"There is no such thing, O king, as alms or sacrifice, or offerings … there is no such thing as this world or the next …

A human being is made up of the four elements. When he dies the earthy in him returns to the earth, the fluid to water, the heat to fire, the windy to air, and his senses pass into space …

The talk of gifts is a doctrine of fools, an empty lie … fools and wise alike are cut off and perish. They do not survive after death."

The first teacher belonged to the tradition of the Ajivikas. They have often been described as fatalists: those who believe that everything is predetermined. The second teacher belonged to the tradition of the Lokayatas, usually described as materialists. Texts from these traditions have not survived, so we know about them only from the works of other traditions.

(i) From where has this excerpt been taken? What does it describe?

(ii) How many elements is a human being made-up of ? What happens after his death?

(iii) Distinguish in brief between fatalists and materialists.

Ans (i) This excerpt has been taken from *Sutta Pitaka.* The excerpt described the dialogue between Ajatasattu and Lord Buddha.

(ii) A human being is made-up of four elements. When he passes away i.e., dies the earthy in him return to earth, the fluid to water, the heat to fire, the winds to air and his sense pass into space.

(iii) The differences between fatalists and materialists are

- Fatalists belonged to the Ajivika tradition, while the materialists belonged to Lokayata tradition.
- According to fatalists, everything in life was pre-destined and could not be changed.
- Materialists considered the talk of gift and donation as a doctrine of fools. They did not believe in alms sacrifice or offerings.

5. Buddhism in Practice CBSE 2024

This is an excerpt from the *Sutta Pitaka* and contains the advice given by the Buddha to a wealthy householder named Sigala :

In five ways should a master look after his servants and employees.... by assigning them work according to their strength, by supplying them with food and wages, by tending them in sickness; by sharing delicacies with them and by granting leave at times...

In five ways should the clansmen look after the needs of *samanas* (those who have renounced the world) and Brahmanas : by affection in act and speech and mind, by keeping open house to them and supplying their worldly needs.

There are similar instructions to Sigala about how to behave with his parents, teacher and wife.

(i) Explain the significance of *Sutta Pitaka* in Buddhism.

(ii) How did Buddha advise the wealthy householders to be humane and ethical?

(iii) What was the advice given by Buddha to Sigala on how to behave with his parents and teachers?

Or

(i) How did Buddha highlight the significance of compassion in social hierarchy ?

(ii) Why did Buddha emphasise righteous action ?

(iii) Explain any two tenets of Karma according to Buddha.

Ans. (i) The *Sutta Pitaka* contains the Buddha's teachings, forming the foundation of Buddhist doctrine and guiding practitioners on the path to enlightenment.

(ii) Buddha advised kings and *gahapatis* to be humane and ethical. Buddha regarded the social world as the creation of humans rather than of divine origin.

(iii) The advice given by Buddha to Sigala on parents and teachers was that they ought to be respected and their needs should be fulfilled with grace and dignity.

Or

(i) Buddha emphasised compassion in social hierarchy by advising those in authority, like Sigala, to care for their servants, teachers, and family with kindness, fairness, and respect. He taught that all individuals, regardless of their social status, deserve empathy, support, and dignity, promoting mutual care and equality in relationships.

(ii) Buddha emphasised righteous action to promote ethical conduct, fairness, and compassion in all relationships. By advising Sigala on how to care for servants, teachers, and family, Buddha highlighted that righteous actions, based on kindness and respect, foster harmony and well-being in society.

(iii) Two key tenets of karma according to Buddha are

(a) Buddha emphasised that the intention behind an action is crucial in shaping its consequences. Positive intentions lead to good karma, while harmful intentions result in bad karma.

(b) Every action, whether physical, verbal, or mental, has an impact on one's future. Buddha taught that righteous actions, such as treating servants and others with respect and compassion, lead to favorable outcomes and the accumulation of good karma.

6. Rules for Monks and Nuns

These are some of the rules laid down in the *Vinaya Pitaka*:

When a new felt (blanket/rug) has been made by a *bhikkhu*, it is to be kept for (at least) six years. If after less than six years he should have another new felt (blanket/rug) made, regardless of whether or not he has disposed of the first, then – unless he has been authorised by the *bhikkhus* – it is to be forfeited and confessed.

In case a *bhikkhu* arriving at a family residence is presented with cakes or cooked grain-meal, he may accept two or three bowlfuls if he so desires. If he should accept more than that, it is to be confessed. Having accepted the two or three bowlfuls and having taken them from there, he is to share them among the *bhikkhus*.

This is the proper course here. Should any *bhikkhu*, having set out bedding in a lodging belonging to the *sangha* – or having had it set out – and then on departing neither put it away nor have it put away, or should he go without taking leave, it is to be confessed.

(i) What is the importance of *Vinaya Pitaka*?

(ii) Why do you think men and women joined *sangha*? Give two reasons.

(iii) What was the Bodh *sangha*?

Ans (i) The *Vinaya Pitaka* is one of the three *pitakas* of Buddhism. The importance of *Vinaya Pitaka* is that the rules for Buddhist monks and nuns are laid down in it.

(ii) Men and women joined *sangha* due to the two reasons given below

(a) They wanted to live a simple and disciplined life in *sangha*.

(b) They wanted to remain away from wordly pleasures.

(iii) The Bodh *sangha* was an organisation of monks, who served as teachers of Dhamma. They lived a simple life and possessed only those essential goods which were required in daily routine life.

7. Why were Stupas built?

This is an excerpt from the *Mahaparinibbana Sutta*, part of the *Sutta Pitaka*.

As the Buddha lay dying, Ananda asked him, "What are we to do Lord, with the remains of the Tathagata (another name for the Buddha)?" The Buddha replied, "Hinder not yourselves Ananda by honouring the remains of the Tathagata. Be zealous, be intent on your own good."

But when pressed further, the Buddha said, "At the four crossroads, they should erect a *thupa* (Pali for stupa) to the Tathagata. And whosoever shall there place garlands or perfume.... or make a salutation there, or become in its presence calm of heart, that shall long be to them for a profit and joy."

(i) Why were the stupas built?

(ii) What Asoka did with the relics of Buddha?

(iii) Describe the structure of the stupas.

Ans (i) Stupas were built because the relics of Buddha such as his bodily remains or objects used by him were buried there.

(ii) Asoka distributed portions of Buddha's relics to every important town and ordered the construction of stupas over them.

(iii) Structure of stupas is as follows

- ***Anda*** It is a semi-circular mound of Earth called *anda*.
- ***Harmika*** It is located above *anda*.
- **Yashti** It was a mast arising from *harmika*.
- **Railing** It is located around the mound and separated the sacred place from the secular world.

Map Based Questions

1 **In the outline map of India, two places which are major Buddhist sites have been marked as A and B.**

Identify them and write their correct names on the lines drawn near them.

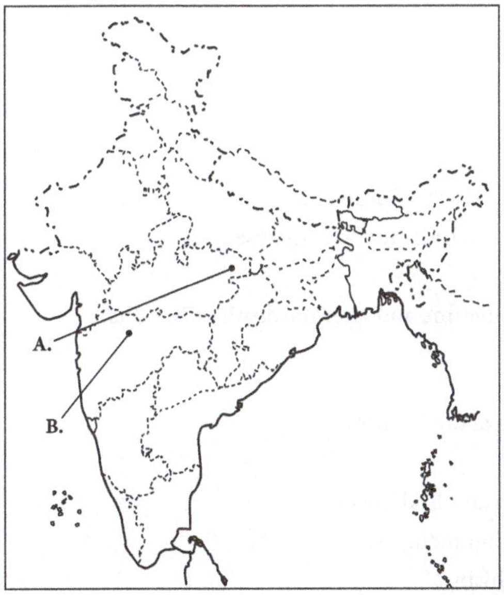

Ans

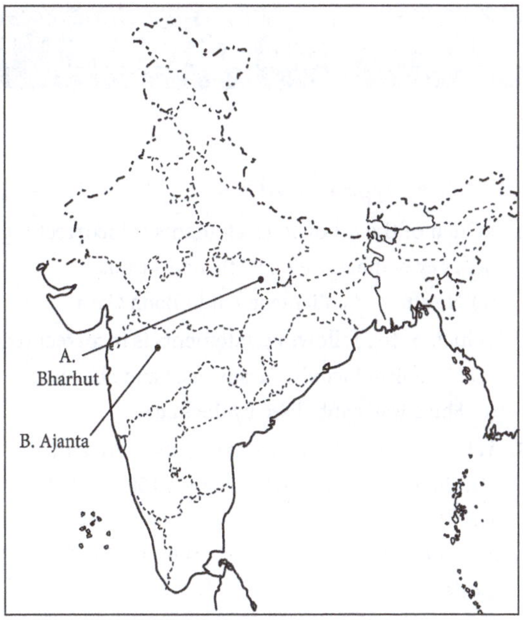

2 **On the given political map of India, locate and label the following.**

(i) Bodh Gaya **(ii) Lumbini**

(iii) Sanchi CBSE SQP 2024

(iv) Nagarjunakonda

(v) Amaravati CBSE 2024, 2025 CBSE SQP 2022

(vi) Nasik

(vii) Bharhut CBSE 2024

Ans

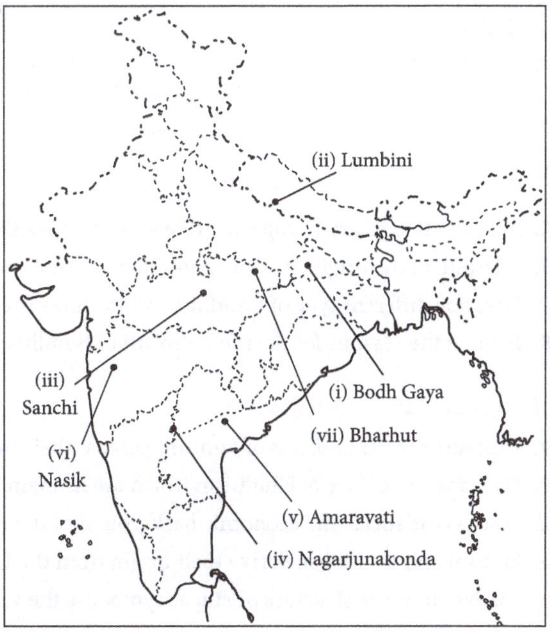

SELF ASSESSMENT TEST

Objective Type Questions

1. Which of the following statements is incorrect regarding Buddhism?
   (a) They emphasised on metta and karuna.
   (b) Buddha was born in Lumbini.
   (c) He attained enlightenment in Bodh Gaya.
   (d) He attained *nibbana* at Sarnath.
2. Which of the following statements is incorrect regarding Hinduism?
   (a) Hinduism include Vaishnavism and Shaivism.
   (b) Vishnu was worshipped in Vaishnavism.
   (c) Shiva was symbolised by the linga.
   (d) In Vaishnavism sixteen avatars were recognised.
3. Which of the following statements is/are correct?
   (i) *Rigveda* compiled between c. 1500 and 1000 BCE.
   (ii) It consists of hymns.
   (iii) It praises the deities like Agni, Indra and Soma, etc.

   Codes
   (a) (i) and (ii)
   (b) (ii) and (iii)
   (c) (i) and (iii)
   (d) All of these
4. Match the Following.

	List I (Places associated with Buddha)		List II (Events)
A.	Birth	1.	Kushinagara
B.	Enlightenment	2.	Sarnath
C.	First Sermon	3.	Lumbini
D.	*Nibbana*	4.	Bodh Gaya

Codes

	A	B	C	D		A	B	C	D
(a)	3	4	2	1	(b)	2	3	1	4
(c)	4	2	1	3	(d)	1	2	3	4

Short Answer Type Questions

5. Nineteenth century Europeans were very interested in the stupa at Sanchi. Comment.
6. "Despite of the origin of Jainism in India, it is not majorily present in India today". Analyse.
7. Describe different type of Buddhist architectures present in India.
8. Explain the reasons for the rapid growth of Buddhism during the lifetime and after the death of Buddha.

Long Answer Type Questions

9. Describe the *tirthankaras* of Jainism. Discuss their main teachings about Jainism.
10. Describe the nature of Hinduism which are its main sects.
11. Discuss the social and economic background of the rise of Jainism and Buddhism.
12. Jainism and Buddhism derive their origin from the Upanishads. Comment
13. Analyse how the structure of stupas symbolise the values of Buddhism.

5 CHAPTER

This chapter deals with various foreign travellers who visited India in the past. Al-Biruni, Ibn Battuta and Francois Bernier wrote books about India which help us in reconstructing our Indian history.

▼ **YOUR STUDY GOALS**

5.1 Al-Biruni
5.2 Ibn Battuta
5.3 Francois Bernier
5.4 Other European Travellers
5.5 Women : Slaves, Sati and Labourers

▼ **YOUR PRACTICE GOALS**

- Objective Type Questions (53 Qs ; MCQs, A-R, Matching, Picture Based)
- Subjective Questions (22 SAs, 4 LAs)
- Source Based Questions (13 Qs)

Through the Eyes of Travellers

(Perceptions of Society)

- People including both men and women have travelled to different places due to various reasons.
- These travellers found differences in terms of landscape or physical environment, customs, beliefs and languages, etc. wherever they visited. While some adapted to these differences, others noted them in their accounts.
- Women used to travel, but their accounts have not been found.
- The accounts that have survived deal with subjects such as affairs of the court, religious issues or architecture. In this chapter, we will focus mainly on the travel accounts of
  - Al-Biruni (11th century)
  - Ibn Battuta (14th century)
  - Francois Bernier (17th century).
- These authors focused on everyday activities, unlike local writers who viewed daily activities as routine tasks.

5.1 Al-Biruni

From Khwarizm to the Punjab

- Al-Biruni was born in 973 CE, in **Khwarizm** (present-day Uzbekistan). It was an important centre of learning.
- He was well versed in languages like **Syriac, Arabic, Persian, Hebrew** and **Sanskrit.**

- He did not know Greek, but read the works of Plato and other Greek philosophers in Arabic translations.
- He was taken to Ghazni by **Sultan Mahmud** when he invaded Khwarizm in 1017 CE. Though Al-Biruni came to Ghazni as a hostage (prisoner), he later developed a liking for the city and spent the rest of his life there.
- The objectives of Al-Biruni's work as described by him were
  - A help to those who wanted to discuss religious questions with them (the **Hindus**[1]) .
  - A repertory (storehouse) of information to those who want to associate with them.
  - Al-Biruni developed interest about India in Ghazni as from the eighth century onwards, Sanskrit works on astronomy, mathematics and medicine were already translated into Arabic.
  - When Punjab became a part of the Ghaznavid Empire, contacts with the local population created a friendly environment.
  - Al-Biruni spent many years with Brahmana priests and scholars. He learnt Sanskrit and studied religious and philosophical texts. He travelled widely in the Punjab and other parts of Northern India.
  - Al-Biruni translated several Sanskrit works including *Patanjali's* work on grammar into Arabic. For his Brahmana friends, he translated the works of **Euclid**, a Greek mathematician, into Sanskrit.
  - Literature on travelling was already established as a recognised field in Arabic literature. It dealt with far away lands like the Sahara desert in the West and river Volga in the North.

Al-Biruni and the *Kitab-ul-Hind*

- Al-Biruni wrote Kitab-ul-Hind in Arabic in simple and easy language. It is divided into **80 chapters** on subjects such as
  - Religion and philosophy
  - Festivals
  - Astronomy
  - Alchemy
  - Manners and customs
  - Social life
  - Weights and measures
  - Iconography
  - Laws and **metrology**[2]
- Al-Biruni's writing style was different as
  - He used to start with a question.
  - The questions were followed with a description based on Sanskritic traditions.
  - The conclusion was based on comparison with other cultures.
- Present-day scholars thought that geometric structures, remarkable precision and predictability in his writings were the result of his interest in mathematics.
- Al-Biruni wrote his work for people living along the boundaries of the subcontinent. He also became familiar with the translations and adaptations of Sanskrit, Pali and Prakrit texts into Arabic.
- These texts were about different subjects like **fables** (fictitious stories), **astronomy** and **medicine**. He wanted to improve these texts as he was not happy with the way these texts were written earlier.

Al-Biruni and the Sanskritic Tradition

Al-Biruni discussed the problems in understanding the local practices. These problems were

- Learning Sanskrit was difficult as it had a wide range and forms of words. It was different from Arabic and Persian. The ideas and concepts could not be easily translated from one language into another.
- There were differences in religious beliefs and practices.
- According to him, the local population's narrow-mindedness was the third barrier.

1 **Hindu** The term 'Hindu' was derived from an old Persian word, used in c. sixth-fifth centuries BCE. It refers to the region East of the river Sindhu (Indus).

2 **Metrology** It is the science of measurement.

Despite these problems, Al-Biruni was depend exclusively on the works of Brahmanas. He often cited passages from the Vedas, the Puranas, the Bhagavad Gita, the works of Patanjali, the Manusmriti, etc. to provide an understanding of Indian society.

Al-Biruni' Description of the Caste System

- Al-Biruni explained the caste system by noting that in ancient **Persia**, four social categories were recognised. These were

(i) Knights and princes
(ii) Monks, fire-priests and lawyers
(iii) Physicians, astronomers and other scientists
(iv) Peasants and artisans

- He also pointed out that within Islam all men were considered equal. They differed only in their practices of worship that reflect one's faith.
- His description was influenced by his study of Sanskrit texts. These texts laid down the rules governing the system from the point of view of the Brahmanas. However, in real life these rules were not so rigid. For example, the categories defined as antyaja[3] were often expected to provide cheap labour to both peasants and zamindars.
- ***Antyajas*** often faced social oppression, but they were included within economic networks.

Al-Biruni's Views on Social Pollution

- Al-Biruni disapproved the idea of social pollution.
- He pointed out that every impure thing tries to come back to its original condition of purity.
- For Al-Biruni, the concept of social pollution in the caste system is against the laws of nature.

Al-Biruni's Account on Varna System

- The highest caste was the **Brahmana**. They were created from the head of Brahman, Since the head was the highest part of the body, the Brahmana were considered the best caste in the world among the Hindus.
- The next caste were the **Kshatriya**, who were created from the shoulders and hands of **Brahman**.
- **Vaishya** were created from the thigh of Brahman.
- The **Shudra** were created from the feet of Brahman.

According to Al-Biruni, these classes differed from each other, but they lived together in the same towns and villages and mixed together in the same houses and lodgings.

Quick Test 1

1 Al-Biruni came to India from which place?
2 Name two languages in which Al-Biruni was well versed?
3 Which subjects were included in the Kitab-ul-Hind?
4 What were the four social categories of caste system in ancient Persia according to Al-Biruni?
5 Which caste considered the best among Hindus?

5.2 Ibn Battuta

- Ibn Battuta was born into one of the most respectable and educated families in **Tangier, Morocco**. His family was known for their expertise in Islamic religious law or *sharia*. He received literary and scholastic education at a young age.
- His book of travels, called ***The Rihla***, was written in **Arabic**. It has interesting details about the social and cultural life in the subcontinent in the fourteenth century.

3 Antyaja People who are born outside the caste system.

- For Ibn Battuta, experience through travels was more important source of knowledge than books.
- Before travelling to India in 1332-33, he had made pilgrimage trips to Mecca. He had already travelled to different countries like Syria, Iraq, Persia, Yemen, Oman and a few trading ports on the coast of East Africa.
- Ibn Battuta was an inveterate (habitual) traveller. He is often referred to as a **globe-trotter**[4].
- He spent several years travelling through North Africa, West Asia and parts of Central Asia, the Indian subcontinent and China.
- He returned to his home in 1354, about 30 years after he left.

Ibn Battuta's Travel to India

- Ibn Battuta reached Sind in 1333 CE, by travelling overland through Central Asia.
- To meet Muhammad Bin Tughlaq he travelled to Delhi, passing through Multan and Uch.
- The Sultan was impressed by his scholarship and appointed him the ***qazi*** or **judge of Delhi**. Later due to some misunderstanding between Sultan and Ibn Battuta, he was imprisoned. When this issue was resolved, he was restored to imperial service by the Sultan.

Ibn Battuta's Travel to China

- The Sultan ordered Ibn Battuta in 1342 CE to travel to China as the Sultan's representative to the Mongol ruler.
- Ibn Battuta proceeded to the Malabar coast through Central India. From Malabar, he went to the Maldives. He stayed in Maldives for eighteen months as the *qazi* and then decided to travel to Sri Lanka.

▲ *A boat carrying passengers, a terracotta sculpture from a temple in Bengal (c. seventeenth-eighteenth centuries)*

- Before going to China, he once again went to the Malabar coast and the Maldives and also visited Bengal and Assam. He took a ship to Sumatra and from there, he took another ship for the Chinese port town of Zaytun (now known as **Quanzhou**).
- He travelled extensively in China and went to Beijing, but did not stay for long. He decided to return home in 1347 CE.
- Ibn Battuta's account is often compared to the accounts of **Marco Polo**, who visited China and India in the late thirteenth century from his home country Venice.

Analysis of Ibn Battuta's Travel

- Ibn Battuta recorded his observations about new cultures, peoples, beliefs, values, etc.
- In the 14th century, travelling was more difficult and dangerous than present times.
- According to Ibn Battuta, it took forty days to travel from Multan to Delhi; about fifty days from Sind to Delhi; about forty days from Daulatabad to Delhi and about ten days from Gwalior to Delhi.
- Ibn Battuta was attacked by groups of robbers several times while travelling. He preferred travelling in a caravan along with companions, but highway robbers attacked these caravans also.
- On his journey from Multan to Delhi, Ibn Battuta's carvan was attacked and many travellers lost their lives. The survivors, including him were badly injured.

4 **Globe-trotter** A person who travels a lot.

Ibn Battuta and the Excitement of the Unfamiliar

- Ibn Battuta reached Delhi in the 14th century. The subcontinent was part of a global network of communication from China in the East to North-West Africa and Europe in the West.
- He visited sacred shrines and spent time with learned men and rulers. He enjoyed the vibrant culture which accepted people who spoke Arabic, Persian, Turkish and other languages. They shared ideas, information and real life stories.

The Coconut and the *Paan*

- Ibn Battuta described that the coconut trees were similar to date-palms. The difference was that while date-palms produce dates, coconut trees produce nuts.
- The coconut's fibre was used for making **cords** which were used to sew ships instead of using iron nails and cables for vessels were also made using this fibre.
- He also described *paan*. According to him, betel is a tree without any fruit which was grown only for its leaves.

Ibn Battuta and Indian Cities

- According to Ibn Battuta, Indian cities had a lot of opportunities for those who had the necessary interest, resources and skills.
- The cities were densely populated and prosperous, but were destroyed during wars and invasions.
- Most cities had crowded streets and bright and colourful markets filled with a wide variety of goods.

Ibn Battuta's Views about Delhi

- Ibn Battuta described **Delhi** as a vast city, having the largest population in India.
- There was a defensive wall around Delhi. The breadth of the wall was eleven cubits.
- There were houses inside for night watchmen and gatekeepers. There were store-houses for storing edibles, magazines, ammunition, ballistas and siege machines. The stored grains could last long without rotting.
- There were wide windows in the wall through which light entered inside. The lower part of the defensive wall was built of stone and the upper part with bricks. It also had many towers close to one another.
- There were many gates called as ***darwaza*** and the ***Budaun Darwaza*** was the greatest among them.
- There was a grain market inside the **Mandwi *darwaza*** and an orchard near ***Gul darwaza***.
- City of Delhi also had a fine cemetery in which graves had domes over them and those without dome had an arch.

▲ *An arch in Daulatabad*

Ibn Battuta's Views about Daulatabad

- Daulatabad (in Maharashtra) was equal in size with Delhi. There was a marketplace for male and female singers in Daulatabad which was known as **Tarabad.** It was one of the greatest and most beautiful bazaars.
- It had many shops, each having a door which led into the house of the owner. These shops were decorated with carpets and there was a swing at the centre on which a female singer sits.
- In the middle of the marketplace, there was a **cupola**[5] which was carpeted and decorated. Every Thursday after dawn (morning) prayers, the chief musician and his servants would gather there.
- There were mosques in the bazaars where prayers were offered. Whenever a Hindu or Muslim ruler arrived at the domed building and pass by the market places, female singers would sing before them.

5 **Cupola** A large domed building

Ibn Battuta's Views about the Economy, Agriculture and Trade

- The bazaars were important places of economic transactions, as well as hubs of social and cultural activities.

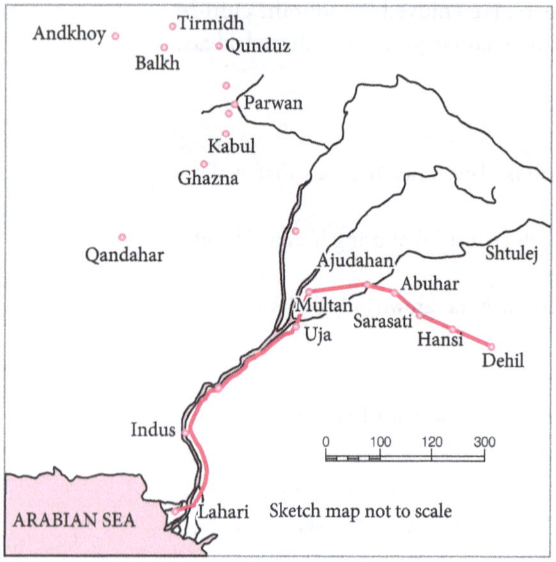

- Most bazaars had mosque and temples. In some bazaars, spaces were marked for public performances by dancers, musicians and singers.
- Historians used Ibn Battuta's accounts and explained about the prosperity of the towns. The towns derived a significant part of its wealth from the surplus of villages.
- Ibn Battuta found Indian agriculture very productive because of the soil fertility which allowed farmers to cultivate two crops a year.
- The subcontinent was well connected and integrated with inter-Asian networks of trade and commerce.
- The Indian manufacturers were in great demand in both West Asia and South-East Asia which bought huge profits for artisans and merchants.
- There was a great demand for Indian textiles like **cotton cloth, fine muslins, silks, brocade** and **satin.**
- Few varieties of fine muslin were so expensive that only nobles and the rich could afford it.

Ibn Battuta's Description about Indian Postal System

- Ibn Battuta was surprised by the efficient postal system of India. The postal system enabled merchants to send information, transfer credit over long distances and also deliver goods on short notice.
- It took fifty days to reach Delhi from Sind, but it took just five days for the postal system to send news reports of spies to the Sultan.
- The Indian postal system was of two types: ***uluq***[6] and ***dawa***[7].
- At every third mile, there was a well-populated village with men available to carry the courier.
- When a courier starts from the city, each of the men holds the letter in one hand and the rod with copper bells on the other, and runs as fast as they can.
- In the next *dawa*, when the other men hear this bell, he gets ready and as soon as the courier reaches him, he takes it and transfers it to the next dawa. This continues till it reaches its destination.
- The foot-post was quicker than the horse-post and was used to transport fruits of Khurasan which were much desired in India.

Followers of Ibn Battuta

Many writers and travellers followed the journey of Al-Biruni and Ibn Battuta. Among the best known of these writers were

- **Abdur Razzaq Samarqandi,** who visited South India in the 1440s.
- **Mahmud Wali Balkhi** travelled widely in the 1620s.
- **Shaikh Ali Hazin** who came to North India in the 1740s.

Some of them were fascinated by India. Mahmud Balkhi even became a sort of *sanyasi* for a time. Others like Hazin were disappointed and disgusted with India because they expected to receive good treatment. Most of them saw India as a **land of wonders.**

6 **Uluq** A horse-post service run by royal horses stationed every four miles.
7 **Dawa** Foot-post which has three stations per mile.

Quick Test 2

1 Who was Ibn Battuta?
2 Ibn Battuta's book of travel was written in which language?
3 Which city was described by Ibn Battuta as having the largest population?
4 What does the marketplace for male and female singers in Daulatabad known as?
5 Name the two types of Indian Postal System?

5.3 Francois Bernier

- Francois Berneir was a doctor, political philosopher and historian from **France**. He came to the Mughal Empire in search of opportunities and was in India between 1656 and 1668 CE.
- He was associated with the Mughal court. He was physician to **Prince Dara Shukoh**, the eldest son of Emperor Shah Jahan. Later he also worked as an intellectual and scientist with **Danishmand Khan** (an Armenian noble) at the Mughal court.

▲ *Bernier in European Clothes*

Comparing East and West

- Bernier travelled to several parts of India. He wrote accounts about what he saw and compared them with the situation in Europe in general and France in particular.
- He dedicated his major writing to **Louis XIV** and many of his other works were written in the form of letters to influential officials and ministers.
- For Bernier, the situation in India was not hopeful and was discouraging compared to the developments in Europe.
- Bernier wanted to influence the policy makers and the intellectuals to make right decisions.

Publishing of Bernier's Works

- Bernier's works were published in France in 1670-71 CE and translated into English, Dutch, German and Italian within the next five years.
- His account was reprinted in French eight times between 1670 and 1725 CE.
- By 1684 CE, it was reprinted three times in English. As compared to it, Arabic and Persian accounts were circulated as manuscripts and were not published before 1800 CE.

Bernier's 'Travels in the Mughal Empire'

- Bernier's book **Travels in the Mughal Empire** has detailed observations, critical insights and reflection of Mughal society.
- He compared Mughal India with contemporary Europe and stressed on the superiority of Europe.

The Question of Land Ownership

- According to Bernier, ownership of land was a major difference between Mughal India and Europe.
- In India, there was a lack of private property in land. He strongly believed that it was good to have private property for both the state and its people.
- He thought that in the Mughal Empire, the emperor owned all the land and distributed it among his nobles. This method had negative consequences for the economy and society.
- These views were also found in other travellers' accounts of the sixteenth and seventeenth centuries.

Disadvantages of Ownership of Land System in India

- According to Bernier, in crown ownership of land, landholders could not pass on the land to their children which discouraged landholders from investing in the maintenance and expansion of production.
- The absence of private property in land prevented the emergence of the class of landlords who focussed on improving their lands as in Western Europe.
- This led to the uniform destruction of agriculture, excessive oppression of the peasantry and continuous decline in the living standards of all sections of society, except the ruling aristocracy.

Truth about Ownership of Land

- Mughal official documents do not show that the state was the sole owner of land.
- The sixteenth century official chronicler, **Abu'l Fazl** describes the land revenue as **remunerations of sovereignty** during the Akbar's reign.
- Remunerations of sovereignty meant that a ruler could claim revenue from his subjects for the protection he provided for the land, rather than as rent on land he owned.
- European travellers assumed this claim to be rent because land revenue demands were very high in those times. But in reality this was not a rent or a land tax, it was a tax on crop.

Bernier's Views on Peasantry

- Bernier described the exploitation of peasants in his travel accounts. He pointed out that there were vast tracts of land in Hindustan and most of the land was barren, badly cultivated and sparsely populated.
- A large portion of fertile land remained untilled (wasted) because of the lack of labourers.
- When poor people could not meet the demands of their cruel and greedy lords, they were not only deprived of their means of livelihood but their children also were carried away as slaves. This cruelty disturbed the peasantry, forcing them to leave the country.

Bernier's Views about Towns

- During the 17th century, about 15 per cent of the population lived in towns. This was higher than the percentage of urban population in Western Europe in the same period.
- Bernier described Mughal cities as camp towns[8]. He believed that these towns came into existence when the imperial court come to town and rapidly declined when it moved out.
- These towns did not have viable social and economic foundations and were dependent on imperial patronage (protection).
- Bernier had drawn an oversimplified picture about towns. In reality, there were all kinds of towns like manufacturing towns, trading towns, port-towns, sacred centres, pilgrimage towns, etc. The existence of these towns indicated the prosperity of merchant communities and professional classes.

Complex Social Reality

- Bernier portrays the Mughal state as cruel, but his descriptions represent a more complex society.
- He believed that artisans lacked motivation to improve their work because the state took their profits, which leads to a decline in quality. However, he acknowledged that India received large amounts of precious metals through exports.
- He also observed a successful merchant community involved in long-distance trade.

Merchants and Other Professionals in Towns

- Merchants formed a strong community and were organised into caste-based occupational groups. In Western India, these groups were called ***Mahajans*** and their chief, the ***sheth***.
- In urban centres such as Ahmedabad, the *Mahajans* were collectively represented by the chief of the merchant community who was called the ***Nagarsheth***.

8 Camp towns Those towns which owed their existence and survival to the imperial camp.

- There were other professionals in towns like physicians (*hakim or vaid*), teachers (*pundit* or *mulla*), lawyers (*wakil*), painters, architects, musicians, calligraphers, etc. Some of these professionals depended on imperial patronage. Many of them earned by serving other patrons and some others served ordinary people in crowded markets or bazaars.

Criticism of Indian Society by Bernier

- Bernier criticised Indian society as it had undefined masses of poor people which was suppressed by a minority of the rich and powerful ruling class.
- He stated that there was no middle state in India. In between the poorest of the poor and the richest of rich, there was no social group or class.
- The king of the Mughal Empire was the king of beggars and barbarians.
- The cities and towns were ruined and polluted with bad air and its fields were overspread with bushes and full of infectious waterlogged areas. Crown ownership of land was responsible for all this bad state of affairs.
- A Dutch traveller, **Pelsaert** visited the subcontinent during the early decades of the 17th century. Like Berneir, he was also shocked to see poverty in the Indian society.

Ideas about India

- European travelers shaped the image of India in Europe through their published books and writings.
- After 1750, Indian figures like **Shaikh Itisamuddin** and **Mirza Abu Talib** visited Europe and challenged these perceptions by sharing their own views on Indian society.

Bernier's Account on Imperial Karkhanas[9]

- Bernier was the **only historian** to provide a detailed account of the working of the imperial *karkhanas* or workshops.
- These were large halls for artisans seen at many places.
- Each hall had various craftsmen, supervised by a master, including embroiderers, goldsmiths, painters, joiners, turners, tailors, shoemakers and makers of silk, brocade and fine muslins.
- The artisans came to their *karkhanas* every morning. They remain employed the whole day and return to homes in the evening. In this way, their time passes away and no one aspires for any improvement in their living standards.

Influence of Bernier's Account on Other Scholars

Bernier's descriptions about the Indian sub-continent influenced Western theorists from the 18th century onwards. These theorists were

Montesquieu

- He was a French philosopher. He used Bernier's account to develop the idea of **oriental despotism**, which means rulers of Asia (the Orient or the East) enjoyed absolute authority over their subjects.
- People were suppressed and kept in poverty by making all land under ownership of the king and not allowing private property. Apart from the emperor and his nobles, all people hardly managed to survive.

Karl Marx

- He developed Bernier's idea as the concept of the **Asiatic mode of production** in the 19th century.

---

9 Karkhanas Large halls or workshops for artisans.

- According to him, before colonialism, surplus was kept by the state in India and other Asian countries. This system led to the emergence of a society that had a large number of independent and democratic village communities.
- The Imperial court respected the autonomy of these villages till the flow of surplus was not disturbed. Thus, this system was regarded as a stagnant system.

Reality of Rural Society

- The picture depicted by Western thinkers about the subcontinent's rural society was not real. Rural society was characterised by considerable social and economic differentiation during the 16th and 17th centuries.
- On one hand, there were big zamindars with superior rights in land and on the other, there were untouchable landless labourers. Between them, there was the big peasant who used hired labour and engaged in commodity production and the smaller peasant who struggled to produce enough for their survival.

Abdur Razzaq's Account on India

- The travelogue of Abdur Razzaq written in the 1440s was an interesting mixture of emotions and perceptions about India.
- He was not impressed by what he saw in the port of Calicut, Kerala, as the people there were very different from what Abdur Razzaq had imagined. He described them as a **strange nation.**
- Later, when he visited Mangalore, he admired the temple that he saw there. He described the temple as an idol house. He was amazed by the craft and artisanship of the temple.

5.4 Other European Travellers

- After the Portuguese arrived in India in about 1500, many European scholars wrote detailed accounts regarding Indian customs and religious practices.
- **Jesuit Roberto Nobili** translated Indian texts into European languages.
- **Duarte Barbosa** was the best known among the Portuguese writers, who wrote a detailed account of trade and society in South India.
- After 1600 CE, there were many Dutch, English and French travellers who came to India.
- The French jeweller **Jean-Baptiste Tavernier** travelled to India at least six times. He was impressed with the trading conditions and compared India to Iran and the Ottoman empire.
- Some travellers like Italian doctor **Manucci**, settled down in India and never returned to Europe.

5.5 Women : Slaves, Sati and Labourers

- Travellers who left written accounts were generally men, but they were attracted by the condition of women in the subcontinent.
- Sometimes, they took social inequalities for granted as a natural state of affairs. For example, slaves were openly sold in markets, like other commodities and were exchanged as gifts.
- According to Ibn Battuta, most female slaves were captured in raids and expeditions.
- Ibn Battuta himself bought slaves along with horses and camels when he reached Sind, as gifts for Sultan Muhammad bin Tughlaq. After reaching Multan, he gifted a slave and horse along with raisins and almonds to the Governor.
- Muhammad bin Tughlaq became so happy with the religious speech of a preacher named **Nasiruddin** that he gave him a hundred thousand *tankas* (coins) and two hundred slaves.

- Ibn Battuta's account shows that there was considerable differentiation among slaves.
- Some female slaves in the service of the Sultan were experts in music and dance. Female slaves were also employed by the Sultan to keep a watch on his nobles.
- Slaves were also used for domestic labour and Ibn Battuta found their services necessary for carrying women and men on palanquins or *dola.*
- Price of female slaves for domestic labour was very low, therefore most families who could afford slaves, kept at least one or two of them.

European Traveller's Views on Condition of Women

- Many contemporary European travellers and writers often highlighted the treatment of women as an important marker of difference between Western and Eastern societies.
- Bernier described about the practice of Sati. He noted that while some women seemed to accept death cheerfully, others were forced to die.
- Women were also involved in other things. Their labour was important in both agricultural and non-agricultural production.
- Women from merchant families participated in commercial activities, sometimes even taking **mercantile** (trade and commerce) disputes to the court of law.

Conclusion

The accounts of travellers give us a good idea of the lives of men and women during these centuries. However, the place where the travellers came from influenced their observations. Various spheres of social life were not noticed by them. The experiences of people from the subcontinent who moved beyond the subcontinent are also unknown.

Quick Test 3

1. Francois Bernier was associated with which Mughal Court noble after serving as a physician?
2. Francois Bernier dedicated his work to whom?
3. Who was the historian that provided a detailed account of the imperial karkhanas?
4. Which idea of Bernier was developed by Karl Marx?
5. Name the Italian traveller who came and settled in India.

TIMELINE

Some Travellers who left Accounts

973-1048	Muhammad Ibn Ahmad Abu Raihan al-Biruni (from Uzbekistan)	1518 (visit to India)	Duarte Barbosa, d.1521 (from Portugal)
1254-1323	Marco Polo (from Italy)	1562 (year of death)	Seydi Ali Reis (from Turkey)
1304-77	Ibn Battuta (from Morocco)	1536-1600	Antonio Monserrate (from Spain)
1413-82	Abd-al-Razzaq Kamal al-Din ibn Ishaq al-Samarqandi (from Samarqand)	1626-31 (years spent in India)	Mahmud Wali Balkhi (from Balkh)
1466-72 (years spent in India)	Afanasii Nikitich Nikitin (From Russia)	1600-67	Peter Mundy (from England)
		1605-89	Jean-Baptiste Tavernier (from France)
		1620-88	François Bernier (from France)

Mind Map

THROUGH THE EYES OF TRAVELLERS

1 Al-Biruni

From Khwarizm to the Punjab
- Al-Biruni was born in 1973, in Khwarizm, Uzbekistan.
- Sultan Mahmud bought Al-Biruni to Ghazni in 1017.

The Kitab-ul-Hind
Al-Biruni's Kitab-ul-Hind covers religion, philosophy, astronomy and customs.

2 Al-Biruni and the Sanskritic Tradition

Overcoming Barriers to Understanding
- Al-Biruni faced barriers like language differences in understanding India.
- Religious beliefs and narrow-mindedness of the local population were also challenges for Al-Biruni.

Al-Biruni's Description of the Caste System
- He compared caste system to social divisions in Persia.
- His caste descriptions were influenced by Brahmanical texts.

3 Ibn Battuta and the Excitement of the Unfamiliar

A Unique System of Communication
- State encouraged trade with inns, guest horses.
- Ibn Battuta admired the efficiency of the Postal system

The Coconut and the Paan
Ibn Battuta introduced coconut and the paan that were completely unfamiliar to his audience.

An Early Globe Trotter
- Ibn Battuta wrote Rihla, a book about 14th century India.
- He valued travel experience over book knowledge for learning.

Ibn Battuta and Indian cities
Ibn Battuta described Delhi and Daulatabad as large, prosperous cities.

4 Francois Bernier: A Doctor with a Difference

The Question of Landownership
- Bernier believed that crown ownership of land harmed economy and society.
- Widespread poverty resulted from excessive oppression of peasants.

Comparing East and West
Bernier compared India unfavourably with Europe in his writings.

A More Complex Social Reality
- Bernier saw artisans as lacking incentive due to state profits.
- He acknowledged India's prosperity from exports of gold and silver.

5 Women: Slaves, Sati and Labourers

- Slaves were sold openly in markets and exchanged as gifts.
- Bernier criticised the practice of Sati.

NCERT Folder

Intext Questions

1. If Al-Biruni lived in the twenty-first century, which are the areas of the world where he could have been easily understood, if he still knew the same languages? (Pg. 117)

Ans. If Al-Biruni lived in the twenty-first century, he would be easily understood in areas of the world like South Asia (particularly Pakistan, India and Afghanistan), the Middle East, Central Asia (including Uzbekistan and Tajikistan) and parts of North Africa due to his fluency in languages like Arabic, Persian, Sanskrit and Hebrew, which are still widely spoken in these areas today.

2. Compare the objectives of Al-Biruni and Ibn Battuta in writing their accounts. (Pg. 121)

Ans. The primary objective of Al-Biruni was to provide a comprehensive analysis of Indian society, religion and culture. He aimed to foster understanding between different civilisations through detailed comparisons.

On the other hand, Ibn Battuta focused on narrating his personal travel experiences, highlighting the exciting aspects of the places he visited to engage a wider audience with his stories and observations about diverse cultures.

3. How important is knowledge of the language of the area for a traveller from a different region? (Pg. 125)

Ans. Knowledge of the local language is very important for a traveller from a different region because it helps in proper communication, improves navigation, helps with safety. It also leads to more positive interactions with locals, making the travel experience richer and more fulfilling.

4. How did Ibn Battuta handle the problem of describing things or situations to people who had not seen or experienced them? (Pg. 129)

Ans. Ibn Battuta handled the problem of describing unfamiliar sights and experiences to his audience by using vivid metaphors, comparisons to familiar objects, detailed descriptions of everyday life, incorporating local terms with explanations and drawing on his own cultural context to create relatable similarity whenever possible.

5. Why do you think scholars like Bernier chose to compare India with Europe? (Pg. 134)

Ans. Scholars like François Bernier compared India with Europe to highlight contrasts in social structures, land ownership, and governance. Such comparisons aimed to critique and reflect on European systems by showing India as an inferior country. This helped shape European perspectives on India while potentially influencing European policymakers and intellectual circles.

6. Why do you think the lives of ordinary women workers did not attract the attention of travellers such as Ibn Battuta and Bernier? (Pg. 136)

Ans. The lives of ordinary women workers did not attract the attention of travellers like Ibn Battuta and Bernier because they mainly focussed on the elite, political, and religious aspects of societies. They often neglected the daily lives of common people, particularly women who were largely confined to the domestic sphere and considered socially invisible in many cultures at the time.

Answer in 100-150 words

1. Write a note on the Kitab-ul-Hind.

Ans. Al-Biruni wrote Kitab-ul-Hind in Arabic, in very simple and easy to understand language. It is divided into 80 chapters on subjects such as religion and philosophy, festivals, astronomy, alchemy (magic), manners and customs, social life, weights and measures, iconography, laws and metrology. He followed a different structure in each chapter. He started with a question in each chapter, followed with a description based on Sanskritic traditions and concluding with a comparison with other cultures. Some scholars praised about this structure and compared it with geometric structure known for its precision and predictability. This was due to Al-Biruni's mathematical orientation.

2. Compare and contrast the perspectives from which Ibn Battuta and Bernier wrote their accounts of their travels in India. CBSE Diksha

Ans. Ibn Battuta's perspective in his accounts of travel in India was

- He was very much excited about the new and unfamiliar things. He wrote a detailed description about coconut and *paan* that was used in India.
- He wrote stories about men known for their devotion, kings who could be both cruel and generous and about lives of ordinary men and women.
- He wrote about anything that was unfamiliar and particularly highlighted in order to ensure that the listener or the reader was suitably impressed by accounts of far but accessible worlds.

Bernier's perspective in his accounts of his travel in India was

- Bernier compared the situations he saw in India with those of Europe in general and France in particular. He mainly focussed on the depressing things of India. He wanted to influence the European policy makers to make the right decisions.
- Bernier compared Mughal Empire with that of Europe and stressed on the superiority of the Europe. He showed India to be inferior to that of Europe.

3. Discuss the picture of urban centres that emerges from Bernier's account.

Ans. The picture of urban centres from Bernier's account was as follows

- The cities and towns were ruined with polluted air, its fields overspread with bushes and full of dirty still water.
- Bernier described Mughal cities as camp towns. This means these towns owed their existence and depended on the imperial court for their survival. He believed that these came into existence when imperial court moved in and they will decline when imperial court moves out.
- Bernier suggested that urban centres did not have viable social and economic foundations and were dependent on imperial protection.

4. Analyse the evidence for slavery provided by Ibn Battuta.

Ans. The evidences of slavery provided by the account of Ibn Battuta were

- Ibn Battuta account mentions that slaves were openly sold in markets.
- When Ibn Battuta reached Sind, he purchased slaves along with horses and camels, as gifts for Sultan Muhammad bin Tughlaq.
- He presented Governor of Multan with a slave and horse together with raisins and almonds.
- Muhammad bin Tughlaq informed Ibn Battuta that he gave a preacher named Nasiruddin, a thousand tankas and two hundred slaves.
- As per the Ibn Battuta's account, there was significant differentiation among slaves. Some female slaves in the service of Sultans were experts in music and dance. Female slaves were also employed by Sultan to spy on his nobles.
- Slaves were generally used for domestic labour and Ibn Battuta found their services absolute necessary. Price of female slaves required for domestic labour was very low and most families who could afford to do kept at least one or two of them.

5. What were the elements of the practice of sati that drew the attention of Bernier?

Ans. The practice of sati according to Bernier showed the difference in the treatment of women in Western and Eastern society. He noticed how a child widow were forcefully burnt screaming on the funeral pyre while many of the older women accepted death willingly. Following elments drew his attention

(i) Under this cruel practices an alive widow was forcibly made to sit on the pyre of her husband.

(ii) Hands and feet of the widow were tied and she was burnt alive. People had no sympathy for her.

(iii) The widow was an unwilling victim of the sati-practice. She was forced to be a sati.

Write a short Essay (about 250-300 words) on the following

6. Discuss Al-Biruni's understanding of the caste system. **CBSE Diksha**

Ans. Al-Biruni tried to explain the caste system by looking for similar systems in other societies. According to his accounts caste system can be understood as

- He noted that social divisions were not unique to India and pointed out that similar system existed in ancient Persia. There were four social categories present in Persia. Knights and princes belonged to first, monk, fire-priests and lawyers belonged to second, physicians, astronomers and other scientists belonged to third and finally peasants and artisans belonged to fourth.
- Al-Biruni accepted Brahmanical description of the caste system, but he disapproved the notion of pollution. He stated that social pollution which is part of the caste system was against the laws of nature.
- He also described about the hierarchy present in the caste system which he learnt from various Sanskritic texts.
- He described that highest castes were the Brahmanas who were created from the head of Brahman and thus Hindus considered them as the very best of mankind. Next caste are the Kshatriyas who were created from the shoulders and hands of Brahman. They are followed by Vaishyas who were created from the thigh of Brahman and Shudras were created from feet of Brahman. Al-Biruni stated that these classes live together in the same towns and villages, mixed together in the same houses and lodgings.

7. Do you think Ibn Battuta's account is useful in arriving at an understanding of life in contemporary urban centres? Give reasons for your answer. **Competency Based Que**

Ans. Yes, Ibn Battuta's account is useful for understanding life in contemporary urban centres. He has described about Indian urban centres in a positive way which was as follows

- He found cities in the subcontinent full of exciting opportunities for those who have necessary resources and skills.
- The cities were densely populated and prosperous, except for the occasional disruptions caused by wars and

invasions. Most cities were crowded and had bright colourful markets that were arranged with wide range of goods.

- He described Delhi as a big city, with a great population, the largest in India. He also described that Daulatabad was also equally big as Delhi.
- He stated that bazaars in urban centres were not just places of economic transactions but also hub of social and cultural activities. Most bazaars had a mosque and a temple and some of them also had specific places marked for public performances by dancers, musicians and singers. Ibn Battuta suggested that towns derived significant portion of their wealth through the appropriation of surplus from villages.

8. Discuss the extent to which Bernier's account enables historians to reconstruct contemporary rural society. CBSE Diksha

Ans. Bernier's account on India is not completely true in reality but few of his findings are true. Some of his findings which enabled historians to reconstruct contemporary rural society are

- Mughal emperor owned all the land and distributed it to his nobles. This crown ownership had disastrous consequences for the economy and society.
- Since land was under crown ownership, landholders could not pass on their land to their children and hence they were not interested in any long-term investment in the sustenance and expansions of production. This kind of system prevented the emergence of improving landlord class.
- It also led to destruction of agriculture, excessive oppression of the peasantry and a continuous decline in the living standards of all sections of society, except the ruling aristocracy.
- He pointed out that vast land of empire was left waste, badly cultivated, and thinly populated. Many of the poor peasants experienced bad treatment from their Governors and were unable to fulfil the demands of the greedy lords.
- Poor people's children were taken away as slaves when they could not satisfy the demands of their lords.
- Bernier also pointed out that Indian society is full of poor and needy people who are controlled and suppressed by a small minority of very rich and powerful ruling class.
- Indian society has only two extreme classes i.e. poorest of the poor and richest of the rich and there was no middle class in between them.
- He stated that Mughal empire and its king was the king of beggars and uncivilised people.

9. Read this excerpt from Bernier

Numerous are the instances of handsome pieces of workmanship made by persons destitute of tools and who can scarcely be said to have received instruction from a master. Sometimes they imitate so perfectly articles of European manufacture that the difference between the original and copy can hardly be discerned. Among other things, the Indians make excellent muskets, and fowling-pieces, and such beautiful ornaments that it may be doubted if the exquisite workmanship of those articles can be exceeded by any European goldsmith.

I have often admired the beauty, softness and delicacy of their paintings. List the crafts mentioned in the passage. Compare these with the descriptions of artisanal activity in the chapter.

Ans. The list of crafts mentioned in the passage are excellent muskets, fowling pieces, beautiful ornaments and paintings.

Comparison of these with descriptions of artisanal activity in the chapter is discussed below

- In this chapter, boat manufacturing, terracotta sculpture and temple construction have been mentioned.
- Painting was also mentioned in this chapter, depicting travellers around a campfire. Another painting of Bernier with European clothes and Tavernier in Indian clothes are also depicted in this chapter.
- Artisanal activities related to arch, cemeteries are also mentioned in this chapter.
- Ikat weaving patterns and other textile related artisanal activities are described.
- Arts like dance, music are also mentioned in this chapter.
- Artisanal activity of goldsmiths is also mentioned. For instance, gold spoon with emeralds and rubies shows the skill of Mughal artisans.
- Various artisanal works that happened in *karkhanas* or workshops were mentioned in the chapter. They are embroiders, goldsmiths, painters, varnishers in lacquer work, joiners, turners, tailors, shoemakers, silken weavers and fine muslin manufacturers.

10. On an outline map of the world mark the countries visited by Ibn Battuta. What are the seas that he may have crossed?

Ans. The countries visited by Ibn Battuta are

(i) India (ii) Sri Lanka (iii) Maldives
(iv) China (v) Sumatra (vi) Morocco
(vii) Iraq (viii) Yemen (ix) Syria

(x) Persia
(xi) Oman

The seas he may have crossed are
- Indian Ocean
- Arabian Sea
- Bay of Bengal
- South China Sea
- East China Sea
- South Atlantic Ocean
- North Atlantic Ocean
- Red Sea

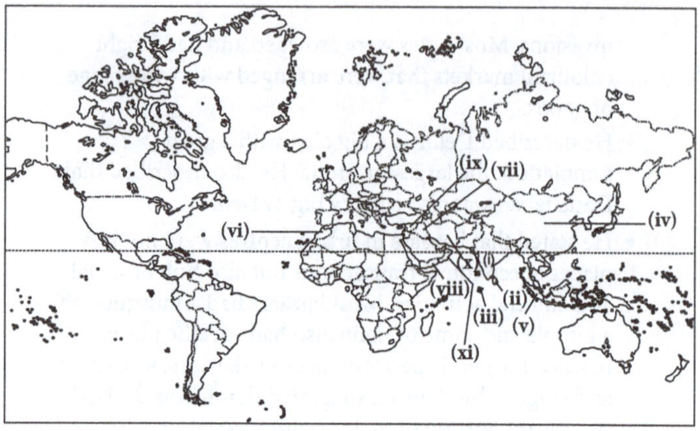

Exam Pattern Questions

Objective Type Questions

Multiple Choice Questions (MCQs)

1. When and where Al-Biruni was born ?
(a) 873 CE, Uzbekistan (b) 973 CE, Uzbekistan
(c) 873 CE, Morocco (d) 973 CE, Morocco

2. Who was the author of Kitab-ul-Hind ? CBSE Diksha
(a) Ibn Battuta (b) Al-Biruni
(c) Francois Bernier (d) None of these

3. Who brought Al-Biruni as hostage to Ghazni? CBSE Diksha
(a) Sultan Mahmud
(b) Sultan Muhammad Bin Tughlaq
(c) Akbar
(d) Danishmand Khan

4. Al-Biruni discussed several barriers that he felt obstructed his understanding. What were those barriers? CBSE Diksha
(a) Language and religious beliefs
(b) Language and administration
(c) Population and customs
(d) Religion and polity

5. ....means born outside the system, were often expected to provide inexpensive labour to both peasants and zamindars.
(a) Caravans
(b) Antyaja
(c) Zaytun
(d) None of the above

6. Which of the following is related to the Al-Biruni's concept of pollution ?
(a) Concept of energy generation
(b) Sustainable development
(c) Destroying tree cover of earth
(d) Concept of social pollution

7. Al-Biruni's major work Kitab-ul-Hind' is significant for its comprehensive study of India. Which of the following was the primary aim of this work? CBSE 2025
(a) Promote Islamic teaching
(b) Map geographical locations
(c) Critique culture and traditions
(d) Document Indian culture

8. Which of the following category of society of ancient Persia was not recognised by the Al-Biruni ?
(a) Knights and princes (b) Monks and fire-priests
(c) Peasants and artisans (d) Children and women

9. In which of the following languages has Al-Biruni translated Sanskrit, Pali and Prakrit texts in India ? CBSE 2024
(a) Persian (b) Arabic
(c) Urdu (d) Hindavi

10. Which of the following travellers was appointed as the Qazi of Delhi by the Sultan Muhammad Bin Tughlaq? CBSE Diksha
(a) Abdur Razzaq (b) Al-Biruni
(c) Ibn Battuta (d) Barbosa

11. **Where was market place for male and female singers was situated?**
(a) Delhi (b) Agra
(c) Daulatabad (d) Sind

12. **Which of the following is the greatest gate ?**
(a) Gurl Darwaza
(b) Mandwi Darwaza
(c) Budaun Darwaza
(d) None of the above

13. **There is a ....at the centre of the shop on which a female singer sits.**
(a) Chair (b) Throne
(c) Stone (d) Swing

14. **During Ibn Battuta's travels in India, which prominent city did he visit and describe as 'a vast city, with a great population, the largest in India ?** CBSE 2024
(a) Daulatabad (b) Agra
(c) Calcutta (d) Delhi

15. **Name the French traveller who visited India 6 times and was fascinated with the trading conditions in India.** CBSE Diksha
(a) Tavernier (b) Al-Biruni
(c) Ibn Battuta (d) Francois Bernier

16. **Who dedicated his travel account to Louis XIV, the King of France?** CBSE Diksha
(a) Tavernier (b) Ibn Battuta
(c) Barbosa (d) Francois Bernier

17. **Who used the travel account of Bernier to develop the idea of oriental despotism?** CBSE Diksha
(a) Montesquieu (b) Karl Marx
(c) Barbosa (d) Abul Fazl

18. **To whom among the following did François Bernier dedicate his writing "Comparing East and West" ?** CBSE 2024
(a) Louis XIV (b) Charles IX
(c) Louis IX (d) Phillip II

19. **Identify the foreign traveller who wrote about the ill-effects of the Mughal crown's ownership of land in his book** CBSE 2024 C
(a) Al-Biruni (b) François Bernier
(c) Ibn Battuta (d) Domingo Paes

20. **Among the following, whose description of 'degenerated East' inspired Western theorists to develop the idea of 'oriental despotism' ?** CBSE 2024
(a) Peter Mundy (b) François Bernier
(c) Duarte Barbosa (d) Marco Polo

21. **Which of the following countries 'Duarte Barbosa' belonged to?** CBSE 2023
(a) Russia (b) Portugal
(c) Spain (d) France

22. **Identify the things purchased by Ibn Battuta from Sind for giving gifts?** CBSE Diksha
(a) Horses, camels, textiles
(b) Horses, slaves and camels
(c) Horses, camels and muslin
(d) Horses, slaves and elephants

23. **Which one of the following distinct styles did Al-Biruni adopt in each chapter of his book 'Kitab-ul-Hind' ?** CBSE 2024 C
(a) Beginning with a question
(b) Beginning with a poem
(c) Beginning with a picture
(d) Beginning with a quote

24. **Which of the following skills can be identified from Al-Biruni's writings?** SQP 2024-25
(a) Proficiency in diplomacy and political negotiation.
(b) Fluency in multiple languages and a broad intellectual curiosity.
(c) Expertise in military strategy and warfare tactics.
(d) Exceptional talent for storytelling and vivid descriptions.

25. **Throughout his extensive travels, Ibn Batuta was able to explore unfamiliar cultures and societies. Which of the following competencies did he most likely develop?** CBSE 2025
(a) Leadership and Judicial Management
(b) Cultural Competencies and Skills
(c) Knowledge of Administration and Army
(d) Scientific and Technical expertise

26. **Which of the following statements regarding Ibn Battuta is incorrect?** CBSE Diksha
(a) Ibn Battuta commenced his journey to India in 1232-33.
(b) Ibn Battuta was born in Tangier into one of the most respected and educated families.
(c) Ibn Battuta found Indian agriculture very productive because of the fertility of the soil which allowed farmers to cultivate two crops a year.
(d) Indian textiles, particularly cotton cloth, fine muslins, silks, brocade and satin were in great demand.

27. **According to Ibn Battuta, Indian postal system was used for which of the following activities?**
(a) To send information.
(b) To remit credit across long distances.
(c) To dispatch goods required at short notice.
(d) All of the above

28. **Which of the following statements is correct regarding the traveller Ibn Battuta?**
(a) He was born in France.
(b) His book Rihla is written in Persian language.
(c) He was not travelled much before came to India.
(d) He travelled to different countries like Syria, Iraq, Persia, etc.

29. **Which of these is a notable feature about the Italian doctor, Manucci, who travelled to India?**

(a) He came and treated many people in India and improved the healthcare system.
(b) He found India so impressive that he did not go back to his home country in Europe.
(c) He observed and wrote detailed accounts on India's agricultural system.
(d) He was closely associated with the Mughal court.

30. **What insights did Francois Bernier provide about the economic structure of Mughal India?** SQP 2024

Choose the best suitable option from the following.

(a) The prevalence of private land ownership and equitable distribution of wealth.
(b) The dominance of state-controlled resources and limitations on private property.
(c) The absence of trade networks and economic isolation from global markets.
(d) The reliance on foreign investments and the absence of indigenous industries.

31. **Identify the traveller with the help of information given below.**

(i) He was born in Khwarizm.
(ii) He translated Patanjali's grammer into Arabic.
(iii) He was well versed in several languages : Syriac, Arabic, Persian, Hebrew and Sanskrit.
(iv) He was familiar with the works of Plato and other Greek philosophers, having read them in Arabic translations.

Options

(a) Al-Biruni (b) Barbosa
(c) Pelsaert (d) Ibn Battuta

32. **As per Al-Biruni account of the system of varnas, arrange them according to the order of precedence.**

(i) Shudra (ii) Vaishya
(iii) Brahmana (iv) Kshatriya

Codes

(a) (iii), (iv), (ii), (i) (b) (iv), (i), (iii), (ii)
(c) (iv), (iii), (ii), (i) (d) (i), (ii), (iii), (iv)

33. **Arrange the journey of Ibn Battuta in chronological order.**

(i) Maldives (ii) Sri Lanka
(iii) Malabar (iv) China

Codes

(a) (i), (ii), (iii), (iv) (b) (iii), (i), (ii), (iv)
(c) (ii), (iii), (i), (iv) (d) (iii), (ii), (iv), (i)

34. **Arrange the following visitors of India as per the chronology.**

(i) Marco Polo (ii) Francois Bernier
(iii) Ibn Battuta (iv) Al-Biruni

Codes

(a) (iii), (ii), (iv), (i) (b) (iv), (i), (iii), (ii)
(c) (iv), (iii), (ii), (i) (d) (i), (ii), (iii), (iv)

35. **Which one of the following pairs is correctly matched?**

(a) Domingo Paes - Italian traveller CBSE Term I 2021
(b) Abdur Razzak - Russian traveller
(c) Nicolo de Conti - Persian Ambassador
(d) Duarte Barbosa - A Portuguese traveller

36. **Identify the name of the person from the information given below.**

(i) He considered experience gained through travels to be a more important source of knowledge than books.
(ii) He had travelled extensively in Syria, Iraq, Persia, Yemen, Oman and a few trading ports on the coast of East Africa.
(iii) He wrote a book named Rihla.

Options

(a) Al-Biruni (b) Tavernier
(c) Ibn Battuta (d) Barbosa

37. **Identify the medieval globe-trotter with the help of the following information.** CBSE 2024

(a) Before he set-off for India he made pilgrimage trips to Mecca before 1332-33 C.E.
(b) The Delhi Sultan Muhammad Bin Tughlaq made him Qazi or the judge of Delhi.

Options

(a) Abd-al-Razzaq (b) Al-Biruni
(c) Ibn Battuta (d) Seydi Ali Reis

38. **Identify the traveller with the help of information given below.**

(i) He was doctor, political philosopher and historian.
(ii) He was in India from 1656 to 1668 CE.
(iii) He was closely associated with Mughal Prince Dara Shukoh.
(iv) He was later associated with Danishmand Khan.

Options

(a) Al-Biruni (b) Ibn Battuta
(c) Francois Bernier (d) Abul Fazl

39. **Complete the following with the correct option regarding the travellers and their respective birth places.**
Al-Biruni : Khwarizm :: Ibn Battuta : ....

(a) Tangier (b) Bukhara
(c) Samarkand (d) Baghdad

40. **Complete the following with the correct option regarding the travellers and the languages in which they translated Indian texts.**

Jesuit Roberto Nobili : European :: Al-Biruni : ....

(a) Arabic (b) German
(c) Mandarin (d) Portuguese

Assertion-Reason

41. **Assertion** (A) Ibn Battuta travelled to different countries.

Reason (R) He considered experience gained through travel.

Codes

(a) Both A and R are true and R is the correct explanation of A
(b) Both A and R are true, but R is not the correct explanation of A
(c) A is true, but R is false
(d) A is false, but R is true

42. **Assertion** (A) Ibn Battuta found Indian agriculture very productive. **CBSE 2024**

Reason (R) The soils were fertile which allowed the farmers to produce two crops a year.

Codes

(a) Both A and R are true and R is the correct explanation of A
(b) Both A and R are true, but R is not the correct explanation of A
(c) A is true, but R is false
(d) A is false, but R is true

43. **Assertion** (A) Bernier was a firm believer in the virtues of private property. He saw crown ownership of land in the Mughal empire as being harmful to both State and the people.

Reason (R) Landlords could not pass on their land to their children, so they were averse to any long time investment in the expansion of production.

Codes

(a) Both A and R are true and R is the correct explanation of A
(b) Both A and R are true, but R is not the correct explantion of A
(c) A is true, but R is false
(d) A is false, but R is true

44. **Assertion** (A) There was lack of private property in land in India.

Reason (R) The emperor owned all the land distributed it among his nobles.

Codes

(a) Both A and R are true and R is the correct explanation of A
(b) Both A and R are true, but R is not the correct explanation of A
(c) A is true, but R is false
(d) A is false, but R is true

Match the Following

45.

List I	List II
A. Al Biruni	1. Uzbekistan
B. Francois Bernier	2. Italy
C. Duarte Barbosa	3. France
D. Manucci	4. Portugal

Codes

	A	B	C	D		A	B	C	D
(a)	1	2	3	4	(b)	2	1	4	3
(c)	3	1	2	4	(d)	1	3	4	2

46.

List I	List II
A. Al-Biruni	1. Physician to Dara Shukoh.
B. Mahmud Balkhi	2. Translated Patanjali's work on grammer.
C. Francois Bernier	3. Pointed about the poverty in India.
D. Pelsaert	4. Became a Sanyasi.

Codes

	A	B	C	D		A	B	C	D
(a)	1	3	2	4	(b)	2	4	1	3
(c)	3	1	2	4	(d)	1	3	4	2

47.

List I	List II
A. Brahmana	1. Thigh
B. Kshatriya	2. Feet
C. Vaishya	3. Hands
D. Shudra	4. Head

Codes

	A	B	C	D		A	B	C	D
(a)	2	1	3	4	(b)	4	3	1	2
(c)	4	1	3	2	(d)	3	2	1	4

48.

List I	List II
A. The horse-post	1. Dawa
B. The foot-post	2. Nagarseth
C. Domed building	3. Uluq
D. Community merchant	4. Cupola

Codes

	A	B	C	D		A	B	C	D
(a)	1	2	3	4	(b)	3	2	1	4
(c)	3	1	4	2	(d)	4	3	2	1

49.

List I		List II	
A.	Abu'l Fazl	1.	Travels in the Mughal Empire
B.	Ibn Battuta	2.	Kitab-ul-Hind
C.	Al-Biruni	3.	Rihla
D.	François Bernier	4.	Ain-i-Akbari

Codes **CBSE 2024**

	A	B	C	D		A	B	C	D
(a)	4	3	2	1	(b)	3	2	1	4
(c)	2	1	4	3	(d)	1	3	2	4

Picture Based Questions

50. **Who among the following foreign traveller was attacked by the robbers in the picture below?**

(a) Francois Bernier
(b) Duarto Barbosa
(c) Ibn Battuta
(d) AI-Biruni

51. **Identify the picture given below and choose the correct the option.**

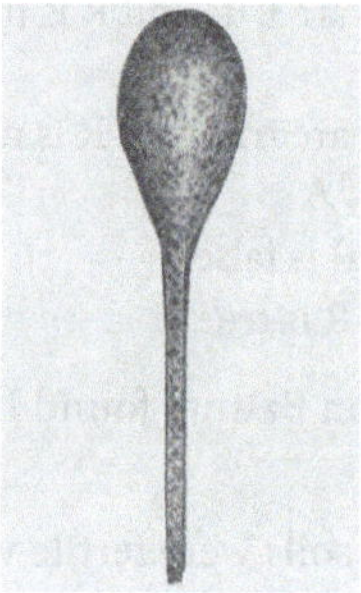

(a) A bronze spoon
(b) A gold spoon used by Akbar
(c) A gold spoon of Gupta period
(d) A gold spoon studded with emeralds.

52. **Identify which of the following options refers to the image given below.**

(a) A sculpted panel from Mathura depicting travellers
(b) A raid by the Mughal army
(c) A wedding procession
(d) A royal ceremony

Answers

1. (b) 973 CE, Uzbekistan
2. (b) Al-Biruni
3. (a) Sultan Mahmud
4. (a) Language and religious beliefs
5. (b) Antyaja
6. (d) Concept of social pollution
7. (d) Document Indian culture
8. (d) Children and women
9. (b) Arabic
10. (c) Ibn Battuta
11. (c) Daulatabad
12. (c) Budaun Darwaza
13. (d) Swing
14. (d) Delhi
15. (a) Tavernier
16. (d) Francois Bernier
17. (a) Montesquieu
18. (a) Louis XIV
19. (b) François Bernier
20. (b) François Bernier

21. (b) Portugal
22. (b) Horses, slaves and camels
23. (a) Beginning with a question
24. (b) Fluency in multiple languages and a broad intellectual curiosity.
25. (b) Cultural Competencies and Skills
26. (a) Ibn Battuta commenced his journey to India in 1232-33.
27. (d) All of the above
28. (d) He travelled to different countries like Syria, Iraq, Persia, etc.
29. (b) He found India so impressive that he did not go back to his home country in Europe.
30. (b) The dominance of state-controlled resources and limitations on private property.
31. (a) Al-Biruni
32. (a) (iii), (iv), (ii), (i)
33. (b) (iii), (i), (ii), (iv)
34. (b) (iv), (i), (iii), (ii)
35. (d) Duarte Barbosa - A Portuguese traveller
36. (c) Ibn Battuta
37. (c) Ibn Battuta
38. (c) Francois Bernier
39. (a) Tangier
40. (a) Arabic
41. (a) Both A and R are true and R is the correct explanation of A
42. (a) Both A and R are true and R is the correct explanation of A
43. (b) Both A and R are true, but R is not the correct explantion of A
44. (a) Both A and R are true and R is the correct explanation of A
45. (d)
46. (b)
47. (b)
48. (c)
49. (a)
50. (c) Ibn Battuta
51. (d) A gold spoon studded with emeralds.
52. (a) A sculpted panel from Mathura depicting travellers

Subjective Questions

Short Answer Type Questions

1. Examine the causes that made Al-Biruni visit India.

Ans. The causes that made Al-Biruni visit India were

- Al-Biruni was among the several scholars taken away by Sultan Mahmud from invaded Khwarizm to his capital Ghazni.
- Al-Biruni developed an interest in India during his stay in Ghazni.
- Al-Biruni wanted to learn more of mathematics, astronomy and medicine, so he visited India. After visiting India, he contacted local people and learnt Indian philosophy. He also learnt Sanskrit and studied religious and philosophical texts.

2. State the inherent problems faced by Al-Biruni in the task of understanding Indian social and Brahmanical practices. Mention any two sources that provided him the support.

Ans. The inherent problems faced by Al-Biruni in the task of understanding Indian social and Brahminical practices were

- First problem was the, language as Sanskrit was so different from Arabic and Persian that ideas and concepts could not be easily translated from one language to another.
- Second was difference in religious beliefs and practices.
- Third was self-absorption and consequent intolerance of the local population.

The main sources that provided him the support are the Vedas, the Puranas, the *Bhagavad Gita*, the works of Patanjali, the *Manusmriti*, etc to provide an understanding of Indian society.

3. Discuss briefly about Al-Biruni.

Ans. Al-Biruni was born in 973 CE, in Khwarizm (Present day Uzbekistan). He attained his early education in Khwarizm, which was the famous centre of learning at that time. He was well versed in different languages like Arabic, Persian, Hebrew, Sanskrit and Syriac. Due to his immense capability, he became the member of council of Khwarizm.

In 1017, Sultan Mahmud invaded Khwarizm and took Al-Biruni to his capital. At first Al-Biruni was a hostage, but he later liked the city and stayed there until he died at 70.

4. Generally Al-Biruni adopted a distinctive structure in each chapter. Justify the statement. Competency Based Que

Ans. Al-Biruni adopted a distinctive structure in each chapter. He started his chapter with a question which was followed up with a description based on Sanskritic traditions. In conclusion, he used a comparison with other cultures. Some present-day scholars have argued that this structure is remarkable for its precision and predictability, and because of his interest in mathematics.

5. "Travellers often compared what they saw in the subcontinent with practices with which they were familiar". Explain the observations of Al-Biruni in context of the above statement. CBSE 2024 C

Ans. Al-Biruni, a Persian scholar who visited India in the 11th century, made observations based on his own cultural and religious background. He compared Indian practices with those he was familiar with to understand the Indian social structure, especially the caste system. Here are the key points of his observations

- **Comparing Practices** Al-Biruni compared Indian customs with those from other societies he knew, especially Persia, to explain what he saw.
- **Caste System Understanding** He tried to understand the caste system by looking for similar social divisions in other cultures, like ancient Persia, where there were four main social groups: knights, priests, scientists, and peasants/artisans.
- **Social Divisions Are Common** By comparing the caste system to other societal structures, Al-Biruni suggested that such divisions were not a unique or particularly Indian phenomenon but were found across different cultures.
- **Islamic Equality and Caste** He pointed out that Islam sees all people as equal, contrasting it with the hierarchical caste system in India.
- **Disagreement with Pollution** Al-Biruni disagreed with the idea of pollution in the caste system, believing it went against natural laws.

6. How did the term 'Hindu' derive?

Ans. The term 'Hindu' was derived from an old Persian word used around 6th - 5th century BCE, to refer to the region to the East of the river Sindhu (Indus). The Arabs continued the Persian usage and called this region 'al-Hind' and its people 'Hindi'.

Later, the Turks referred to the people East of Indus as 'Hindu' and their land as 'Hindustan' and their language as 'Hindavi'. These expressions did not indicate the religious identity of the people. It was much later that the term developed religious implications.

7. Discuss about the travel plans of Ibn Battuta, after his new assignment of going to China as Sultan's envoy.

Ans. The travel plan of Ibn Battuta was as follows

- Ibn Battuta after his new assignment, proceeded to the Malabar coast through Central India. From Malabar, he went to the Maldives, where he stayed for eighteen months as the *qazi*, but then he decided to proceed to Sri Lanka.
- He then went back again to the Malabar coast and the Maldives and before resuming his mission to China, he visited Bengal and Assam.
- He took a Ship to Sumatra and from there another ship for the Chinese port town of Zaytun.
- He travelled extensively in China, going as far as Beijing, but did not stay for long. He decided to return home in 1347 CE.

8. Discuss about initial days of Ibn Battuta in the subcontinent.

Ans. Ibn Battuta reached Sind in 1333 CE. He was attracted by the reputation of Muhmmad bin Tughlaq, the Sultan of Delhi, as a generous patron of arts and letters and thus set off for Delhi. The Sultan was impressed by his scholarship and appointed him the *qazi* or judge of Delhi. He remained in that position for several years, until he fell out of favour and was imprisoned.

Once the misunderstanding was cleared, he was restored to the imperial service and was sent in 1342 CE as the Sultan's representative to the Mongol ruler in China.

9. Discuss about the Ibn Battuta's description of Indian economy.

Ans. The views of Ibn Battuta on Indian economy were

- Ibn Battuta found Indian agriculture very productive because of the fertility of the soil. This fertility allowed farmers to cultivate two crops a year.
- He described that the subcontinent was well connected and integrated with inter-Asian networks of trade and commerce.
- He also pointed out that Indian manufacturers were in great demand in both West Asia and South-East Asia and this brought huge profits for artisans and merchants. There was great demand for Indian textiles like cotton cloth, fine muslins, silks, brocade and satin.

10. **"India had a unique system of communication during the fourteenth century". Examine the statement of Ibn Battuta.** Competency Based Que

Ans. Ibn Battuta was quite amazed with the efficiency of the communication system present in India during fourteenth century. He described that Indian postal system was of two kinds

(i) **Horse post** (Uluq) It was run by royal horses stationed at a distance of every four miles.

(ii) **Foot post** (dawa) It had three stations per mile.

The postal system allowed merchants to not only send information and remit credit across long distance, but also to dispatch goods required at short notice.

The postal system was so efficient that while it took fifty days to reach Delhi from Sind, the news reports of spies would reach the Sultan through the postal system in just five days.

11. **Ibn Battuta travelled in the fourteenth century, when it was much more arduous and hazardous to travel than it is today. Discuss** Competency Based Que

Ans. Ibn Battuta travelled in the fourteenth century, when it was much more arduous and hazardous to travel than it is today because of limited means of transportation available at that time. According to Ibn Battuta, it took forty days to travel from Multan to Delhi and about fifty days from Sind to Delhi. The distance from Daulatabad to Delhi was covered in forty days, while that from Gwalior to Delhi took ten days.

12. **"Ibn Battuta found cities in the subcontinent full of exciting opportunities for those who had the necessary drive, resources and skills." Explain this statement.** CBSE 2024 C

Ans. Ibn Battuta, a famous Moroccan traveller, found the cities in the Indian subcontinent during his visits to be bustling with opportunities for those who had the necessary drive, resources, and skills. He felt this due to the following reasons

- **Colourful Markets** The markets were lively and colourful, offering a wide variety of goods, showing the richness and diversity of products available.
- **Economic Transactions in Bazaars** Bazaars were central to the economy, where merchants and buyers engaged in active trade.
- **Social and Cultural Activities in Bazaars** These markets were not just places for buying and selling but also centers for socialising and cultural exchanges.
- **Bazaars with Mosques and Temples** Many bazaars included mosques and temples, often with spaces for public performances, blending economic, religious, and cultural life.
- **Towns' Wealth from Villages** Towns derived their wealth from the surplus produce brought in from surrounding villages, emphasising the agrarian basis of urban prosperity.
- **Demand for Indian Textiles** India's strong trade networks meant that its textiles, highly valued in the global market, were in great demand.

13. **Examine Ibn-Battuta's views on Daulatabad during his Travel.** CBSE 2024

Ans. Ibn-Battuta's views on Daulatabad during his Travel are as follows

- Ibn Battuta described Daulatabad as a city with a vibrant and unique market known as *Tarabad*, dedicated to male and female singers. He found it to be one of the most beautiful and bustling *bazaars*, where each shop was richly decorated with carpets, and the female singers, dressed in fine clothes, performed on swings.
- In the center of the market, there was a large, decorated structure (cupola) where the chief musician, accompanied by servants, held performances every Thursday. The bazaar also had mosques for prayer.
- Interestingly, even Hindu and Muslim rulers visited this market, where the singers would perform for them. This highlights the cultural richness and entertainment in Daulatabad during Ibn Battuta's visit.

14. **What was the reality about rural society in sixteenth and seventeenth centuries in contradiction to Karl Marx's view?**

Ans. The picture depicted by Karl Marx about subcontinent's rural society was not real. The reality was as follows

- Rural society was characterised by considerable social and economic differentiation during sixteenth and seventeenth centuries.
- On one hand, there were big zamindars with superior rights on land and on the other, there were untouchable landless labourers.
- There was the big peasant who used hired labour and engaged in commodity production and the smaller peasant who could barely produce for his livelihood.

15. **How did crown ownership of land effect the living standards of all sections of society according to Bernier?**

Or **Examine Bernier's description of crown ownership of land and lack of private property during Mughal India.** CBSE 2024

Ans. According to Bernier, the crown ownership of land effect the living standards of society in the following ways

- Bernier argued that due to crown ownership of land, landholders could not pass on their land to their children. So they were not interested in any long-term investment in the sustenance and expansion of production.

- The absence of private property in land prevented the emergence of the class of landlords with a concern to maintain or improve the land.
- This led to the uniform abolition of agriculture, excessive oppression of the peasantry and a continuous decline in the living standards of all sections of society, except the ruling aristocracy.

16. Describe briefly about imperial *karkhanas*.

Ans. Bernier provided a detailed account of the working of the imperial *karkhanas* or workshops. They were large halls located at many places for the artisans. In one hall, there were embroiders supervised by a master and similarly other artisans in other halls like goldsmiths, painters, varnishers in lacquer work, joiners, turners, tailors and shoe makers, manufacturers of silk, brocade and fine muslins.

The artisans came every morning to their *karkhanas* and remain employed the whole day and returned to their homes in the evening.

17. Explain the views of Bernier about a more complex social reality of the Mughal Empire.

Ans. Bernier's descriptions give hint about a more complex social reality. His views about this were as follows :

- He felt that artisans had no incentive to improve the quality of their manufactures, since profits were kept by the state. Manufactures were thus everywhere in decline.
- He also pointed that large quantities of the world's precious metals flowed into India, as manufactures were exported in exchange of gold and silver.
- He also noticed the existence of a prosperous merchant community, engaged in long-distance exchange.

18. "Bernier's description of imperial land ownership influenced Western theorists like French philosopher Montesquieu and German Karl Marx." Justify it with suitable arguments. **Competency Based Que**

***Or* Analyse the concept of the Asiatic mode of production as stated by Karl Marx.**

Ans. Bernier's description about imperial land ownership influenced Western theorists. These Western theorists like Montesquieu and Karl Marx have developed new theories based on this.

Montesquieu's Oriental Despotism Montesquieu developed the idea of oriental despotism, which means that the rulers in Asia enjoyed absolute authority over their subjects, and were kept under control and poverty.

Karl Marx's Asiatic Mode of Production Karl Marx developed the concept of Asiatic mode of production. He argued that in India and other Asian countries before colonialism, surplus was appropriated by the state. This led to the emergence of a society that was composed of a large number of independent and internally democratic village communities.

19. Describe the perspectives of Ibn Battuta and Francois Bernier on the condition of women in the Indian subcontinent.

Ans. **Perspective of Ibn Battuta**

- According to Ibn Battuta, female slaves were expert in music and dance and they served for Sultan. Some were employed to keep watch on his nobles.
- According to Battuta, the price of female slave was very low and most of the family could afford to keep at least one or two of them.

Perspective of Francois Bernier

- According to Francois Bernier, some women seemed to embrace death cheerfully during 'Sati', but others were forced to die.
- Bernier pointed out that women were also involved in other activities of the society. Their labour was crucial in both agricultural and non-agricultural production. Women from merchant families participated in commercial activities, sometimes even taking mercantile disputes to the court of law.

20. Bernier made this statement with reference to the ownership of land in the Mughal empire. Explain the observations that led him to this conclusion. **Competency Based Que**

Ans. The observations that led him to this conclusion were as follows

- Bernier noticed the absence of private property in the empire and was against crown ownership of land.
- He thought that the emperor distributed the lands amongst a few nobles.
- Since landowners could not pass their land to their children, they were hesitant to make investments. As a result, landowners were not improving the land.
- It led to oppression of the peasantry and continuous decline in the living standards.
- There was a class of extremely poor people and a minority of the powerful ruling class. There was absence of middle class.

21. Highlight the complex reality of women in India around the time Bernier came to India. **Competency Based Que**

Ans. The complex reality of women in India around the time Bernier came to India are

- There was widespread inequality between men and women.
- Inequity in the genders was considered 'natural'.

- Female slaves were employed by the Sultan to keep a watch over the nobles and entertain them with music and dance.
- Slaves were employed in domestic work and also to carry palanquins of nobles.
- Slaves were also sold at a very low cost, so most families could afford to keep one.
- It was noted that Sati was practiced widely. Some women were forced into it.
- Women's contribution to agriculture and non-agricultural production was important. It suggests that they were not confined just to their homes.

22. A number of travellers wrote detailed accounts regarding Indian social customs and religious practices. Comment. **Competency Based Que**

Ans. Beginning with the arrival of Portuguese in India in 1500, many travellers wrote detailed accounts regarding Indian social customs and religious practices. These included

- Jesuit Roberto Nobili who translated Indian texts into European languages.
- Duarte Barbosa is among the best known of the Portuguese writers. He wrote a detailed account of trade and society in South India.
- The French jeweller Jean-Baptiste Tavernier, travelled to India at least six times. He was particularly excited with the trading conditions in India and compared India to Iran and the Ottoman Empire.

Long Answer Type Questions

1. "Ibn Battuta found Delhi as a city full of exciting opportunities." Support your answer with evidences given by him. **Competency Based Que**

Or **Explain the observations of Ibn Battuta about the cities of India, with special reference to Delhi.**

Or **Explain how Ibn Battuta described the Indian cities.** **CBSE 2024**

Ans. Ibn Battuta found cities in the subcontinent full of exciting opportunities for those who had the necessary drive, resources and skills.

Some of the evidences given by him were

- Cities were densely populated and prosperous. Though they sometimes faced disruptions by wars and invasions.
- Most cities had crowded streets and bright and colourful markets that were arranged with a wide variety of goods.
- Ibn Battuta described Delhi as a vast city, with the largest population in India. Daulatabad in Maharashtra was also as big as Delhi.
- Ibn Battuta account gives a detailed description about Delhi. He describes Delhi covers a wide area and had a large population. The defensive wall around the city was very unique. The breadth of the wall was eleven cubits and inside it there were houses for the night sentry (watchman) and gatekeepers. Inside the defensive wall there were store houses for storing edibles, magazines, ammunition, missile and siege machines. The grains stored could last for a long time without rotting.
- In the interior of the defensive wall, horseman and infantrymen moved from one end of the city to another. The wall had windows from which light entered inside.
- The lower part of the wall was built with stone and the upper part with bricks. City had many towers close to one another.
- There were twenty eight gates for the city of Delhi which were called *darwaza*, and the Budaun *darwaza* was the greatest. Inside the Mandwi *darwaza*, there was a grain market and adjacent to the Gul *darwaza*, there was an orchard.
- The city of Delhi also had a fine cemetery in which graves had domes over them and those that do not had a dome, had an arch.

2. "Ibn Battuta's strategies of representation were evident in the ways in which he described the coconut and the *paan*". Look at the statement and give the description of Ibn Battuta on coconut and paan. **Competency Based Que**

Ans. Ibn Battuta was interested in writing about anything that was unfamiliar and exciting. Following were his descriptions about coconut and the *paan*

Coconut Ibn Battuta described the coconut, as trees that were most peculiar and most astonishing in habit. He described that they look exactly like date-palms, without any difference between them except that the one produces nuts as its fruits and other produces dates. He compared the nut of a coconut tree to a man's head and said that it looks like it had two eyes and a mouth and inside of it when it was green, it looks like the human brain. Attached to it was a fibre which looks like hair. They made fibre from this, the rope with which they sew up ships, instead of using iron nails. They also made cables for vessels from it.

The Paan Ibn Battuta described that the betel was a tree which was cultivated in the same manner as the grapevine. The betel had no fruit and was grown only for the sake of its leaves. The manner of its use was that before eating it, one takes areca nut which was like a nutmeg. It was broken up until it was reduced to small pellets, and one places these in his mouth and chews them. Then he took the leaves of betel, puts a little chalk on them and chews them along with the betel.

3. Discuss about the travellers, other than Al-Biruni, Ibn Battuta and Bernier, who travelled to India and wrote their accounts.

Ans. Many writers and travellers followed the footsteps of Al-Biruni and Ibn Battuta. Among the best known writers were

Abdur Razzaq Samarqandi

He visited South-India in the 1440s.

The travelogue of Abdur Razzaq written in the 1440s was an interesting mixture of emotions and perceptions about India. He did not appreciate what he saw in the port of Calicut in Kerala which was populated by people, and their likes were very different from the Abdur Razzaq's imagination.

He described it as a strange nation. Later, when he visited India, he arrived in Mangalore and crossed the Western Ghats. Here when he saw a temple, he was full of admirations. He described the temple that, such a kind of idol house could not be found anywhere in the world. He was amazed by the craft and artisanship of the temple.

Portuguese Writers

After Portuguese arrived in India in about 1500, number of scholars wrote detailed accounts regarding Indian customs and religious practices. A few of them, like Jesuit Roberto Nobili, translated Indian texts into European languages.

Duarte Barbosa was the best known among the Portuguese writers, he wrote a detailed account of trade and society in South India.

Other Travellers

After 1600 CE, there were many Dutch, English and French travellers who come to India. Among them famous was the French jeweller Jean-Baptiste Tavernier, who travelled to India at least six times. He was especially fascinated with the trading conditions in India and compared India to Iran and the Ottoman empire. Some travellers like Italian doctor Manucci settled down in India.

4. "Travellers who left written accounts were generally men who were interested in and sometimes intrigued by the condition of women in the subcontinent. Sometimes they took social inequities for granted as a natural state of affairs". Discuss about the condition of slaves and women in subcontinent.

Competency Based Que

Ans. Many travellers have written about the condition of slaves and women in their travel accounts. These are discussed below

- Slaves were openly sold in markets, like any other commodity, and were regularly exchanged as gifts. Ibn Battuta himself purchased horses, camels and slaves when he reached Sind, to gift to Sultan Muhammad bin Tughlaq. He gifted a slave along with horse, raisins and almonds to Multan's Governor.
- Muhammad bin Tughlaq was so happy with the sermon of a preacher named Nasiruddin that he gave him a hundred thousand tankas and two hundred slaves. He also kept his slaves to spy on his nobles.
- According to Ibn Battuta, there was considerable differentiation among slaves. Some female slaves in the service of the Sultan were experts in music and dance. They were generally used for domestic labour, and Ibn Battuta found their services very important for carrying women and men on palanquins or *dola*.
- Price of female slaves required for domestic labour was very low, and most families who could afford to do so kept at least one or two of them.
- Bernier described about the practice of sati and said that while some women embraced death cheerfully, others were forced to die.
- In reality, there was much more that happened in women's lives. For instance, their labour was important in both agricultural and non-agricultural production. Women from merchant families participated in commercial activities, sometimes even taking mercantile disputes to the court of law.

Source Based Questions

Read the sources given below and answer the following questions.

1. Al-Biruni's Objectives and Translating Texts, Sharing Ideas

Al-Biruni described his work as a help to those who want to discuss religious questions with them (the Hindus) and as a repertory of information to those who want to associate with them.

Al-Biruni's expertise in several languages allowed him to compare languages and translate texts. He translated several Sanskrit works, including Patanjali's work on grammar, into Arabic. For his Brahmana friends, he translated the works of Euclid Greek mathematician into Sanskrit.

(i) How did Al-Biruni described his work?

(ii) What is the meaning of word 'repertory'? How did expertise in several languages help Al-Biruni?

(iii) How did Al-Biruni's linguistic skills contribute to his cultural and intellectual exchanges in India?

Or

(i) Analyse the advantage Al-Biruni gained from his expertise in multiple languages?

(ii) **Analyse the significance of Al-Biruni translating Patanjali's work on grammar into Arabic?**

(iii) **How did Al-Biruni's translations contribute to the mutual understanding and appreciation between Islamic and Indian Civilisations?**

Ans. (i) Al-Biruni stated that his work was to help those who wanted to discuss religious questions with them.

(ii) Repertory means 'collection'. Expertise in several languages helped Al-Biruni to compare languages and translate texts.

(iii) Al-Biruni's knowledge of multiple languages enabled him to bridge cultures by translating significant works. His translations of Sanskrit texts into Arabic and Euclid's works into Sanskrit reflect his dedication to mutual understanding and scholarly exchange, fostering intellectual connections between Indian and Islamic scholarly traditions.

Or (i) Al-Biruni's proficiency in several languages allowed him to compare languages and translate texts, facilitating cross-cultural exchange and the dissemination of knowledge across different regions.

(ii) Al-Biruni's translation of Patanjali's grammar into Arabic was crucial for preserving and transferring Indian linguistic knowledge to the Islamic world, fostering cross-cultural intellectual exchange and enriching both traditions.

(iii) Al-Biruni's translations contribute to the mutual understanding and appreciation between Islamic and Indian civilisations in the following ways

- **Facilitated Exchange** Al-Biruni's translations enabled the exchange of knowledge and ideas between Islamic and Indian civilisations, introducing Indian concepts to Islamic scholars and vice versa.
- **Promoted Dialogue** This intellectual exchange enriched both traditions, fostering mutual respect and cooperation, and enhancing cultural and scholarly dialogue between the two civilisations.

2. The Bird Leaves its Nest

This is an excerpt from the Rihla.

My departure from Tangier, my birthplace, took place on Thursday... I set out alone, having neither fellow-traveller...nor caravan whose party I might join, but swayed by an overmastering impulse within me and a desire long-cherished in my bosom to visit these illustrious sanctuaries. So I braced my resolution to quit all my dear ones, female and male, and forsook my home as birds forsake their nests... My age at that time was twenty-two years.

Ibn Battuta returned home in 1354, about 30 years after he had set out.

(i) **What is the source of the passage? At what age Ibn Battuta leave his home and when did he return?**

(ii) **What is the birthplace of Ibn Battuta? What was the motivation behind Ibn Battuta's journey?**

(iii) **Discuss how did Ibn Battuta's journey start.**

Ans. (i) The passage is an extract from the book Rihla written by Ibn Battuta. Ibn Battuta left his home at the age of twenty two years and returned after 30 years in 1354 CE.

(ii) Tangier is the birthplace of Ibn Battuta.
Ibn Battuta had strong urge within him and a desire to visit the respected holy places which was the motivation behind his journey.

(iii) Ibn Battuta started his journey alone and had no companion or fellow traveller. He also did not join any caravan. So he decided to leave all his dear ones and his home just like birds leave their nests.

3. The Lonely Traveller

Robbers were not the only hazard on long journeys: the traveller could feel homesick, or fall ill. Here is an excerpt from the Rihla.

I was attacked by the fever and I actually tied myself on the saddle with a turban-cloth in case I should fall off by reasons of my weakness...So at last we reached the town of Tunis, and the townsfolk came out to welcome the *shaikh*...and...the son of the *qazi*... On all sides they came forward with greetings and questions to one another, but not a soul said a word of greeting to me, since there was none of them I knew. I felt so sad at heart on account of my loneliness that I could not restrain the tears that started to my eyes, and wept bitterly. But one of the pilgrims, realising the cause of my distress, came up to me with a greeting.

(i) **What were the other hazards on long journeys other than robbers? What is the source of this passage and who is the author of the book?**

(ii) **Why did author tie himself with turban cloth?**

(iii) **What was the town where author reached?**

Ans. (i) The other hazards for travellers on a journey are that they could feel homesick, or fall ill. The source of the passage is Rihla. It was written by Ibn Battuta.

(ii) As author was suffering from fever, he tied himself on the saddle with turban cloth so that he does not fall off due to weakness.

(iii) The town's name was Tunis. Once author reached the town Tunis, all the townsfolk came out to welcome the *shaikh* and the son of the *qazi*.

4. Travelling with the Mughal Army

Bernier often travelled with the army. This is an excerpt from his description of the army's march to Kashmir.

I am expected to keep two good Turkoman horses and I also take with me a powerful Persian camel and driver, a groom for my horses, a cook and a servant to go before my horse with a flask of water in his hand, according to the custom of the country.

I am also provided with every useful article, such as a tent of moderate size, a carpet, a portable bed made of four very strong but light canes, a pillow, a mattress, round leather table-clothes used at meals, some few napkins of dyed cloth, three small bags with culinary utensils which are all placed in a large bag and this bag is again carried in a very capacious and strong double sack or net made of leather thongs. This double sack likewise contains the provisions, linen and wearing apparel, both of master and servants. I have taken care to lay in a stock of excellent rice for five or six days' consumption, of sweet biscuits flavoured with anise (a herb), of limes and sugar. Nor have I forgotten a linen bag with its small iron hook for the purpose of suspending and draining *dahi* or curds; nothing being considered so refreshing in this country as lemonade and *dahi*.

(i) Who was Bernier? Give his brief introduction.

(ii) What was the purpose of his travel and what was expected of him while going on travel?

(iii) What things would you like to take with you while going on travel? Explain.

Ans. (i) Francois Bernier was a French doctor, a political philosopher and historian. He was closely associated with the Mughal Court.

(ii) His purpose of travel was to seek opportunities in the Mughal Empire. He was expected to keep two good Turkoman horses, a powerful Persian camel and driver, a groom for his horses, a cook and a servant.

(iii) While going to travel I would prefer to take clothes as per the weather condition of that place. I would keep necessary items like toothpaste, brush, medicines, soap, water bottle, blanket, etc.

5. The creation and circulation of ideas about India **CBSE 2024**

The writings of European travellers helped produce an image of India for Europeans through the printing and circulation of their books. Later, after 1750, when Indians like Shaikh Itisamuddin and Mirza Abu Talib visited Europe and confronted this image that Europeans had of their society, they tried to influence it by producing their own version of matters and described India as a great nation.

(i) In what way did Shaikh Itisamuddin and Mirza Abu Talib challenge the version of Europeans towards India ?

(ii) Give any one example of a book authored by European writers on Medieval India.

(iii) Explain the significant difference between the image of India presented by Europeans and the versions of Indians.

Ans. (i) Shaikh Itisamuddin and Mirza Abu Talib challenged the negative views of Europe by offering a more positive and respectful perspective of India. Instead of focusing on its differences, they appreciated the richness of Indian culture, its traditions, and impressive craftsmanship, especially in temples.

(ii) One example of a book by a European writer on Medieval India is "The Travels of Marco Polo", where Marco Polo described his journey to India and other parts of Asia.

(iii) European travellers often depicted India as strange and backward, focusing on its differences. In contrast, Indians like Shaikh Itisamuddin and Mirza Abu Talib, who visited Europe, presented India as a great and prosperous nation, challenging these negative views and offering a more positive perspective.

6. A Language with and Enormous Range

Al-Biruni described Sanskrit as follows

If you want to conquer this difficulty (i.e. to learn Sanskrit), you will not find it easy, because the language is of an enormous range, both in words and inflections, something like the Arabic, calling one and the same thing by various names, both original and derivative, and using one and the same word for a variety of subjects, which, in order to be properly understood, must be distinguished from each other by various qualifying epithets.

(i) How did Al-Biruni compare Sanskrit with Arabic? **CBSE 2023**

(ii) Give an example of the work Al-Biruni translated in Arabic from Sanskrit.

(iii) Analyse the reason of Sanskrit being considered as a language with enormous range.

Or **(i) What motivated Al-Biruni to study Sanskrit?**

(ii) How did Al-Biruni's observations about Sanskrit contribute to cross cultural understanding?

(iii) What challenges did Al-Biruni identify in learning Sanskrit, and how did he compare it to other languages?

Ans. (i) Al-Biruni compared Sanskrit with Arabic and noted similarities and differences in their grammatical structures and vocabulary, as well as in their literary and philosophical traditions.

(ii) Al-Biruni translated Patanjali's Sanskrit work on grammar into Arabic. He also translated works of Euclid, Greek mathematician, into Sanskrit.

(iii) Sanskrit is considered a language with an enormous range because it has a vast and complex vocabulary, with a variety of synonyms, antonyms, and homonyms, and a rich tradition of literature and philosophical texts. It also has a sophisticated grammatical structure, with intricate rules for syntax, tense, and mood, which allows for precise and nuanced expression.

Or (i) Al-Biruni was motivated to study Sanskrit to understand Hindu thought, religion and culture.

(ii) Al-Biruni's observations highlighted Sanskrit's complexity, fostering cross-cultural understanding by emphasising the linguistic richness and nuances inherent in the language, promoting appreciation and respect for diverse linguistic traditions.

(iii) Al-Biruni found Sanskrit challenging due to its vast vocabulary, complex inflections, and multiple meanings for single terms, which required specific qualifiers for clarity. He compared it to Arabic, highlighting both languages' richness and linguistic complexity. His observations underscore the intellectual rigor needed to accurately understand and translate Sanskrit texts.

7. The System of Varnas

This is Al-Biruni's account of the system of *varnas.*

The highest caste are the Brahmana, of whom the books of the Hindus tell us that they were created from the head of Brahman. And as the Brahman is only another name for the force called nature, and the head is the highest part of the...body, the Brahmana are the choice part of the whole genus. Therefore the Hindus consider them as the very best of mankind.

The next caste are Kshatriya, who were created, as they say, from the shoulders and hands of Brahman. Their degree is not much below that of the Brahmana.

After them follow the Vaishya, who were created from the thigh of Brahman. The Shudra, who were created from his feet.

Between the latter two classes there is not very great distance. Much, however, as these classes differ from each other, they live together in the same towns and villages, mixed together in the same houses and lodgings.

(i) Why do Hindus consider Brahmanas as best of mankind?

(ii) What are the four castes that Al-Biruni mentioned in the source? Which body parts of Brahman represent castes other than Brahmanas?

(iii) How do you know that there is cohesiveness between different castes?

Ans. (i) The Brahmana is the other name for the force called nature. The Brahmana are made from head and the head is the highest part of the body. Therefore Hindus consider them as best of mankind.

(ii) The four castes that were mentioned by Al-Biruni are Brahmanas, Kshatriya, Vaishya and Shudra.

Kshatriyas were created from the shoulders and hands of Brahman, Vaishyas were created from the thigh and Shudras from the feet of the Brahman.

(iii) There is cohesiveness between different castes because they live together in same towns and villages, mixed together in the same houses and lodgings.

8. Music in the Market

Read Ibn Battuta's description of Daulatabad.

In Daulatabad, there was a market place for male and female singers, which was known as Tarababad. It was one of the greatest and most beautiful bazaars. It had numerous shops and every shop had a door which leads into the house of the owner. The shops were decorated with carpets and at the centre of a shop there was a swing on which sits the female singer. She was decked with all kinds of finery and her female attendants swing her. In the middle of the market place there stands a large cupola, which was carpeted and decorated and in which the chief of the musicians takes his place every Thursday after the dawn prayers, accompanied by his servants and slaves. The female singers come in successive crowds, sing before him and dance until dusk after which he withdrews.

In this bazaar there were mosques for offering prayers. One of the Hindu rulers alighted at the cupola every time he passed by this market place, and the female singers would sing before him. Even some Muslim rulers did the same.

(i) What was Tarababad? How were shops decorated and who sits in the centre of the shop?

(ii) What was cupola? What happened when Hindu rulers visited the cupola?

(iii) What happens every Thursday?

Ans. (i) In Daulatabad, there was a market place for male and female singers, which was known as Tarababad.

The shops were decorated with carpets and at the centre of a shop there was a swing on which the female singer sit.

(ii) Cupola was a rounded dome forming or adorning a roof or ceiling.

Whenever the Hindu rulers came to the cupola, he would pass the market place and the female singers would sing before him.

(iii) There is a large cupola, in the middle of the market place, which is carpeted and decorated. Every Thursday the chief of the musicians takes his place in the middle of the market place after the dawn prayers, accompanied by his servants and slaves.

9. A strange nation ? **CBSE 2024**

The travelogue of Abdur Razzaq written in the 1440s is an interesting mixture of emotions and perceptions. On the one hand, he did not appreciate what he saw in the port of Calicut (present-day Kozhikode) in Kerala, which was populated by "a people the likes of whom I had never imagined", describing them as "a strange nation". Later in his visit to India, he arrived in Mangalore, and crossed the Western Ghats. Here he saw a temple that filled him with admiration : Within three leagues (about nine miles) of Mangalore, I saw an idol-house the likes of which is not to be found in all the world. It was a square, approximately ten yards a side, five yards in height, all covered with cast bronze, with four porticos. In the entrance portico was a statue in the likeness of a human being, full stature, made of gold. It had two red rubies for eyes, so cunningly made that you would say it could see. What craft and artisanship!

(i) Why did Abdur Razzaq call India a 'strange nation' ?
(ii) How do emotions and perceptions reflect in this source ?
(iii) How did Abdur Razzaq describe the temples of the Western Ghats in Mangalore ?

Ans. (i) Abdur Razzaq called India a 'strange nation' because he was shocked by the unfamiliar customs and people he saw, especially in Calicut (Kozhikode). However, his view changed when he visited Mangalore and saw a beautiful temple with a golden statue and ruby eyes, which impressed him with its craftsmanship. This made him appreciate India's rich culture.

(ii) In his travelogue, Abdur Razzaq first expressed surprise and discomfort with the people he saw in Calicut, calling them 'a strange nation'. However, his feelings change when he visits Mangalore and sees a beautiful temple. He admires the craftsmanship of the temple, especially the golden statue with ruby eyes, and is filled with awe. His emotions shift from confusion to appreciation as he experiences different aspects of India.

(iii) Abdur Razzaq was impressed by a temple near Mangalore, describing it as unique with a golden statue having lifelike ruby eyes. He admired its beautiful bronze structure and fine craftsmanship.

10. The Poor Peasant

An excerpt from Bernier's description of the peasantry in the countryside.

Of the vast tracts of country constituting the empire of Hindustan, many were little more than sand or barren mountains, badly cultivated and thinly populated. Even a considerable portion of the good land remains untilled for want of labourers; many of whom perish in consequence of the bad treatment they experience from Governors.

The poor people, when they become incapable of discharging the demands of their rapacious lords, were not only often deprived of the means of subsistence, but were also made to lose their children, who were carried away as slaves. Thus, it happens that the peasantry, driven to despair by so excessive a tyranny, abandon the country. In this instance, Bernier was participating in contemporary debates in Europe concerning the nature of state and society and intended that his description of Mughal India would serve as a warning to those who did not recognise the 'merits' of private property.

(i) Name the book written by Francois Bernier on the critical insight and reflection on the empire of Hindustan.
(ii) What description Bernier had given on the condition of Indian peasantry during the Mughal Empire?
(iii) Which fundamental differences he found between Mughal India and Europe during 16th and 17th century?

Or **(i) How the tracts of Hindustan been described by Bernier?**
(ii) Why did the land remain untilled? Explain.
(iii) What happened when the poor peasants were unable to fulfil the demands of their landlords?

Or **(i) What were the problems about cultivating the land, according to Bernier?**
(ii) Why did the peasantry abandon the land?
(iii) Explain the reasons given by Bernier for the exploitation of the peasants.

Ans. (i) Francois Bernier wrote a book named '*Travels in the Mughal Empire*' which had critical insights and reflection on the empire of Hindustan.

(ii) Bernier said that peasants faced excessive oppression and when they were not able to fulfill the demands of their greedy lords, they were then not only deprived of their means of subsistence, but were also made to lose their children, who were carried away as slaves.

(iii) The fundamental differences between Mughal India and Europe was the lack of private property in land in the Mughal India. There were also no class of improving landlords and middle class in India unlike Europe.

Or (i) Bernier described that vast tracts of country constituted the empire of Hindustan. Many were little more than sand, or barren mountains, badly cultivated, and thinly populated.

(ii) The land remained untilled because of shortage of labourers, many of whom suffer the consequence of the bad treatment they get from Governors.

(iii) When poor peasants were unable to fulfil the demands of their landlords, they were not only deprived of their means of livelihood, but also they were made to lose their children who were carried away as slaves.

Or(i)The problems about cultivating the land according to Bernier were that most of it was sand, barren mountains and shortage of labourers and greedy demands from the landlords.

(ii) Peasantry abandoned the land because they were driven to hopelessness by excessive cruelty and oppressive government. Even the landlords made the excessive greedy demands.

(iii) The reasons for the exploitation of the peasants was that they could not satisfy the greedy demands of their landlords. They were driven to despair by the excessive tyranny of the state.

11. A Warning for Europe

Bernier warned that if European kings followed the Mughal model, their kingdoms would be very far from being well-cultivated and people, so well built, so rich, so polite and flourishing. Our kings were otherwise rich and powerful and we must knew that they were much better and more royally served. They would soon be kings of deserts and solitudes, of beggars and barbarians, such as those whom I have been representing (the Mughals)... We should find the great cities and the great Burroughs (boroughs) rendered uninhabitable because of ill air and to fall to ruine (ruin) without any bodies (anybody) taking care of repairing them; the hillocks abandoned and the fields overspread with bushes or filled with pestilential marishes (marshes), as hath been already intimated. **CBSE 2025**

(i) Mention any one prominent contribution of Bernier.

(ii) How did Bernier describe the difference between European kingdom and the Mughal territories?

(iii) Explain Bernier's views on the socio-economic status of people under Mughal rule.

Ans. (i) François Bernier contributed significantly by documenting his travels in Mughal India, comparing it with Europe, and highlighting political, economic, and social differences, which influenced European perceptions of India.

(ii) Bernier described European kingdoms as well-organised, wealthy, and prosperous, whereas he depicted Mughal territories as poorly maintained, with declining cities, depopulated lands, and ineffective governance, leading to economic and social stagnation.

(iii) Bernier viewed the socio-economic status of people under Mughal rule as deteriorating. He believed excessive state control, lack of private land ownership, and poor infrastructure led to widespread poverty, depopulation, and economic decline, making cities uninhabitable and agriculture inefficient.

12. **The Imperial Karkhanas**

Bernier is perhaps the only historian who provides a detailed account of the working of the imperial *karkhanas* or workshops:

Large halls are seen at many places, called *karkhanas* or workshops for the artisans. In one hall, embroiderers are busily employed, superintended by a master. In another, you see the goldsmiths; in a third, painters; in a fourth, varnishers in lacquer work; in a fifth, joiners, turners, tailors and shoe makers; in a sixth, manufacturers of silk, brocade and fine muslins. The artisans come every morning to their *karkhanas* where they remain employed the whole day; and in the evening return to their homes. In this quiet regular manner, their time glides away; no one aspiring for any improvement in the condition of life wherein he happens to be born.

(i) What was so unique about Bernier according to the passage? Why did Bernier criticise artisans?

(ii) Discuss about karkhanas.

(iii) How do you know that artisans were not aspiring for better lives?

Ans. (i) The unique thing about Bernier is that he is the only historian who provided the detailed account of the working of the imperial *karkhanas* or workshops. Bernier criticised artisans because they were not aspiring for any improvement of their lives.

(ii) Large halls were seen at many places, called *karkhanas* or workshops for the artisans.

In halls, the artisans were employed who were supervised by a master.

(iii) It is known from the fact that artisans were doing routine work daily, by coming to *karkhanas* and returning to homes in evening in a quiet regular manner and passing the time.

13. The Child Sati

This is perhaps one of the most poignant descriptions by Bernier.

At Lahore, I saw a most beautiful young widow sacrificed, who could not, I think, have been more than twelve years of age.

The poor little creature appeared more dead than alive when she approached the dreadful pit; the agony of her mind cannot be described; she trembled and wept bitterly; but three or four of the Brahmanas, assisted by an old woman who held her under the arm, forced the unwilling victim towards the fatal spot, seated her on the wood, tied her hands, feet and lest she should run away, and in that situation the innocent creature was burnt alive.

I found it difficult to repress my feelings and to prevent their bursting forth into clamorous and unavailing rage.

(i) Why did Bernier consider this treatment as a crucial marker of the difference between Western and Eastern societies?

(ii) What role did the Indian patriarchal society play towards this social evil?

(iii) Compare the conditions of the women of the era mentioned above to that of today.

Or **(i) How has Bernier described the practice of sati?**

(ii) Describe the feelings of Bernier that he has expressed in the passage.

(iii) What does Bernier's account of the sati ritual reveal about his views on Indian society and customs?

Or **(i) Describe what Bernier saw at Lahore.**

(ii) How had the agony of the girl been described?

(iii) How and why was the girl forced towards the fatal spot?

Ans. (i) Bernier described the practice of sati, in which women were forced to die and this kind of brutal act was absent in Western societies. Thus, this treatment of women was used as a crucial marker of difference between Western and Eastern societies.

(ii) Indian society is basically patriarchal and it always kept women next only to men. Men always considered women as their property and thus the customs like sati were developed out of this mentality, in which women was made to die along with husband after his death.

(iii) The condition of women in those days was not very satisfying. They had lot of restrictions and inhuman practices like sati were practised with justification. After independence, women also were given right to vote and were given equal rights in property. Successive governments also introduced many reforms and changing mindsets of people towards women also help to bring in lot of change in the status of women.

Or (i) Bernier noted that practice of sati had two dimensions, while some women seemed to embrace death cheerfully, others were forced to die.

(ii) Bernier felt so confused and had uncontrollable anger when he saw the practice of sati. He was in anger after looking at the condition of women which was different in West.

(iii) Bernier's account of sati reveals his deep disapproval of certain Indian customs, which he viewed as oppressive and inhumane. His description of the young widow's forced sacrifice underscores his belief that such practices symbolised a broader societal cruelty, reinforcing his perception of Indian society as regressive compared to European values of individual rights and freedom.

Or (i) At Lahore, Bernier saw a beautiful young widow who was hardly twelve years old and who looked more dead than alive as she approached the dreadful pit. There were three to four Brahmanas, assisted by an old woman who held her under the arm, forced the unwilling victim towards the fatal spot and was burnt alive.

(ii) Bernier described the agony of the girl by telling how she was trembling with fear and wept bitterly when she was taken near to the pyre.

(iii) She was forced because she was unwilling to go towards the fatal spot. Three to four of the Brahmanas assisted by an old woman who held her under the arm, forced her towards the fatal spot, seated her on the wood and tied her hands and feet to prevent her from running away.

SELF ASSESSMENT TEST

Objective Type Questions

1. When was Sultan Mahmud Invaded Khwarizm?
   (a) 1018 CE (b) 1207 CE (c) 1017 CE (d) None of these
2. Which of the following statement is correct regarding the Ibn Battuta?
   (a) He described about the mango and the people.
   (b) He described that people tree leaves used for making cords.
   (c) He described betal is a tree.
   (d) None of these
3. Which of the following is incorrect regarding the Francois Bernier?
   (a) He was a doctor. (b) He was a historian.
   (c) He was a political philosopher. (d) He came in the the Court of Shah Jahan.
4. Match the Following

List I		List II	
A.	Peter Mundi	1.	Turkey
B.	Antonio Monserrate	2.	Italy
C.	Marco Polo	3.	Spain
D.	Seyedi Ali Reis	4.	England

Codes

	A	B	C	D		A	B	C	D
(a)	1	3	2	4	(b)	2	4	1	3
(c)	4	3	2	1	(d)	1	3	4	2

Short Answer Type Questions

5. Analyse Al-Biruni's linguistic skills and how they influenced his work on Indian texts.
6. Comment on Ibn Battuta's observations of the social and cultural activities in Indian marketplaces.
7. Explain why Bernier was critical of the lack of private land ownership in Mughal India.
8. Justify why Al-Biruni saw the study of Sanskrit as essential for understanding Indian society.
9. Comment on the reasons why Ibn Battuta found the Indian postal system impressive.

Long Answer Type Questions

10. Analyse Al-Biruni's understanding of the caste system and how it shaped his portrayal of Indian society.
11. Comment on how Bernier's comparison of Indian and European societies reflects his own biases and assumptions.
12. Justify the significance of Bernier's critique of Mughal land policies for European readers of his time.
13. Discuss about Ibn Battuta's description of Indian cities focussing in Delhi and also discuss about Bernier's views on Indian cities.
14. Discuss about the status of women and slaves through the eyes of travellers. Were there any progressive elements present in the status of women in India? Mention if any.

6

CHAPTER

This chapter deals with Bhakti and Sufi traditions prevalent during the eighth to eighteenth century in the Indian subcontinent. This period saw the emergence of famous saints like Kabir, Mirabai, Guru Nanak, etc.

Bhakti-Sufi Traditions

(Changes in Religious Beliefs and Devotional Texts)

YOUR STUDY GOALS

6.1 Development of Religious Beliefs and Practices
6.2 Early Traditions of Bhakti
6.3 The Virashaiva and Lingayats of Karnataka
6.4 Islamic Traditions
6.5 The Growth of Sufism
6.6 The Chishti in the Subcontinent
6.7 Poet-Saints of Devotional Paths
6.8 Reconstructing Histories of Religious Traditions

YOUR PRACTICE GOALS

- Objective Type Questions (52 Qs ; MCQs, A-R, Matching, Picture Based)
- Subjective Questions (21 SAs, 7 LAs)
- Source Based Questions (6 Qs)

The various religious beliefs of the subcontinent were reconstructed from textual traditions which included compositions by poet-saints. These traditions were modified and sometimes left by the next generations, posing a challenge to historians. Historians also used sources like hagiographies or biographies of saints written by their followers or members of their religious sect.

6.1 Development of Religious Beliefs and Practices

- The most important feature of the phase between eighth and eighteenth centuries was that many new Gods and Goddesses were visible in sculpture and texts.
- The worship of the major deities like Vishnu, Shiva and the Goddess which were visualised or depicted in various forms, also became important.

The Integration of Cults

During this phase, there were two religious processes which were

(i) The spread of Brahmanical ideas. Its main objective was **composition, compilation** and **preservation of Puranic texts**. These texts were written in simple Sanskrit. They were easily accessible to women and Shudras, who were generally excluded from the Vedic learning.

(ii) The acceptance of the beliefs and practices of other social categories by the Brahmanas. Many beliefs and practices were reconstructed through a **continuous interaction** between 'great' Sanskritic Puranic traditions and 'little' traditions throughout the country.

'Great' and 'little' traditions

- The terms great and little traditions were coined by a sociologist, **Robert Redfield** in the twentieth century to describe the cultural practices of peasant societies.
- **Great Tradition** Peasants observed rituals and customs that originated from dominant social categories, including priests and rulers.
- **Little Tradition** Peasants followed local practices that did not necessarily match with those of the great tradition.
- Robert Redfield also noticed that both great and little traditions changed over time, through a process of interaction.
- Scholars recognise these ideas but dislike the hierarchy suggested by the term great and little, so they use quotation marks to show 'great' and 'little'.

Example of Second Process

- The example of the second process was evident at **Puri, Orissa**, where the main deity was identified as *Jagannatha*, a form of Vishnu.
- Here, the deity is represented in a very different way. A local god, made of wood by local tribal artisans, was identified as a form of Vishnu. At the same time, Vishnu was depicted differently than in other regions of the country.
- Goddess were worshipped simply in the form of a stone with some colour pigment on it like ochre. These local deities were given identities as the wives of major male deities, such as Lakshmi, the wife of Vishnu, and Parvati, the wife of Shiva, etc.

▲ *Jagannatha with his sister Subhadra and his brother Balarama*

Difference and Conflict

- New forms of worship which developed around c. tenth century were classified as **Tantric**.
- Tantric practices were associated with the Goddess. They were prevalent in various parts of the subcontinent. These practices were open to both men and women.
- The followers of tantric did not discriminate against people based on caste and class within the ritual.
- Buddhism and Shaivism especially in the Eastern, Northern and Southern parts of the subcontinent were influenced by many of these ideas.
- All these different beliefs and practices including worship of Vishnu, Shiva, Goddesses and tantric practices etc, were later grouped together as Hinduism over the next thousand years. The differences are especially clear in comparison between Vedic and Puranic traditions.
- The popularity of main deities of Vedic pantheon (religion), i.e, Agni, Indra and Soma, reduced and they became marginal figures which were rarely visible in textual or visual forms.
- On the other hand, the popularity of Gods like Vishnu, Shiva and Goddesses increased. However, this popularity did not mean that the Vedas were not valued. Vedas continued to be superior.
- There were some conflicts as well. Those who valued the Vedic tradition, often criticised practices that extended beyond God, sacrifies and mantras. While those engaged in tantric practices, frequently ignored the authority of the Vedas.
- The devotees often projected their chosen deity, either Vishnu or Shiva, as supreme.
- Relationships with other traditions, like Buddhism and Jainism, were often tense and sometimes led to open conflict.

- During the tenth century, devotion varied from regular temple worship to ecstatic adoration (intense happiness), which led devotees to enter a trance-like state (an abnormal state of wakefulness).
- The singing and chanting of devotional compositions was part of worship especially for Shiva and Vaishnava sects.

6.2 Early Traditions of Bhakti

- During the evolution of different forms of worship, the poet-saints emerged as leaders.
- Brahmanas remained as intermediaries between Gods and devotees in several forms of bhakti.
- Women and lower caste were also allowed to worship, which was prohibited earlier.
- Historians of religion classify bhakti traditions into *saguna* (with attributes) and *nirguna* (without attributes).
  - **Saguna tradition** It means the worship of specific deities such as Shiva, Vishnu and his avatars or incarnations and forms of the Goddess or Devi which were seen as having human forms.
  - **Nirguna bhakti** It means the worship of an abstract form i.e. existing in thought or as an idea but not having a physical or concrete existence of God.

The Alvars and Nayanars of Tamil Nadu

- Earliest bhakti movements around the sixth century were led by the **Alvars** (devotees of Vishnu) and **Nayanars** (devotees of Shiva).
- Alvars and Nayanars sang hymns in Tamil in praise of their Gods and travelled from one place to another.
- During their travels, the Alvars and Nayanars identified some shrines as residences of their chosen deities. Later, very large temples were built at these places which were developed as centres of pilgrimage.
- Singing compositions of these poet-saints became a part of temple rituals in these shrines and saint's images were also worshipped.
- The compositions of these people were as important as the Vedas. For example, one of the major collections of poems composed by the Alvars, the ***Nalayira Divyaprabandham***, was often described as the **Tamil Veda**.

Attitudes towards Caste

▲ *A twelfth century bronze image of Karaikkal Ammaiyar*

- As per historians, the Alvars and Nayanars started a movement to protest against the caste system.
- Devotees or bhaktas came from different social backgrounds like Brahmanas, artisans, cultivators and even from castes considered as 'untouchable'.
- An Alvar, ***Tondaradippodi***, mentioned no difference between *Chaturvedins* (Brahmana) and the outcastes in his writings. This indicates that he opposed the caste system.
- Appar, a Nayanar saint questioned the use of *gotra* and *kula* in his composition, and suggested that one should just devote himself to Marperu's lord (Shiva).

Women Devotees

- The compositions of **Andal**, a woman Alvar, were widely sung and even now they are sung. She saw herself as the beloved of Vishnu and her verses expressed her love for the deity.

- Another woman, **Karaikkal Ammaiyar** was a devotee of Shiva. She adopted the path of extreme self-discipline to attain her goal. Her compositions were preserved within the Nayanar tradition.
- These women renounced their social obligations and posed a challenge to patriarchal norms.

Relations with the State

- There were several important chiefdoms in the Tamil region in the early first millennium CE.
- From the second half of the first millennium, there is evidence of states like the **Pallavas** and **Pandyas.** (c. sixth to ninth centuries CE).
- Buddhism and Jainism had been prevalent in these states for several centuries, which had support from merchant and artisan communities. They also received royal patronage.
- The poet's opposition to Buddhism and Jainism was one of the major themes in Tamil bhakti hymns. This was marked in the compositions of the **Nayanars.**
- Powerful Chola rulers of the ninth to thirteenth centuries supported Brahmanical and bhakti traditions by making land grants and constructing temples for Vishnu and Shiva.
- Some of the grand Shiva temples, like those at **Chidambaram, Thanjavur** and **Gangaikondacholapuram** were constructed with the support of Chola rulers.
- In tenth century, bronze sculpture of Shiva was produced after inspiration from the Nayanars artists.
- Both Nayanars and Alvars were respected by Vellala peasants and got their support.
- Chola rulers also tried to get support from the divine by building temples with stone and metal sculpture.
- Chola kings introduced the singing of Tamil Shaiva hymns in temples with royal support and took the initiative to collect and organise them into a text called ***Tevaram***.
- According to inscriptions, around 945 CE, Chola ruler **Parantaka** I had dedicated the metal images of Appar, Sambandar and Sundarar in a Shiva temple. These were also carried in processions during the festivals of these saints.

▲ *An image of Shiva and Nataraja*

6.3 The Virashaiva and Lingayats of Karnataka

- A new movement emerged in Karnataka in the twelfth century, led by a Brahmana named **Basavanna** (1106-68 CE).
- Basavanna was a minister in the court of a Kalachuri king. His followers were known as *Virashaivas* (heroes of Shiva) and *Lingayats* (wearers of the *linga*).
- The Virashaiva tradition is derived from ***vachanas***[1] composed in Kannada by women and men who joined the movement.
- Lingayats worship Shiva in the form of *linga* and men wear a small *linga* in a silver case on a thread strung over the left shoulder. These men were admired as *Jangama* or wandering monks.
- Lingayats believe that devotees unite with Shiva after death and do not return to this world. Therefore, they do not follow traditional cremation practices and instead bury their dead.
- Some practices like post-puberty marriage and the remarriage of widows which were disapproved in the Dharmashastras, were encouraged by the Lingayats.
- The Lingayats challenged the idea of caste and its pollution related to certain groups by Brahmanas. They also questioned the theory of rebirth.

1 Vachanas It means Sayings

Religious Agitation in North India

- North India deities like Vishnu and Shiva were worshipped in temples which were mainly built with the support of rulers.

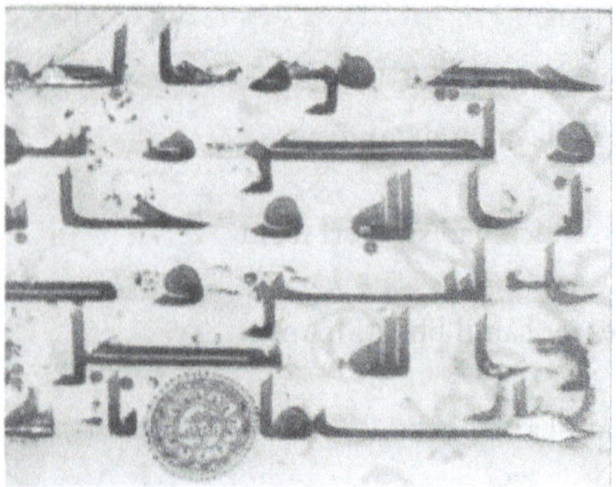

▲ *Fragment of a page from the Qur'an*

- Many Rajput states emerged in North India. Brahmanas occupied important positions and performed secular and ritual functions in most of these states.
- During the twelfth century, other religious leaders emerged. They were the **Naths, Jogis** and **Siddhas**.
- Most of them came from artisanal groups like weavers, who became important due to the development of organised craft production.
- These leaders questioned the authority of the Vedas and expressed themselves in languages spoken by ordinary people.
- The coming of Turks in North India led to the establishment of Delhi Sultanate. The power of many Rajput states and Brahmanas slowly weakened, thus leading to cultural and religious changes.
- One of the most important change was the coming of the Sufis.

Quick Test 1

1. What was the main objective of the spread of Brahmanical ideas?
2. Who were the major deities of Vedic pantheon?
3. In which tradition were Karaikkal Ammaiyar's compositions preserved?
4. Which grand Shiva temples were constructed with the support of Chola rulers?
5. Who were Naths, Jogis and Siddhas?

6.4 Islamic Traditions

- When Central Asian people settled in the North-Western parts of the subcontinent, Arab merchants visited ports along the Western coast in the first millennium CE.
- With the advent of Islam from the seventh century, these regions became a part of Islamic world.

Faiths of Rulers and Subjects

- In 711 CE, an Arab general named **Muhammad Qasim** conquered Sind, which became part of the Caliph's territory.
- Later in the thirteenth century, the Turks and Afghans established the Delhi Sultanate, which was followed by the formation of Sultanates in the Deccan and other parts of the subcontinent.
- Islam was an acknowledged religion of rulers in several areas. This continued with the establishment of the Mughal Empire in the sixteenth century and regional states in the eighteenth century.
- A category of the ***zimmi*** (protected) was developed for people who followed revealed scriptures. These included Jews and Christians. They paid a tax called ***jizya*** and got the right to be protected by Muslims.
- Rulers adopted a fairly flexible policy towards their Muslim and non-Muslim subjects. They expressed devotion towards non-Muslim religious leaders.
- Several grants were made for subjects by Akbar and Aurangzeb and many other Mughal rulers.

Ulama and Shari'a

- Muslim rulers were to be guided by the *ulama*[2]. Ulamas were expected to ensure that Muslim rulers ruled according to shari'a.
- As preservers of this tradition, *ulama* perform various religious, judicial and teaching functions. Whereas, shari'a is the law governing the Muslim community.
- Shari'a is based on the *Quran* and the *hadis*, traditions of the Prophet including a record of his remembered words and deeds.
- With the expansion of Islamic rule outside Arabia, *qiagas* (reasoning by analogy) and *ijma* (consensus of the community) were reorganised as two other sources of legislation.
- Shari'a was evolved from the *Qur'an, hadis, qiyas* and *ijma*.

Popular Practice of Islam

- Those who have adopted Islam, also accepted the five pillars of the faith. They are
  - (i) There is one God, Allah and Prophet Muhammad is his messenger (*shahada*)
  - (ii) Offering prayers five times a day (*namaz/salat*)
  - (iii) Giving alms (*zakat*)
  - (iv) Fasting during the month of Ramzan (*sawm*)
  - (v) Performing the pilgrimage to Mecca (*hajj*)
- These features were practiced differently among different sects like Sunni and Shi'a. They were also influenced by the local customs.
- For example, the **Khojahs**, a branch of the Ismailis (Shi'a sect) developed new modes of communication, spreading ideas derived from the Qur'an.
- Khojahs included the *ginan* (knowledge), devotional poems in Punjabi, Multani, Sindhi, Kachchi, Hindi and Gujarati.
- Arab Muslim traders who settled along the Malabar coast (Kerala) adopted the local language, Malayalam. They also adopted local customs such as **matriliny**[3] and **matrilocal residence**[4].
- The blend of Islam with local traditions was evident in the architecture, especially construction of the mosque. Some architectural features of mosques are common, like their direction towards Mecca, shown by the *mihrab* (prayer niche) and the minbar (pulpit). However their features like roof and building materials varied.

Names for Islamic Communities

- People were identified from the region they came from like Turkish rulers were called Turushka, Tajikistan people were Tajika and people from Persia were called Parashika.
- New migrants were referred to with terms used for other people, like the Turks and Afghans were referred to as **Shakas** and **Yavanas**.
- ***Mlechchha*** was the more general term used for the migrant communities, which indicated that they did not observe the rules of caste society and spoke languages that were not derived from Sanskrit.

---

2 **Ulama** They were scholars of Islamic studies.

3 **Matriliny** Practice of tracing descent through the mother's line.

4 **Matrilocal Residence** It is a practice where women after marriage remain in their natal home with their children and the husbands may come to stay with them.

6.5 The Growth of Sufism

- Sufis were a group of religious-minded people in Islam. They believed in **asceticism** (severe self-discipline) and **mysticism** (spiritual belief of union with god) in protest against the growing materialism of the Caliphate.
- The English word Sufism was coined in the nineteenth century. The original word used in Islamic texts was *tasawwuf.*
- According to some scholars, the word **'sufism'** was derived from, 'suf', meaning wool, referring to the rough woollen clothes worn by sufis. Some others derived it from 'safa', meaning purity.
- It might also have been derived from 'suffa', the platform outside the Prophet's Mosque, where a group of close followers assembled to learn about faith.
- Sufis focussed on seeking salvation through intense devotion and love for God by following his commands.
- The sufis interpret the *Qur'an* on the basis of their personal experience.

Khanqahs and Silsilas

- Sufism evolved into a well-developed movement by the eleventh century. It had a body of literature based on Quranic studies and sufi practices.
- The sufis started creating institutions by organising communities for travellers called ***khanqah***[5] (Persian). These institutions were controlled by a teaching master known as ***shaikh*** (in Arabic), ***pir*** or ***murshid*** (in Persian).
- The master would enroll disciples (murids) and appoint a successor (*khalifa*). He also established rules for spiritual conduct and interaction between group members as well as between lay persons and the master.

Sufi Silsilas

- Around the twelfth century, sufi *silsilas* began to take form in different parts of Islamic world.
- The word *silsila* means chain, which indicates the continuous link between master (*Shaikh*) and disciple. This chain formed a continuous spiritual connection to the Prophet Muhammad, passing spiritual power and blessings to devotees through it.
- Special rituals to admit people into the group were developed in which persons who wanted to enter the group took an oath of commitment, wore a piece of cloth and shaved their hair.
- When the *shaikh* died, his tomb-shrine called ***dargah*** (Persian term meaning court) became the centre of religious worship for his followers. This encouraged the practice of pilgrimage or ***ziyarat*** to his grave, especially on his death anniversary or ***urs*** or marriage.
- People believed that saints were more closer to God during life-time and are united with God in death, so they worshipped such saints.

Outside the *Khanqah*

- Some sufis disrespected *khanqah* and adopted mendicancy (the practice of begging) and observed celibacy (self-restraint). These sufis were known as mystics.
- They ignored rituals and observed a strict and simple way of living. They were known by different names like **Qalandars, Madaris, Malangs, Haidaris**, etc.
- Those who did not obey the shari'a were often referred to as **be-shari'a** and those who obeyed shari'a were called ***ba-shari'a*** sufis.

---

5 **Khanqah** It is a hospice/lodging for travellers, especially one run by a religious order.

Quick Test 2

Which Mughal ruler regarded himself as the emperor of all peoples, not just Muslims?

In the context of Muslim rule in India, the category of "zimmi" was extended to which religious groups?

What kind of religious poetry did the Khojahs use to communicate ideas from the Qur'an?

Which term referred to people who did not observe the norms of caste society and spoke non-Sanskrit languages?

Who was responsible for controlling a Sufi hospice or khanqah?

6.6 The Chishtis in the Subcontinent

The Chishtis were the most influential among the groups of sufis. They migrated to India in the later twelfth century, and adapted to the local environment and various features of Indian devotional traditions.

Life in the Chishti *Khanqahs*

- The *khanqah* (hospice) was the centre of social life of the Chishtis.
- The *khanqah* of Shaikh Nizamuddin's was on the banks of the river Yamuna in Ghiyaspur, on the outskirts of the city of Delhi.
- It had many small rooms and a big hall called *jama'at khana*, where the inmates and visitors lived and prayed. The inmates included family members of the Shaikh, his attendants and disciples.
- The Shaikh lived in a small room on the roof of the hall where he met visitors in the morning and evening.
- The courtyard was surrounded by a veranda and a boundary wall was present around the complex. There was an open kitchen called *langar* which ran on *futuh* (voluntary charity).
- People from different fields like soldiers, slaves, singers, merchants, poets, travellers, rich and poor, Hindu *jogis* (yogi) and *qalandars* came to seek guidance and help of the Shaikh in different matters.
- Poets like **Amir Hasan Sijzi** and **Amir Khusrau** and the court historian Ziyauddin Barani also visited and wrote about the Shaikh.

Chishti Devotionalism : *Ziyarat* and *Qawwali*

- Shaikh Nizamuddin appointed several spiritual successors and sent them to set up religious institutions in various parts of the subcontinent.
- This resulted in the rapid spread of the teachings, practices and organisation of the Chistis and also the fame of the Shaikh.
- This practice attracted the pilgrims to his shrine and also to the shrines of his spiritual ancestors.

▲ *A seventeenth-century painting of Shaikh Nizamuddin Auliya and his disciple Amir Khusrau*

Ziyarat

- Ziyarat[6] was the practice used as an occasion to seek the sufi's spiritual grace (*barakat*).
- The shrine of Khwaja Muinuddin who was popularly known as **Gharib Nawaz** (comforter of the poor) is the most respected. The earliest textual reference to Khwaja Muinuddin' *dargah* belong to fourteenth century.
- **Muhammad bin Tughlaq** was the first Sultan to visit the shrine, but the construction to house the tomb was funded by **Sultan Ghiyasuddin Khalji** of Malwa, in the late fifteenth century.
- The shrine had become popular by the sixteenth century. Akbar visited the tomb, and was inspired by the spirited singing of pilgrims in the shrine of Ajmer.

6 *Ziyarat* It means pilgrimage.

▲ *Qawwali at the dargah of Nizamuddin Auliya*

Qawwali

- The use of music and dance was also a part of ***ziyarat***. It included spiritual chants performed by specially trained musicians called ***qawwals*** to feel divine happiness.
- The sufis remember God either by reciting the ***zikr*** (the Divine Names) or call his presence through ***sama'*** (interview) or performance of spiritual music.
- ***Sama'*** was essential to the Chistis, and it is an example of interaction with indigenous or local devotional traditions.
- **Amir Khusrau** who was a great poet, musician and disciple of Shaikh Nizamuddin Auliya, gave a unique form to the Chishti *sama'* by introducing the *qaul* (Arabic word meaning "saying") i.e. a hymn sung at the beginning or ending of *qawwali*.
- Today *qawwali* is performed in shrines all over the subcontinent.

Languages and Communication

- In Delhi, the Chishti *silsila* conversed in the language of the people i.e. Hindavi.
- Sufis such as **Baba Farid** composed verses in the local language, which were put in the *Guru Granth Sahib*.
- Others composed long poems or *masnavis* to express ideas of divine love using human love as a symbol. For example, the *prem-akhyan* (love story) *Padmavat* composed by Malik Muhammad Jayasi depicted the romance of Padmini and Ratansen, the king of Chittor.
- A different type of sufi poetry was composed in and around the town of Bijapur, Karnataka which were short poems in Dakhani (a form of Urdu). They were dedicated to Chisti sufis who lived in this region during the seventeenth and eighteenth centuries.
- ***Lurinama*** or lullabies and ***shadinama*** or wedding songs were other forms of compositions.
- The sufis of Karnataka must have been inspired by the existing bhakti tradition of the Kannada *vachanas* of the Lingayats and the Marathi *abhangs* of the *sants* of Pandharpur.

Sufis and the State

- Simplicity and maintaining a distance from worldly power were major features of the Chisti tradition. For example, once Shaikh Nizamuddin Auliya was gifted land and gardens by a local ruler, but he declined it and instead asked for money to distribute it to the needy.
- The sufis accepted voluntary grants and donations from political persons.
- The Sultans set up charitable trusts (*auqaf*) as an income for hospices and granted tax-free land (*inam*).
- The Chistis accepted donations in cash and kind. They preferred to use donations for immediate needs like food, clothes, living quarters and ritual necessities like *sama'* instead of accumulating donations.
- The sufis became popular among the masses due to their charity, scholarship, and people's belief in their magical powers.
- When the Turks set up the Delhi Sultanate, they were under the pressure of the *ulama* to implement *shari'a* as state law. This was because they expected opposition from their non-Muslims subjects against Muslim rule.
- Sultans depended on sufis who derived authority directly from God, to interpret the sharia.
- Sometimes there were conflicts between the Sultans and the sufis. To assert their authority, both expected that rituals like **prostration**[7] and kissing of the feet, should be performed.
- Sufi shaikh often used grand titles. For example, the disciples of Nizamuddin Auliya called him as ***Sultan-ul-mashaikh*** (means Sultan amongst Shaikhs).

7 **Prostration** State of lying on the ground with one's face downwards.

Major Teachers of the Chisti Silsila

Sufi Teachers	Year of Death	Location of Dargah
Shaikh Muinuddin Sijzi	1235	Ajmer (Rajasthan)
Khwaja Qutbuddin Bakhtiyar Kaki	1235	Delhi
Shaikh Fariduddin Ganj-i Shakar	1265	Ajodhan (Pakistan)
Shaikh Nizamuddin Auliya	1325	Delhi
Shaikh Nasiruddin Chiragh-i Delhi	1356	Delhi

Quick Test 3

1. Name the shrine which was visited by Akbar in the sixteenth century?
2. Which mughal rulers made grants for subjects?
3. What local customs did the Arab Muslim traders adopt in Kerala?
4. Which language did the Chishti Silsila use to communicate in Delhi?
5. Nizamuddin Auliya was given which title by his disciples?

6.7 Poet-Saints of Devotional Paths

Many poet-saints were engaged in direct and indirect discussion with the new social situations, ideas and institutions. The detail description of these poets-saints is given below

Kabir

- Kabir (c. fourteenth-fifteenth centuries) is an Arabic name meaning **great**.
- Kabir was born Hindu, but he was brought up by a poor Muslim family belonging to a community of weavers or *julahas*, who were recently converted to Islam.
- Kabir was taught bhakti by a guru named ***Ramananda***.
- Kabir became an inspiration for those people who challenged the existing religious and social beliefs in the search for God.

Kabir's Compositions

- Verses that belonged to Kabir have been compiled in three different but overlapping traditions. These were
  (i) The ***Kabir Bijak*** which was preserved by the Kabirpanth (the path or sect of Kabir) in Varanasi, Uttar Pradesh.
  (ii) The ***Kabir Granthavali*** which is related with the Dadupanth in Rajasthan.
  (iii) ***Adi Granth Sahib*** which included many of Kabir's compositions.
- All these text compilations were made long after the death of Kabir.
- By the nineteenth century, collections of poems and writings belonging to Kabir were circulated in print in Bengal, Gujarat and Maharashtra.
- Kabir's poems have survived in different languages and forms. Some of them are composed in the special language of *nirguna* poets, the *sant bhasha*.
- Others known as *ulatbansi* (upside-down sayings), are written in a form in which everyday meanings are inverted.

Importance of Kabir's Poems

- Kabir described the Ultimate Reality in Islam as *Allah, Khuda, Hazrat* and *Pir.*
- He used terms from Vedantic traditions such as *alakh* (the unseen), *nirakar* (formless), *Brahman, Atman*, etc.
- Spiritual ideas such as *shabda* (sound) or *shunya* (emptiness) belonged to yogic traditions.
- Sometimes diverse and opposing ideas were expressed in Kabir's poems.
- Some poems took Islamic ideas and used concepts like **monotheism** (belief in one God) and **iconoclasm** (the destruction of religious images) to attack Hindu polytheism (belief in many Gods) and idol worship.
- Some other poems use the *sufi* concept of *zikr* and *ishq* (love) to express the Hindu practice of *nam-simaran* (remembrance of God's name).

Baba Guru Nanak

- Baba Guru Nanak (1469 - 1539) was born in a Hindu merchant family in a village called Nankana Sahib near the river Ravi, in the predominantly Muslim Punjab.
- He was trained as an accountant and studied Persian. He was married at a young age, but he spent most of his time among sufis and bhaktas. He also travelled widely.

Teachings of Guru Nanak

- Baba Guru Nanak supported a form of *nirguna bhakti.* He rejected sacrificies, ritual baths, image worship, simplicity and the scriptures of both Hindus and Muslims.
- For Baba Guru Nanak, the Absolute or *rab* had no gender or form.
- He proposed a simple way to connect to the Divine i.e. by remembering and repeating the Divine Name, conveying his ideas through hymns called *shabad* in Punjabi (the language of the region).
- *Shabad* were sung by Baba Guru Nanak in various ragas. His attendant **Mardana** played the *rabab.*
- Baba Guru Nanak organised his followers into a community. He framed rules for group worship (*sangat*) involving collective recitation (repeating hymns).
- Angad, one of his disciples, was appointed by him as the teacher (*guru*) to succeed him. This practice was followed for nearly 200 years.
- Baba Guru Nanak did not wish to create a new religion, but after his death, his followers distinguished themselves from both Hindus and Muslims, and maintained their religious practices separately.
- The fifth Sikh Guru, **Guru Arjan Dev**, collected hymns of Baba Guru Nanak along with his four successors and religious poets like Baba Farid, Ravidas (also known as Raidas) and Kabir in the ***Adi Granth Sahib.*** These hymns, called *gurbani*, are composed in various languages.
- The tenth teacher, **Guru Gobind Singh** included the compositions of the ninth guru, **Guru Tegh Bahadur** in the late seventeenth century and his scripture was called the *Guru Granth Sahib.*
- Guru Gobind Singh also laid the foundation of the *Khalsa Panth* (army of the pure) and defined its five symbols

  (i) uncut hair (ii) a dagger (iii) a pair of shorts
  (iv) a comb (v) a steel bangle
- The community became a socio-religious and military force under Guru Gobind Singh.

Mirabai

- Mirabai (c. fifteenth-sixteenth century) was the best-known woman poet within the bhakti tradition.
- She was a Rajput princess from Merta in Marwar. She was married against her wishes to a prince of the Sisodia clan of Mewar in Rajasthan.
- She opposed her husband and did not accept the traditional role of wife and mother. She recognised Krishna, the *avatar* of Vishnu, as her lover.
- She left his husband's palace and lived as a wandering saint and wrote songs.
- As per some traditions, her teacher was **Raidas**, a leather worker which indicates that she challenged the norms of caste society.
- She did not form a sect or had a group of followers, but she was recognised as a source of inspiration for many centuries.
- Both women and men sing her songs, especially those who are poor and belong to low caste in Gujarat and Rajasthan.

▲ *Krishna playing the flute, a form of the deity worshipped by Mirabai*

Shankaradeva

- He was a fifteenth century saint who promoted **Vaishnavism** in Assam.
- His teachings were often known as the Bhagavati dharma. They were based on the *Bhagavad Gita* and the *Bhagavata Purana.*
- He emphasised the need for ***naam kirtan*** i.e. recitation of the names of the lord in *sat sanga* or groups of devotees.
- He also encouraged the establishment of ***satra*** or monasteries for the spread of spiritual knowledge and ***naam ghar*** or prayer halls.
- His major compositions include the ***Kirtana-ghosha***.

6.8 Reconstructing Histories of Religious Traditions

Various texts were produced in and around sufi *khanqahs* that give us knowledge about the history of sufi traditions. These sources are

Treaties or Manuals

- Treaties or manuals dealing with sufi thought and practices included the ***Kashf-ul-Mahjub*** of **Ali bin Usman Hujwiri**. It helps historians to see how traditions outside the subcontinent influenced sufi thought in India.

Malfuzat

- *Malfuzat* means uttered i.e. conversations of sufi saints. *Malfuzats* were compiled by different *sufi silsilas* with the permission of the *shaikhs.*
- The aim of these texts was to teach moral values. Several such texts have been found from different parts of the subcontinent, including the Deccan.
- An early text on *malfuzat* is the ***Fawa'id-al-Fu'ad***. It is the collection of conversations of Shaikh Nizamuddin Auliya, compiled by Amir Hasan Sijzi Dehlavi, a Persian poet.

Maktubat

- *Maktubat* means written collections of letters by sufi masters to their disciples and associates. It gives us information about the shaikh's experience of religious truth that he wanted to share with others.
- It also shows the life conditions of the recipients of letter and response to their difficulties ***Maktubat-i Imam Rabbani*** by Naqshbandi Shaikh Ahmad Sirhindi is an example of *maktubat*.

Tazkiras

- *Tazkiras* means to mention and memorialise biographical accounts of saints.
- The fourteenth century ***Siyar-ul-Auliya*** of Mir Khwurd Kirmani was the ***first* sufi tazkira** written in India. It was about Chishti saints.
- The most famous *tazkira* was the **Akhbar-ul-Akhyar** of Abdul Haqq Muhaddis Dehlavi.

Quick Test 4

1. Name the three most influential poet-saints of devotional paths.
2. Which place did Shankardeva belong to?
3. What was the language of *Nirguna* poets known as?
4. What were the main forms of worship of sufism?
5. Who was the most famous *tazkira*?

TIMELINE

c. 500-800 CE	Appar, Sambandar, Sundaramurti in Tamil Nadu
c. 800-900	Nammalvar, Manikkavachakar, Andal, Tondaradippodi in Tamil Nadu
c.1000-1100	Al Hujwiri, Data Ganj Bakhsh in the Punjab; Ramanujacharya in Tamil Nadu
c.1100-1200	Basavanna in Karnataka
c.1200-1300	Jnanadeva, Muktabai in Maharashtra; Khwaja Muinuddin Chishti in Rajasthan; Bahauddin Zakariyya and Fariduddin Ganj- i Shakar in the Punjab; Qutbuddin Bakhtiyar Kaki in Delhi
c.1300-1400	Lal Ded in Kashmir; Lal Shahbaz Qalandar in Sind; Nizamuddin Auliya in Delhi; Ramananda in Uttar Pradesh; Chokhamela in Maharashtra; Sharafuddin Yahya Maneri in Bihar
c.1400-1500	Kabir, Raidas, Surdas in Uttar Pradesh; Baba Guru Nanak in the Punjab; Vallabhacharya in Gujarat; Abdullah Shattari in Gwalior; Muhammad Shah Alam in Gujarat; Mir Sayyid Muhammad Gesu Daraz in Gulbarga, Shankaradeva in Assam; Tukaram in Maharashtra
c.1500-1600	Sri Chaitanya in Bengal; Mirabai in Rajasthan; Shaikh Abdul Quddus Gangohi, Malik Muhammad Jaisi, Tulsidas in Uttar Pradesh
c.1600-1700	Shaikh Ahmad Sirhindi in Haryana; Miyan Mir in the Punjab

Mind Map

BHAKTI-SUFI TRADITIONS

1 Development of Religious Beliefs and Practices

The Integration of Cults
- Puranas made Brahmanical ideas accessible to women and Shudras.
- Brahmanas adapted local beliefs into Sanskritic traditions.

Difference and Conflict
- Tantric practices ignored caste, class and Vedic authority which led to conflicts.

2 Poems of Prayer: Early Traditions of Bhakti

Relations with the States
- Tamil Bhakti poets opposed Buddhism and Jainism due to competition.
- Chola rulers supported Brahaminical traditions by constructing grand temples.
- Nayanars and Alvars inspired temple art and worship practices.

The Alvars and Nayanars of Tamil Nadu
- Alvars praised Vishnu and Nayanars devotedly worshipped Shiva through Hymns
- Alvars and Nayanars protested against caste and Brahmana dominance.

Women Devotees
- Women like Andal and Karaikkal Ammaiyar played key devotional roles.

3 The Virashaiva Tradition in Karnataka

- Basavanna led the Virashaiva movement. Virashaivas were also called Lingayats.
- Vachanas composed in Kannada explain Virashaiva beliefs and practices.

4 Religious Ferment in North India

- In North India, deities such as Vishnu and Shiva were worshipped in temples.
- Naths, Jogis, Siddhas emerged, questioning vedic authority, influencing common people.

5 New Stands in the Fabric: Islamic Traditions

Faiths of Rules and Subjects
- Muslims rulers were guided by the Ulama to follow Shari'a law.
- Zimmi policy protected non-Muslims who paid the Jizya tax.
- Akbar promoted religious tolerance.

The Popular Practice of Islam
- The five pillars of Islam were practiced universally but with local variations.
- Khojahs used indigenous genres to spread Quranic knowledge.

6 The Growth of Sufism

- Sufism developed institutions like Khanqah and leadership roles for masters.
- Mystics interpreted Sufi ideals radically, rejecting khanqah and rituals.
- They were known as Qalandars, Madaris, Malangs, Haidaris.

7 The Chishtis on the Sub-continent

Language and Communication
Chishtis used local languages like Hindavi to connect culturally.

Sufis and the State
Chishtis maintained austerity but accepted donations from state.

Chishti Devotionalism: Ziyarat and Qawwali
- Ziyarat involves pilgrimage to Sufi tombs for spiritual blessings.
- Chisti *sama* mixes mystical music with indigenous devotional traditions.

8 Poet-Saints of Devotional Paths

- **Mirabai** She devoted herself to Krishna, rejecting traditional family roles.
- **Baba Guru Nanak** He promoted Nirguna bhakti, rejecting religious rituals.
- **Kabir** His verses challenged religious divisions and idol worship practices. His poems used islamic vedantic and yogic terms for God.

9 Reconstructing Histories of Religious Traditions

Historians use sculpture architecture and texts to study religious traditions.

NCERT Folder

Intext Questions

1. Why do you think kings were interested in proclaiming their connections with bhaktas? (Pg. 146)

Ans. The kings were interested in proclaiming their connections with bhaktas to gain spiritual legitimacy and moral authority among their followers. By associating themselves with bhaktas, the kings could significantly enhance their image as just and righteous leaders.

2. What are the potential sources of conflict in the relationship between religious and political leaders? (Pg. 160)

Ans. The potential sources of conflict in the relationship between religious and political leaders are as follows

- Conflicts can arise when religious leaders claim moral authority that challenges the legitimacy of political leaders or vice versa.
- Policy making can be the priority of political leaders, while religious leaders may focus on moral or spiritual principles, leading to disagreements on key issues.
- Tensions can occur when religious groups attempt to influence laws and policies related to secular governance.

3. Why do you think the traditions of Kabir, Baba Guru Nanak and Mirabai remain significant in the twenty-first century? (Pg. 165)

Ans. The traditions of Kabir, Baba Guru Nanak and Mirabai remain significant in the twenty-first century due to the following reasons

- Their teachings promote universal values like love, equality and compassion.
- They challenged social norms, including caste and gender discrimination which makes their messages relevant in contemporary times.

Answer in 100-150 words

1. Explain with example what historians meant by the integration of cults.

Ans. Historians use the term 'integration of cults' to describe the blending of diverse local religious practices into mainstream traditions. In ancient India, this process involved incorporating local deities and rituals into broader Brahmanical traditions, making religious beliefs accessible to a wider range of social groups.

For example, the deity Jagannatha in Puri was originally a local god worshipped by tribal communities; by the 12th century, he was integrated as a form of Vishnu. Similarly, various goddesses worshipped locally were recognised within the Puranic framework, often as consorts of major deities like Vishnu and Shiva.

This integration demonstrates how Brahmanical traditions adapted and expanded by including regional beliefs and practices.

2. To what extent do you think the architecture of mosques in the subcontinent reflects a combination of universal ideals and local traditions?

Ans. The complex mixture of a universal faith with local traditions can be seen in the architecture of mosques in subcontinent. Universal features like Mosques' orientation towards Mecca, placement of the *mihrab* (prayer place) and the *minbar* (raised platform) were common but there were variations in roofs and building materials.

Following mosques show how local traditions were included in the architectural style of mosques

- A mosque in Kerala of thirteenth century, with a *shikhara*- like roof unlike a normal mosque where it was dome.
- Atiya Mosque, Mymensingh district, Bangladesh, built with brick, in 1609 CE.
- The Shah Hamadan Mosque in Srinagar, on the banks of the Jhelum is often regarded as 'jewel in the crown' of all the existing mosques of Kashmir. It was built in 1395 CE and is one of the best examples of Kashmiri wooden architecture.

3. What were the similarities and differences between the *be-shari'a* and *ba-shari'a* sufi traditions?

or **Point out one difference and one similarity between *be-shari'a* and *ba-shari'a* sufi traditions.**

Ans. The differences between the be-shari'a and ba-shari'a sufi traditions were

The *shari'a* is the law governing the Muslim community. Based on radical interpretation of sufi ideals, some mystics started movements. They were known as be-shari'a. They disrespected *khanqah*, took to begging and did not marry. They ignored rituals and observed extreme form of strict and simple way of living. They were known by different names like Qalandars, Madaris, Malangs, Haidaris, etc. On the other hand, sufis who obeyed *shari'a* were called *ba-shari'a* sufis. They were adhered to Islamic sacred law. They mostly lived in shrines or *khanqahs*.

The similarities between the be-shari'a and ba-shari'a sufi traditions were

The similarity between be-shari'a and ba-shari'a was that both are related to sufi traditions. Both are critical of the strict methods of interpretation of Quran and Sunnah adopted by religious people. They laid stress on seeking salvation.

4. Discuss the ways in which the Alvars, Nayanars and Virashaivas expressed critiques of the caste system.

Ans. The Alvars, Nayanars and Virashaivas expressed critiques of the caste system in the following ways

- **The Alvars and Nayanars** started a movement to protest against the caste system and the dominance of Brahmanas or at least attempted to reform the system. The devotees or *bhaktas* came from different social backgrounds ranging from Brahmanas to artisans and cultivators and even from castes considered 'untouchable'.

  An Alvar named *Tondaradippodi*, who was a Brahmana, in his writings described that there was no difference between *Chaturvedins* (Brahmana) and the outcastes. This indicates that he opposed caste system.
- Appar, a Nayanar saint in his composition questioned the use of *gotra* and *kula* and suggests that one should just devote himself to Marperu's lord (Shiva).
- **The Virashaivas** or **Lingayats** challenged the idea of caste and the pollution attributed to certain groups by Brahmanas. They also questioned the theory of rebirth. Some practices like post-puberty marriage and the remarriage of widows which were disapproved in the Dharmashastras, were encouraged by the Lingayats.

5. Describe the major teachings of either Kabir or Baba Guru Nanak, and the ways in which these have been transmitted.

Or **Describe the philosophy and teachings of Kabir.** **CBSE 2024**

Ans. The major teachings of Kabir were

- He described the Ultimate Reality as *Allah, Khuda, Hazrat* and *Pir*.
- He also used terms from Vedantic traditions, *alakh* (the unseen), *nirakar* (formless), Brahman, Atman, etc. Other spiritual ideas such as *shabda* (sound) or *shunya* (emptiness) were from yogic traditions.
- He, through his poems, promoted the concepts like belief in one God and the destruction of religious images to attack Hindu's belief in many Gods and idol worship.
- He promoted the sufi concept of *zikr* and *ishq* (love) to express the Hindu practice of *nam-simaran* or (remembrance of God's name) through his poems.

The major teachings of Baba Guru Nanak were

- Baba Guru Nanak's hymns and teachings suggest that he supported a form of *nirguna* bhakti.
- He strongly refused to accept the external practices of the religions he saw around him.
- He rejected sacrifices, ritual baths, image worship, simplicity and the scriptures of both Hindus and Muslims.
- According to Baba Guru Nanak, the Absolute or *'rab'* has no gender or form.
- He proposed a simple way to connect to the Divine i.e. by remembering and repeating the Divine Name, conveying his ideas through hymns called *'shabad'* in Punjabi, which was the language of the region.

Write a Short Essay (about 250-300 words) on the following

6. Discuss the major beliefs and practices that characterised Sufism.

Ans. The major beliefs and practices that characterised Sufism were

- Sufis believed in severe self-discipline and spiritual belief of union with God.
- Sufism evolved into a well-developed movement by eleventh century. It had a literature on Quranic studies and Sufi practices.
- The Sufis started creating institutions by organising communities around rest places meant for travellers called *khanqah*, controlled by a teaching master known as *shaikh, pir* or *murshid.*
- *Silsilas* were used as link between master and disciple. This link was stretched as an unbroken spiritual link to the Prophet Muhammad. The spiritual power and blessings were transmitted to devotees through this channel.
- The person who wanted to enter the group took an oath of commitment, wore a piece of cloth and shaved their hair. The *silsilas* were named after their founding figure.
- When *shaikh* died, his tomb-shrine called *dargah* became the centre of religious worship for his followers. Thus encouraging the practice of pilgrimage or *ziyarat* to his grave, especially on his death anniversary or urs or marriage.

- For economic and spiritual benefits, people sought Shaikh's blessings. This led to evolution of the cult of the *shaikh* referred as *wali*. *Wali* means friend of God, who was a sufi who claimed closeness to Allah, acquiring his grace to perform miracles.

7. Examine how and why rulers tried to establish connections with the traditions of the Nayanars and the Sufis?

Ans. Rulers tried to establish connections with the traditions of the Nayanars and the Sufis by building very impressive temples. These were made by using beautiful stones and metal sculptures to recreate the visions of the popular saints who sang in the language of the people.

The Chola kings tried to claim divine support and proclaim their own power and status. These kings also introduced the singing of Tamil Shaiva hymns in the temples under royal patronage, taking the initiative to collect and organise them into a text called *Tevaram*.

Around 945 CE, Chola ruler Parantaka I, had dedicated the metal images of Appar, Sambandar and Sundarar in a Shiva temple for religious purpose. These were also carried in processions during the festivals of these saints.

Rulers like Muhammad bin Tughlaq and Mughal emperor Akbar visited the Khwaja Muinuddin's *dargah* many times. Akbar offered a huge cauldron *(degh)* to facilitate cooking for pilgrims and also had a mosque constructed within the compound of *dargah*. In this way, the rulers showed their connection with the Nayanars and the Sufis.

The kings tried to establish connections because kings wanted their support as Sufi's charity and scholarship, and people's belief in their magical powers made them famous among the masses. Kings had to not only show that they are associated with sufis but also required acceptance from sufis.

For instance, when Turks set up the Delhi Sultanate, they resisted the pressure of the *ulama* on implementing *shari'a* as state law because they expected opposition from their subjects, the majority of whom were non-Muslims.

Now Sultans asked for sufi's help, who derived authority directly from God and did not depend on jurists to interpret the *shari'a*.

8. Analyse, with illustrations, why bhakti and sufi thinkers adopted a variety of languages in which to express their opinions.

Ans. The bhakti and sufi thinkers used the languages of the common people to express their opinions. They often spoke in local languages. So, they were well-understood by the common people.

This is shown in the examples below

- Sanskrit was used by traditional bhakti saints to sing hymns at different occasions, places of worship and ceremonies.
- Bhakti thinkers in Tamil Nadu region like Alvars and Nayanars used Tamil language. Even kings supported by introducing the singing of Tamil Shaiva hymns in the temples under royal patronage, and took the initiative to collect and organise them into a text called *Tevaram*.
- *Vachanas* meaning sayings, composed in Kannada by Lingayats.
- *Quran* through local literature and devotional poems expressed their opinion.
- Devotional poems in Punjabi, Multani, Sindhi, Kachchi, Hindi and Gujarati, were sung in special *ragas* during daily prayer meetings. Malayalam was adopted by Muslims in Kerala.
- Local languages were not adopted in *sama* by the Chishtis. In Delhi, those linked with the Chishti *silsila* conversed in the language of the people i.e Hindavi. Sufis such as Baba Farid composed verses in the local language, which were put in the *Guru Granth Sahib*.
- A different type of sufi poetry was composed in and around Bijapur, Karnataka. These were short poems in Dakhani (a form of Urdu).
- Kabir's poems have survived in different languages and different forms of languages, and some are composed in the special language of *nirguna* poets, the *sant bhasha*. Others known as *ulatbansi* (upside-down sayings), are written in a form in which everyday meanings are reversed.
- Baba Guru Nanak conveyed his ideas through hymns called *'shabad'* in Punjabi, which was the language of the region.

9. Read any five of the sources included in this chapter and discuss the social and religious ideas that are expressed in them.

Ans. The different social and religious ideas that are expressed are

(i) An Alvar named *Tondaradippodi*, who was a Brahmana, in his writings finds that Vishnu likes those servants who express love for Vishnu's feet even though, they might have born as outcastes. Vishnu like these people more than the *Chaturvedins*.

(ii) In other instance, Appar, a Nayanar saint in his composition questions the use of *gotra* and *kula*, and suggests that one should just devote himself to Marperu's lord (Shiva).

(iii) Karaikkal Ammaiyar in a poem describes herself as a demoness who was roaming in the forest of Alankatu, which was the home of Shiva. She rejects the idea of the feminine beauty that was traditionally attributed to women.

(iv) Basavanna in his *vachana* says that people pray to a snake carved on stone and pour milk on it, but in real life if they see a snake, they want to kill it. Also if a servant of the god was served food, people show their disliking, but the image of a God who cannot eat was offered food by the people.

(v) An extract from a *farman* issued by Akbar in 1598 CE suggests that, the city of Kambayat in Gujarat, was allowed to build a Church by the Holy society of Jesus. He ordered officials of the city of Kambayat not to create problem in building the Church and allow Christians to practice their religion. This shows Akbar was tolerant to all the religions.

Map Work

10. **On an outline map of India, plot three major sufi shrines, and three places associated with temples (one each of a form of Vishnu, Shiva and the goddess).**

Ans.

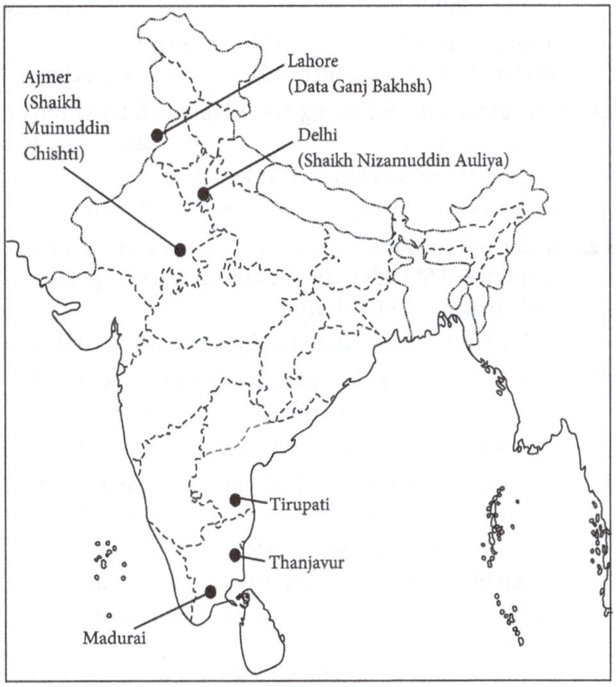

Exam Pattern Questions

Objective Type Questions

Multiple Choice Questions (MCQs)

1. **Historians of religion classify bhakti traditions into two broad categories ...... and ....**
(a) *Saguna* and *Viguna* (b) *Saguna* and *Nirguna*
(c) *Nirguna* and *Sarvaguna* (d) None of these

2. **The '*Nalayira Divyprabandham*' was frequently described as the**
(a) Tamil Veda (b) Vedas of North India
(c) Kannada Vedas (d) Dharmashastras

3. **Which Alvar woman's songs were sung widely?**
(a) Pindal (b) Andal
(c) Priyasi (d) Prajapati

4. **Who consecrated metal images of Appar, Sambandar and Sundarar in a Shiva temple?** CBSE Diksha
(a) Parantaka I (b) Parantaka II
(c) Rajaraja Chola (d) Rajendra Chola

5. **Which of the following sects did not practice funerary rites such as cremation prescribed in the Dharmashastras?** CBSE Diksha
(a) Nathpanthis (b) Lingayats
(c) Nayanars (d) Bhagvats

6. **Basavanna was a minister in the court of**
(a) Kalachuri ruler (b) Chola ruler
(c) Pandaya ruler (d) None of these

7. **Which branch of Ismailis developed new modes of communication?**
(a) Khojahs (b) *Jizya* (c) Chishtis (d) *Salat*

8. **Who among the following was the mentor of Amir Khusrau ?** CBSE 2024
(a) Shaikh Nasiruddin Chiragh-i-Delhi
(b) Shaikh Muinuddin Chishti
(c) Shaikh Salim Chishti
(d) Shaikh Nizamuddin Auliya

9. **Who among the following Sikh Gurus compiled 'Adi Granth Sahib'?** **CBSE 2024**

(a) Guru Nanak Dev ji (b) Guru Arjan Dev ji
(c) Guru Hargobind Sahib ji (d) Guru Gobind Singh ji

10. **Who among the following gurus laid the foundation of 'Khalsa Panth' ?** **CBSE Term I 2021**

(a) Guru Hargobind Sahib (b) Guru Arjan Dev
(c) Guru Gobind Singh (d) Guru Tegh Bahadur

11. **Which of the following is a collection of conversations of Sufi Saint Shaikh Nizamuddin Auliya, compiled by Amir Hasan Sijzi Dehlavi?**

(a) *Malfuzat* (b) *Tazkiras* (c) *Ziyarat* (d) *Maktubat*

12. **Which term is used for collections of letters written by sufi masters to their disciples and associates?**

(a) *Malfuzat* (b) *Tazkiras* (c) *Ziyarat* (d) *Maktubat*

13. **'The bhakti movement in India played an important role in laying the foundation for a reconfiguration of society on more equitable lines.'**

Which of the following supports this statement?

(a) The rich were forced to redistribute their wealth to the poor.
(b) Rituals and practices like idol worshipping were highly encouraged.
(c) Insisted on using only Sanskrit as their medium to write songs and hymns.
(d) Women and people from lower castes were acknowledged and accommodated.

14. **In a modern city, a group of friends discusses the relevance of Kabir's teachings in today's society. Some believe these are outdated, while others see their significance in promoting equality and love. Which of the following scenario best reflects Kabir's relevance today?** **CBSE 2025**

(a) A debate on Kabir's historical context
(b) A discussion dismissing spirituality irrelevant
(c) Focus on societal norms and traditions only
(d) Seeking simple connection with the divine

15. **Which of the following statements is incorrect about Andal?** **CBSE SQP 2024**

(a) Andal was a woman Alvar, the most striking features of her compositions were widely sung.
(b) Andal was a woman Nayanar, she incorporated the prevailing caste system in the society.
(c) Andal saw herself as the beloved of Vishnu; her verses express her love for the deity.
(d) Andal saw herself as the beloved of Krishna; her verses express her love for the deity

16. **Which of the following statements is correct regarding Virashaivas?**

(a) It means 'heroes of Shiva'.
(b) They question the theory of birth.
(c) They question casticism and its pollution.
(d) They believed in theory of death.

17. **Choose the correct option regarding Virashaiva tradition from the following.** **CBSE 2024**

(a) This tradition emerged in Karnataka.
(b) They are the followers of Vishnu.
(c) They believed in the theory of rebirth.
(d) They practice funerary rites.

18. **Which of the following statements regarding 'Nath' sect of Medieval India is not correct?** **CBSE 2023**

(a) Nath sect mostly came from artisans groups.
(b) They expressed themselves in common language.
(c) They were the devotional people from North India.
(d) Amir Khusran was the prominent one from this sect.

19. **Which of the following is common between Sufism and the Bhakti tradition?**

(a) Both did not consist of music and singing.
(b) Both literary traditions did not adopt local languages.
(c) Both believed in reviving rituals and orthodox practices.
(d) Both did not appeal only to the higher ranks of the society.

20. **Which of the following is correct regarding Vaishanavism ?** **CBSE Term I 2021**

(a) Vaishanavism developed around various avtars of Vishnu and Shiva.
(b) Ten *avtars* are recognised within this tradition.
(c) The ten forms are assumed as Brahma.
(d) The different forms of deity are not represented in sculpture.

21. **Which of the following is correct regarding the Lingayats?**

(i) They challenged the idea of caste.
(ii) They questioned the theory of rebirth.
(iii) They encouraged the practices approved in Dharmashastras.
(iv) They did not practice funerary rites.

Codes

(a) (i), (ii) and (iii) (b) (ii) and (iii)
(c) (i), (ii) and (iv) (d) All of the above

22. **Read the following statements regarding Sufism in India.** **CBSE SQP Term I 2021**

(i) They turned to asceticism and mysticism in protest against the growing materialism.
(ii) They sought an interpretation of Quran on the basis of their experience.
(iii) Amir Khusrau was the disciple of Shaikh Nizamuddin Aulia.
(iv) Shaikh Muinuddin Sijzi was from Delhi.

Which of the following statements are correct?

(a) (i), (ii) and (iii) (b) (iii), (iv) and (i)
(c) (i), (iii) and (iv) (d) (ii) and (iv)

23. Read the following statements regarding Kabir and choose the correct option. **Compartment 2024**

(i) Verses ascribed to Kabir have been compiled in four distinct traditions.
(ii) Kabir's poems are available only in the Urdu language.
(iii) Kabir used many traditions to describe the ultimate reality.
(iv) Kabir called ultimate reality as Allah, Khuda, Hazrat and Pir.

Options

(a) (i) and (ii) (b) (iii) and (iv)
(c) (ii) and (iii) (d) (i) and (iv)

24. Which of the following statements regarding Mirabai are correct? **CBSE Term I 2021**

(i) She was a Rajput princess from Marwar.
(ii) She defied her husband and did not submit to the role of a wife and mother.
(iii) She recognised Lord Krishna as her lover.
(iv) Surdas was her preceptor.

Choose the correct option

(a) Only (i) and (ii) (b) Only (i), (ii) and (iii)
(c) Only (i), (iii) and (iv) (d) Only (i), (ii) and (iv)

25. Which one of the following pairs is correctly matched ? **CBSE 2024**

	Saints		Their Region
(a)	Kabirdas	—	Karnataka
(b)	Mirabai	—	Rajasthan
(c)	Basavanna	—	Assam
(d)	Shankaradeva	—	Uttar Pradesh

26. Which one of the following pairs is correctly matched? **CBSE 2024**

	Sufi teachers		Location of Dargah
(a)	Shaikh Moinuddin Chishti	—	Ajodhan (Pakistan)
(b)	Khwaja Qutubuddin Bakhtiyar Kaki	—	Agra
(c)	Shaikh Nizamuddin Auliya	—	Delhi
(d)	Shaikh Fariduddin Ganj-i-Shakar	—	Ajmer

27. Arranged them in chronological order.

(i) Sambandar (ii) Ramanujacharya
(iii) Basavanna (iv) Sri Chaitanya

Codes

(a) (i), (iv), (iii), (iv) (b) (i), (ii), (iii), (iv)
(c) (iv), (i), (ii), (iii) (d) (iv), (ii), (iii), (i)

28. Find out the correct chronological order of 'The Chishti *Silsila*' from the following options. **CBSE SQP 2022**

(i) Shaikh Nizamuddin Auliya
(ii) Shaikh Fariduddin Ganj-i Shakar
(iii) Shaikh Nasiruddin Chiragh-i Delhi
(iv) Shaikh Muinuddin Sijzi

Codes

(a) (i), (ii), (iii), (iv) (b) (ii), (iii), (iv), (i)
(c) (iii), (ii), (i), (iv) (d) (iv), (ii), (i), (iii)

29. Arranged them in chronological order.

(i) Kabir (ii) Mirabai
(iii) Guru Nanak (iv) Shankaradeva

Codes

(a) (i), (iii), (ii), (iv) (b) (i), (ii), (iii), (iv)
(c) (iv), (iii), (i), (ii) (d) (iii), (ii), (i), (iv)

30. Identify the name of a woman devotee of early Bhakti tradition with the help of information given below. **CBSE 2024**

- She was a devotee of Lord Shiva.
- She adopted a path of extreme asceticism to attain her goal.

(a) Karraikal Ammaiyar (b) Mirabai
(c) Andal (d) Muktabai

31. Identify the Sufi saint with the help of following information. **Compartment 2024**

- His dargah is in Delhi.
- Amir Khusrau was his disciple

(a) Shaikh Muinuddin Chishti
(b) Khwaja Qutbuddin Bakhtiyar Kaki
(c) Shaikh Fariduddin Ganj-i Shakar
(d) Shaikh Nizamuddin Auliya

32. Identify the disciple of Shaikh Nizamuddin Auliya with the help of the following information. **CBSE 2024**

- He was a great poet and musician of medieval period.
- He gave a unique form to Chishti sama.
- He introduced qawwali.

(a) Baba Farid
(b) Data Ganj Bakhsh
(c) Amir Khusrau
(d) Ziyauddin Barani

33. Read the following information carefully and choose the correct location for this dargah from the given options. **CBSE 2024**

(i) It is a dargah of Shaikh Salim Chishti.
(ii) Akbar visited this dargah many times.

Options

(a) Ajmer (b) Delhi
(c) Agra (d) Fatehpur Sikri

34. **Identify the religious saint with the help of following information**

(i) He was raised by a poor Muslim family.

(ii) He was introduced into bhakti by a *guru* named Ramananda.

(iii) Some of his poems are composed in the *sant bhasha*.

(a) Guru Tegh Bahadur (b) Kabir
(c) Shaikh Salim Chishti (d) Baba Farid

35. **Identify and name the preceptor or Guru of the Sikh community whose works and contributions are given below.**

- He laid the foundation of the Khalsa Panth.
- He bestowed the Sikhs with five distinct symbols.
- He consolidated the community as a socio-religious and military force.
- He compiled the compositions of the ninth guru, Guru Tegh Bahadur in *Guru Granth Sahib.*

Options

(a) Guru Gobind Singh (b) Guru Tegh Bahadur
(c) Baba Farid (d) Kabir

36. **Read the following information given below carefully.**

Identify and name the devotee of *Saguna* Bhakti.

- She was Rajput princess from Merta in Marwar.
- She was married against her wishes to a prince of the Sisodia clan of Mewar.
- She defied her husband and did not submit to the traditional role of a wife and mother.
- She considered Lord Krishna as her lover.

Options

(a) Mirabai (b) Kabir
(c) Guru nanak (d) Andal

37. **Complete the following with the correct option regarding the saints and their respective groups.**
Tondaradippodi: Alvar :: Appar : ....

(a) Nayanar (b) Sufi
(c) Chishti (d) Virashaiva

38. **Complete the following with the correct option regarding the saints and their respective groups.**

Shaikh Muinuddin Sijzi: Ajmer :: Shaikh Nizamuddin Auliya: ....

(a) Kerala (b) Delhi
(c) Ajodhan (Pakistan) (d) Sind

Assertion-Reason

39. **Assertion** (A) Both Nayanars and Alvars were revered by the Vella peasants.
Reason (R) Earliest Bhakti movements were led by the Alvars and Nayanars.

Codes

(a) Both A and R are true and R is the correct explanation of A
(b) Both A and R are true, but R is not the correct explanation of A
(c) A is true, but R is false
(d) A is false, but R is true

40. **Assertion** (A) One of the major themes in Tamil Bhakti hymns is the poet's opposition to Buddhism and Jainism.

Reason (R) It was due to competition between members of other religious traditions for royal patronage.

Codes

(a) Both A and R are true and R is the correct explanation of A
(b) Both A and R are true but R is not the correct explanation of A
(c) A is true but R is false
(d) A is false but R is true

41. **Assertion** (A) The twelfth-century north India saw a rise of religious leaders who did not particularly belong to the orthodox Brahminical backgrounds.

Reason (R) People began valuing the sermons of sages who belonged to the prospering artisans and trading communities of the time.

Codes

(a) Both A and R are true and R is the correct explanation of A
(b) Both A and R are true but R is not the correct explanation of A
(c) A is true but R is false (d) A is false but R is true

42. **Assertion** (A) Lingayats did not practise funerary rites.
Reason (R) Lingayats believed that on death the devotee will be united with Shiva and will not return to this world.

Codes

(a) Both A and R are true and R is the correct explanation of A
(b) Both A and R are true, but R is not the correct explanation of A
(c) A is true, but R is false (d) A is false, but R is true

Match the Following

43.

	List I		List II
A.	There is one God	1.	*Hajj*
B.	Protected non-muslims under Islamic rule	2.	*Ulma*
C.	Scholars of Islamic law and teachings.	3.	*Zimmi*
D.	Performing the pilgrimage to Mecca	4.	*Allah*

Codes

	A	B	C	D		A	B	C	D
(a)	1	3	2	4	(b)	2	4	1	3
(c)	4	3	2	1	(d)	3	1	2	4

44.

List I	List II
A. Shahada	1. Offering prayers
B. Salat	2. Messenger
C. Zakat	3. Fasting
D. Sawm	4. Giving alms

Codes

	A	B	C	D		A	B	C	D
(a)	2	3	4	1	(b)	1	2	3	4
(c)	4	3	2	1	(d)	2	1	4	3

45.

List I	List II
A. Pilgrimage	1. Hospice
B. Barakat	2. Tomb-shrine
C. *Khanqah*	3. *Ziyarat*
D. *Dargah*	4. Sufi's spiritual grace

Codes

	A	B	C	D		A	B	C	D
(a)	1	2	3	4	(b)	2	1	4	3
(c)	3	4	1	2	(d)	1	3	4	2

46.

List I	List II
A. Guru Nanak	1. Assam
B. Kabir	2. Marwar
C. Shankaradeva	3. Nankana Sahib
D. Mirabai	4. Varanasi

Codes

	A	B	C	D		A	B	C	D
(a)	3	2	1	4	(b)	3	4	1	2
(c)	2	3	1	4	(d)	1	2	4	3

47.

List I	List II
A. Conversations of sufi saints	1. *Tazkiras*
B. Written collections of letters by sufi masters	2. *Malfuzat*
C. To mention and memorialise biographical accounts of saints	3. *Maktubat*

Codes

	A	B	C		A	B	C
(a)	2	3	1	(b)	1	3	2
(c)	3	2	1	(d)	1	2	3

Picture Based Questions

48. This picture is one of the most striking example of

(a) Nayanar bhakti movement
(b) Lingayat sect
(c) Integration of cults
(d) Alvar bhakti movement

49. Identify the sculpture given in the image below.

(a) A Buddhist goddess Marich
(b) A Nayanar saint Appar
(c) Karaikkal Ammaiyar
(d) Mirabai

50. Shiva in this image, through his left leg is crushing

(a) the demons of ignorance
(b) all humanity
(c) the demon of enmity among all.
(d) All of the above

51. What can be inferred by the postures of Shaikh Nizamuddin Auliya and Amir Khusrau in the image below?

(a) Amir Khusrau is the *murid* (disciple), while the Shaikh Nizamuddin Auliya is the *pir*.

(b) Amir Khusrau is seeking spiritual grace (*barakat*) from the Shaikh.

(c) Amir Khusrau is evoking the presence of his *pir* by creating a *'rama'* or performance of mystical music.

(d) All of the above

52. Identify the picture.

(a) Atiya Mosque

(b) Shah Hamadon Mosque

(c) Dargah of Shaikh Bahauddin Zakaiya Multan

(d) A Mosque in Kerala

Answers

1. (b) *Saguna* and *Nirguna*
2. (a) Tamil Veda
3. (b) Andal
4. (a) Parantaka I
5. (b) Lingayats
6. (a) Kalachuri ruler
7. (a) Khojahs
8. (d) Shaikh Nizamuddin Auliya
9. (b) Guru Arjan Dev ji
10. (c) Guru Gobind Singh
11. (a) *Malfuzat*
12. (d) *Maktubat*
13. (d) Women and people from lower castes were acknowledged and accommodated.
14. (d) Seeking simple connection with the divine
15. (b) Andal was a woman Nayanar, she incorporated the prevailing caste system in the society.
16. (a) It means 'heroes of Shiva'.
17. (a) This tradition emerged in Karnataka.
18. (d) Amir Khusran was the prominent one from this sect.
19. (d) Both did not appeal only to the higher ranks of the society.
20. (b) Ten *avtars* are recognised within this tradition.
21. (c) (i), (ii) and (iv)
22. (a) (i), (ii) and (iii)
23. (b) (iii) and (iv)
24. (b) Only (i), (ii) and (iii)
25. (b) Mirabai–Rajasthan
26. (c) Shaikh Nizamuddin Auliya–Delhi
27. (b) (i), (ii), (iii), (iv)
28. (d) (iv), (ii), (i), (iii)
29. (a) (i), (iii), (ii), (iv)
30. (a) Karraikal Ammaiyar
31. (d) Shaikh Nizamuddin Auliya
32. (c) Amir Khusrau
33. (a) Ajmer
34. (b) Kabir
35. (a) Guru Gobind Singh
36. (a) Mirabai
37. (a) Nayanar
38. (b) Delhi
39. (b) Both A and R are true, but R is not the correct explanation of A
40. (a) Both A and R are true and R is the correct explanation of A
41. (a) Both A and R are true and R is the correct explanation of A
42. (a) Both A and R are true and R is the correct explanation of A
43. (c)
44. (d)
45. (c)
46. (b)
47. (a)
48. (c) Integration of cults
49. (a) A Buddhist goddess Marich
50. (a) the demons of ignorance
51. (d) All of the above
52. (a) Atiya Mosque

Subjective Questions

Short Answer Type Questions

1. What was the meaning of the terms "great" and "little" traditions that Robert Redfield coined in the 20th century? Why do historic scholars use quotation marks while referring to these terms?

Ans. Robert Redfield found that the peasants observed rituals and customs that emerged from dominant social categories, which he referred to as the great traditions. The peasants also practiced local traditions that do not correspond with those of great traditions, which were coined as the little traditions by Robert.

Historic scholars use quotation marks while referring to these terms because it is the only way to indicate that the words great and little do not signify the hierarchy suggested by them.

2. State three ways in which the Alvars and Nayanars created social change.

Ans. The Alvars and Nayanars brought about social changes in the following ways

- **Challenging the Caste System** They came from diverse backgrounds, including lower castes, and emphasised devotion over social status, promoting a more inclusive society.
- **Promoting Gender Equality** Female saints like Andal and Karaikkal Ammaiyar played a significant role, challenging patriarchal norms through their devotion and compositions.
- **Integrating Local Practices** They popularised temple rituals and hymns, making temples and shrines central to social and religious life, and integrated local customs into religious practices.

3. Explain the ideas of Alvars and Nayanars. **CBSE 2024**

Ans. The Alvars, devoted to Vishnu, and the Nayanars, devoted to Shiva, were key figures in the early Bhakti movement around the sixth century. They travelled, singing hymns in Tamil, and identified sacred shrines, leading to the establishment of temples and pilgrimage centers. Their hymns became central to temple rituals. The Alvars and Nayanars challenged the caste system, as their followers came from diverse social backgrounds. Their compositions were considered as significant as the Vedas.

Women like Andal and Karaikkal Ammaiyar, who composed devotional hymns, also played a significant role in challenging patriarchal norms.

4. Discuss the importance of women devotees during bhakti period.

Ans. Women devotees played a significant role during the Bhakti period, with several becoming revered poet-saints who challenged social norms.

For example, Andal, a Tamil Alvar, composed passionate hymns expressing her devotion to Vishnu, viewing herself as his beloved. Her poetry continues to be celebrated in temple rituals. Another prominent figure, Karaikkal Ammaiyar, was a Shaiva devotee known for her intense asceticism and spiritual songs.

These women not only contributed to devotional literature but also defied traditional gender roles, as they renounced family obligations yet remained outside formal monastic orders, challenging patriarchal norms through their devotion and literary works.

5. Around the fourteenth century, religious leaders who did not function within the orthodox Brahmanical framework, were gaining ground. Justify the statement. **Competency Based Que**

Ans. Around the fourteenth century, religious leaders who did not function within the orthodox Brahmanical framework, were gaining ground which included the Naths, Jogis and Siddhas. Many of these leaders came from artisanal groups, including weavers. They were becoming increasingly important with the development of organised craft production. There was a rise in demand for such production with the emergence of new urban centres, and long-distance trade with Central Asia and West Asia. Many of these new religious leaders questioned the authority of the Vedas, and expressed themselves in languages spoken by ordinary people. However, in spite of their popularity these religious leaders could not win the support of the ruling elites.

6. "The Lingayats challenged the idea of caste and the 'pollution' attributed to certain groups by Brahmanas." Critically examine the statement. **Competency Based Que**

Ans. The Lingayats challenged the idea of caste and the pollution attributed to certain groups by Brahmanas. They also questioned the theory of rebirth.

Some practices like post-puberty marriage and the remarriage of widows which were disapproved in the Dharmashastras, were encouraged by the Lingayats. Lingayats also believed that devotee will be united with Shiva and will not return to this world after the death. Thus, they do not practice funeral practices like cremation as per Dharmashastras and instead they ceremonially bury their dead.

7. Explain the major features of Virashaiva tradition. CBSE 2024

Ans. The major features of Virashaiva traditions were

- The Virashaivas or Lingayats worship Shiva in his *linga* form, often wearing a small *linga* in a silver case over the left shoulder.
- Respected Lingayat saints are known as jangamas or wandering monks.
- Lingayats believe in unity with Shiva after death, rejecting cremation for ceremonial burial.
- They refuse caste norms and Brahmanical concepts like rebirth, attracting marginalised individuals.
- Lingayats endorse practices like post-puberty marriage and widow remarriage, diverging from traditional Dharmashastras.

8. One of the major themes in Tamil bhakti hymns is the poets' opposition to Buddhism and Jainism. Discuss. Competency Based Que

Ans. One of the major themes in Tamil bhakti hymns is the poets' opposition to Buddhism and Jainism. This has been primarily found in the compositions of the Nayanars. Historians have explained this hostility by suggesting that it was due to competition between members of other religious traditions for royal patronage. There has been evidence of powerful Chola rulers (ninth to thirteenth centuries) supporting Brahmanical and bhakti traditions, making land grants and constructing temples for Vishnu and Shiva. Some of the most magnificent Shiva temples at Chidambaram, Thanjavur and Gangaikondacholapuram, were constructed under the patronage of Chola rulers.

9. Explain the features of Islamic religion which contributed to its spread through the subcontinent.

Ans. The features of Islamic religion which contributed to its spread through the sub-continent are

- The development of Islam were not confined to ruling elites. They spread to far and wide amongst different social groups–peasants, artisans, warriors, merchants, etc.
- All those who adopted Islam also accepted the five 'pillars' of the faith which include

(i) There is one God, Allah and Prophet Muhammad is his messenger (*shahada*).

(ii) Offering prayers five times a day (namaz/salat).

(iii) Giving alms (*zakat*).

(iv) Fasting during the month of Ramzan (*sawm*).

(v) Performing the pilgrimage to Mecca (*hajj*).

- Arab Muslim traders who settled along the Malabar coast adopted the local language. They also adopted local customs such as matriliny and matrilocal residence.
- Universal practices were changed with diversities in practices derived from sectarian groups like Sunni, Shi'a and from the influence of local customary practices of converting people from different social environments.

10. Mention any two universal architectural features of the mosque. CBSE Diksha

Ans. Two universal architectural features of the mosque are

(i) Mosque is regarded as the basis of Islamic religious life. It has an open compound and pillars on all sides. The roof stands on all these pillars. In the middle of the compound, there is an artificial pond. Here, devotees can take bath before offering namaz.

(ii) Some architectural features of the mosque are their orientation towards Mecca. It is evident in the placement of the *minrab* (prayer niche) and the *minbar* (pulpit). Mosque blends a universal faith with local traditions. In Kerala, we find the shikara like roof and in Bangladesh, we find dome like roof. In Kashmir, Shah Hamadan mosque is the best example of Kashmiri wooden architecture, decorated with paper mache.

11. Rulers such as the Mughals came to regard themselves as emperors of not just Muslims but of all peoples. Discuss. Competency Based Que

Ans. Rulers such as the Mughals came to regard themselves as emperor of not just Muslims but of all peoples. This is evident from the adoption of a fairly flexible policy by the rulers towards their subjects. For example, many rulers gave land grants and granted tax relief to Hindu, Jaina, Zoroastrian, Christian and Jewish religious institutions. They also expressed respect and devotion towards non-Muslim religious leaders. These grants were made by several Mughal rulers, including Akbar and Aurangzeb.

12. "Sufism evolved as a reaction to the growing materialism of the caliphate as a religious and political institution." Elucidate Competency Based Que

Ans. In the early centuries of Islam, a group of religious-minded people called sufis protested against the growing materialism of the Caliphate. They were critical of the orthodox definitions and scholastic methods of interpreting the Qur'an and Sunna (traditions of the prophet) adopted by theologians.

Instead, they laid emphasis on seeking salvation through intense devotion and love for God. They followed Prophet Mohammad whom they regarded as a perfect human being.

13. Discuss in brief about the Sufi poetry and their compositions.

Ans. A different type of Sufi poetry was composed in and around the town of Bijapur, Karnataka. These were short poems in Dakhani (a form of Urdu) attributed to Chishti sufis who lived in this region during the seventeenth and eighteenth centuries. These poems were sung by women while performing household tasks.

Apart from these *lurinama* or lullabies and *shadinama* or wedding songs were other forms of compositions. The sufis of Karnataka are supposed to have been inspired by the existing bhakti tradition of the Kannada Vachanas of the Lingayats.

14. Write a brief note on Chishti *khanqah*.

Ans. The *khanqah* was the centre of social life. Shaikh Nizamuddin's *Khanqah* was on the banks of the river Yamuna in Ghiyaspur, on the outskirts of the city of Delhi. It had many small rooms and a big hall called *jama'at khana*, where the inmates and visitors lived and prayed.

The inmates included family members of the *shaikh*, his attendants and disciples. The *shaikh* lived in a small room on the roof of the hall where he met visitors in the morning and evening. The courtyard was surrounded by a veranda and a boundary wall was present around the complex.

15. (a) **'The khanqah built by Shaikh Nizamuddin was 'the centre of social life'. Justify this statement.**

Competency Based Que

(b) **List two initiatives that the Shaikh Nizamuddin's *khanqah* undertook to help the community.**

Ans. (a) The *khanqah* built by Shaikh Nizamuddin was 'the centre of social life' as

- People from various walks of life came to seek advice and discipleship from the Shaikh in various matters.
- It was a centre for social gathering where people from all walks of life would socialise.

(b) Two initiatives that the Shaikh Nizamuddin's *khanqah* undertook to help the community were

(i) During the Mongol invasion, the *khanqah* acted as a place of refuge to the local people.

(ii) Open *langars* were organised free of cost to all the people in need.

16. 'Kabir is known as one of the saints whose philosophy has greatly influenced the bhakti movement.' Justify the statement with suitable points.

Competency Based Que, CBSE 2023

Ans. Kabir is one of the most important examples of a poet-saint. His philosophy has greatly influenced the bhakti movement as in the following ways

- He coordinated the Hinduism and Islam by giving a universal path which could be followed by both Hindus and Muslims.
- He composed poems in a clear and simple style resonating the admire for guru. Being an illiterate, he had written his poems in Hindi mixing with Awadhi, Braj and Bhojpuri languages.
- He had given the people an authentic fact about what is the religion of human beings that one should have. This has helped the common people to understand his message very easily.

17. Kabir's work reflected elements of various religions and traditions. Support the assertion that Kabir drew from the traditions of varied religions for his art.

Competency Based Que

Ans. Kabir drew from the traditions of varied religions for his art. This assertion can be supported by the following points

- Kabir's verses have been compiled in three distinct but overlapping traditions.
- Kabir's poems have survived in several languages and dialects.
- Kabir used terms drawn from Islam such as Allah, Pir and Hazrat as well as Hindu terms drawn from Vedantic traditions such as Atman, Brahman, etc.

18. Describe the teachings of Guru Nanak Dev ji emphasising his philosophy of oneness. **CBSE 2024**

Ans. The teachings of Guru Nanak Dev Ji emphasise his philosophy of oneness and a simple, direct connection to the Divine. His teachings are discussed below

- Guru Nanak believed in the oneness of God, whom he referred to as 'Rab'. This God was beyond gender and form, and cannot be limited by rituals or external practices.
- Guru Nanak rejected the rituals and practices of both Hinduism and Islam, such as sacrifices, image worship, and austerities. He opposed the focus on external practices and instead emphasised inner devotion.
- Guru Nanak expressed his spiritual ideas through hymns, called 'shabad', which were sung in various ragas. These hymns conveyed his teachings and the importance of remembering and repeating the Divine Name.
- He organised his followers into a community and established congregational worship, where collective recitation of hymns became a central practice (sangat).

19. Who was the instructor of Mirabai? How did she challenge the norms of society?

Ans. Mirabai's instructor was Raidas, a leather worker. Mirabai (c. fifteenth – sixteenth century) was the best known woman poet within the bhakti tradition. She was a Rajput princess from Merta in Marwar who was married against her wishes to a prince of the Sisodia clan of Mewar in Rajasthan. She opposed her husband and did not accept the traditional role of wife and mother. She instead, recognised Krishna who was the *avatar* of Vishnu, as her lover. After leaving his husband's palace she lived as a wandering saint and composed songs.

She did not form a sect or had group of followers, but she was recognised as a source of inspiration for many centuries. Both women and men sing her songs, especially those who are poor and considered low caste in Gujarat and Rajasthan.

20. Examine the impact of Bhakti and Sufi poetry on the development of regional languages and literature. CBSE SQP 2024

Ans. The impact of Bhakti and Sufi poetry on the development of regional languages and literature are as follows

- Bhakti and Sufi poetry profoundly influenced regional languages and literature by promoting the use of vernacular languages in devotional and mystical expression.
- The Tamil Bhakti tradition, exemplified by the Nayanar and Alvar poets, enriched Tamil literature with hymns like Tevaram and Nalayira Divya Prabandham.
- Similarly, Sufi poets, writing in Persian and local languages, expressed deep mystical love and spiritual need, enriching regional literature and promoting cultural and linguistic exchange.

21. Examine how music and devotional songs in Bhakti and Sufi traditions serve spiritual expression and community unity. CBSE SQP 2024

Ans. Music and devotional songs in Bhakti and Sufi traditions serve spiritual expression and community unity in the following ways

- **Spiritual Expression** Bhakti and Sufi traditions use music and devotional songs to express deep spiritual feelings and connect with the divine. The Tamil Shaiva hymns of Appar, Sambandar, and Sundarar, gathered in the Tevaram, show how music deepens the devotional experience.
- **Community Unity** Royal patronage in Tamil temples helped standardise and popularise Shaiva hymns, fostering communal worship and unity.
- **Mystical Practices** Sufi ziyarat uses music, dance, and mystical chants by qawwals to create divine ecstasy, strengthening community bonds and spiritual connection.

Long Answer Type Questions

1. Discuss about the Tantric worship. What were the different beliefs and practices that were emerged during this bhakti period? What were the conflicts in belief system during bhakti period ?

Ans. Tantric practices were the forms of worship that were often associated with the goddess. Tantric practices were prevalent in various parts of the subcontinent. These were open to both men and women, and practitioners did not discriminate people based on caste and class within the ritual context.

Emergence of Different Beliefs and Practices

Buddhism and Shaivism especially in the Eastern, Northern and Southern parts of the subcontinent were influenced by many of these ideas of Tantric practice.

Over the next millennium, all these divergent and even completely different beliefs and practices were classified as Hindu. In Vedic times, the main deities were *Agni*, *Indra* and *Soma* and these deities became marginal figures and rarely visible in textual and visual representations.

Conflicts in Belief System

We could see conflicts sometimes, like people who valued the Vedic traditions often condemned practices like performance of sacrifices or accurate chanting of *mantras*. People who were engaged in Tantric practices often ignored the authority of the Vedas. Even devotees protected their chosen deity like Vishnu or Shiva, as supreme. Though, the relations with other traditions like Buddhism or Jainism did not lead to open conflict, but there were tensed conditions.

Expressions of devotion ranged from the routine worship of deities within temples to extremely high love and respect where devotees attained a meditative state. This could be seen in both Vaishnava and Shaiva sects.

2. Explain the major beliefs and teachings of Chishtis during medieval India. CBSE 2025

Ans. The Chishti Sufi order played a crucial role in shaping the religious and cultural landscape of medieval India. Their teachings emphasized devotion, humility, universal brotherhood, and service to humanity, blending Islamic principles with local traditions.

Core Beliefs of the Chishtis

Universal Brotherhood and Religious Tolerance The Chishtis preached the idea of universal brotherhood, promoting love and respect for people of all faiths. Their teachings aligned with the Mughal rulers' policies of religious tolerance, as seen in the land grants and tax exemptions given to various religious institutions.

Simplicity and Renunciation of Wealth The Chishti saints followed a life of simplicity and detachment from material wealth, emphasising service to humanity over personal gain. This belief echoed broader Islamic teachings such as zakat (charity) and devotion to spiritual knowledge.

Integration of Local Cultural Expressions The Chishtis embraced local music, poetry, and languages to spread their message. Their practice of devotional singing (Sama) and poetry was similar to the ginans, the devotional songs of the Khojahs, which blended Islamic spiritual themes with indigenous traditions.

Teachings of the Chishtis

Love and Compassion for All The Chishtis emphasised compassion, selfless service, and love for humanity, encouraging their followers to serve people regardless of religion or social status.

Spiritual Devotion Through Music and Poetry The order promoted Sama (devotional music gatherings) as a way to experience divine love and attain spiritual closeness. They believed that music had the power to elevate the soul and deepen devotion.

Charity and Helping the Needy Inspired by Islamic principles of charity, the Chishtis encouraged feeding the poor, caring for the sick, and supporting those in need, making service a central aspect of their spiritual path.

3. Identify the relationship of the Alvars and Nayanars of Tamil Nadu with the state from the 8th to the 18th century. **CBSE Diksha**

Or **Elucidate how Alvars and Nayanars established their relations with the states.** **CBSE 2024**

Ans. The relationship of the Alvars and Nayanars of Tamil Nadu with the state is discussed below

- The Alvars (literally, those who were immersed in devotion to Vishnu) and Nayanars (who were devotees of Shiva) preached their message in Tamil. During their travel they identified certain shrines as abodes of their chosen deities and these were developed as centres of pilgrimage. One of the major themes in Tamil bhakti hymns was the opposition to Buddhism and Jainism. The main reason for this opposition was competition between members of other religious traditions for royal patronage.
- The Chola rulers (ninth to thirteenth centuries) supported Brahmanical and Bhakti traditions, making land grants and constructing temples for Vishnu and Shiva. The Chola rulers constructed many Shiva temples e.g. Chidambram, Thanjavur and Gangaikandacholapuram. They done this to proclaim their own power and status. This was also the period when some of the most spectacular representations of Shiva in bronze scuplture were produced.
- Both Nayanars and Alvars were revered (admire) by the Vellala peasants. Rulers also tried to win their support as well.

Thus, we can say that the Chola rulers had intimate relations with the both Alvars and Nayanars as they had much honour and status in the society.

4. Explain the causes of the growth of Sufism and also explain the Sufis relations with the state. **CBSE 2024**

Ans. Growth of Sufism

Sufism grew due to its reaction against materialism, dogmatic theology, and its emphasis on personal experience of God.

Early Sufis were unhappy with the growing focus on material wealth in the Islamic world. They believed it distracted from the true spiritual essence of Islam and chose asceticism and mysticism as a way to protest against this corruption.

Sufis were not happy with the strict, academic ways theologians interpreted the Qur'an and teachings of the Prophet. Instead, they focused on a personal, spiritual understanding of religion, seeking a direct connection with God.

Sufis believed salvation came from deep devotion and love for God, following the example of Prophet Muhammad. This personal, heartfelt approach to religion attracted many followers who wanted a closer relationship with God.

By the 11th century, Sufism became more organised with its own literature and practices. Sufis started forming communities around khanqahs (spiritual centers) where people gathered for learning and worship.

Sufis' Relations with the State

- Sufis, especially in the Chishti tradition, lived simply and avoided getting involved in politics. However, they still interacted with the state and were not fully isolated from political power.
- Sufis accepted donations from rulers and elites, which helped support their spiritual centers (khanqahs). These donations included money, land, and tax-free land (inam), as well as charitable trusts (auqaf) set up by the state.
- Kings valued Sufis' moral authority and popularity as it helped legitimise their rule and win the support of the people. In return, Sufis received resources to continue their spiritual practices.
- Sufis were believed to have special spiritual power from God, not based on academic knowledge or laws. Kings often asked Sufis to pray for them, believing their prayers could improve their lives and reigns.
- Some kings wanted to be buried near famous Sufi tombs, as they believed this would bring blessings and divine favor, strengthening the bond between political power and Sufism.
- Although Sufis generally supported rulers, there were disagreements, especially over rituals and authority. Both kings and Sufis tried to assert their power through rituals like prostration and high titles for Sufi leaders (e.g., Sultan-ul-Mashaikh for Nizamuddin Auliya).

These instances reflected the complex and sometimes contentious relationship between the Sufi order and political authority.

5. Explain the teachings of Kabir. How did he describe the Ultimate Reality through his poems?

Or **Explain the significance of Kabir's poems and the traditions he drew to describe the Ultimate Reality.** **CBSE Diksha**

Ans. Kabir is one of the most important examples of a poet-saint. He used the range of traditions to describe the Ultimate Reality.

In Islam, he described the ultimate Reality as Allah, *Khuda, Hazrat* and Pir. He also used terms from Vedantic traditions such as, *alakh* (the unseen), *nirakar* (formless), *Brahman*, Atman, etc.

Other spiritual ideas such as *shabda* (sound) or *shunya* (emptiness) were from yogic traditions.

Diverse and sometimes opposing ideas were expressed in his poems. Some poems took Islamic ideas and used the concepts like belief in one God and the destruction of religious images to attack Hindu's belief in many Gods and idol worship. Some other poems used the sufi concepts of *zikr* and *ishq* (love) to express the Hindu practice of *nam-simaran* (remembrance of God's name). Kabir's poems have survived in different languages and different forms of languages, and some are composed in the special language of *nirguna* poets, the *sant bhasha*. Other compositions known as *ulatbansi* (upside-down sayings), are written in a form in which everyday meanings are reversed.

These show the difficulties of getting the character of the Ultimate Reality in words and expressions such as 'the lotus which blooms without flower' or the 'fire raging in the ocean' show a sense of Kabir's spiritual experiences.

The rich collection of written texts also signifies that Kabir was a source of inspiration. Kabir's ideas might have formed through discussion and debate with the traditions of Sufis and Yogis in the region of Awadh.

6. Explain the main beliefs and teachings of Guru Nanak Dev. **CBSE 2025**

Ans. Guru Nanak Dev's beliefs and teachings form the core of Sikhism, emphasizing nirguna bhakti-devotion to a formless and genderless Divine. He rejected external rituals and promoted a simple, direct connection with God through remembrance and devotion.

Beliefs of Guru Nanak Dev

Devotion to a Formless Divine Guru Nanak emphasized nirguna bhakti, which means devotion to a formless, omnipresent God. He opposed idol worship, ritual sacrifices, and austerities, considering them unnecessary for spiritual enlightenment.

Rejection of Rituals and Religious Formalities He criticised ritual baths, scriptural dogma, and priestly dominance, advocating for personal devotion and ethical living over religious formalities.

Singing Hymns (Shabad Kirtan) as Worship Guru Nanak conveyed his teachings through shabads (hymns), which he sang in different ragas, accompanied by his attendant Mardana on the rabab. This method emphasized music and poetry as a means of spiritual connection.

Formation of a Devotional Community He organised his followers into a spiritual community (Sangat), where people gathered to recite, meditate, and worship collectively. This practice promoted unity, social equality, and devotion.

Teachings of Guru Nanak Dev

Succession and Preservation of Teachings Guru Nanak established a lineage of successors, appointing Guru Angad to continue his mission. This tradition ensured the preservation of Sikh teachings for nearly 200 years.

Compilation of Hymns in the Adi Granth Sahib The fifth Guru, Guru Arjan, compiled Guru Nanak's hymns along with those of other saints like Kabir, Ravidas, and Baba Farid into the Adi Granth Sahib, laying a strong scriptural foundation for Sikhism.

Formation of the Khalsa and Sikh Identity In the seventeenth century, Guru Gobind Singh included the hymns of Guru Tegh Bahadur in the Sikh scripture, renaming it the Guru Granth Sahib. He also established the Khalsa Panth and introduced five symbols (uncut hair, a dagger, a pair of shorts, a comb, and a steel bangle), strengthening the distinct identity of Sikhs.

Thus, Guru Nanak Dev's teachings emphasized devotion to a formless Divine, rejection of rituals, community worship, and spiritual equality, laying the foundation of Sikhism as a distinct religious tradition.

7. Explain how the biography of the saint poetess Mirabai has been primarily constructed. **CBSE Diksha**

Ans. The reconstruction of biographies of Mirabai has been done from the bhajans composed by her, which were transmitted orally for centuries

- From the bhajans, it has been reconstructed that she was a Rajput princess from Merta in Marwar. She was married against her wishes to a prince of the Sisodia clan of Mewar, Rajasthan.
- She refused her husband and did not agree to the traditional role of wife and mother. She recognised Krishna, the avatar of Vishnu, as her lover.
- Because of her behaviour, her in-laws tried to poison her, but she managed to escape from the palace to live as a wandering saint composing the songs of bhakti and love for Krishna. Her compositions are known for intense expressions of emotion.
- In some traditions, Mirabai has been mentioned as a disciple of Raidas, a leather worker. This indicates that she defied the norms of caste society.

- For her intense love for Krishna, she rejected the comforts of her husband's palace and accepted to wore the white robes of a widow or the saffron robe of the saint.
- Mirabai has been recognised as a source of inspiration for centuries. However, she did not attract a sect or group of followers. Her songs continue to be sung by women and men, especially those who are poor and considered "low caste" in Gujarat and Rajasthan.

Source Based Questions

Read the sources given below and answer the following questions

1. Shastras or devotion ? **Compartment 2024**

This is a verse composed by Appar, a Nayanar saint
O people who quote the law books,
Of what use are your gotra and kula ?
Just bow to Marperu's lord (Shiva who resides in Marperu in Thanjavur, Tamil Nadu) as your sole refuge.

(i) Who were the Nayanars ?
(ii) Who was considered as the sole refugee ?
(iii) Explain the views of Appar on Bhakti.

Ans. (i) The Nayanars were a group of early bhakti saints and poets who were devoted to Shiva. They lived around the 6th century and travelled from place to place, singing hymns in Tamil to praise Shiva.

(ii) In the verse composed by Appar, the Nayanar saint, Shiva (referred to as the 'lord of Marperu') is considered the sole refuge.

(iii) Appar, a Nayanar saint, expresses his views on Bhakti by emphasising that true devotion to God transcends social distinctions such as caste and religious law. In the verse, Appar advocates for surrendering to Shiva as the sole refuge, highlighting the importance of personal devotion (Bhakti) over rituals or social status.

2. A Demon

This is an excerpt from a poem by Karaikkal Ammaiyar in which she described herself
The female Pey (demoness) :
with... bulging veins,
protruding eyes, white teeth and shrunken stomach,
red haired and jutting teeth
lengthy shins extending till the ankles,
shouts and wails
while wandering in the forest.
This is the forest of Alankatu,
which is the home of our father (Shiva)
who dances... with his matted hair
thrown in all eight directions, and with cool limbs.

(i) Who is the author of this excerpt and what is it about?
(ii) How did the author describe herself in the poem?
(iii) What did author try to convey through the poem?

Ans. (i) Karaikkal Ammaiyar is the author of this excerpt. In this poem she described herself.

(ii) Karaikkal Ammaiyar in the poem described herself as a demoness having bulging veins, eyes that were popping out, white teeth, smaller stomach, red hair and teeth coming out, lengthy part of the leg below knee.

(iii) Author is trying to go against the established traditional norms where women are shown beautifully with feminine characteristics.

3. Church in Khambat

This is an excerpt from a *farman* (imperial order) issued by Akbar in 1598. Whereas, it reached our eminent and holy notice that the *padris* (fathers) of the Holy Society of Jesus wish to build a house of prayer (Church) in the city of Kambayat (Khambat, in Gujarat); therefore an exalted mandate... is being issued... that the dignitaries of the city of Kambayat should in no case stand in their way but should allow them to build a Church so that they may engage themselves in their own worship. It is necessary that the order of the Emperor should be obeyed in every way.

(i) What did the *padris* want to do? How did Akbar ensure that their desire was fulfilled?
(ii) Who guided the Muslim rulers?
(iii) How was the situation complicated in the subcontinent?

Ans. (i) The *padris* wanted to build a house of prayer i.e. Church in the city of Kambayat.
Akbar directed the officials of the city of Kambayat to not obstruct *padris* in building Church. In this way, he ensured that the desire of *padris* was fulfilled.

(ii) Muslim rulers were guided by *ulama*. They made sure that they followed *shari'a*. But some rulers also followed Sufi saints.

(iii) The situation became complicated because most of the population was non-Muslim in the sub-continent. The Mughal ruler adapted themselves to the situation by honouring the wishes of non-Muslim.

4. The Story of Data Ganj Bakhsh

In 1039 Abu'l Hasan al Hujwiri, a native of Hujwir near Ghazni in Afghanistan, was forced to cross the Indus as a captive of the invading Turkish army. He settled in Lahore and wrote a book in Persian called the *Kashf-ul-Mahjub* (Unveiling of the Veiled) to explain the meaning of *tasawwuf*, and those who practised it, that is, the sufi.
Hujwiri died in 1073 and was buried in Lahore. The grandson of Sultan Mahmud of Ghazni constructed a

tomb over his grave, and this tomb-shrine became a site of pilgrimage for his devotees, especially on his death anniversary. Even today Hujwiri is revered as Data Ganj Bakhsh or "Giver who bestows treasures" and his mausoleum is called Data Darbar or 'Court of the Giver'.

(i) Who is Abu'l Hasan al Hujwiri? Where did Abu'l Hasan settle and what was his book's name?

(ii) When did Abu'l Hasan die? Who built Abu'l Hasan's tomb?

(iii) How is Abu'l Hasan revered even today?

Ans. (i) Abu'l Hasan al Hujwiri was a native of Hujwir near Ghazni in Afghanistan. Abu'l Hasan settled in Lahore and wrote a book in Persian called the *Kashf-ul-Mahjub* to explain the meaning of *tasawwuf.*

(ii) Abu'l Hasan al Hujwiri died in 1073 and was buried in Lahore. The grandson of Sultan Mahmud of Ghazni constructed a tomb over his grave, and this tomb-shrine became a site of pilgrimage for his devotees, especially on his death anniversary.

(iii) Even today Abu'l Hasan Hujwiri is revered as Data Ganj Bakhsh or 'Giver who bestows treasures' and his mausoleum is called Data Darbar or 'Court of the Giver'.

5. The One Lord

Here is a composition attributed to Kabir :
Tell me, brother, how can there be
No one lord of the world but two?
Who led you so astray?
God is called by many names : Names like Allah, Ram, Karim, Keshav, Hari and Hazrat.
Gold may be shaped into rings and bangles.
Isn't it gold all the same?
Distinctions are only in words that we invent.
Kabir says, they are both mistaken.
Neither can find the only Ram. One kills the goat, the other cows.
They waste their lives in disputation.

(i) Name any two scriptures, in which verses, ascribed to Kabir, have been complied.

(ii) How did Kabir describe the 'Ultimate Reality'?

(iii) Explain the arguments given by Kabir against the lords of the world of different communities.

Or **(i) How does Kabir's philosophy contribute to a broader understanding of spiritualism ?** CBSE 2024

(ii) How has Kabir advocated an inclusive and compassionate view of humanity ? CBSE 2024

(iii) What does Kabir criticise in his composition "The One Lord"?

Ans. (i) *Kabir Bijak* and *Kabir Granthavali* are the two scriptures that were ascribed to Kabir.

(ii) In Islam, he described the Ultimate Reality as *Allah, Khuda, Hazrat* and *Pir.* He also used terms from Vedantic traditions such as *alakh* (the unseen), *nirakar* (formless), Brahman, Atman, etc. Other spiritual ideas such as *shabda* (sound) or *shunya* (emptiness) were from yogic traditions.

(iii) Kabir argued that just like gold is shaped into rings and bangles and the gold being same, similarly God is called by different names like Allah, Ram, Karim, Keshav, Hari and Hazrat.

Or (i) Kabir's philosophy contributes to spiritualism by emphasising the oneness of God, no matter what name people use for him (e.g., Allah, Ram, Karim). He believes that all these names refer to the same Divine. Kabir rejects religious divisions and argues that differences between religions are created by humans.

(ii) Kabir teaches that all people are united by the same God, no matter their religion. He believes God is one, called by different names like Allah, Ram, or Hari, and these differences are just human-made labels. He compares these names to gold in different shapes, showing that everyone is the same at heart. Kabir's message promotes unity, compassion, and understanding, encouraging people to rise above religious divisions.

(iii) In "The One Lord" Kabir criticises the decision between religions. He belived God is one, called by different names and argues that people waste time fighting over religious differences instead of seeking truth.

6. Love for the Lord

This is part of a song attributed to Mirabai :
I will build a funeral pyre of sandalwood and aloe;
Light it by your own hand
When I am burned away to cinders;
Smear this ash upon your limbs.
....let flame be lost in flame.
In another verse, she sings:
What can Mewar's ruler do to me?
If God is angry, all is lost.
But what can the Rana do? CBSE SQP 2022

(i) Examine the reason of calling Mirabai as an ascetic figure.

(ii) Analyse Mirabai's relation with Mewar.

(iii) How was Mirabai unique among the poet-saints of the bhakti movement?

Ans. (i) The reason of calling Mirabai as an ascetic figure is because she lived a life of asceticism and showed absolute devotion to Krishna all her life.

(ii) Mirabai was married to crown prince of Mewar, but after few years Rana of Mewar died.

(iii) Mirabai was unique among the poet-saints of the bhakti movement owing to her socio-economic background as well as her gender. Even after being born as a princess, she opted for the life of a saint.

SELF ASSESSMENT TEST

Objective Type Questions

1. Which of the following is incorrect regarding Mirabai ?
   (i) She was married against her wishes.
   (ii) Her husband belongs to Sisodia clan of Mewar Rajasthan.
   (iii) She accepted all the comforts of her husband's palace initially.
   (iv) She was a Rajput princess.
2. Who among the following were early Bhakti saints in Tamil Nadu known for their devotion to Vishnu and Shiva, respectively?
   (a) Alvars and Nayanars
   (b) Virashaivas and Lingayats
   (c) Sufis and Yogis
   (d) Buddhists and Jains
3. Match the Following

	List I		List II
A.	Atiya Mosque	1.	Srinagar
B.	Shah Hamdam Mosque	2.	Delhi
C.	Dargah of Nizamuddin Auliya	3.	Bangladesh
D.	Dargah of Shaikh Muinuddin Chishti	4.	Ajmer

Codes

	A	B	C	D
(a)	1	2	3	4
(b)	2	4	1	3
(c)	3	1	2	4
(d)	1	3	4	2

Short Answer Type Questions

4. Analyse the significance of the integration of local deities within the Puranic framework. How did this impact regional religious practices?
5. Explain how the Alvars and Nayanars challenged the caste system. Provide examples of their practices that promoted inclusivity.
6. Comment on the role of women in the Bhakti movement. How did figures like Andal and Karaikkal Ammaiyar influence Bhakti traditions?
7. Justify the importance of the Chola dynasty's support for Bhakti traditions. How did their patronage shape the worship of Vishnu and Shiva?
8. Analyse how the architecture of mosques in the subcontinent represents a fusion of Islamic ideals with local artistic traditions.

Long Answer Type Questions

9. Discuss about Sufis and Sufism development in subcontinent. What kind of support did it get from the state and people?
10. Who are Alvars and Nayanars ? How did they influence the bhakti traditions ? What kind of changes in the society were initiated due to their preachings?

7

CHAPTER

This chapter deals with the Vijayanagara Empire which was the largest Hindu empire established in the Southern India in Medieval times. It was known for its large temples like Brihadishvara Temple.

An Imperial Capital : Vijayanagara

▼ **YOUR STUDY GOALS**

7.1 Vijayanagara
7.2 Rayas, Nayakas and Sultans
7.3 Vijayanagara : The Capital and its Surroundings
7.4 The Royal Centre of Vijayanagara
7.5 The Sacred Centre of Vijayanagara
7.6 Plotting Palaces, Temples and Bazaars

▼ **YOUR PRACTICE GOALS**

- Objective Type Questions (49 Qs ; MCQs, A-R, Matching, Picture Based)
- Subjective Questions (21 SAs, 8 LAs)
- Source Based Questions (5 Qs) Map Based Questions (2 Qs)

7.1 Vijayanagara

- Vijayanagara (city of victory) was both a city and an empire. It was founded in the fourteenth century and was ruined in the seventeenth-eighteenth centuries.
- It stretched from the river Krishna in the North to the extreme South in the peninsula during its successful days.
- People remembered it as Hampi, the name derived from a local mother Goddess, **Pampadevi**. While historians use the term Vijayanagara empire, contemporaries described it as the ***Karnataka samrajyamu***.

The Discovery of Hampi

- **Colonel Colin Mackenzie**, an engineer, antiquarian[1], surveyor and cartographer[2] discovered the ruins at Hampi in 1800 CE. He prepared the first survey map of the Hampi site.
- The initial information he collected was based on the memories of priests of the Virupaksha temple and the shrine of Pampadevi.
- In 1836 CE, epigraphists[3] started collecting many inscriptions found in the temples at Hampi. Later from 1856, photographers started to record the monuments which helped scholars to study them.

---

1 Antiquarian A person who studies or collects antiquities i.e. objects belonging to past times.

2. Cartographer A person who draws and produces maps.

3. Epigraphists The people who study and interpret ancient inscriptions.

- Historians collected all the information from these sources along with travel accounts of foreign travellers and other literature written in Telugu, Kannada, Tamil and Sanskrit to reconstruct the history of the city and the empire.

Colin Mackenzie

- Colin Mackenzie was born in 1754 CE and became a famous engineer, surveyor and cartographer.
- He was appointed as the **First Surveyor General of India** in 1815 CE and held this post till his death in 1821 CE.
- He started collecting local histories and surveying historic sites to better understand India's past and make governance of India easier.
- He believed that South India had struggled a lot due to bad management, before the South came under the gentle and kind influence of the British Government.

7.2 Rayas, Nayakas and Sultans

- According to ancient inscriptions, two brothers, **Harihara** and **Bukka** founded the Vijayanagara Empire in 1336.
- People of this empire spoke different languages and followed different religious traditions.
- In the North, the Vijayanagara kings competed with contemporary rulers, like the Sultans of the Deccan and the Gajapati[4] rulers of Orissa, for control of the fertile river valleys and the resources generated by overseas trade.
- The interaction between these states also helped in sharing of ideas, especially in the field of architecture.
- In the popular traditions of Vijayanagara, the Deccan Sultans were termed as *ashvapati*[5].
- Vijayanagar rulers borrowed concepts and building techniques and developed them further.
- Some of the areas that were made part of the empire had witnessed the development of powerful states like the Cholas in Tamil Nadu and the Hoysalas in Karnataka.

▲ *The gopuram or gateway of the Brihadishvara temple at Thanjavur*

- Rulers in these areas had provided support to develop the temples such as the **Brihadishvara temple** (Thanjavur) and the **Chennakeshvara temple** (Belur).
- The rulers of Vijayanagara, who called themselves *rayas* are also called narapati or lord of men.

Kings and Traders

- In medieval India, cavalry was crucial for warfare, making the import of horses from Arabia and Central Asia essential for rival kingdoms. This trade was initially managed by Arab traders.
- Local communities of merchants known as ***kudirai chetties*** (horse merchants) also participated in these exchanges.
- From 1498, Portuguese arrived on the West coast of the subcontinent and tried to establish trading and military stations. They had superior military technology, especially in the use of **muskets** (long guns).
- Vijayanagara Empire was known for its markets dealing in **spices, textiles** and **precious stones**.

---

4 Gajapati It means lord of elephants.
5 Ashvapati It means lord of horses.

- Trade was regarded as a status symbol in cities with wealthy populations that demanded high-value exotic goods, especially precious stones and jewellery.
- The revenue derived from trade helped in improving the prosperity of the state.

The Rise and Decline of the Empire

- The **Sangama dynasty** was the first dynasty that exercised control till 1485.
- They were replaced by the **Saluvas**, who were military commanders and remained in power till 1503. They were replaced by the Tuluvas.
- The most famous ruler of the Tuluva dynasty was **Krishnadeva Raya**.

Krishnadeva Raya

- Krishnadeva Raya's rule was known for expansion and strengthening the empire.
- During his rule, the land between the Tungabhadra and Krishna rivers (the Raichur doab) was acquired in 1512, the rulers of Orissa were brought under control in 1514, and the Sultan of Bijapur suffered severe defeats in 1520.
- Krishnadeva Raya was credited with building some fine temples and adding impressive *gopurams*[6] to many important South Indian temples.
- He founded a suburban township near Vijayanagara called **Nagalapuram**, named after his mother. He was also known for his literacy skills.
- His work on statecraft in Telugu is known as ***Amuktamalyada***.

The Rayas and the Nayakas

- Military chiefs who exercised power in the empire were known as ***nayakas***. They usually controlled forts and had armed supporters.
- They were usually accompanied by peasants seeking fertile land to settle. They usually spoke Telugu or Kannada.
- **Nayakas** accepted the authority of the kings of Vijayanagara but they often rebelled and had to be brought under control by military action.
- After the death of Krishnadeva Raya in 1529, his successors were troubled by rebellious ***nayakas***.

The Amara-Nayaka System

The **amara-nayaka** system was a major political innovation of the Vijayanagara Empire. Most of its features were derived from the ***iqta* system** of the Delhi Sultanate. They were as follows

- The *amara-nayakas* were military commanders who were given territories to govern by the *raya*.
- They collected taxes and other dues from peasants, craftspersons and traders in the area.
- They kept part of the revenue for personal use and for maintaining a required group of horses and elephants. Some of the revenue was also used for the maintenance of temples and irrigation works.
- These military groups helped the Vijayanagara kings gain control over the entire Southern peninsula.
- The *amara-nayakas* sent tribute to the king annually and personally appeared in the royal court with gifts to express their loyalty.
- Kings occasionally asserted their control over them by transferring them from one place to another.
- In the seventeenth century, many of these *nayakas* established independent kingdoms, which accelerated the collapse of the kingdom and its structure.

6 **Gopuram** It is a big gateway tower, usually decorate with carvings, at the entrance of any temple, especially in Southern India.

Vijayanagara Empire after Krishnadeva Raya

- By 1542, control of the empire shifted to the **Aravidu** ruling family, which stayed in power until the end of the seventeenth century.
- During this time, the military goals of the Vijayanagara rulers and the Deccan Sultanates caused a change in alliances, leading to an alliance of the Sultanates against Vijayanagara.
- In 1565, **Rama Raya**, the Chief Minister of Vijayanagara, fought a battle at **Rakshasi-Tangadi** also known as **Talikota**. The combined armies of Bijapur, Ahmadnagar and Golconda defeated the forces of Rama Raya.
- The victorious armies looted and destroyed the city of Vijayanagara. Within a few years, this city was totally abandoned.
- Now the focus of the empire shifted to the East where the Aravidu dynasty ruled from Penukonda and later from Chandragiri near Tirupati.

Sultans

- The armies of the Sultans of Deccan were responsible for the destruction of the city of Vijayanagara.
- Relations between the Sultans and the *rayas* were not always tensed despite their religious differences. For example, Krishnadeva Raya supported the people who claimed power in the Sultanates and took the title of establishment of the Yavana[7] kingdom.
- Similarly, the Sultan of Bijapur was involved in resolving the succession disputes in Vijayanagara after the death of Krishnadeva Raya.
- The Vijayanagara kings and the Sultanates both wanted stability, but Rama Raya's strategy of turning one Sultan against another caused the Sultans to unite and decisively defeat him.

Quick Test 1

1. When was the Vijayanagara Empire founded?
2. In which year was Hampi discovered?
3. Who was appointed as the first Surveyor General of India?
4. Who led the army of Vijayanagara in the Battle of Talikota?
5. From where the *amara-nayaka* system was derived?

7.3 Vijayanagara : The Capital and its Surroundings

- Many travellers such as, **Nicolo de Conti**, an Italian trader, **Abdur Razaaq** an ambassador sent by ruler of Persia, **Afanasii Nikitin**, a merchant from Russia, **Duarte Barbosa**, **Domingo Paes** and **Fernao Nuniz** from Portugal visited the Vijayanagara city.
- Domingo Paes described Vijayanagara as very beautiful and large as Rome. He pointed out that the city had many trees, gardens and many water channels and some lakes.
- Vijayanagara is known for its distinctive physical layout and building style.

Water Resources of Vijayanagara

- The most important feature about the location of Vijayanagara is the natural basin formed by the river Tungabhadra, flowing in North-Easterly direction.
- City was surrounded by the Granite hills through which river flow down. Embankments were built along these streams to create reservoirs of different sizes.

---

7 Yavana It is a Sanskrit word used for the Greeks and other people who entered the subcontinent from the North-West.

- This region is one of the most arid zones of the peninsula, so arrangements were made to store rainwater and transmit it to the city.
- In the fifteenth century, the most important tank was built known as **Kamalapuram tank**. The water from this tank was used both to irrigate fields and transmit to the royal centre through a channel.
- One of the most important waterworks was the **Hiriya canal**. This was built by the kings of the Sangama dynasty.
- Water for the canal was drawn from a dam across the Tungabhadra and it irrigated the cultivated valley, that separated the 'sacred centre' from the 'urban core'.

Fortifications and Roads

- The great fortress walls surrounded the city.
- **Abdur Razzaq**, an ambassador sent by the ruler of Persia to Calicut in the fifteenth century, was impressed by the fortifications of Vijayanagara and mentioned the **seven lines of forts**.
- These fortifications not only surrounded the city but also remote agricultural areas and forests. The hills surrounding the city were linked with the outermost wall.
- The large structure was slightly thinner at one end. The mortar or cementing agent were not used in the construction.
- The stone blocks were wedge shaped (thick at one end and thin at another end) which held them in place.
- The inner walls were filled with Earth and rubble, while the fortifications extended outward in a square or rectangular shape.
- Archaeologists have studied roads within the city and those leading out from it.
- Roads generally turn around through the valleys (i.e. low area of land present between hills or mountains) and avoided rocky lands.
- Some of the most important roads extended from temple gateways, and were bordered by bazaars.

Fortification of Agricultural Lands

- The fortification surrounded agricultural lands. Abdur Razzaq noted that between the first, second and the third walls, there were cultivated fields, gardens and houses.
- Domingo Paes noted different things about these three walls. According to him, from the first outer wall to the city entrance, there was a great distance in which fields existed. In these fields rice was sown. It had many gardens and much water, which comes from two lakes.
- There was evidence of agricultural land between the sacred centre and the urban core. This land was supplied with water from a canal system built on the Tungabhadra river.
- In the medieval time, armies often try to make their armies surrender by blocking food supplies.
- Rulers usually build big storage rooms inside their forts to keep grains in case of an attack.
- The Vijayanagara rulers protected the agriculture fields within the fortified walls.

The Inner Core of the Urban Complex

- Urban complex was surrounded by a second line of fortification and the royal centre was surrounded by a third line. Within this, there were major buildings which were surrounded by their own high walls.
- The well-guarded gates which were linked to major roads of the city were used to enter the fort.

Gateways

- These were unique architectural features that defined the structure of city.
- The arch on the gateway leading to the fortified settlement and dome over the gate were regarded as typical features of the architecture introduced by the Turkish Sultans.
- This style is referred as **Indo-Islamic** by art historians, because it developed through the interaction with local building practices in different regions.

▲ *A gateway in the fortification wall*

The Urban Core

- Archaeologists found little archaeological evidence of the houses of ordinary people.
- They have found fine **Chinese porcelain** (Chinaware) in some areas in the North-Eastern corner of the urban core which shows that these areas might have been occupied by rich traders.
- This area was also the Muslim residential quarter. Tombs and mosques present here have different functions but their architecture resembles the *mandapas* that were found in temples of Hampi.
- Sixteenth-century Portuguese traveller **Duarte Barbosa** described the houses of ordinary people. The houses had roofs made of straw and palm leaves, but were well built. They were arranged along long streets, organised by occupation, and had many open spaces.
- Field surveys show that the entire area was scattered with many shrines and small temples. This shows that different cults were present there, which might be supported by different communities.
- The surveys also indicate that wells, rainwater tanks, temple tanks were used as sources of water by the ordinary town people.

7.4 The Royal Centre of Vijayanagara

- The royal centre was located in the South-Western part of the settlement. It had over 60 temples. It shows that rulers valued the support of temples and cults to establish their authority, and gain approval by associating themselves with the gods and goddesses in the shrines.
- Around thirty building complexes were identified as palaces. These were relatively large structures that do not seem to be associated with ritual functions.
- The difference between these structures and temples was that the temples were constructed by using stones, while the superstructure of the secular buildings were made of materials that would decay after some time.

The Buildings in Royal Centres

- On the basis of the form of buildings and their functions, different structures were assigned their names.
- The **king's palace** was the largest building but there was no strong evidence that it was a royal residence. It had two impressive platforms, called the **audience hall** and the ***mahanavami dibba***.
- The entire complex was surrounded by high double walls with a street running between them.
- The audience hall was a high platform having slots for wooden pillars to be placed at close and regular intervals. On these pillars, a staircase was present which went to the second floor. There was no or little space between these pillars.

▲ *Interior of the audience hall at Madurai*

- ***Mahanavami dibba*** was located at one of the highest points in the city. It was a massive platform or stage rising from a base of about 11,000 sq ft to a height of 40 ft.

▲ The mahanavami dibba

▲ Carvings on the mahanavami dibba

- There was evidence that it supported a wooden building. The base of the platform was covered with relief designs or carvings.
- Rituals associated with the building probably coincided with Mahanavami. It is known as **Dussehra** in North India, **Durga Puja** in Bengal and **Navaratri** or **Mahanavami** in peninsular India. The Vijayanagara kings showed their prestige, power and control over the empire on this occasion.

Ceremonies on Occasion of Mahanavami

- Various ceremonies were performed on this occasion like
  - Worship of the image, worship of the state horse and the sacrifice of buffaloes and other animals.
  - Dances, wrestling matches, processions of highly decorated horses, elephants, chariots and soldiers.
  - Ritual presentations before the king and his guests by the chief *nayakas* and subordinate kings.
- The ceremonies had deep symbolic meanings. On the last day of the festival, the king inspected his army and the armies of the *nayakas* in a grand ceremony in an open field. The *nayakas* brought rich gifts for the king on this occasion.

Other Buildings in the Royal Centre

▲ A photograph of the Lotus Mahal

The Lotus Mahal

- The Lotus Mahal, named by British travellers in the nineteenth century, was one of the most beautiful buildings in the royal centre.
- A map drawn by Mackenzie suggested that it might have been a **council chamber**, a place where the king met his advisers.

Hazara Rama Temple

- It was one of the grandest temples which might have been used only by the king and his family.
- The scenes from the *Ramayana* are sculpted on the inner walls of the shrine.

Quick Test 2

1. Name some travellers whose accounts give information about Vijayanagara.
2. What is the most important feature about the location of Vijayanagara?
3. Hiriya Canal was built by which dynasty?
4. Give one feature of the houses of ordinary people in Vijayanagara as described by Duarte Barbosa.
5. The rituals associated with *Mahanavami dibba* coincided with which festival?

7.5 The Sacred Centre of Vijayanagara

- The rocky northern end of the city was located on the banks of the Tungabhadra.
- Local traditions suggest that these hills had the monkey kingdom of Vali and Sugriva mentioned in the *Ramayana*.

- Some other traditions suggested that Pampadevi did penance (*tapasya*) in these hills to marry Virupaksha, the God who protected the kingdom and also recognised as a form of Shiva. This marriage is celebrated even today every year in the Virupaksha temple.
- In these hills, Jaina temples of the pre-Vijayanagara period are also found. It implies that this area was associated with different sacred traditions.

Tradition of Temple Building

- The Pallavas, Chalukyas, Hoysalas and Cholas started building temples in the Northern region.
- The rulers were encouraged to build temples to associate themselves with the divine. The deity was often identified directly or indirectly with the king.
- Temples also acted as the centres of learning. Rulers and others frequently donated land and resources for temple maintenance, which turned temples into significant religious, social, cultural, and economic centers.
- Rulers viewed constructing, repairing and maintaining temples as important means to win support and recognition of their power, wealth and being religious.
- The rulers of Vijayanagara innovated and developed new traditions like display of royal portrait sculpture in temples.
- The king's visits to temples were treated as important state occasions, and thus the king was accompanied by the important *nayakas* of the temple.

Gopurams and Mandapas

The new features of temple architecture in this period were

- **Raya *gopurams*** or **royal gateways** which made the towers on the central shrines appear smaller and indicated the temple's presence from a great distance. They could also symbolise the power of kings, who controlled the resources, techniques and skills required to build these towering gateways.
- Construction of ***mandapas***[8] or **pavilions**.
- **Long, pillared corridors** which surrounded the shrines within the temple complex.

The Virupaksha Temple

- The Virupaksha temple was built over centuries. The inscriptions indicate that the earliest shrine dates back to the ninth-tenth centuries. It was expanded with the rise of the Vijayanagara Empire.
- Krishnadeva Raya built the hall in front of the shrine to mark his accession to the throne. It was decorated with intricately carved pillars. He also constructed the Eastern *gopuram*.
- The central shrine was a small part of the complex.
- The halls in the temple were used for various purposes. Some spaces had images of Gods for special programmes of music, dance, drama, etc. Other spaces were used for marriages of deities, and some others were meant for the deities to swing in.

▲ *An aerial view of the Virupaksha temple*

8 *Mandapa* It is a pillared outdoor hall or pavilion for public rituals.

Virupaksha Temple's Influence on Vijayanagara

- The site of Vijayanagara was influenced by the presence of the Virupaksha and Pampadevi shrines.
- Vijayanagara kings claimed that they ruled on behalf of the god Virupaksha. The royal orders were signed **Shri Virupaksha**, in the Kannada script.
- Kings used titles like **Hindu Suratrana** to show their close links with the gods. This title was the Sanskritisation of the Arabic term Sultan, meaning king. It literally meant Hindu Sultan.

▲ *The chariot of the Vitthala temple*

The Vitthala Temple

- The main deity in this temple was **Vitthala**, a form of Vishnu generally worshipped in **Maharashtra**.
- Like other temples, Vitthala temple also had several halls and a unique shrine designed as a chariot.
- One of the important features was the chariot streets which extended from the temple *gopuram* in a straight line. These streets were paved with stone slabs and lined with pillared pavilions in which merchants set up their shops.

7.6 Plotting Palaces, Temples and Bazaars

- Photographs, plans, designs of structures and sculpture provide a lot of information on Vijayanagara.
- The Vijayanagara site was preserved by the Archaeological Survey of India and the Karnataka Department of Archaeology and Museums in the twentieth century.
- Hampi was recognised as a site of national importance in 1976.
- A project was launched in early 1980s to document and record the material remains at Vijayanagara in detail.

Contribution of Scholars

- The scholars have recovered and documented traces of thousands of structures from tiny shrines and residences to large temples. They also recovered the traces of roads, paths, bazars, etc.
- Scholars like **John M. Fritz**, **George Michell** and **MS Nagaraja Rao** had to imagine a whole set of disappeared wooden parts, pillars, beams, ceilings, overhanging roofs, and towers decorated with plaster and painted brightly.

Contribution of Travellers

- Some travellers, like **Paes**, described Vijayanagara as one of the best-equipped cities in the world. Its markets were filled with rice, wheat, grains, Indian corn, barley, beans, moong, pulses and horse-gram.
- All these were readily available and inexpensive.
- According to **Fernao Nuniz**, the markets of Vijayanagara had large quantities of fruits, grapes and oranges, limes, pomegranates, jackfruit and mangoes which are all very cheap.
- Meat was also sold in excesive quantities in the marketplaces. Mutton, pork, deer meat, partridges, hares, doves, quail and all kinds of birds, rats, cats and lizards were also sold in the market of Bisnaga (Vijayanagara).

Information Acquired from Buildings

- Buildings provide insights into how spaces were organised and used, as well as the materials and techniques used in their construction. For example, the defence requirements and military preparedness of a city can be identified by studying its fortifications.

- Buildings also give information about spread of ideas and cultural influences by comparing them with other places.
- They convey the ideas desired by the builders or their patrons to projects. They often have symbols that arise from their cultural context.
- Architectural features do not give information about ordinary men, women and children, comprising the vast majority of the people who lived in the city and its outskirts.

Conclusion

In Vijayanagara, rulers made all key decisions about construction. However, information about the designers of the buildings, wages of the construction workers, sources of raw materials etc. is not yet clear. These questions cannot be answered by just examining the buildings or their remains, further research may offer more information.

Quick Test 3

1 The marriage of Pampadevi is celebrated in which temple?
2 Who constructed the Eastern *gopuram* of the Virupaksha Temple?
3 The form of Vishnu, Vitthala was worshipped in which state?
4 When was Hampi recognised as a site of national importance?
5 Which traveller has described Vijayanagara as the best provided city?

TIMELINE

Major Political Developments

c. 1200-1300	Establishment of the Delhi Sultanate in 1206
c. 1300-1400	Establishment of the Vijayanagara Empire in 1336; Establishment of the Bahmani kingdom in 1347, Sultanates in Jaunpur, Kashmir and Madura
c. 1400-1500	Establishment of the Gajapati kingdom of Orissa in 1435; Establishment of the Sultanates of Gujarat and Malwa; Emergence of the Sultanates of Ahmadnagar, Bijapur and Berar in 1490

Landmarks in the Discovery and Conservation of Vijayanagara

1800	Colin Mackenzie visits Vijayanagara
1856	Alexander Greenlaw takes the first detailed photographs of archaeological remains at Hampi.
1876	J.F. Fleet begins documenting the inscriptions on the temple walls at the site
1902	Conservation begins under John Marshall
1986	Hampi declared a World Heritage site by UNESCO.

Mind Map

AN IMPERIAL CAPITAL: VIJAYANAGARA

1 The Discovery of Hampi

Hampi ruins were discovered in 1800 by Colin Mackenzie.

2 Rayas, Nayakas and Sultans

Kings and Traders
- Import of horses from Arabia and Central Asia were crucial for warfare in kingdoms.
- Krishnadeva Raya emphasised supporting trade for state prosperity and security.

The Rise and Decline of the Empire
- Krishnadeva Raya expanded Vijayangara empire and built temples adding Gopurams.
- In 1565, Vijayanagara was destroyed after defeat at Talikota.

The Rayas and the Nayakas
- Nayakas were military chiefs controlling forts and leading peasants.
- Amara-Nayakas were military commanders appointed by the Rayas.

3 Vijayanagara: The Capital and its Environs

Water Resources
- Vijayanagara is surrounded by granite hills and the Tungabhadra River.
- Hiriya Canal irrigated valleys between sacred centre and urban core.

The Urban Core
- Chinese porcelain found in the urban core suggests rich traders lived there.
- Wells, rainwater tanks and temple tanks served as sources of water.

Fortifications and Roads
- Seven lines of fortifications protected city, fields and forests.
- Roads winding through valleys connected temples and bazaars.

4 The Royal Centre

- King's palace had two platforms: Audience Hall and Mahanavami Dibba.
- Mahanavami Dibba is a high platform, likely used for rituals.
- Other buildings in the royal centre included the Lotus Mahal and the Hazara Rama Temple.

5 The Sacred Centre

Gopurams and Mandapas
- Royal gateways (Raya Gopurams) symbolised king's power and authority.
- Mandapas (Pavillions) and long, pillard corridors encircle the shrines within the temple complex.

Choosing a Capital
- The Northern hills sheltered the monkey kingdom of Vali and Sugriva.
- Pampadevi, the local mother Goddess did penance in these hills to marry Virupahsha, the guardian diety of the kingdom.
- Dynasties such as the Pallavas, Chalukyas, Hoysalas and Cholas, encouraged temple building as a means of associating themselves with the divine.

6 Plotting Palaces, Temples and Bazaars

- Detailed surveys documented Vijayanagara's structures, roads and market places.
- Hampi was recognised as a site of national importance in 1976.

7 Questions in Search of Answers

Insights from Buildings and their Context
- Buildings reveal space organisation, materials, techniques and cultural influences.
- Fortifications reflect city's defence strategies and military preparedness.

NCERT Folder

Intext Questions

1. Why did the *nayakas* continue with the building traditions of the rulers of Vijayanagara? (Pg. 183)

Ans. The *nayakas* continued the building traditions of the Vijayanagara rulers primarily because it served as a way to demonstrate their loyalty, power and religious beliefs. It also helped them in consolidating their own regional influence by patronising grand temple construction projects within their territories, which were often extensions of the architectural style established by the Vijayanagara kings.

The *nayakas* were maintaining the established cultural and political fabric of the region by continuing the architectural legacy of their predecessors.

2. How and why did the rulers of Vijayanagara adopt and adapt earlier traditions of ritual architecture? (Pg. 188)

Ans. The rulers of Vijayanagara adopted and adapted earlier traditions of ritual architecture. They included elements from pre-existing temple styles, particularly from the Chalukya and Hoysala dynasties, to demonstrate their power and legitimacy as Hindu rulers.

They expanded existing temples and also built new ones with grand features like big *gopurams* and intricate pillared halls. While doing this, they focussed on maintaining the main principles of Hindu temple design to connect with their subjects' religious beliefs.

Answer in 100-150 words

1. What have been the methods used to study the ruins of Hampi over the last two centuries? In what way do you think they would have complemented the information provided by the priests of the Virupaksha temple?

Or **How and when were the ruins of Hampi brought to light? Explain briefly.**

Or **Describe the various efforts made by scholars to reconstruct the history of the city and the empire from the ruins of Hampi upto the century.**

Ans. Colonel Colin Mackenzie had discovered the ruins at Hampi in 1800 CE. The methods used to study the ruins of Hampi were

- Mackenzie prepared the first Survey Map of the Hampi site.
- In 1836 CE, epigraphists started collecting many inscriptions found at this and other temples at Hampi.
- From 1856, photographers started to record the monuments which helped scholars to study them.
- Historians collected all the information from these sources along with travel accounts of foreign travellers and other literature written in Telugu, Kannada, Tamil and Sanskrit to reconstruct the history of city and the empire.

These methods complemented the information given by the priests of Virupaksha temple because the information was based on the memories of priests.

2. How were the water requirements of Vijayanagara met?

Ans. The water requirements of Vijayanagara were met through the following ways

- In Vijayanagara, the natural basin was formed by the river Tungabhadra which flows in North-Easterly direction. This natural basin met the water requirements of Vijayanagara.
- A number of streams flow down to the river from the rocky mountains. In many cases, check-dams were built along these streams to create reservoirs of different sizes.
- This region was among the most arid zones of the peninsula, so arrangements were made to store rainwater and transmit to the city.
- In the fifteenth century, the most important tank was built which is now called as Kamalapuram tank. The water from this tank was used both to irrigate fields and transmit to the royal centre through a channel.
- One of the most important waterworks was the Hiriya canal. This was built by the kings of the Sangama dynasty. The canal got water from a dam across the Tungabhadra and irrigated the cultivated valley that separated the sacred centre from the urban core.

3. What do you think were the advantages and disadvantages of enclosing agricultural land within the fortified area of the city?

Ans. The advantages of enclosing agricultural land within the fortified area of the city were

- Since siege (military) operations sometimes lasts for many months, this kind of system enables farmers to produce grains even during the siege operation.
- Agricultural lands were often destroyed first during war, which were outside the forts. But in this case, that was not possible because they were well protected inside the fortification.

The disadvantage of enclosing agricultural land within the fortified area of the city were

- This was more expensive and complicated strategy of protecting the agricultural belt itself.

- Expansion of agriculture to other areas beyond the fortified area becomes difficult. Agriculture has to confined within this area.

4. What do you think was the significance of the rituals associated with the *mahanavami dibba*?

Ans. *Mahanavami dibba* was located at one of the highest points in the city. It was a massive platform or stage rising from a base of about 11,000 sq ft. to a height of 40 ft. It supported a wooden building and the base of the platform was covered with relief designs or carvings.

Rituals associated with the *mahanavami dibba* probably coincided with Mahanavami i.e. the ninth day of the ten-day Hindu festival during the autumn months of September and October. It is known as Dussehra in North India, Durga Puja in Bengal and Navaratri or Mahanavami in peninsular India. The Vijayanagara kings showed their prestige, power and control over the empire on this occasion. Various ceremonies were performed on this occasion like worship of image and state horse, and the sacrifices of animals like buffaloes.

The main attractions of this occasion were dances, wrestling matches, processions of horses, elephants etc.

These rituals were presented before the king and his guests by the chief *nayakas* and subordinate kings. Thus, the rituals associated with the *Mahanavami dibba* were significant.

5. The below figure is an illustration of another pillar from the Virupaksha temple. Do you notice any floral motifs? What are the animals shown? Why do you think they are depicted? Describe the human figures shown.

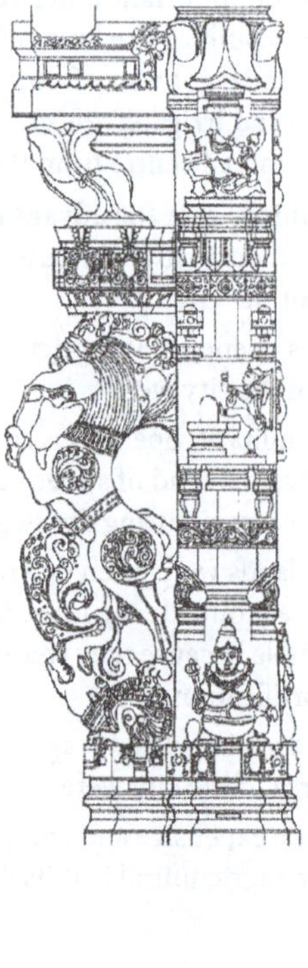

Ans. The illustration of pillar from the Virupaksha temple contains floral motifs i.e. flower images which can be noticed on the pillars.

The animals shown include horse, peacock, duck, etc. They were depicted to add more beauty to the pillars of the temple. Animals like horses are symbolic to royal power, because they were used in wars as cavalry.

The human figures are also depicted on the pillar. At the top, there is a human figure which looks like it was in kneeling position.

The middle human figure was praying to Shiva linga, but he was using legs instead of hands. The below human figure mostly belongs to some deity, which has crown, a weapon in one hand and necklaces around the neck.

Write a Short Essay (about 250-300 words) on the following

6. Discuss whether the term 'royal centre' is an appropriate description for the part of the city for which it is used.

Ans. The royal centre is an appropriate description for the part of the city for which it is used due to its royal features which are as follows

- The royal centre was located in the South-Western part of the settlement. It had over 60 temples. It shows that support of temples and cults was important for rulers who tried to establish and get approved of their authority through association with the gods and goddesses housed in the shrines.
- Around 30 building complexes were identified as palaces. There were relatively large structures that do not seem to be associated with ritual functions.
- The difference between these structures and temples was that the temples were constructed by using stones, while the superstructure of the secular buildings were made of materials that would get decayed after some time.
- The king's palace was the largest of the buildings but there is no strong evidence that it was a royal residence. It had two impressive platforms, called the audience hall and the *Mahanavami Dibba*.
- The audience hall was a high platform which had slots for wooden pillars to be placed at close and regular intervals.
- *Mahanavami Dibba* was a massive platform or stage rising from a base of about 11,000 sq ft to a height of 40 ft.
- The Lotus Mahal, named by British travellers in the nineteenth century was one of the most beautiful buildings in the royal centre.

- Hazara temple was meant to be used by the king and his family. The sculpted panels which survive include scenes from the Ramayana.

Thus, all the buildings and the activities present in the royal centre shows that it is an appropriate description. Though there are many temples present in the royal centre, we should remember that, temples at that time were symbol of power and they were centres of many other activities other than rituals.

7. What does the architecture of buildings like the Lotus Mahal and elephant stables tell us about the rulers who commissioned them?

Ans. The architecture of buildings like Lotus Mahal and elephant stables show that Indian rulers tried to use native symbols and innovatively mix them with other cultures. Though, they were related to Hindu religion but it had features of other religions also.

Lotus Mahal

The Lotus Mahal, named by British travellers in the nineteenth century was one of the most beautiful buildings in the royal centre. But, historians are not sure about the use of the building.

A map drawn by Mackenzie suggested that it might have been a council chamber, a place where the king met his advisors.

Lotus Mahal had arches, which might be inspired by Indo-Islamic techniques. It had nine towers, a high central one and eight along sides.

Elephant Stables

Elephant stable was constructed near the Lotus Mahal which had many rooms. There were a large number of elephants in the army. To keep these elephants, stable was constructed.

8. What are the architectural traditions that inspired the architects of Vijayanagara? How did they transform these traditions?

Ans. The rulers of Vijayanagara were known for their innovations and beautifully carved architectural traditions. The architectural traditions that inspired the architects of Vijayanagara were

- Temple building had a long history in the Vijayanagara region. Rulers very often encouraged temple building as a means of associating themselves with the divine. Often the deity was explicitly or implicitly identified with the king.
- The Vijayanagara kings claimed to rule on behalf of the God Virupaksha- the guardian royal orders were signed 'Shri Virupaksha'.
- Rulers also indicated their close links with God by using the title 'Hindu Suratrana' which meant Hindu Sultan.

Vijayanagara rulers transformed some traditions in the following ways

- Royal portrait sculpture was now displayed in temple and the king's visit to the temples was treated as important state occasions on which he was accompanied by the royal *nayakas* of the empire.
- In terms of temple architecture, certain new features were added. These included 'the *gopurams*' or the royal gateways. These *gopurams* were very tall structures which even dwarfed the towers on the central shrine. It signalled the presence of the temple from a great distance. They were probably a mark of imperial authority and power of the king. For example, Krishnadeva Raya built the Eastern *gopurams* of the Virupaksha temple.
- Other distinctive features that were added were the *mandapas* or pavilions and long, pillared corridors that often ran around the shrines within the temple complex.
- Krishnadeva Raya, to mark his accession, also built a hall in front the main shrine. This hall was decorated with delicately carved pillars. These halls were used for a variety of deities.
- A characteristic feature is the 'Chariot Street' that extended from the temple *gopurams* in a straight line. These streets were paved with stone slabs and lined with pillared pavilions in which the merchants set up their shops.

9. What impression on the lives of the ordinary people of Vijayanagara can you collect from the various descriptions in the chapter?

Ans. The impression on the lives of the ordinary people of Vijayanagara can be explained through the following points

- Sixteenth century Portuguese traveller Duarte Barbosa described that the houses of ordinary people had roofs made of straw, palm leaves, etc, but were well built and were arranged according to the occupations, in long streets with many open places.
- Field surveys show that the entire area of Vijayanagara was scattered with number of shrines and small temples. This shows that different cults were present there, which might be supported by different communities.
- The surveys also indicate that wells, rainwater tanks, temple tanks were used as sources of water by the ordinary town people.

- Archaeologists found little archaeological evidence of the houses of ordinary people. They have found fine Chinese porcelain (Chinaware) in some areas in the North-Eastern corner of the urban core and this shows that these areas might have been occupied by rich traders.
- This area was also the Muslim residential quarter. Tombs and mosques present here have different functions but their architecture resembles the *Mandapas* that were found in temples of Hampi.

10. On an outline map of the world, mark approximately Italy, Portugal, Iran and Russia. Trace the routes the travellers mentioned in fig. 7.4 (NCERT) would have taken to reach Vijayanagara.

Ans.

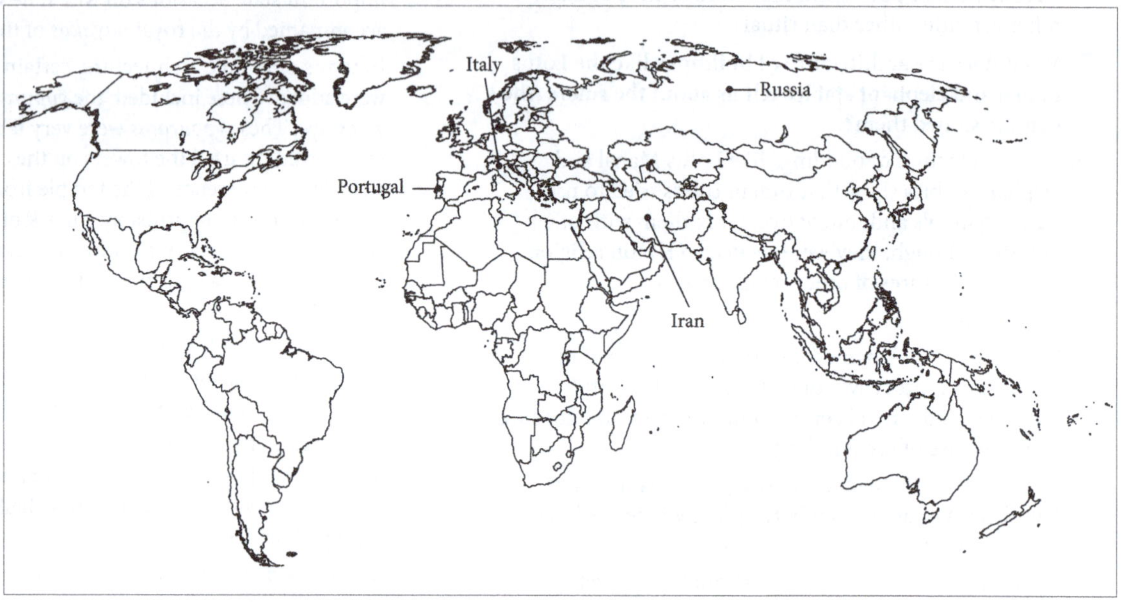

The routes the travellers would have taken to reach Vijayanagara were

- The Italian travellers crossed the Arabian Sea and then Indian Ocean, and through Malabar Coast they would have reached Vijayanagara.
- The Portugal travellers would have crossed Atlantic Ocean touching the Cape of Good Hope and then Indian Ocean to reach Malabar of India. From here, they took land route to reach Vijayanagara.
- The travellers from Iran *via* Afghanistan and modern Pakistan would have taken land route upto Karnataka, India.
- The Russian travellers would have came to India *via* Afghanistan. They would have crossed modern Punjab in Pakistan, central India crossing Vindhyachal, Satpura to Karnataka.

Exam Pattern Questions

Objective Type Questions

Multiple Choice Questions (MCQs)

1. **Who among the following brought the ruins of Hampi to light in 1800 ?**

(a) Thomas Hickey (b) Colin Mackenzie
(c) J.F. Fleet (d) Alexander Greenlaw

2. **Who among the following, as the tradition goes, founded the empire of Vijayanagara?** **CBSE Term I 2021**

(a) Sadasiva Raya (b) Ramadeva Raya
(c) Harihara and Bukka (d) Krishnadeva Raya

3. **Which of the following empires was called "Karnataka Samrajyamu" ?** **CBSE 2024**

(a) Chera (b) Pallava
(c) Chola (d) Vijayanagara

4. **Gajapati rulers ruled which of the following states?**

(a) Orissa (b) Deccan states
(c) Assam (d) West Bengal

5. **Who among the following was the author of Amuktamalyada ?** **Compartment 2024**

(a) Krishnadeva Raya (b) Rama Raya
(c) Harihara (d) Bukka

6. **Where Brihadishvara temple is situated?**

(a) Madurai (b) Chennai
(c) Thanjavur (d) Cochin

7. **Where is Chennakeshava temple situated?**

(a) Madurai (b) Thanjavur
(c) Belur (d) Chennai

8. **What according to Colin Mackenzie was the purpose of the Lotus Mahal?** **CBSE Diksha**

(a) Administrative Block (b) Council Chamber
(c) Cremation ground (d) Queens Palace

9. **The walls of the Hazara Rama temple has scenes sculpted from** **CBSE Diksha**

(a) *Mahabharata* (b) *Ramayana*
(c) *Jataka stories* (d) *Panchatantra*

10. **Fill in the blank.** **CBSE 2024**

The most striking feature about the location of Vijayanagara was the natural basin formed by river .... which flows in a North-easterly direction.

(a) Narmada (b) Godavari
(c) Kaveri (d) Tungabhadra

11. **Why was Vijayanagara named as Hampi? Select the appropriate option from the following.** **CBSE 2023**

(a) This name was given by Krishnadeva Raya to Vijayanagara.
(b) This name was derived by Colin Meckenzie, an antiquarian.
(c) This name was derived from the local Goddess named Pampadevi.
(d) This name was devoted to Vitthala and Virupaksha deities.

12. **Vijayanagara city was situated between which of the following rivers?**

(a) Krishna in North and Tungabhadra in South.
(b) Krishna in the South and Cauvery in North.
(c) Tungabhadra in North and Krishna in South.
(d) Kaveri in the North and Tungabhadra in South.

13. **Who among the following were known as '*kudirai chettis*' ?** **CBSE Term I 2021**

(a) A group of Portuguese who traded in military technology.
(b) A local community of horse traders.
(c) A group of Arab traders trading in horses.
(d) A local community of traders trading in muskets.

14. **Which of the following statements from the given options is true?** **CBSE Diksha**

(a) Krishnadeva Raya belonged to the Saluva dynasty.
(b) Krishnadeva Raya founded Nagalapuram suburban township in the name of his mother.
(c) Krishnadeva Raya died in 1530 CE.
(d) Gajapati rulers of Orissa were defeated in 1520 by Krishnadeva Raya.

15. **Which one of the following was the main factor that led to the decline of the Vijayanagara empire ?** **CBSE 2024**

(a) Internal conflicts and alliance with the Sultanates against Vijayanagara.
(b) Defeat of Bijapur, Ahmadnagar and Golconda in Talikota.
(c) Heavy decline in trade and economy of the Vijayanagara empire.
(d) Invasion of Portuguese and French on Vijayanagara.

16. **Choose the correct statement from the following options with reference to Vijayanagara empire.** CBSE 2024

(a) This empire was founded by the rulers of Saluva dynasty.
(b) This empire became powerful after the death of Krishnadeva Raya.
(c) The battle of Talikota proved disastrous for Vijayanagara Empire.
(d) Their land revenue system was taken from Mansabdari system.

17. **Imagine you are analysing a historical document from the Vijayanagara Empire. Which of the following documents would be most helpful in understanding the relationship between the empire and religious institutions?** CBSE SQP 2024

(a) A military chronicle detailing the conquests of a Vijayanagara rulers.
(b) A record of diplomatic exchanges with traders and foreign ambassadors.
(c) A legal code outlining the rights and responsibilities of urban classes.
(d) An imperial decree granting land or privileges to a sacred organisation.

18. **Which one of the following facts regarding Vijayanagara city is incorrect?** CBSE Diksha

(a) The surrounding landscape of Vijayanagara is characterised by stunning granite hills .
(b) Vijayanagara has seven lines of forts which encircled not only the city but also its agricultural hinterland and forests .
(c) Gateways of the fort were distinctive architectural features that often defined the structures to which they regulated access.
(d) Only Hindus resided in the urban core of the city .

19. **Why were the agricultural tracts in Vijayanagara included within the fortified area?** CBSE Diksha

(a) To ensure proper tax collection
(b) To avoid starvation during a siege
(c) To keep an eye on the farmers and labourers
(d) To reduce the wastage of grains

20. **Which of the following statements is correct regarding *Mahanavami dibba*?** CBSE SQP Term I 2021

(a) *Mahanavami dibba* was part of 'The King's Palace Complex'.
(b) *Mahanavami dibba* was a part of Sacred Centre.
(c) *Mahanavami dibba* was a 'Counselling Hall'.
(d) *Mahanavami dibba* was a 'Discussion Hall'.

21. **Read the following statements**

(i) Krishnadeva Raya's rule was characterised by expansion and consolidation.
(ii) There was peace and prosperity in his empire.
(iii) He was credited with building some fine temples.
(iv) He belonged to the Sangama dynasty.

Which of the above statements are related to Krishnadeva Raya?

(a) Only (i)
(b) (i), (ii) and (iii)
(c) (ii), (iii) and (iv)
(d) (i), (iii) and (iv)

22. **Which of the following statements regarding Colonel Colin Mackenzie are correct? Choose the correct option:** CBSE 2025

I. The ruins of Hampi were brought to light in 1800 by him.
II. He was an official of East India Company.
III. He prepared the first survey maps of the site.
IV. He received information of Vijayanagara empire from the Duarte Barbosa.

Options

(a) I, II and III
(b) II, III and IV
(c) I, III and IV
(d) I, II and IV

23. **Read the following statements about Rama Raya carefully and choose the correct option.** CBSE Term I 2021

(i) He led the army into battle at Talikota in 1565.
(ii) His army was routed by the combined armies of the Sultans.
(iii) Rama Raya was the Sultan of Vijayanagara.
(iv) The city was totally abandoned by him.

Codes

(a) Only (i) and (ii) are correct
(b) Only (i), (ii) and (iii) are correct
(c) Only (i), (ii) and (iv) are correct
(d) Only (iii) is correct

24. **Which one of the following pairs is correctly matched ?** CBSE 2024

	Temple		Location
(a)	Chidambaram Temple	–	Thanjavur
(b)	Brihadishvara Temple	–	Vijayanagara
(c)	Chennakeshava Temple	–	Belur
(d)	Hazara Rama Temple	–	Tamil Nadu

25. **Which one of the following pairs is correctly matched?** CBSE Term I 2021

(a) Shrine of Pampadevi - Belur
(b) Brihadishvara Temple - Thanjavur
(c) Virupaksha Temple - Tamil Nadu
(d) Lotus Mahal - Golconda

26. **Which one of the following pairs is correctly matched?** CBSE Term I 2021

(a) Vitthala Temple - Devoted to Pampadevi
(b) Virupaksha Temple - Chariot Temple
(c) Hazara Rama Temple - Temple of Krishnadeva Raya
(d) Nagalapuram - Suburban city

27. **Identify the name of the text with the help of following information**

(i) It was composed by Krishnadeva Raya.
(ii) It is a work on statecraft in Telugu.
(iii) It contains descriptions about traders.

Options

(a) *Amuktamalyada* (b) Tevaram
(c) Pattuppattu (d) Marai

28. **Identify the structure of Vijayanagara with the help of following information.**

(i) The complex is surrounded by high double walls.
(ii) It is a high platform with slots for wooden pillars.
(iii) It had a staircase going up to the second floor.
(iv) The pillars are being closely spaced.

Options

(a) Audience hall (b) Lotus Mahal
(c) An Aqueduct (d) Elephant stables

29. **Arrange the following dynasties of Vijayanagara in chronological order.** CBSE Term I 2021

(i) Aravidu (ii) Tuluva
(iii) Sangama (iv) Saluva

Codes

(a) (i), (ii), (iv), (iii) (b) (ii), (iii), (i), (iv)
(c) (iii), (iv), (ii), (i) (d) (iv), (i), (iii), (ii)

30. **Complete the following with the correct option regarding the travellers with their respective countries.**

Abdur Razzaq : Persia :: Domingo Paes: ....

(a) USA (b) Portugal
(c) France (d) Canada

31. **Complete the following with the correct option regarding the buildings in Vijayanagara and their respective functions.**

Mahanavami dibba **: Festivals :: Nagalapuram**

(a) Suburban city
(b) Religious Meetings
(c) Ritual Bath
(d) Military Practices

Assertion-Reason

32. **Assertion** (A) The ruins of Hampi were brought to light in 1800 AD by an engineer and antiquarian named Colonel Colin Mackenzie. CBSE 2024 C

Reason (R) Dozens of inscriptions were found from the Virupaksha temple and other temples at Hampi.

Codes

(a) Both A and R are true and R is the correct explanation of A
(b) Both A and R are true, but R is not the correct explanation of A
(c) A is true, but R is false
(d) A is false, but R is true

33. **Assertion** (A) Sangama dynasty was the first dynasty, exercised control till 1400.

Reason (R) Krishnadeva Raya belonged to the Tuluva dynasty.

Codes

(a) Both A and R are true and R is the correct explanation of A
(b) Both A and R are true, but R is not the correct explanation of A
(c) A is true, but R is false
(d) A is false, but R is true

34. **Assertion** (A) Military chiefs were also known as nayakas.

Reason (R) *Amara-nayaka* system was a major political innovation of the Vijayanagara *Empire*.

Codes

(a) Both A and R are true and R is the correct explanation of A
(b) Both A and R are true, but R is not the correct explanation of A
(c) A is true, but R is false
(d) A is false, but R is true

35. **Assertion** (A) Local communities of merchants known as kudirai chettis.

Reason (R) *kudirai chettis* were also known as horse merchants.

Codes

(a) Both A and R are true and R is the correct explanation of A
(b) Both A and R are true, but R is not the correct explanation of A
(c) A is true, but R is false
(d) A is false, but R is true

36. **Assertion** (A) The *amara-nayaka* system was a major political innovation of the Vijayanagara Empire.

Reason (R) *Amara-nayaka* system provided the Vijayanagara Kings with an effective fighting force with which they brought the entire southern peninsula under their control .

Codes

(a) Both A and R are true and R is the correct explanation of A
(b) Both A and R are true, but R is not the correct explanation of A
(c) A is true, but R is false
(d) A is false, but R is true

37. **Assertion** (A) The Vijayanagara Empire was known for its advanced water management system.

Reason (R) The rulers of Vijayanagara constructed embankments and reservoirs along streams flowing from the surrounding hills to store rainwater.

Codes

(a) Both A and R are true and R is the correct explanation of A

(b) Both A and R are true, but R is not the correct explanation of A

(c) A is true, but R is false

(d) A is false, but R is true

Match the Following

38.

List I	List II
A. Harihara and Bukka	1. Tuluva Dynasty
B. Krishnadeva Raya	2. Saluva Dynasty
C. Narsimha Deva Raya	3. Sangama Dynasty
D. Rama Deva Raya	4. Aravidu Dynasty

Codes

	A	B	C	D		A	B	C	D
(a)	1	2	3	4	(b)	2	1	4	3
(c)	3	1	2	4	(d)	1	3	4	2

39.

List I	List II
A. Lord of elephants	1. *Narapati*
B. Lord of horses	2. *Gajapati*
C. Lord of men	3. *Ashvapati*

Codes

	A	B	C		A	B	C
(a)	1	2	3	(b)	2	3	1
(c)	3	2	1	(d)	3	1	2

40.

List I	List II
A. Mahanavi Dibba	1. A council chamber or meeting hall
B. Lotus Mahal	2. Platform used for royal ceremonies and celebrations
C. Audience Hall	3. A high platform with slots for wooden pillars
D. Hiriya Canal	4. Canal that brought water from the Tungabhadra River

Codes

	A	B	C	D		A	B	C	D
(a)	2	1	3	4	(b)	2	4	1	3
(c)	3	1	2	4	(d)	1	3	4	2

41.

List I	List II
A. 1800	1. Conversation begins under John Marshal
B. 1876	2. Colin Mackenzie vists Vijayanagara
C. 1902	3. Hampi declared a World Heritage Site by UNESCO
D. 1986	4. J.F. Fleet begins documenting inscriptions at the site.

Codes

	A	B	C	D		A	B	C	D
(a)	1	2	3	4	(b)	2	4	1	3
(c)	3	1	2	4	(d)	1	3	4	2

42.

List I	List II
A. Nayakas	1. Merchants engaged in horse trade
B. Kudirai Chettis	2. Military chiefs who governed territories for the king
C. Raya Gopurams	3. Large gateways symbolising royal authority in temples
D. Virupaksha Temple	4. Sacred center associated with the guardian deity of the city

Codes

	A	B	C	D		A	B	C	D
(a)	1	3	2	4	(b)	2	1	3	4
(c)	3	4	2	1	(d)	4	2	1	3

43.

List I	List II
A. Afanasi Nikitin	1. Persia
B. Domingo Paes	2. Russia
C. Abdur-Razzak	3. Portugal
D. Nicolo de Conti	4. Italy

Codes **CBSE SQP 2024**

	A	B	C	D		A	B	C	D
(a)	3	4	1	2	(b)	2	3	1	4
(c)	1	2	4	3	(d)	2	1	3	4

Picture Based Questions

44. **The *mahanavami dibba* in the picture below was enclosed within**

(a) Royal centre
(b) Sacred centre
(c) Compound of Brihadishvara temple.
(d) Outside the main fortification of capital of Vijayanagara Empire.

45. **The sculptures of this temple shows scenes from which of the following ancient epic of India?**

(a) Ramayana
(b) Mahabharata
(c) Panchtantra
(d) Jataka stories

46. **The aerial view of which temple is shown in the picture below?**

(a) Brihadishvara Temple
(b) Hazara Rama Temple
(c) Virupaksha Temple
(d) Vitthala Temple

47. **Which temple of Vijayanagara is shown in the picture below?**

(a) Lotus Mahal
(b) Hazara Rama Temple
(c) Virupaksha Temple
(d) Vitthala Temple

Answers

1. (b) Colin Mackenzie
2. (c) Harihara and Bukka
3. (d) Vijayanagara
4. (a) Orissa
5. (a) Krishna deva Raya
6. (c) Thanjavur
7. (c) Belur
8. (b) Council Chamber
9. (b) *Ramayana*
10. (d) Tungabhadra
11. (c) This name was derived from the local Goddess named Pampadevi.
12. (a) Krishna in North and Tungabhadra in South.
13. (b) A local community of horse traders.
14. (b) Krishnadeva Raya founded Nagalapuram suburban township in the name of his mother.
15. (b) Defeat of Bijapur, Ahmadnagar and Golconda in Talikota.
16. (c) The battle of Talikota proved disastrous for Vijayanagara Empire.
17. (d) An imperial decree granting land or privileges to a sacred organisation.
18. (d) Only Hindus resided in the urban core of the city.
19. (b) To avoid starvation during a siege

20. (a) *Mahanavami dibba* was part of 'The King's Palace Complex'.
21. (b) (i), (ii) and (iii)
22. (a) (ii) and (iii)
23. (c) Only (i), (ii) and (iv) are correct
24. (c) Chennakeshava Temple –Belur
25. (b) Brihadishvara Temple - Thanjavur
26. (d) Nagalapuram - Suburban city
27. (a) *Amuktamalyada*
28. (a) Audience hall
29. (c) (iiii), (iv), (ii), (i)
30. (b) Portugal
31. (a) Suburban city
32. (a) Both A and R are true and R is the correct explanation of A
33. (d) A is false, but R is true
34. (b) Both A and R are true, but R is not the correct explanation of A
35. (b) Both A and R are true, but R is not the correct explanation of A
36. (a) Both the statements are true and R is correct explanation of A.
37. (a) Both A and R are true and R is the correct explanation of A
38. (c)
39. (b) 40. (a)
41. (b) 42. (b)
43. (b)
44. (a) Royal centre
45. (a) *Ramayana*
46. (c) Virupaksha Temple
47. (d) Vitthala Temple

Subjective Questions

Short Answer Type Questions

1. Why did the imperial power of Vijayanagara decline after the death of Krishnadeva Raya?

Ans. After the death of Krishnadeva Raya in 1529 CE, the imperial power of Vijayanagara declined due to following reasons

- The successors of Krishnadeva were troubled by rebellious *nayakas* or military chiefs. By 1542, control at the centre was shifted to another ruling family of the Aravidu, which remained in power till the end of the seventeenth century.
- During the rule of Aravidu, there was shift in alliances due to shift in the military goals of the rulers of Vijayanagara and Deccan Sultanates. This led to an alliance of the Sultanates against Vijayanagara.
- In 1565 CE, Rama Raya, the Chief Minister of Vijayanagara, led the army into battle at Rakshasi-Tangadi also known as Talikota. Here, Rama Raya's forces were decisively defeated by the combined armies of Bijapur, Ahmadnagar and Golconda. The victorious armies looted and destroyed the city of Vijayanagara.

2. Highlight the contribution of Krishnadeva Raya in the expansion of Vijaynagara Empire. CBSE Diksha

Or **Analyse the role of Krishnadeva Raya as the ruler of Vijayanagara Empire.** CBSE 2024

Ans. Contribution of Krishnadeva Raya in the expansion of Vijaynagar Empire is as follows

- He acquired land between the Tungabhadra and Krishna rivers (the Raichur doab) and defeated the rulers of Odisha in 1514 and the Sultan of Bijapur in 1520.
- His kingdom was well-prepared for military challenges.
- It also enjoyed a period of peace and prosperity.
- Krishnadeva Raya is also known for building beautiful temples and enhancing many with impressive *gopurams*.
- Additionally, he founded a suburb near Vijayanagara called Nagalapuram in honor of his mother.
- Many detailed accounts of Vijayanagara date from his time, highlighting its significance.

3. Discuss about the relation between Sultans and Vijayanagara kings.

Ans. The relations between the Sultans and the *rayas* were not always of hatred, despite their religious differences.

For example, Krishnadeva Raya, supported the people who claimed power in the Sultanates and took pride in the title of establisher of the Yavana kingdom. Similarly, the Sultan of Bijapur involved in resolving the succession disputes in Vijayanagara after the death of Krishnadeva Raya. Both Vijayanagara rulers and Sultanates wanted to ensure stability of each other. It was due to the aggressive policy of Rama Raya who tried to engage one Sultan against another. This led the Sultans to come together and decisively defeat him.

4. Describe the trade during the Vijayanagara Empire and its impact on their society.

Ans. Trade during the Vijayanagara Empire and its impact on their society are as follows

- *Kudirai chettis* or horse merchants participated in the trade of horses which was crucial for warfare.
- Vijayanagara was also noted for its markets that dealt in spices, textiles and precious stones.
- Trade was often regarded as a status symbol for such cities, which boasted of a wealthy population that demanded high-value exotic goods, especially precious stones and jewellery.
- The revenue derived from trade in turn contributed significantly to the prosperity of the state.

5. 'The *amara-nayaka* system was the major political innovation of the Vijayanagara Empire.' Elaborate.

Or **Analyse the main features of *amara–nayaka* system which was introduced in Vijayanagara Empire.**

Or **"The *amara-nayaka* system was a political innovation of Vijayanagara Empire." Justify the statement with suitable arguments.** Competency Based Que

Or **Analyse why was Amaranayaka system considered as a major political invovation of the Vijayanagara empire.** CBSE 2025

Ans. The *amara-nayaka* system was a major political innovation of the Vijayanagara Empire. This can be explained in following ways

- The *amara-nayakas* were military commanders who were given territories to govern by the *raya*. Most of its features were derived from the *iqta* system of the Delhi Sultanate.
- They collected taxes and other dues from peasants, craftspersons and traders in the area. They kept part of the revenue for personal use and for maintaining a required group of horses and elephants. Some of the revenue was also used for the maintenance of temples and irrigation works.
- The *amara-nayakas* sent tribute to the king annually and personally appeared in the royal court with gifts to show their loyalty. They were transferred from one place to another by kings to prove their control over *amara-nayakas*.

6. Control of the military was decentralised in the Vijayanagara Empire. Justify this statement. Competency Based Que

Ans. The military power of the Vijayanagara Empire rested on the *amara-nayaka* system. The *amara-nayakas* were military commanders who were given territories to govern and collect revenue from the king. They used part of the revenue for personal use and for maintaining a contingent of horses and elephants. These provided the Vijayanagara kings with an army. Thus, the *amara-nayakas* had autonomy and power over the military which shows that the military was decentralised in the Vijayanagara Empire.

7. Explain the water resource management of Vijayanagara Empire with Examples. CBSE 2024

Ans. The Vijayanagara Empire had a well-organised water resource management system. It employed sophisticated water management techniques, such as reservoirs, channels, and canals, to ensure a steady water supply for both agricultural and urban needs in a challenging, arid environment. Some of the examples are

- **Natural Basin and Embankments** The empire was located in a natural basin formed by the Tungabhadra River, surrounded by granite hills. Streams flowing from these hills were dammed to create reservoirs of varying sizes, helping to store and manage water effectively.
- **Kamalapuram Tank** One of the most important water resources was the Kamalapuram tank, built in the early 15th century. This tank not only irrigated nearby fields but also supplied water to the royal center through a channel.
- **Hiriya Canal** Another significant waterworks was the Hiriya canal, which was fed by a dam across the Tungabhadra River. It irrigated the valley between the "sacred center" and the "urban core", supporting agriculture and providing water to the city.

8. 'One of the most prominent features of the Vijayanagara Empire is the way in which they utilised their strategic location and access to water resources.' Discuss. Competency Based Que

Ans. One of the most prominent features of the Vijayanagara Empire is the way in which they utilised their strategic location and access to water resources.

Vijayanagara is the natural basin formed by the river Tungabhadra which flows through it. A number of streams flow down to the river from the adjacent granite hills. Embankments were built along these streams to create reservoirs of varying sizes. As this is one of the most arid zones of the peninsula, huge tanks had to be built to store rainwater and carry it to the city. A sophisticated system of canal was also built that helped in carrying the water from the tank to different locations. A dam was built across Tungabhadra which helped in the irrigation of the agricultural fields.

9. Highlight any four aspects observed by Abdur Razzaq on the fortification of the Vijayanagara Empire.

Ans. Abdur Razzaq, observed following aspects after looking at the fortifications of Vijayanagara Empire

(i) These fortifications not only surrounded the city but also remote agricultural areas and forests.

(ii) The hills surrounding the city were linked with the outermost wall.

(iii) The large construction was slightly reduced in thickness at one end.

(iv) The mortar or cementing agent was not used in the construction. The stone blocks were wedge shaped, which held them in place. Square or rectangular fortification was projected outwards.

10. Describe the features of water resources of Vijayanagara Empire. **CBSE SQP 2022**

Ans. The features of water resources of Vijayanagara Empire are

- Vijayanagara is the natural basin formed by the river Tungabhadra which flows in North-Easterly direction.
- Granite hills surround the city and a number of streams flow down to the river from these rocky mountains. Embankments were built along these streams to create reservoirs of different sizes.
- This region is among the most arid zones of the peninsula, so arrangements were made to store rainwater and transmit it to the city.

11. Highlight the aspects observed by Domingo Paes on the *mahanavami dibba* of the Vijayanagara Empire.

Ans. Domingo Paes had made following observations on the *mahanavami dibba* of the Vijayanagara Empire

- He called *mahanavami dibba* along with audience hall as the house of victory.
- These buildings have two platforms one above the other, which were beautifully sculpted.
- On the upper platform of house of victory, king had a room made of cloth. In this room shrine of idol was present. Throne of state, crown and royal anklet was present in the middle of the house of victory.

12. 'Vijayanagara was characterised by a distinct building style'. Support this statement with the sacred architectural examples of Vijayanagara. **Competency Based Que**

Or **Describe briefly about the buildings that survive and tell us about the way, spaces were organised and used in Vijayanagara.**

Ans. Vijayanagara was characterised by a distinct building style as Vijayanagara rulers were known for their buildings and architecture. Some of the examples of their achitecture were

- Krishnadeva Raya built some fine temples and added *gopurams* to many important South Indian temples. He found Nagalapuram, a suburban township named after his mother, near Vijayanagara.
- Other features like audience hall and *mahanavami dibba* were also built.
- *Mandapas* or pavilions, and long pillared corridors that often ran around the shrines within the temple complex were built.

13. Highlight any four aspects observed by the Portuguese traveller Duarte Barbosa on the urban core of the Vijayanagara Empire.

Ans. Sixteenth century Portuguese traveller Duarte Barbosa described following aspects on the urban core of the Vijayanagara Empire.

(i) The houses had roofs made of straw, palm leaves, etc.

(ii) They were well built and were arranged according to the occupations, in long streets.

(iii) Field surveys show that the entire area was scattered with number of shrines and small temples. This shows that different cults were present there which might be supported by different communities.

(iv) The field surveys also indicate that wells, rainwater tanks, temple tanks were used as sources of water by the ordinary town people.

14. Give three pieces of archaeological evidence that supports the claim that patronage of temples and cults was important for the rulers of the Vijayanagara Empire.

Ans. Three pieces of archaeological evidence that supports the claim that patronage of temples and cults was important for the rulers of the Vijayanagara Empire are as follows

- Around 60 temples have been found in the place designated as the royal centre indicating that the temples were a major part of the king's life.
- The *mahanavami dibba* is also found in the royal centre. Scholars have argued that this place was used in celebrating the Mahanavami festival and displayed their prestige, power and supremacy on this occasion.
- It is likely that the very choice of the site of Vijayanagara was inspired by the existence of the shrines of Virupaksha and Pampadevi. In fact, the Vijayanagara kings claimed to rule on behalf of the god Virupaksha.

15. 'The *mahanavami dibba* in the royal centre of Vijayanagara has been assigned name on the basis of its form of building as well as functions.' Elaborate. **Competency Based Que**

Ans. It is true that *mahanavami dibba* has been assigned name on the basis of building and functions.

Rituals associated with the building might have coincided with Mahanavami i.e. the ninth day of the ten-day Hindu festival during the autumn months of September and October, known as Dusshera in North India, Durga Puja in Bengal and Navaratari or Mahanavami in peninsular India. The Vijayanagara kings showed their prestige, power and control over the empire on this occasion. Various ceremonies were performed on this occasion like worship of image, worship of the state horse and the sacrifice of buffaloes and other animals.

The ceremonies had a deep symbolic meanings. On the last day of the festival, king's army and the armies of the *nayakas* were inspected by the king in a grand ceremony in an open field.

16. Discuss about the Hazara Rama temple. What happened to different buildings after Vijayanagara kings?

Ans. Hazara Rama temple was one of the most spectacular among the temples. This might have been used only by the king and his family. Images in the central shrine of this temple are missing, but sculpted panels on the walls are still present. These include scenes from the *Ramayana* sculpted on the inner walls of the shrine. When the Vijayanagara city was looted and destroyed, many of the structures or buildings were destroyed. Later, the practice of building large structures were continued by the *nayakas*. Now many of these buildings have survived.

17. Describe the significance of temple building in the sacred centre of Vijayanagara.

Ans. The temples were developed as significant religious, social, cultural and economic centres. Rulers viewed constructing, repairing and maintaining temples as important means to win support and recognition of their power, wealth and being religious. Vijayanagara rulers were inspired by the rulers of Cholas, Hoysalas in temple building, and took them to the new heights.

The rulers of Vijayanagara innovated and developed new traditions like, display of royal portrait sculpture in temples. The king's visits to temples were treated as important state occasions, and thus king was accompanied by the important *nayakas* of temple.

18. Discuss about the sacred centre briefly with respect to legends and other temples.

Ans. The rocky Northern end of city which was located on the banks of the Tungabhadra was referred to as sacred centre. As per the local traditions, these hills had the monkey kingdom of Vali and Sugriva mentioned in the *Ramayana*.

Some other traditions suggested that Pampadevi, the local mother Goddess, did penance (*tapasya*) in these hills to marry Virupaksha, the god who protected the kingdom and also recognised as a form of Shiva. This marriage was celebrated even today every year in the Virupaksha temple.

In these hills, Jaina temples of the pre-Vijayanagara period were also found. It implies that this area was associated with different sacred traditions.

19. 'The rulers of Vijayanagara innovated and developed new traditions in the Virupaksha temple'. Elaborate. **Competency Based Que**

Ans. The rulers of Vijayanagara developed new traditions in Virupaksha temple. These new traditions were

- Krishnadeva Raya to indicate his accession to throne had built the hall in front of the shrine. He also constructed the Eastern *gopuram*. Central shrine occupied a small part of the complex with these additions.
- The halls in the temple were started to be used for various purposes. Some spaces had images of gods to witness special programmes of music, dance, drama, etc. Other spaces were used for marriages of deities and some other were meant for the deities to swing in.

20. Analyse the causes that led to the ruin of Vijayanagara empire. **CBSE 2025**

Ans. The following were the causes that led to the ruin of the Vijayanagara Empire

(i) **Battle of Talikota (1565)** The decisive defeat by the combined forces of the Deccan Sultanates led to large-scale destruction.

(ii) **Weak Successors** Inefficient rulers after Krishna Deva Raya failed to maintain the empire's stability.

(iii) **Court Intrigues** Internal conflicts and power struggles weakened governance.

(iv) **Continuous Wars** Frequent battles drained resources and military strength.

(v) **Economic Decline** Loss of trade routes and wealth weakened the empire.

(vi) **Military Exhaustion** Overburdened forces and lack of strong leadership accelerated the empire's downfall.

21. What were the contributions of scholars in reconstructing the history of Vijayanagara Empire?

Ans. Many scholars from all over the world worked to compile and preserve the information about Vijayanagara Empire. The contributions of these scholars were

- Some scholars have recovered and documented traces of thousands of structures from tiny shrines and residences to large temples in the Vijayanagara site. They also recovered the traces of roads, paths, bazaars, etc.
- Scholars like John M. Fritz, George Michell and MS Nagaraja Rao, who worked for years at the site, have described that they had to imagine a whole set of disappeared wooden parts, pillars, beams, ceilings, overhanging roofs and towers decorated with plaster and painted brightly.

- Though these wooden structures are lost and only stone structures have survived, the descriptions of travellers allowed them to reconstruct some aspects of the energetic life of those times.

Long Answer Type Questions

1. Why did strain begin to show within the imperial structure after the death of Krishnadeva Raya in 1529?

Ans. Strain began to show within the imperial structure of the Vijayanagara Empire after the death of its notable ruler, Krishnadeva Raya, in 1529. Krishnadeva Raya's reign had been marked by successful expansion and consolidation, particularly through the conquest of fertile lands and control over significant trade routes. His military strategies and alliances had fostered stability and growth, but his death created a power vacuum and exposed underlying tensions.

One major source of strain was the rivalry among military chiefs, or nayakas, who held considerable power within the empire. These nayakas, who were initially loyal and governed territories on behalf of the king, began to assert greater independence. With Krishnadeva Raya's central authority no longer uniting them, many sought to expand their own power and territories. This led to frequent rebellions and challenges to the central authority, putting pressure on the ruling structure to maintain control over these regional powers.

Moreover, Krishnadeva Raya's successors struggled to maintain his level of political and military influence. The Aravidu dynasty eventually assumed control, but the empire's cohesion was increasingly compromised by shifting alliances and internal conflicts. Without a strong, unifying leader, the Vijayanagara rulers found it difficult to manage the empire's vast territories and multi-ethnic populace, which included different languages, religions, and cultural practices.

Simultaneously, the Deccan Sultanates, which had been restrained by Krishnadeva Raya's strong military presence, took advantage of the weakened empire. This external threat culminated in the Battle of Talikota in 1565, where a coalition of Sultanates defeated the Vijayanagara forces and sacked the capital. This decisive loss marked the empire's rapid decline, as it could no longer sustain the political and military structure that had once held it together. Thus, the combination of internal fragmentation, weakened leadership, and external pressures led to the gradual unraveling of the Vijayanagara Empire after Krishnadeva Raya's death.

2. Amara-Nayaka system was a major political innovation of Vijayanagar Empire. Justify the statement. Competency Based Que

Or Examine the 'Amara-Nayaka system' in the military and administrative structure of the Vijayanagara empire. CBSE 2024

Ans The Amara-Nayaka system was a major political innovation of the Vijayanagara Empire. This can be justified through the following

- It is likely that many features of this system were derived from the iqta system of the Delhi Sultanate.
- The Amara-Nayakas were military commanders who were given territories to govern by the raya. They collected taxes and other dues from peasants, craftspersons and traders in the area.
- They retained part of the revenue for personal use and for maintaining a stipulated contingent of horses and elephants. These contingents provided the Vijayanagara kings with an effective fighting force with which they brought the entire Southern peninsula under their control.
- Some of the revenue was also used for the maintenance of temples and irrigation works.
- The Amara-Nayakas sent tribute to the king annually and personally appeared in the royal court with gifts to express their loyalty.
- Kings occasionally asserted their control over them by transferring them from one place to another.

However, during the course of the seventeenth century, many of these Nayakas established independent kingdoms. This hastened the collapse of the central imperial structure

3. Examine the distinctive aspects of the fortification of the Vijayanagara Empire. CBSE 2024

Ans. The fortification of the Vijayanagara Empire exhibited several distinctive aspects as follows

- **Seven Lines of Forts** The empire boasted seven lines of forts, encompassing not only the Vijayanagara city but also the surrounding farmland and forests, providing extensive protection.
- **Use of Wedge-Shaped Stones** The tallest wall, connecting the city's hills, was constructed using wedge-shaped stones without mortar. Despite the absence of cementing materials, the stones adhered well to one another, showing advanced engineering techniques.
- **Incorporation of Agricultural Areas** The fortification integrated agricultural areas, gardens, cultivated fields and wooded areas within its boundaries.

- **Multiple Lines of Defence** Distinct lines of defence encircled different sections of the empire, including the metropolitan complex and the royal centre, enhancing the overall security and fortification strategy.
- **Heavily Guarded Gates** The gates leading into the fort were heavily guarded, with architectural features such as arches and domes distinguishing them.

4. Explain why Abdur Razzaq, a Persian ambassador, was greatly impressed by the fortification of Vijayanagara Empire during the 15th century.

Ans. Abdur Razzaq, an ambassador sent by the ruler of Persia to Calicut in the fifteenth century was impressed after looking at the fortifications due to its following features

- The fortifications not only surrounded the city but also remote agricultural areas and forests.
- The hills surrounding the city were linked with the outermost wall. The large construction was slightly reduced in thickness at one end.
- The mortar or cementing agent was not used in the construction. The stone blocks were wedge shaped, which held them in place.
- The inner portion of walls was packed with waste parts of Earth like remains of stone, brick, etc and square or rectangular fortification was projected outwards.
- The most important thing about this fortification was that it surrounded agricultural lands. Between the first, second and the third walls, there were cultivated fields, gardens and houses.
- There is an evidence of an agricultural land between the sacred centre and the urban core, and this land was supplied water from a canal system which drew water from the river Tungabhadra.
- The inner core of the urban complex was surrounded by second line of fortification and the royal centre was surrounded by a third line. Within this, there were major buildings present which were surrounded by their own high walls.
- The well-guarded gates which were linked to major roads of the city were used to entered the fort.

5. Examine the main reasons for the rise and decline of the Vijayanagara Empire. CBSE 2024

Ans. The main reasons for the rise of the Vijayanagara Empire are as follows

- The empire benefited from strong central authority under capable rulers like Krishnadeva Raya.
- The empire's strategic location helped in smooth trade and cultural exchange, contributing to its growth and influence in South India.

The main reasons for the decline of the Vijayanagara empire are as follows

- Decentralisation of powers to provincial governments by weak central governments. It led to inefficiency and instability.
- Weak and incompetent successors to capable rulers further weakened the empire's control.
- The luxurious lifestyle of the people led to moral decay and societal instability.
- Internal conflict caused by the rule of different dynasties and continuous conflicts with neighbouring powers like the Bahmani Sultanate drained the empire's resources and weakened its military strength.
- The Battle of Talikota in 1565 marked the decisive defeat of Vijayanagara's army, leading to the empire's downfall.

6. "Vijayanagara was characterised by its distinctive building style." Support this statement with the sacred architectural examples of Vijayanagara. CBSE Diksha

Or **Vijayanagara Empire was characterised by a distinctive architecture and building styles. 'Justify the statement.** CBSE SQP 2024

Ans. Temple building in the region had a long history going back to the period of Pallavas, Chalukyas, Hoysalas and Cholas. The temples had distinct features such as Raya *gopurams* or royal gateways which indicated the presence of the temple from a distance. Gopurams were reminders of the power of kings, ability to command resources, techniques and skills needed to construct these towering gateways. Other distinctive features include *mandapas* or pavilion along a pillared corridor that often ran around the shrines within the temple complex.

Sacred architectural examples of Vijayanagara are as follows

- **Virupaksha temple** It was built over centuries. The hall in front of the main shrine was built by Krishnadeva Raya to mark his accession. This was decorated with delicately carved pillars. The halls in the temple were used for a variety of purposes. Some were spaces in which the images of gods were placed to witness special programmes of music, dance, drama, etc. Others were used to celebrate the marriages of deities, and yet others were meant for the deities to swing in. Special images, distinct from those kept in the small central shrine, were used on these occasions.
- **Vitthala temple** there were several halls and a unique shine designed like a chariot in this temple. The principal deity was Vitthala, a form of Vishnu generally worshipped in Maharashtra.

7. Why was the South-Western part of Vijayanagara settlement designated as royal centre? Explain.

Ans. The South-Westen part of the Vijayanagara settlement was designated as royal centre due to its following features

- It had over 60 temples. It shows that support of temples and cults was important for rulers who tried to establish and get approved of their authority through association with the gods and goddesses housed in the shrines.
- It was designated as royal centre because most of the buildings belonged to the royal family and administration were present here.
- Around thirty building complexes were identified as palaces. There were relatively large structures that do not seem to be associated with ritual functions.
- On the basis of the form of the buildings and their functions, different structures were assigned names. The king's palace was the largest of the buildings. It had two impressive platforms, called the audience hall and the *mahanavami dibba*.
- The entire complex was surrounded by high double walls with a street running between them.
- The audience hall was a high platform and it had slots for wooden pillars to be placed at close and regular intervals. On these pillars, a staircase was present which went to the second floor.
- At *mahanavami dibba*, various ceremonies were performed on the occasion of Mahanavami, like worship of image, worship of the state horse and the sacrifice of buffaloes and other animals. Dances, wrestling matches, procession of highly decorated horses, elephants and chariots and soldiers, as well as ritual presentations before the king and his guests by the chief *nayakas* and subordinate kings were the main events that took place on this day.

8. 'The establishment of the Vijayanagara Empire is considered significant in the history of the Indian sub-continent'. Justify the statement. **CBSE SQP 2024**

Ans. The establishment of the Vijayanagara Empire is significant in the history of the Indian sub-continent because of the following reasons

- **Cultural Synthesis** The Vijayanagara Empire promoted cultural blending by combining different traditions. It brought together Hindu, Jain, and Islamic influences, creating a vibrant mix of art, literature, and religious practices that showed the empire's inclusive way of governing and living.
- **Architectural Marvels** The empire's architecture, including temples, palaces, and fortifications, is known for combining local Dravidian styles with influences from nearby regions. This fusion can be seen in structures like the Virupaksha Temple and the Lotus Mahal, which mix local and external design elements.
- **Trade Dominance** Vijayanagara's strategic control over key trade routes made it a major commercial hub. The empire attracted merchants from across the Indian Ocean region, facilitating vibrant trade networks that included the exchange of goods and cultural ideas, further enhancing its significance.
- **Economic Prosperity** Its strategic location on the trade routes with the Arab, Persian, and European merchants contributed significantly to its economic prosperity. This trade brought great wealth to the empire, increasing its power and allowing it to support large architectural and cultural projects.
- **Control of Commodities** The Vijayanagara Empire's control over important trade routes and valuable goods like horses, spices, textiles, and gemstones highlighted its economic power. This control boosted its wealth and strengthened its influence in regional politics and trade.
- **Expansion and Consolidation** The Vijayanagara rulers focused on expanding and strengthening the empire. They extended their influence across South India, including taking over Orissa, and launched major military campaigns against regional powers like the Sultan of Bijapur.

Source Based Questions

Read the sources given below and answer the following questions.

1. Colin Mackenzie

Born in 1754 CE, Colin Mackenzie became famous as an engineer, surveyor and cartographer. In 1815, he was appointed the First Surveyor General of India, a post he held till his death in 1821. He embarked on collecting local histories and surveying historic sites in order to better understand India's past and make governance of the colony easier. He says that "it struggled long under the miseries of bad management... before the South came under the benign influence of the British government." By studying Vijayanagara, Mackenzie believed that the East India Company could gain "much useful information on many of these institutions, laws and customs whose influence still prevails among the various Tribes of Natives forming the general mass of the population to this day."

(i) Explain about the first surveyor General of India.

(ii) Mention what Mackenzie did to make governance of the colony easier.

(iii) According to him what benefits would the East India Company gain after studying Vijayanagara? Explain in brief.

Ans. (i) Colin Mackenzie was born in 1754 CE. He became famous as an engineer, surveyor and cartographer. In 1815, he was appointed as the first Surveyor General of India, he held this post till his death in 1821.

(ii) Colin Mackenzie embarked on collecting local histories and surveying historic sites in order to better understand India's past and make governance of the colony easier.

(iii) By studying Vijayanagara, Mackenzie believed that the East India Company could gain much useful information on many of the institutions, laws and customs whose influence still prevails among the various tribes of natives forming the general mass of the population.

2. Kings and Traders

Krishnadeva Raya (ruled 1509-29), the most famous ruler of Vijayanagara, composed a work on statecraft in Telugu known as the *Amuktamalyada*. About traders he wrote:

A king should improve the harbours of his country and so encourage its commerce that horses, elephants, precious gems, sandalwood, pearls and other articles are freely imported... He should arrange that the foreign sailors who land in his country on account of storms, illness and exhaustion are looked after in a suitable manner... Make the merchants of distant foreign countries who import elephants and good horses be attached to yourself by providing them with daily audience, presents and allowing decent profits. Then those articles will never go to your enemies.

(i) Explain the responsibility of king mentioned by Krishnadeva Raya.

(ii) In what ways Krishnadeva Raya protected articles from going to his enemies?

(iii) Explain the measures taken by the king to improve the conditions of his country.

Or **(i) Who was the most famous ruler of Vijayanagara and why?**

(ii) Mention the name and theme of the work compiled by him.

(iii) Why do you think the king was interested in encouraging trade? Explain.

Ans. (i) A king should have the responsibility to improve the harbours of his country and so encourage its commerce that horses, elephants, precious gems, sandalwood, pearls and other articles are freely imported.

(ii) Krishnadeva Raya protected articles by providing the merchants of distant foreign countries with daily audience, presents and decent profits. These merchants imported elephants, goods and horses from Vijayanagara Empire.

(iii) The measures taken by the king to improve the condition of his country were

- Fortifications of city
- Raising an efficient and effective army
- Importing good horses and elephants
- Improve trade and commerce and thus generating wealth

Or (i) Krishnadeva Raya of Tuluva dynasty was the most famous ruler of Vijayanagara because during his rule, the land between the Tungabhadra and Krishna rivers (the Raichur doab) was acquired in 1512 CE.

(ii) Krishnadeva Raya composed a work on statecraft in Telugu known as the *Amuktamalyada*. He talked about trade and traders and the ways to improve them.

(iii) The king was interested in encouraging trade to bring prosperity and improve the lives of the people in the kingdom. He improved harbours of the kingdom and encouraged trade and commerce. He allowed horses, elephants, precious gems, sandalwood, pearls and other articles to be freely imported.

3. How tanks were built ? **CBSE 2024**

About a tank constructed by Krishnadeva Raya, Paes wrote

The king made a tank ... at the mouth of two hills so that all the water which comes from either one side or the other collects there; and, besides this, water comes to it from more than three leagues (approximately 15 kilometres) by pipes which run along the lower parts of the range outside. This water is brought from a lake which itself overflows into a little river. The tank has three large pillars handsomely carved with figures; these connect above with certain pipes by which they get water when they have to irrigate their gardens and rice-fields. In order to make this tank the said king broke down a hill ... In the tank I saw so many people at work that there must have been fifteen or twenty thousand men, looking like ants ...

(i) Why did Krishnadeva Raya construct a tank ?

(ii) Why did Krishnadeva Raya choose the location at the mouth of two hills for building the tank?

(iii) In what ways was the water from the tanks used ?

Ans. (i) Krishnadeva Raya constructed a tank to manage water for irrigation and ensure a steady supply. Located between two hills, the tank collected water from both sides and was fed by pipes from a lake about 15 kilometers away.

(ii) Krishnadeva Raya chose the location at the mouth of two hills for the tank to collect water from both sides naturally. This site also allowed water to be brought from a distant lake through pipes, ensuring a steady supply for irrigation.

(iii) The water from the tank constructed by Krishnadeva Raya was primarily used for irrigation. It supplied water to irrigate gardens and rice fields, ensuring agricultural productivity. Additionally, the water was collected from multiple sources, including streams and a distant lake, and was channeled through pipes connected to the tank, providing a steady water supply for the region.

4. A Sprawling City

This is an excerpt from Domingo Paes's description of Vijayanagara:

The size of this city I do not write here, because it cannot all be seen from any spot, but I climbed a hill hence I could see a great part of it; I could not see it all because it lies between several ranges of hills. What I saw from thence seemed to me as large as Rome, and very beautiful to the sight; there are many groves of trees within it, in the gardens of the houses, and many conduits of water which flow into the midst of it, and in places there are lakes; and the king has close to his palace a palm-grove and other rich fruit-bearing trees.

(i) Who is the author of the passage? What is the theme of it? What did king had close to his palace?

(ii) Why could Paes not describe the size of city in the first instance?

(iii) What was the description of the city by Paes later?

Ans. (i) Domingo Paes is the author of the passage.

The theme is description of Vijayanagara.

The king had a palm-grove and other rich fruit-bearing trees close to his palace.

(ii) Paes had not described the size of city because he could not see the whole of city from the point where he was studying. The city was lying between several ranges of hill.

(iii) Later, when Paes climbed a hill, he described a great part of the city. He described it as large as Rome and very beautiful to the sight. He saw many groups of trees in the gardens of the houses. He saw water conduits flowing in the middle of them. He also saw lakes in some places.

5. The Bazaar

Paes gives a vivid description of the bazaar:

Going forward, you have a broad and beautiful street... In this street many merchants live and there you will find all sorts of rubies, and diamonds, emeralds, pearls, and seed-pearls and cloths, and every other sort of thing there is on earth and that you may wish to buy. Then you have there every evening, a fair where they sell many common horses and nags, and also many citrons, and limes, and oranges, and grapes, and every other kind of garden stuff, and wood; you have all in this street.

More generally, he described the city as being "the best-provided city in the world" with the markets "stocked with provisions such as rice, wheat, grains, Indian corn and a certain amount of barley and beans, moong, pulses and horse-gram" all of which were cheaply and abundantly available.

According to Fernao Nuniz, the Vijayanagara markets were "overflowing with abundance of fruits, grapes and oranges, limes, pomegranates, jackfruit and mangoes are all very cheap." Meat too was sold in abundance in the marketplaces. Nuniz describes "mutton, pork, venison, partridges, hares, doves, quail and all kinds of birds, sparrows, rats and cats and lizards" as being sold in the market of Bisnaga (Vijayanagara).

(i) Who is the author of the passage? What is the theme? What all can you find in the market street?

(ii) How did Paes describe the city?

(iii) What did Fernao Nuniz tell about Vijayanagara markets?

Ans. (i) The author of the passage is Domingo Paes.

The theme is about bazaar i.e. market street.

We can find in the market street all sorts of rubies, diamonds, emeralds, pearls, seed-pearls, cloths and every other sort of thing that exist on earth and that you may wish to buy.

(ii) Paes described the city as being the best-provided city in the world. It had markets stocked with provisions such as rice, wheat, grains, Indian corn and a certain amount of barley and beans, moong, pulses and horse-gram all of which were cheaply and abundantly available.

(iii) According to Fernao Nuniz, the Vijayanagara markets have abundance of fruits, grapes, oranges, limes, pomegranates, jackfruit and mangoes. Meat too was sold in abundance in the marketplaces. Mutton, pork, venison, partridges, hares, doves, quail and all kinds of birds, sparrows, rats, cats and lizards were also sold in the market of Bisnaga (Vijayanagara).

Map Based Questions

1. **On the given political outline map of India, locate and label the following with appropriate symbols.**

(i) Mysore (ii) Thanjavur
(iii) Bidar (iv) Golconda
(v) Bijapur

CBSE 2024

Ans.

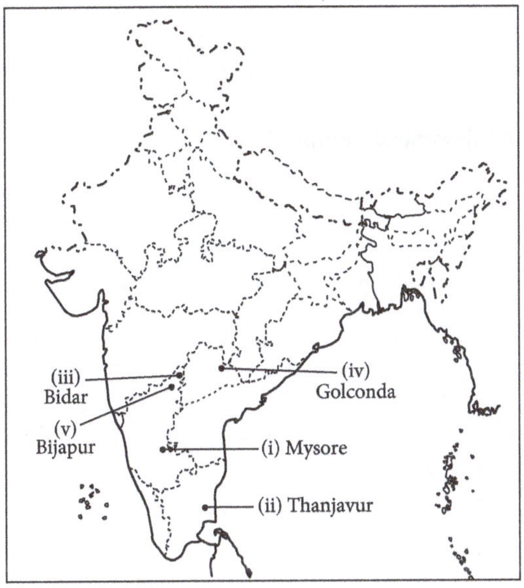

2. **On a political outline map of India, locate and label the following with appropriate symbols.**

(i) Chandragiri (ii) Kanchipuram
(iii) Kolar (iv) Tirunelveli
(v) Vijayanagara

CBSE SQP 2024

Ans.

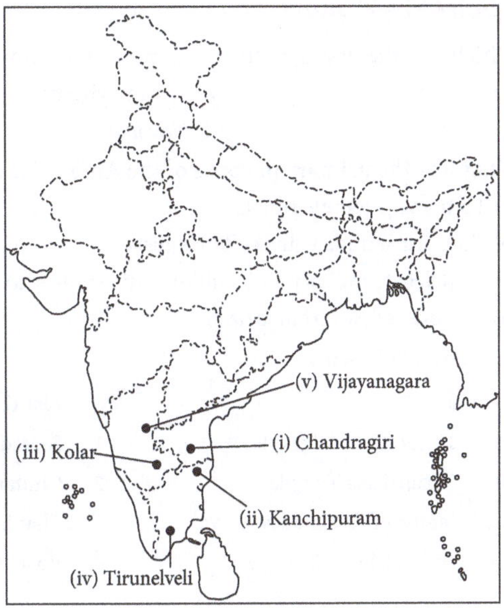

SELF ASSESSMENT TEST

Objective Type Questions

1. Which was the first dynasty of Vijayanagara Empire?
   (a) Tuluva dynasty (b) Saluva dynasty
   (c) *Rayas* (d) *Nayakas*

3. **What was the primary purpose of the Amara-Nayaka system in the Vijayanagara Empire?**
   (a) To manage temple rituals
   (b) To control trade with the Portuguese
   (c) To delegate military and administrative power to commanders
   (d) To collect taxes from artisans

3. Match the Following.

	List I		List II
A.	Hazara Rama Temple	1.	Sacred centre
B.	Virupaksha Temple	2.	Chidambram
C.	Statue of Krishnadeva Raya	3.	Thanjavur
D.	Brihadishvara Temple	4.	Royal Centre

Codes

	A	B	C	D		A	B	C	D
(a)	4	2	3	1	(b)	4	1	2	3
(c)	1	3	2	4	(d)	2	1	4	3

Short Answer Type Questions

4. Explain the conditions in Vijayanagara after the death of Krishnadeva Raya.
5. The relationship between Vijayanagara rulers and Sultans always hostile? Discuss.
6. What was the importance of temples in Vijayanagara Empire?
7. How did scholars reconstruct the history of Vijayanagara Empire? Discuss.
8. Give features of the roads in Vijayanagara as studied by the archaeologists.
9. The Virupaksha temple was built over centuries. Discuss.
10. Analyse the reasons for the rise and decline of the Vijayanagara Empire.

Long Answer Type Questions

11. How was the plotting of palaces, bazaars and temples of Vijayanagara possible?
12. Discuss about the importance of royal centre and sacred centre in the Vijayanagara Empire.
13. Comment on the architectural innovations and cultural synthesis in the Vijayanagara Empire.

8

CHAPTER

This chapter deals with social and economic conditions of the Mughal Empire. *Ain- i Akbari* written by Abu'l Fazl is the main source to reconstruct the history of Mughal Empire.

YOUR STUDY GOALS

8.1 Peasants and Agricultural Production
8.2 The Village Community
8.3 Women in Agrarian Society
8.4 Forests and Tribes
8.5 The Zamindars
8.6 Land Revenue System
8.7 The Flow of Silver
8.8 The *Ain-i Akbari* of Abu'l Fazl Allami

YOUR PRACTICE GOALS

- Objective Type Questions (38 Qs ; MCQs, A-R, Matching, Picture Based)
- Subjective Questions (20 SAs, 6 LAs)
- Source Based Questions (8 Qs)
- Map Based Questions (2 Qs)

Peasants, Zamindars and the State

(Agrarian Society and the Mughal Empire)

In the sixteenth and seventeenth centuries, both peasants and elites participated in agricultural production and claimed their rights to a share of the harvest. This created relationships of cooperation, competition and conflict among them.

States also derived a large portion of their income from agriculture production. Revenue assessors, collectors, record keepers were the agents of the state. These agents controlled society to ensure that cultivation took place and the state got its regular share of taxes from the produce.

8.1 Peasants and Agricultural Production

- The basic unit of agricultural society was the village, where peasants lived and performed different tasks that made up agricultural production throughout the year.
- Peasants were involved in tilling the soil, sowing seeds and harvesting the crop when it was ripe. They also performed labour for the production of agro-based goods like sugar and oil.
- Areas like large tracts of dry land or hilly regions were not cultivable in the same way as the more fertile expanses of land.

Looking for Sources

- Major sources for the agrarian history of the sixteenth and early seventeenth centuries are chronicles and documents from the Mughal Court.
- ***Ain-i Akbari*** was the most important chronicle authored by Akbar's court historian **Abu'l Fazl.**
- The *Ain-i-Akbari* documented the measures taken by the state to ensure cultivation and facilitate revenue collection by state agencies and zamindars.
- The main goal of the *Ain* was to showcase Akbar's empire as one where social harmony was maintained by a strong ruling class.
- According to the author of the *Ain*, any revolt against the Mughal state could not succeed.
- The *Ain* account can be supported by descriptions from areas outside the Mughal capital, including detailed revenue records from **Gujarat**, **Maharashtra** and **Rajasthan** from the seventeenth and eighteenth centuries.
- The records of the East India Company provide us descriptions of agrarian relations in Eastern India. They also record instances of conflicts between peasants, zamindars and the state.

Peasants and their Lands

- In the Mughal period, the terms most commonly used to refer to a peasant were ***raiyat*** (plural: *riaya*) or ***muzarian***. Other terms used for peasants were *kisan* or *asami*[1].
- The seventeenth century sources referred to two kinds of peasants
  (i) ***Khud-kashta*** These were the residents of the village in which they held their lands.
  (ii) ***Pahi-kashta*** These were non-resident cultivators who belonged to some other village, but cultivated lands elsewhere on a contractual basis.
- There were different reasons for people to become *pahi-kashta* such as
  - By choice i.e. when the taxes were lower in far away villages.
  - By compulsion i.e. forced by economic loss after a famine or other natural calamity.
- The average peasant of North India had more than a pair of bullocks and two ploughs, whereas most had even less.
- In Gujarat, peasants with about six acres of land were regarded as wealthy.
- In Bengal, five acres was the maximum size for an average peasant farm, while ten acres would make someone a wealthy *asami*.
- Cultivation was based on the principle of individual ownership. Peasant lands were bought and sold in the same way as the lands of other property owners.

Irrigation and Technology

- The reasons for the constant expansion of agriculture were the plenty of land, available labour and the mobility of peasants.
- As the primary purpose of agriculture was to feed people, basic food sources like rice, wheat or millets were the most cultivated crops.
- The rice producing zones were those areas receiving 40 inches or more of rainfall in a year. This was followed by wheat and millets with decreasing amounts of rainfall.
- Monsoons were the backbone of Indian agriculture. But some crops needed extra water for which artificial systems of irrigation had to be made.
- The state also supported irrigation projects. In Northern India, state dug new canals (*nahr, nala*) and also repaired old ones like the *shahnahr* in the Punjab during Shah Jahan's rule.

---

1 *Asami* It refers to rich peasant with ten or more acres of land.

- Peasants used technologies that often harnessed cattle energy. For example,
  - Wooden plough, which was light and easily assembled with an iron tip. But it did not make deep furrows which preserved the moisture better during hot months.
  - A drill was used to plant seeds which were pulled by a pair of giant oxen. Scattering seeds to different areas was the most prevalent method.
  - Hoeing and weeding were done simultaneously using a narrow iron blade with a small wooden handle.

An Abundance of Crops

- The ***kharif*** (autumn) and the ***rabi*** (spring) were the two major agricultural seasons.
- Most regions other than arid or dry or harsh areas produced a minimum of two crops a year (*do-fasla*). Some areas where rainfall or irrigation provided a continuous supply of water produce three crops.
- According to *Ain-i-Akbari*, Mughal provinces of Agra produced 39 varieties of crops and Delhi produced 43 over the two seasons. Bengal produced 50 varieties of rice alone.
- The Mughal state also encouraged peasants to cultivate *jins-i kamil*[2], for more revenue. For example, crops like cotton and sugarcane.
- Cotton was widely grown in central India and the Deccan plateau, while Bengal was known for its sugar.
- These cash crops also included different types of oilseeds and lentils. This shows that subsistence and commercial production were closely linked in an average peasant's holdings.
- During the seventeenth century, new crops from different parts of the world reached the Indian subcontinent. Maize (*makka*) was introduced into India *via* Africa and Spain and it became one of the major crops of Western India.
- Vegetables like tomatoes, potatoes and chillies, as well as fruits like pineapple and papaya, were introduced from the New World during this time. This indicates that peasants grew crops for both subsistence and commercial purposes.

Agricultural Prosperity and Population Growth

- The main result of diverse and flexible agricultural practices was slow population growth.
- Despite periodic disruptions caused by famines and epidemics, India's population increased.
- According to calculations by economic historians, there were about 50 million people between 1600 and 1800, which is an increase of about 33 per cent over 200 years.

The Spread of Tobacco

- Tobacco arrived first in the Deccan and it spread to Northern India in the early years of the seventeenth century.
- The *Ain-i-Akbari* does not mention tobacco in the lists of crops in Northern India.
- In 1604, Akbar and his nobles came across tobacco for the first time. Smoking tobacco in *hookahs* or *chillums* became a big fashion at that time.
- Jahangir was so worried about tobacco addiction that he banned it, but the ban was ineffective. By the end of the seventeenth century, tobacco had become a major product for consumption, cultivation and trade across India.

Quick Test 1

1. What was the basic unit of agricultural society of the Mughal empire?
2. Who is the author of *Ain-i-Akbari*?
3. The *shahnahr* was repaired during the rule of which Mughal emperor?
4. Name two *jins-i-kamil* crops.
5. Who banned the use of tobacco?

2 ***Jins-i kamil*** It means perfect crops.

8.2 The Village Community

- The peasants were mostly involved in agricultural production. They held their lands in individual ownership.
- At the same time, they were part of a collective village community in many aspects of their social lives.
- This village community has three parts i.e. **the cultivators**, **the panchayat** and **the village headman**.

Caste and the Rural Environment

- The cultivators were a diverse group due to significant inequalities based on caste and similar distinctions.
- Among those who tilled the land, there was a large number who worked as menials or agricultural labourers (*majur*).
- Despite the availability of a large amount of cultivable land in the Mughal empire, some caste groups were given low-status jobs, keeping them in poverty.
- These groups made up a large part of the village population, had minimal resources, and were limited by their position in the caste hierarchy, such as Dalits in modern India.
- Such distinctions had begun spreading into other communities also.
- In Muslim communities, menials (low status) like the *halalkhoran* (scavengers) were made to stay outside the boundaries of the village. Similarly, the **mallahzadas** (sons of boatmen) in Bihar were comparable to slaves.

▲ *A rural scene during Mughal rule*

- There was a direct correlation between caste, poverty and social status at the lower level of society. The same correlations were not so visible at the intermediate levels.
- A seventeenth century manual from Marwar mentions Rajputs as peasants, sharing the same status as Jats, who were placed lower in the caste hierarchy.
- The Gauravas, who cultivated land around Vrindavan (Uttar Pradesh), wanted Rajput status.
- Castes like **Ahirs, Gujars** and **Malis** moved to higher positions in the hierarchy because of the profitability of cattle rearing and horticulture.
- In the Eastern regions, intermediate pastoral and fishing castes like the Sadgops and Kaivartas gained the status of peasants.

Panchayats and Headmen

- The village panchayat was an assembly of elders, usually important people of the village with hereditary rights over their property.

▲ *Meeting of village elders and tax collectors*

- The panchayats in some village consists of mixed caste populations.
- The decisions made by these panchayats were binding on the members.
- The panchayat was headed by a headman known as *muqaddam* or *mandal*. The headman was selected by agreement among the village elders, which had to be approved by the zamindar.
- Headmen held office as long as they enjoyed the confidence of the village elders. They could be dismissed by them also.
- The main function of the headman was to look after the preparation of village accounts. He was assisted by the **accountant** or ***patwari*** of the panchayat.

Sources of Funds for Panchayat

- The panchayat received funds from contributions made by individuals to a collective fund. These funds were used for entertaining revenue officials who visited the village periodically.
- Other expenses for community welfare, such as addressing challenges from natural disasters like floods, were also covered by these funds.
- These funds were also used for construction of bund (structure to control the flow of water) or digging a canal which peasants usually could not afford to do on their own.

Role of Panchayat

- The panchayat ensured that the caste boundaries among the various communities residing in the village were maintained.
- In Eastern India, all marriages were held in the presence of the *mandal.*
- The village headmen had to oversee the conduct of the members of the village community, mainly to prevent any offence against their caste.
- Panchayats had the authority to levy fines and impose serious punishments like expulsion from the community. Expulsion meant that the punished person was forced to leave the village, become an outcaste, and lose the right to practice their profession.

Petitions in Panchayat

- Petitions were submitted collectively by a caste group or community protesting against unjust demands of elite groups. For example, excessive tax demands during drought or other disasters.
- For the petitioners, the right to the basic minimum for survival was sanctioned by the custom. They regarded the village panchayats as the court of appeal that would ensure that the state carried out its moral obligations and guaranteed justice.
- In Western India, particularly Maharashtra, petitions were submitted to the panchayat regarding complaints about taxation or demands for unpaid labour (*begar*) imposed by higher castes or state officials. These petitions were usually made by villagers, from the lowest levels of rural society.

Decisions of Panchayat

- The decision of the panchayat in conflicts between lower-caste and the state officials or the local zamindar could vary from case to case.
- In case of excessive revenue demands, the panchayat often suggested compromise. In cases where reconciliation failed, peasants adopted extreme forms of resistance like deserting the village.

Jati Panchayats

- In addition to the village panchayat, each caste or jati in the village had its own jati panchayat.
- In **Rajasthan,** jati panchayats settled civil disputes between members of different castes.
- Jati panchayats mediated in land disputes like
  - when different persons claimed same piece of land,
  - deciding whether marriages were performed according to the rules laid down by a particular caste group
  - deciding who had more religious importance in village functions, etc.
- State respected the decisions of jati panchayats in most cases, except in the matters of criminal justice.

Village Artisans

- According to Marathi documents and village surveys made in the early years of British rule, there were huge numbers of artisans, sometimes as high as 25 per cent of the total households in the villages.
- Cultivators and their families would also participate in craft production like dyeing, textile printing, baking and firing of pottery, making and repairing agricultural implements.
- Cultivators were engaged in artisanal production when there was a gap in between agricultural activities, like the period between sowing and weeding or between weeding and harvesting.
- Village artisans like potters, blacksmiths, carpenters, barbers, even goldsmiths provided specialised services and in return they were paid by villagers through different means. The most common way of paying was giving them a share of the harvest, or an allotment of land. In Maharashtra, such lands became the artisans' ***miras*** or ***watan***, which were their hereditary holdings.
- ***Jajmani*** **System** was prevalent where artisans and peasant households were paid a small daily allowances by the zamindars.

Villages as a Little Republic

- In the nineteenth century, some British officials saw the village as a 'little republic' where people with common interests shared resources and labour collectively. But this was not a symbol of rural equality.
- Individual ownership of assets and deep inequities based on caste and gender differences were present in villages.
- A group of powerful individuals decided the affairs of the village and exploited the weaker sections. They also had the authority to deliver justice.
- A cash network had already developed through trade between villages and towns.
- In the central region of the Mughal Empire, revenue was assessed and collected in cash.
- Artisans working for the export market, as well as producers of commercial products like cotton, silk or indigo, received their advances or wages in cash.

Quick Test 2

1. Who were *halalkhorans* and *mallahzadas*?
2. How were the headmen of the village panchayat chosen?
3. Which cases were settled by jati panchayats in Rajasthan?
4. What term refers to the hereditary holdings of artisans in Maharashtra?
5. What was the *jajmani* system?

8.3 Women in Agrarian Society

▲ *A woman spinning thread*

- In many societies, men and women had specific roles in the production process. They worked together in the fields, with men ploughing and women sowing, weeding, threshing and winnowing.
- In medieval India, the development of small villages and individual peasant farming depended on the labour and resources of the whole household, leading to the impracticality of strict gender roles.
- Menstruating women were often prohibited from touching the plough or potter's wheel in Western India or entering betel-leaf (*paan*) groves in Bengal.
- Artisanal tasks such as spinning yarn, sifting and kneading clay for pottery, and embroidery relied heavily on female labour.

- Peasant and artisan women not only worked in the fields but also went to the houses of their employers or to the markets if needed.
- Women were considered an important resource in agrarian society also because they gave birth to children in a society dependent on labour.
- Many women also died because of malnutrition, frequent pregnancies and death during childbirth.
- There was often a shortage of wives. Marriages in many rural communities required the payment of bride-price rather than dowry to the bride's family. Remarriage was accepted both among divorced and widowed women.

Atrocities Against Women

- Households were typically headed by men, leading to strict control over women by male family members and the community.
- Harsh punishments could be imposed if women were suspected of infidelity (having a sexual relationship with somebody else).
- In Western India, documents from Rajasthan, Gujarat and Maharashtra show that women submitted petitions to the village panchayat seeking compensation and justice.
- Wives protested against the unfaithfulness of husbands or the neglect of the wife and children by the male head of the household.
- The panchayat often excluded women's names from the petitions, referring to them as the mother, sister, or wife of the male head of the household.

Property Rights of Women

- Among the landholding class, women had the right to inherit property. For example, in Punjab, women, including widows, participated in rural land markets as sellers of their inherited property.
- The zamindaris were inherited by both Hindu and Muslim women, which they were free to sell or mortgage.
- In the eighteenth century, there were women zamindars in Bengal, including a notable woman leader of the Rajshahi zamindari.

8.4 Forests and Tribes

Beyond Settled Villages

- In Northern and North-Western India, large areas of forests, including dense forests (*jangal*) and scrubland (*kharbandi*), were common in Eastern India, Central India, Northern India (including the Terai on the Indo-Nepal border), Jharkhand, and in peninsular India down the Western Ghats and the Deccan plateau.
- Forest cover was about 40% during the Mughal period.
- Forest dwellers, called *jangli*, depended on gathering forest produce, hunting and shifting agriculture, with seasonal activities. For example, the Bhil tribe collected forest produce in spring, fish in summer, cultivated during the monsoon and hunted in autumn and winter.
- Forests were seen as refugees for troublemakers. Mughal Emperor Babur noted that jungles provided good defense, allowing rebellious villagers to avoid paying taxes.

Inroads into Forests

- External forces entered forests in various ways, such as the state's demand for elephants for the army, which led to ***peshkash*** (a form of tribute) demanded from forest people. It often included a supply of elephants.

- In Mughal ideology, hunting symbolised the state's concern for all subjects. Regular hunting expeditions allowed emperors to address grievances of its inhabitants.
- The spread of commercial agriculture negatively impacted forest dwellers' lives.
- Forest products like honey, beeswax and gum lac were in great demand, with gum lac becoming a key overseas export by the seventeenth century.
- Elephants were also captured and sold. The state required elephants for the army.
- Trade included the exchange of goods through barter. Some tribes, like the Lohanis in Punjab, engaged in overland trade with Afghanistan and local trade within Punjab.
- The lives of forest people were also affected by social factors. Tribes had their chieftains just like the 'big men' of the village community.
- Many tribal chiefs became zamindars or even kings. To do this, they built armies by recruiting relatives and demanding military service from their tribes.
- Tribes in the Sind region had armies which were 6000 cavalry and 7000 infantry.
- Ahom kings in Assam had *paiks*, people who provide military service in exchange for land.
- The Ahom kings declared a royal monopoly (ownership) over the capture of wild elephants.

Transition from Tribal to Monarchy

- In the sixteenth century, the transition from tribal to **monarchical systems** fully developed, which was based on earlier changes.
- The *Ain-i Akbari* noted the existence of tribal kingdoms in the North-East.
- Wars were common; for example, the Koch kings fought against neighbouring tribes to gain control over them during the sixteenth and seventeenth centuries.
- New cultural influences began to enter forested areas.
- Some historians suggest that sufi saints (*pirs*) significantly contributed to the gradual acceptance of Islam among agricultural communities in newly colonised regions.

7.5 The Zamindars

- Zamindars were a rural class that depended on agriculture but did not directly farm the land.
- They owned land and enjoyed social and economic privileges due to their higher status. Their high status was because of caste and services (*khidmat*) they provided to the state.
- Zamindars held large personal lands, called ***milkiyat***[3], which they cultivated for private use with hired or slave labour. The zamindars could sell, leave or mortgage these lands at their will.
- Zamindars collected revenue for the state and controlled military resources, often having fortresses (*qilachas*) and armed forces, including cavalry and infantry.
- Abu'l Fazl's account shows that an 'upper caste' Brahmana-Rajput alliance had already gained strong control over rural society, with significant representation from the so-called intermediate castes.
- Contemporary documents indicate that some people became zamindars through military force, often by seizing land from weaker individuals with the support of an imperial order (*sanad*).
- The gradual unification of zamindari also led to the rise of new zamindars due to land colonisation, rights transfers and purchases.
- Other factors also contributed to the strengthening of the clan or zamindaris based on heredity. For example, clans like the Rajputs and Jats used these strategies to centralise control in Northern India, while peasant-pastoralists such as the Sadgops established powerful zamindaris in Central and South-Western Bengal.

3 **Milkiyat** It refers to the lands cultivated for the private use of zamindars.

- Zamindars led the process of colonisation of agricultural land and helped cultivators to settle down by providing them the means of cultivation, like cash loans.
- The buying and selling of zamindaris increased the circulation of money in the village side.
- Zamindars also sold the produce from their *milkiyat* lands. Zamindars often set up markets (*haats*) where peasants would come to sell their produce.

Relationship between Zamindars and Peasants

The zamindar's relationship with the peasantry involved mutual benefit, authority, a subordinate role, and patronage. This view can be supported by the following aspects

- Bhakti saints criticised caste-based oppression but did not label zamindars or moneylenders as exploiters of peasants; instead, they criticised state revenue officials.
- Zamindars often received support from peasants in agrarian revolts against the state in North India.

Quick Test 3

1. Name some activities that were dependent on female labour.
2. Which Mughal emperor stated that jungles provided a good defence?
3. Who declared a royal monopoly over the capture of wild elephants?
4. Who were *paiks*?
5. How did zamindars contribute to the monetisation of rural economies?

8.6 Land Revenue System

- The Mughal Empire's economy depended on land revenue. Thus, it was essential for the state to create an administrative system to manage agriculture and collect taxes as the empire expanded.
- This system included the *diwan's* office (*daftar*), which managed the empire's budget.
- Revenue officials and record keepers played key roles in agricultural management and shaping land relations.
- The land revenue arrangements consisted of two stages, first assessment and then actual collection. The **jama** was the amount assessed and ***hasil*** was the collected amount.
- Akbar in his order mentioned ***amil-guzar***[4] should collect the revenue from the cultivators either in cash or kind.
- The main motto of the state while fixing revenue was to maximise its claims, but sometimes it was prevented because of the local conditions.
- Both cultivated and cultivable lands were measured in each province. The *Ain* recorded land details during Akbar's reign, and land measurement efforts continued under later emperors.
- In 1665, Aurangzeb directed his revenue officials to keep yearly records of cultivators in each village. However, many areas, especially forests, remained unmeasured.
- The Emperor Akbar classified the lands and fixed a different revenue to be paid by each. These land systems were
  - ***Polaj*** is a land that is cultivated every year for different crops and is never left fallow.
  - ***Parauti*** is a land that is left uncultivated for a period to regain its fertility.
  - ***Chachar*** is a land that has been left fallow for three or four years.
  - ***Banjar*** is a land uncultivated for five years and more.

4 *Amil-guzar* It refers to the revenue collector.

- There were several systems for land revenue collection
  - ***kankut*** the word *kan* signifies grain, and *kut* means to estimate or appraisal. This system refers to estimating grain, where crops are cut and assessed in three categories: good, middling and inferior. This estimation provides an accurate return.
  - ***batai***, also known as *bhaoli*, involves harvesting and collecting the crops, which are then divided by agreement in front of all parties.
  - ***khet-batai*** is the system in which the fields are divided after they are sown.
  - ***lang batai*** is a system where, after cutting the grain, the crops are arranged in heaps and divided. Each person takes their share home to profit from it.

The Mansabdari System

- The Mughal administrative system included a military and bureaucratic structure (*mansabdari*) at the top that managed both civil and military matters. This was called *mansabdari* system.
- Some *mansabdars* were paid in cash (*naqdi*), while the majority of them were paid through revenue assignments (*jagirs*) from different regions, which were changed periodically.

8.7 The Flow of Silver

- The Mughal Empire was among the large territorial empires in Asia that had managed to consolidate power and resources during the sixteenth and seventeenth centuries. The other empires were the **Ming** (China), **Safavid** (Iran) and **Ottoman** (Turkey).

▲ *A silver rupya issued by Akbar*

▲ *A silver rupya issued by Aurangzeb*

- The political stability established by these empires created active overland trade networks from China to the Mediterranean Sea.
- The exploration journeys and the opening of the New World greatly increased India's trade with Europe. This led to greater geographical diversity and a wider variety of goods in India's overseas trade.
- This growing trade brought large amounts of silver into Asia to pay for goods from India, with a significant portion going to India.
- The period between the sixteenth and eighteenth centuries was also marked by a remarkable stability in the availability of metal currency, mainly the *silver* rupya in India.
- Italian traveller **Giovanni Careri**, visited India around 1690. He gave details about how silver circulated globally to reach India. His accounts highlight the huge cash and commodity transactions taking place in India in seventeenth-century India.

8.8 The Ain-i Akbari of Abu'l Fazl Allami

- The *Ain-i Akbari* was a significant historical and administrative project compiled by Abu'l Fazl under Emperor Akbar's order. It was completed in 1598.
- The *Ain-i Akbari* was part of a broader history writing project commissioned by Akbar called the ***Akbar Nama***. It consists of three books.
- The first two books of the *Akbar Nama* offer a historical narrative, while the *Ain-i Akbari*, the third book, contains imperial regulations and an overview of the empire.

Importance of *Ain-i Akbari*

- The *Ain-i Akbari* gave detailed accounts of the organisation of the court, administration and army, the sources of revenue, the physical layout of the provinces of Akbar's empire and the literary, cultural and religious traditions of the people.
- It also gave the description of the various departments of Akbar's government and detailed descriptions of the various provinces (*subas*) of the empire.
- It informed the emperor about the different and diverse customs and practices that existed across his large empire in different regions.
- The *Ain-i Akbari* recorded information about the empire and the people of India. It sets a standard reference for studying India in the seventeenth century.

The Five Books of *Ain-i Akbari*

The *Ain-i Akbari* was made up of five books (*daftars*), out of which the first three books describe about administration

(i) ***Manzil-abadi*** was the first book which concerned about the imperial household and its maintenance.

(ii) ***Sipah-abadi*** was the second book, which covers the military and civil administration and the establishment of servants. It also included notices and short biographical sketches of imperial officials (*mansabdars*), learned men, poets and artists.

(iii) ***Mulk-abadi***, the third book, dealt with the financial matters of the empire, providing detailed quantitative data on revenue rates. It included an **Account of the Twelve Provinces** which offered statistical insights into geography, economy and administrative divisions. This section provided a detailed view of agrarian society in Northern India.

The fourth and fifth books (*daftars*) dealt with the religious, literary and cultural traditions of the people of India and also contained a collection of Akbar's auspicious sayings.

The Details of *Ain-i Akbari* about *Sarkars*

The *Ain-i Akbari* provides a detailed overview of the *sarkars* after presenting information at the *suba* level. This information was organised in tables with eight columns that provide the following details

(i) *Parganat/mahal*

(ii) *Qila* (forts)

(iii) *Arazi* and *zamin-i paimuda* (measured area)

(iv) *Naqdi*, revenue assessed in cash

(v) *Suyurghal*, grants of revenue in charity

(vi) Zamindars

(vii) Details of the castes of the zamindars

(viii) Details of the troops including horsemen (*sawar*), foot-soldiers (*piyada*) and elephants (*fil*) of the zamindars.

Authenticity of *Ain-i Akbari*

- The *Ain-i Akbari* manuscript was revised **five times** by Abu'l Fazl, indicating his careful approach to ensuring accuracy.
- Oral testimonies were cross-checked and verified before being included as facts in the chronicle.
- All numeric data were written out in words to reduce **transcription**[5] errors.

5 **Transcription** The act or process of representing something in a written or printed form.

Limitations of Ain-i Akbari

- Many errors in totals were caused by simple arithmetic mistakes or transcription errors by assistants of Abu'l Fazl.
- Another limitation of the *Ain* was the biased nature of the quantitative data. Data was not collected uniformly from all provinces. For many *subas*, detailed information about the caste composition of zamindars was available, but this data was not given for Bengal and Orissa.
- The financial data from the *subas* was remarkable for its richness, but other important parameters such as prices and wages from these same areas were not recorded.
- The detailed list of prices and wages in the *Ain-i Akbari* came from data about the areas near the imperial capital of Agra. Therefore, this data is of limited relevance for the rest of the country.

Conclusion

Despite its limitations, the *Ain* remains an important document of its times. It gives valuable insights into the structure and organisation of the Mughal empire.

Unlike earlier chroniclers who focused mainly on political events, Abu'l Fazl recorded detailed information about the empire and its people. The insights of the *Ain* into professions, trades, and the imperial establishment help historians reconstruct the social structure of Mughal era.

Quick Test 4

1. What was the main motto of the Mughal state while fixing revenue?
2. Name the Italian traveller who provided a clear account of the flow of silver across India?
3. Which book of the *Ain-i-Akbari* deals gives the idea of a fiscal account of the Mughal state?
4. How many times the manuscript of *Ain-i-Akbari* revised?
5. Give any one limitation of *Ain-i-Akbari*.

TIMELINE

1526	Babur defeats Ibrahim Lodi, the Delhi Sultan, at Panipat, becomes the first Mughal emperor
1530-40	First phase of Humayun's reign
1540-55	Humayun defeated by Sher Shah, in exile at the Safavid court
1555-56	Humayun regains lost territories
1556-1605	Reign of Akbar
1605-27	Reign of Jahangir
1628-58	Reign of Shah Jahan
1658-1707	Reign of Aurangzeb
1739	Nadir Shah invades India and sacks Delhi
1761	Ahmad Shah Abdali defeats the Marathas in the third battle of Panipat
1765	The *diwani* of Bengal transferred to the East India Company
1857	Last Mughal ruler, Bahadur Shah II, deposed by the British and exiled to Rangoon (present-day Yangon, Myanmar)

Mind Map

PEASANTS, ZAMINDARS AND THE STATE

1 Peasants and Agricultural Production

Looking for sources
- Ain-i-Akbari recorded state arrangements for cultivation and revenue collection.
- Supplementary sources include regional revenue records and East India Company accounts.

Irrigation and Technology
- State supported irrigation projects like canals during Shah Jahan's reign.
- Peasants used cattle energy with technologies like plough and drills.

An Abundance of Crops
- Mughal provinces produced diverse crops such as 39 varieties in Agra, 43 varieties in Delhi and 50 varieties in Bengal.
- New crops like maize, tomatoes and papaya introduced in India.

Peasants and their Lands
- Peasants in Mughal period were called Raiyat, Muzarian, Kisan or Asami.
- There were two kinds of peasants: Khud-Kashta (residents of the village) and Pahi-kashta (non-residents cultivators).
- Affluent peasants in Gujarat owned 6 acres and in Bengal has 5 acres of land.

2 The Village Community

Village Artisans
- Artisans provided specialised services in exchange for goods.
- Artisans were compensated with a share of the harvest of land.
- Artisan's land in Maharashtra were known as miras or watan.

A Little Republic
- Village was seen as a collective but not equalitarian (equality for all people).
- Individual ownership existed with caste and gender inequalities.

Panchayats and Headmen
- Panchayats were assemblies of elders with hereditary property rights.
- Headmen also known as Muqaddam or mandal supervised village accounts and activities.

Caste and the Rural Milieu
- Caste based inequalities led to a diverse group of cultivators, including agricultural labourers.
- In Muslim communities, menials like Halalkhoran and Mallahzadas faced social exclusion.

3 Women in Agrarian Society

- Men and women worked together in agricultural production.
- Gender roles persisted despite share household in agriculture.
- Women's labour was essential for both agriculture and artisanal tasks.

4 Forests and Tribes

Beyond Settled Villages
- Forest dwellers were called *jangli*, living off forest resources.
- Activities included gathering, hunting, fishing and shifting agriculture.

Inroads into Forests
- State required elephants for the army, so *peshkash* levied from forest people which included a supply of elephants.
- Mughal hunting symbolised state concern and emperor's justice.
- Forest products like gum lac, honey were in high demand.

5 The Zamindars

- Zamindars held personal lands (milkiyat) cultivated with hired labour.
- They collected revenue for the state and controlled military resources.
- Colonisation, land transfer and purchase led to Zamindari consolidation.

6 Land Revenue System

- Revenue from land was crucial for Mughal empire's economy.
- Administrative system ensured control over agriculture production which included the office of the diwan.
- The land revenue arrangements consisted of two stages: Jana (the assessmet of amount) and hasil (the actual collection of amount).

7 The Flow of Silver

Trade, Currency and Global Exchange
- Mughal Empire consolidated power, fostering overland trade networks.
- Voyagaes of discovery expanded India trade with Europe.
- Giovanni Careri's account reveals global cash flow in India.

8 The Ain-i Akbari of Abu'l Fazl Allami

- Ain-i Akbari consists detailed account of empire's administration, revenue and provinces.
- It provides quantitative data on Subas, Sarkars and Mahals.
- Ain was revised five times for accuracy and authenticity.
- Oral testimonies were cross-checked before inclusion in the manuscript.
- Price and wage data was limited to Agra region, not nationwide.

NCERT Folder

Intext Questions

1. In what ways do you think the panchayats described in this section were similar to or different from present-day gram panchayats? (Pg. 206)

Ans. The panchayats described in historical texts are similar to present-day gram panchayats in their core function of managing village affairs and resolving local disputes. But they differ significantly in terms of their structure, election process, and the composition of members, which are now mandated to be more inclusive and representative with the introduction of the 73rd Constitutional Amendment. The Act guarantees reservations for women and lower castes in modern Gram Panchayats.

2. The zamindari system was abolished in India after Independence. Read through this section and identify reasons why this was done. (Pg. 213)

Ans. The zamindari system was abolished in India after independence primarily because it was seen as a system of extreme exploitation of peasant farmers by the zamindars (landlords), leading to widespread poverty and social injustice.

The government aimed to redistribute land ownership to the actual tillers by ending the intermediary role of the zamindars, promoting economic development and social equality in rural India.

3. Would you consider the land revenue system of the Mughals as a flexible one? (Pg. 215)

Ans. Yes, the land revenue system of the Mughals is generally considered to be flexible, particularly due to its ability to adapt to different regions and agricultural practices. It had features like land classification based on fertility, the option to pay in cash or kind, and a system of periodic reassessment of land revenue based on actual crop yields.

Answer in 100-150 words

1 What are the problems in using the *Ain* as a source for reconstructing agrarian history? How did historians deal with this situation?

Or **"There are some limitations of *Ain-i-Akbari*". Examine the statement.** **CBSE 2024**

Ans. *Ain-i Akbari* was written by Abu'l Fazl who was the court historian of Akbar. The problems in using the *Ain-i Akbari* as a source for reconstructing agrarian history are

- All the information about peasants in the *Ain-i Akbari* was the view from the top i.e. written by the ruling class in favour of ruling class.
- Another problem of the *Ain-i Akbari* was the biased nature of the quantitative data. Data was not collected uniformly from all provinces.
- The detailed list of prices and wages that the *Ain-i Akbari* provided were mainly derived from data related to the areas in and around the imperial capital of Agra, and is therefore of limited relevance for the rest of the country.

The historians deal with this situation by acquiring information from

- The detailed revenue records from Gujarat, Maharashtra and Rajasthan from the seventeenth and eighteenth centuries.
- The East India Company's numerous records which provide useful descriptions of agrarian relations in Eastern India.

2. To what extent is it possible to characterise agricultural production in the sixteenth- seventeenth centuries as subsistence agriculture? Give reasons for your answer.

Ans. It is not justified to characterise the agricultural production in the sixteenth-seventeenth centuries as subsistence agriculture because the agriculture in medieval India was not only for subsistence. This can be explained through the following reasons

- Terms like *jins-i kamil* meaning perfect crops, suggested that other crops were also grown other than food crops.
- The Mughal state encouraged peasants to cultivate crops which brought more revenue. Cotton and sugarcane crops were *jins-i kamil* i.e. they were the excellent crops for revenue.
- Cotton was grown over a large area of territory spread over Central India and the Deccan plateau, whereas Bengal was famous for sugar.
- Cash crops also included various kinds of oilseeds like mustard and lentils.
- This shows that peasants cultivated crops both for subsistence and commercial production.

3. Describe the role played by women in agricultural production.

Ans. The role played by women in agricultural production was

- Men tilled and ploughed, while women sowed, weeded, threshed and winnowed the harvest.
- The artisanal tasks like spinning yarn, sifting (removing lumps and large particles) and kneading (moulding) clay for pottery, and embroidery were dependent on female labour.
- Peasant and artisan women not only worked in the fields but also went to the houses of their employers or to the markets if needed.
- The women had the right to inherit property among the landed class of people. For example, in Punjab, women including widows participated in the rural land markets as sellers of property inherited by them.

4. Discuss with examples, the significance of monetary transactions during the period under consideration.

Ans. The significance of monetary transactions during the Mughal period were as follows

- Cash connections had already developed through trade between villages and towns during the Mughal period. In the most important part of Mughal empire, revenue was evaluated and collected in cash.
- Artisans such as weavers who produced for the export market received their advances or wages in cash.
- The producers of commercial products like cotton, silk or indigo also got payments in cash.
- The seventeenth century French traveller Jean-Baptiste Tavernier pointed out that the villages had money changer called Shroff. They acted as bankers to make settlements of monetary transactions.

5 Examine the evidence that suggests that land revenue was important for the Mughal fiscal system.

***Or* How revenue from land was the economic mainstay of the Mughal Empire? Explain with examples.** CBSE 2023

Ans. The Mughal Empire economy or fiscal system was based on the revenue from the land. So it was very important for Mughal state to create an administrative machinery to have control over agricultural production and to fix and collect revenue from the large empire which was expanding rapidly. This administrative machinery included the office (*daftar*) of the *diwan* who was responsible for looking after budget system of the empire.

Thus, revenue official and record keepers entered the agricultural domain and became important people in shaping agrarian relations.

Before fixing and collecting taxes from people, Mughal state first tried to gather specific information about the total area of the agricultural lands in the empire and what these lands produced. The land revenue arrangements consisted of two stages – first was assessment and then actual collection. The *jama* was the amount assessed and *hasil* is the amount collected.

Akbar in his order mentioned that, the revenue can be paid by the cultivators to *amil-guzar* in cash or in kind. The main motto of the state while fixing revenue was to maximise its claims, but sometimes it was prevented because of local conditions.

Write a short Essay (about 250-300 words) on the following

6. To what extent do you think caste was a factor influencing social and economic relations in agrarian society?

Ans. Caste was a factor influencing social and economic relations in agrarian society in the following ways

- Certain caste groups were assigned tasks which lacked prestige and thus pushed to poverty.
- Some caste groups had the least resources and were forced and restricted by their position in the caste hierarchy, much like the Dalits of modern India. These kind of distinctions passed on to other communities also.
- In Muslim communities, menials like the *halalkhoran* (scavengers) were made to stay outside the boundaries of the village. Similarly, the *mallahzadas* (sons of boatmen) in Bihar were compared to slaves.
- There was a direct correlation between caste, poverty and social status at the lower level of society. The same correlations were not so visible at the intermediate levels.
- From a manual belonging to seventeenth century Marwar, Rajputs are mentioned as peasants, sharing the same space with Jats, who were given a lower status in the caste hierarchy.
- Castes like Ahirs, Gujars and Malis moved to higher positions in the hierarchy because of the profitability of cattle rearing and horticulture.
- In the Eastern regions, intermediate pastoral and fishing castes like the Sadgops and Kaivartas acquired the status of peasants.

7 How were the lives of forest dwellers transformed in the sixteenth and seventeenth centuries?

Or Describe the life of forest dwellers in the Mughal Era.

Or Describe the life led by the forest dwellers during the Mughal Era in sixteenth-seventeenth centuries.

Ans. The lives of forest dwellers transformed in the sixteenth and seventeenth centuries in the following ways

- The lives of people those who lived in forests was effected negatively by the external factors like the spread of commercial agriculture. Forest products like honey, beeswax and gum lac were in great demand. In the seventeenth century, products like gum lac, became the important items of overseas export from India.
- Elephants were also captured and sold. Barter system was also used in trade by exchanging commodities. Some tribes like Lohanis in the Punjab were involved in overland trade, between India and Afghanistan. They also traded in the town-country trade in the Punjab itself.
- The lives of forest people too were manipulated and changed by the social factors. Tribes had their chieftains just like the 'big men' of the village community.
- Many tribal chiefs had become zamindars and some even became kings. They had to build an army for this and thus they recruited people from their relatives or demanded that their brotherhood i.e. people of their tribes provide military service.
- Tribes in the Sind region had armies comprised of 6000 cavalry and 7000 infantry. Ahom kings, in Assam had their paiks, people who were morally bound to render military service in exchange for land. The Ahom kings declared a royal monopoly over the capture of wild elephants.
- In the sixteenth century only, transition from a tribal to a monarchical system become fully developed though it had started earlier. This could be seen from the *Ain-i Akbari's* observations on the existence of tribal kingdoms in the North-East.
- War was common, for example, the Koch kings fought and brought a number of neighbouring tribes under control, after a long series of wars through the sixteenth and seventeenth centuries.

8. Examine the role played by zamindars in Mughal India.

Ans. Zamindars were class of people in the countryside that lived on agriculture but did not participate directly in the processes of agricultural production.

The role played by zamindar was as follows

- The zamindars held large areas of personal lands known as *milkiyat*, meaning property. *Milkiyat* lands were cultivated for the private use of zamindars, often with the help of hired or slave labour. The zamindars could sell, leave or mortgage these lands at their will.
- Zamindars got their power because they could often collect revenue on behalf of the state, a service for which they were paid financially. They also controlled military resources which was another source of power. Most of them also had fortresses (*qilachas*) as well as an armed group comprising units of cavalry, artillery and infantry.
- Zamindars led from the front in the process of colonisation of agricultural land and helped cultivators to settle down by providing them the means of cultivation, like cash loans. The buying and selling of zamindaris increased the process of monetisation in the village side. Zamindars also sold the produce from their *milkiyat* lands. These are proofs to show that zamindars often established markets to which peasants also came to sell their produce.
- Zamindars were an exploitative class. Their relationship with the peasantry had an element of mutual benefit, authority and subordinate relation and patronage. This view can be supported by two aspects
  (i) Bhakti saints who fearlessly condemned caste-based and other forms of oppression did not show the zamindars or moneylender as exploiters or oppressors of the peasantry. They criticised the revenue official of the state.
  (ii) Zamindars were often supported by the peasantry in their struggle against the state in many agrarian revolts that arose in North India.

9. Discuss the ways in which panchayats and village headmen regulated rural society.

Or "The village panchayat during the Mughal period regulated rural society." Explain the statement.

Or Assess the role played by panchayats in the villages during Mughal period.

Or Examine the role of panchayat as the main constituent of the Mughal village community.

Or Describe the role of village panchayats and headmen during the Mughal period in the sixteenth and seventeenth centuries.

Ans. Panchayat and Village Headmen

The village panchayat was an assembly of elders, usually important people of the village with hereditary rights over their property. The panchayat was a mixed body in the villages which had mixed-caste populations. A headman known as *muqaddam* or *mandal* headed the panchayat.

The headman was chosen through the consensus of the village elders, and this choice had to be accepted by the zamindar. Headmen held office as long as they enjoyed the confidence of the village elders. They could be dismissed by the village elders.

Role of Panchayat and Village Headmen

- One of the important functions of the panchayat was to ensure that the caste boundaries among the various communities residing in the village were maintained. In Eastern India, all marriages were held in the presence of the *mandal*.
- Panchayats also had the authority to levy fines and impose serious punishments like expulsion from the community. Expulsion meant that the person who was given punishment was forced to leave the village, become an outcaste and lose his right to practise his profession. Such punishments were meant to discourage violation of caste systems.
- The panchayat got its funds from the contributions made by the individuals to a common financial pool. These funds were used to pay for the costs of entertaining revenue officials who visited the village from time to time. These funds were also used for construction of a bund or digging a canal which peasants usually could not afford to do on their own.
- For petitioners, village panchayat was a court of appeal which could ensure that the state carried out its moral duties and guaranteed justice.
- The main function of the headman was to look after the preparation of village accounts. He was assisted by the accountant or *patwari* of the panchayat.

10 On an outline map of the world, mark the areas which had economic links with the Mughal Empire and trace out possible routes of communication.

Ans.

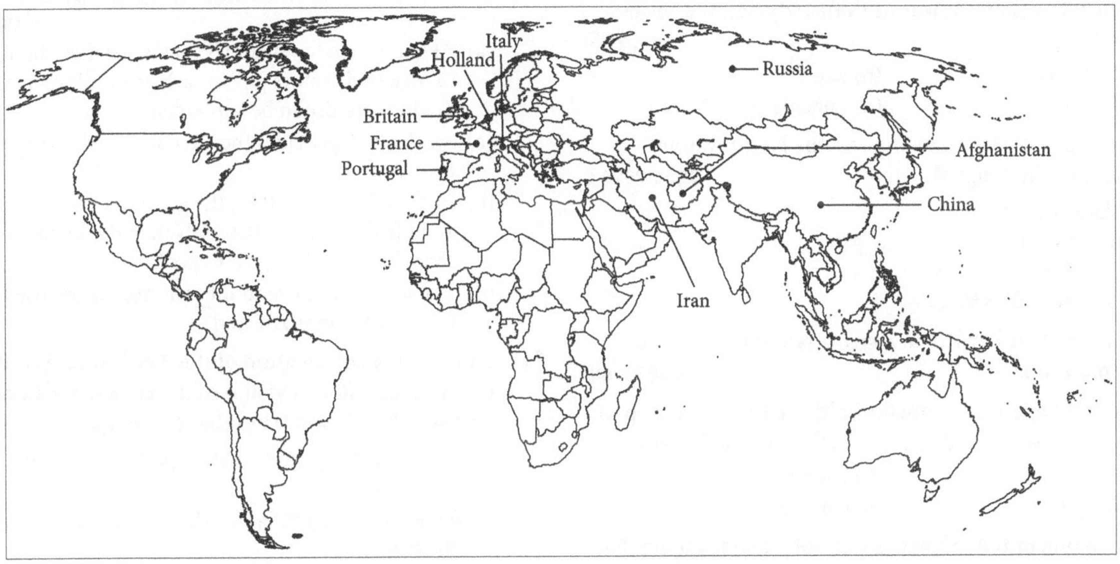

Their possible routes for communication could have been

- Sea route *via* Atlantic Ocean to Cape of Good Hope (South Africa), Arabian Sea and Indian Ocean.
- Land Route from Central Asia to Afghanistan through modern Pakistan upto Kerala or Goa.

Exam Pattern Questions

Objective Type Questions

Multiple Choice Questions (MCQs)

1. Abu'l Fazl was a court historian of which Mughal emperor?

(a) Humayun (b) Babur
(c) Akbar (d) Jahangir

2. The term used for village headman was

(a) *kamil* (b) *muqaddam*
(c) *shahnahr* (d) *asamis*

3. Which one of the following tribes was engaged in overland trade between India and Afghanistan and in the villages and towns in Punjab during the Mughal era ? **CBSE 2024**

(a) Mundas (b) Koch
(c) Ahoms (d) Lohanis

4. Which one of the following was the land revenue system of the Mughals ? **CBSE 2024 C**

(a) Ijaradari System
(b) Iqta System
(c) Mansabdari System
(d) Mahanayak System

5. Fill in the blank with the appropriate word from the given options **CBSE 2024**

The land which was annually cultivated for each crop in succession was called .... in the Mughal Empire.

(a) Polaj (b) Parauti
(c) Banjar (d) Chachar

6. Which one of the following was not a major factor that accounted for the constant expansion of agriculture in the Mughal state ? **CBSE 2024**

(a) Abundance of land
(b) Availability of labour
(c) Mobility of peasants
(d) Availability of tractors

7. Which of the following is a major source to understand agrarian history of 16th and 17th century India? **CBSE 2025**

(a) Revenue records of Agra & Delhi
(b) Relationship between peasants and zamindars
(c) Important chronicle - the Ain-e-Akbari
(d) Types of agricultural crops grown at that time

8. Which one of the following statements is most appropriate regarding the zamindars of 16th and 17th century India? **CBSE 2025**

(a) The zamindars were the exploitative class for the peasants.
(b) The zamindars collected revenue on behalf of the state.
(c) They always maintained cordial relations with the villagers.
(d) The zamindars had small piece of lands for personal use.

9. Choose the correct statement from the given options. **CBSE Diksha**

(a) Akbar decreed to mandals that while they should strive to make cultivators pay in cash, the option of payment in kind was also to be kept open .
(b) *Mulk-abadi* provides the "Account of the Twelve Provinces".
(c) In *'Bhaoli'*, after cutting the grain ,they form it in heaps and divide it among themselves, and each takes his share home and turns it to profit.
(d) The *jama* was the amount collected, as opposed to hasil,the amount assessed.

10. How did the compilation of the Ain-i Akbari contribute to Emperor Akbar's vision of governance? Choose the best suitable option from the following. **SQP 2024**

(a) By emphasising military strategies for territorial expansion.
(b) By documenting religious rituals and practices across the empire.
(c) By providing information on administrative and cultural traditions.
(d) By focusing on trade routes and economic policies.

11. Which of the following statements is correct regarding Ain-i-Akbari ? **CBSE 2024**

(a) Akbar Nama was the third book of Ain-i-Akbari.
(b) Manzil-abadi deals with the civil administration of the Mughals.
(c) Sipah-abadi deals with the imperial household of the Mughals.
(d) Mulk-abadi deals with the fiscal side of the Mughal Empire.

12. **Select the incorrect statement using the codes given below.**

(i) The peasants were mostly involved in the agricultural production.
(ii) *Khud-kashta* were non-residents cultivator of the village.
(iii) *Pahi-kashta* were the residents of the village in which they held their lands.

Codes

(a) (i) and (ii) (b) (ii) and (iii)
(c) (i) and (iii) (d) All of these

13. **Select the correct statement using the codes given below.**

(i) In sixteenth century, transition from a tribal to a monarchical system became partially developed.
(ii) War was common during this phase.
(iii) The Ahom kings declared a royal monopoly over the capture of wild elephants.

Codes

(a) (i) and (ii) (b) (i) and (iii)
(c) (i), (ii) and (iii) (d) (ii) and (iii)

14. **Select the correct statements about the *Ain-i Akbari*.**

(i) The first book is called *manzil-abadi.*
(ii) The second book is *mulk-abadi.*
(iii) The third book is *sipah-abadi.*
(iv) The fourth book deal with the religious traditions of people of India.

Codes

(a) (i) and (ii) (b) (ii) and (iii)
(c) (i) and (iv) (d) (iii) and (iv)

15. **Select the correct statements.**

(i) Men and women worked together in the fields.
(ii) Agricultural production was based on the labour.
(iii) The commercialised product decreased the demand of women's labour.
(iv) Women tilled and ploughed the fields.

Codes

(a) (i) and (ii) (b) (ii) and (iii)
(c) (iii) and (iv) (d) (i) and (iv)

16. **Which of the following tribal kingdoms exerted considerable influence and played a significant role in the Mughal Empire during the 16th and 17th centuries?** **CBSE 2024**

(i) Lohanis in Punjab
(ii) Ahoms in Assam
(iii) Koch in Bengal
(iv) Kols in Singhbhum

Options

(a) (ii), (iiii) and (iv) (b) (i), (ii) and (iii)
(c) (i), (ii) and (iv) (d) (i), (iii) and (iv)

17. **Which one of the following descriptions of Mughal rural society is correctly matched?** **CBSE 2024**

(Rural-people)		**(Profession)**
(a) Raiyat	-	Boatsman
(b) Mallah	-	Banker
(c) Shroff	-	Peasant
(d) *Mansabdar*	-	Military-Bureaucrat

18. **Choose the correct pair regarding the profile of rural people during the Mughal period** **CBSE 2024**

	List I (Name)		**List II** (Profile)
(a)	Mallahzadas	–	Village Headman
(b)	Muqaddam	–	Banker
(c)	Shroff	–	Boatmen
(d)	Muzarian	–	Peasant

19. **Which of the following pairs is correctly matched regarding the classification of lands under Akbar ?** **CBSE 2024**

(a) Polaj - Land which was cultivated annually.
(b) Parauti - Land uncultivated for five years.
(c) Chachar - Land left uncultivated for a year.
(d) Banjar - Land laid fallow for three years.

20. **Arrange the following in sequence**

(i) Reign of Shah Jahan (ii) Reign of Akbar
(iii) Humayun's reign (iv) Reign of Aurangzeb

Codes

(a) (iii), (iv), (ii), (i) (b) (iii), (ii), (i), (iv)
(c) (iv), (ii), (iii), (i) (d) (i), (ii), (iii), (iv)

21. **Arrange the following in sequence**

(i) Bahadur Shah (ii) Nadir Shah
(iii) Ahmad Shah Abdali (iv) Reign of Jahangir

Codes

(a) (iv), (ii), (iii), (i) (b) (iv), (iii), (ii), (i)
(c) (i), (ii), (iii), (iv) (d) (i), (iii), (iv), (ii)

22. **Identify the name of the chronicle from the information given below.**

(i) It was authored by Akbar's court historian Abu'l Fazl.
(ii) It recorded the arrangements made by the state to ensure cultivation, to enable the collection of revenue and to regulate the relationship between the state and the zamindars.
(iii) The central purpose of this chronicle was to present a vision of Akbar's empire where social harmony was provided by a strong ruling class.
(iv) It was completed in 1598, the forty-second regional year of the emperor.

Options

(a) *Ain-i-Akbari* (b) *Babar Nama*
(c) *Padshahnama* (d) *Akbar Nama*

23. **Identify the forest tribe during the sixteenth and seventeenth century with the help of following information.** **CBSE 2024**

(i) In Assam, these tribal chiefs became kings.
(ii) They rendered military service in exchange of land.
(iii) They declared their monopoly on catching wild elephants.

Options

(a) Lohani tribe (b) Santhal tribe
(c) Ahom tribe (d) Munda tribe

24. **Complete the following with the correct option regarding the terms with their respective meanings.**

Scrubland: ***Kharbandi*** **:: Fortress: ....**

(a) *Qilacha* (b) *Mawas* (c) *Sanad* (d) *Peshkash*

Assertion-Reason

25. **Assertion** (A) The peasants were mostly involved in the agricultural production.
Reason (R) Peasants held their lands in individual ownership.

Codes

(a) Both A and R are true and R is the correct explanation of A
(b) Both A and R are true, but R is not the correct explanation of A
(c) A is true, but R is false
(d) A is false, but R is true

26. **Assertion** (A) Maize was introduced in India *via* Africa and Spain.
Reason (R) Several new crops from different parts of the world reached the Indian subcontinent during the seventeenth century.

Codes

(a) Both A and R are true and R is the correct explanation of A
(b) Both A and R are true, but R is not the correct explanation of A
(c) A is true, but R is false
(d) A is false, but R is true

27. **Assertion** (A) State dug new canals and also repaired old ones.
Reason (R) The state supported irrigation projects.

Codes

(a) Both A and R are true and R is the correct explanation of A
(b) Both A and R are true, but R is not the correct explanation of A
(c) A is true, but R is false
(d) A is false, but R is true

28. **Assertion** (A) People became *pahi-kashta* out of compulsion.
Reason (R) They were forced by economic distress after a famine. **CBSE Diksha**

Codes

(a) Both A and R are true and R is the correct explanation of A
(b) Both A and R are true, but R is not the correct explanation of A
(c) A is true, but R is false
(d) A is false, but R is true

29. **Assertion** (A) The village panchayat was an assembly of elders.
Reason (R)*Muqaddam* or *mandal* headed the panchayat.

Codes

(a) Both A and R are true and R is the correct explanation of A
(b) Both A and R are true, but R is not the correct explanation of A
(c) A is true, but R is false
(d) A is false, but R is true

Match the Following

30.

	List-I (Lands in Mughal Empire)		List-II (Features)
A.	*Polaj*	1.	Land always being cultivated
B.	*Parauti*	2.	Land fallow for three to four years
C.	*Chachar*	3.	Land fallow a year
D.	*Banjar*	4.	Land uncultivated for five years

Codes **CBSE 2023**

	A	B	C	D		A	B	C	D
(a)	1	3	2	4	(b)	2	3	4	1
(c)	3	4	1	2	(d)	4	3	2	1

31.

	List I	List II
A.	To estimate or appraisal of grain.	1. *Lang batai*
B.	The grain is divided by agreement in the presence of the parties.	2. *Khet batai*
C.	The fields are divided after they are sown.	3. *Bhaoli*
D.	The crops are arranged in heaps and divided.	4. *Kankut*

Codes

	A	B	C	D		A	B	C	D
(a)	1	2	3	4	(b)	4	3	2	1
(c)	4	3	1	2	(d)	3	2	1	4

32.

	List I		List II
A.	Jama	1.	The amount actually collected
B.	Khet Batai	2.	After cutting the crops, putting it in heaps and divided equally
C.	Lang Batai	3.	Field is divided when it is sown for levying revenue
D.	Hasil	4.	The amount of revenue assessed

	A	B	C	D		A	B	C	D
(a)	4	3	2	1	(b)	1	2	3	4
(c)	4	3	1	2	(d)	3	2	1	4

33.

	List I		List II
A.	Pargana	1.	Administrative subdivison
B.	*Peshkash*	2.	Money exchanger
C.	Shroff	3.	Tribute collected by the Mughal state
D.	*Patwari*	4.	Maintenance of land records

Codes

	A	B	C	D		A	B	C	D
(a)	1	2	3	4	(b)	2	1	4	3
(c)	1	3	2	4	(d)	4	1	3	2

34.

	List I		List II
A.	*Diwan*	1.	Imperial regulation in the province
B.	*Amin*	2.	Supervision of the fiscal system of the empire
C.	*Amil-guzar*	3.	Village headmen
D.	*Muqaddam*	4.	Revenue collection

	A	B	C	D		A	B	C	D
(a)	1	3	2	4	(b)	2	1	4	3
(c)	3	4	1	2	(d)	4	1	2	3

Picture Based Question

35. The meetings of elders in the image below is known as

(a) Panchayat (b) *Mandal*
(c) *Miras* (d) *Kharbandi*

36. The construction of which historical monument is shown in the image below?

(a) Red Fort (b) Jama Masjid
(c) Fatehpur Sikri (d) Buland Darwaza

37. The couple represented in the image below has dressed in accordance with

(a) European style (b) Indian style
(c) Both (a) and (b) (d) None of these

38. What does the gesture of king in the image below towards Abu'l Fazl suggests?

(a) His recognition of the efforts put fourth by Abu'l Fazl for completion of the manuscript.
(b) His disinterest towards his pupil, Abu'l Fazl.
(c) His anger as depiction of images in the Islam is strictly forbidded.
(d) None of the above

Answers

1. (c) Akbar
2. (b) *muqaddam*
3. (d) Lohanis
4. (a) Ijaradari System
5. (a) Polaj
6. (d) Availability of tractors
7. (c) Important chronicle - the Ain-e-Akbari
8. (b) The zamindars collected revenue on behalf of the state.
9. (b)*Mulk-abadi* provides the "Account of the Twelve Provinces".
10. (c) By providing information on administrative and cultural traditions.
11. (d) Mulk-abadi deals with the fiscal side of the Mughal empire.
12. (d) All of these
13. (d) (ii) and (iii)
14. (c) (i) and (iv)
15. (a) (i) and (ii)
16. (a) (ii), (iii) and (iv)
17. (d) *Mansabdar* - Military-Bureaucrat
18. (d) Muzarian-Peasant
19. (a) Polaj : Land which was cultivated annually.
20. (b) (iii), (ii), (i), (iv)
21. (a) (iv), (ii), (iii), (i)
22. (a) *Ain-i-Akbari*
23. (a) Lohani tribe
24. (a) *Qilacha*
25. (b) Both A and R are true, but R is not the correct explanation of A
26. (a) Both A and R are true and R is the correct explanation of A
27. (a) Both A and R are true and R is the correct explanation of A
28. (a) Both A and R are true and R is the correct explanation of A
29. (a) Both A and R are true and R is the correct explanation of A
30. (a)
31. (b)
32. (a)
33. (c)
34. (b)
35. (a) Panchayat
36. (c) Fatehpur Sikri
37. (c) Both (a) and (b)
38. (a) His recognition of the efforts put fourth by Abu'l Fazl for completion of the manuscript.

Subjective Questions

Short Answer Type Questions

1. The basic unit of agricultural society was the village. Discuss. Competency Based Que

Ans. The basic unit of agricultural society was the village. It was inhabited by peasants who performed different seasonal tasks like tilling the soil, sowing seeds, harvesting the crop when it was ripe. They also contributed their labour to produce agro-based goods such as sugar and oil. However, rural India was not characterised by settled peasant production alone. Several kinds of areas such as large tracts of dry land or hilly regions were not cultivable as the more fertile areas. Additionally, forest areas comprised a significant part of the landscape.

2. The account of the *Ain* can be supplemented by descriptions contained in sources found from regions away from the Mughal capital. Justify the statement. Competency Based Que

Ans. The central purpose of the *Ain* was to present Akbar's empire as a society where social harmony was provided by a strong ruling class. However, the account of the *Ain* can be supplemented by descriptions contained in sources found from regions away from the Mughal capital. These include detailed revenue records from Gujarat, Maharashtra and Rajasthan dating from the seventeenth and eighteenth centuries. Further, the extensive records of the East India Company provide useful descriptions of agrarian relations in Eastern India. All these sources record conflicts between peasants, zamindars and the state.

3. Describe the condition of an average peasant of North India during the seventeenth century.

Ans. The condition of an average peasant of North India during the seventeenth century was as follows

- The average peasant of North India did not possess more than a pair of bullocks and two ploughs and most of them had even less.
- In Gujarat, peasants were considered affluent or rich, if they had about six acres of land.
- In Bengal, five acres was the upper limit of an average peasant farm and 10 acres of land would make one a rich *asami*.

- Cultivation was based on the principle of individual ownership. Peasant lands were bought and sold in the same way as the lands of other property owners.

4. How did state help peasants in irrigation sector? How did peasants help themselves by using different technologies?

Ans. The state helped peasants in irrigation sector by supporting irrigation projects. In Northern India, state dug new canals (*nahr, nala*) and also repaired old ones like the *shahnahr* in the Punjab during Shah Jahan's rule.

Peasants helped themselves by using technologies that often produced cattle energy. For example, using wooden plough, which was light and easily combined with an iron tip or iron blade. This did not make deep furrows which save the moisture better during the very hot months.

A drill, pulled by a pair of giant oxen, was used to plant seeds, but scattering the seeds by hand was the most used method. Hoeing and weeding were done together using a narrow iron blade with a small wooden handle.

5. What were the major seasonal cycles in agriculture?

Ans. The *kharif* (autumn) and the *rabi* (spring) were the two major seasonal cycles around which agriculture was organised in Mughal India. This means that most regions, other than areas that were the most arid or dry or harsh, produced a minimum of two crops a year.

Some areas where there was good amount of rainfall or irrigation provided a continuous supply of water gave three crops. The *Ain-i-Akbari* pointed out that Mughal provinces of Agra produced 39 varieties of crops and Delhi produced 43 over the two seasons. Bengal produced 50 varieties of rice alone.

6. What role did cattle play in the agrarian economy, particularly in labour-intensive regions? Explain with an example. Competency Based Que

Ans. The cattle played an important role in the agrarian economy as though agriculture was labour intensive, peasants did use technologies that often harnessed cattle energy. For example, the wooden plough, which was light and easily assembled with an iron tip or coulter (cutting tool used in agriculture). It therefore did not make deep furrows, which preserved the moisture better during the intensely hot months.

A drill, pulled by a pair of giant oxen, was used to plant seeds, but broadcasting of seed was the most prevalent method. Hoeing and weeding were done simultaneously using a narrow iron blade with a small wooden handle.

7. Discuss about the spread of tobacco crop in the Northern India.

Ans. Tobacco arrived first in the Deccan and it spread to Northern India in the early years of seventeenth century. The *Ain-i Akbari* does not mention tobacco in the lists of crops in Northern India. In 1604, Akbar and his noble came across tobacco for the first time.

Smoking tobacco in *hookahs* or *chillums* became a big fashion at that time. Jahangir was so concerned about its addiction that he banned it. However, the ban was ineffective because by the end of the seventeenth century, tobacco had become a major article of consumption, cultivation and trade all over India.

8. How were the subsistence and commercial production closely intertwined in an average peasants holding during the Mughal period in sixteenth and seventeenth centuries? Explain. CBSE Diksha

Ans. Subsistence and commercial production were closely intertwined in an average peasants holding in the following ways

- **Subsistence crops** Agriculture was organised around two major seasonal cycles, the *kharif* (autumn) and the *rabi* (spring). Arid or non-cultivable areas produced at least two crops in a year, while regions with sufficient rainfall and irrigation could produce three crops. For example, Mughal provinces of Agra produced 39 varieties of crops, Delhi produced 43 and in Bengal 50 varieties of rice were produced over two seasons according to the *Ain-i Akbari*.
- **Commercial Production** Mughal state encouraged crops which gave more revenue such as cotton and sugarcane. Such crops were *jins-i-kamil* which meant that their quality was the best. Cotton was grown over the large parts of Central India and Deccan Plateau Bengal was famous for its sugar. Cash crops (*jins-i-kamil*) also included various kinds of oil seeds and lentils.

9. Discuss about the relation between caste, poverty and social status during Mughal India.

Ans. There was a direct correlation between caste, poverty and social status at the lower level of society. From a manual belonging to seventeenth century Marwar, Rajputs are mentioned as peasants, sharing the same space with Jats, who were given a lower status in the caste hierarchy.

In the seventeenth century, the Gauravas, who cultivated land around Vrindavan (Uttar Pradesh), wanted Rajput status. Castes like Ahirs, Gujars and Malis moved to higher positions in the hierarchy because of the profitability of cattle rearing and horticulture. In the Eastern regions, intermediate pastoral and fishing castes like the Sadgops and Kaivartas acquired the status of peasants.

10. Examine the major sources of income of the panchayats during the sixteenth and seventeenth centuries. CBSE 2024

Ans. The major sources of income of the panchayats during the sixteenth and seventeenth centuries were

- **Land Revenue** One of the main sources of income for panchayats was land revenue which was collected from the farmers in the village. This revenue was often shared with the local rulers or zamindars.
- **Taxes and Levies** Panchayats imposed various local taxes and levies on agricultural produce, livestock, and goods traded in the village. This included market fees for goods sold in local *haats* (markets).
- **Fines and Penalties** Panchayats collected fines and penalties for local disputes, violations of village rules and misconduct. These fines contributed to the financial resources of the Panchayat.
- **Common Resources** Panchayats managed common resources such as forests, water bodies and grazing lands. They generated income through the regulated use of these resources, including fishing rights or timber collection.

11. "Jati panchayats were formed during sixteenth and seventeenth centuries." Explain their functions and authority.

Ans. Jati panchayats were formed during sixteenth and seventeenth centuries in the villages. Each caste or jati in the village had its own jati panchayat apart from village panchayat.

The functions and authority of jati panchayats were as follows

- They had considerable power in the rural society. In Rajasthan, jati panchayats settled civil disputes between members of different castes.
- They mediated in land disputes like
  (i) Different persons claiming same piece of land
  (ii) When deciding whether marriages were performed according to the rules laid down by a particular caste group.
  (iii) Determined who had more religious importance in village functions.

State respected the decisions of jati panchayats in most cases, except in the matters of criminal justice.

12. Examine the role of Panchayat in advocating for the rights of common people during the Mughal era. CBSE 2025

Ans. During the Mughal era, the village panchayat played a crucial role in advocating for the rights of common people by acting as a mediator between villagers and state authorities. It addressed grievances related to excessive taxation, forced labour (beggar), and caste-based oppression. Peasants, especially from lower castes, often approached the panchayat to seek justice against unjust demands by zamindars or officials. The panchayat could suggest compromises or, in extreme cases, support resistance like village desertion, ensuring that customary rights and basic subsistence were upheld.

13. Explain the term "Little Republics" as applied to villages during the Mughal Period. CBSE SQP 2024

Ans. The term "Little Republics" as applied to villages during the Mughal period is explained in given below points

- The village as a "little republic" made up of fraternal partners sharing resources and labour in a collective. However, this was not a sign of rural egalitarianism. There was individual ownership of assets and deep inequities based on caste and gender distinctions.
- A group of powerful individuals decided the affairs of the village, exploited the weaker sections and had the authority to deliver justice.
- More importantly, a cash network had already developed through trade between villages and towns. Revenue was assessed and collected in cash. Artisans working for the export market as well as producers of commerical products like cotton, silk or indigo, received their advances or wages in cash.

14. Examine the status and role played by the women in the agrarian society during Mughal period. CBSE Diksha

Or **Analyse the role of women as a resource in the agrarian society of the Mughal Empire.** CBSE 2024 C

Or **Explain why were women considered an important resource in agrarian society during sixteenth and seventeenth centuries.** CBSE 2024

Ans. The status of the women during Mughal period is as follows

- They were considered an important resource as they gave birth to child in a society dependent on labour.
- Marriages in many rural communities required the payment of bride price rather than dowry. Remarriage was considered legitimate.
- They were kept under strict control by the family and the community.
- Women found committing infidelity were severely punished.
- In some parts of India, rich women had the right to inherit property.

The role played by the women in the agrarian society during Mughal period is as follows

- Women worked together with the men in fields. Men tilled and ploughed, while women sowed, weeded, threshed and winnowed the harvest.

- Artisanal tasks such as spinning yarn, sifting and kneading clay for pottery, and embroidery work depended on female labour. They even went to the houses of the employees or to the markets if necessary.

15. What were the atrocities committed against women during the period of Mughal India?

Ans. The atrocities committed against women during the period of Mughal India were

- The women were kept under strict control by the male members of the family and the community.
- Women were given very harsh and inhuman punishments if they were suspected of being unfaithful to husband. But on the other hand, husband's unfaithfulness was not always punished.
- Menstruating women, were not allowed to touch the plough or the potter's wheel in Western India, or enter the groves where betel-leaves (*paan*) were grown in Bengal.

16. How did Mughals organise their land revenue system? Explain. CBSE 2024

Ans. The Mughal land revenue system was a key component of the empire's economy, based on agricultural production. The system involved two main stages assessment and collection. The Diwan oversaw the fiscal system, while amil-guzars (revenue collectors) handled local tax collection.

First, officials assessed the land by measuring both cultivated and cultivable lands to determine the jama (assessed revenue). The hasil was the actual amount collected, often in cash but sometimes in kind, depending on local conditions. The system aimed to maximise revenue, though local factors, like forests, sometimes made accurate measurement and collection difficult. Efforts to document land and its productivity were made throughout the Mughal period, with records compiled in works like the *Ain* during Akbar's reign.

17. State some features of Akbar Nama.

Ans. Some features of Akbar Nama are

- It was authored by Abu'l Fazl, Akbar's court historian, and completed in 1598.
- Akbar Nama consists of three books: the first two books give detail about Akbar's reign and significant historical events, while the third book, known as the *Ain-i Akbari*, records administrative regulations and a gazetteer of the empire.
- The text includes extensive quantitative information on Akbar's empire, detailing provincial layouts, military, revenue, and administrative structures.
- Abu'l Fazl compiled information from a wide range of sources, including imperial orders, reports and oral testimonies.
- The *Ain-i Akbari* portion provides insights into the social, cultural and economic aspects of Akbar's empire, serving as a major historical source for Mughal India.

18. Discuss briefly about the five books of *Ain-i Akbari*.

Ans. The *Ain-i Akbari* is made up of five books (*daftars*). The first three books describe about the administration. These are

(i) The first book is called *manzil-abadi*. It is concerned about the imperial household and its maintenance.

(ii) The second book, *sipah-abadi*, covered the military and civil administration and the establishment of servants.

(iii) The third book, *mulk-abadi*, deals with the financial matters of the empire and provided rich quantitative information on revenue rates, followed by the 'Account of the Twelve Provinces'.

The fourth and fifth books (*daftars*) dealt with the religious, literary and cultural traditions of the people of India and also contained a collection of Akbar's 'auspicious sayings'.

19. Why was *Ain-i-Akbari* translated? Explain.

Ans. The *Ain-i Akbari* was translated to make its rich historical content accessible to a broader audience, particularly scholars who did not read Persian, the original language of the text. This document offers a detailed account of Mughal administrative practices, social customs, and economic data, which provides valuable insights into Akbar's empire.

The translation was also essential for historical and academic studies, as it allowed historians to analyse Mughal governance, military organisation, and agrarian society. The translation, first by Henry Blochmann and later by H.S. Jarrett, preserved the precision of Abu'l Fazl's work. This enabled detailed research on Mughal India and facilitated further studies on pre-colonial South Asian history and society.

20. Analyse the growth of the Mughal Empire in managing their economic resources. CBSE 2024 C

Ans. The growth of the Mughal Empire in managing their economic resources is discussed below

- **Revenue from Land** Land revenue was the main economic source for the Mughal Empire. A well-organised administrative system was created to manage agricultural production and collect taxes.
- **Land Measurement and Taxation** Revenue collection involved two stages: assessment (jama) and collection (hasil). Efforts were made to measure both cultivated and cultivable lands across provinces.

- **Flexible Tax Collection** Taxes were primarily collected in cash, but payment in kind was also allowed based on local conditions.
- **Trade and Currency** The Mughal Empire benefitted from expanding trade networks, especially with Europe and Asia. A significant inflow of silver bullion stabilised currency and enabled extensive minting of silver rupya.
- **Detailed Fiscal Records** Records like Mulk-Abadi and "Account of the Twelve Provinces" provided detailed information on land, revenue rates, and local economies, aiding in effective resource management.
- **Global Trade Influence** Trade expansion contributed to economic growth, bringing in commodities and cash, particularly boosting India's economy.

Long Answer Type Questions

1. Examine the ways in which panchayats and village headmen regulated Mughal rural society. CBSE SQP 2022

Ans. The ways in which panchayats regulated Mughal rural society were

- The village panchayat was an assembly of elders, usually important people of the village with hereditary rights over their property. The panchayat was a mixed body in the villages which had mixed caste populations.
- The headman was chosen through the consensus of the village elders and this choice had to be ratified by the zamindar. Headmen held office as long as they enjoyed the confidence of the village elders. They could be dismissed by them also. The headman was known as *muqaddam* or *mandal.*
- The main function of the headman was to look after the preparation of village accounts. He was assisted by the accountant or *patwari* of the panchayat.
- The panchayat got its funds from the contributions made by the individuals to a common financial pool. These funds were used to pay for the costs of entertaining revenue officials who visited the village from time to time.
- One of the important functions of the panchayat was to ensure that the caste boundaries among the various communities residing in the village were maintained.
- Panchayats had the authority to levy fines and impose serious punishments like expulsion from the community. Expulsion meant that the person who was given punishment was forced to leave the village, become an outcaste and lose his right to practice his profession.
- The duties of the village headmen was to oversee the conduct of the members of the village community and to prevent any offence against their caste.

2. Discuss in detail about the village artisans in India during Mughal period. Also discuss about the *jajmani* system related to village artisans.

Ans. Village Artisans

Marathi documents and village surveys made in the early years of British rule pointed out the existence of huge numbers of village artisans, sometimes as high as 25 per cent of the total households in the villages.

Sometimes the difference between artisans and peasants in village society was not fixed because many groups performed both the tasks. Cultivators and their families would also participate in craft production like dyeing, textile printing, baking and firing of pottery, making and repairing agricultural implements. Cultivators engaged in artisanal production when there is a gap in between agricultural activities, like the period between sowing and weeding or between weeding and harvesting.

Village artisans like potters, blacksmiths, carpenters, barbers, even goldsmiths provided specialised services and in return they were paid by villagers using different means. The most common way of paying them was by giving them a share of the harvest, or an allotment of land, perhaps cultivable wastes, which was most likely decided by the panchayat. In Maharashtra, such lands became the artisans' *miras* or *watan* i.e. their hereditary holding.

Relationship between Village Artisans and *Jajmani* System

There was a different kind of system where artisans and individual peasant households entered into a mutually agreed system of remuneration, most of the time it was goods for services. This system was called *jajmani system.* For example, eighteenth century records suggested that zamindars in Bengal paid blacksmiths, carpenters, goldsmiths for their work by paying them a small daily allowance and diet money.

The term *jajmani* was not popular during sixteenth and seventeenth centuries. It indicated the complicated ways in which exchange networks worked at the micro-level of the village.

3. "Revenue was the economic mainstay of the Mughal Empire". Explain the statement in the context of agriculture and trade. Competency Based Que

Or **"Revenue from the land was the economic mainsay of the Mughal Empire". Support the statement with examples.** CBSE 2024

Ans. Revenue was the economic mainstay of the Mughal Empire due to several critical factors

- **Primary Source of State Income** Land revenue, derived from agricultural production, was the principal source of income for the Mughal state. This income enabled the empire to finance its extensive administration, maintain the royal court, and fund military campaigns.

- **Organised Revenue Collection System** The Mughal Empire developed an elaborate system to assess and collect revenue. Revenue officials, including the *diwan* and *amils* (revenue collectors), were assigned to calculate the annual agricultural yield of lands, known as *jama*, and oversee collections, ensuring regular contributions from each province.
- **Administrative Structure** To support revenue collection, the empire established a detailed administrative structure, with records of cultivable land, productivity and dues. Documents like the *Ain-i Akbari* provide insight into how meticulously the Mughals categorised land types, production, and corresponding revenue expectations.
- **Cash Transactions and Monetisation** Revenue from land was often collected in cash, which facilitated the monetisation of the rural economy. This cash flow linked villages to broader market networks, as peasants needed to generate cash by selling surplus crops.
- **Control Over Local Power Structures** Revenue collection also allowed the Mughals to exert influence over zamindars (landowners) who collected taxes on behalf of the empire. This strengthened Mughal authority over rural and agrarian communities.
- **Support for Expansion and Consolidation** The steady revenue provided the resources needed to expand the empire's territories and consolidate its control across diverse regions, enabling it to maintain a stable administration and military presence.

Thus, the Mughal economy heavily relied on an efficient land revenue system, which underpinned the empire's stability, governance and territorial growth.

4. Discuss in detail about the flow of silver in India during Mughal period. How did it help in growth of silver currency in India?

Ans. The flow of silver in India during the Mughal period played a crucial role in the growth and stability of the silver currency system. Key aspects include

- **International Trade and Demand for Indian Goods** India's export of highly demanded goods like textiles, spices, and other manufactured items to Europe and Asia brought in large quantities of silver as payment. European powers, especially the Portuguese, Dutch and English, imported Indian products, which led to an influx of silver bullion into the country.
- **Silver as a Global Commodity** With the discovery of silver mines in the America, silver became a major global currency, with a substantial amount of it making its way to India *via* Middle Eastern and Central Asian trade routes. This influx strengthened India's reserves, as the country itself had limited silver mines.
- **Role of Mughal Empire in Trade** The political stability and extensive territory under Mughal rule allowed the empire to facilitate and control trade networks. Mughal ports and trade centers along the coasts enabled the efficient movement of silver through exports.
- **Impact on Currency and Economy** The steady inflow of silver boosted the Mughal currency system by increasing the availability of silver rupya coins. This abundance allowed the Mughal Empire to establish a stable silver based currency, which facilitated trade and taxation.
- **Enhanced Monetisation and Economic Growth** The availability of silver coins promoted cash transactions across the empire. Artisans, merchants, and peasants alike could engage in monetised exchanges, stimulating economic activity at both rural and urban levels.
- **Integration into Local and Global Economies** The silver flow into India integrated the Mughal economy with global trade networks and strengthened the empire's financial base. This growth of a silver currency in India set a strong foundation for the empire's fiscal policies and allowed for a stable revenue collection system.

5. Explain the organisation of the administration and army during the rule of Akbar as given in '*Ain-i-Akbari*'.

Ans. The organisation of administration and the army during Akbar's rule, as detailed in the *Aini-Akbari*, reflects a highly structured and efficient system designed to maintain order and support the vast Mughal Empire. It is discussed below

- **Centralised Administration** Akbar implemented a centralised administrative system with various departments overseeing governance. The emperor held supreme authority, with officials and advisors appointed to manage specific functions such as revenue collection, law, and local administration. This ensured that all regions adhered to the policies set by the central government.
- **Mansabdari System** A core feature of Akbar's administration and military organisation was the mansabdari system, where officials, known as mansabdars, were granted ranks (mansabs) that determined their responsibilities, pay, and the number of troops they had to maintain. This hierarchical system streamlined military organisation and established loyalty to the emperor.
- **Civil and Military Responsibilities of Mansabdars** Mansabdars were required to perform both civil administrative tasks and military duties. They were

responsible for maintaining troops and overseeing land assigned to them (jagir) in return for their services. Higher ranking mansabdars commanded larger forces and played significant roles in military campaigns and provincial administration.

- **Revenue and Fiscal Organisation** The diwan, or finance minister, was in charge of the fiscal administration, including revenue assessment and collection. The revenue system was designed to ensure that the empire could sustain its administrative and military expenditures. Regular assessments ensured that land revenue was fairly calculated and collected, allowing the empire to support its extensive military structure.
- **Standing Army and Cavalry** The Mughal military was known for its strong cavalry and use of artillery. The *Ain-i Akbari* details that Akbar maintained a standing army, including infantry, cavalry, artillery, and war elephants. The horses and equipments were carefully inspected to maintain quality.
- **Artillery and Technological Advancement** Akbar emphasised the use of artillery and the latest military technology, which enhanced the effectiveness of his forces. This focus on advanced weaponry helped the Mughals defend their empire and expand their territory.

6. Inspite of the limitations, the *Ain-i -Akbari* remains an extraordinary document of its time. Explain the statement. Competency Based Que

Ans. The *Ain-i Akbari* was the collection of a large historical, administrative project of classification undertaken by Abu'l Fazl at the order of emperor Akbar. It was completed in 1598, the forty second ruling year of the emperor, after going through five revisions. The *Ain-i Akbari* was part of a larger project of history writing commissioned by Akbar, which was known as the *Akbar Nama*.

The *Ain-i Akbari* is made up of five books (*daftars*). The first three books describe about the administration. The fourth and fifth books (*daftars*) dealt with the religious, literary and cultural traditions of the people of India and also contained a collection of Akbar's auspicious sayings.

Though there are many problems in the *Ain-i Akbari* but it remains an extraordinary document of its times.

Its importance is as follows

- It provided the interesting views into the structure and organisation of the Mughal Empire and gave us quantitative information about its products and people.
- It provided information about the important political events like wars, conquests, political machinery and dynastic disturbances.
- Information about the country, its people and its products is mentioned in it.
- The *Ain-i Akbari* introduced a standard of reference for studying India during the seventeenth century.
- It is possible for the historians to reconstruct the social fabric of India at that time by its information on people their professions and trade and on the imperial establishment and people of high ranks of the empire.

Source Based Questions

Read the sources given below and answer the following questions.

1. Peasants on the Move

This was a feature of agrarian society which struck a keen observer like Babur, the first Mughal emperor, forcefully enough for him to write about it in the *Babur Nama*, his memories:

In Hindustan hamlets and villages, towns indeed, are depopulated and set up in a moment! If the people of a large town, one inhabited for years even, flee from it, they do it in such a way that not a sign or trace of them remains in a day and a half. On the other hand, if they fix their eyes on a place to settle, they need not dig water courses because their crops are all rain-grown, and as the population of Hindustan is unlimited it swarms in. They make a tank or well; they need not build houses or set up walls ... *khas-grass* abounds, wood is unlimited, huts are made, and straightaway there is village or a town!

(i) Who is the author of this passage? What is the source of passage?

(ii) Who was Babur? What did Babur say about hamlets, villages and towns?

(iii) How do people flee from a large town?

Ans. (i) Babur is the author of the passage.

The source of the passage is *Babur Nama*, the biography of Babur.

(ii) Babur was the first Mughal emperor of India. He was the founder of Mughal dynasty in India.

Babur observed that, in Hindustan, hamlets and village, towns indeed, are depopulated and set up in a very short time.

(iii) People of a large town, even after living there for years, flee in such a way that not a sign or trace of them remains in a day and a half.

2. Irrigating Trees and Fields

This is an excerpt from the *Babur Nama* that describes the irrigation devices the emperor observed in Northern India.

The greater part of Hindustan country is situated on level land. Many though its towns and cultivated lands are, it nowhere has running waters...For...water is not at all a necessity in cultivating crops and orchards. Autumn crops grow by the downpour of the rains themselves; and strange it is that spring crops grow even when no rains fall. (However) to young trees water is made to flow by means of buckets or wheels...

In Lahore, Dipalpur (both in present-day Pakistan) and those other parts, people water by means of a wheel. They make two circles of rope long enough to suit the depths of the well, fix strips of wood between them, and on these fasten pitchers. The ropes with the wood and attached pitchers are put over the wheel-well. At one end of the wheel-axle a second wheel is fixed, and close to it another on upright axle. The last wheel the bullock turns; its teeth catch in the teeth of the second (wheel), and thus the wheel with the pitchers is turned. A trough is set where the water empties from the pitchers and from this the water is conveyed everywhere.

In Agra, Chandwar, Bayana (all in present-day Uttar Pradesh) and those parts again, people water with a bucket... At the well-edge they setup a fork of wood, having a roller adjusted between the forks, tie a rope to a large bucket, put the rope over a roller, and tie its other end to the bullock. One person must drive the bullock, another empty the bucket.

(i) What were the different irrigation devices observed by Babur?

(ii) What did Babur observe in relation to water usage in cultivating crops?

(iii) Discuss about how the water was supplied through the wheel for cultivation.

Ans. (i) Babur observed that water is made to flow by means of buckets or wheels. In Lahore, Dipalpur and other parts, people watered using a wheel. In Agra, Chandwar, Bayana and other parts, people watered with a bucket.

(ii) Babur observed that, many of the towns and cultivated lands of India do not have running waters. Water is not a necessity in cultivating crops and orchards. Autumn crops grow by the downpour of the rains themselves, and strange thing was that spring crops grow even wihout rain.

(iii) The excerpt from the Babur Nama describes irrigation methods using bullock-powered wheels and buckets to lift water from wells for crop cultivation. The Persian wheel, with pitchers attached to ropes, was used in places like Lahore and Dipalpur, while simpler bucket systems were used in Agra and Bayana, ensuring water supply even in the absence of consistent rainfall.

3. Clearance of Forests for Agricultural Settlements

This is an excerpt from a sixteenth century Bengali poem, *Chandimangala*, composed by Mukundaram Chakrabarti. The hero of the poem, Kalaketu, set up a kingdom by clearing forests :

Hearing the news, outsiders came from various lands.
Kalaketu then bought and distributed among them Heavy knives, axes, battle-axes and pikes.

From the North came the Das (people)
One hundred of them advanced.

They were struck with wonder on seeing Kalaketu
Who distributed betel-nut to each of them.
From the South came the harvesters
Five hundred of them under one organiser.
From the West came Zafar Mian,
Together with twenty-two thousand men.
Sulaimani beads in their hands.
They chanted the names of their *pir* and *paighambar* (Prophet).

Having cleared the forest
They established markets.

Hundreds and hundreds of foreigners
Ate and entered the forest.
Hearing the sound of the axe,
Tigers became apprehensive and ran away, roaring.

(i) What is the source of this passage and name of the author?

(ii) Who are the people identified as 'foreigners' from the perspective of the forest dwellers? What kind of tools did Kalaketu distributed to outsiders?

(iii) Who is the hero of the poem? How did he set up his kingdom? Why did tigers run away?

Ans. (i) The source of the passage is a sixteenth century Bengali poem, *Chandimangala*. The name of the author is Mukundaram Chakrabarti.

(ii) People from North, the Das, harvesters from South, from the West, Zafar Mian along with twenty-two thousand men were all identified as foreigners from the perspective of the forest dwellers.

Heavy knives, axes, battle-axes and pikes were distributed by Kalaketu to the outsiders.

(iii) The hero of the poem is Kalaketu. He set up a kingdom by clearing forests. After hearing the sound of the axe, tigers were frightened and ran away.

4. Trade between the Hill Tribes and the Plains,c. 1595

This is how Abu'l Fazl describes the transactions between the hill tribes and the plains in the *suba* of Awadh (part of present-day Uttar Pradesh) :

From the Northern mountains quantities of goods are carried on the backs of men, of stout ponies and of goats, such as gold, copper, lead, musk, tails of the *kutas* cow (the yak), honey, *chuk* (an acid composed of orange juice and lemon boiled together), pomegranate seed, ginger, long pepper, *majith* (a plant producing a red dye) root, borax, zedoary (a root resembling turmeric), wax, woollen stuffs, wooden ware, hawks, falcons, black falcons, merlins (a kind of bird), and other articles. In exchange they carry back white and coloured clothes, amber, salt, asafoetida, ornaments, glass and earthen ware.

(i) **What is this passage about? What are the modes of transport described in this passage?**

(ii) **What are the products that were taken from Northern mountains?**

(iii) **What did people from Northern mountains carry back in exchange of their goods? Guess the uses of any three products that were transacted in the passage.**

Ans. (i) Abu'l Fazl in this passage describes about the transactions between the hill tribes and the plains in the *suba* of Awadh (part of present-day Uttar Pradesh).

The modes of transport mentioned in the passage are the goods that are carried on the backs of men, of stout ponies and of goats.

(ii) From the Northern mountains, that are carried on the backs of men, of stout ponies and of goats, were gold, copper, lead, musk, tails of the *kutas* cow (the yak), honey, pomegranate seed, ginger, long pepper, woollen stuffs, wooden ware, hawks, falcons, black falcons, etc.

(iii) In exchange, people from Northern mountains carried back white and coloured clothes, amber, salt, asafoetida, ornaments, glass and earthen ware.

The three products that were transacted in the passage were gold, which must have been used to make ornaments, copper must have been used to make utensils. Ginger, long pepper must have been used in cooking.

5. Classification of Lands under Akbar

The following is a listing of criteria of classification excerpt from the *Ain-i Akbari*.

The Emperor Akbar in his profound sagacity classified the lands and fixed a different revenue to be paid by each. *Polaj* is a land which is annually cultivated for each crop in succession and is never allowed to lie fallow. *Parauti* is land left out of cultivation for a time that it may recover its strength. *Chachar* is land that has lain fallow for three or four years. *Banjar* is land uncultivated for five years and more. Of the first two kinds of land, there are three classes, good, middling, and bad. They add together the produce of each sort, and the third of this represents the medium produce, one-third part of which is exacted as the royal dues.

(i) **Why was *Chachar* land left uncultivated for some three to four years?**

(ii) **Explain the basis of this classification.**

(iii) **Do you think it was a sound basis to assess the revenue? Explain.**

Ans. (i) *Chachar* was the land that was laid fallow for three or four years. This land was not used for growing crops as it was believed that the quality of land would improve within three or four years and then it would be suitable for futher cultivation.

(*ii*) Emperor Akbar classified lands in the following ways

Polaj The land which is annually cultivated for each crop in succession and is never allowed to lie fallow.

Parauti The land that is left out for cultivation for some time to recover its fertility.

Chachar The land that has been left fallow for three or four years.

Banjar The land which is uncultivated for five years and more.

(*iii*) I do not think that the above mentioned system to assess the revenue was proper. Kankut system which was prevalent during the reign of Akbar was a better method than this. The term Kankut was a combination of two terms *viz*, Kan which signified grain and Kut signified estimates. The estimate was made on the basis of an actual inspection on the spot and one-third of the estimated produce was fixed as the state demand.

6. The *Ain-i Akbari* on land revenue collection

Let him (the *amil-guzar*) not make it a practice of taking only in cash but also in kind. The latter is effected in several ways.

First, *kankut* : in the Hindi language *kan* signifies grain, and *kut*, estimates... If any doubts arise, the crops should be cut and estimated in three lots, the good, the middling and the inferior, and the hesitation should be removed. Often, too, the land taken by appraisement, gives a sufficiently accurate return. Secondly, *batai*, also called *bhaoli*, the crops are reaped and stacked and divided by agreement in the presence of the parties. But in this case several intelligent inspectors are required; otherwise, the evil-minded and false are given to deception. Thirdly, *khet-batai*, when they divide the fields after they are sown.

Fourthly, *lang batai*, after cutting the grain, they form it in heaps and divide it among themselves, and each takes his share home and turns it to profit.

(i) **Explain the *kankut* system of land revenue.**
(ii) **How was the land revenue assessed in the case of *batai* or *bhaoli*?**
(iii) **Do you think that the land revenue system of the Mughals was flexible?**

Ans. (i) In the *kankut* system, the crops should be cut and estimated in three lots, the good, the middling and the inferior.
(ii) In *batai*, also called *bhaoli*, the crops are reaped, stacked and divided by agreement in the presence of the parties. But in this case, several intelligent inspectors are required to collect revenue.
(iii) Yes, the land revenue system of the Mughals was flexible. It did not strictly practiced collecting revenue only in cash but instead gave provision of collecting in kind also. There were also various systems of estimation like *kankut, batai, khet-batai* and *lang batai*, which show that land revenue system of the Mughals was very flexible.

7. How Silver came to India?

This excerpt from Giovanni Careri's account (based on Bernier's account) gives an idea of the enormous amount of wealth that found its way into the Mughal Empire :

That the reader may form some idea of the wealth of this (Mughal) empire, he is to observe that all the gold and silver, which circulates throughout the world at last centres here.

It is well known that as much of it comes out of America, after running through several Kingdoms of Europe, goes partly into (Turky) Turkey, for several sorts of commodities; and part into Persia, by the way of Smirna for Silk.

Now the Turks not being able to abstain from coffee, which comes from Hyeman (Oman), and Arabia... nor Persia, Arabia, and the Turks themselves to go without the commodities of India, send vast quantities of Mony (money) to Moka (Mocha) on the Red sea, near Babel Mandel; to Bassora (Basra) at the bottom of the Persian Gulgh (Gulf);... which is afterwards sent over in ships to Indostan (Hindustan).

Besides the Indian, Dutch, English, and Portuguese ships, that every year carry the commodities of Indostan, to Pegu, Tanasserri (parts of Myanmar), Siam (Thailand), Ceylon (Sri Lanka)... the Maldive islands, Mozambique and other places, must of necessity convey much gold and silver thither, from those countries. All that the Dutch fetch from the Mines in Japan, sooner or later, goes to Indostan; and the goods carry'd hence into Europe, whether to France, England, or Portugal, are all purchas'd for ready Mony, which remains there.

(i) **What is the source of the passage and what is it about?**
(ii) **How reader form an idea about the wealth of Mughal Empire? What are Turks addicted to and where does that commodity come from?**
(iii) **From where did much of silver come from? How do silver get into Persia?**

Ans. (i) This passage is from Giovanni Careri's account, based on Bernier's account, which gives an idea of the huge amount of wealth that found its way into the Mughal Empire.
(ii) The reader may form some idea of the wealth of Mughal empire, by observing that all the gold and silver, which circulates throughout the world at last come and centres in Mughal Empire.
Turks are addicted to coffee which comes from Hyeman (Oman) and Arabia.
(iii) Much of the silver comes out of America, after running through several Kingdoms of Europe.
Silver got into Persia, after exchanging it with Smirna for silk.

8. "Moistening the Rose Garden of Fortune"

In this extract Abu'l Fazl gives a vivid account of how and from whom he collected his information :

...to Abu'l Fazl, son of Mubarak... this sublime mandate was given. "Write with the pen of sincerity the account of the glorious events and of our dominion-conquering victories... Assuredly, I spent much labour and research in collecting the records and narratives of His Majesty's actions and I was a long time interrogating the servants of the State and the old members of the illustrious family. I examined both prudent, truth-speaking old men and active-minded, right-actioned young ones and reduced their statements to writing.

The Royal commands were issued to the provinces, that those who from old service remembered, with certainty or with adminicle of doubt, the events of the past, should copy out the notes and memoranda and transit them to the court. (Then) a second command shone forth from the holy Presence-chamber; to wit – that the materials which had been collected should be ... recited in the royal hearing, and whatever might have to be written down afterwards, should be introduced into the noble volume as a supplement, and that such details as on account of the minuteness of the inquiries and the minutae of affairs, (which) could not then be brought to an end, should be inserted afterwards at my leisure. Being relieved by his royal order – the interpreter of the Divine ordinance – from the secret anxiety of my heart, I proceeded to reduce into writing the rough draughts (drafts) which were void of the grace of arrangement and style. I obtained the chronicle of events beginning at the Nineteenth Year of the Divine Era, when the Record Office was established by the enlightened intellect of His Majesty, and from its rich pages, I gathered the accounts of many events.

Great pains too, were taken to procure the originals or copies of most of the orders which had been issued to the provinces from the Accession up to the present-day... I also took much trouble to incorporate many of the reports which ministers and high officials had submitted, about the affairs of the empire and the events of foreign countries. And my labour-loving soul was satiated by the apparatus of inquiry and research. I also exerted myself energetically to collect the rough notes and memoranda of sagacious and well-informed men. By these means, I constructed a reservoir for irrigating and moistening the rose garden of fortune (the *Akbar Nama*).

(i) List some sources that Abu'l Fazl used to compile his work.

(ii) Which of these sources would have been most useful for arriving at an understanding of agrarian relations?

(iii) Where did Abu'l Fazl get his chronicle of events?

Ans. (i) The sources that Abu'l Fazl used to compile his work are

- Records and narratives of Majesty's actions, from the servants of the state and the old members of the illustrious family.
- Reports which ministers and high officials had submitted.
- Originals or copies of most of the orders which had been issued to the provinces from the accession up to the present-day.

(ii) Royal commands issued to the provinces and originals or copies of most of the orders which had been issued to the provinces must have been most useful in understanding agrarian relations.

(iii) Abu'l Fazl obtained the chronicle of events beginning at the Nineteenth Year of the Divine Era, when the Record Office was established by the emperor, and from its rich pages, he gathered the accounts of many events.

Map Based Questions

1. Draw the boundaries of Mughal Empire under various rulers.

(i) Babur's rule, 1530

(ii) Akbar's rule, 1605

(iii) Aurangzeb's rule, 1707

Or **On the given political outline map of India, located and label the following wih appropriate symbols**

(i) Ajmer (Territory under the Mughals)

(ii) Panipat (Territory under the Mughals) **CBSE 2024**

Ans.

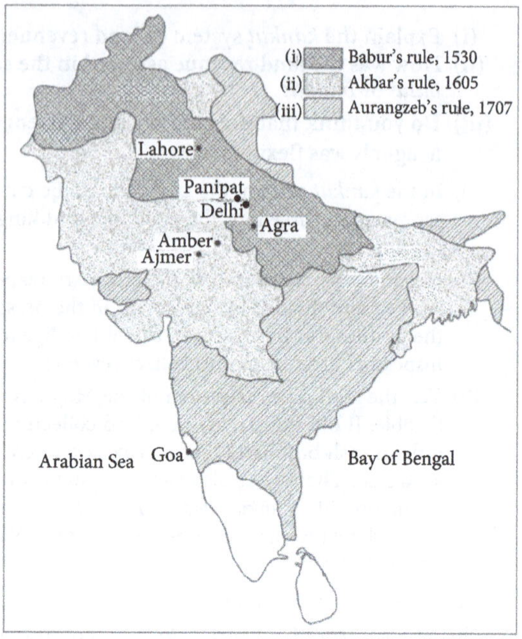

2. On the given political outline map of India, locate and label the following with appropriate signs. **CBSE 2024**

(a) Agra - Territory under Mughal's control

(b) Delhi - Territory under Mughal's control

Ans.

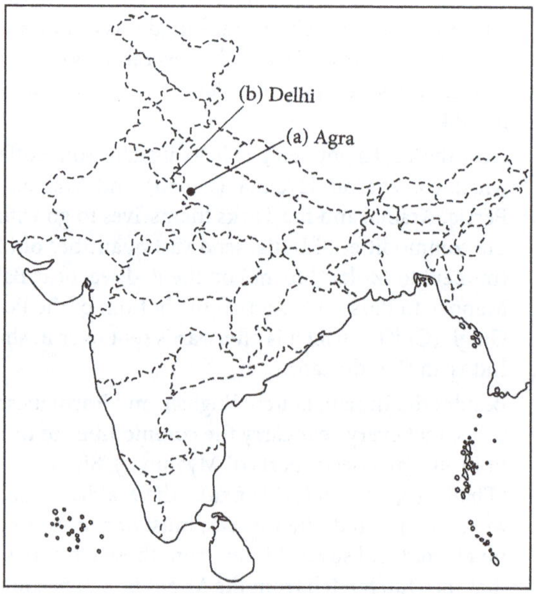

SELF ASSESSMENT TEST

Objective Type Questions

1. Which of the following statements is correct?
   (a) Zamindars were often supported by the peasantry in their struggle.
   (b) Village communities were not depended on the jangli communities.
   (c) Not all but few of the activities were depended on seasons.
   (d) None of the above
2. Which of the following statements is incorrect?
   (a) Cotton and sugarcane crops were *jins-i kamil.*
   (b) They were the excellent crops for revenue.
   (c) Cash crops included various kinds of oilseeds.
   (d) The Emperor Akbar classified the lands and not fixed the revenue to be paid by each.
3. In the Babur Nama, what method was described for lifting water for irrigation in the regions of Lahore and Dipalpur?
   (a) Using hand-held buckets only
   (b) Building channels from nearby rivers
   (c) A wheel system with bullocks turning the wheel
   (d) Rainwater harvesting with storage tanks
4. Match the Following

	List I		List II
A.	*Polaj*	1.	Land which is left fallow for three or four years
B.	*Parauti*	2.	Land which is annually cultivated
C.	*Chachar*	3.	Land uncultivated for five years
D.	*Banjar*	4.	Land left uncultivated to regain its fertility

Codes

	A	B	C	D		A	B	C	D
(a)	1	2	3	4	(b)	2	3	4	1
(c)	4	1	2	3	(d)	2	4	1	3

Short Answer Type Questions

5. Describe the primary unit of agricultural society in Mughal India.
6. What was the role of the village panchayat in rural Mughal society?
7. Analyse how the Mughal revenue system impacted the relationship between the state and rural society.
8. Justify the importance of panchayats in maintaining social order in Mughal villages.
9. Comment on the role of zamindars in the Mughal agrarian structure and their influence over rural society.

Long Answer Type Questions

10. "Revenue was the economic mainstay of the Mughal Empire." Discuss.
11. *Ain-i-Akbari* was part of the large historical, administrateed project of classification. Explain.

9 CHAPTER

This chapter deals with the British rules and revenue policies. It explores how these laws and policies affected different sections of the society such as Zamindars, peasants, forest people, etc.

▼ **YOUR STUDY GOALS**

9.1 Bengal and the Zamindars
9.2 Rural Areas of Bengal
9.3 A Revolt in the Countryside : The Bombay Deccan
9.4 The Deccan Riots Commission

▼ **YOUR PRACTICE GOALS**

- Objective Type Questions (47 Qs ; MCQs, A-R, Matching, Picture Based)
- Subjective Questions (24 SAs, 7 LAs)
- Source Based Questions (2 Qs)

Colonialism and the Countryside

(Exploring official Archives)

The East India company established its rule in the courtryside. It implemented its revenue polices which affected different sections of people. People were not only governed by laws, they also opposed the law.

9.1 Bengal and the Zamindars

- Bengal was the first province in India where colonial rule was established.
- The first efforts to reorganise rural society and create a new system of land rights and revenue took place in Bengal.

The Problem of Unpaid Revenue

- With the advent of colonial rule in Bengal by the 1770's, the rural economy was in crisis due to continuous famines and low agricultural output.
- According to officials, agriculture, trade and the revenue sources could be developed by increasing investment in agriculture. Hence, a new revenue system was introduced in 1793, known as the Permanent Settlement.
- **Charles Cornwallis** or **Lord Cornwallis** was the Governor-General of Bengal when the Permanent Settlement was introduced.
- The settlement was done by securing rights of property and permanently fixing the rates of revenue demand.

- The idea behind Permanent Settlement was to create a class of yeomen (a person who owns a small farm) farmers and rich landowners who would have the capital and enterprise to improve agriculture. They would also be loyal to the Company.
- The British made the settlement with the rajas (powerful zamindars) and *taluqdars*[1] of Bengal classifying them as zamindars. They were supposed to pay the revenue demand that was fixed for a long period of time. Hence, they were just revenue collectors rather than landowners.
- There were several villages (sometimes 400) under one zamindari which, according to the Company, formed one revenue estate.
- The zamindar collected rent from the different villages, paid the revenue to the Company and retained the difference as his income. If he failed to pay the revenue, his estate could be auctioned.

▲ *Charles Cornwallis (1738-1805)*

An Auction in Burdwan

- In 1797, there was an auction in Zamindari of Burdwan (present day Bardhaman).
- The payable revenue of the Zamindars was fixed by the British East India Company.
- The estates of Zamindars who failed to pay, were to be auctioned to recover the revenue.
- As the Raja of Burdwan had accumulated huge arrears, his estate was auctioned.
- A number of *mahals* (estates) of Burdwan were sold. A notable fact was that many buyers were the servants and agents of the Raja, purchasing on their master's behalf.
- The Raja's estates were publicly sold, but he remained in control of his zamindari.

Zamindars Defaulted on Payments

Zamindars regularly failed to pay the revenue demand due to the following reasons

- Firstly, the Company kept revenue prices high.
- Secondly, during the 1790s, the prices of agricultural produce were depressed which made the *ryots* (peasant or farmer) difficult to pay their dues to the zamindar.
- Thirdly, as the revenue was fixed, it had to be paid punctually on time regardless of the harvest. A **Sunset Law** was introduced according to which, if payment did not come in by sunset of the specified date, the zamindari was liable to be auctioned.
- Fourthly, the power of the zamindar was initially limited to collect rent from the *ryots* and manage his zamindari.

Problems Faced by Zamindars

- The zamindars troops were disbanded (dissolved) and custom duties were abolished. Their *cutcheries* (courts) were supervised by a Collector appointed by the Company, which gradually emerged as an alternative source of authority. They also lost the power to organise local justice and the local police.
- Bad harvests and low prices made the *ryots* difficult to pay dues to the zamindars. Sometimes *ryots* deliberately delayed the revenue payment.
- Rich *ryots* and village headmen, *jotedars* and *Mandals* were against the zamindars.
- The judicial process to prosecute defaulters was lengthy. In Burdwan, there were more than 30,000 pending rent arrears cases in 1798.

The Rise of the Jotedars

- Rich peasants known as *jotedars* consolidated their power at village level with the declining position of zamindars, at the end of the eighteenth century.
- **Francis Buchanan** has given a vivid description of *jotedars* in his survey of the Dinajpur district in North Bengal.

---

1 Taluqdar One who holds a taluq or a connection. Taluq refers to a territorial unit.

Factors Responsible for Power of Jotedars

- Zamindars lived in urban areas, whereas the *jotedars* were located in the villages. This gave them direct control over a section of poor villagers.
- They cultivated their land through sharecroppers also known as ***adhiyars*** or ***bargadars***. These people brought their own ploughs, laboured in the field and handed over half of the produce to the *jotedars* after the harvest.
- Local trade and money lending was also controlled by *Jotedars*, so they exercised immense power over poorer cultivators of the region.
- *Jotedars* resisted efforts by zamindars to increase the revenue demand of the village and prevented zamindari officials from doing their duty. They also mobilised dependent *ryots* and delayed payments of revenue to the zamindar.
- The estates of zamindars who failed to pay the revenue were purchased by *jotedars* during auctions.
- There was a growth in the power of the *jotedars*, particularly in North Bengal. In some places, jotedars were known as ***haoladars***, while in others they were known as ***gantidars*** or ***mandals***.

Powers of Zamindars, Jotedars and *Ryots*

- Zamindars were responsible for paying revenue to the Company and distributing the revenue demand (jama) over villages.
- Each village *ryot*, big or small, paid rent to the zamindar.
- *Jotedars* gave out loans to other *ryots* and sold their produce.
- *Ryots* cultivated some land and gave out the rest to under-*ryots* (low level farmers).
- Under-*ryots* paid rent to the *ryots* for that land.

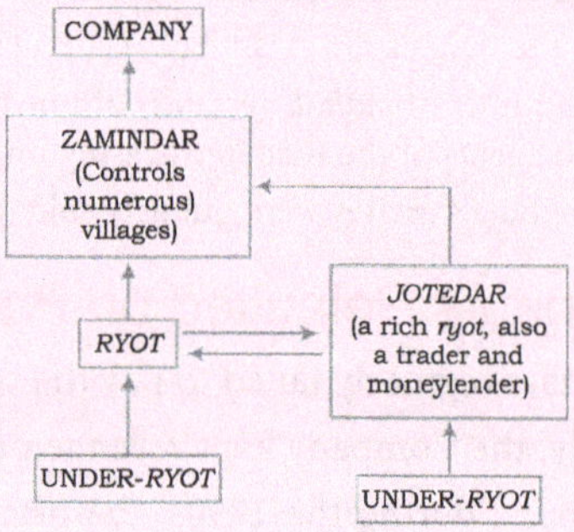

▲ *Power in Rural Bengal*

The Zamindars Resist

Zamindars found ways to deal with high revenue demands and the threat of having their estates auctioned. They adopted new strategies as discussed below

- **Fictitious sale** During auction, the zamindar's men bought the property and refused to pay the purchase money, so that the estate had to be resold. Again it was bought by the zamindar's agents. Such a process was repeated endlessly.
- **Exhaustion of the state and other bidders** The estate was sold at a low price back to the zamindars. Thus, the zamindars never paid the full revenue demand and the Company rarely recovered the balances unpaid. Such transactions took place at a large scale during the period 1793-1801 AD.
- **Attack on outside purchasers** Outside purchasers were attacked by the *lathyals*[2] of the former zamindar or were even opposed by the *ryots* who considered themselves as the *proja* (subjects) of the zamindars. Thus, the zamindars were not easily displaced.

The Fifth Report

- It was the fifth in a series of reports on the Company's administration and activities in India, submitted to the British Parliament in 1813. It contained 1002 pages of which over 800 pages were appendices.
- It reproduced petitions of zamindars and *ryots*, reports of collectors from different districts, statistical tables on revenue returns and notes on the revenue and judicial administration of Bengal and Madras, written by officials.

2 Lathyal One who wields (holds) the lathi or stick, functions as a strongman or the zamindar.

Causes of the Presentation of Report

- Since the establishment of Company's rule in Bengal in the mid 1760s, its activities were watched and debated in England. Many groups in Britain were against the monopoly of the Company over trade with India and China. They wanted a revocation (cancellation) of the Royal Charter which gave the Company this monopoly.
- Many private traders wanted a share in the trade with India and industrialists of Britain wanted to access Indian markets for British manufactures.
- According to some political groups, the conquest of Bengal was not benefitting the British nation as a whole but only the Company.
- The misrule and administration of Company were discussed in Britain and the deeds of greed and corruption by Company officials were publicised in the press.

Hence, the British Parliament passed a series of acts in the late 18th century to regulate and control Company rule in India. The Company was forced to produce regular reports and committees were appointed to enquire into the affairs of the company. The Fifth Report was one such report produced by a Select Committee.

Critical Examination of Fifth Report

- Researchers pointed out that the Fifth Report overstated the collapse of traditional zamindari power.
- It also overestimated the scale on which zamindars were losing their land.

Quick Test 1

1. The colonial rule was first established in which province of India?
2. What was the main purpose of the Permanent Settlement?
3. What steps were taken by the company to control and regulate the zamindars?
4. When did the zamindars finally collapsed?
5. What did the British parliament do to regulate and control company rule in India?

9.2 Rural Areas of Bengal

In the early 19th century, Buchanan travelled through the Rajmahal hills and gave a description about the hills and people living around them.

In the Hills of Rajmahal

- The people living around the Rajmahal hills were known as Paharias. They lived on forest produce and practised shifting cultivation.
- They cleared patches of forest by cutting bushes and burning the undergrowth. These patches were enriched by the potash from the ash.
- They grew a variety of pulses and millets for consumption.
- They scratched the ground lightly with hoes, cultivated the cleared land for a few years and then left it fallow so that it could recover its fertility, and move to a new area.

Life of the Paharias

- The Paharias lived in huts within tamarind groves. They collected *mahua* (a flower) for food, silk cocoons, resin, etc. for sale and wood for charcoal production.
- The patches of grass provided pasture for cattle. Thus, the Paharias were hunters, shifting cultivators, food gatherers, charcoal producers and silkworm rearers.

- For the paharias, the region of Rajmahal hills was their land. It was the basis of their identify and survival as well.
- They had chiefs who maintained the unity of the groups, settled disputes and led the tribe in battles with other tribes and plains people.
- The Paharias used to raid the plains where settled agriculturists lived. These raids were necessary for survival, especially during scarcity. These raids were a way to assert power over settled communities and negotiate political relations with outsiders.
- The zamindars paid tributes to the hill chiefs for peace settlement.
- Traders paid small amounts to the hill people to use the passes they controlled. This served as a toll or tax to the chief, who provided protection to the traders.

British Policies to Control the Paharias

- As agriculture expanded, the areas of forests and pastures declined. This led to conflict among hill folk and settled cultivators. Even the colonial officials tried to control and subdue the Paharias.
- The British in the 1770s, followed a brutal policy of **extermination** (end or finish), **hunting** and **killing** the Paharias.
- By the 1780s, **Augustus Cleveland**, the collector of Bhagalpur, proposed a policy of pacification (attempt to maintain peace). As per the policy, the Paharia chiefs were given annual allowance and were made responsible for the proper conduct of their men. They were expected to maintain order in their localities and discipline their own people.
- Many Paharia chiefs refused the allowance, while those who accepted, lost their authority within the community.
- After receiving payment from the British, they were seen as subordinate employees or paid chiefs rather than independent leaders.

Impact of British Policies

- As the pacifications campaigns grew, the Paharias moved further into mountains to protect themselves from enemies. However, they kept fighting against outsiders.
- They considered every white man as the destructor of their way of life.
- They even viewed Buchanan with suspicion and distrust when he travelled in the region in the winter of 1810-11.

The Battle between Hoe and Plough

- In the 17th century, Santhals were moving into the area around the Rajmahal hills. They cleared forests, cut down timber, ploughed land and produced rice and cotton.
- The Paharias moved deeper into the Rajmahal hills due to Santhals who took over the lower hills.
- If Paharias life was symbolised by the hoe, the settlers represented the power of the plough.

The Santhal : Pioneer Settlers

- The Santhals came into Bengal in the 1780s. They were hired by zamindars to reclaim land and expand cultivation.
- The Britishers invited them to settle in the Jangal Mahals of Rajmahals hills as they failed to change the Paharias into settled agriculturalists.
- For Britishers, Santhals appeared to be ideal settlers who cleared forests and ploughed the land with enthusiasm.
- The Santhals settled down, cultivating a range of commercial crops for the markets and dealing with traders and moneylenders.

Expansion of Santhal Settlements and Effect on Paharias

- A large area of land was provided to the Santhals by 1832 in Rajmahal hills which came to be known as ***Damin-i-Koh***. The Santhals practised plough agriculture there and became settled peasants.
- Santhals were asked to clear and cultivate one-tenth of the area within the first ten years. The area was surveyed and mapped. The area was separated from the world of the settled agriculturists and the Paharias.
- The demarcation (marking off a boundary or setting a limit) of *Damin-i-Koh* resulted into expansion of Santhal settlements. The Santhal population also increased from 3,000 in 1838 to over 82,000 in 1851.
- With the advent of Santhals in the Rajmahal hills, the Paharias were forced to move deeper into the barren and rock hills. This deeply affected their lives.
- As shifting cultivation depended on using new and fertile land, it became inaccessible to the Paharias. The hunters amongst them faced the problems when forests were cleared for cultivation.
- Heavy taxes were imposed by the state on the lands cleared by the Santhals.
- Moneylenders (*dikus*) charged them a high rate of interest and if debt remained unpaid, then zamindars started controlling the Damin area.
- The Santhals decided to revolt against zamindars, moneylenders and colonial state.
- After the Santhal Revolt (1855-56), Santhal Pargana was established, taking 5,500 square miles from the Bhagalpur and Birbhum districts.

▲ *Sidhu Manjhi, the leader of the Santhal Rebellion*

The Accounts of Buchanan

- Francis Buchanan was a physician who came to India and served in Bengal Medical Service. He was an employee of British East India Company. He travelled everywhere with a large army of people.
- Buchanan was a great observer. He obsessed over stones and rocks. He searched for minerals such as iron ore, mica, granite and saltpetre.
- Buchanan described the landscape and even about how to increase its productivity. His assessment was influenced by the Company's commercial requirements.
- He was critical about the lifestyles of forest dwellers and felt that forests had to be turned into agricultural lands.

Quick Test 2

1. Name some of the items collected by the Paharias for food and trade?
2. Who proposed a policy of pacification in the 1780s?
3. Why were the Santhals hired by zamindars?
4. Which type of agriculture did the Santhals practice in Damin-i-Koh?
5. What was one of Buchanan's obsessions during his travels?

9.3 A Revolt in the Countryside : The Bombay Deccan

Peasants in various parts of India rose in revolt against moneylenders and grain dealers through the 19th century. One such revolt occurred in 1875 in the Deccan.

Account Books are Burnt

- The peasant movement began at **Supa**, a large village in Poona (Present-day Pune) district. It was a market centre where moneylenders and shopkeepers lived.

- A large number of *ryots* gathered on 12th May, 1875 and attacked the shopkeepers and demanded their *bahi khatas* (account books) and debt bonds.
- The revolt spread to Ahmednagar and further over an area of 6,500 square km. More than 30 villages were affected.
- The *sahukars*[3] left the villages, leaving behind their property and belongings.
- The British officials were threatened by the revolt spreading so fast. They established police posts in villages to frighten rebellious peasants. It took several months to bring the countryside under control.

A New Revenue System

- As British rule expanded from Bengal to other parts of India, new systems of revenue were imposed.
- A new revenue system **Ryotwari Settlement** was introduced in the Bombay Deccan. Under the ryotwari settlement, the revenue was directly settled with the *ryots.*
- The revenue was fixed according to
  (i) the estimation of average income from different types of soil,
  (ii) the estimation of the ability of the *ryots* to pay revenue.
- Survey of lands was conducted every 30 years and the revenue rates increased. Hence, the revenue demand was no longer permanent.

Revenue Demand and Peasant Debt

- The revenue settlement in the Bombay Deccan was made in the 1820s for the first time. But the demand was kept so high that it was impossible for peasants to pay it. Hence, they left their villages and moved to some other place.
- Less rainfall and poor harvest worsened the situation. However, the collectors continued to demand revenue and enforced payments harshly. If someone failed to pay, then his crops were seized and a fine was imposed on the whole village.
- The prices of agricultural products fell sharply after 1832 and continued for over a decade and a half, which declined the peasants income.
- The countryside was struck with a famine in the years 1832-34. One-third of the cattles of the Deccan were killed and half of the human population died. As a result, unpaid balances of revenue increased.
- With no money left, the peasants had to rely on moneylenders for loans to buy their everyday needs and meet their production expenditure. But once a loan was taken, the ryot found it difficult to pay it back. By the 1840s, officials witnessed increasing levels of peasant indebtedness everywhere.
- In the mid 1840s, there were some signs of economic recovery. The revenue demand was moderated to encourage peasants to expand cultivation.
- Agricultural prices also recovered after 1845. Cultivators moved to new areas and started transforming pasture land into cultivated fields.
- To expand cultivation, they needed more ploughs, cattle, seeds and land, so they had to turn back to moneylenders for loans.

David Ricardo's Idea of Land Ownership

- David Ricardo was an economist, who became a well-known person in England by the 1820s.
- In Maharashtra, the British officials implemented his ideas of revenue settlement.
- According to the Ricardian idea, a landowner was supposed to have a claim only to the 'average rent' prevailing at that time.
- When the land yielded more than this 'average rent', the landowner had a surplus that the state needed to tax.
- If no tax was levied, cultivators might become rentiers and their extra income would likely not be invested in improving the land.

3 Sahukar A person who acted as both a moneylender and a trader.

Cotton and its increasing Demand

- Britain depended on America for cotton. Before the 1860s, 3/4th of raw cotton imports into Britain came from America.
- To ensure continuous supply of cotton from America, the **Cotton Supply Association** was founded in Britain in 1857 by the British and the **Manchester Cotton Company** was formed in 1859.
- The main objective was to encourage cotton production in every part of the world suited for its growth. India was suited for the cotton production as it had a suitable soil, favourable climate for cotton cultivation and cheap labour.

Impact of the American Civil War on the Supply of Cotton

- There was a sharp decline in the supply of cotton from America because of the outbreak of the **American Civil War** (1861).
- Raw cotton imports fell to less than 3% of the normal. Therefore, messages were sent to India and other countries to increase cotton exports to Britain.
- The merchants dealing in cotton in Bombay visited the districts producing cotton.
- The cotton exporters of Bombay started trying to purchase as much cotton as possible to meet the British demand.
- They gave huge advances to the urban *sahukars* who in turn gave loans to the rural moneylenders who promised to secure produce.
- During the American crisis, the cotton production in the Bombay Deccan expanded and it doubled between 1860 and 1864.
- Almost 90% of cotton imports to Britain came from India, but this did not bring prosperity to all cotton producers, as the expansion often led to heavier debts for small producers.

▲ *Cotton bales lying at the Bombay terminus, ready for shipment to England*

Decline in Cotton Export

- As the cotton production increased, the cotton merchants in India thought to replace America in cotton production and capture the world market. But after the civil war ended, cotton production in America revived and Indian cotton exports declined.
- *Sahukars* were no longer providing long-term loans to peasants as the demand for Indian cotton fell and cotton prices too declined.
- Many of them closed their operations, restricted advances to peasants and demanded repayment of debts. On the other side, the revenue demand also increased dramatically from 50 to 100%.

The Experience of Injustice

- Moneylenders were breaking the customary norms of the countryside, which angered the *ryots*. According to such norms, the interest charged, could not be more than the principal.
- In one case investigated by the **Deccan Riots Commission**, the moneylender charged over ₹ 2000 as interest on a loan of ₹100.
- For the *ryots*, moneylenders were dishonest and unethical. In 1859, the British passed a **Limitation Law** stating that loan bonds between moneylenders and *ryots* would be valid for only three years. This was meant to prevent the accumulation of interest over time.
- The moneylenders manipulated the law by forcing the *ryots* to sign a new bond every 3 years.
- With each new bond, the original loan and accumulated interest were treated as the principal for calculating a new set of interest charges.
- Moneylenders employed various ways to cheat the *ryots*, which were described in the petitions collected by Deccan Riots Commission.

- Moneylenders refused to give receipts when the loan was repaid. They entered fictitious figures in bonds, acquire the peasants' harvest at low prices and ultimately take peasants property.
- *Ryots* were made to sign and put thumb impressions on documents without having any knowledge of what they were signing.
- *Ryots* were unaware of the clauses inserted by moneylenders in the bonds. They had no choice but to sign because moneylenders refused to give loans without legal bonds.

9.4 The Deccan Riots Commission

- It was set up by the Government of Bombay to investigate into the causes of the riots.
- The commission submitted its report before the British Parliament in 1878. The report was known as the **Deccan Riots Report**.
- The commission collected many significant information through
    - Enquiries held in riot-affected districts.
    - Statements of *ryots*, sahukars and eyewitnesses were recorded.
    - Statistical data on revenue states.
    - Reports sent by district collectors.

Conclusion

The Deccan Riots Commission was specifically asked to study whether the level of government revenue demand was the cause of the revolt. It submitted its report blaming the moneylenders rather than the anger of peasants for the outbreak of revolt.

Such official reports should be studied with care. The evidence available from them should be checked with evidence from newspapers, unofficial accounts, legal records and oral sources wherever possible.

Quick Test 3

1. When was the revenue settlement in the Bombay Deccan made for the first time?
2. In what ways did Britain depend on America?
3. How did *ryots* generally view moneylenders?
4. What was the purpose of the Limitation Law passed in 1859?
5. What was the name of the commission set up to investigate the riots?

TIMELINE

1765	English East India Company acquires Diwani of Bengal
1773	Regulating Act passed by the British Parliament to regulate the activities of the East India Company
1793	Permanent Settlement in Bengal
1800s	Santhals begin to come to the Rajmahal hills and settle there
1818	First revenue settlement in the Bombay Deccan
1820s	Agricultural prices begin to fall
1840s-50s	A slow process of agrarian expansion in the Bombay Deccan
1855-56	Santhal rebellion
1861	Cotton boom begins
1875	*Ryots* in Deccan villages rebel

Mind Map

COLONIALISM AND THE COUNTRYSIDE

1 Bengal and the Zamindars

An auction in Burdwan
- The auction (1797) was a result of 1793 permanent settlement.
- Over 95% of the auction sales were found to be fictitious.

The Problem of Unpaid Revenue
- Permanent settlement came into operation in 1793.
- It fixed zamindar revenue demand permanently.
- Zamindars acted as revenue collectors, not direct landowners.
- Over 75% zamindars changed ownership after permanent settlement.

Zamindars defaulted on Payments
- High revenue demand burdened zamindars after permanent settlement, 1793.
- Zamindars faced resistance, arrears and law suits from defaulters.
- Zamindari collapsed during the 1930s great depression.

The Rise of Jotedars
- Jotedars owned vast lands and controlled trade and moneylending.
- The power of jotedars was more effective than zamindars.
- Jotedars dominated North Bengal.

The Fifth Report
- It documented East India Company's activities extensively.
- British groups opposed the Company's trade monopoly in India.
- The Fifth Report exaggerated zamindari collapse and land loss.

2 Rural Areas of Bengal

In the Hills of Rajamahal
- The hill folks were called paharias. They depended on forest produce and practiced shifting cultivation.
- British expanded agriculture, displacing paharias from their lands.
- Settling of Santhals in the hills intensified conflict between paharias and settlers, symbolising plough verses hoe.

The Santhals: Pioneer Settlers
- Buchanan admired Santhal's efforts in transforming Rajmahal hills.
- Santhal population and villages rapidly expanded between 1832-1851.
- Exploitation by zamindars, moneylenders led to Santhal Revolt (1855).

The Accounts of Buchanan
- Buchanan worked for British East India Company, collecting information.
- His observation focused on landscapes, commercial and agricultural potential.

3 A Revolt in the Countryside: The Bombay Deccan

A New Revenue System
- Permanent settlement not extended beyond Bengal due to fixed revenue.
- Ricardian economic theory influenced revenue policies in colonial India.
- Ryotwari settlement introduced, with taxes directly assessed on ryots.

Accounts Books are Burnt
- Revolt began in 1857 at Supa village in Poona district.
- Ryots destroyed debt bonds, burned account books and looted grain shops.
- Revolts reflect agrarain distress and colonial economic changes.

Credit Dries Up
Export Merchants and Sahukars in Maharashtra were no longer keen on extending long-term credit.

The Experience of Injustice
- Moneylenders charged excessive interest, violating traditional countryside norms.
- The British Limitation Law restricted loan validity to three years.

Revenue Demand and Peasant Debt
- High revenue demand led to peasant migration and distress.
- Famine, crop failure and falling prices worsened peasant conditions.
- After 1845, agricultural recovery led to expanded cultivation and borrowing.

Then Came the Cotton Boom
- American Civil War (1861) halted cotton imports, causing panic in Britain's industry.
- By 1862, over 90% of Britain's cotton imports came from India which benefited wealthy peasants, but also increased debt.

4 The Deccan Riots Comissions
- It was setup to investigate the causes of Deccan Riots.
- The Deccan Riots Report was presented to British Parliament in 1878. It was sent by district collectors.
- Report included data on revenue rates, prices and interest rates in different regions.

NCERT Folder

Intext Questions

1. Compare the account of the zamindars you have just read with that in Chapter 8. (Pg. 235)

Ans. Comparing the account of zamindars in the provided text with Chapter 8, we see that both portray zamindars as powerful landowning elites who collected rent from peasants, but the key difference lies in the degree of autonomy they held under the British rule. Chapter 8 highlighted the increased exploitation of peasants due to the strict revenue demands imposed by the East India Company through the Permanent Settlement, leading to greater hardship for the peasantry compared to the pre-colonial era where zamindars might have had more flexibility in managing their estates.

2. What does Buchanan's description tell us about his ideas of development? Illustrate your argument by quoting from the excerpts. If you were a Paharia forest dweller how would you have reacted to these ideas? (Pg. 245)

Ans. Buchanan's description reflects a colonial idea of development focused on commercial exploitation and transforming landscapes for productivity, aligning with British East India Company interests rather than local needs. He prioritised mineral extraction and converting forests into agricultural lands, disregarding the lifestyles and values of forest dwellers. For example, he described not just what he saw, but also how it could be transformed, what crops could be cultivated, which trees cut down. Buchanan's notion of progress was based on Western commercial values and lacked respect for local customs.

As a Paharia forest dweller, I would likely have felt threatened by Buchanan's ideas. His desire to alter forests into farmlands would disrupt my community's way of life, harming our environment, resources and cultural ties to the land.

Answer in 100-150 words

1. Why was the *jotedar* a powerful figure in many areas of rural Bengal?

Ans. The *jotedars* was a powerful figure in many areas of rural Bengal due to the following factors

- *Zamindars* used to live in urban areas, whereas the *Jotedars* were located in the villages which helped them to have direct control over a section of poor villagers.
- Local trade and moneylending was also controlled by them, hence exercising immense power over poorer cultivators of the region.
- *Jotedars* resisted efforts by zamindars to increase the revenue demand of the village and prevented zamindari officials to do their duty. They also organised dependent *ryots* and delayed payments of revenue to the zamindar.

2. How did zamindars manage to retain control of their zamindaris?

Ans. Even after the power of zamindars declined, they did not collapse. They planned several ways to retain control of their zamindaris

- Fake sale or fictious sale was one strategy adopted by them. Their own men would make highest bid and later refused to pay up. After repeating this method, the government would be tired and sell it back to zamindar at lesser rate.
- Zamindari was transferred to female members due to the rule that property of women would not be taken over by the government.
- It was difficult for an outsider to take into possession of the zamindari bought in the auction as they were attacked by the *lathyals* of the former zamindar.
- Sometimes even *ryots* who considered themselves as the subjects of the zamindars opposed such auction.

3. How did the Paharias respond to the coming of outsiders?

Ans. The Paharias who lived in the hills of Raj Mahal were replaced by the Santhals. The Britishers invited Santhals to settle in the Jangal Mahals. Hence, the response of the Paharias to the coming of outsiders is as follows

- The Paharias were moved deeper into the hills.
- They were confined to the dry interior and more barren and rocky upper hills.
- The shifting cultivation done by the Paharias became more difficult due to proper and stable settlements.
- The hunters amongst them faced problems due to clearance of forests for cultivation.

Thus, the lifestyle and living of Paharias underwent change due to coming of outsiders.

4. Why did the Santhals rebel against British rule?

Ans. By 1832, a large area of land was provided to the Santhals which came to be known as Damin-i-Koh. The Santhals were asked to live within it, practise plough agriculture and become settled peasants. However, problems started between the Santhals and the Britishers which led to the Santhal revolt in 1855-56.

Following are the main causes for their rebellion against British rule

- The Santhals realised that the land under them was slipping away from their hands.
- The tax rates imposed on the land were high and exploitative.
- Moneylenders also charged them high rate of interest and took away lands if debt remained unpaid.
- The zamindars began to exercise greater control on the areas brought under cultivation by Santhals.
- The British created the Santhal Pargana from the districts of Bhagalpur and Birbhum.
- It was believed that the creation of a new state and passing of special laws for their protection would calm down the Santhals.

5. What explains the anger of the Deccan *ryots* against the moneylenders?

Ans. The reasons for the anger of the Deccan *ryots* against the moneylenders were

- It was a customary norm that the interest will always remain less than the principal amount. But in many cases interest payable was more than the principal itself. For example, in one case the moneylender charged over ₹ 2000 as interest on a loan of ₹ 100.
- According to a Limitation Law (1859), the loan bonds signed between moneylenders and *ryots* would have validity for only three years. But the moneylenders turned the law which forced the *ryot* to sign a new bond every three years.
  With every new bond, the original loan and the accumulated interest was entered as the principal on which a new set of interest charges was calculated.
- Moneylenders also refused to give receipts when loans were repaid.
- *Ryots* complained about forging of documents and other fraudulent activity by the moneylenders.

Write a short Essay (about 250-300 words) on the following

6. Why were many zamindaris auctioned after the Permanent Settlement?

Ans. The reasons for auctioning of zamindaris even after the Permanent Settlement were

- Company kept the revenue price high as it believed that if the initial price would be low, then they would never be able to claim a share of increased income from land when prices rose and cultivation expanded. Hence, the Company argued that the burden on zamindars would decline with expanded agricultural production and price rise.
- During the 1790s, the prices of agricultural produce were depressed which made the *ryots* difficult to pay their dues to the zamindars.
- The revenue was fixed and it had to be paid punctually on time regardless of the harvest. A law was introduced which came to be known as the Sunset Law. According to the law, if payment did not come in by sunset of the specified date, the zamindari was liable to be auctioned.
- The power of zamindars were reduced. Their troops were disbanded, custom duties were abolished and their power to meet out local justice was restricted. This made it difficult for zamindars to assert their power over the peasants and *jotedars* to ensure timely payment.

7. In what way was the livelihood of the Paharias different from that of the Santhals?

Ans. The people living around the hills were known as Paharias. **The life of Paharias**

- They lived on forest produce and practised shifting cultivation.
- They grew a variety of pulses and millets.
- They collected *mahua* (a flower) for food, silk cocoons and resin for sale and wood for charcoal production.
- They used the patches of grass on the land as pasture for the cattle.
- They also raided the plains where the settled agriculturalists lived. It was necessary for survival specially during scarcity.
- They used to get tributes from the zamindars for peace settlement.
- Traders too gave small amount to them to use the passes controlled by them.
- The Paharias were hunters, shifting cultivators, food gatherers, charcoal producers and silkworm rearers.

On the other hand, the Santhals came into Bengal in the 1780s. **The life of Santhals**

- They cleared forests and cut down timber.
- They ploughed land and grew rice and cotton.
- They settled down cultivating a range of commercial crops for the market.
- They also dealt with traders and moneylenders.

8. How did the American Civil War affect the lives of *ryots* in India?

or Explain the impact of American Civil War of 1861 on Indian peasants.

Ans. American Civil War affected the lives of *ryots* in India in the following ways

- Britain was depended on America for cotton. Before the 1860s, 3/4th of raw cotton imports into Britain came from America. To reduce this dependency, Britain always looked for alternative sources of supply.

- To solve this issue, they established the Cotton Supply Association in 1857 and the Manchester Cotton Company in 1859. The main objective was to encourage cotton production in every part of the world suited for its growth specially in India.
- When the American Civil War broke out in 1861, there was a steep decline in the supply of cotton. Many attempts were made to increase cotton exports to Britain.
- The cotton exporters of Bombay started trying to purchase as much cotton as possible in order to meet the British demand. They gave huge advances to the urban *sahukars* who in turn gave loans to the rural moneylenders who made promise to secure produce.
- The *ryots* were now getting loans from the *sahukars* very easily. They were being given ₹ 100 as advance for every area they planted with cotton. However, while rich peasants benefitted by these developments, cotton expansion meant heavier debt.
- After the civil war ended, cotton production in America revived and Indian cotton exports declined. *Sahukars* began to restrict advances to peasants and demanded repayment of debts. The revenue demand also got increased. When the peasants once again turned to *sahukars*, they refused to give them loans. This enraged the poor peasants and fuelled the outbreak of the peasant revolts in Deccan.

9. What are the problems in using official sources in writing about the history of peasants?

Ans. The problems in using official sources in writing about the history of peasants are as follows

(i) The official sources reflect the concerns of British officials only. The interpretation of all events is as per the British outlook. For example, the Deccan Riots Commission was specifically asked to judge whether the level of government revenue demand was the cause of the revolt.

(ii) Most of the events, revolts, and happenings have been presented in a biased manner. The colonial government and officials had their own political, economic, religious, cultural and social interests. They had always tried to present an inferior picture of Indian society, people, tradition, culture and even the achievements.

(iii) The sources have been presented and recorded by such clever people who have intentionally presented things with false evidence also. For example, the Deccan Riot Commission altered presenting all the findings with such evidence, which was utilised to give authenticity to the report of the commission. The commission has presented this wrong fact that the government demand was not the cause of the peasants' anger. It was the moneylenders who were responsible for the Deccan Riots. Such arguments are found very frequently in British colonial records. This shows that there was a constant effort on the part of the colonial government to admit that popular discontent was ever on account of government action.

(iv) Official reports are thus invaluable sources for the reconstruction of history. But they have to always read the case and just be opposed with evidence called from newspapers, unofficial accounts, legal records, and, where possible, oral sources.

10. On an outline map of the subcontinent, mark out the areas described in this chapter. Find out whether there were other areas where the Permanent Settlement and the ryotwari system were prevalent and plot these on the map as well.

Ans. Following areas were mentioned in this chapter

(a) Bengal (b) Bombay presidency

(c) Madras (f) Rajmahal hills retain it

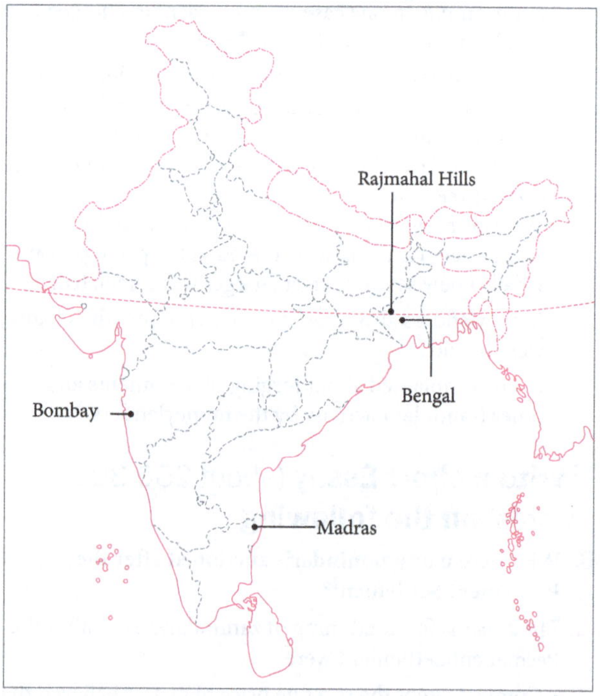

Exam Pattern Questions

Objective Type Questions

Multiple Choice Questions (MCQs)

1. What was being auctioned in Burdwan in 1797?
(a) Estates (b) Jewelleries
(c) Paintings (d) Clothes

2. Who was Governor General of Bengal when the Permanent Settlement was introduced?
(a) Lord Irwin (b) Lord Buchanan
(c) Lord Cornwallis (d) Lord William

3. When did Permanent Settlement came into operation?
(a) 1891 (b) 1793 (c) 1792 (d) 1893

4. Zamindars were responsible for
(a) extraction of minerals from the hills.
(b) cotton trade with the British.
(c) maintaining *bahi khatas* for the British.
(d) paying revenue to the British.

5. Why couldn't *ryots* pay dues to the Zamindars?
(a) Bad harvest (b) Low prices
(c) Both (a) and (b) (d) None of these

6. What do you mean by cutcheries?
(a) Court (b) Police Station
(c) Zamindar's house (d) Hospital

7. What were rich *ryots* called?
(a) Mandals (b) *Jotedars*
(c) Zamindars (d) All of these

8. When did the *jotedars* becomes powerful?
(a) End of 18th century (b) Late 19th century
(c) Early 18th century (d) None of these

9. To save their property, whom did the zamindar transferred it to?
(a) Children (b) Servants
(c) Women (d) None of these

10. When was the Fifth Report submitted?
(a) 1810 (b) 1811
(c) 1813 (d) 1815

11. Who travelled through Rajmahal Hills in the 19th Century?
(a) Buchanan (b) William
(c) Cleveland (d) Ricardo

12. Who lived in Rajmahal Hills?
(a) Bengals (b) Paharias
(c) Singhal (d) Rajputs

13. Which of the following explains Paharias?
(a) Hunters (b) Shifting cultivator
(c) Food gatherers (d) All of these

14. Who among the following proposed a 'Policy of Pacification' with the Paharias in 1770 in Bhagalpur ? **CBSE 2024**
(a) William Hodge (b) Augustus Cleveland
(c) George Chinray (d) Captain Cook

15. Who came into Bengal in the 1780s?
(a) Santhals (b) Paharias
(c) Rajputs (d) None of these

16. What was created after Santhals revolt?
(a) Damin-i-Koh
(b) Santhal Pargana
(c) Dikus
(d) Ryotwari

17. What did Buchanan searched for?
(a) Mineral (b) Iron ore
(c) Mica (d) All of these

18. Where did the revolt started in Deccan?
(a) Supa (b) Mumbai
(c) Boriwalli (d) Hyderabad

19. In which of the following districts did the ryots revolt against sahukars of the Ryotwari system ? **CBSE 2024**
(a) Awadh (b) Barrackpore
(c) Bhagalpur (d) Poona

20. Under the Ryotwari system, the lands were surveyed every
(a) 10 years (b) 20 years
(c) 30 years (d) 40 years

21. Which one of the following was the main cause of the Santhal Rebellion of 1855? **CBSE 2025**
(a) Imposition of the Summary Settlement
(b) Cultural suppression by the British
(c) Imposition of Western education
(d) Heavy taxes and land annexation

22. Why is the Santhal rebellion considered significant in the Indian history ? Choose the most suitable option from the following CBSE 2024 C

(a) It marked the beginning of National Freedom Movement.
(b) It led to the immediate abolition of Permanent Settlement.
(c) It directly sparked the Revolt of 1857 through sepoys.
(d) It highlighted the exploitative nature of the British towards people of Damin-e-Koh.

23. Which of the following was the primary characteristic of the Ryotwari system implemented by the British in 'Bombay Deccan' ? CBSE 2024

(a) Indirect revenue collection through zamindars
(b) Collective ownership of land by village community
(c) The Britishers settled revenue directly with the peasants
(d) Lands were given to the Jotedars to promote equality

24. Find the odd one out regarding the Permanent Settlement of 1793. CBSE 2025

(a) The Sunset law
(b) The Burdwan's Auction
(c) The Fifth Report
(d) The Deccan Riots Commission

25. Compare and contrast the impacts of the American Civil War on cotton production in India and the United States. Choose the best suitable option from the following. CBSE SQP 2024

(a) Both countries experienced a decline in cotton production due to the war.
(b) India's cotton production increased while the United States experienced a decline.
(c) The United States saw increased cotton production while India's remained stagnant.
(d) Both countries saw a surge in cotton exports during the war period.

26. Which of the following statement is true?

(i) Auction of estate was held in Burdawan in 1797.
(ii) The Raja of Burdawan failed to pay his dues.
(iii) The Britishers purchased the estates.

Codes

(a) Only (iii) (b) (i) and (ii)
(c) (i) and (iii) (d) (ii) and (iii)

27. Which of the following statement is true?

(i) Paharias followed jhoom cultivation.
(ii) They lived in huts within tamarind groves.
(iii) They collected *Mahua* flower for food.

Codes

(a) Only (i) (b) (i), (ii) and (iii)
(c) (i) and (ii) (d) (i) and (iii)

28. Which of the following statement is true?

(i) Santhals were hired by zamindars.
(ii) They settled in Burdawan.
(iii) A large area was provided to Santhal known as Damin-i-Koh.

Codes

(a) Only (i) (b) (i) and (ii)
(c) (i) and (iii) (d) Only (iii)

29. Arrange the following in chronological order and select the correct order from the following options. CBSE 2023

(i) Santhal Rebellion
(ii) Riots in Deccan Villages
(iii) Permanent Settlement in Bengal
(iv) First Revenue Settlement in Bombay Deccan

Codes

(a) (i), (ii), (iii) and (iv) (b) (ii), (iii), (iv) and (i)
(c) (iii), (iv), (i) and (ii) (d) (iv), (i), (ii) and (iii)

30. Which of the following represents the correct chronological order of events related to agrarian developments in India during the 19th century? CBSE SQP 2024

(i) The Permanent Settlement in Bengal
(ii) The Deccan Riots Commission
(iii) The Santhal Rebellion
(iv) The Fifth Report by a Select Committee

Options

(a) (i), (ii), (iii) and (iv)
(b) (ii), (iii), (iv) and (i)
(c) (iii), (ii), (i) and (iv)
(d) (i), (iv), (iii) and (ii)

31. Arrange the following in chronological order and choose the correct option : CBSE 2024

(i) Limitation Law
(ii) Sunset Law
(iii) Santhal Rebellion
(iv) Bombay-Deccan Riots

Options

(a) (ii), (iii), (i), (iv) (b) (i), (ii), (iv), (iii)
(c) (iii), (iv), (ii), (i) (d) (iv), (iii), (i), (ii)

32. Arrange the following in chronological order and choose the correct option. CBSE 2024

(i) Limitation Law passed by the British
(ii) Starting of Permanent Settlement in Bengal
(iii) Santhal Rebellion
(iv) Ryotwari settlement in Bombay Deccan

Options

(a) (i), (ii), (iii), and (iv) (b) (i), (iii), (i) and (iv)
(c) (ii), (iv), (iii) and (i) (d) (iii), (iv), (i) and (ii)

33. **Identify the primary purpose of Britishers to implement Permanent Settlement in Bengal.** CBSE 2024

Choose the best suitable option from the following.

(a) To empower peasants of the region.
(b) To abolish land ownership in the region.
(c) To increase agricultural productivity of jotedars.
(d) To provide financial stability to the British government.

34. **Identify the name of the person from the information given below**

(i) He was a physician who came to India and served in the Bengal Medical Service from 1794 to 1815.
(ii) For few years, he was surgeon to the Governor-General of India, Lord Wellesley.
(iii) During his stay in Calcutta, he organised a Zoo that became the Calcutta Alipore Zoo.
(iv) He was also incharge of the Botanical Gardens for a short period.

Options

(a) Francis Buchanan (b) James Buchanan
(c) John Fryer (d) Francois Bernier

35. **Identify the name of the law from the information given below:**

(i) It was passed by British in 1859.
(ii) According to this law, the loan bonds signed between moneylenders and ryots would have validity for only three years.
(iii) This law was meant to check the accumulation of interest over time.

(a) Sunset Law (b) Limitation Law
(c) Resistance Law (d) No Tax Law

36. **Complete the following with the correct option regarding the revenue settlements and their respective areas of operation.**

Permanent settlement: Bengal :: Ryotwari Settlement: ....

(a) Awadh (b) Bombay Deccan
(c) Rajmahal (d) Lucknow

Assertion-Reason

37. **Assertion** (A) Zamindars in the Permanent Settlement failed to pay the revenue demand and unpaid balances accumulated. CBSE 2024

Reason (R) According to the Sunset Law, if payment did not come in by Sunset of the specified date, the zamindari was liable to be auctioned.

Codes

(a) Both A and R are true and R is the correct explanation of A
(b) Both A and R are true, but R is not the correct explanation of A
(c) A is correct, but R is incorrect
(d) A is incorrect, but R is correct

38. **Assertion** (A) Ryotwari Settlement was a new revenue system introduced in Bombay Deccan.
Reason (R) The revenue was fixed for every *ryot*.

Codes

(a) Both A and R are true and R is the correct explanation of A
(b) Both A and R are true, but R is not the correct explanation of A
(c) A is true, but R is false
(d) A is false, but R is true

39. **Assertion** (A) After American Civil War, there was steep decline in the supply of cotton.
Reason (R) Britain started imports cotton from India.

Codes

(a) Both A and R are true and R is the correct explanation of A
(b) Both A and R are true, but R is not the correct explanation of A
(c) A is true, but R is false
(d) A is false, but R is true

40. **Assertion** (A) Deccan Riot Commission was formed by government of Bengal.
Reason (R) It submitted its report in 1878.

Codes

(a) Both A and R are true and R is the correct explanation of A
(b) Both A and R are true, but R is not the correct explanation of A
(c) A is true, but R is false
(d) A is false, but R is true

Match the Following

41.

	List I		List II
A.	Deccan Riot Report	1.	1813
B.	Policy of Pacification	2.	1878
C.	Fifth Report	3.	1793
D.	Permanent Settlement	4.	1780

Codes

	A	B	C	D		A	B	C	D
(a)	1	3	2	4	(b)	2	4	1	3
(c)	4	2	1	3	(d)	1	3	4	2

42.

List I	List II
A. Lord Cornwallis	1. Observer
B. Augustus Cleveland	2. Economist
C. Francis Buchanan	3. Governor General of Bengal
D. David Ricardo	4. Policy of Pacification

Codes

	A	B	C	D		A	B	C	D
(a)	2	1	4	3	(b)	3	1	2	4
(c)	3	4	1	2	(d)	2	4	3	1

43.

List I	List II
A. Francis Buchanan	1. Introduced Permanent Settlement
B. Charles Cornwallis	2. Surveyed North Bengal
C. David Ricardo	3. Land records management
D. Sidhu Manjhi	4. Santhal revolt

Codes

	A	B	C	D		A	B	C	D
(a)	2	1	3	4	(b)	1	2	3	4
(c)	3	1	4	2	(d)	2	3	1	4

44.

List I	List II
A. *Mahals*	1. Peasants
B. *Ryots*	2. Estates
C. *Mandals*	3. Strongmen of the zamindar
D. *Lathyals*	4. Village headmen

Codes

	A	B	C	D		A	B	C	D
(a)	1	2	3	4	(b)	2	1	4	3
(c)	3	4	1	2	(d)	4	1	2	3

Picture Based Questions

45. The image given below was painted by which artist?

(a) Thomas Gainsborough (b) Wilson Adam
(c) Robert Kim (d) Carl Magson

46. Who is shown in the image below?

(a) Mehtab Chand (b) Tejchand
(c) Amar Singh (d) Raja Dham

47. The stock of cotton bales in Bombay as depicted in figure were transported to

(a) textile factories in Lancashire and Manchester.
(b) textile factories in Boston city of USA.
(c) textile manufacturing hub of Kanpur.
(d) All of the above

Answers

1. (a) Estates
2. (c) Lord Cornwallis
3. (b) 1793
4. (d) paying revenue to the British.
5. (c) Both (a) and (b)
6. (a) Court
7. (b) *Jotedars*
8. (a) End of 18th century
9. (c) Women
10. (c) 1813
11. (a) Buchanan
12. (b) Paharias
13. (d) All of these
14. (b) Augustus Cleveland
15. (a) Santhals
16. (a) Damin-i-Koh
17. (d) All of these
18. (a) Supa
19. (d) Poona
20. (c) 30 years
21. (d) Heavy taxes and land annexation
22. (d) It highlighted the exploitative nature of the British towards people of Damin-e-Koh.
23. (c) The Britishers settled revenue directly with the peasants
24. (d) The Deccan Riots Commission
25. (b) India's cotton production increased while the United States experienced a decline.
26. (b) (i) and (ii)
27. (b) (i), (ii) and (iii)
28. (c) (i) and (iii)
29. (c) (iii), (iv), (i) and (ii)
30. (d) (i), (iv), (iii) and (ii)
31. (a) (ii), (iii), (i), (iv)
32. (b) (ii), (iii), (i) and (iv)
33. (d) To provide financial stability to the British government.
34. (a) Francis Buchanan
35. (b) Limitation Law
36. (b) Bombay Deccan
37. (b) Both A and R are correct, but Reason (R) is not the correct explanation of the A.
38. (c) A is true, but R is false
39. (a) Both A and R are true and R is the correct explanation of A
40. (d) A is false, but R is true
41. (b)
42. (c)
43. (a)
44. (b)
45. (a) Thomas Gainsborough
46. (a) Mehtab Chand
47. (a) textile factories in Lancashire and Manchester.

Subjective Questions

Short Answer Type Questions

1. How did the auction in Burdwan took place?

Ans. The auction in the Burdwan can be explained from the following events

- The auction was held in Burdwan (present day Bardhaman) in 1797. A number of *mahals* (estates) held by the Raja of Burdwan were being sold because the raja had accumulated huge arrears.
- Many purchasers came to the auction and the estates were sold to the highest bidder. But it was later realised that over 95 per cent of the sale at the auction was fictitious.
- Many purchasers turned out to be servants and agents of the raja in the auction. Hence, publicly the estates were sold but raja remained in control of his zamindari.

2. In introducing the Permanent Settlement, British officials hoped to resolve the problems they had been facing since the conquest of Bengal. Discuss

Competency Based Que

Ans. In introducing the Permanent Settlement, British officials hoped to resolve the problems they had been facing since the conquest of Bengal.

This was because

- By the 1770s, the rural economy in Bengal was in crisis, with recurrent famines and declining agricultural output.
- Officials felt that agriculture, trade and the revenue resources of the state could all be developed by encouraging investment in agriculture.
  This could be done by securing rights of property and permanently fixing the rates of revenue demand.
- If the state's revenue demand was fixed, the Company could expect a steady income and entrepreneurs could be confident in making a profit from their investments, knowing the state would not take more money later.

3. Why did British introduce the Permanent Settlement in Bengal? Explain. **CBSE Term II 2022**

Ans. By introducing the Permanent Settlement, British officials hoped to resolve the problems they had been facing since the conquest of Bengal. By the 1770s, the rural economy in Bengal was in crisis, with recurrent famines and declining agricultural output. Officials felt that agriculture, trade and the revenue resources of the state could all be developed by encouraging investment in agriculture. This could be done by securing rights of property and permanently fixing the rates of Raja.

4. Examine the different aspects of the 'Permanent Settlement' introduced in Bengal by the British. CBSE 2024 C

Ans. The different aspects of the 'Permanent Settlement' introduced in Bengal by the British are as follows

- The British East India Company fixed the revenue that each zamindar (landowner) had to pay. This revenue was set permanently, meaning it wouldn't change over time. If zamindars failed to pay, their estates could be auctioned to recover the revenue.
- The British aimed to resolve Bengal's economic crisis, which was marked by recurrent famines and declining agricultural output. By fixing the revenue permanently, they hoped to encourage investment in agriculture, improve agricultural output, and ensure a steady flow of revenue for the Company.
- The zamindars were not landowners in the traditional sense but were revenue collectors for the Company. They were given control over several villages (sometimes up to 400), which formed a single revenue estate. Zamindars collected rent from peasants, paid the fixed revenue to the Company, and kept the difference as their income.
- The revenue demands were initially set very high. The British did this to prevent losing out on potential future profits when land prices rose or cultivation expanded. However, this made it difficult for zamindars to pay, especially since agricultural prices were low at the time.

5. Explain two reasons for the failure of the Permanent Settlement of the land revenue introduced by the British in Bengal.

Ans. The reasons for the failure of the Permanent Settlement of the land revenue introduced by the British in Bengal are as follows

(i) The early revenue demands fixed by the Company were very high. Under Permanent Settlement, the state revenue demand was fixed in perpetuity.
It meant that Company was not claiming an additional share of increased income from land with rising prices and expanding cultivation. Therefore, the Company wanted huge revenue for high demand in order to minimise this anticipated loss.

(ii) High demand of land revenue was fixed in 1790s. The price of agricultural produce were depressed during this period. Consequently, it became difficult for the *ryots* to pay their dues to the zamindars.
Thus, the zamindars could not collect the rent and were unable to pay their fixed amount to the Company.

6. The East India Company had recognised the zamindars importance but wanted to control and regulate them. Explain the steps taken by them to subdue their authority in the 18th century.

Or **Explain how the East India Company subdued the authority of zamindars in Bengal during 18th century?**

Ans. The East India Company recognised the importance and significance of zamindars but it also wanted to control, regulate and subdue their authority. The Company took the following steps:

- To limit the authority of zamindars, the Company disbanded the troop organised by zamindars.
- Custom duties were abolished and *'cutcheries'* or local court organised by zamindars were brought under supervision of the Company.
- The Company appointed collectors and gave them power to supervise these courts. Over the period of time collectorate emerged as centre of authority.
- The power to organise local justice and the local police, was also abolished. The Permanent Settlement system also limited the power of the zamindars to collect rent from the *ryots* and manage their zamindari.

7. "*Jotedars* inevitably weakened zamindars in Bengal by the end of the 18th century." Give arguments to support the statement. Competency Based Que

Or **Describe the position of the *jotedars* at the end of the 18th century.**

Or **During the late eighteenth century, while many zamindars faced crises, a group of affluent peasants, known as jotedars, were consolidating their power in rural villages. Justify the statement.** CBSE SQP 2024

Or **"The jotedars become powerful figures in many areas of North Bengal during the end of the 18th century". Examine the statement.** CBSE 2024

Ans. *Jotedars* inevitably weakened the power of zamindars in Bengal by the end of the 18th century because

- *Jotedars* lived in villages and thus, had good influence on village population.
- *Jotedars* had acquired vast areas of land. They controlled local trade, moneylending, exercising immense power over the poorer cultivators and their land was cultivated through *adhiyars* or *bargadars* (share croppers).
- They resisted the effects of zamindars to increase the *jama* of the village, prevented zamindari officials from executing their duties. They deliberately delayed payments of revenue to the zamindars.
- When the estates of the zamindars were auctioned for failure to make revenue payment, *jotedars* bought their estate. This made the *jotedars* most powerful in the North Bengal.

8. Evaluate the main aspects of the Fifth Report on the administration and activities of East India Company, submitted to the British Parliament. **Competency Based Que**

Ans. The Fifth Report was a significant report. It continued shaping our conception for over a century and a half about the nature and consequences of East India Company's Rule in Bengal in the late 18th century. It served as basis for intense parliamentary debates on the nature of company's rule in India. It described what happened in rural Bengal in the late 18th century.

The evidence contained in the 'Fifth Report' is considered to be of great importance. But as it is an official report, it should be read and anaylsed very carefully.

The major shortcomings of this report included

- The Fifth Report exaggerated the collapse of traditional zamindari power and the rate at which zamindar were losing their lands. Zamindars were not always displaced given the indigenous methods they used to retain their lands.
- The report was biased because it wanted to highlight the maladministration of the East India Company in India.

9. Analyse the economic and social conditions of the Paharias (hill folk) of Rajmahal hills during the late eighteenth century.

Ans. The economic and social conditions of the Paharias of Rajmahal hills during the late eighteenth century were

- They cleared patches of forests and grew a variety of pulses and millets for consumption. They cultivated land for a few years, then left it fallow, so that it could recover its fertility and moved to a new area.
- They collected mahua for food, silk cocoons and resins for sale and wood for charcoal production from the forest.
- They lived as hunters, shifting cultivators, food gatherers, charcoal producers and silkworm rearers. They consider the entire region as their land and resisted the intrusion of the outsiders.

10. Which policy was adopted by British officials towards Paharias in the decade of 1770? What was its result?

or Analyse the impact of the 'policy of pacification' on the Paharias, proposed by Augustus Cleveland in 1780. **CBSE Term II 2022**

Ans. The policies adopted by British towards Paharias in the decade of 1770s are as follows

- By the 1770s, the British embarked on a brutal policy of extermination, hunting the Paharias down and killing them.
- By the 1780s, Augustus Cleveland, the Collector of Bhagalpur, proposed a policy of pacification.
- Paharia chiefs were given an annual allowance and made responsible for the proper conduct of their men. They were expected to maintain order in their localities and discipline their own people.

Result of British policies towards Paharias was

- Many Paharia chiefs refused the allowances. Those who accepted, most often lost authority within the community.
- Being paid by the colonial government, they came to be perceived as subordinate employees or stipendiary chiefs.
- As the pacification campaign continued, Paharias went deep into mountain to save themselves from hostile forces. However, they continued their war against outsiders.
- The experience of pacification and memories of brutal repression shaped their perception of British infiltration into their area. They saw every white man as a power who wants to destroy their lifestyle.

11. The battle between the hoe and the plough was a long one. Substantiate the statement with reference to the Santhals and Paharias of Rajmahal hills during 18th century. **Competency Based Que**

Ans. The Paharias represented the hoe whereas the plough was represented by Santhals. The battle between these was a long one. The British wanted to bring more land under cultivation for increasing agricultural produce and revenue. They failed to convince the Paharias to practice settled agriculture.

The Paharias were depended on forest produce and shifting cultivation for their living and grew a variety of pulses for consumption. The British gave land to Santhals (Damin -i-Koh) to settle and cultivate. The Santhals cleared land and converted it into cultivable land. Santhals displaced the Paharias. They practiced plough agriculture and ploughed land to grow rice and cotton.

12. Analyse the circumstances under which the British officials invited Santhals to settle in the peripheries of Rajmahal hills during the nineteenth century.

Ans. The circumstances under which the British officials invited Santhals to settle in the peripheries of Rajmahal hills during the nineteenth century are given below

- To the British, extension of settled agriculture was necessary to enlarge the sources of land revenue, produce crops for export, and establish the basis of a settled, ordered society.
- People who live around the Rajmahal hills were known as Paharias. They were dependent on forest produce and shifting agriculture. The British wanted that forest people should adopt plough agriculture. As settled agriculture expanded, the area under forests and pastures contracted. This sharpened the conflict between hill folk and settled cultivators. The British could not subdue Paharias despite several efforts.

- The Santhals had begun to come into Bengal around the 1780s. To the British, the Santhals appeared ideal settlers who could clear forest and plough the land with enthuisiasm.

13. What was Damin-i-Koh? How it came into being?

Or **Analyse how Santhals settled in the periphery of Raj Mahal hills in the beginning of nineteenth century.** **CBSE 2024**

Ans. A large area of land was provided to the Santhals by 1832 in Rajmahal hills which came to be known as Damin-i-Koh.

The Santhals were asked to live within it, practise plough agriculture and become settled peasants. They were asked to clear and cultivate one-tenth of the area within the first ten years. The area was surveyed and mapped. The area was separated from the world of the settled agriculturists and the Paharias. The demarcation resulted into expansion of Santhal settlements. From 40 Santhal villages in the area in 1838, around 1437 villages had come up by 1851. The Santhal population also increased from 3,000 to 82,000.

14. What were the accounts of Buchanan?

Or **Examine the role of Francis Buchanan as an extraordinary observer of British East India Company.** **CBSE Term II 2022**

Ans. Buchanan was an employee of the British East India Company. The Company was looking for natural resources to control and exploit. It surveyed landscapes and revenue sources, organised voyages of discovery and sent its geologists and geographers, botanists and medical men to collect information. Buchanan was one such individual sent by Company for survey.

He observed the stones and rocks and the different strata and layers of soil. He searched for minerals and stones which were commercially valuable. All signs of iron ore and mica, granite and saltpetre were recorded by him. He also observed local practices of salt-making and iron ore-mining.

15. East India Company commissioned Buchanan with specific instructions about what he had to look for and what he had to record. Justify the statement with three suitable arguments. **Competency Based Que**

Ans. East India Company commissioned Buchanan with specific instructions. The arguments in justification of the statement are as follows

- Buchanan during his travels was always accompanied by specialists who helped in collecting data about the place and people. The East India Company required him to collect data so that decisions about where to invest and how to make a profit out of these places could be made.
- The Company looked for natural resources it could control and exploit and Buchanan observed stones, rocks, different strata and layers of soil. He searched for minerals that were commercially valuable. All the data Buchanan collected about natural resources helped the East India Company in making profits.
- When Buchanan wrote about a landscape he explained extensively how it could be transformed and made more productive like what crops could be cultivated, which trees to cut down and which ones should be grown. All such information that the East India Company sought in order to make profits Buchanan with his observation and data collection was able to provide.

16. How did the Deccan Riots take place?

Ans. The Deccan Riots took place as a response of *ryots* against the high revenue demand by the British and exploitation by the moneylenders.

The movement began at Supa, a large village in Poona district. On 12th May, 1875, *ryots* from surrounding rural areas gathered and attacked the shopkeepers, demanding their *bahi khatas* (account books) and debt bonds. They burnt the *khatas*, looted grain shops, and in some cases set fire to the houses of *sahukars*.

From Poona, the revolt spread to Ahmednagar. Then over the next two months it spread even further, over an area of 6,500 square km. More than thirty villages were affected.

Ryots attacked on *sahukars*, burned account books and destroyed debt bonds. Terrified by peasant attacks, the *sahukars* fled the villages, very often leaving their property and belongings behind.

17. Which economic ideas of David Ricardo influenced British officials in Maharashtra during the 1820s?

Ans. By the 1820s, the economist David Ricardo was a well-known figure in England. The economic ideas of David Ricardo which influenced British officials in Maharashtra during the 1820s are as follows

- According to Ricardian ideas, a landowner should have a claim only to the "average rent" that prevailed at a given time.
- When the land yielded more than the "average rent", the landowner had a surplus that the state needed to tax.
- If tax was not levied, cultivators were likely to turn into rentiers, and their surplus income was unlikely to be productively invested in the improvement of the land.
- Many British officials in India thought that the history of Bengal confirmed Ricardo's theory. There the zamindars seemed to have turned into rentiers, leasing out land and living on the rental incomes.

18. Examine the different aspects of 'Ryotwari system' introduced in the Bombay Deccan by the British. CBSE 2024 C

Ans. The Ryotwari system, introduced in the Bombay Deccan by the British, was a revenue collection system directly settled with individual peasants, or ryots. Here are the different aspects of the Ryotwari system

- The British assessed land revenue directly from the peasants. The income potential of different soils was estimated, and based on the ryot's capacity to pay, a share of the revenue was fixed as the state's demand.
- Lands were resurveyed every 30 years, and revenue rates were increased. This meant the revenue demand was not fixed and became variable over time.
- When peasants failed to pay their dues, revenue collectors would seize crops, impose fines on entire villages, and use severe methods to extract payments.
- To meet their needs, peasants had to borrow money from moneylenders. As their debts grew, they got stuck in a cycle of borrowing and repaying. By the 1840s, their debts were so high that it worsened their poverty and increased their dependence on moneylenders.

19. How was the Permanent Settlement different from Ryotwari Settlement?

Ans. Difference between Permanent and Ryotwari Settlements were as follows

	Permanent Settlement	Ryotwari Settlement
1.	The Permanent Settlement was introduced in 1793 in Bengal under the Governor-General of Lord Cornwallis.	The Ryotwari Settlement was introduced in the Bombay Deccan.
2.	In Permanent Settlement, the Taluqdars were the owners of the land. They paid a fixed rent to the Company.	Under the Ryotwari system, the government received tax from the peasants directly.
3.	In Permanent Settlement, land was distributed among the peasants. They earned the desire interests.	In Ryotwari system, the government estimated the average income from different types of soil.
4.	The state was unable to claim its share in the enhanced income of the farmers as per permanent settlement.	In Ryotwari system, a proportional amount of the share was fixed as the share of the state.

20. Explain how the deeds and bonds appeared as symbols of the new oppressive systems.

Ans. Deeds and bonds became the symbols of the new oppressive system. The British did not believe in transactions based on informal understanding. For them, transactions had to be clearly stated in contracts. Deeds and bonds are regulated by law. For the *ryots*, deeds and bonds were misery to their lives. They were made to sign and put thumb impressions on documents without having any knowledge of what they were signing.

Ryots were unaware of the clauses inserted by moneylenders in the bonds. They had no choice but to sign because moneylenders refused to give loans without legal bonds.

21. When the American Civil War broke out in 1861, a wave of panic spread through cotton circles in Britain. Discuss. Competency Based Que

Ans. When the American Civil War broke out in 1861, a wave of panic spread through cotton circles in Britain. Raw cotton imports from America fell to less than three percent of the normal: from over 2,000,000 bales (of 400 lbs each) in 1861 to 55,000 bales in 1862. Urgent messages were sent to India and other places to boost cotton exports to Britain. In Bombay, cotton merchants travelled to cotton growing areas to evaluate supplies and promote cultivation. As cotton prices fell, export merchants in Bombay were eager to acquire as much cotton as possible to meet the British demand. They provided advances to urban sahukars, who in turn extended credit to those rural moneylenders who promised to secure the produce.

While the American crisis continued, cotton production in the Bombay Deccan expanded. By 1862 over 90 per cent of cotton imports into Britain were coming from India.

22. Explain the impact of refusal by moneylenders to extend loans to ryots, around 1865, under the colonial rule in India.

Ans. The condition of the cotton market changed in 1865 when American Civil War came to an end and *ryots* started producing cotton.

The merchants profit were lowered so they were not able to pay the peasants whatever dues were left.

Under these circumstances, moneylenders and merchants were no longer keen on providing to the *ryots*. The impact of this on *ryots* was

- They were caught into the deeper and deeper debt.
- The *ryots* were completely dependent upon the moneylenders for their survial. The moneylenders charged the *ryots* with heavy interest and violated the customary norms of countryside by even charging interest of ₹ 2000 on the actual amount of ₹100.

23. What was the Limitation Law? Why was this considered as a symbol of oppression against the *ryots* of 19th century? Give two reasons.

Ans. In 1859, British passed Limitation Law which stated that the loan bond signed between moneylenders and *ryots* would have validity for only three years.

This law was considered as a symbol of oppression due to the following reasons

- When new bond was signed, the unpaid balance, i.e. original loan and interest was entered as principal and this principal interest was charged.
- Moneylenders refused to give receipt when loans were repaid, entered fictitious figures in bond, acquired the peasant's harvest at low price and ultimately took over the property of peasants.

24. Critically examine the Deccan Riots Commission Report.

Ans. The Deccan Riots Commission Report can be examined through the following points

- Proper enquiries were held in the riot affected districts and the statement of the *ryots*, *sahukars* and eyewitnesses were recorded. Statistical data on revenue rates, prices and interest rates were compiled in various regions.
- In the Deccan Riots Commission Report, there the official sources and reflect concerns and interpretations of events. For example, the commission was specifically asked to judge whether the level of the government revenue demand was the cause of the revolt. After presenting all the evidences, the commission reported that the government demand was not the cause of anger of the peasants. It was the moneylenders who were to blame.

Long Answer Type Questions

1. Examine the factors that influenced the implementation of the Permanent Settlement in Bengal and its consequences. CBSE 2024

Ans. The Permanent Settlement of Bengal was introduced by the British East India Company in 1793. The factors that influenced the implementation of the Permanent Settlement in Bengal are as follows

- By the 1770s, Bengal faced recurrent famines, declining agricultural output, and an unstable rural economy. British officials believed that fixing the revenue demand would provide economic stability and promote investment in agriculture.
- The Company aimed for a steady, predictable revenue stream. By fixing the revenue demand permanently, they hoped to secure a fixed amount each year without the risk of the state increasing its claims.
- Officials believed that securing property rights for zamindars and offering a fixed revenue rate would encourage them to invest in improving agricultural productivity. The British hoped this would lead to a class of wealthy, loyal landowners.
- The British decided to make the Permanent Settlement with rajas and taluqdars of Bengal, recognising them as zamindars. They were made responsible for collecting revenue and paying it to the Company. This allowed the Company to avoid direct involvement in the agrarian sector.

The consequences of the Permanent Settlement are as follows

- The Company fixed the revenue demand at a high level to prevent future claims on increasing land revenues. This burdened zamindars, especially since agricultural prices were low during the 1790s.
- Zamindars struggled to collect sufficient rent from peasants (ryots) due to low agricultural prices and the fixed, high revenue demand. As a result, many zamindars failed to pay the required revenue, leading to unpaid balances and financial distress.
- The revenue was fixed irrespective of the harvest, meaning that zamindars had to pay the same amount even in years of poor harvests. The Sunset Law added pressure, stating that failure to pay by sunset could lead to the auctioning of the zamindari.
- Initially, zamindars had authority over their estates, but the Permanent Settlement gradually diminished their power. The British reduced their control over local justice, law enforcement, and military, transferring these functions to the Collector, a British-appointed official.

2. 'After introducing the Permanent Settlement in Bengal, the zamindars regularly failed to pay the land revenue demand." Examine the causes and consequences of it. Competency Based Que

Ans. Even after the surety of revenue, zamindars regularly failed to pay the revenue demand and unpaid balances accumulated. The causes behind such default includes

- Firstly, Company kept the revenue price high with an idea that if the initial price would be low, then they would never be able to claim a share of increased income from land when prices rose and cultivation expanded. Hence, the Company argued that the burden on zamindars would decline with expanded agricultural production and price rise.
- Secondly, during the 1790s, the prices of agricultural produce were depressed which made the *ryots* difficult to pay their dues to the zamindar.
- Thirdly, as the revenue was fixed, it had to be paid punctually on time regardless of the harvest. A law was introduced which came to be known as the Sunset Law. According to the law, if payment did not come in by sunset of the specified date, the zamindari was liable to be auctioned.
- Fourthly, the power of the zamindar was initially limited to collect rent from the *ryot* and manage his zamindari.

The duty of collecting revenue was under zamindars, but they were brought under some consequences. These were

- The zamindars troops were disbanded, custom duties abolished and their *cutcheries* (courts) were brought under the supervision of a collector appointed by the Company.

- They lost the power to organise local justice and the local police. The collectorate emerged as an alternative centre of authority.
- An officer of the zamindar, the *amlah,* came to the village at the time of rent collection to keep an eye on the process.
- Bad harvests and low prices made the *ryots* difficult to pay dues to the zamindars.
- Sometimes *ryots* deliberately delayed the revenue payment.
- Rich *ryots* and village headmen, *jotedars* and *Mandals* were against the zamindars.
- The judicial process was long drawn to prosecute defaulters. In Burdwan, there were over 30,000 pending suits for arrears of rent payment in 1798.

3. Faced with an exorbitantly high revenue demand and possible auction of their estates, zamindars in rural areas devised ways of surviving the pressures. Justify the statement. **Competency Based Que**

Ans. The ways that the zamindars in rural areas devised to survive the pressure were

- Zamindars transferred their zamindari to their women. The company had decreed that property of women could not be taken over. For example, the Raja of Burdwan transferred some of his zamindari to his mother.
- Zamindars used the strategy of fictious sale or fake sale. As per this strategy, zamindar's men brought the property, outbidding other purchasers. Subsequently, they refused to pay up the purchase money so that the estate had to be resold.
- Men of zamindars would participate in every auction to manipulate it. They brought property and later refused to pay. This process was repeated endlessly, exhausting the state, and the other bidders at the auction. At last, the estate was sold at a low price back to the zamindar.
- The zamindar never paid the full revenue demand; the Company rarely recovered the unpaid balances that had piled up.
- When people from outside the zamindari bought an estate at an auction, they could not always take possession. At times their agents would be attacked by lathyals of the former zamindar.
- Sometimes even the ryots resisted the entry of outsiders. They felt bound to their own zamindar through a sense of loyalty and perceived him as a figure of authority and themselves as his *praja* (subjects). The sale of the zamindari disturbed their sense of identity and pride. The zamindars therefore were not easily displaced.

4. Examine the main aspects of the Fifth Report which was submitted to the British Parliament in 1813.

***Or* Critically examine the Fifth Report of 1813.** **CBSE 2024**

Ans. Many of the changes occured at the time of the East India Company were documented in detail in a report that was submitted to the British Parliament in 1813. It was the Fifth Report on the administration and activities of the East India Company in India. The main aspects of the Fifth Report are discussed below

- The Fifth Report had been covered into 1002 pages of which over 800 pages were appendices that reproduced petitions of zamindars and *ryots* reports of collectors from different districts, statistical tables on revenue returns, and notes on the revenue and judicial administration of Bengal and Madras (present-day Tamil Nadu) written by officials.
- The British Parliament passed a series of acts in the late 18th century to regulate and control Company rule in India. It forced the Company to produce regular reports on committees to enquire into the affairs of the Company. The Fifth Report was one such report produced by a Select Committee. It became the basis of intense Parliamentary debates on the nature of the East India Company's rule in India.
- The evidence contained in the Fifth Report is invaluable. But the recent researches show that the arguments and evidences offered by the Fifth Report cannot be accepted uncritically.
- After careful examination of the archives of various Bengal zamindars and the local records of the districts, researchers found that the report exaggerated the collapse of traditional zamindari power and also overestimated the scale on which zamindars were losing their land. When zamindaris were auctioned, zamindars were not always displaced. They used ingenious methods to retain their zamindaris.

Thus, the Fifth Report had been proved to be a good source to understand the India's economy in the colonial times.

5. Explain the causes that led to the conflict between the Paharias of Rajmahal Hills and the Santhals. **CBSE 2024**

Ans. The causes that led to the conflict between the Paharias of Rajmahal Hills and the Santhals are discussed below

- As British colonial rule expanded, settled agriculture grew, leading to the contraction of forests and pastures that the Paharias depended on for their traditional livelihood. The Paharias practiced shifting cultivation, which required access to forests and fertile lands. The spread of permanent settlements by the Santhals disrupted their mobility and encroached on their resources.
- The Paharias used hoes for shifting cultivation, while the Santhals introduced plough agriculture, which was more permanent and intensive. The Paharias viewed this as a

threat to their way of life, symbolised by the clash between the "hoe" (Paharias) and the "plough" (Santhals).

- The British initially tried to control the Paharias through violent repression, particularly in the 1770s. This policy only deepened the mistrust between the Paharias and the British.
- The British, failing to pacify the Paharias, turned to the Santhals, encouraging them to settle in the Rajmahal Hills. In 1832, the land of Damin-i-Koh was demarcated specifically for the Santhals, further isolating the Paharias and limiting their access to fertile lands.
- The Paharias, unable to compete with the growing number of Santhal settlements, were forced to retreat deeper into the hills, away from the fertile land. This confinement led to a long-term impoverishment of the Paharias, as their traditional agricultural practices could no longer be sustained.

6. Examine the land revenue system that was introduced in Bombay Deccan. How did the peasants fall into the debt-trap of the moneylenders? Explain.

Ans. Ryotwari Settlement was introduced in the Bombay Deccan by the British. It has the following features

Direct Settlement with the *Ryots* The revenue was settled directly with the *ryots*.

Calculation of Revenue Unlike the Permanent Settlement, the revenue was estimated taking into consideration all types of soil and the average income of the harvest was estimated. It assessed how much revenue a *ryot* could pay.

Share of State The share of the state was fixed in proportion to the income of the *ryot*.

Re-survey of Land After every 30 years, the lands were re-surveyed and the rates of revenue were increased accordingly.

Temporary Demand The demand for revenue was not permanent but temporary.

As the moneylenders were much insensitive to the plight of the peasants, they got deeper and deeper into debt trap and were dependent on the moneylenders for their survival. This can be understood by the following points

- In ryotwari system, one general norm was that the interest charged could not be more than the principle. But when the Deccan Riots Commission investigated, they found the law broken by the moneylenders as they had charged over ₹ 2000 as interest on a loan of ₹ 100. Ater complain of this manipulation by *ryots*, the British passed a Limitation Law in 1859, which meant to check the accumulation of interest over time and give 3 years validity of loan bonds signed between moneylenders and *ryots*.
- Moneylenders manipulated the Limitation Law and forced *ryots* to sign a new bond every 3 years. When a new bond was signed, the unpaid balance, the original loan and accumulated interest was entered as principle on which a new set of interest charges was calculated.
- Moneylenders refused to give receipts when loans were repaid, entered fictitious figures in bonds, acquired peasants harvest at low prices, made peasants to sign and put thumb impression on documents and did not allow peasants to know what is inside the documents.

This way the *ryots* faced injustice in the hands of the moneylenders and lost their harvest and properties as well.

7. How were Britain and the Bombay Deccan affected by the American civil war? Discuss.

Ans. The American civil war affected both Britain and Bombay Deccan.

Effect of the Amrican Civil War on Britain

- Before the 1860s, three-fourth of raw cotton imports into Britain came from America.
- When the American Civil War broke out in 1861, a wave of panic spread through cotton circles in Britain. Raw cotton imports from America fell to less than three percent of the normal: from over 2,000,000 bales (of 400 lbs each) in 1861 to 55,000 bales in 1862.
- Urgent messages were sent to India and elsewhere to increase cotton exports to Britain.

Effect of the American Civil War on the Bombay Deccan

- In Bombay, cotton merchants visited the cotton districts to assess supplies and encourage cultivation. As cotton prices increased, export merchants in Bombay were keen to acquire as much cotton as possible to meet the British demand.
- Cotton merchants of Bombay gave advances to urban sahukars, who in turn gave credit to those rural moneylenders who promised to secure the produce.
- The *ryots* in the Deccan villages suddenly found access to seemingly limitless credit. They were being given Rs 100 in advance for every acre they planted with cotton. Sahukars were more willing to extend long-term loans.
- While the American crisis continued, cotton production in the Bombay Deccan expanded. Between 1860 and 1864, cotton fields doubled. By 1862, over 90 percent of cotton imports into Britain were coming from India. But these boom years did not bring prosperity to all cotton producers. Some rich peasants did gain, but for the large majority, cotton expansion meant heavier debt.

Source Based Question

Read the sources given below and answer the following questions.

1. On clearance and settled cultivation

Passing through one village in the lower Rajmahal hills, Buchanan wrote: The view of the country is exceedingly fine, the cultivation, especially the narrow valleys of rice winding in all directions, the cleared lands with scattered trees, and the rocky hills are in perfection; all that is wanted is some appearance of progress in the area and a vastly extended and improved cultivation, of which the country is highly susceptible. Plantations of Asan and Palas, for Tessar (Tassar silk worms) and Lac, should occupy the place of woods to as great an extent as the demand will admit; the remainder might be all cleared, and the greater part cultivated, while what is not fit for the purpose, might rear Plamira (palmyra) and Mowa (mahua). **CBSE 2025**

(i) **How did Buchanan describe the view of the lower Rajmahal hills?**

(ii) **Why did Buchanan believe that the area had high potential for improved cultivation?**

(iii) **How did Buchanan propose utilising the land for economic benefits?**

Ans. (i) Buchanan described the lower Rajmahal hills as an exceptionally beautiful landscape with winding rice valleys, scattered trees, and rocky hills but lacked visible progress and extensive agricultural development.

(ii) Buchanan believed the area had high potential for improved cultivation due to its fertile land, suitability for expanding plantations of commercial trees, and the possibility of clearing forests for better agricultural use.

(iii) Buchanan proposed utilising the land for economic benefits by promoting commercial plantations like Asan and Palas for silk and lac production, clearing forests for extensive farming, and cultivating Palmyra and Mahua in non-arable areas.

2. A Ryot Petition **CBSE 2024**

This is an example of a petition from a ryot of the village of Mirajgaon, Taluka Karjat, to the Collector Ahmednagar, Deccan Riots Commission. The *sowkars* (*sahukars*) have of late begun to oppress us. As we cannot earn enough to defray our household expenses, we are actually forced to beg of them to provide us with money, clothes and grain, which we obtain from them not without great difficulty, nor without their compelling us to enter into hard conditions in the bond.

Moreover the necessary clothes and grain are not sold to us at cash rates. The prices asked from us are generally twenty-five or fifty per cent more than demanded from customers making ready money payments. The produce of our fields is also taken by the soiwkars, who at the time of removing it assure us that it will be credited to our account, but they do not actually make any mention of it in the accounts. They also refuse to pass us any receipts for the produce so removed by them.

(i) **In what ways the moneylenders oppressed the ryots?**

(ii) **Why was the harvest taken away by the money-lenders?**

(iii) **Explain any two features of the *Ryotwari* system.**

Ans. (i) Moneylenders oppressed *ryots* by forcing them into debt, providing loans with harsh conditions, overcharging for goods and misappropriating produce without documentation.

(ii) The moneylenders took away the harvest to exploit the ryots, ensuring dependence and profiting from inflated prices and debts.

(iii) Two features of the Ryotwari system were

(i) **Direct Land Settlement** Under *Ryotwari*, individual peasants (*ryots*) had direct ownership and cultivation rights over their land, paying revenue directly to the British government.

(ii) **Absence of Intermediaries** The system eliminated intermediaries like zamindars, giving *ryots* direct interaction with government officials regarding land revenue matters.

SELF ASSESSMENT TEST

Objective Type Questions

1. Which among the following statement is correct about the Permanent Settlement?

(a) The Permanent Settlement was introduced by Augustus Cleveland in Bengal.

(b) Zamindars became more powerful under Permanent Settlement.

(c) The Permanent Settlement became successful in Bengal and the British extended to other parts of India.

(d) The revenue demand was too high in the Permanent Settlement.

2. What did Fifth Report contain?

(a) Petitions of zamindar (b) *Ryot* report of collector

(c) Statistical table (d) All of these

3. Who were the *Dikus*?

(a) Zamindars (b) Moneylender

(c) Peasants (d) *Jotedars*

4. Match the Following.

	List I		List II
A.	Deccan *Ryots*	1.	1765
B.	British East India acquired the Diwani of Bengal.	2.	1832
C.	First Revenue Settlement in Bombay Deccan.	3.	1875
D.	Declaration of Damin-i-Koh.	4.	1818

Codes

	A	B	C	D		A	B	C	D
(a)	1	2	3	4	(b)	3	1	2	4
(c)	3	1	4	2	(d)	4	1	3	2

Short Answer Type Questions

5. How did the Permanent Settlement lead to the decline of zamindars?

6. 'Deeds and bonds appeared as symbols of the new oppressive system'. Analyse the statement.

7. How can you say that the Deccan Riots Report was not accurate? Justify your answer.

Long Answer Type Questions

8. 'In the early decades after the Permanent Settlement, however, zamindars regularly failed to pay the revenue demand and unpaid balances accumulated'. Analyse the statement.

9. Differentiate between the lives of Santhals and Paharias.

10 CHAPTER

This chapter deals with the causes, spread and repression of the revolt of 1857. It also explores how 1857 revolt is remembered in the British and Indian sources.

YOUR STUDY GOALS

10.1 Emergence of Revolt of 1857
10.2 Pattern of the Rebellion
10.3 Awadh in Revolt
10.4 Objectives of the Revolt
10.5 Repression of the Revolt
10.6 Images of the Revolt

YOUR PRACTICE GOALS

- Objective Type Questions (40 Qs ; MCQs, A-R, Matching, Picture Based)
- Subjective Questions (20 SAs, 7 LAs)
- Source Based Questions (6 Qs)
- Map Based Questions (4 Qs)

Rebels and the Raj

(The Revolt of 1857 and its Representations)

10.1 Emergence of Revolt of 1857

- On 10th May 1857, the sepoys at the Meerut cantonment (military camps) began to **revolt**[1]. The **mutiny**[2] started among the native infantry first which quickly spread to the cavalry, and then to the city.
- The sepoys began the mutiny with a signal, such as the firing of the evening gun or the sounding of a bugle. They seized and robbed the British treasury and weapons.
- The sepoys captured the armory where weapons and ammunition (bullets) were stored. They also attacked government buildings including the jail, treasury, telegraph office, record room, bungalows, etc and burnt all the records. The telegraph line to Delhi was also cut.

Arrival in Delhi

- The sepoys reached the gates of the Red Fort on 11th May 1857. Many other sepoys also entered Delhi and people of the city joined them.
- The rich people of Delhi were attacked, and looted and Europeans were killed.

1 **Revolt** A rebellion of people against established authority and power.

2. **Mutiny** A collective disobedience of rules and regulations within the armed forces.

▲ *Mughal Emperor Bahadur Shah*

- Sepoys entered the Red Fort and demanded the support of Mughal emperor Bahadur Shah to which he agreed. The revolt gained legitimacy, as it was now fought in the mughal emperor's name.
- Cantonments in the Gangetic valley and to the West of Delhi joined the revolt.
- Everything and everybody related to white men were targeted. The targets also included moneylenders and the rich in towns like Lucknow, Kanpur and Bareilly.
- The targets of attack expanded as ordinary people joined the revolt.
- The mutiny among the sepoys quickly turned into a rebellion.

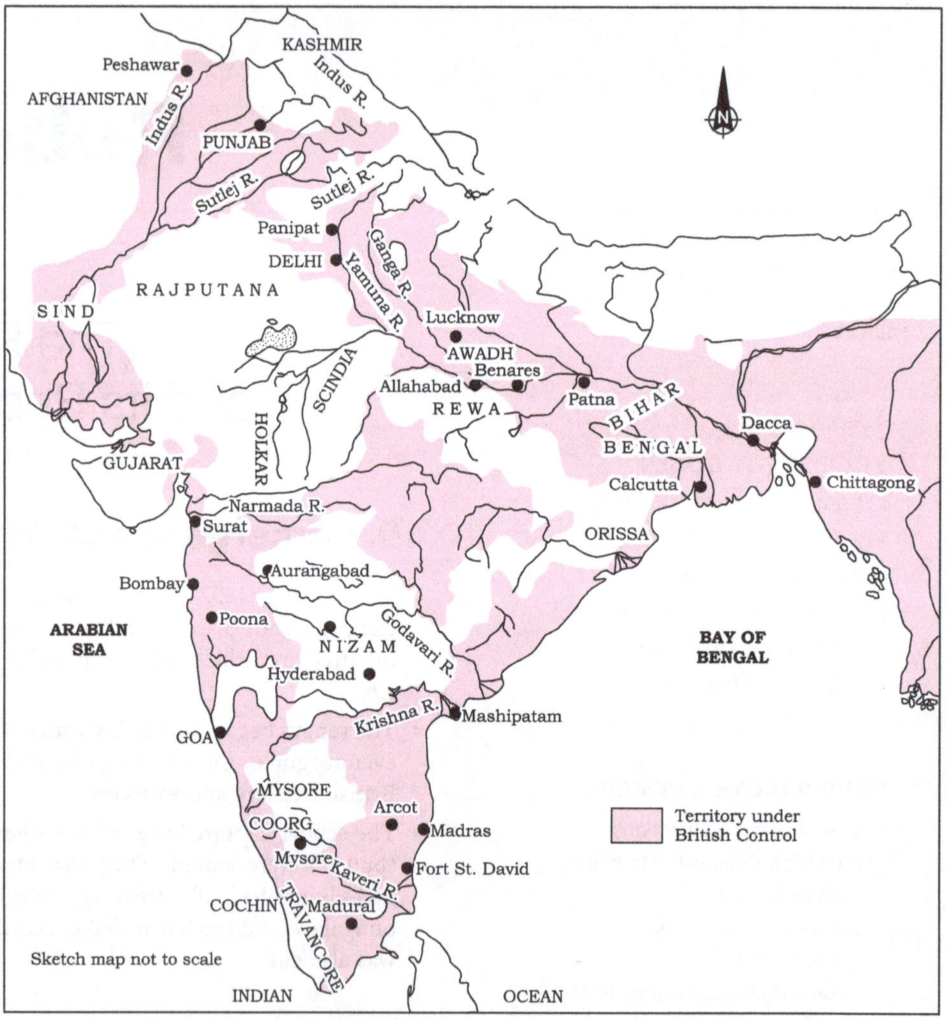

▲ *Territories under British control in 1857*

10.2 Pattern of the Rebellion

- News of the mutiny spread quickly, with many cantonments rebelling against the British.
- The sequence of events in every cantonment followed a similar pattern.

Lines of Communication

- The similarity in the pattern of the revolt in different places was due to its planning and coordination.
- Sepoys or their agents moved from one station to another communicating about the rebellion. For example, in early May, the **7th Awadh Irregular Cavalry** refused to use the new cartridges. It informed the 48th Native Infantry about this incident and awaited their orders.
- **Captain Hearsey** of the Awadh military police was protected by his Indian subordinates during the mutiny against the 41st Native Infantry.
- Historian Charles Ball noted that panchayats were held every night in the Kanpur sepoy lines. This suggests that some decisions were taken collectively.

Leaders and Followers of the Revolt

▲ *Rani Lakshmi Bai*

- In Delhi, the sepoys of Meerut appealed to the old Mughal emperor **Bahadur Shah** to accept the leadership of the revolt.
- In Kanpur, the sepoys selected **Nana Sahib**, the successor to Peshwa Baji Rao II as their leader.
- **Rani Lakshmi Bai**, the Queen of Jhansi, led the revolt in Jhansi.
- **Kunwar Singh** was the leader of the revolt in Bihar.
- The people elected **Birjis Qadr**, the young son of the Nawab as their leader in Awadh.
- In some places, local leaders emerged who encouraged peasants, zamindars and tribals to revolt. For example,
  - **Shah Mal** became the leader of Pargana Barout in Uttar Pradesh.
  - **Gonoo**, a tribal cultivator of Singhbhum in Chotanagpur became a rebel[3] leader of the Kol tribals of the region.
  - **Maulvi Ahmadullah** of Faizabad kept the city free from British rule for almost a year until his death.

Rumours and Prophecies Leading to Revolt

- **Issue of Cartridges** A rumour spread among the sepoys that the cartridges of the new enfield rifles were coated with the fat of cows and pigs. The sepoys believed that using these cartridges would corrupt the caste and religion of Hindus and Muslims.
- **Conspiracy to Destroy the Caste and Religion** There were rumours that the British had mixed cow and pig bone dust into market flour, which the sepoys and the public refused to eat. Many feared the British aimed to convert Indians to Christianity.
- **Circulation of Chapattis** Reports from North India indicated that chapattis were being distributed from village to village at night. This distribution was believed to be a signal of an uprising.

Reasons for Acceptance of Rumours

- The British policies aimed to reform Indian society by introducing Western education, ideas and institutions under Governor General **Lord William Bentinck.**
- Laws were enacted by the British to abolish customs like sati (1829) and to allow the remarriage of Hindu widows.
- The British started annexing (taking over) the Indian states on issues like misgovernment and the refusal to recognise adoption. After annexing states like **Awadh, Jhansi, Satara**, etc on these grounds, the British introduced their land settlement and land revenue collection methods.
- Socio-religious customs and landholding patterns were replaced by an impersonal and oppressive system.

3 **Rebels** It means rise in opposition or armed resistance to an established government or leader.

Quick Test 1

1 When did the sepoys in Meerut break out in mutiny?
2 What did Bahadur Shah do when he was surrounded by the sepoys?
3 Who provided protection to Captain Hearsey during the mutiny?
4 Whom did the people of Awadh elected as their leader?
5 Which Indian states were annexed by the British on issues like misgovernment?

10.3 Awadh in Revolt

The kingdom of Awadh was formally annexed to the British Empire in **1856**. The conquest happened in stages which are as follows

Subsidiary Alliance

- The Subsidiary Alliance was introduced by **Lord Wellesley** in 1798. It was imposed on Awadh in **1801**.
- All those who entered into subsidiary alliance with the British had to accept the following terms and conditions
  - The British would be responsible for protecting their ally from external and internal threats to their power.
  - A group of British armed would be placed in the ally's territory.
  - The ally would have to provide the resources for maintaining this contingent.
  - The ally could enter into agreements with other rulers or engage in warfare only with the permission of the British.
- Under this alliance, the Nawab had to disband his military, allow the British to position their troops within the kingdom, and follow the orders of the British Resident[4] at court. This made the Nawab dependent on the British for maintaining law and order and weakened his control over rebellious chiefs and *taluqdars*.

Growing Interest in Awadh and Removal of Nawab

- The British gradually became more interested in acquiring Awadh, as its fertile soil was suitable for growing indigo and cotton.
- The annexation of Awadh by **Lord Dalhousie**, Governor General of India, on the basis of misgovernance created disaffection in all the annexed areas and principalities.
- Nawab Wajid Ali Shah was removed and sent to Calcutta. His removal dissolved the Court and its culture.
- People including musicians, dancers, poets, artisans, cooks, retainers, administrative officials lost their livelihood.

Circumstances after Annexation of Awadh

Grievances of *Taluqdars*

- The *taluqdars* had many estates and forts in the countryside of Awadh for many generations. They controlled land and power, maintained armed followers and built forts. They also had some freedom as long as they accepted the Nawab's authority and paid taxes on their *taluqs*.
- The bigger *taluqdars* had about **12,000 foot soldiers** and the small taluqdars had about 200 soldiers. But their position declined as the Britishers disarmed the *taluqdars* and destroyed their forts.

4 British Resident It refers to a designation of a representative of the Governor General who lived in a state which was not under directly to British rule.

Summary Settlement : A Land Revenue Policy

- After the annexation of Awadh, the British introduced a land revenue policy known as Summary Settlement in 1856. It was based on the belief that *taluqdars* had no rightful claim to the land, and they had taken control through force and fraud.
- The Summary Settlement aimed to remove *taluqdars* whenever possible. As a result, those who once controlled 67% of the villages in Awadh before British rule were reduced to 38%.
- Some of the *taluqdars* of Southern Awadh lost more than half of the total number of villages they held previously.

Grievances of Peasants

- British officials believed that removing *taluqdars* and settling land with actual owners would reduce peasant exploitation and increase revenue.
- In some areas, revenue demands rose from 30% to 70%. The revenue increased for the state, but the pressure on peasants remained high.
- The relationship between peasants and *taluqdars* was disrupted by the removal of *taluqdars*. Under direct British control, peasants faced heavy taxation and rigid collection methods.
- There was no guarantee of reduction of revenue demand or postponement of collection during hardship and crop failure.
- Even during the festivities, the peasants were uncertain about getting the loan and support that the *taluqdars* had earlier provided.
- Many *taluqdars* in Awadh were loyal to the Nawab of Awadh. They joined **Begum Hazrat Mahal** (the wife of the Nawab) in Lucknow to fight the British.

Grievances of Sepoys

- The salaries of the sepoys were low. They also faced difficulty in getting leaves.
- Earlier, white officers had friendly ties with sepoys. However, later the officers started treating the sepoys as their inferiors. Abuse and physical violence became common and trust was replaced by doubts.
- Many sepoys of the Bengal Army were recruited from the villages of Awadh and Eastern Uttar Pradesh. Many of them were Brahmins or from the 'upper castes'. Therefore, Awadh was popularly known as the **Nursery of the Bengal Army**.

▲ *Bengal Sepoys in European style uniform*

10.4 Objectives of the Revolt

The objective of the revolt can be explained from the proclamations and *ishtahars* (notifications) issued by rebels in 1857. These are discussed below

The Vision of Unity

- The proclamation of revolt in 1857 appealed to all sections of the population, irrespective of caste and creed.
- The proclamations issued by Muslim princes or in their name, also took care of the sentiments of Hindus.
- The *ishtahars* represented the presence of different communities under the Mughal empire.
- The proclamation issued in Bahadur Shah's name asked people to join the fight in the names of both Muhammad and Mahavir.
- During the uprising, there were no religious divisions between Hindus and Muslims despite British attempts to create such divisions.

Against the Symbols of Oppression

- The proclamations rejected everything related to British rule or *firangi*[5] *raj*.
- People were against British land revenue settlements which dispossessed both large and small landholders, and foreign trade which destroyed artisans and weavers.
- The proclamations claimed that the British were trying to convert Hindus and Muslims to Christianity. People were urged to unite and fight to protect their livelihoods, faith, honour, identity and the greater good.
- In villages, houses of moneylenders were ransacked (looted) and account books were destroyed.

The Search for Alternative Power

- In Delhi, Lucknow and Kanpur, the rebels tried to establish authority and administration once British rule had collapsed.
- They tried to restore the pre-British world of the Eighteenth century in the following ways
  - The court culture was re-established.
  - Appointments were made to various posts.
  - Arrangements were made for the collection of land revenue and the payment of troops.
  - Orders were issued to stop loot and stealing.
  - Plans were made to fight battles against the British.
  - Chains of command were established in the army.
- These structures established by the rebels aimed at meeting the demands of war but they did not survive the British attack.

10.5 Repression of the Revolt

Enactment of New Laws

- The British passed several laws to help the troops before sending them to reoccupy North India.
- The Acts passed in May and June 1857, placed North India under **martial law**. The acts also allowed military officers and ordinary Britons (local Britain people) to try and punish Indians suspected of rebellion.
- The common process of law and trial were suspended and death was the only punishment for the rebels.

Conquest of Delhi

- A two pointed attack was organised to conquer Delhi. One force moved from Calcutta into North India and the second force moved from the Punjab.
- Delhi was finally captured in late September 1857. The difficulty in capturing Delhi was due to rebels from across North India who had gathered in Delhi to defend it.

Capture of the Gangetic Plains

- The Gangetic area was captured **village by village** by the British forces. By this time, the Britishers realised that it was not merely a revolt but an uprising that had huge popular support.
- As per a British official in Awadh, about three-fourths of the adult male population was rebel.
- The area was brought under control only in March 1858 after a long and tough fighting.

Other Strategies

- In many parts of present-day Uttar Pradesh, the British tried to weaken the unity of large landholders and peasants by promising to return estates to loyal landholders.
- Rebel landholders were dispossessed, while loyal ones were rewarded.
- Many landholders died fighting the British, while others escaped to Nepal, where they died from illness or starvation.

5 Firangi It is a term of Persian origin, often used to refer foreigners.

Quick Test 2

1 What was one of the key responsibilities of the British under the Subsidiary Alliance?
2 What happened to Nawab Wajid Ali Shah after the annexation of Awadh?
3 Why was Awadh known as the "Nursery of the Bengal Army"?
4 What did the *ishtahars* represent during the uprising?
5 When did the British aim to capture Delhi?

10.6 Images of the Revolt

- There are various sources available to know about the Revolt of 1857 including written documents and pictorial images.
- Official messages, notes and reports help us to know the mindset and the changing British attitudes. Many of these have now been collected in a set of volumes on mutiny records. These reveal the fears of officials and their views of the rebels.
- Stories of the revolt in British newspapers described the violence of the rebels which sparked demands for revenge.
- The pictorial images produced by the British and Indians includes paintings, pencil drawings, sketchings, posters, cartoons, bazaar prints, etc.

▲ *A picture of mosque on the Delhi Ridge*

Celebrating the Saviours

- **'Relief of Lucknow'**, painted by Thomas Jones Barker in 1859, represents the British heroes as saviours. It depicts the incident when Lucknow was taken over by the rebels as follows
  - **Henry Lawrence**, the Commissioner of Lucknow took refuge in fortified residency with other Christians. He was killed but the residency was defended by **Colonel Inglis.**
  - On 25th September, James Outram and Henry Havelock fought through the rebel forces to support the British troops.
  - After 20 days, Colin Campbell, the new Commander of British forces in India, rescued the trapped British troops.

▲ *Relief of Lucknow*

English Women and the Honour of Britain

- **Joseph Noel Paton** painted **'In Memoriam'** after two years of revolt. In this painting, English women and children are gathered in a circle, appearing helpless and innocent as they await dishonour, violence and death.
- Other paintings depict women courageously defending themselves from rebel attacks, such as **Miss Wheeler** protecting herself against sepoys.
- Some paintings show a symbolic female figure of justice holding a sword in one hand and a shield in the other.

▲ *"In Memoriam"*

Vengence and Retribution

- Pictures, paintings and news about the mutiny in Britain created a condition where revenge and retribution (punishment) were seen as important.
- The desire for revenge was shown in the brutal executions of the rebels, who were either blown from guns or hanged. Images of these executions were widely spread in popular journals.

No Time for Mercy

- In a cartoon from the British journal of comic satire, Punch, Canning is portrayed as a father figure, with his protective hand over a sepoy who holds a sword in one hand and a dagger in the other, both covered with blood.
- The British press made fun of General Canning for believing that showing lenient and mercy would win back the loyalty of the sepoys.

▲ *Rani Lakshmi Bai as a masculine warrior*

Nationalist Imageries

- The Revolt of 1857 inspired the National Movement in the twentieth century. The revolt was called the **First War of Independence**. All sections of the society participated in it.
- The memory of 1857 was preserved in art and literature. Leaders of the revolt were depicted as heroes who inspired the public to fight against British rule.
- **Rani Lakshmi Bai** of Jhansi became an iconic figure, fighting the enemy until her last breath. Heroic poems were written about her. For example, the famous lines by **Subhadra Kumari Chauhan** *"Khoob lari mardani woh to Jhansi wali rani thi"* (Like a man she fought, she was the Rani of Jhansi).
- She is also depicted in popular prints on the battlefield, holding a sword and riding a horse. It is seen as a symbol of her determination to resist injustice and foreign rule.

Conclusion

The images show how the artists viewed events, what they felt, and what they wanted to express. Through these paintings, we learn about the public who appreciated or criticised them and bought copies to display in their homes. These images also influenced public attitudes. The images circulating in Britain supported harsh repression of the rebels. In contrast, nationalist depictions of the revolt helped shape the nationalist imagination.

Quick Test 3

1. What types of pictorial images were produced during the mutiny?
2. What items does the allegorical female figure hold?
3. Who was the commissioner of Lucknow during the Revolt of 1857?
4. In the cartoon published in 'Punch', how is Canning depicted?
5. What does Rani Lakshmi Bai symbolise in the context of the revolt?

TIMELINE

1801	Subsidiary Alliance introduced by Wellesley in Awadh
1856	Nawab Wajid Ali Shah deposed; Awadh annexed
1856-57	Summary revenue settlements introduced in Awadh by the British
1857	
10 May	Mutiny starts in Meerut
11-12 May	Delhi garrisons revolt; Bahadur Shah accepts nominal leadership
20-27 May	Sepoys mutiny in Aligarh, Etawah, Mainpuri, Etah
30 May	Rising in Lucknow
May-June	Mutiny turns into a general revolt of the people
30 June	British suffer defeat in the battle of Chinhat
July	Shah Mal killed in battle
25 Sept	British forces under Havelock and Outram enter the Residency in Lucknow
1858 June	Rani Jhansi killed in battle

Mind Map

REBELS AND THE RAJ

1 Pattern of the Rebellion

Leaders and Followers
- Bahadur Shah became the symbolic leader of the revolt.
- Religious leaders inspired rebellion in several regions.
- Local leaders like Shah Mal and Gonoo mobilised villagers and tribals.

Rumors and Prophecies
- Rumours of cow and pig fat on cartridges angered sepoys.
- Rumours claimed that British mixed bone dust in flour to destroy caste and religion.
- Prophecies predicted the end of British rule on 23rd June, 1857.

The Mutinies Began
- Sepoys started the revolt with signals like evening gunfire.
- Rebels seized weapons, plundered treasuries and burned records.
- Proclamations united Hindus and Muslims against the British.

Lines of Communication
Sepoys coordinated rebellion through letters and emissaries.

2 Awadh in Revolt

- Awadh was annexed by the British Empire in 1856.
- The Subsidiary Alliance weakened the control of Nawab of Awadh.
- British positioned troops in Awadh under the alliance terms.
- Nawab Wajid Ali Shah was dethroned and exiled in 1856.
- Many artisans, poets and workers lost their livelihoods.

Circumstances after Annexation of Awadh
- Grievances in Awadh connected prince, taluqdars, peasants and sepoys, fueling rebellion.

3 Objectives of the Revolt

The Vision of Unity
- The rebel proclamations of 1857 appealed to all people, regardless of caste or religion.
- Rebels emphasised Hindu-Muslim unity, glorifying coexistence under the Mughal Empire.

Against the Symbols of Oppression
- Proclamations completely rejected everything associated with British rule of Firangi Raj.
- British land policies angered people, dispossessing land holders and artisans.
- The rebellion targeted British allies and local oppressors, seeking to disrupt hierarchies.

The Search for Alternative Power
- Rebels in Delhi, Lucknow and Kanpur sought to restore pre-British authority.
- System for land revenue, troop payments and military command were established by rebels.
- Rebels worked to restore order and prevent looting and plunder.

4 Repression by British

- The British passed laws to put North India under martial law and punished rebels.
- The British launched a two-pronged attack from Calcutta and Punjab to recapture Delhi.
- Many landholders died fighting the British or they escaped into Nepal.

5 Images of the Revolt

English Women and the Honour of Britain
- Newpaper reports shaped public feelings in Britain.
- In the painting 'In Memoriam', painted by Joseph Noel Paton, women and children were painted as helpless victims.
- British artist portrayed women as heroic figures.

The Performance of Terror
- The rebels were executed in brutal way.
- They were blown from guns or hanged from the gallows.

Nationalist Imageries
- The 1857 revolt inspired India's 20th century nationalist movement.
- Leaders of revolt were depicted as heroic figures.

No time for Clemency
- When there was call for vegeance, requests for moderation were mocked.
- Governor-General canning's plea for leniency was mocked in the British Press.

Vengeance and Retribution
- Anger and shock in Britain encouraged demands for violent retribution against rebels.
- Visual representations depicted violent repression as necessary to restore British honour.
- The urge for vengeance and retribution was expressed in the brutal way.

NCERT Folder

Intext Questions

1. Read the section once more and explain the similarities and differences you notice in the ways in which leaders emerged during the revolt. For any two leaders, discuss why ordinary people were drawn to them. (Pg. 265)

Ans. During the revolt of 1857, leaders emerged from various sections of society. There are some similarities as well as differences in the ways in which leaders emerged during the revolt.

Similarities between leaders

- Leaders of the revolt shared a common thread of resentment against British rule.
- Most of the leaders emerged due to local support.

Differences between leaders

- Leaders of the 1857 revolt belonged to different social backgrounds. Some were nawabs, taluqdars, etc., whereas some were common people like cultivators.
- Leaders had different motives to join the revolt. Some joined the revolt as per their wish. However, some leaders were forced to join the revolt, like Bahadur Shah Zafar.

Impact of leaders on ordinary people

- Bahadur Shah Zafar was the Mughal emperor. People were drawn to him due to his status as the emperor of India. So, rebels wanted the blessings and support of Zafar to provide legitimacy to the revolt.
- Maulvi Shah Alam was famous for his courage and power. Many people believed that he was unconquerable, had magical powers, and could not be killed by the British. It was this belief that partly formed the basis of his authority.

2. What do you think are the major problems faced by historians in reconstructing the point of view of the rebels? (Pg. 274)

Ans. Some major problems faced by historians in reconstructing the view of the 1857 rebels include

- **Biased British Records** Since most documentation was by British officials, the records often portray the rebels as chaotic or disloyal, lacking an objective view of their intentions.
- **Lack of Rebel Accounts** Few written records from the rebels themselves exist, limiting insight into their motivations, objectives, and leadership.
- **Suppression of Rebel Documents** The British actively suppressed or destroyed many rebel documents during and after the conflict, creating significant gaps in historical evidence.
- **Reliance on Oral History** Oral accounts are subject to memory distortions and changes over generations, complicating efforts to form an accurate view. These challenges make it difficult to capture the rebels' true aims, which historians seek to understand.

Answer in 100-150 words

1. Why did the mutinous sepoys in many places turn to erstwhile rulers to provide leadership to the revolt?

Ans. There are many reasons for the mutinous sepoys to turn to erstwhile rulers to provide leadership to the revolt. These were as follows

- Native rulers were defeated by the East India Company. But many mutineers believed that the native Indian rulers had the legal and legitimate authority to regain power in their respective kingdoms.
- The erstwhile rulers had substantial resources at their command. They had wealth and private armies too. The rebels waited to get the support of resources from them.
- Most rulers were popular at the local level. Their subjects often sympathised with them. Hence, choosing these rulers was a chance to win more support for the cause.

2. Discuss the evidence that indicates planning and coordination on the part of the rebels.

Or **"The similarities in the pattern of Revolt of 1857 in different places lay partly in its planning and coordination." Explain the statement.** CBSE Term II 2022

Ans. The two pieces of evidence that show the coordination in the revolt are given below

(i) **Communication** It is clear that there was communication between the sepoy lines of various cantonments. After the 7th Awadh Irregular Cavalry had refused to accept the new cartridges in early May, they wrote to the 48th Native Infantry that "they had acted for the faith and awaited the 48th's orders". Sepoys or their emissaries moved from one station to another. People were thus planning and talking about the rebellion.

(ii) **Collective decision making** Some of the decisions were taken collectively. For example, Captain Hearsey of the Awadh Military Police was protected by native officers. Native officers did not cooperate with rebel soldiers of the 41st Native Infantry. Then it was decided that the matter would be settled by a panchayat composed of native officers drawn from each regiment.

3. Discuss the extent to which religious beliefs shaped the events of 1857.

Ans. To a large extent religious beliefs shaped the events of 1857. Some of them are discussed below

- The issue of the cartridges was the most important incidence. It was believed that the new cartridges of the Enfield rifles were made up of fat of cows and pigs.
- Another incident was regarding the mixing of bone dust of cows and pigs mixed into the flour sold in the market. Hence, sepoys and common people refused to touch the *atta*. It was feared that the British wanted to convert Indians to Christianity.
- The British adopted policies aimed at reforming Indian society by introducing Western education, ideas and institutions under the rule of Governor General Lord William Bentick. English-medium schools, colleges and universities were opened where Western sciences and the liberal arts were taught. Laws to abolish customs like *sati* and to permit widow remarriage were introduced.
- Many people felt that the British were destroying their sacred ideals that they had long cherished. Many Hindus were enraged when the Christian missionaries criticised their scriptures or religious books.

4. What were the measures taken to ensure unity among the rebels?

Or **Explain any three aspects of the vision of unity reflected in the 1857 Revolt.** **CBSE 2024 C**

Ans. The following measures were taken to ensure unity among the rebels

- Rebels repeatedly appealed to all sections of the population, irrespective of their caste and creed.
- Rebels tried to take care of the religious sentiments of people. Many of the proclamations were issued by Muslim princes or in their names, but even these took care to address the sentiments of Hindus.
- Pre-British Hindu-Muslim part was recalled in *ishtahars*. The coexistence of different communities under the Mughal Empire was glorified in *ishtahars*.
- Rebels appealed to people to join the revolt on the basis of religion also. The proclamation that was issued under the name of Bahadur Shah appealed to the people to join the fight under the standards of both Muhammad and Mahavir.

5. What steps did the British take to quell the uprising?

Ans. The British had to take many harsh measures in order to quell (finish) the revolt. These were

- The British passed several laws to help the troops before sending them to reoccupy North India. A number of acts were passed in May and June 1857 which also put North India under Martial law.
- The army officers as well as common English men were empowered to try and punish Indians on mere suspicion.
- The common process of law and trial were suspended and it was made clear that death was the only punishment for the rebels.
- Recognising the symbolic value of Delhi, the British mounted a two-pronged attack on the city. One force moved from Calcutta into North India and the other from the Punjab. The city was finally captured by September 1857.
- The Gangetic area was captured village by village and more military power was used there. British also tried to broke the unity among the landholders and peasants by promising to give back to the big landholders their estates.

Write a short Essay (about 250-300 words) on the Following

6. Why was the revolt particularly widespread in Awadh? What prompted the peasants, *taluqdars* and zamindars to join the revolt?

Or **Why was the Revolt of 1857 specially widespread in Awadh? Explain.** **CBSE 2024**

Ans. Revolt was much widespread in Awadh due to wider participation of peasants, *taluqdars* and zamindars. The reasons that prompted them to join revolt are discussed below

Annexation of Awadh

- Awadh was annexed by the British on grounds of maladministration and wrong assumption that the nawab was an unpopular ruler. On the contrary, he was greatly loved and his departure from Lucknow was marked by widespread grief and sorrow.
- The removal of the nawab led to the dissolution of the court and its culture. A whole range of people including musicians, dancers, poets, artisans, cooks, retainers, administrative officials lost their livelihood.
- The annexation of Awadh created disaffection among the *taluqdars* of the region. They had many estates and

forts in the countryside of Awadh and controlled land and power. But their position was declined as the Britishers disarmed the *taluqdars* and destroyed their forts.

- The British introduced a land revenue policy known as Summary Settlement in 1856. It was believed that taluqdars had no legal right over land. They controlled the land through force and fraud. The settlement sought to remove *taluqdars* whenever possible and the number of *taluqdars* come down. Many *taluqdars* of Southern Awadh lost more than half of the total number of villages they held previously.

Tussle between Peasant and *Taluqdars*

- The relation between the peasant and the *taluqdars* was also disrupted. Now, when the peasants were under direct control of British, they were directly exposed to over assessment of revenue and inflexible methods of collection.

Crop Failure

- At times of hardship and crop failure, there was no guarantee of reduction or postponement of collection. Even during the festivities, the peasants were not sure of getting the loan and support that the *taluqdars* had earlier provided.

7. What did the rebels want? To what extent did the vision of different social groups differ?

Ans. The rebels wanted the following

- The rebels wanted to uproot the rule of the Britishers.
- They did not want their rulers, nawabs, *taluqdars* and zamindars to be removed. Apart from this, they also did not want the princely states to be annexed to the company empire.
- The rebels wanted unity among Hindus and Muslims. They wanted good wishes of Mughal emperor as well as other kings and rulers for the success of revolt.
- They were against imposing English language and Western civilisation on their country. They did not like to disturb their social tradition, customs and life.

The vision of different social groups and their differences are as follows

Zamindars The zamindars did not like the putting up of their land estate for public auctions just for due payment of rent. They did not like their summon into court time to time due to some case filed against them by the *ryot* or a slave.

Merchants This section of the society did not like British Government monopoly over the trade, particularly all the fine and valuable merchandise such as indigo cloth and other articles of shipping. Besides this, the profits of the traders were taxed with postage, tolls and subscriptions for schools, etc.

Public Servants Natives employed in the civil and military services have little respect, low pay and no manner of influence. All the posts of dignity and evolvement in both the departments were exclusively bestowed on Englishmen.

Artisans The Europeans, by the introduction of English articles into India, have thrown the weavers, the cotton dressers, the carpenters, the blacksmiths and the shoemakers, etc of India out of employment. But it was believed that under the Badshahi Government they will no doubt ensure their prosperity.

Pandits, *Fakirs* and Other Learned Persons The pandits and *fakirs* being the guardians of the Hindu and the Muslim religions respectively viewed the Europeans as the enemies of both the religions. Hence, they thought to take part in the holy war against their enemy.

8. What do visual representations tell us about the revolt of 1857? How do historians analyse these representations?

Or **Examine the visual representations of the revolt of 1857 that provoked a range of different emotions and reactions.**

Ans. The visual representations produced by the British and Indians is one important record of the mutiny. They include paintings, pencil drawings, sketchings, posters, cartoons, bazaar prints, etc. The visual representations are helpful to us in the study of the revolt by the following ways

Relief of Lucknow The paintings painted by the British artists present the British heroes, saving the English and repressing the rebels, as saviours.

'Relief of Lucknow', painted by Thomas Jones Barker in 1859, is an example of this type.

Account of Barker's Painting The painting by Thomas Jones Barker depicts the incidence when Lucknow was sieged by the rebels.

Henry Lawrence, the Commissioner of Lucknow took refuge in fortified residency with other Christian population. Lawrence was killed but the residency was defended under Colonel Inglis.

On 25th September, James Outram and Henry Havelock cut through the rebel forces and reinforced the British garrisons. After 20 days, the new Commander of British forces in India, Colin Campbell, rescued the besieged British garrison. The incident became a story of survival, heroic resistance and the ultimate triumph of British power.

Celebrating the Saviours Thomas Jones Barkers painting celebrates the entry of Colin Campbell. The three heroes, Campbell, Dutrain and Havelock are shown at the centre of the canvas. The gestures of the hands of those around lead the speclator's eyes towards the centre. The heroes are standing on a well lit ground with shadows in the foreground and the damaged residency in the background. The dead and injured in the foreground indicates suffering. During the siege, the victorious figures of horses indicates the reestablishment of British power and control.

Paintings on Women Honour Joseph Noel Paton painted 'In Memoriam' after two years of revolt. In the Painting, English women and children can be seen huddled in a circle, looking helpless and innocent, seemingly waiting for the inevitable dishonour, violence and death. The painting disturbs spectators imagination and provokes anger and fury. Rebels are represented as violent and cruel whereas British are represented as saviours.

On the other hand, in another set of paintings women are shown heroic defending themselves against the attack of rebels. One such woman Miss Wheeler, is shown standing firmly at the centre defending her honour single handedly killing the attacking rebels. The woman struggles to save her honour and her life which also represents a deeper religious meaning i.e. a battle to save the honour of Christianity.

9. Examine any two sources presented in the chapter, choosing one visual and one text, and discuss how these represent the point of view of the victor and vanquished.

Ans. Do it yourself.

10. On an outline map of India, mark Calcutta (Kolkata), Bombay (Mumbai) and Madras (Chennai), three major centres of British power in 1857. Refer to Maps 1 and 2 and plot the areas where the revolt was most widespread. How close or far were these areas from the colonial cities?

Ans. Some areas where the revolt was most widespread were Delhi, Meerut, Mathura, Kanpur, Jhansi, Allahabad, Agra, etc. These areas were very far from the colonial cities.

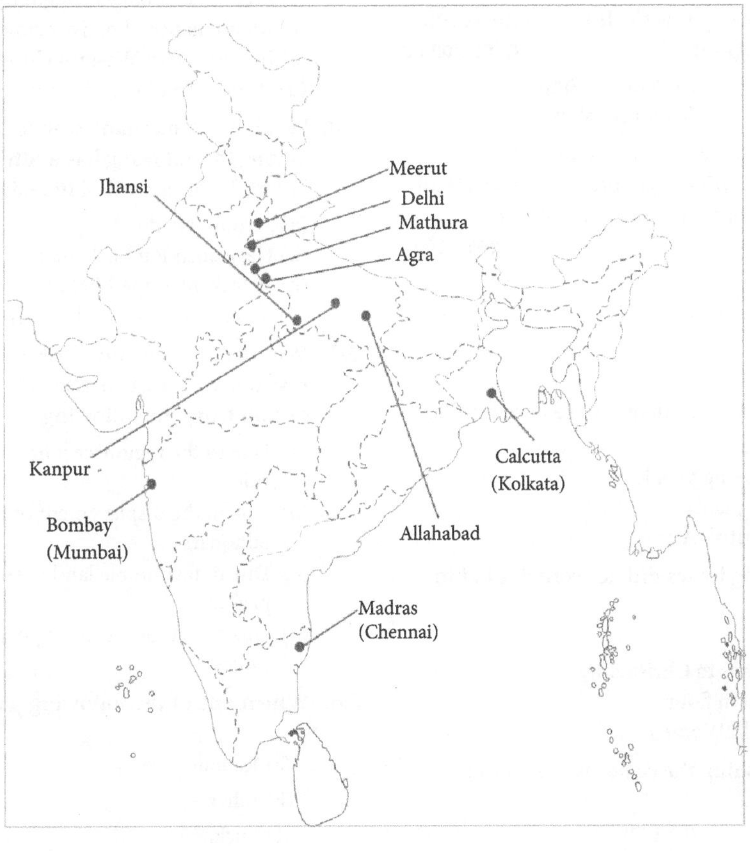

Exam Pattern Questions

Objective Type Questions

Multiple Choice Questions (MCQs)

1. **At which of the following places the mutiny broke out on the 10th day of May 1857?** **CBSE 2024**

(a) Barrakpore (b) Delhi
(c) Meerut Cantt (d) Lucknow

2. **From which one of the following regions did Bahadur Shah Zafar II represent the Revolt of 1857?** **CBSE 2024 C**

(a) Delhi (b) Lucknow
(c) Awadh (d) Barrackpore

3. **Captain Hearsey was given protection by**

(a) Bengal Military Police
(b) Sikh Military Police
(c) Gorkha Forces
(d) Awadh Military Police

4. **Who among the following was the leader of the revolt of 1857 from Bihar region?** **CBSE 2024 C**

(a) Shah Mal (b) Kunwar Singh
(c) Gonoo (d) Nana Sahib

5. **Who among the following rebels took over the bungalow of a British official and turned it into a 'hall of justice' to settle disputes during 1857 in Uttar Pradesh ?** **CBSE 2024**

(a) Shah Mal
(b) Maulvi Ahmadullah Shah
(c) Gonoo
(d) Kunwar Singh

6. **Distribution of chapattis in villages were percieved as**

(a) signal of an upheaval
(b) sign of solidarity among people
(c) sign of resisting inequality
(d) invitation to join British Army

7. **Which of the following issues did not contributed in spread of revolt?**

(a) Issue of Cartridges
(b) Conversion of Indians to Christianity
(c) Mixing of bone dust in flour
(d) Dishonouring Hindu Women

8. **Laws related to abolishing the customs of *sati* were passed in the year ....**

(a) 1832 (b) 1875
(c) 1829 (d) 1825

9. **Who among the following described the following line for the Kingdom of Awadh?** **CBSE 2024**

"A cherry that will fall into our mouth one day."

(a) Lord Cornwallis (b) Lord Wellesley
(c) Lord Dalhousie (d) Lord Canning

10. **In 1856, the kingdom which was formally annexed to the British empire was ....**

(a) Awadh (b) Satara (c) Mysore (d) Jhansi

11. **Summary Settlement was introduced by British in**

(a) Awadh (b) Sindh (c) Bengal (d) Madras

12. **Which one of the following was a key feature of the 'Subsidiary Alliance introduced by Lord Wellesley in 1798?** **CBSE 2025**

(a) Free Trade Policy brought by British
(b) Maintenance of native army by British
(c) Imposition of Western Customs by British
(d) Protection of native territory by British

13. **"Khoob ladi mardani, woh to Jhansi wali rani thi." Who among the following has written these lines and portrayed Laxmi Bai as a symbol to resist injustice ?** **CBSE 2024**

(a) Sarojini Naidu
(b) Harivansh Rai Bachchan
(c) Suryakant Tripathi Nirala
(d) Subhadra Kumari Chauhan

14. **Why did the rebellion in Awadh become a symbol of resistance against British rule? Choose the best suitable option from the following.** **CBSE SQP 2024**

(a) Due to the region's economic prosperity under native rule
(b) Due to the displacement of Nawab Wajid Ali Shah and taluqdars
(c) Due to favourable land revenue policies towards the peasantry
(d) Due to Awadh's central position for organising rebel forces.

15. **Which one of the following pairs is correctly matched ?** **CBSE 2024**

(a) Kanpur – Kunwar Singh
(b) Bihar – Gonoo
(c) Lucknow – Birjis Qadr
(d) Singhbhum – Nana Saheb

16. **Find out from the following pairs which one is correctly matched.**

(a) Relief of Lucknow – Joseph Noel Paton
(b) In Memoriam – Thomas Jones Barker
(c) The Clemency of Canning – A journal named 'Punch'
(d) Henry Hardinge – Adam Grant

17. **Consider the following statements regarding revolt of 1857.**

(i) Mughal emperor Bahadur Shah was declared as the leader of sepoys.
(ii) There was no participation of common people.
(iii) Moneylenders and the rich were attacked.

Which of the above statements is/are correct?

(a) (i) and (ii) (b) (ii) and (iii)
(c) (i) and (iii) (d) (i), (ii) and (iii)

18. **British started annexing the Indian states on the pretext of**

(i) misgovernance
(ii) anarchy
(iii) refusal to recognise adoption
(iv) treachery

Which of the following options is/are correct?

(a) Only (i) (b) (i) and (ii)
(c) (i) and (iii) (d) (i), (ii) and (iii)

19. **Consider the following statements regarding Subsidiary Alliance.**

(i) This system was devised by William Bentinck in 1798.
(ii) A British force was stationed in the territory of the ally.
(iii) Ally could enter into agreements with other rulers without any interference.
(iv) A British Resident was attached to the court of ally.

Which of the above statements is/are correct?

(a) (i) and (ii) (b) (ii) and (iii)
(c) (ii) and (iv) (d) (i), (ii), (iii) and (iv)

20. **Arrange the following events in chronological order and select the correct answer from the option below**

(i) Mutiny starts in Meerut
(ii) Subsidiary Alliance introduced in Awadh
(iii) Defeat of British at Chinhat
(iv) Rani Jhansi was killed in battle

Codes

(a) (i), (ii), (iii), (iv) (b) (ii), (i), (iii), (iv)
(c) (i), (ii), (iv), (iii) (d) (ii), (i), (iv), (iii)

21. **Arrange the following events regarding the Revolt of 1857 in chronological order and choose the correct option from the following** **CBSE 2024**

(i) Summary Settlement in Awadh
(ii) Subsidiary Alliance in Awadh
(iii) Reforming policies of William Bentinck
(iv) Azamgarh Proclamation

Options

(a) (ii), (iii), (i), (iv) (b) (i), (iii), (iv), (ii)
(c) (iii), (ii), (iv), (i) (d) (iv), (i), (ii), (iii)

22. **Identify the name of the person from the information given below.**

- **He lived in a large village in Pargana Barout in Uttar Pradesh.**
- He belonged to a clan of Jat cultivators whose kinship ties extended over *chaurasee des* (eighty-four villages).
- He mobilised the headmen and cultivators of *chaurasee des*, moving at night from village to village.
- He took over the bungalow of an English officer turned it into a hall of justice, settling disputes and dispensing judgements.

Options

(a) Shah Mal (b) Nana Sahib
(c) Birjis Qadr (d) Gonoo

23. **Identify the name of the person from the information given below.**

- He was one of the many *maulvis* who played an important part in the revolt of 1857.
- He was popularly called Danka Shah – the *maulvi* with the drum (*danka*).
- He fought in the famous Battle of Chinhat in which the British forces under Henry Lawrence were defeated.
- He was invincible, had magical powers and could not be killed by the British.

Options

(a) Bahadur Shah (b) Shah Alam
(c) Wajid Ali Shah (d) Ahmadullah Shah

24. **Read the given information and identify the leader of 1857 Revolt from the following options.** **CBSE 2023**

- Nawab of Awadh
- Was dethroned and exiled to Calcutta
- British wrongly assumed him as unpopular ruler.

Options

(a) Birjis Qadr
(b) Shah Alam
(c) Wajid Ali Shah
(d) Bahadur Shah

25. **Identify the ruler of India in the 1850s from the given options using the provided information.** **SQP 2024**

(i) He was the successor to Peshwa Baji Rao II.

(ii) He was compelled by sepoys and the towns people to join the revolt as their leader from Kanpur.

(a) Nana Sahib
(b) Kunwar Singh
(c) Birjis Qadr
(d) Maulvi Ahmadullah Shah

26. **Identify the name of a British official from the information given below.** **CBSE 2024**

(i) He adopted policies of reforming Indian society by introducing Western education.

(ii) He established laws to abolish Sati system.

(iii) He permitted remarriage of Hindu widows

Options

(a) Lord Mountbatten
(b) Lord William Bentinck
(C) Lord Wellesley
(d) Lord Ripon

27. **Complete the following with the correct option regarding the paintings with their respective artists.**

Relief of Lucknow: Thomas Jones Barker :: In Memoriam: ....

(a) Joseph Noel Paton (b) MF Husain
(c) Arunima Roy (d) Wilson Hunt

Assertion-Reason

28. Assertion (A) There was similarity in the pattern of the revolt of different places.

Reason (R) There was proper planning and coordination between these revolts.

Codes

(a) Both A and R are true and R is the correct explanation of A
(b) Both A and R are true, but R is not the correct explanation of A
(c) A is true, but R is false
(d) A is false, but R is true

29. Assertion (A) The British interest in acquiring the territory of Awadh increased with passage of time.

Reason (R) Soil of Awadh was good for indigo and cotton cultivation and could be developed into a principal market.

Codes

(a) Both A and R are true and R is the correct explanation of A
(b) Both A and R are true, but R is not the correct explanation of A
(c) A is true, but R is false
(d) A is false, but R is true

30. Assertion (A) Despite severe suppression of revolt, common process of law and trail were not suspended.

Reason (R) The army officers as well as the common Englishmen were empowered to try and punish Indians on mere suspicion.

Codes

(a) Both A and R are true and R is the correct explanation of A
(b) Both A and R are true, but R is not the correct explanation of A
(c) A is true, but R is false
(d) A is false, but R is true

Match the Following

31.

	List I (Leadership of the Revolt of 1857)		List II (Regions)
A.	Shah Mal	1.	Lucknow
B.	Kunwar Singh	2.	Kanpur
C.	Birjis Qadr	3.	Baraut
D.	Nana Sahib	4.	Arrah

Codes

	A	B	C	D		A	B	C	D
(a)	2	3	4	1	(b)	3	4	1	2
(c)	4	2	3	1	(d)	4	2	3	1

32.

	List I		List II
A.	Delhi	1.	Hazrat Mahal
B.	Jhansi	2.	Kunwar Singh
C.	Arrah	3.	Bahadur Shah
D.	Lucknow	4.	Rani Lakshmi Bai

Codes

	A	B	C	D		A	B	C	D
(a)	2	3	1	4	(b)	3	4	2	1
(c)	1	2	3	4	(d)	4	2	3	1

33.

	List I		List II
A.	Lord Wellesley	1.	Commander of British Forces in India
B.	Lord Dalhousie	2.	Introduced Doctrine of Lapse
C.	Lord Canning	3.	Introduced Subsidiary Alliance
D.	Colin Campbell	4.	Governor-General during Revolt of 1857

Codes

	A	B	C	D		A	B	C	D
(a)	1	2	3	4	(b)	2	1	3	4
(c)	4	1	3	2	(d)	3	2	4	1

34.

	List I		List II
A.	Lord Wellesley	1.	Introduced annexation policies
B.	Lord Dalhousie	2.	Introduced Subsidiary Alliance
C.	Lord Bentinck	3.	Introduced greased cartridges
D.	Lord Hardinge	4.	Introduced reformative polices

Codes

	A	B	C	D		A	B	C	D
(a)	3	2	1	4	(b)	4	3	2	1
(c)	2	1	4	3	(d)	1	4	3	2

35.

	List I		List II
A.	Nana Sahib	1.	Awadh
B.	Kunwar Singh	2.	Kanpur
C.	Wajid Ali Shah	3.	Bihar
D.	Birjis Qadr	4.	Lucknow

Codes

	A	B	C	D		A	B	C	D
(a)	3	1	2	4	(b)	2	3	1	4
(c)	4	2	3	4	(d)	1	4	2	3

36.

	List I		List II
A.	1857 10 May	1.	Mutiny Starts in Meerut
B.	1857 30 June	2.	British Suffer defeat in the battle of Chinhat
C.	1857 July	3.	Shah Mal killed in battle
D.	1858 June	4.	Rani Jhansi killed in battle

Codes

	A	B	C	D		A	B	C	D
(a)	1	2	3	4	(b)	3	2	4	1
(c)	2	3	4	1	(d)	4	2	3	1

Picture Based Questions

37. The leader in the image below, Nana Sahib escaped to which place at the end of 1858?

(a) Nepal (b) Rangoon
(c) Assam (d) Karnataka

38. The famous monument Secundra Bagh was

(a) Pleasure garden built by Nawab Wajid Ali Shah in Lucknow.
(b) Royal mosque built by Nawab Safdar Jung in Lucknow.
(c) Pleasure garden built by Nawab Alivardi Khan in Calcutta.
(d) None of the above

39. Who among the following was the painter of 'Relief of Lucknow'?

(a) Thomas Jones Barker (b) Joseph Noel Paton
(c) Henry Lawrence (d) Colin Campbell

Answers

1. (c) Meerut Cantt
2. (a) Delhi
3. (d) Awadh Military Police
4. (b) Kunwar Singh
5. (a) Shah Mal
6. (a) signal of an upheaval
7. (d) Dishonouring Hindu Women
8. (c) 1829
9. (c) Lord Dalhousie
10. (a) Awadh
11. (a) Awadh
12. (d) Protection of native territory by British
13. (d) Subhadra Kumari Chauhan
14. (b) Due to the displacement of Nawab Wajid Ali Shah and taluqdars
15. (c) Lucknow – Birjis Qadr
16. (c) The Clemency of Canning – A journal named 'Punch'
17. (c) (i) and (iii)
18. (c) (i) and (iii)
19. (c) (ii) and (iv)
20. (b) (ii), (i), (iii), (iv)
21. (a) (ii), (iii), (i), (iv)
22. (a) Shah Mal
23. (d) Ahmadullah Shah
24. (c) Wajid Ali Shah
25. (a) Nana Sahib
26. (b) Lord William Bentinck
27. (a) Joseph Noel Paton
28. (a) Both A and R are true and R is the correct explanation of A
29. (a) Both A and R are true and R is the correct explanation of A
30. (d) A is false, but R is true
31. (b)
32. (b)
33. (d)
34. (c)
35. (b)
36. (a)
37. (a) Nepal
38. (a) Pleasure garden built by Nawab Wajid Ali Shah in Lucknow.
39. (a) Thomas Jones Barker

Subjective Questions

Short Answer Type Questions

1. Discuss the nature of revolt of 1857.

Ans. Nature of revolt of 1857 was as follows

- The revolt of 1857 started as a sepoy mutiny. Later, people of different sections of the society joined the rebels.
- The main ground for the uprising had been prepared by the soldiers.
- Important and immediate cause of the revolt was that the soldiers refused to use the greased cartridges.
- It was the First War of Independence. Lakhs of artisans, farmers and soldiers united against the British rule.
- Hindus and Muslims took active part in the movement. The masses took active part in the struggle against the British at almost all centres of uprisings.

2. Under what circumstances did Bahadur Shah Zafar bless the rebellion of 1857? Explain. CBSE 2024

Ans. The sepoys in the cantonment of Meerut started mutiny on 10th May, 1857. The sepoys arrived at the gates of the Red Fort in early morning on 11th May. The sepoys told Bahadur Shah Zafar that they have killed all Englishmen in Meerut. They also told him about bullets coated with fat of cows and pigs. Another group of sepoys also entered Delhi. Europeans were killed in large numbers; the rich people of Delhi were attacked and looted. It was clear that the British had lost control of Delhi. Some sepoys rode into the Red Fort, without observing the elaborate court etiquette expected from them. They demanded the blessings from the emperor. Surrounded by the sepoys, Bahadur Shah had no other option but to submit so, he blessed the rebellion of 1857.

3. With the help of specific examples, examine the nature of Indian leadership that emerged against British in the revolt of 1857.

Ans. The nature of Indian leadership that emerged against British in the Revolt of 1857 was complex. During the revolt, few leaders participated as per their own will. While some other participated because they had no choice. They had to participate in the revolt for the sake of their reputation. Examples of Indian leadership that emerged during the Revolt of 1857 were

Bahadur Shah

Bahadur Shah was reluctant to join the rebellion but due to demands of sepoy, he joined the revolt and it was fought under his name. Similarly, sepoys and people of Kanpur choose Nana Sahib as their leader and he joined the revolt.

Rani Lakshmi Bai

Rani Lakshmi Bai of Jhansi participated because her kingdom had been annexed to empire by 'Doctrine of Lapse' and there was also popular pressure on her to take the leadership.

Apart from the royal families, local leaders also emerged during the revolt like Kunwar Singh in Arrah, Fakir in Lucknow, Shah Mal in Barout and Gonoo, a tribal cultivator in Singhbhum. Although the leaders of 1857 revolt participated in this war, but they had separate goals which made the revolt unsuccessful against British.

4. 'Rumours and prophecies played a part in moving people to action.' Explain the statement in the context of the Revolt of 1857. Competency Based Que

Or **How did the rumors play a role in moving the people to revolt against the British during 1857? Explain.** CBSE 2024

Ans. Rumours and prophecies played a part in moving people to action. There was a rumour among sepoys that bullets are coated with the fat of cows and pigs. They believed that biting those bullets would corrupt their caste and religion. There was another rumour that the British government had hatched a massive conspiracy to destroy the caste and religion of Hindus and Muslims. To this end, the rumours said, the British had mixed the bone dust of cows and pigs into the flour that was sold in the market. These fears inspired men to action. The response to the call for action was reinforced by the prophecy that British rule would come to an end on the centenary of the Battle of Plassey, on 23rd June 1857.

5. Why were the British so keen to acquire Awadh ? Explain. CBSE 2024

Ans. The British were keen to acquire Awadh for several key reasons

- **Strategic Importance** Awadh was seen as strategically important due to its fertile soil and potential for agricultural production, particularly of crops like indigo and cotton. This made it an economically valuable region for the British.
- **Market Potential** The British recognised that Awadh could serve as a major market for goods in Upper India, further strengthening their control over the region's economy.
- **Completion of Territorial Annexation** By the mid-19th century, the British had already conquered most major regions of India, including the Maratha lands, Doab, Carnatic, Punjab, and Bengal. Annexing Awadh was seen as the final step in their territorial expansion, completing their control over the subcontinent.
- **Weakening of the Nawab's Power** Since 1801, the British had imposed the Subsidiary Alliance on Awadh, which severely weakened the Nawab's authority. This made it easier for the British to eventually annex Awadh, as the Nawab could not resist British control effectively.

6. Examine how Lord Dalhousie's policy of annexation created dissatisfaction amongst the people of Awadh.

Or **Critically examine Lord Dalhousie's policy of annexation in Awadh.**

Or **How did British dispossess *taluqdars* of Awadh during 1857. Explain with examples.**

Or **"The annexation of Awadh displaced not just the nawab, but also dispossessed the *taluqdars* of the region, causing breakdown of an entire social order." Critically examine the statement.**

Ans. The British, especially Lord Dalhousie used a number of ways to annex the Awadh and dispossess *taluqdars*. For example,

- On 13th February, 1856, Awadh was annexed to the British empire on the grounds of maladministration. Nawab Wazid Ali Shah was sent to Calcutta with an annual pension of ₹ 12 lakh. With the dissolution of the royal administration, large number of courtiers, officials and *taluqdars* became jobless.
- With the removal of nawab, all *taluqdars* of the Awadh were dispossessed, disarmed and their forts were destroyed.
- With a new revenue system i.e. Summary Settlement, *taluqdars* lost their very large share of revenue from land. Wherever possible, *taluqdars* were removed and settlement was done directly with peasant.

Thus, these methods of annexation created dissatisfaction amongst the people of Awadh.

7. Examine the provisions of 'Subsidiary Alliance system' devised by Lord Wellesley in 1798 for India.

Or **Explain the provisions of the Subsidiary Alliance imposed on Awadh in 1801 by the British.**

Ans. The Subsidiary Alliance was introduced by Lord Wellesley in 1798. All those who entered into such an alliance with the British had to accept certain terms and conditions.

These were

- The British would be responsible for protecting their ally from external and internal threats to their power. In the territory of the ally, a British armed contingent would be stationed.
- The ally would have to provide the resources for maintaining the contingent.
- The ally could enter into agreements with other rulers or engage in warfare only with the permission of the British.

8. Examine the participation of the *taluqdars* of Awadh in the Revolt of 1857.

Ans. The annexation of Awadh created disaffection among the *taluqdars*, peasants and sepoys as their positions were declined by the Britishers who disarmed the *taluqdars* and destroyed their forts. The British officials increased the land revenue in some places from 30 to 70 per cent. Neither *taluqdars* nor peasants had any reason to be happy with the annexation.

During 1857, revolt in Awadh was intense and long lasting. The revolt was carried out by *taluqdars* and their peasants. Many *taluqdars* were loyal to the Nawab of Awadh and joined Begum Hazrat Mahal in Lucknow to fight against the British. Even after Begum's defeat, some of these continued to fight against the British.

9. Discuss Summary Settlement. What was its impact?

Ans. After the annexation of Awadh, the British introduced a land revenue policy known as Summary Settlement in 1856. It was believed that the taluqdars had established their hold on land through force and fraud with no permanent stakes in land. Summary Settlement proceeded to remove the taluqdars wherever possible.

Impact of Summary Settlement

Both peasants and taluqdars were affected by the summary settlement. Taluqdars lost villages held by them. The taluqdars of Southern Awadh were the hardest hit, and some lost more than half of the total number of villages they had previously held. Peasants faced high revenue demand from the British due to overestimation of revenue.

10. The dispossession of *taluqdars* meant the breakdown of an entire social order. Justify the statement. Competency Based

Ans. The dispossession of *taluqdars* meant the breakdown of an entire social order as

- The ties of loyalty and patronage that had bound the peasant to the *taluqdar* were disrupted. .
- Before British rule, *taluqdars* were often oppressive but also acted like generous father figures. They collected various dues from peasants but showed consideration during times of need.
- When taluqdars lost their rights and power, peasant became directly exposed to high revenue demand and inflexible methods of collection.
- There was no longer guarantee that in times of hardship or crop failure the revenue demand of the state would be reduced or collection postponed; or that in times of festivities the peasant would get the loan and support that the *taluqdar* had earlier provided.

11. Describe the aspirations and objectives of the rebels during the Indian Rebellion of 1857, as reflected in their proclamations and actions. CBSE SQP 2024

Ans. The aspirations and objectives of the rebels during the Indian Rebellion of 1857, as reflected in their proclamations and actions are given below

- **Opposition to Annexations** Rebels condemned British annexations and broken treaties, seeking to restore sovereignty to dethroned rulers and reinstate traditional governance structures.
- **Rejection of Revenue Policies** They criticised British land revenue settlements, which they felt exploited local farmers and disrupted traditional agricultural practices.
- **Defense of Tradition** The rebels attacked various aspects of British rule, accusing the British of undermining cherished cultural and social norms, and aiming to preserve their familiar way of life.

12. What was the importance of proclamations of the revolt of 1857?

Ans. The importance of proclamations of the revolt of 1857 can be understood by the following points

- The proclamations were a medium for the rebels to spread their ideas to people.
- Proclamation called upon people, both Hindus and Muslims, to unite, rise and kill the British.
- The proclamation tried to ensure religious unity by taking care of the religious sentiments of the population.
- The proclamations completely rejected everything associated with British rule, or *firangi raj* as they called it. They condemned the British for the annexations they had carried out and the treaties they had broken.
- The proclamations expressed the widespread fear that the British were bent on destroying the caste and religions of Hindus and Muslims and converting them to Christianity-a fear that led people to believe many of the rumours that circulated at the time.

13. How did the rebels of 1857 give emphasis on the vision of unity? Explain with examples. CBSE 2023

Ans. The rebels of 1857 had given emphasis on the vision of unity in the following ways

- The proclamation of revolt in 1857 appealed to all sections of the population irrespective of caste and creed. Even if the proclamations were issued by Muslim princes or in their name, they took care of the sentiments of Hindus.
- The revolt was a loss or a gain equally to both Hindus and Muslims.
- The *ishtahars* were a symbol to show the existence of different communities under the Mughal empire.
- The proclamation issued in the name of Bahadur Shah appealed to the people to join the fight under the standards of both Muhammad and Mahavira.
- During the uprising, religious divisions between Hindus and Muslims were absent despite British attempts to create such divisions.

  For example, the British spent ₹ 50,000 to incite the Hindu population against the Muslims in Bareilly, Western Uttar Pradesh in December 1857, but the attempt failed.

14. "The rebellion of 1857 was seen as a war in which both Hindus and Muslims had equally to lose or gain." Analyse the statement. CBSE 2025

Ans. The rebellion of 1857 was seen as a war in which both Hindus and Muslims had equally to lose or gain. The proclamations issued during the rebellion repeatedly appealed to all sections of the population, irrespective of their caste and creed. Even proclamations issued by Muslim princes took care to address the sentiments of Hindus. The rebels glorified the coexistence of different communities under the Mughal Empire and sought unity in their fight against British rule. Despite British attempts to create religious divisions, such as spending money to incite Hindus against Muslims, these efforts largely failed.

15. Examine the repressive measures undertaken by the British Govt. to control the rebellion of 1857. CBSE 2025

Ans. The British government took several repressive measures to control the 1857 rebellion, some of them were

(i) **Martial Law** Military officers and civilians were given the authority to punish suspected rebels, often sentencing them to death.

(ii) **Recapture of Delhi** The British launched intense battles to regain control of Delhi, the symbolic center of the revolt.

(iii) **Brutal Suppression in Awadh** Entire villages were destroyed, and rebels were executed to crush resistance.

(iv) **Punitive Actions** Rebels were publicly executed, including hangings and being blown from cannons, to instill fear.

(v) **Divide and Rule Policy** Loyal landowners were rewarded, while rebel supporters were dispossessed to weaken further uprisings.

16. What is the significance of visual representations?

Ans. The significance of visual representation is as follows

- The visual representations of the revolt indicates the feelings of the painters and their messages.
- The paintings and cartoons tells us about the public that looked at the paintings, appreciated or criticised the images.
- The paintings not only reflects the emotions and feelings of the times but also shapes sensibilities.
- Nationalist imageries of the revolt helped shape the nationalist imagination.

17. "The relationship of the sepoys with the superior white officers underwent a significant change in the years preceding the uprising of 1857". Support the statement with examples. Competency Based Que

Ans. The relationship between the sepoys and their superior white officers underwent a significant change. Earlier during 1820s, there was friendly relation among the sepoys and the white officers. They would take part in the fun activities, wrestled with each other and played games with each other. Many officers were fluent in Hindustani and were familiar with the customs and culture of the country.

But during the 1840s, this relation underwent a change. Officers developed a sense of superiority and treated sepoys as inferiors. Abuse and physical violence became common due to which distance between sepoys and officers grew and the trust was replaced by suspicion.

18. Mention any three sources to know about the Revolt of 1857. CBSE Term II 2022

Or **Explain any three sources to know about the Revolt of 1857.** CBSE 2024

Ans. We can know about the revolt of 1857 by the following sources

- Few rebel proclamations and notifications, and letters that rebel leaders wrote.
- Official accounts, colonial administrators and military men who have left their versions in letters and diaries, autobiographies and official histories.

- Innumerable memos and notes, assessments of situations, and reports that were produced. Many of these have now been collected in a set of volumes on mutiny records.
- The stories of the revolt that were published in British newspapers and magazines are some sources.

19. "Art and literature helped in keeping alive the memory of 1857." Explain with examples from Indian perspective. CBSE SQP 2022, Competency Based Que

Or Examine how art and literature have helped in keeping the memories of 1857 alive? CBSE 2025

Ans. Art and literature, as much as the writing of history, have helped in keeping alive the memory of 1857. The leaders of the revolt were presented as heroic figures who inspired public against oppressive British rule.

Rani Lakshmi Bai of Jhansi became an iconic masculine figure chasing the enemy till her last breath. Heroic poems were written about the queen. The famous lines of Subhadra Kumari Chauhan "*Khoob lari mardani woh to Jhansi wali rani thi*" (Like a man she fought, she was the Rani of Jhansi) is one such example.

Rani Lakshmi Bai is also portrayed in popular prints in the battlefield with a sword in hand and riding a horse, a symbol of the determination to resist injustice and alien rule. The paintings not only reflects the emotions and feelings of the times, but also shapes sensibilities.

20. "Visual images and literature as much as the writing of history have helped in keeping alive the memory of the revolt of 1857." Assess this statement. Competency Based Que

Ans. The visual images and literature as well as the writing of history contributed remarkably to immortalise the sacred memory of the struggle of 1857. The leaders of revolt were presented as heroes taking the country towards the battlefield. They were depicted as heroes inspiring the common masses to begin struggle against the oppressive colonial power.

Many heroic poems were composed narrating the bravery of Laxmi Bai. She was usually portrayed in battle armour with a sword in hand and riding a horse symbolising the determination to resist injustice and alien rule.

Thus, it becomes clear that visual representations produced various images of the revolt. These images were not a mere expression of contemporary ideas and sentiments, but they also reflected the contemporary sensibilities.

Long Answer Type Questions

1. "Rumours and prophecies played a part in moving the people into action during the revolt of 1857." Examine the statement with rumours and reasons for its belief. Competency Based Que

Ans. There were a number of rumours and prophecies which led to spread of revolt. Some of them include

Issue of Cartridges It was believed that the cartridges of the enfield rifles were coated with the fat of cows and pigs which corrupt the caste and religion of Hindus and Muslims.

Conspiracy to Destroy the Caste and Religion A news was spread that the British had mined the bone dust of cows and pigs into the flour that was sold in the market. Hence, sepoys and the common people refused to touch the *atta*. It was feared that the British wanted to convert Indians to Christianity.

Circulation of Chapattis The rumour was that chapattis were being distributed from village to village. A person would come at night and give a chapatti to the watchman of the village and ask him to make five more and distribute to the next village and so on. The people believed it to be a signal of an upheaval.

There were various reasons for the acceptance of such rumours by the common people. It can be seen in the context of the policies, the British pursued from the late 1820s. These include

Reforming Indian Society The British adopted policies aimed at 'reforming' Indian society by introducing Western education, ideas and institutions. Under the rule of Governor General Lord William Bentinck. English-medium schools, colleges and universities were opened where Western sciences and the liberal arts were taught. Laws were established to abolish customs like sati (1829) and to permit the remarriage of Hindu widows.

Annexation of States The British started annexing the Indian states on issues like misgovernment and the refusal to recognise adoption. States like Awadh, Jhansi, Satara, etc were annexed on these grounds. Once the territories were annexed, the British introduced their own methods of land settlement and land revenue collection.

Changes in Indian Society Socio-religious customs, patterns of land holding and revenue payment were destroyed and replaced by a more impersonal, alien and oppressive system. This perception was further aggravated by the activities of Christian missionaries. In such a situation of uncertainty, rumours spread with remarkable swiftness.

2. The rumours in 1857 begin to make sense when seen in the context of the policies the British pursued from the late 1820s. Evaluate. Competency Based Que

Ans. The rumours in 1857 begin to make sense when seen in the context of the policies the British pursued from the late 1820s due to the following reasons

- Under the leadership of Governor General Lord William Bentinck, the British adopted policies aimed at 'reforming' Indian society by introducing Western education, ideas and institutions.
- With the cooperation of sections of Indian society they set up English-medium schools, colleges and universities which taught Western sciences and the liberal arts.
- The British established laws to abolish customs like *sati* (1829) and to permit the remarriage of Hindu widows.
- On a various basis, the British annexed not only Awadh, but many other kingdoms and principalities like Jhansi and Satara.
- Once these territories were annexed, the British introduced their own system of administration, their own laws and their own methods of land settlement and land revenue collection.
- The overall impact on the people of North India was significant. They felt that everything they valued like their kings, traditions, and land ownership was being destroyed and replaced by a more impersonal and oppressive system.
- This feeling was worsened by the actions of Christian missionaries. In this uncertain situation, rumours spread quickly.

3. Explain the stages of conquest of Awadh by the British from 1801 onwards. CBSE Term II 2022

Ans. The conquest of Awadh by British happened in stages. The Subsidiary Alliance had been imposed on Awadh in 1801. By the terms of this alliance the nawab had to disband his military force, allow the British to position their troops within the kingdom, and act in accordance with the advice of the British Resident who was now to be attached to the court. Deprived of his armed forces, the nawab became increasingly dependent on the British to maintain law and order within the kingdom.

He could no longer assert control over the rebellious chiefs and *taluqdars*. In the meantime, the British became increasingly interested in acquiring the territory of Awadh. They felt that the soil there was good for producing indigo and cotton, and the region was ideally located to be developed into the principal market of upper India.

By the early 1850s, moreover, all the major areas of India had been conquered: the Maratha lands, the Doab, the Carnatic, the Punjab and Bengal. The takeover of Awadh in 1856 was expected to complete a process of territorial annexation that had begun with the conquest of Bengal almost a century earlier.

4. Why did *taluqdars* and sepoys of Awadh join the Revolt of 1857? Explain.

Ans. Since 18th century, Awadh faced a number of grievances which linked the princes, *taluqdars*, peasants and sepoys. They united against the British in the revolt of 1857. The grievances of taluqdars and sepoys are given below

Grievances of *Taluqdars* The annexation of Awadh dispossessed the *taluqdars* of the region. Before the advent of the British, they were powerful and maintained armed retainers, built forts and enjoyed degree of autonomy. The British were unwilling to tolerate the power of *taluqdars*.

Immediately after the annexation, the *taluqdars* were disarmed and their forts destroyed. The first revenue settlement, known as the 'Summary Settlement', further undermined the position and authority of the *taluqdars*. This settlement proceeded to remove the *taluqdars* wherever possible. The *taluqdars* of Southern Awadh were the hardest hit and some lost more than half of total number of villages.

Grievances of Sepoys Before 1820, the British were very gentle with the sepoys but in 1840 this began to change. The officers developed sense of superiority and started treating the sepoys as their inferiors. Abuse and physical violence became common. Trust was replaced by suspicion. The episode of the greased cartridges was a classic example of this. Most of the sepoys were from Awadh and Eastern Uttar Pradesh. Now, the fears of the sepoys about the new cartridges, their grievances about leave and the increasing misbehaviour and racial abuse on the part of their white officers were the responsible factors for their rage.

A whole complex of emotions and issues, traditions and loyalities worked themselves out in the revolt of 1857. In Awadh, more than anywhere else, the revolt became an expression of popular resistance of an alien order.

5. "A chain of grievances in Awadh linked the prince, *taluqdars*, peasants and sepoy to join hands in the revolt of 1857 against the British ". Examine the statement.

Or "Chain of grievances of *taluqdars*, and peasants led them to join the revolt of 1857." Elucidate the statement. Competency Based Que

Ans. Since eighteenth century, Awadh faced a number of grievances which linked the princes, *taluqdars*, peasants and sepoys to join hands in the revolt of 1857 against the British. The factors which were responsible for generating grievances are discussed below

Annexation of Awadh The Subsidiary Alliance had been imposed on Awadh in 1801, which confined the power of the nawab over his territory as his military force disbanded. The British troops took position in the kingdom and he could not take any decision without the advice of the British resident who was attached to the Court of Awadh. The British became increasingly interested in acquiring the territory of Awadh as it was economically and geographically important for them.

Dispossession of *Taluqdars* This annexation also dispossessed the *taluqdars* of the region.

Immediately after the annexation, the *taluqdars* were disarmed and their forts destroyed. The first revenue settlement, known as the Summary Settlement, further undermined the position and authority of the *taluqdars*.

Suppression over Peasants By removing the *taluqdars*, the British wanted to reduce the level of exploitation and increase the revenue demand.

Under the British rule, there was no guarantee that in times of hardship or crop failure the revenue demand of the state would be reduced or collection postponed, or that in times of need they would get any loan or support that the *taluqdars* had earlier provided. Thus, with this suppression, neither *taluqdars* nor peasants had any reasons to be happy with the annexation.

Rage of Sepoys There was also anger in sepoys towards the British. Before 1820, the British were very polite with the sepoys but in 1840 this began to change. The officers developed sense of superiority and started treating the sepoy as inferiors. Abuse and physical violence became common and trust was replaced by suspicion.

6. Examine the repressive measures adopted by British to subdue the rebels of 1857.

Ans. It was not easy for the Britishers to suppress the revolt. Even then they took various steps to crush the rebels.

These steps were as follows

Passing of Laws to help the Troops The British passed several laws to help the troops before sending them to re-occupy North India.

The military officers were also empowered to try and punish the rebel Indians. The ordinary process of law and trial were ignored by them.

With the help of new laws and the new reinforcements coming from Britain, the British started the process of suppressing the revolt. British thought to reconquer Delhi which was most important to suppress the revolt. Therefore, in June 1857, the British attacked Delhi from two directions.

Resorting to Diplomacy The British while resorting to diplomacy kept away the educated Indians and zamindars from the rebels. The British created a rift between rebels and the zamindars by promising the latter to give back their estates.

Use of Military Power The British used military power on a huge scale. Their absolute control over the means of communication and their control over the railways enabled them to send quick military support to different parts of the country.

Communication System The telegraph system helped the British to get timely information about the incidents occurring in different parts of the country. Consequently, they were successful to workout plans to take immediate action against rebels. Thus, the British tried their best to maintain their absolute control over the means of communication in order to suppress the revolt.

7. Describe how the British celebrated those, who they believed saved the English and repressed the rebels during the revolt of 1857?

Ans. The British celebrated those who they believed saved the English and repressed the rebels during the revolt of 1857 by the various types of paintings which were meant to provide a range of different emotions and reactions also. 'Relief of Lucknow', which has been painted by Thomas Jones Barker in 1859 is particularly remarkable in this regard.

In this painting, it is depicted that Henry Lawrence, the Commissioner of Lucknow, gathered all the Christians and took refuge along with them in heavily fortified residency after the rebel forces besieged Lucknow. Lawrence was killed, but the residency continued to be defended under the command of Colonel Inglis.

On 25th September, James Outram and Henry Havelock arrived out through the rebel forces and reinforced the British Garrisons.

Twenty days later, Collin Campbell who had been appointed as new commander of the British forces in India, reached with huge reinforcements and rescued the besieged British Garrison. In British accounts, the siege of Lucknow became a story of survival heroic resistance and the ultimate triumph of British power. The arrival of Collin Campbell has been depicted as an event of celebration in Jones Barker's painting. Campbell, Havelock and Outram, the three British heroes have been painted in the middle of the canvas. The gestures of the hands of the persons standing around them forcefully attract visitors to the middle of the painting.

The victorious figures of the heroes in the middle symbolising the re-establishment of British power and control is the main objective of these paintings and was to reassure the English in the power of their government. These paintings clearly conveyed the message that crisis was over and the revolt had been finished and the British had succeeded in re-establishment of their power and authority.

Source Based Questions

Read the sources given below and answer the following questions.

1. Ordinary Life in Extraordinary Times

Read these reports from the Delhi *Urdu Akhbar*, 14th June 1857: The same thing is true for vegetables and *saag* (spinach). People have been found to complain that even *kaddu* (pumpkin) and *baingan* (brinjal) cannot be found in the bazaars. Potatoes and *arvi* (yam) when available are of stale and rotten variety, stored from before by farsighted *kunjras* (vegetable growers). From the gardens inside the city some produce does reach a few places but the poor and the middle class can only lick their lips and watch them (as they are earmarked for the select)... There is something else that needs attention which is causing a lot of damage to the people which is that the water-carriers have stopped filling water. Poor *Shurfas* (gentility) are seen carrying water in pails on their shoulders and only then the necessary household tasks such as cooking, etc can take place. The *halalkhors* (righteous) have become *haramkhors* (corrupt), many *mohallas* have not been able to earn for several days and if this situation continues then decay, death and disease will combine together to spoil the city's air and an epidemic will spread all over the city and even to areas adjacent and around.

(i) How did the breakdown of routine activities impact daily lite in the city during the revolt?

(ii) What was the condition of poor and the middle class during the revolt of 1857?

(iii) How did Delhi *Urdu Akhbar* view the actions of the people?

Ans. (i) The revolt disrupted daily life. Causing good shortages, lack of clean water halted earnings and fear of disease spreading across the city.

(ii) During the revolt of 1857 as the prices of essential goods increased, it became impossible for the poor and the middle class to avail them.

(iii) The Delhi Urdu Akhbar recorded that the poor *Shurfas* (gentility) were seen carrying water in pails on their shoulders because water carriers had stopped filling water. The *halalkhors* have became *haramkhors* (corrupt).

2. Shah Mal

Shah Mal lived in a large village in Pargana Barout in Uttar Pradesh. He belonged to a clan of Jat cultivators whose kinship ties extended over *chaurasee des* (eighty-four villages). The lands in the region were irrigated and fertile, with rich dark loam soil. Many of the villagers were prosperous and saw the British land revenue system as oppressive: the revenue demand was high and its collection inflexible. Consequently cultivators were losing land to outsiders, to traders and moneylenders who were coming into the area.

Shah Mal mobilised the headmen and cultivators of *chaurasee des*, moving at night from village to village, urging people to rebel against the British. As in many other places, the revolt against the British turned into a general rebellion against all signs of oppression and injustice. Cultivators left their fields and plundered the houses of moneylenders and traders.

Displaced proprietors took possession of the lands they had lost. Shah Mal's men attacked government buildings, destroyed the bridge over the river, and dug up metalled roads – partly to prevent government forces from coming into the area, and partly because bridges and roads were seen as symbols of British rule. They sent supplies to the sepoys who had mutinied in Delhi and stopped all official communication between British headquarters and Meerut. Locally acknowledged as the Raja, Shah Mal took over the bungalow of an English officer, turned it into a "hall of justice", settling disputes and dispensing judgements. He also set up an amazingly effective network of intelligence. For a period the people of the area felt that *firangi raj* was over, and their raj had come. Shah Mal was killed in battle in July 1857.

CBSE Term II 2022

(i) Why did Shah Mal raise his voice against the Britishers?

(ii) How did Shah Mal support rebels of the Revolts of 1857?

(iii) How did Shah Mal Show his network of intelligence?

Ans. (i) Shah Mal belonged to a clan of Jat cultivators whose kinship ties extended over *chaurasee des* (eighty-four villages). Many of the villagers were prosperous and saw the British land revenue system as oppressive: the revenue demand was high and its collection inflexible. Consequently cultivators were losing land to outsiders, to traders and moneylenders who were coming into the area. Hence, he raised voice against the Britishers.

(ii) In order to help the rebels in the Revolt of 1857, Shah Mal and his men sent supplies to the sepoys who had mutinied in Delhi and stopped all official communication between British headquarters and Meerut. Shah Mal took over the bungalow of an English officer, turned it into a "hall of justice", settling disputes and dispensing judgements. He also set up an amazingly effective network of intelligence.

(iii) Shah Mal set up an amazingly effective network of intelligence. Shah Mal and his men stopped all official communication between British headquarters and Meerut. Locally acknowledged as the Raja, Shah Mal took over the bungalow of an English officer, turned it into a "hall of justice", settling disputes and dispensing judgements.

3. Maulvi Ahmadullah Shah

Maulvi Ahmadullah Shah was one of the many *maulvis* who played an important part in the revolt of 1857. Educated in Hyderabad, he became a preacher when young. In 1856, he was seen moving from village to village preaching *jehad* (religious war) against the British and urging people to rebel. He moved in a palanquin, with drumbeaters in front and followers at the rear. He was therefore popularly called Danka Shah – the *maulvi* with the drum *(danka)*. British officials panicked as thousands began following the *maulvi* and many Muslims began seeing him as an inspired prophet.

When he reached Lucknow in 1856, he was stopped by the police from preaching in the city. Subsequently, in 1857, he was jailed in Faizabad.

When released, he was elected by the mutinous 22nd Native Infantry as their leader. He fought in the famous Battle of Chinhat in which the British forces under Henry Lawrence were defeated.

He came to be known for his courage and power. Many people in fact believed that he was invincible, had magical powers, and could not be killed by the British. It was this belief that partly formed the basis of his authority.

(i) Who was Maulvi Ahmadullah Shah?

(ii) Why Maulvi Ahmadullah Shah was popular?

(iii) Which battle was fought by Shah and what were the consequences?

Ans. (i) Maulvi Ahmadullah Shah was one of the many *maulvis* who played an important part in the revolt of 1857.

(ii) He used to move from village to village preaching *jehad* (religious war) against the British and urging people to rebel, so he became popular.

(iii) He fought the famous Battle of Chinhat in which the British forces under Henry Lawrence were defeated.

4. The Nawab has left **CBSE 2024**

Another song mourned the plight of the ruler who had to leave his motherland : Noble and peasant all wept together and all the world wept and wailed Alas! The chief has bidden adieu to his country and gone abroad.

(i) What was the immediate impact of the removal of the Nawab ?

(ii) Why was there emotional upheaval at the dethroning and departure of the Nawab ?

(iii) How did the annexation of Awadh fit into the British colonial strategy ? Explain.

Ans. (i) The immediate impact of Nawab Wajid Ali Shah's removal was both emotional and material. His removal caused widespread grief, as he was loved by his subjects, and many mourned his departure. The town of Lucknow was described as "lifeless" without him. Additionally, the dissolution of the court culture led to the loss of livelihoods for many, including musicians, dancers, poets, and administrative officials.

(ii) The emotional upheaval following the dethroning of Nawab Wajid Ali Shah was due to his widespread popularity. Contrary to British assumptions, he was deeply loved by his people, and his exile caused great grief.

(iii) The annexation of Awadh in 1856 was a key part of the British strategy to expand their control in India. After imposing the Subsidiary Alliance in 1801, the British gradually weakened the Nawab by reducing his military power and making him dependent on British forces. By the 1850s, after conquering other regions like Punjab and Bengal, the British annexed Awadh to complete their territorial control over India.

5. The Azamgarh Proclamation, 25th August 1857

Section III – *Regarding Public Servants.* It is not a secret thing, that under the British Government, natives employed in the civil and military services have little respect, low pay, and no manner of influence; and all the posts of dignity and emolument in both the departments are exclusively bestowed on Englishmen, ... Therefore, all the natives in the British service ought to be alive to their religion and interest, and abjuring their loyalty to the English, side with the Badshahi Government, and obtain salaries of 200 and 300 rupees a month for the present, and be entitled to high posts in the future....

Section IV – *Regarding Artisans.* It is evident that the Europeans, by the introduction of English articles into India, have thrown the weavers, the cotton dressers, the carpenters, the blacksmiths, and the shoemakers, etc., out of employ, and have engrossed their occupations, so that every description of native artisan has been reduced to beggary. But under the Badshahi Government the native artisans will exclusively be employed in the service of the kings, the rajas, and the rich; and this will no doubt ensure their prosperity. Therefore these artisans ought to renounce the English services, ...

(i) **How did the introduction of English affect the artisans?**

(ii) **How would the condition of the artisans improve under the Badshahi Government?**

(iii) **Why were the public servants dissatisfied with the British Government?**

Ans. (i) The effect on artisans was that they lost their employment as the cheap machine made goods of Britain captured the Indian markets.

(ii) Under the Badshahi government, the condition of native artisans would improved as they would exclusively be employed in the service of the kings, the *rajas* and the rich.

(iii) Under the British Government, natives employed in the civil and military service had no respect. Their salaries were low and they had no power or influence so, they were dissatisfied with the British Government.

6. What the Sepoys Thought?

This is one of the *arzis* (petition or application) of rebel sepoys that have survived:

A century ago the British arrived in Hindostan and gradually entertained troops in their service and became masters of every state. Our forefathers have always served them, and we also entered their service ... By the mercy of God and with our assistance the British also conquered every place they liked, in which thousands of us, Hindostani men were sacrificed, but we never made any excuses or pretences nor revolted ...

But in the year eighteen fifty seven the British issued an order that new cartridges and muskets which had arrived from England were to be issued; in the former of which the fats of cows and pigs were mixed; and also that *attah* of wheat mixed with powdered bones was to be eaten; and even distributed them in every Regiment of infantry, cavalry and artillery ...

They gave these cartridges to the *sowars* (mounted soldiers) of the 3rd Light Cavalry, and ordered them to bite them; the troopers objected to it, and said that they would never bite them, for if they did, their religion and faith would be destroyed ... upon this the British officers paraded the men of the 3 Regiments and having prepared 1,400 English soldiers and other Battalions of European troops and Horse Artillery, surrounded them, and placing six guns before each of the infantry regiments, loaded the guns with grape and made 84 new troopers prisoners, and put them in jail with irons on them...

The reason that the *sowars* of the Cantonment were put into jail was that we should be frightened into biting the new cartridges. On this account we and all our country-men having united together, have fought the British for the preservation of our faith ... we have been compelled to make war for two years and the rajahs and Chiefs who are with us in faith and religion, are still so, and have undergone all sorts of trouble; we have fought for two years in order that our faith and religion may not be polluted. If the religion of a *Hindoo* or *Mussalman* is lost, what remains in the world?

(i) **Give one reason for the mutiny as stated in the *arzi*.**

(ii) **State one grievance of the sepoys.**

(iii) **What according to the sepoys was against their religion?**

Ans. (i) The reason for the mutiny was to protect and preserve faith and religion from being polluted by British rule.

(ii) The grievance of sepoys was that there was racial discrimination in matters of promotion, pension and terms of service.

(iii) According to the sepoys, the issue of the cartridges which were filled by the fats of cows and pigs was hurting the sentiments of the sepoys and was against their religion.

Map Based Questions

1. On the political outline map of India, three places related to the centres of the revolt of 1857 have been marked as A, B and C. Identify them and write their correct names on the lines drawn near them.

Or On the political outline map of India, two places have been marked as A and B, as the centres of the Revolt of 1857. Identify them and write their correct names on the lines drawn near them. **CBSE SQP 2024**

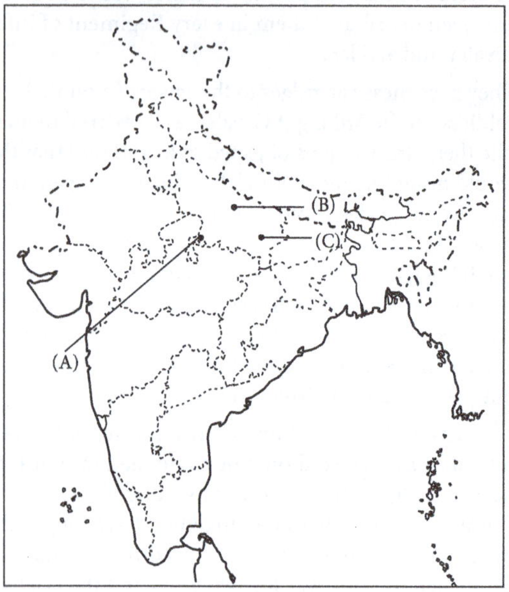

Ans.

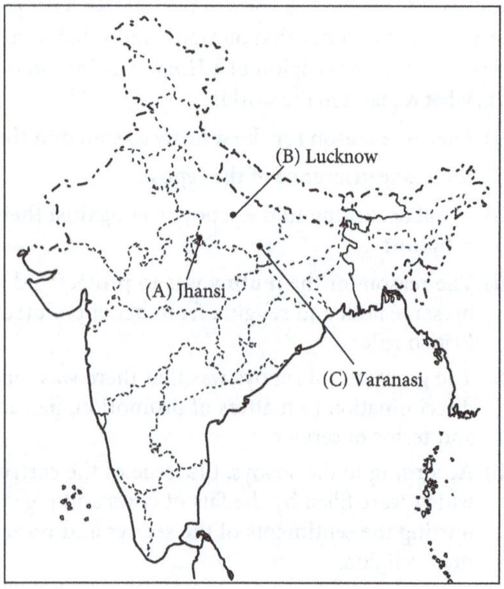

2. On an outline map of India, mark the following as territories under British control in 1857.

(i) Punjab (ii) Bombay
(iii) Fort St David (iv) Bengal
(v) Awadh (vi) Lucknow

Ans.

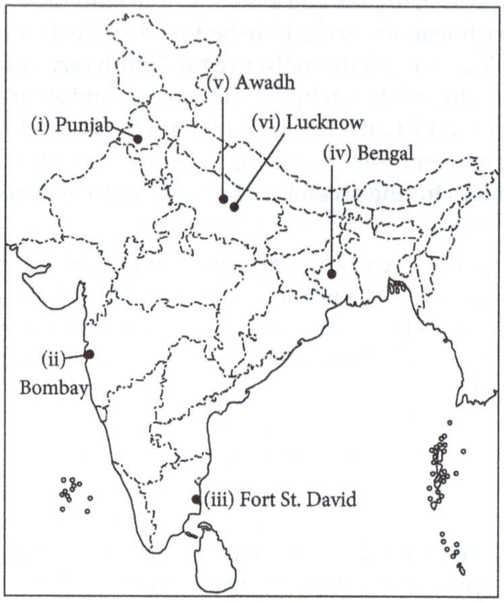

3. On the given political map of India, the important centres of Indian National Movement have been marked as A, B, C, D, E, F, G, H, I and J. Identify them and write their names on the lines drawn near them.

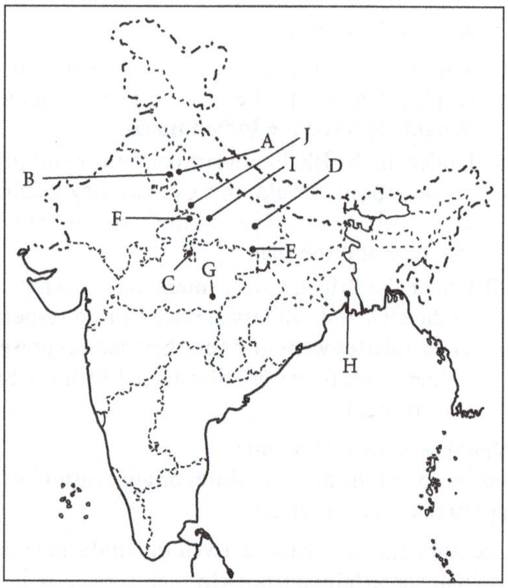

Ans.

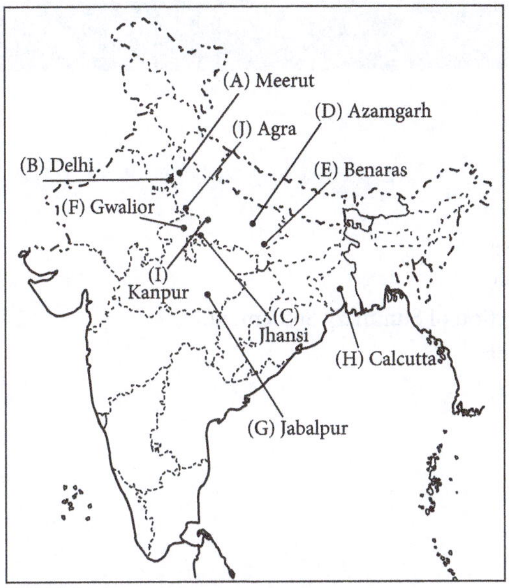

4. On an outline map of India, mark the following territories / cities under British control in 1857.

(i) Sindh	**(ii) Masulipatnam**
(iii) Berar	**(iv) Bihar**
(v) Orissa	**(vi) Surat**
(vii) Patna	**(viii) Madras**
(ix) Allabhabad	

Ans.

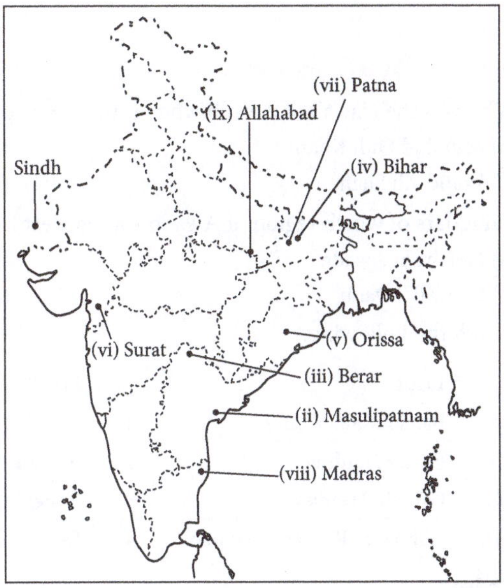

SELF ASSESSMENT TEST

Objective Type Questions

1. Who was the Nawab of Awadh when it was annexed by the British?
   (a) Murshid Quli Khan
   (b) Waris Ali Mirza
   (c) Wajid Ali Shah
   (d) Amjad Ali Shah

2. Taluqdars of which region of Awadh was hardest hit due to introduction of Summary Settlement.
   (a) Northern Awadh
   (b) Southern Awadh
   (c) Central Awadh
   (d) Eastern Awadh

3. Match the Following.

	List I		List II
A.	Bahadur Shah Zafar	1.	Rani Lakshmi Bai
B.	Henry Hardinge	2.	Awadh
C.	Captain Hearsey	3.	Enfield Rifle
D.	Subhadra Kumari Chauhan	4.	Delhi

Codes

	A	B	C	D
(a)	4	3	2	1
(b)	4	2	3	1
(c)	3	4	1	2
(d)	3	4	2	1

Short Answer Type Questions

4. 'The sepoys were the makers of their own rebellion'. Explain this statement with help of an example.
5. How are proclamations an important source to understand the revolt of 1857? Explain.
6. Why did Delhi become a centre of conflict between the British and the rebels?

Long Answer Type Questions

7. Examine the causes of the revolt of 1857.
8. 'It is clear from all accounts of 1857 that the British did not have an easy time in putting down the rebellion'. Analyse the statement.
9. 'The historians till now have continued to discuss rebel actions primarily through accounts written by the British'. Discuss.

11

CHAPTER

This chapter deals with Gandhiji's activities from 1915-1948 with special focus on movements like Non-Cooperation, Salt Satyagraha and Quit India Movement. It also explores sources used by historians to reconstruct his life and the social movements that he was associated with.

YOUR STUDY GOALS

11.1 The Making of a Nation
11.2 The Salt Satyagraha : A Case Study
11.3 Quit India Movement
11.4 Sources about Gandhiji

YOUR PRACTICE GOALS

- Objective Type Questions (38 Qs ; MCQs, A-R, Matching, Picture Based)
- Subjective Questions (11 SAs, 13 LAs)
- Source Based Questions (4 Qs)
- Map Based Questions (4 Qs)

Mahatma Gandhi and the Nationalist Movement

(Civil Disobedience and Beyond)

11.1 The Making of a Nation

- The making of a nation is often identified with a single individual. Examples include Garibaldi, who is associated with the making of Italy, George Washington with the American War of Independence and Ho Chi-Minh with the Vietnam freedom struggle.
- The Indian national struggle is identified with **Mahatma Gandhi**, who is regarded as the **Father of the Indian Nation**.
- Gandhiji was the most influential and respected of all the leaders in the freedom struggle.

Arrival of Gandhiji in India

- Mohandas Karamchand Gandhi came back to India in **January 1915** after spending two decades abroad.
- He spent most of his time in South Africa, where he started as a lawyer and became a leader of the Indian community.
- South Africa was 'the making of the Mahatma' according to historian Chandran Devanesan.
- Mahatma Gandhi practiced a non-violent protest, satyagraha in South Africa. It encouraged religious harmony and raised awareness among upper-caste Indians about the discrimination faced by low castes and women.

Congress in 1915

- The India that Mahatma Gandhi returned to in 1915 was rather different from the one he had left in 1893. Even though it was still a British colony, it was more active politically.

▲ *Mahatma Gandhi in Johannesburg, South Africa*

- There were branches of the Indian National Congress in most major cities and towns.
- The Congress widened its appeal among the middle classes through the **Swadeshi Movement (1905-1907)**.
- There was a rise of leaders like **Bal Gangadhar Tilak (Maharashtra)**, **Bipin Chandra Pal (Bengal)** and **Lala Lajpat Rai (Punjab)**. These leaders, also known as *Lal, Bal* and *Pal* preferred militant opposition to colonial rule.
- **Moderates** was another group which followed a slow and convincing approach. This group included Gandhiji's political mentor, **Gopal Krishna Gokhale** and **Mohammad Ali Jinnah**, a lawyer of Gujarati lineage trained in London.

Gandhiji on National Front

- On the advice of Gokhale, Gandhiji travelled around British India for a year.
- Gandhiji's first public appearance was at the opening of the **Banaras Hindu University (BHU)** in February 1916. The princes and philanthropists[1] who contributed to the founding of the BHU and Congress leaders such as **Annie Besant** were also invited.
- Gandhiji was concerned about the gap between the rich men present and the poor Indians who were not there. According to him, there was no salvation (process of being saved) until the privileged people gave up jewellery.
- Gandhiji emphasised more on the peasants and workers who constituted a majority of the Indian population.
- The opening of BHU was a celebratory event as the university was funded and initiated by Indians.
- Gandhiji in his speech, accused the Indian elite of ignoring the needs of the labouring poor. He highlighted that Indian nationalism was mainly an elite movement, created by lawyers, doctors and landlords.
- In **December 1916**, during the Lucknow Congress Session, a peasant from Champaran (Bihar) informed Gandhiji about the harsh treatment by the Britishers to the Indigo farmers.

Non-Cooperation : A Mass Movement

- Before launching a mass movement, Gandhiji had proved himself a nationalist leader through struggles like Champaran, Ahmedabad and Kheda.
- These localised struggles and Rowlatt satyagraha with wider participation, gave Gandhiji a strong foundation to launch the Non-cooperation movement.

Early Struggles

- In **1917**, Mahatma Gandhi worked to secure land rights for peasants in Champaran and their freedom to grow the crops they wanted.
- In **1918**, his campaigns in Gujarat were
  - **Ahmedabad Mill strike** where he demanded better working conditions for the textile mill workers.
  - **Kheda Satyagraha** in which he asked the state for the cancellation of taxes of peasants after the failure of harvest.

---

1 Philarthropist A rich person who helps poor and needy people, especially by giving money.

Rowlatt Satyagraha

- The British imposed censorship on the press during the First World War (1914-18). Accordingly, the political prisoners could be kept in prison for two years without any trial. These measures were continued after the recommendation of a committee chaired by **Sir Sidney Rowlatt**.
- Gandhiji called for a countrywide campaign against the Rowlatt Act in 1919. Shops and schools were closed in response to the *bandh* call.
- The protest in Punjab was strong because many men had served the British during the war. They expected rewards but were instead given the Rowlatt Act.
- Gandhiji was arrested while proceeding to the Punjab. Prominent Congressmen were also arrested.
- In Amritsar, a British Brigadier ordered the troops to open fire on a nationalist meeting in April 1919. Over four hundred people were killed. This incident is known as the **Jallianwala Bagh massacre**.

Integrating Non-cooperation with Khilafat

- Gandhiji became a true national leader after the Rowlatt satyagraha. Inspired by the success of the satyagraha, he announced 'Non-cooperation' with British rule.
- To expand the struggle, Gandhiji collaborated with the Khilafat Movement. He believed that by integrating Non-cooperation with Khilafat, Hindus and Muslims could collectively bring an end to colonial rule.
- These movements encouraged people to go for popular action against the British. These actions were
  - Students boycotted schools and colleges run by the government.
  - Lawyers refused to attend court.
  - Strikes were organised by the working class in many towns and cities. There were 396 strikes in 1921 involving 600,000 workers and a loss of seven million workdays.
  - Forest laws were violated by hill tribes in Northern Andhra.
  - Farmers in Awadh refused to pay taxes.
  - Peasants in Kumaun refused to carry loads for colonial officials.

Khilafat Movement (1919-1920)

It was a movement of Indian Muslims, led by **Muhammad Ali** and **Shaukat Ali**. It demanded that

- The Turkish Sultan or *Khalifa* must retain control over the Muslim sacred places in the erstwhile Ottoman empire;
- The *jazirat-ul-Arab* (Arabia, Syria, Iraq, Palestine) must remain under Muslim sovereignty;
- The *Khalifa* should have sufficient territory to defend the Islamic faith.

End of the Non-Cooperation Movement

- According to **Louis Fischer**, Mahatma Gandhi's American biographer, non-cooperation was significant in both India's history and Gandhiji's life. It involved denial, renunciation (act of rejecting) and self-discipline. It was a training for self-rule.
- The movement shook the British Raj to its foundation for the first time since the Revolt of 1857. But the movement stopped after the **Chauri Chaura incident**.
- In February 1922, a group of peasants attacked and burned police station in Chauri Chaura in the United Provinces (now, Uttar Pradesh).

▲ *Non-cooperation Movement*

- Several constables died in the incident which forced Gandhiji to put an end to the movement.
- Thousands of Indians were put in jail. Gandhiji was also arrested in March 1922 and charged with **sedition**[2].

Gandhiji as a People's Leader

- By 1922, Gandhiji had transformed Indian nationalism by involving peasants, workers and artisans in the struggle.
- Gandhiji was popularly called **Gandhi Baba**, **Gandhi Maharaj** or simply as **Mahatma**.

▲ *Mahatma Gandhi with Charkha*

- For peasants, Gandhiji was a saviour who would rescue them from high taxes and oppressive officials.
- His simple lifestyle and clever use of symbols such as the ***dhoti*** and the ***charkha*** enhanced his appeal among the poor.
- Mahatma Gandhi's success in expanding nationalism was also based on careful organisation.
- A series of *'Praja Mandals'* were established in the princely states to promote nationalist theory.
- Gandhiji encouraged communicating the nationalist messages in the mother tongue rather than in colonial language. Thus, the provincial committees of the Congress were organised on linguistic basis.
- Gandhiji was also admired by many businessmen and industrialists. Indian entrepreneurs believed that after the end of colonial era, the favours enjoyed by their British competitors would come to an end. Entrepreneurs like **G.D. Birla** supported the national movement openly.
- Gandhiji was also followed by a group of highly talented Indians between 1917 and 1922. They included Mahadev Desai, Vallabh Bhai Patel, J.B. Kripalani, Subhas Chandra Bose, Abul Kalam Azad, Jawaharlal Nehru, Sarojini Naidu, Govind Ballabh Pant and C. Rajagopalachari.

Quick Test 1

1 Name the person who is often identified with the making of Italy.
2 The Indian National Congress widened its appeal among the middle classes with which movement?
3 Which approach did the moderates prefer in the Indian National Congress?
4 What incident led to the suspension of the Non-cooperation Movement in 1922?
5 Who was one of the prominent entrepreneurs that openly supported the national movement?

11.2 The Salt Satyagraha : A Case Study

- After being released from prison in February 1924, Gandhiji promoted home-spun cloth (*khadi*) and worked against untouchability. In 1928, he thought about entering politics again.
- In 1928, there was a nationwide campaign against the Simon Commission, which was sent from England to investigate conditions in the colony. Gandhiji did not participate in this campaign as he was involved in peasant satyagraha in **Bardoli (1928)**.

Re-entry of Gandhiji in Active Politics

- In December, **1929**, a Congress session was held in **Lahore** which announced
  (i) The election of **Jawaharalal Nehru** as President, indicating the passing of leadership to the younger generation.

2 **Sedition** The use of words or actions that encourage people to act against a government

(ii) Commitment of **Purna Swaraj** or complete independence.

- On 26th January, 1930, Independence Day was celebrated across India. Gandhiji gave clear instructions for the day, starting with raising the national flag, followed by a focus on constructive work.

Dandi March

- After observing independence day, Gandhiji announced that he would lead a march to break the law that gave the state a monopoly in the manufacture and sale of salt.
- People were restricted from making salt even for domestic use and were forced to buy from shops at a high price. Thus, Gandhiji wanted to organise dissatisfaction against British rule.
- Before the Salt March, Gandhiji gave advance notice to the viceroy Lord Irwin.
- Gandhiji started marching from his ashram at **Sabarmati** towards the ocean on 12th March, 1930.

▲ *On the Dandi March, March 1930*

- After three weeks, Gandhiji reached his destination. He broke the law by making a fistful of salt. Similar salt marches were also organised in other parts of the country.
- The **dissenters**[3] were detained by the rulers. Nearly 60,000 Indians were arrested alongwith Gandhiji in the wake of the Salt March in 1930.
- Other forms of protest apart from nationalist campaigns were
  - Peasants went against the colonial forest laws that kept them and their cattle out of the woods.
  - Factory workers went on strike.
  - Lawyers boycotted British courts.
  - Students refused to attend government-run educational institutions.

Significance of the Salt March

- It brought Mahatma Gandhi to the world's attention. The European and American press widely covered the march.
- It became the first nationalist activity in which women participated in large numbers. Kamaladevi Chattopadhyay persuaded Gandhiji for the involvement of women in the march.
- The British understood that their Raj would not last forever and they would have to share some power with the Indians.

Round Table Conferences

- At the end of the Salt March, the British government organised a series of Round Table Conferences in London.
- The first meeting was held in **November 1930**, but it was unsuccessful as important political leaders of India did not participate.

Gandhi-Irwin Pact

- In 1931, several meetings were held between Gandhiji and Viceroy Irwin resulting in the **Gandhi-Irwin Pact**.
- The terms of the Gandhi-Irwin Pact were to end the Civil Disobedience Movement, release all the prisoners and allow salt manufacture along the coast.

---

3 Dissenter A person who does not agree with opinions that are officially or generally accepted.

Second Round Table Conference

- The Second Round Table Conference was held in London in the latter part of 1931 in which the Congress was represented by Gandhiji.
- Gandhiji was challenged by the following three parties for his claim that Congress represented all of India.

▲ *At the Second Round Table Conference, London, November 1931*

(i) **Muslim League** which represented the Muslim minority.

(ii) **Princes** who represented the princely states and claimed that the Congress had no role in their territories.

(iii) **B.R. Ambedkar** who represented lower castes.

- This conference also remained inconclusive. Gandhiji returned to India and resumed his civil disobedience.
- In **1935, the Government of India Act** promised some form of representative government.
- After two years, elections were held with a limited franchise. Congress won in eight out of eleven provinces which had a Congress Prime Minister working under the supervision of a British Governor.

The Second World War and India

- The Second World War started in **September 1939**.
- Both Mahatma Gandhi and Jawaharlal Nehru were critical of Hitler and the Nazis. They promised that if the British government granted independence to India after the war, the Congress would consider joining them. This offer was refused which resulted in the resignation of the Congress Ministries in October 1939.
- A series of **individual satyagrahas** were organised by the Congress through 1940 and 1941.

Cripps Mission

- By **March 1940**, the Muslim League demanded some autonomy for the Muslim-majority areas of the subcontinent.
- Now it was a three-way struggle between the Congress, the Muslim League and the British.
- In 1942, the Prime Minister **Winston Churchill** sent Sir Stafford Cripps to India to compromise with Gandhiji and the Congress. The mission failed because Congress insisted that it would support the British against the Axis powers only if an Indian was appointed as the Defence Member of the Viceroy's Executive Council.

Quick Test 2

1. In which year did Mahatma Gandhi begin to think of re-entering in politics?
2. What law did Mahatma Gandhi target during his campaign in 1930?
3. How long did it take Gandhi to reach the ocean during his Salt March?
4. Who persuaded Gandhiji to allow women to participate in the Salt March protests?
5. When was Gandhiji released from jail, allowing him to attend the Round Table Conferences?

11.3 Quit India Movement

- After the failure of Cripps Mission, Mahatma Gandhi launched the Quit India Movement in 1942. Gandhiji was in jail, but younger activists organised strikes and acts of sabotage (destruction) all over the country.
- The socialist members of the Congress such as Jayaprakash Narayan, were active in the underground resistance[4].
- **Independent governments** were formed in districts such as Satara in the West and Medinipur in the East. It took a year for the British to suppress the rebellion.
- Quit India was a mass movement as it involved participation of hundreds of thousands of ordinary Indians. Many young people left their colleges to go to jail.

▲ *Women's procession in Bombay during the Quit India Movement*

- Jinnah and his followers in the Muslim League worked at expanding their influence. The League started making a mark in Punjab and Sind where it had no presence.

Satara, 1943

- From the late nineteenth century, a non-Brahman movement, which opposed the caste system and landlordism, had developed in Maharashtra. This movement established links with the national movement by the 1930s.
- In 1943, younger leaders in the Satara district of Maharashtra set up a parallel government (*prati sarkar*), with volunteer corps (*seba dals*) and village units (*tufan dals*). They ran people's courts and organised constructive work.
- Dominated by *kunbi* peasants and supported by dalits, the Satara *prati sarkar* worked till the elections of 1946.

Efforts for Peace between Congress and League

- Gandhiji was released from jail in June 1944. He held many meetings with Jinnah to bring peace between the Congress and the League.
- The new Labour Government of Britain in 1945, wanted to grant independence to India.
- The Viceroy, **Lord Wavell**, brought the Congress and the League together for a series of talks.

1946 Elections and Direct Action Day

- Fresh elections were held in the provincial legislatures in early 1946.
- The Congress won in the General category and the League won a majority in the seats reserved for Muslims.
- A **Cabinet Mission** was sent in 1946 which failed to bring compromise between the Congress and the League. Jinnah declared **Direct Action Day** to support the League's demand for Pakistan.
- On **16th August 1946**, riots started in Calcutta which spread to rural Bengal, Bihar, the United Provinces and the Punjab.

Declaration of Independence

- **Lord Mountbatten** became the new Viceroy in February 1947 replacing Wavell. He announced that India would be freed by the British but it will be divided.
- **15th August** was fixed as the date for the formal transfer of power. The day was celebrated with delight in different parts of India.
- The Constituent Assembly in Delhi held a meeting where the President referred to Mahatma Gandhi as the Father of the Nation.

4 Underground resistance Underground organisations involved in a struggle for independence in a country

The Last Heroic Days

- On 15th August, 1947, Gandhiji was not present for the independence celebrations as he was in Calcutta and marked the day with a 24-hour fast.
- According to biographer DG Tendulkar, Gandhiji went to hospitals and refugee camps giving consolation to people. He appealed to the Sikhs, the Hindus and the Muslims to forget the past and live in peace.
- After bringing peace in Bengal, he shifted to Delhi and from there to Punjab. His meetings were sometimes disrupted by refugees who protested against readings from the Koran. They wanted him to address the sufferings of Hindus and Sikhs still living in Pakistan.

Death of Gandhiji

- Gandhiji was shot dead by **Nathuram Godse**, a young Brahman from Pune on the evening of **30th January**. His death caused a huge wave of grief, with heartfelt tributes from all political groups in India. International figures like George Orwell and Albert Einstein also appreciated Gandhiji.
- The martyrdom of Gandhiji was compared to that of Abraham Lincoln by the Times magazine.

11.4 Sources about Gandhiji

Many sources are available which helps us to understand the political career of Gandhiji and the history of the nationalist movement.

Public Voice and Private Scripts

- This includes writings and speeches of Mahatma Gandhi and his associates and political adversaries.
- Speeches help us to understand the public voice of an individual whereas private letters give an idea of his or her private thoughts.
- Letters express anger, pain, dismay, anxiety, hopes and frustrations as they can not be expressed in public statements. Mahatma Gandhi published the letters written to him in his journal, *Harijan.*
- Nehru also edited letters written to him during the national movement and published A Bunch of Old Letters.

Autobiographies

- Autobiographies give us an account of the past. They are often rich in human detail.
- They are to be read and interpreted carefully as they are retrospective (backward-looking) accounts written very often from memory.

Government Records

- The letters and reports written by policemen and other officials are now available in **archives**[5].
- For example, the fortnightly reports were prepared by the Home Department from the early twentieth century. In this report, Salt March was seen as a drama, an effort of Gandhiji to mobilise happy people against British rule.

Newspapers

- Newspapers published in both English and different Indian languages inform about Mahatma Gandhi's movements and his activities. However, newspaper accounts should not be seen as **unprejudiced**[6]. Newspapers were published by people who had their own political opinions and world views.

5 **Archives** A collection of historical documents.
6 **Unprejudiced** A dislike or distrust based on fixed or preconceived ideas.

- The ideas were shaped by the way events were published and reported. Therefore, it is important to look into these reports carefully while interpreting them.

Conclusion

These reports need to be studied carefully. Not everything can be taken literally as a true reflection of events. They often express the fears of officials who felt unable to control the movement and were uncertain about how to handle Gandhi. The more the colonial state monitored the public, the more it became anxious about its own authority.

Quick Test 3

1 In February 1947, who replaced Wavell as Viceroy of India?
2 In which districts were independent governments proclaimed during the Quit India Movement?
3 How did Mahatma Gandhi mark Independence Day on 15th August 1947?
4 Name the government records which can serve as valuable historical sources.

TIMELINE

1915	Mahatma Gandhi returns from South Africa
1917	Champaran Satyagraha Movement
1918	Peasant movements in Kheda (Gujarat), and workers' Movement in Ahmedabad
1919	Rowlatt Satyagraha (March-April)
1919	Jallianwala Bagh massacre (April)
1921	Non-cooperation and Khilafat Movements
1928	Peasant movement in Bardoli
1929	"Purna Swaraj" accepted as Congress goal at the Lahore Congress (December)
1930	Civil Disobedience Movement begins; Dandi March (March-April)
1931	Gandhi-Irwin Pact (March); Second Round Table Conference (December)
1935	Government of India Act promises some form of representative government
1939	Congress ministries resign
1942	Quit India Movement begins (August)
1946	Mahatma Gandhi visits Noakhali and other riot-turn areas to stop communal violence.

Mind Map

MAHATMA GANDHI AND THE NATIONALIST MOVEMENT

1 Arrival of Gandhiji in India

- Mahatma Gandhi returned in India in 1915 from South Africa.
- He developed the concept of non-violent protest (Satyagraha) in South Africa.
- Gandhiji aimed to make Indian nationalism more inclusive for peasants and workers.

2 The Making and Unmaking of Non-cooperation

Gandhiji as a People's Leader

- Gandhiji transformed Indian nationalism by including peasants, workers and artisans.
- His simple lifestyle including wearing a dhoti and spinning the charkha connected him with people.
- Both poor peasants and wealthy industrialists supported Gandhiji.

Integrating Non-Cooperation with Khilafat

- Gandhiji hoped that non-cooperation and Khilafat could unite Hindus and Muslims against British rule.
- Non-cooperation movement was a peaceful yet effective form of resistance, fostering self-discipline and denial.

National Struggles and the Rowlatt Satyagraha

- Gandhiji focused on securing rights for peasants in Champaran, Ahmedabad and Kheda.
- In 1919, Gandhiji launched Nationwide Protest against the repressive Rowlatt Act.
- The Rowlatt Act protests led to the Jallianwala Bagh Massacre.

3 The Salt Satyagraha: A Case Study

Dandi or Salt March

- Gandhiji led the Salt March to protest the British monopoly on salt.
- Gandhiji's call encouraged Indians of all classes to oppose colonial rule.
- Nearly 60,000 Indians, including Gandhiji, were arrested after the Salt March.

Gandhi-Irwin Pact and Second Round Table Conference

- Gandhiji and the British Government signed the Gandhi-Irwin Pact in 1931.
- The Second Round Table Conference faced challenges from Muslims, Princes and Ambedkar.
- In 1939, Congress ministries resigned.

4 The Quit India Movement

- The movement began in August 1942.
- The movement gained support from youth and activists.
- British India was partitioned and independence was granted on 15th August, 1947.

5 The Last Heroic Days

- Gandhiji marked Independence day with a fast.
- He focused on the suffering of minorities in both India and Pakistan.
- Gandhiji was assasinated on 30th January, 1948 by Nathuram Godse.

6 Sources about Gandhiji

Public Voice and Private Scripts

- Gandhiji's writing and speeches reveal both public and private aspects of his thoughts.
- Public speeches expresses an individual's voice, while private letters show personal emotions.

From Newspapers

- Contemporary newspapers tracked Gandhi's activities and public opinions about him.
- Newspapers were influenced by political views.

Government Records

- Government records, like reports from officials, offer insights into colonial rule.
- Reports during the Salt March minimised its popular response among the masses.
- Officials saw Gandhiji's Salt March as a useless effort, ignoring mass mobilisation.

NCERT Folder

Intext Question

1. What was Non-cooperation? Find out about the variety of ways in which different social groups participated in the movement. (Pg. 295)

Ans. Non-cooperation was an important movement in the Indian independence struggle. It was launched by Mahatma Gandhi in 1920 in response to the Rowlatt Act and the Jallianwala Bagh massacre. The movement aimed to resist British rule through non-violent means, encouraging Indians to withdraw from British institutions and refuse cooperation with the colonial government.

Different social groups participated in the movement in the following ways

- **Middle Class** The educated middle class boycotted British institutions, adopted *khadi* and organised protests. They used newspapers and pamphlets to spread the message.
- **Farmers and Peasants** Many rural communities participated by refusing to pay taxes and protesting against oppressive policies.
- **Women** They actively participated in the movement by spinning *khadi*, organising rallies, and supporting boycotts.
- **Students** Young students boycotted schools and colleges, joining the movement in large numbers. Their energy and enthusiasm mobilized larger sections of society
- **Workers** Trade unions organised strikes and demonstrations, integrating their struggles with the national movement.

Answer in 100-150 Words

1. How did Mahatma Gandhi seek to identify with the common people?

Ans. Mahatma Gandhi identified himself with the common people of India in the following ways

- He did not behave like professional or an intellectual. He rather mixed with thousands of peasants, workers and artisans.
- He, unlike other nationalist leaders, dressed himself like the common man. He wore simple *dhoti* or loincloth.
- He worked on the *charkha* (spinning wheel) everyday. He also encouraged other nationalists to do the same.
- He did not believe in the traditional caste system.
- He often spoke in the mother-tongue.

2. How was Mahatma Gandhi perceived by the peasants?

Ans. Mahatma Gandhi was perceived by the peasants in the following ways

- The peasants respected Gandhiji referring to him as their 'Mahatma'. Stories spread that those who opposed him suffered bad consequences. Rumours spread off how villagers who criticised Gandhiji found their houses falling apart and their crops failing.
- In some places, peasants believed that Gandhi's power was superior to that of the English monarch and that with his arrival, the British rulers would leave the district.
- In other places, peasants believed that he had been sent by the king to help the farmers and has the power to overrule the local officials.
- The popular perception of Gandhi was that of a saviour who would rescue peasants from high taxes, oppressive officials and restore dignity and autonomy to their lives.

3. Why did the salt laws become an important issue of struggle?

Ans. The salt law became an important issue of struggle due to the following

- The salt laws gave the state a monopoly in the manufacture and sale of salt. This was thus, one of the most disliked laws in British India.
- Salt was an important commodity in any household but people were forbidden from making salt even for domestic use. They were forced to buy from shops at a high price. The salt laws deprived the people of the benefits of valuable village industry.
- Moreover, to prevent people from having access to natural salt, tonnes of salt were destroyed. Destroying the extra natural salt involved national expenditure and the salt tax itself was a heavy burden on the people.

Thus, the salt laws were deeply unpopular and making these laws his target, Gandhi sought to mobilise a wider discontent against British rule.

4. Why are newspapers an important source for the study of the national movement?

Ans. Newspapers published in both English and different Indian languages are important sources as they inform us about Mahatma Gandhi's movements and his activities. However, newspaper accounts should not be seen as unprejudiced. They were published by people who had their own political opinions and world views.

These ideas shaped what was published and the way events were reported. There will be difference in the accounts published in a London newspaper and an Indian nationalist paper. Therefore, it is important to look into these reports carefully while interpreting them. Every statement can not be accepted literally. Sometimes, they represented fear and anxiety of those officials who were not able to control movement.

5. **Why was the *charkha* chosen as a symbol of nationalism?**

Ans. Gandhiji made *charkha* a symbol of nationalism because of the following reasons

- It symbolised manual labour. Mahatma Gandhi always believed in the dignity of labour.
- Gandhiji opposed machines as they enslaved human beings. He adopted *charkha* as he wanted to glorify the dignity of manual labour.
- He believed that *charkha* could make a man self-reliant as it added to his income.
- The act of spinning at *charkha* enabled Gandhiji to break the boundaries of traditional caste system.

Write a short Essay (about 250-300 words) on the Following

6. **How was non-cooperation a form of protest?**

Or **"Mahatma Gandhi's role was vital in the Non-Cooperation Movement." Explain the statement.**

CBSE 2024, 2024 C

Ans. Gandhiji joined Non-Cooperation Movement with the Khilafat Movement in hope to bring two major religious communities, Hindus and Muslims together. It brought a surge of popular action which was unprecedented in colonial India.

Following were some actions took place during the Non-cooperation Movement

- Peaceful demonstrations were carried out under the leadership of Gandhiji.
- Students boycotted schools and colleges run by the government.
- Lawyers refused to attend court on Gandhiji's call.
- Strike by working class in many towns and cities. There were 396 strikes in 1921 involving 600,000 workers and a loss of seven million workdays.
- Forest laws were violated by hill tribes in Northern Andhra.
- Farmers in Awadh refused to pay taxes.
- Peasants in Kumaun refused to carry loads for colonial officials.

Peasants, workers and others interpreted and acted upon the call to 'non-cooperate' with colonial rule in ways best suited their interests. According to Louis Fischer, Mahatma Gandhi's American biographer, 'non-cooperation became the name of an epoch in the life of India and of Gandhiji. The movement shook the foundation of British rule in India for the first time.

7. **Why were the dialogues at the Round Table Conference inconclusive?**

Ans. Two Round Table Conferences were held in London but both of them are inconclusive.

Inconclusiveness of First Round Table Conference

The First Round Table Conference was held in November 1930 but, it was held without any pre-eminent political leader in India, thus, making it a useless effort. Meanwhile, Gandhiji was released from jail in January 1931 and had meetings with the Viceroy. It led to the signing of Gandhi–Irwin Pact. The British government agreed to withdraw salt law partly.

Inconclusiveness of Second Round Table Conference

The Second Round Table Conference was held in London in latter part of 1931. The Congress was represented by Gandhiji. But, he was challenged by three parties for his claim that Congress represented all of India.

The three parties who challenged Gandhiji were

(i) Muslim League which represented the Muslim minority.

(ii) Princes who represented the princely states and claimed that the Congress had no stake in their territories.

(iii) BR Ambedkar, a brilliant lawyer and thinker who represented lower castes.

Thus, unfair attitude of the British Government, stubbornness of Muslim League and wrong attitude of princely states, rulers as well as of Dr Bhimrao Ambedkar were the main reasons for Round Table failure of the conference.

8. **In what way did Mahatma Gandhi transform the nature of the national movement?**

Ans. Gandhiji transformed the national movement of the masses by following his new technique of struggle based on the principle of satyagraha and civil disobedience.

The ways in which Mahatma Gandhi transform the nature of the national movement were as follows

- The mass appeal of Gandhiji was undoubtedly genuine. His qualities of efficient leadership made a remarkable contribution in making the base of Indian Nationalism wider.
- The provincial committees of the Congress were formed on linguistic regions and not on the artificial boundaries of the British India. These different ways contributed greatly to take nationalism to the distant corners of the country.
- The social groups previously untouched by nationalism, now became an important part of it. Thousands of peasants, labourers and artisans started participating in the national movement. Similarly, the common masses participated in

the Civil Disobedience Movement significantly. In Delhi, some 1600 women picketed the liquor shops.

- In the same way, Quit India Movement became genuinely a Mass Movement as hundreds of thousands of ordinary Indians participated in it.
- Besides the common Indian, some very prosperous businessmen and industrialists too became supporters of the Indian National Congress. They realised that the favours enjoyed by their British competitors would come to them in free India.
- Some renowned industrialists such as GD Birla started supporting the national movement openly, whereas some others began to do so tactfully. The followers and admirers of Gandhiji included both the peasants and the rich industrialists.
- Thus, under Gandhiji, the national movement was transformed into a mass movement.

9. What do private letters and autobiographies tell us about an individual? How are these sources different from official accounts?

Ans. Private letters and autobiographies give significant information about an individual. With these, an accurate estimate of the concerned individual's ideology and career can be made. For example, Gandhiji's letters and his autobiography help us significantly in understanding Gandhiji and his ideology.

Autobiographies give an account of the past that is rich in human detail. Autobiographies are retrospective accounts written very often from memory. They tell us what the author would be able to recollect, what he or she saw as important or was recounting or how a person wanted his or her life to be viewed by others.

Private letters give a glimpse of the private thoughts of an individual. In letters, people can be seen expressing their anger and pain, their dismay and anxiety, their hopes and frustrations, in a way in which they may not express themselves in public statements. Gandhiji regularly published in his journal *Harijan*, letters written to him during the national movements. Nehru edited a collection of letters called *A Bunch of Old Letters*.

Official Accounts differ from Other Sources

Government records or official accounts are different from autobiographies and private letters as government records include letters and reports written by policemen and other officials. One such source is the fortnightly report prepared by the home department from early twentieth century.

These reports were based on information given to the police by the localities, but often expressed what the officials saw or wanted to believe. For example, in fortnightly reports for the period of the salt march, it is noticed that the home department was unwilling to accept that Mahatma Gandhiji's actions had evolved any enthusiastic response from the masses. On the contrary, Dandi March was seen as a drama, to mobilise unwilling people against the British rule by Gandhiji.

10. Find out about the route of the Dandi March. On a map of Gujarat plot the line of the march and mark the major towns and villages that it passed along the route.

Ans.

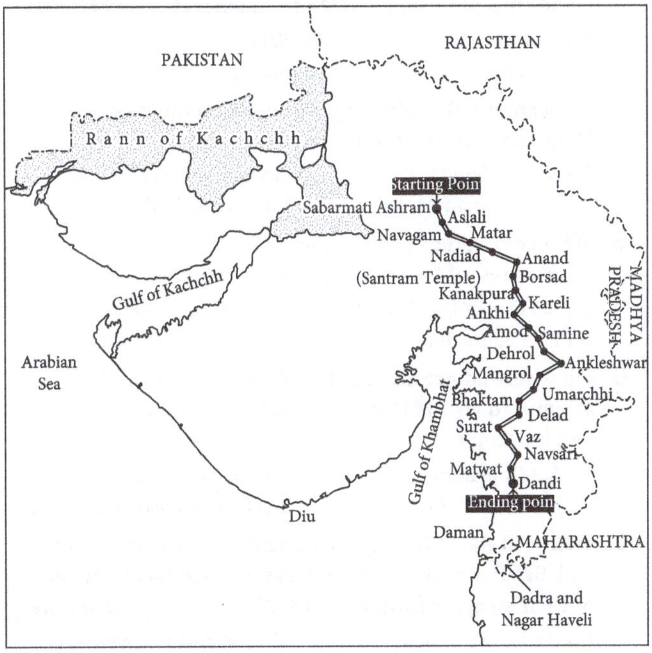

Exam Pattern Questions

Objective Type Questions

Multiple Choice Questions (MCQs)

1. **In which year Mahatma Gandhi returned to India?**
(a) 1915 (b) 1914
(c) 1916 (d) 1910

2. **Mahatma Gandhi for the first time experimented with satyagraha in ....**
(a) Britain (b) India
(c) South Africa (d) Africa

3. **Which of the following terms is used to describe Gandhiji's philosophy of 'Non-violence' ?** CBSE 2024
(a) Swaraj (b) Sarvodaya
(c) Boycott (d) Satyagraha

4. **Who among the following was not a member of Moderate Group of National movement?**
(a) Bipin Chandra Pal (b) Gopal Krishna Gokhale
(c) Mohammad Ali Jinnah (d) Pherozeshah Mehta

5. **Who among the following belonged to the group of 'Moderates' of the Indian National Congress ?** CBSE 2024
(a) Bal Gangadhar Tilak (b) Bipin Chandra Pal
(c) Lala Lajpat Rai (d) Gopal Krishna Gokhale

6. **On whose advice among the following did Gandhiji attempt to visit British India and learn about the land and its people ?** CBSE 2024
(a) Bal Gangadhar Tilak (b) Bipin Chandra Pal
(c) Lala Lajpat Rai (d) Gopal Krishna Gokhale

7. **Which of the following movements was broadened by 'Lal-Bal-Pal' and conveyed it as the all-India character of their struggle from 1905-1907?** CBSE 2024
(a) Gadar Movement (b) Swadeshi Movement
(c) Satyagraha Movement (d) Peasant Movement

8. **Gandhiji made his first public appearance in India at**
(a) Champaran Satyagraha
(b) Opening of Banaras Hindu University
(c) Kheda Satyagraha
(d) Foundation of Indian National Congress

9. **Banaras Hindu University was opened in the year ....**
(a) 1910 (b) 1915
(c) 1916 (d) 1917

10. **In which satyagraha, Gandhiji asked for the remission of taxes for peasants following the failure of their harvest?**
(a) Rowlatt Satyagraha
(b) Champaran Satyagraha
(c) Kheda Satyagraha
(d) Individual Satyagraha

11. **Who was the Viceroy of the British in India at the time of Dandi March?**
(a) Lord Curzon
(b) Lord Canning
(c) Lord William Bentinck
(d) Lord Irwin

12. **Who among the following was active in underground resistence during Quit India Movement?**
(a) Jawaharlal Nehru
(b) Jayaprakash Narayan
(c) Subhas Chandra Bose
(d) Dr Rajendra Prasad

13. **Mahatma Gandhi used to publish the letters written to him in his journal ....**
(a) *Harijan* (b) Young India
(c) New India (d) Indian Opinion

14. **Which one of the following was the Gandhi's main demand for the peasants in Champaran?** CBSE SQP 2024
(a) Increase in minimum wages of workers
(b) Freedom to cultivate the crops of their choice.
(c) Reduction in government taxes for social classes
(d) Indian education for all farmers' children

15. **What was the main demand of Khilafat Movement?**
(a) Dominion Status for India
(b) Self Rule to India
(c) Restoration of Caliphate of Turkey
(d) Revival of Orthodox Culture of Islam

16. **The reason for which Simon Commission visited India was**
(a) enquiring the conditions in the colony.
(b) granting special privileges to minorities.
(c) granting separate electorate to dalits.
(d) enquiring the excesses of Jallianwala Bagh massacre.

17. **Why was the Charkha chosen as a national symbol by Gandhiji ? Choose the most suitable option from the following.** **CBSE 2024 C**

(a) Gandhiji saw the Charkha as a symbol of truth.
(b) Gandhiji saw the Charkha as a symbol of the poor.
(c) Gandhiji saw the Charkha as a symbol of human society.
(d) Gandhiji saw the Charkha as a symbol of self-reliance.

18. **Which of the following statements is not correct regarding 'Quit India Movement'?** **CBSE 2024**

(a) Quit India Movement was a mass movement.
(b) Thousands of Indians took part in this movement.
(c) 'Independent' governments were proclaimed in Satara and Medinipur.
(d) A series of 'Praja Mandals' were established in princely states.

19. **Consider the following statements regarding Gandhiji's first public appearance at Banaras Hindu University.**

(i) He was invited due to his status in India.
(ii) He charged Indian elite with a lack of concern for the poor.
(iii) He was invited due to his work in South Africa.
(iv) Congress leaders like Annie Besant were in attendance.

Which of the above statements are correct?

(a) (i) and (ii) (b) (ii), (iii) and (iv)
(c) (i), (ii) and (iv) (d) All of these

20. **Consider the following statements regarding Rowlatt Satyagraha.**

(i) Rowlatt Act was passed in the year 1915.
(ii) It was passed on the recommendation of a committee chaired by Justice CN Broomfield.
(iii) This act permitted detention without trial.
(iv) Gandhiji called for a countrywide campaign against this act.

Which of the above statements are not correct?

(a) (i) and (ii)
(b) (ii) and (iii)
(c) (i) and (iii)
(d) (i), (ii) and (iii)

21. **Which of the following pairs is correctly matched?** **CBSE SQP 2022**

	Viceroy		Event
(a)	Lord Irwin	–	Salt Satyagraha
(b)	Lord Willington	–	Outbreak of World War II
(c)	Lord Linlithgow	–	Second Round Table Conference
(d)	Lord Mountbatten	–	1946 provincial legislatures elections

22. **Arrange the following in chronological order and select the correct answer from the options given below**

(i) 'Purna Swaraj' Accepted as Congress goal
(ii) Congress Ministries Resign
(iii) Government of India Act
(iv) Quit India Movement begins

Codes

(a) (i), (ii), (iii), (iv) (b) (i), (iv), (iii), (ii)
(c) (i), (iii), (ii), (iv) (d) (i), (iii), (iv), (ii)

23. **Arrange the following historical events in a correct chronological order and choose the correct option**

I. Making of the Constituent Assembly **CBSE 2025**
II. Jallianwala Bagh Massacre
III. Quit India Movement
IV. Gandhi-Irwin Pact

Options

(a) II, III, I and IV (b) II, IV, III and I
(c) III, II, I and IV (d) IV, III, I and II

24. **Identify the name of the movement from the information given below.**

- It was a movement of Indian Muslims.
- It was led by Mohammad Ali and Shaukat Ali.
- It demanded that the Turkish Sultan or Khalifa must retain control over the Muslim sacred places in the erstwhile Ottoman empire.
- The Congress supported this movement and Mahatma Gandhi sought to conjoin it to the Non-cooperation Movement.

Options

(a) Non-cooperation Movement
(b) Quit India Movement
(c) Salt Satyagraha
(d) Khilafat Movement

25. **Identify the name of the person from the information given below.**

- He was the most influential and revered of all the leaders who participated in the freedom struggle.
- He had been invited on account of his work in South Africa rather than his status within India.
- At the Second Round Table Conference, he opposed the demand for separate electorates for lower castes.
- He first forged the distinctive techniques of non-violent protests known as satyagraha.

Options

(a) Sardar Patel
(b) Mahatma Gandhi
(c) Jawaharlal Nehru
(d) Mohammad Ali Jannah

26. **Complete the following with the correct option regarding the movements with their respective leaders.**

Non-cooperation: Gandhi :: Khilafat movement: ....

(a) Sardar Patel (b) Mohammad Ali Jinnah
(c) Maulana Abul Kalam Azad (d) Shaukat Ali

27. **Complete the following with the correct option regarding the role of leaders in the history of nationalism of their respective countries.** CBSE SQP 2024

Ho Chi Minh: Vietnam, George Washington: ....

(a) USA (b) UK
(c) France (d) Canada

Assertion-Reason

28. **Assertion** (A) In 1917, Mahatma Gandhi was struggling for peasants in Champaran.

Reason (R) Peasants of Champaran did not have freedom to cultivate the crops of their choice.

Codes

(a) Both A and R are true and R is the correct explanation of A
(b) Both A and R are true, but R is not the correct explanation of A
(c) A is true, but R is false
(d) A is false, but R is true

29. **Assertion** (A) To broaden the Non-Cooperation Movement, Gandhiji had joined hands with the Khilafat Movement. CBSE 2024

Reason (R) Gandhiji hoped that coupling Non-Cooperation and Khilafat could collectively bring an end to the Colonial rule.

Options

(a) Both Assertion (A) and Reason (R) are true and Reason (R) is the correct explanation of the Assertion (A).
(b) Both Assertion (A) and Reason (R) are true, but Reason (R) is not the correct explanation of the Assertion (A).
(c) Assertion (A) is correct, but Reason (R) is incorrect.
(d) Assertion (A) is incorrect, but Reason (R) is correct.

30. **Assertion** (A) Lahore Session of Congress in 1929 was significant.

Reason (R) Proclamation of commitment to 'Purna Swaraj' or complete independence was passed. CBSE 2023

Codes

(a) Both A and R are true and R is the correct explanation of A
(b) Both A and R are true, but R is not the correct explanation of A
(c) A is true, but R is false
(d) A is false, but R is true

31. **Assertion** (A) First Round Table Conference remains fruitless.

Reason (R) Three parties challenged Gandhiji's claim that Congress represents all of India.

Codes

(a) Both A and R are true and R is the correct explanation of A
(b) Both A and R are true, but R is not the correct explanation of A
(c) A is true, but R is false
(d) A is false, but R is true

32. **Assertion** (A) Cripps Mission failed in its aim.

Reason (R) Congress demanded to appoint an Indian as Defence Member to help British in war.

Codes

(a) Both A and R are true and R is the correct explanation of A
(b) Both A and R are true, but R is not the correct explanation of A
(c) A is true, but R is false
(d) A is false, but R is true

Match the Following

33.

	List I		List II
A.	Peasant Movement in Bardoli	1.	1917
B.	Jallianwala Bagh Massacre	2.	1918
C.	Ahmedabad Mill Strike	3.	1919
D.	Champaran Satyagraha	4.	1928

Codes

	A	B	C	D		A	B	C	D
(a)	4	2	1	3	(b)	4	3	2	1
(c)	1	2	3	4	(d)	3	4	1	2

34.

	List I		List II
A.	Non-Cooperation Movement	1.	1931
B.	Arrival of Mahatma Gandhi	2.	1921
C.	Kheda Satyagraha	3.	1915
D.	Second Round Table Conference	4.	1918

Codes

	A	B	C	D		A	B	C	D
(a)	1	2	3	4	(b)	2	3	4	1
(c)	3	4	1	2	(d)	1	3	4	2

35.

	List I		List II
A.	Parallel government	1.	Dandi
B.	Assassination of Mahatma Gandhi	2.	Amritsar
C.	Salt Satyagraha	3.	Delhi
D.	Jallianwala Bagh Massacre	4.	Satara

Codes

	A	B	C	D		A	B	C	D
(a)	1	2	3	4	(b)	2	3	4	1
(c)	3	4	1	2	(d)	4	3	1	2

Picture Based Questions

36. The people seen in this image are seen indulged in

(a) collection of foreign clothes.
(b) empathetically listening to the speech of their leader.
(c) Both (a) and (b)
(d) None of the above

37. The image below shows the beginning of which act by Gandhiji?

(a) Dandi March
(b) Protest against Simon Commission
(c) Satyagraha against Rowlatt Act
(d) Quit India Movement

38. This women procession in Quit India reflects

(a) broadening the base of nationalist struggle.
(b) they were completely free from seclusion and were employed at large scale.
(c) participation of women from every section of the society.
(d) All of the above

Answers

1. (a) 1915
2. (c) South Africa
3. (d) Satyagraha
4. (a) Bipin Chandra Pal
5. (d) Gopal Krishna Gokhale
6. (d) Gopal Krishna Gokhale
7. (b) Swadeshi Movement
8. (b) Opening of Banaras Hindu University
9. (c) 1916
10. (c) Kheda Satyagraha
11. (d) Lord Irwin
12. (b) Jayaprakash Narayan
13. (a) *Harijan*
14. (b) Freedom to cultivate the crops of their choice.
15. (c) Restoration of Caliphate of Turkey
16. (a) enquiring the conditions in the colony.
17. (c) Gandhiji saw the Charkha as a symbol of human society.
18. (d) A series of 'Praja Mandals' were established in princely states.
19. (b) (ii), (iii) and (iv)
20. (a) (i) and (ii)
21. (a) Lord Irwin-Salt Satyagraha
22. (c) (i), (iii), (ii), (iv)
23. (b) II, IV, III and I
24. (d) Khilafat Movement
25. (b) Mahatma Gandhi
26. (d) Shaukat Ali
27. (a) USA
28. (a) Both A and R are true and R is the correct explanation of A
29. (a) Both A and R are true and R is the correct explanation of A
30. (a) Both A and R are true and R is the correct explanation of A
31. (b) Both A and R are true, but R is not the correct explanation of A
32. (a) Both A and R are true and R is the correct explanation of A
33. (b)
34. (b)
35. (d)
36. (c) Both (a) and (b)
37. (a) Dandi March
38. (a) broadening the base of nationalist struggle.

Subjective Questions

Short Answer Type Questions

1. India in which Gandhiji came back to in 1915 was rather different from the one that he had left in 1893. Substantiate the statement. Competency Based Que

Ans. India in which Gandhiji came back to in 1915 was rather different than the one that he had left in 1893 as

- India, though a colony of the British, was far more active in political sense in 1915.
- The Indian National Congress had branches in most major cities and towns.
- The Swadeshi Movement of 1905-07 had broadened its appeal amongst the middle classes. That movement introduced leaders like Bal Gangadhar Tilak of Maharashtra, Bipin Chandra Pal of Bengal and Lala Lajpat Rai of Punjab. Together, the three were known as 'Lal, Bal and Pal'. These leaders advocated militant opposition to the colonial rule.
- A group called the 'Moderates' preferred a more gradual and persuasive approach.

2. "The initiatives in Champaran, Ahmedabad and Kheda marked Gandhiji out as a nationalist with a deep sympathy for the poor". Substantiate the statement. Competency Based Que

Ans. The initiatives in Champaran, Ahmedabad and Kheda marked Gandhiji out as a nationalist with a deep sympathy for the poor. This statement can be justified in the following ways

- In 1917, Mahatma Gandhi was busy in seeking security of tenure for peasants as well as freedom to cultivate the crops of their choice.
- In 1918, he intervened in a labour dispute in Ahmedabad, demanding better working conditions for the textile mill workers.
- In the same year, he joined peasants in Kheda asking the state for the remission of taxes following the failure of their harvest, this movement was known as Kheda Satyagraha.

All these movements made him as the most popular nationalist leader who had a deep sympathy for the poor of our country.

3. What actions took place during the Non-cooperation Movement?

Ans. Following were some actions that took place during the Non-cooperation Movement

- Students boycotted schools and colleges run by the government.
- Lawyers refused to attend court.
- Strike was organised by working class in many towns and cities. There were 396 strikes in 1921 involving 600,000 workers and a loss of seven million workdays.
- Forest laws were violated by hill tribes in Northern Andhra.
- Farmers in Awadh refused to pay taxes.
- Peasants in Kumaun refused to carry loads for colonial officials.

4. What were the consequences of the Non-cooperation Movement?

Ans. The consequences of Non-cooperation movement were

- The most important consequence of the movement was it shooked the British Raj to its foundations for the first time since the Revolt of 1857. But the movement ended after the Chauri Chaura incident.
- In February 1922, a group of peasants attacked and torched a police station in the hamlet of Chauri Chaura, in the United Provinces (now, Uttar Pradesh and Uttaranchal). Several constables lost their lives in the incident. This forced Gandhiji to call off the movement altogether.
- Thousands of Indian were put in Jail. Gandhiji was arrested in March 1922 and charged with sedition. Gandhiji was sentenced for six years imprisonment.

5. 'Wherever Gandhiji went rumours spread of his miraculous powers.' Explain with examples. Competency Based Que

Ans. The peasants regarded Gandhiji as their *'Messiah'* and considered him to be having many beneficial and miraculous powers. Many rumours were in circulation at various places regarding his miraculous powers. These were

- At some places, the common masses came to believe that he had been sent by the king to remove their miseries and resolve their problems and he had such power that he could even reject the orders of all the officials.
- At some other places, it was affirmed that Gandhiji's power was greater than even the English king and it was claimed that with his arrival the colonial rulers would run away out of fear.
- In many villages, the rumour spread that the persons criticising Gandhiji got their houses mysteriously caved and their standing crops getting destroyed without any reason.
- Gandhiji became popular with many names such as 'Gandhi Baba', 'Gandhi Maharaj' or 'Mahatma' among the peasants. They considered him as their saviour and believed that only he could save them from the excessive rate of land revenue and the oppressive activities of British officials.

6. Gandhiji was a social reformer. Explain.

Or **Describe the role of Gandhiji as a social reformer.** CBSE 2024

Ans. Gandhiji is considered to be a social reformer due to the following reasons

- He believed that it is important to get rid of social evils like child marriage and untouchability in order to be worthy of freedom.
- There should be tolerance of one religion towards the other hence he emphasised on Hindu-Muslim harmony.
- He also believed that Indians should become self-reliant. He stressed on the significance of wearing *khadi* rather than mill made cloth imported from overseas.

7. Describe the role of Gandhiji as a saviour of the peasants of India.

Ans. India is a country of villagers and a large number of its population is engaged in farming. Gandhi knew that during the freedom struggle, his focus was to address the issues of farmers. His involvement in Indian politics began in Champaran when he successfully resolved the issues of farmers. He stood for farmers against excesses of the British government like high tax rates. Apart from this, there were certain mysterious rumours that surrounded the personality of Mahatma Gandhi. Many believed he had supernatural powers. Stories spread that those who spoke against Mahatma Gandhi faced natural calamities.

8. Discuss in brief about the Salt March and other forms of protests alongwith it.

Ans. On 12th March 1930, Gandhiji began Salt March by walking from his ashram at Sabarmati towards the ocean. He reached his destination three weeks later, making a fistful of salt as he did and thereby making himself a criminal in the eyes of the law. Meanwhile, similar salt marches were being conducted in other parts of the country.

Similar to Non-Cooperation, there were numerous other streams of protest. Across large parts of India, peasants opposed colonial forest laws that kept them and their cattle out of the woods in which they had once roamed freely. In some towns, factory workers went on strike while lawyers boycotted British courts and students refused to attend government-run educational institutions.

9. Assess the significance of Salt March in India's freedom struggle. How did the British Government react to it?

Ans. The salt satyagraha is a significant event in India's freedom struggle due to its widespread participation across India, symbolising unity and defiance against colonial rule. Salt Satyagraha drew international attention towards the Indian freedom struggle. It showed the power of non-violent resistance. The British realised that their rule will not last forever due to salt satygraha. So, they decided to share some powers with Indians.

Initially, the British government did not take the advance notice of Gandhi for the salt march seriously. The Home Department considered the Salt March as a drama. After the success of the Salt March, the British government arrested all protestors along with Gandhiji.

10. (a) **Explain the reasons of initiating the Non-cooperation Movement by Gandhiji.**

(b) **Explain the reasons that led to the Civil Disobedience Movement of 1930.** CBSE Term II 2022

Ans. (a) The Non-cooperation Movement was a movement organised by Mahatma Gandhi in an attempt to persuade the British government in India to grant self-government, or swaraj, to India. Gandhiji hoped that by joining Non-Cooperation with Khilafat, India's two major religious communities, Hindus and Muslims, could collectively bring an end to colonial rule. Factors that led to formation of this movement was the oppressive policies of Britishers such as the Rowlatt Act and the Jallianwala Bagh incident in Amritsar.

(b) Some of the reasons for launching Civil Disobedience was the formation and rejection of all white Simon Commission as well as the rejection of the demand for Dominion Status. The British government's lack of genuine interest in giving Dominion Status was evident to the nationalist leaders. In an emergency meeting held in Lahore in December 1929, the INC announced Purna Swaraj, or 'Complete Independence,' as the Congress's main objective. At Sabarmati Ashram in 1930, Gandhi was given full authority to start the Civil Disobedience Movement whenever and wherever he chose.

11. "Quit India Movement was genuinely a mass movement bringing into its ambit hundreds or thousands ordinary Indians". Analyse the statement. Competency Based Que

Ans. The 'Quit India Movement' against the British rule was a mass movement, that included hundreds or thousands of ordinary Indians. It especially energised the young who, were in very large numbers, left their colleges to join the Congress leaders suffering in jails.

After the failure of the Cripps Mission, Mahatma Gandhi launched his third major movement the 'Quit India' campaign which began in August 1942. Gandhiji was jailed at once, but the young activists organised strikes and acts of disruption all over the country.

On the other hand, there were socialist members of the Congress such as Jayaprakash Narayan who were active in the underground resistance. Independent governments were proclaimed in several districts such as Satara in the West and Medinipur in the East.

Long Answer Type Questions

1. Explain the ideas expressed by Gandhiji in his address at the time of opening of Banaras Hindu University in February 1916. Did he put his principles into practice? Give examples. Competency Based Que

Ans. Gandhi's first major public appearance in India was at the opening of Banaras Hindu University (BHU) in February 1916. When his turn came to speak, Gandhi charged the Indian elites with a lack of concern for the labouring poor. The opening of the BHU he said was, "certainly a most gorgeous show". But, he worried about the contrast between the richly bedecked noblemen present and "millions of the poor Indians who were absent."

He put his precepts into practice in the following ways

- Gandhiji favoured the opening of the BHU as it was an occasion for celebration, marking as it did the opening of a nationalist university, sustained by Indian money and initiative. But rather than adopt a tone of self-congratulation, Gandhi chose instead to remind those present of the peasants and workers who constituted a majority of the Indian population.
- By 1922, Gandhi had transformed Indian nationalism, thereby deeming the promise he made in his BHU speech of February 1916. It was no longer a movement of professionals and intellectuals, now hundreds of peasants, workers and artisans also participated in it. Many of them respected Gandhiji, referring to him as their Mahatma. The Indians appreciated the fact that he dressed like them, lived like them, and their language. Unlike other leaders, he did not stand apart from the common folk, but empathised and even identified with them.
- Mahatma Gandhi was released from prison in February 1924, and now devoted his attention to the promotion of home-spun cloth (*khadi*) and the abolition of untouchability. Gandhiji was as much a social reformer as he was a politician. He believed that in order to be worthy of freedom, Indians had to get rid of social evils such as child marriage and untouchability.

2. Examine the causes of the Non-Cooperation movement. Why did Gandhiji couple the Non-Cooperation Movement with the Khilafat Movement? How did people participate in the Non-cooperation movement?

Ans. Causes of Non-Cooperation Movement

After Rowlatt Satyagraha, Gandhiji truly became a national leader. Inspired by its success, Gandhiji called for a campaign of "Non-Cooperation" with British rule. Indians who wished colonialism to end were asked to stop attending schools, colleges and law courts, and not pay taxes. If non-cooperation was effectively carried out, said Gandhiji, India would win swaraj within a year.

Combining of Non-Cooperation with Khilafat Movement

To expand the struggle, Gandhiji collaborated with the Khilafat Movement. He believed that by integrating Non-Coopration with Khilafat, Hindus and Muslims could collectively bring an end to colonial rule.

Participation of people in Non-Cooperation Movement

Students stopped going to schools and colleges run by the government. Lawyers refused to attend court. The working class went on strike in many towns and cities. According to official figures, there were 396 strikes in 1921, involving 600,000 workers and a loss of seven million workdays.

Hill tribes in northern Andhra violated the forest laws. Farmers in Awadh did not pay taxes. Peasants in Kumaun refused to carry loads for colonial officials. These protest movements were sometimes carried out in defiance of the local nationalist leadership.

Peasants, workers and others interpreted and acted upon the call to 'non-cooperate' with colonial rule in ways that best suited their interests, rather than following the orders laid down from above.

3. How did 'Salt Satyagraha' of Gandhiji become the All-India campaign in opposition to the British? Explain with examples. Competency Based Que, CBSE 2023

Or **'The Salt March of 1930 was the first event that brought Mahatma Gandhi to world's attention.' Explain significance of this movement for Swaraj.**

Or **Explain the main events of the Dandi March. What is its significance in the history of the Indian National Movement?**

Or **"The salt march was the movement that brought Gandhiji to the world attention." Analyse the statement.** CBSE 2025

Ans. The Salt Satyagraha of Gandhiji became the All-India campaign in opposition to the British as it was a widespread movement. In January 1930, Mahatma Gandhi announced that he would lead a march to break one of the most widely disliked laws in British India. This was the first event that brought Mahatma Gandhi to world's attention. The Salt Law gave the state a monopoly in the manufacture and sale of salt.

The conditions in the country had become very favourable to launch a widespread movement against the British. The movement was started with famous Dandi March on 12th March, 1930. Gandhiji alongwith his 78 followers began his foot march from Sabarmati Ashram to Dandi, a village of seashore in Surat district, about 375 km away from Sabarmati Ashram.

The violation of Salt Law by Gandhiji was a signal of the beginning of Civil Disobedience Movement. Soon, this movement spread like wildfire through the length and breadth of the country.

Gandhiji's Dandi March occupies a very significant place in the history of the freedom struggle of India because of several reasons

- This march made Gandhiji a centre of attraction of the whole of the world. The European press and the American press published detailed accounts of the Salt March conducted by Gandhiji.

- Undoubtedly, it was the first national movement in which women participated in large numbers. Kamala Devi Chattopadhyay, the renowned socialist worker advised Gandhiji not to keep the movements limited to men-folk only. A large number of women alongwith Kamala Devi violated the salt and liquor laws and courted arrest collectively.
- As a result of the Salt Movement, the colonial rulers understood clearly that their authority was not going to remain permanent in India and now they will have to give some participation to the Indians in power.

4. Explain the reasons behind Gandhiji's decision to initiate the Salt Satyagraha and why this movement became a significant event. CBSE 2024

Ans. The reasons behind Gandhiji's decision to initiate Salt Satyagraha were as follows

(i) **Challenge to state monopoly in the manufacture and sale of salt** The British government had banned the manufacture and sale of salt. It also banned making salt for domestic use. The salt law established a monopoly of the state in the manufacture and sale of salt. Gandhiji wanted to challenge the state monopoly in the manufacture of salt with his salt satyagraha.

(ii) **Mobilisation of different sections of society** Salt was indispensable for every Indian. The salt law affected every section of society. People were forced to buy salt at a high price. The salt symbolised the British oppression. By choosing the issue of salt, Gandhiji aimed to mobilise widespread discontent against the British rule in different sections of society.

Significance of the Salt Satyagraha

(i) Salt Satyagraha drew international attention to India's freedom struggle, undermining British legitimacy. It created global sympathy for the Indian cause.

(ii) Salt Satygraha showcased the power of non-violent resistance. It also created ground for future mass movements.

(iii) There was a widespread participation of people in salt satyagraha. People from different sections of society like peasants, factory workers, lawyers, students, etc. participated in the movement.

(iv) Salt Satyagraha was the first nationalist activity in which women participated in large numbers. The socialist activist Kamaladevi Chattopadhyay had persuaded Gandhiji not to restrict the protests to men alone. Kamaladevi was herself one of numerous women who courted arrest by breaking the salt or liquor laws.

(v) It was the Salt March that forced upon the British the realisation that their Raj would not last forever and that they would have to share some power with the Indians.

5. Can you consider the Salt Satyagraha a successful movement? Justify your opinion.

Ans. Yes, I can consider Salt Satyagraha a successful movement. The success of Salt Satyagraha can be justified by the following points

(i) **International attention to the Indian freedom struggle** The Salt March was widely covered by the European and American press, such as American news magazine Time. It was the Salt March that first brought Mahatma Gandhi to world attention. It created a global sympathy for Indian independence.

(ii) **Power of non-violent resistance** Salt Satygraha showcased the power of non-violent resistance. It also created ground for future mass movements.

(iii) **Widespread participation** People widely participated in Salt Satyagraha from every section of society. Apart from the officially sanctioned nationalist campaign, there were numerous other streams of protest. Across large parts of India, peasants breached the hated colonial forest laws that kept them and their cattle out of the woods in which they had once roamed freely. In some towns, factory workers went on strike while lawyers boycotted British courts and students refused to attend government-run educational institutions.

(iv) **Participation of women** Salt Satyagraha was the first nationalist activity in which women participated in large numbers. The socialist activist Kamaladevi Chattopadhyay had persuaded Gandhiji not to restrict the protests to men alone. Kamaladevi was herself one of numerous women who courted arrest by breaking the salt or liquor laws.

(v) **Forced British for power sharing** It was the Salt March which forced upon the British the realisation that their Raj would not last forever, and that they would have to give some power to the Indians. To that end, the British government convened a series of 'Round Table Conferences' in London.

6. Explain why the 'Quit India Movement' was considered a mass movement. CBSE 2024

Or **"Quit India Movement challenged the British rule and shaped the course of Indian independence." Justify the statement.** CBSE 2024

Ans. The Quit India Movement is considered a mass movement for the following reasons

- It attracted widespread participation from people all over the country, transcending regional, cultural, and socio-economic boundaries.

- The movement's slogan 'Do or Die' resonated deeply with the masses, urging them into action against British colonial rule.
- It was a leaderless movement. All major leaders were in jail, including Gandhiji. Younger activists organised strikes and acts of destruction all over the country.
- The socialist members of the Congress, such as Jayaprakash Narayan were particularly active in the underground resistance. In several districts, such as Satara in the West and Medinipur in the East, independent governments were proclaimed. The British responded with much force, yet it took more than a year to suppress the rebellion.
- It included hundreds of thousands of ordinary Indians. It especially energised the young, who, in very large numbers, left their colleges to go to jail.
- The movement witnessed active involvement from various segments of society, including students, women, workers, and intellectuals, highlighting its broad-based support.
- The Quit India Movement's massive mobilisation and diverse participation earned it the status of a mass movement in the struggle for India's independence.

7. Gandhiji encouraged the communication of the nationalist message in mother tongue rather than in language of the ruler. Examine how he knitted the Non-cooperation Movement with his philosophy. **Competency Based Que**

Ans. **Communication of Nationalist Message in Mother Tongue**

Gandhiji believed that any struggle can be successful only when masses support it. For participating in any movement, masses must known the aim of movement.

In India, communication with public could be done easily through local languages or mother tongue. So, Gandhiji advised the nationalists to use mother tongue. He believed that mother tongue will play an important role in divided society and will help in bringing masses at single platform. Englishmen during these years believed that their language is superior than other language. Use of Indian language for communication by every Indian will change this notion and alongwith this, it will boost confidence in Indian citizen that their language has its own importance. Therefore, considering all above factors Gandhiji stressed on use of mother tongue.

Knitting the Non-Cooperation Movement

In Non-cooperation Movement, Gandhiji called for renunciation of all voluntary associations with the British and responded very optimistically to it. Students stopped going to the schools and colleges run by the government, lawyers refused to attend courts.

There were strikes in factories, mills and workshops, peasants stopped paying taxes, tribes violated forest laws, forests were burnt and liquor shops were picketed. Non-cooperation Movement was very successful as masses participated in it without any difference of caste, creed, religion, economic and education, status and language. Non-cooperation Movement led by Mahatma Gandhi played an important role in uniting different regions of India as country and promoted a sense of nationhood among the fellow citizens.

8. Analyse the impact of national movement in India from 1915 to 1931 on the Indian masses. **CBSE 2025**

Ans. The period from 1915 to 1931 was a transformative phase in India's national movement, significantly impacting the Indian masses. During this time, the freedom struggle shifted from being an elite-driven movement to a mass-based struggle, deeply influencing various sections of society.

(i) Rise of Mass Participation

- Mahatma Gandhi's arrival in 1915 marked a new era in the Indian national movement. His principles of non-violence and Satyagraha mobilised people from all walks of life.
- The Champaran (1917), Kheda (1918), and Ahmedabad (1918) movements demonstrated the power of non-violent resistance and engaged peasants and workers in the struggle.

(ii) Non-Cooperation Movement (1920-1922)

- The masses boycotted foreign goods, schools, and government jobs, demonstrating their willingness to resist colonial rule.
- Participation of students, women, and traders increased significantly. Khilafat agitation united Hindus and Muslims, creating communal harmony for a brief period.
- However, the movement was withdrawn after the Chauri Chaura incident (1922), leading to disappointment among many followers.

(iii) Peasants and Workers' Involvement

- The 1920s saw growing involvement of peasants through movements like the Bardoli Satyagraha (1928), where Sardar Patel led farmers against increased land revenue.
- Workers organised strikes and protests, as seen in Bombay and Madras, reflecting growing class consciousness against British exploitation.

(iv) Civil Disobedience Movement (1930-1931)

- The Dandi March (1930) symbolised mass resistance, as people across India broke the salt laws.
- Women, students, and rural populations actively participated, broadening the movement's reach.
- British repression through arrests and violence further united the masses in their demand for self-rule.

The period between 1915 and 1931 transformed the Indian masses into active participants in the national struggle. Gandhi's leadership, coupled with movements like Non-Cooperation and Civil Disobedience, awakened a sense of nationalism among diverse sections of society. The impact was irreversible, setting the stage for India's eventual independence.

9. Describe the different source from which we can reconstruct the political career of Gandhiji and the history of national movement.

Or **"There are many different kinds of sources from which we can reconstruct the political career of Gandhiji and the history of the Indian nationalist movement." Examine the statement.** CBSE 2024

Or **How have the different kinds of available sources helped the historians in reconstructing the political career of Gandhiji and the history of the national movement that was associated with it? Explain.**

Or **Explain the sources from which we can reconstruct the political career of Gandhiji and the history of the nationalist movement.**

Or **How do autobiographies, government records and newspapers help us in knowing about Gandhiji? Explain.**

Or **Examine the different kinds of sources from which political career of Gandhiji and the history of the national movement could be reconstructed.**

Ans. Refer to text on pg. no. 316 under Sources about Gandhiji heading.

10. In the history of nationalism, Gandhiji was often identified with the making of a nation. Describe his role in the freedom struggle of India. Competency Based Que

Ans. The period of 1919-1947 occupies a very important place in the history of the Indian freedom struggle. It was the third and the final phase of the Indian freedom struggle.

It was during this period that a great personality entered in the Indian political scene with several weapons like satyagraha, non-cooperation and civil disobedience, based on truth and non-violence and soon became the pioneer of the national movement.

This period is generally known as the 'Gandhian Era', Gandhiji transformed the nature of the national movement and it became a mass movement. His role in the freedom struggle of India was as follows

- Gandhiji transformed the national movement of the masses by following his new technique of struggle based on the principle of satyagraha and civil disobedience.
- Indian Nationalism witnessed a transformation in its nature with the active participation of Gandhiji in Indian National Movement.
- The mass appeal made by Gandhiji was not important. His qualities of efficient leadership made a remarkable contribution in making the base of Indian Nationalism wider.
- Due to Gandhiji's contribution, the provincial committees of the Congress were formed on linguistic regions and not on the artificial boundaries of the British India. These different ways contributed greatly to take nationalism to the distant corners of the country.
- The social groups previously untouched by nationalism, now became an important part of it because of contribution of Gandhiji. Thousands of peasants labourers and artisans started participating in the national movement.
- The common masses participated in the Civil Disobedience Movement significantly. In Delhi, some 1600 women picketed the liquor shop.
- Quit India Movement became genuinely a Mass Movement.
- Hundreds of thousands of ordinary Indians participated in it. Besides the common Indian, some very prosperous businessmen and industrialists too became supporters of the Indian National Congress. They came to realise it well that the favours enjoyed by their British competitors would come to them in free India. Some renowned industrialists such as GD Birla started supporting the national movement openly whereas some others began to do so tactly.

Thus, under Gandhiji, the national movement was transformed into a mass movement.

11. Analyse the role of Gandhiji after independence of India. CBSE 2025

Ans. Mahatma Gandhi played a crucial role even after India gained independence on 15th August, 1947. His efforts were focused on ensuring communal harmony, social upliftment, and guiding the newly independent nation towards peace and stability.

(i) Promoting Communal Harmony

- After independence, India witnessed large-scale communal violence, particularly during the partition. Gandhi undertook fasts and peace marches to restore harmony between Hindus and Muslims.
- His presence in riot-affected areas like Noakhali (in present-day Bangladesh) and Delhi helped in calming tensions.
- He opposed the idea of revenge and insisted on non-violence as the only way forward for a united India.

(ii) Opposition to Partition Violence

- Gandhi was deeply saddened by the partition of India and Pakistan. He worked tirelessly to minimize the impact of violence.
- His fasts in Delhi in January 1948 were aimed at persuading both Hindus and Muslims to coexist peacefully.

(iii) Ensuring Pakistan Received Its Due Share

- A major controversy arose when India withheld ₹ 55 crore, which was owed to Pakistan as part of the partition agreement.
- Gandhi insisted on the release of the funds, believing it was India's moral responsibility. His stance angered radical elements, ultimately leading to his assassination.

(iv) Focus on Village Development and Social Reforms

- Gandhi continued advocating for self-reliant villages, promoting khadi, rural employment, and removal of untouchability.
- He emphasized 'Sarvodaya' (welfare of all), stressing that independence should benefit the poorest sections of society.

(v) His Last Days and Assassination

- Despite the challenges, Gandhi remained committed to his principles of peace and non-violence.
- On January 30, 1948, he was assassinated by Nathuram Godse, who blamed him for appeasing Muslims and supporting Pakistan.

12. Examine the contribution of Mahatma Gandhi towards nation-building after the independence of India. **CBSE 2024**

Ans. Mahatma Gandhi's contribution to nation-building after India's independence was profound and wide-reaching. His efforts focused on promoting unity, and ensuring social and political justice. Some of his main contributions are discussed below

- Gandhiji worked to promote harmony among India's diverse religious communities. He appealed to Hindus, Muslims, and Sikhs to live in peace, especially during the tumultuous period of partition, which saw violence and mass displacement.
- Gandhi was a strong advocate for the rights of Harijans (the untouchables). He sought to improve their social and economic status and fought against their discrimination. He campaigned for their inclusion in society and emphasised their dignity as human beings, encouraging social reforms to end untouchability.
- Gandhi envisioned India as a democratic secular state where people of all faiths and backgrounds would have equal rights and opportunities. He promoted religious tolerance and the separation of religion from the state, which laid the foundation for India's secular Constitution.
- Gandhi strongly believed that every citizen should enjoy full rights, regardless of caste, creed, or religion. He promoted political freedom, social equality, and economic justice as essential components of a democratic society.
- After partition, Gandhi visited riot-affected areas like Bengal and Punjab, where he worked to calm tensions and promote peace. His personal intervention helped in reducing violence and advocating for communal harmony during a time of great turmoil.

13. Explain the activities of the national movement in India during 1905 to 1907. **CBSE 2024**

Ans. The period from 1905 to 1907 was crucial in the history of the Indian National Movement.

The activities during this period were

- This period saw growing political consciousness among the Indian population, especially among the middle classes and educated elites.
- The Indian National Congress (INC) had expanded its presence across the country, with numerous branches in different towns and cities. This growth helped in mobilising people from various regions and communities, creating a more widespread movement for political rights and self-governance.
- The Swadeshi Movement in response to the partition of Bengal by the British, was a significant phase of the national movement. This movement called for the boycott of British goods and the promotion of Indian-made products. It gained popularity, especially among the middle classes, who were inspired to take part in protests, boycotts, and the promotion of Indian industries.
- The Swadeshi Movement introduced important leaders such as Lala Lajpat Rai, Bal Gangadhar Tilak, and Bipin Chandra Pal. These leaders, often referred to as "Lal, Bal, Pal", became symbols of militant opposition to British rule. They advocated for a more assertive stance against colonial rule and called for self-rule (Swaraj) for India.
- **All India Character of the Movement** Despite the geographical and cultural differences between their native provinces, the leaders of the Swadeshi Movement presented an all-India character to the struggle. They united people from various regions and backgrounds under the common cause of national independence and self-governance.

Source Based Questions

Read the sources given below and answer the following questions.

1. Mahatma Gandhi was profoundly critical of the modern age in which machines enslaved humans and displaced labour. He saw the *charkha* as a symbol of a human society that would not glorify machines and technology.

The spinning wheel, moreover, could provide the poor with supplementary income and make them self-reliant. What I object to, is the craze for machinery as such. The craze is for what they call labour-saving machinery.

Men go on "saving labour", till thousands are without work and thrown on the open streets to die of starvation. I want to save time and labour, not for a fraction of mankind, but for all; I want the concentration of wealth, not in the hands of few, but in the hands of all.

Young India, 13th November, 1924

Khaddar does not seek to destroy all machinery but it does regulate its use and check its weedy growth. It uses machinery for the service of the poorest in their own cottages. The wheel is itself an exquisite piece of machinery. ***Young India, 17th March, 1927***

(i) Why *charkha* was given importance by Gandhiji?
(ii) How would spinning wheel help poor?
(iii) How will machines impact the poor?

Or **(i) Why was *charkha* considered sacred by Gandhiji?**
(ii) Why did Gandhiji give importance to Khaddar?
(iii) How had Gandhiji related *charkha* with the spirit of service and foundation of sound village life? **CBSE Term II 2022**

Or **(i) Why was Gandhiji critical of machines ?**
(ii) Why was wheel considered as an exquisite piece of machinery ? **CBSE 2024**
(iii) How did Gandhiji glorify charkha ?

Ans. (i) *Charkha* was symbolised as a symbol of human society. It will diminish the glory of machines and technology, so it was given importance by Gandhiji.

(ii) Gandhiji believed that the spinning wheel could provide the poor with supplementary income and make them self-reliant.

(iii) Gandhiji believed that the poor will be thrown out of their jobs if the machines were introduced. It will leave many people without jobs and increased starvation.

Or (i) According to Gandhiji, *charkha* was sacred because he considered the *charkha* as a symbol of a human society that would not glorify machines and technology. The spinning wheel or the *charkha* provided the poor with supplementary income and made them self-reliant.

(ii) According to Gandhiji, Khaddar is important because, it does not seek to destroy all machinery but it does regulate its use and check its growth. It uses machinery for the service of the poorest in their own cottages. The wheel is itself an exquisite piece of machine.

(iii) Mahatma Gandhi was profoundly critical of the modern age in which machines enslaved humans and displaced labour. Avoiding machines and adapting *charkha* would instill spirit of service among Indians. According to him, the spinning wheel could provide the poor with supplementary income and make them self-reliant thus, leading to foundation of sound and self-reliant village life.

Or (i) Gandhi was critical of machines because he thought machines enslaved human beings and thus human labour has been displaced.

(ii) The wheel was considered an exquisite piece of machinery for many reasons

- **Symbol of Society** It represented human society, emphasising self-reliance and manual craftsmanship.
- **Supplementary Income** The charkha (wheel) could provide poor people with extra income by enabling them to spin cotton and sell it.
- **Self-Reliance** It promoted self-reliance by allowing people to make their own clothes (khadi), reducing dependency on British imports and fostering economic independence.

(iii) Gandhiji glorified the charkha in the following ways

- He promoted the charkha as a tool for people to become self-reliant by producing their own cloth (khadi).
- Gandhi saw the charkha as essential for achieving swaraj (self-rule) and economic independence.
- He encouraged Indians to boycott English products and use indigenous goods like khadi, spun using the charkha.
- Gandhi supported the growth of cottage industries through the widespread use of the charkha in homes.

2. Why the Salt Satyagraha?

Why was salt the symbol of protest? This is what Mahatma Gandhi wrote :

The volume of information being gained daily shows how wickedly the salt tax has been designed. In order to prevent the use of salt that has not paid the tax which is at times even fourteen times its value, the government destroys the salt it cannot sell profitably.

Thus it taxes the nation's vital necessity; it prevents the public from manufacturing it and destroys what nature manufactures without effort.

No adjective is strong enough for characterising this wicked dog-in-the-manager policy. From various sources I hear tales of such wanton destruction of the nation's property in all parts of India. Maunds if not tons of salt are said to be destroyed on the Konkan coast. The same tale comes from Dandi.

Wherever there is likelihood of natural salt being taken away by the people living in the neighbourhood of such areas for their personal use, salt officers are posted for the sole purpose of carrying on destruction.

Thus valuable national property is destroyed at national expense and salt taken out of the mouths of the people.

The salt monopoly is thus a fourfold curse. It deprives the people of a valuable easy village industry, involves wanton destruction of property that nature produces in abundance, the destruction itself means more national expenditure, and fourthly to crown this folly, an unheard of tax of more than 1,000 per cent is exacted from a starving people. This tax has remained so long because of the apathy of the general public. Now that it is sufficiently roused, the tax has to go. How soon it will be abolished upon the strength of the people.

(i) Mention one reason, why salt monopoly introduced by the British was considered as a curse by the Indians?

(ii) How did Gandhiji illustrate his tactical wisdom with regard to salt monopoly?

(iii) Explain the significance of Gandhiji's challenge of salt protest.

Or **(i) What does Gandhi's reference to the "power of peace and non-violence" suggest about his strategic approach to resistance against British colonial rule?**

(ii) What parallels can be drawn between Gandhi's critique of the salt tax and broader movements for social justice and human rights?

(iii) How does Gandhi's reference to the destruction of salt by the government shed light on the broader implications of colonial policies on India's natural resources? **CBSE SQP 2024**

Ans. (i) Indians considered salt monopoly introduced by the British as a curse because it prevented them from manufacturing salt.

(ii) Gandhiji said that as salt is very inevitable for everyone so if any national movement is carried taking salt as medium of protest, it will result in large scale participation of masses.

(iii) As the salt was inevitable for everyone and salt law caused deep resentment, so people responded very enthusiastically to call of march. People's participation was overwhelming and at many places parallel marches were undertaken and salt were made.

Or (i) Gandhi's mention of the "power of peace and non-violence" indicates his belief in the efficacy of non-violent resistance to challenge and ultimately overcome British colonial oppression.

(ii) Gandhi's critique of the salt tax parallels broader social justice movements by exposing systemic injustices and challenging oppressive power structures, illustrating the fight for equality and human rights.

(iii) Gandhi's reference to the destruction of salt by the government shed light on the broader implications of colonial policies on India's natural resources in the following ways

- **Colonial Exploitation** Gandhi's reference highlights how colonial policies prioritised profit over the well-being of Indians by destroying salt, a crucial resource, to control and exploit India's natural wealth.
- **Impact on Development** The destruction of resources like salt exacerbated socio-economic inequalities and stifled local development, as colonial interests prioritised their own gain over India's economic progress and self-sufficiency.

3. "Tomorrow we shall break the Salt Tax Law"

On 5th April, 1930, Mahatma Gandhi spoke at Dandi:

When I left Sabarmati with my companions for this seaside hamlet of Dandi, I was not certain in my mind that we would be allowed to reach this place. Even while I was at Sabarmati there was a rumour that I might be arrested. I had thought that the government might perhaps let my party come as far as Dandi, but not me certainly.

If someone says that this betrays imperfect faith on my part, I shall not deny the charge. That I have reached here is in no small measure due to the power of peace and non-violence: that power is universally felt. The government may, if it wishes, congratulate itself on acting as it has done, for it could have arrested every one of us. In saying that it did not have the courage to arrest this army of peace, we praise it. It felt ashamed to arrest such an army.

He is a civilised man who feels ashamed to do anything which his neighbours would disapprove. The government deserves to be congratulated on not arresting us, even if it desisted only from fear of world opinion. Tomorrow we shall break the salt tax law. Whether the government will tolerate that is a different question. It may not tolerate it, but it deserves congratulations on the patience and forbearance it has displayed in regard to this party...

What if I and all the eminent leaders in Gujarat and in the rest of the country are arrested? This movement is based on the faith that when a whole nation is roused and on the march no leader is necessary.

(i) Why did Gandhiji start the Dandi March?

(ii) Why was the Salt March notable?

(iii) "The power of peace and non-violence are universally felt". Why did Gandhiji said so?

Ans. (i) He started Dandi March to break the salt law. Salt law gave British government monopoly in manufacture and sale of salt.

The state monopoly was very popular and by breaking the salt law Gandhiji hoped to mobilise a wider discontent against British rule.

(ii) Salt March was notable because for first time European and American press started following Indian National Movement and for the very first time large number of women participated in the movement.

(iii) Gandhiji believed that he had come to Dandi along with large number of fellow Indians to break salt law only because of peace and non-violence. British did not arrested them because it lacked the courage to arrest army of peace or may be just because of fear of world opinion. Thus, Gandhiji said that "the power of peace and non-violence are universally felt."

4. Ambedkar on Separate Electorates

In response to Mahatma Gandhi's opposition to the demand for separate electorates for the Depressed Classes, Ambedkar wrote:

Here is a class which is undoubtedly not in a position to sustain itself in the struggle for existence. The religion, to which they are tied, instead of providing them an honourable place, brands them as lepers, not fit for ordinary intercourse. Economically, it is a class entirely dependent upon the high-caste Hindus for earning its daily bread with no independent way of living open to it.

Nor are all ways closed by reason of the social prejudices of the Hindus but there is a definite attempt all through our Hindu Society to bolt every possible door so as not to allow the Depressed Classes any opportunity to rise in the scale of life.

In these circumstances, it would be granted by all fairminded persons that as the only path for a community so handicapped to succeed in the struggle for life against organised tyranny, some share of political power in order that it may protect itself is a paramount necessity.

(i) **Why Mahatma Gandhi was against the separate electorates?**

(ii) **How was the condition of Depressed classes according to Ambedkar?**

(iii) **What was the demand of Ambedkar for Depressed Classes?**

Ans. (i) Gandhi believed that separate electorate would permanently segregate the depressed classes from the mainstream of the society, so, he was against the separate electorates.

(ii) According to Dr BR Ambedkar, the depressed classes were not in a position to sustain themselves. They do not have an honourable place in society. They were totally depended on the upper castes for their living.

(iii) Ambedkar demanded share in political power for Depressed Classes to protect them from organised oppression.

Map Based Questions

1. On the outline map of India three centres related to the Indian National movement have been marked as A, B, C and D. Identify them and write their correct names on the lines drawn near them. **CBSE 2024**

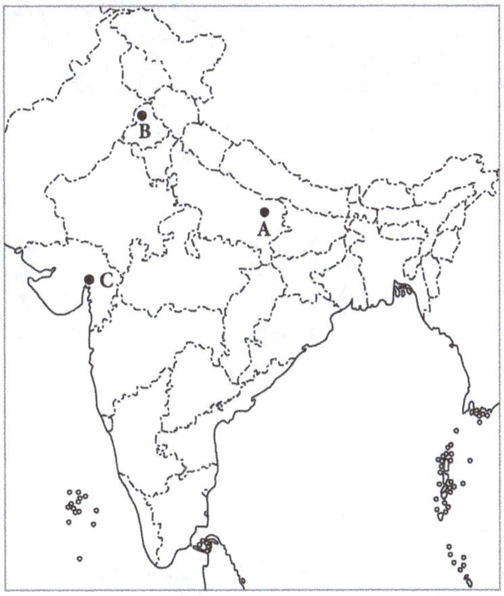

Ans.

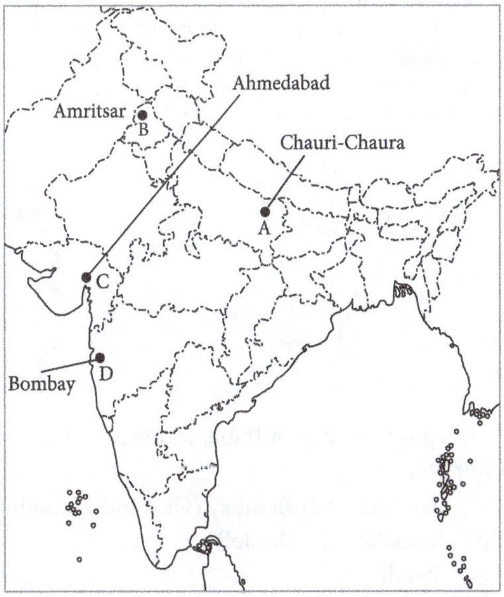

2. On the outline map of India three places related to the Indian National Movement have been marked as A, B and C. Identify them and write their correct names on the lines drawn near them.

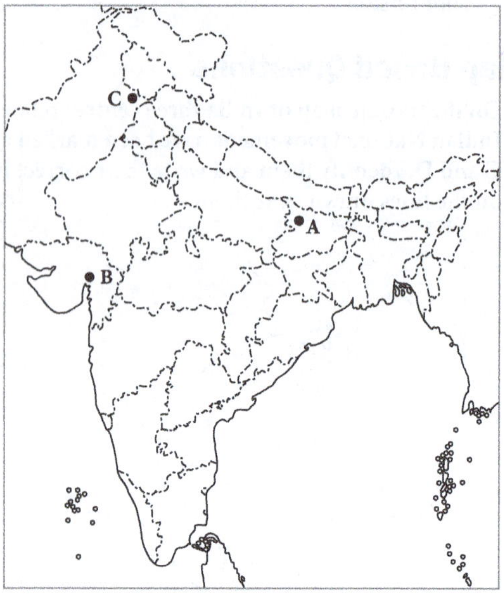

Ans.

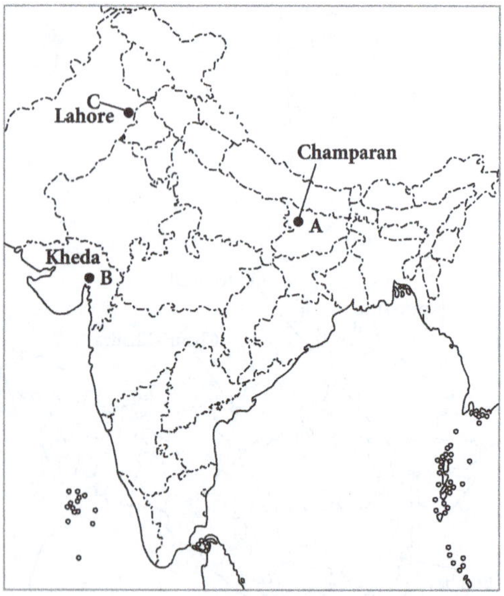

3 On the political map of India, locate and label the following.

(i) Banaras (ii) Bombay (Quit India Resolution)
(iii) Karachi (iv) Bardoli
(v) Dandi

Ans.

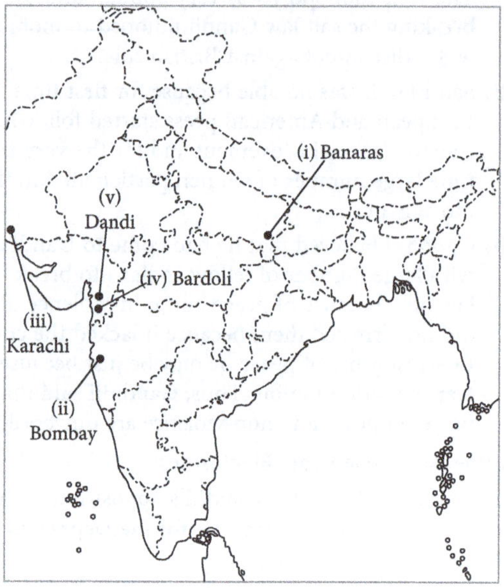

4. (i) The state where Gandhiji withdrew Non-cooperation Movement.
(ii) The state where Gandhiji started satyagraha for the Kheda peasants.
(iii) The place where Gandhiji broke the Salt law.

CBSE Term II 2022

Ans.

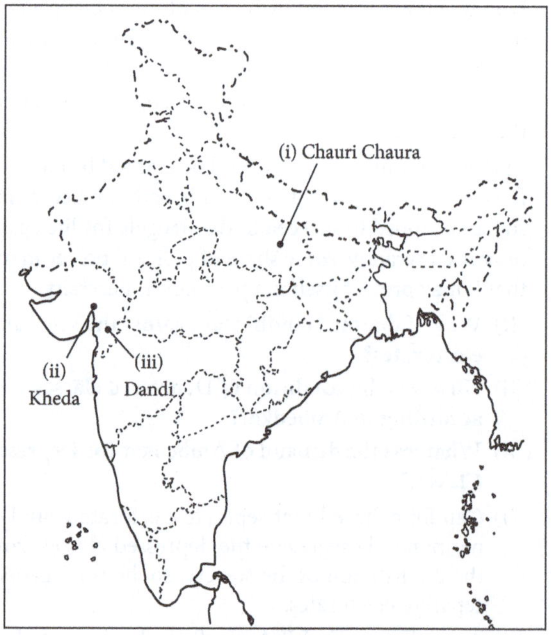

SELF ASSESSMENT TEST

Objective Type Questions

1. According to Louis Fischer, what was a key characteristic of the Non-Cooperation Movement?
   (a) It was violent but effective.
   (b) It was peaceful yet impactful.
   (c) It lacked discipline and organisation.
   (d) It was only a temporary movement with no lasting effects.
2. In which of these, Gandhiji published the letters written to him by others?
   (a) Kesari (b) Young India
   (c) Harijan (d) Time
3. Kamladevi Chattopadhyay was involved in which movement?
   (a) Quit India Movement (b) Non-cooperation Movement
   (c) Individual Satyagraha (d) Salt Satyagraha
4. Second World War broke out in the year ....
   (a) 1939 (b) 1945
   (c) 1914 (d) 1918
5. Match the Following.

	List I		List II
A.	Purna Swaraj adopted as a goal of Congress	1.	London
B.	Round Table Conference	2.	Bombay
C.	Mahatma Gandhi on the eve of Independence	3.	Lahore
D.	Launch of Quit India Movement	4.	Calcutta

Codes

	A	B	C	D		A	B	C	D
(a)	1	2	3	4	(b)	2	3	4	1
(c)	3	1	4	2	(d)	4	3	1	2

Short Answer Type Questions

6. How was India of 1893 different from India of 1915 when Gandhiji came back from abroad? Justify your opinion.
7. Discuss the nationalist activities of Mahatma Gandhi from 1917 to till the launch of Non-Cooperation Movement.
8. Besides a national leader Gandhiji was also a social reformer. Explain with the help of examples.

Long Answer Type Questions

9. Examine the contribution of Mahatma Gandhi in the Indian freedom struggle with the help of the Non-Cooperation Movement and Salt Satyagraha.
10. Do you agree with this view that Mahatma Gandhi was a people's leader? Substantiate your opinion with the help of examples.

12 CHAPTER

This chapter deals with the history that lies beside framing the Constitution. It also explores views of members of the Constituent Assembly on issues like minorities, division of power between the centre and states, language, etc.

YOUR STUDY GOALS

12.1 Constitution of India
12.2 The Vision of the Constitution
12.3 Defining Rights
12.4 The Powers of the State
12.5 The Language of the Nation

YOUR PRACTICE GOALS

- Objective Type Questions (35 Qs ; MCQs, A-R, Matching, Picture Based)
- Descriptive Type Questions (14 SAs, 6 LAs)
- Source Based Questions (6 Qs)

Framing the Constitution

(The Beginning of a New Era)

12.1 Constitution of India

- The Constitution of India came into effect on **26th January, 1950**. It is the longest Constitution in the world. It is lengthy and complex due to India's vast size and diverse population.
- To keep the country together, the Constitution was framed in an elaborative and careful way as the country was divided on various issues.
- The Indian Constitution was framed between December 1946 and November 1949.
- The drafts were discussed clause by clause in the Constituent Assembly of India. The Assembly had 11 sessions which continued for 165 days.
- There were various committees and sub-committees which worked for revision and refining the drafts.
- The objective of framing the Constitution was to unite Indians from various classes, castes and communities, while promoting democratic institutions to eliminate hierarchy and differences.

Events before Making of the Constitution

- Before the making of the Constitution, movements like Quit India struggle of 1942, Subhas Chandra Bose's struggle for free India and uprising of the Royal Indian Navy (1946) in Bombay were popular among people. One similar feature of all these uprisings was **Hindu-Muslim Unity**.

- Political parties like Congress and Muslim League failed to bring religious harmony between Hindus and Muslims in later years.
- With the beginning of the Great Calcutta Killings of August 1946, violence continued across Northern and Eastern India for almost a year.
- Partition left Muslims in India and Hindus and Sikhs in Pakistan with two choices- threat of sudden death or losing their long-standing connections to their homes and communities. Muslims moved to East and West Pakistan and Hindus and Sikhs moved to West Bengal and the Eastern half of the Punjab.
- At the time of independence, the constitutional status of princely states was unclear. These included around one-third of the area of the subcontinent, controlled by nawabs and maharajas who were loyal to the British Crown, but were mostly free to govern their territories as they wished.

The Making of the Constituent Assembly

- The election of the assembly was held in 1946. The members of the assembly were elected by the members of **Provincial Legislatures** instead on the basis of universal franchise.
- The Muslim League boycotted the Constituent Assembly and demanded Pakistan with a separate Constitution. As a result, 82% of the members of the Constituent Assembly were also members of the Congress.
- Some members of Congress supported socialism whereas some supported landlordism. Few of them were close to communal parties while others aimed to exclude religion from the public sphere.

▲ *The Constituent Assembly in Session*

Public Opinions in Constituent Assembly

- Public opinions also influenced the discussions within the Constituent Assembly. Public opinion was given importance to create a sense of collective participation.
- Debates of Assembly members were reported in newspapers and the proposals were publicly debated.
- There were different opinions on different issues. These were
  - The linguistic minorities wanted to protect their mother tongue.
  - Religious minorities asked for special safeguards.
  - Lower caste groups demanded an end to ill-treatment by upper-caste people and reservation of seats in government bodies.

The Dominant Voices of Assembly

- The Constituent Assembly had 300 members, of which role of 6 members was particularly important. These members included Jawaharlal Nehru, Vallabh Bhai Patel, Rajendra Prasad, who were representatives of the Congress and B.R. Ambedkar, K.M. Munshi and Alladi Krishnaswamy Aiyar.
- Jawaharlal Nehru introduced the Objectives Resolution. He also proposed the design of the National Flag of India to be a 'horizontal tricolour of saffron, white and dark green in equal proportion', with a wheel in navy blue at the centre.
- Vallabh Bhai Patel contributed in drafting several reports and in bringing divergent views together.
- As President of the Assembly, Rajendra Prasad guided discussions productively and ensured all members had a chance to speak.
- B.R. Ambedkar, the lawyer and economist, joined the Union Cabinet as Law Minister after Independence. He was the Chairman of the Drafting Committee of the Constitution. He guided the Draft Constitution through the assembly over three years. The discussions were recorded and published in 11 large volumes.

- K.M. Munshi from Gujarat and Alladi Krishnaswamy Aiyar from Madras, were the lawyers who contributed in drafting of the Constitution.
- B.N. Rau was the Constitutional Advisor to the Government of India. He prepared a series of background papers based on a close study of the political systems of other countries.
- S.N. Mukherjee was the Chief Draughtsman who translated complex proposals into clear legal language.

Quick Test 1

1 What was a common feature of the Quit India struggle, Subhas Chandra Bose's efforts and the Royal Indian Navy uprising?
2 How were the members of the Constituent Assembly elected?
3 What percentage of the members of the Constituent Assembly were also members of the Congress?
4 What demand did linguistic minorities make during the discussions?
5 Which two lawyers contributed to the drafting of the Constitution?

12.2 The Vision of the Constitution

- On **13th December, 1946**, Jawaharlal Nehru introduced the 'Objectives Resolution' in the Constituent Assembly. It defined the ideals of the Constitution of Independent India. It also provided the structure for the process of making the Constitution.
- The Objective Resolution proclaimed India to be an Independent, Sovereign and Republic country. It guaranteed its citizens justice, equality and freedom. It assured adequate safeguards for minorities, backward and tribal areas, depressed and Other Backwards Classes.
- Nehru suggested that the Indian Constitution should have a combination of liberal ideas of democracy and socialist ideas of economic justice.

The Will of the People

- According to **Somnath Lahiri**, a Communist member, the discussions in the Constituent Assembly were influenced by the British as they were still in India.
- He argued that despite Jawaharlal Nehru leading the interim government, it was still directed by the British government.

Ideals Influencing the Constituent Assembly

- The Constituent Assembly aimed to represent the aspirations of participants of the independence movement.
- The ideals of democracy, equality and justice were linked with social struggles in India since the nineteenth century.
- The social reformers opposed child marriage and advocated widow remarriage, seeking social justice.
- **Swami Vivekananda** worked to reform Hinduism and make religions more just.
- **Jyotiba Phule** in Maharashtra highlighted the suffering of the depressed castes, while Communists and Socialists organised workers and peasants for economic and social justice.
- The national movement fought against an oppressive government, focusing on democracy, justice, citizens' rights and equality.

Constitutional Reforms by British Government

- The acts passed in 1909, 1919 and 1935 increased opportunities for Indian participation in provincial governments.
- The executive was made partly responsible to the Provincial Legislature in 1919 and entirely responsible under the Government of India Act of 1935.
- Under the 1935 Act, elections were held in 1937, in which the Congress came to power in 8 out of the 11 provinces.
- The legislatures which were elected as per the provision of the 1935 Act, worked within the framework of colonial rule. These legislatures were not responsible to Indian people but were responsible to the Governor appointed by the British.

12.3 Defining Rights

Defining the rights was an important issue before the Constituent Assembly. There were different groups and they expressed their will in different ways and made different demands.

The Problem with Separate Electorates

- On 27th August, 1947, **B. Pocker Bahadur** from Madras appealed to continue with the separate electorate. He emphasised that minorities should get fair representation in the political system, so that they can raise their voice.
- The demand for separate electorates angered and upset the nationalists. **R.V. Dhulekar** believed that the British used these safeguards to mislead minorities.
- According to **Sardar Patel**, separate electorates was a poison that has entered the political body of the country.
- According to **Govind Ballabh Pant**, the demand for separate electorates was not only harmful for the nation but also for the minorities. He also believed that it will permanently isolate the minorities. It will also increase their vulnerability and deprive them of any effective role in the government.
- The idea of separate electorates was also not supported by all Muslims. **Begum Aizaas Rasul** felt that separate electorates were self-destructive as they isolated the minorities from the majority.
- By 1949, most Muslim members of the Constituent Assembly were against the idea of separate electorates. They thought that Muslims must take active part in the democratic process to have a decisive role in the political system.

Issue of Defining Minorities

- The Constituent Asembly discussed the important issue of minorities. It included who should be considered a minority and on what basis.
- **N.G. Ranga**, a socialist, wanted to interpret the term minorities in economic terms. According to him, the real minorities were the poor and the downtrodden.

Views of Jaipal Singh on Tribals

- The tribals were represented in the Assembly by **Jaipal Singh**. He talked about the protection of tribes and ensuring conditions that would bring tribes up to the level of the general population.
- He argued that tribes were displaced from their land, deprived of their forests and pastures, and were forced to settle at a new place. Society did not treat them equally due to their primitiveness and backwardness.
- He demanded reservation of seats in the legislature instead of separate electorates, to allow tribals to represent themselves.

Issue of Rights of Depressed Caste

- **B.R. Ambedkar** had demanded separate electorates for the Depressed Castes during the National Movement. But Gandhiji opposed it and there was a long debate on the issue of the Depressed Caste's rights.
- The Depressed Castes believed that social norms and the moral values of caste society were the main reasons for their disabilities.
- According to **J. Nagappa** from Madras, the Depressed Castes suffered not due to their small number (constituting only 20 to 25 percent of total population) but due to systematic marginalisation[1] which continued for thousands of years.
- After the partition violence, Ambedkar gave up the demand for separate electorates.
- Finally, the Constituent Assembly recommended that
  - Untouchability should be abolished.
  - Hindu temples to be opened to all castes.
  - Seats and jobs should be reserved for the lowest castes, respectively in legislatures and government offices.

Quick Test 2

1. Who highlighted the suffering of the Depressed Castes in Maharashtra?
2. In which year did the executive become partly responsible to the Provincial Legislature?
3. Who expressed concerns about the concept of separate electorates among Muslims?
4. How did NG Ranga interpret the term minorities?
5. Which nationalist leader opposed Ambedkar's demand for separate electorates?

12.4 The Powers of the State

The Draft Constitution provided three lists of subjects for distribution of power

(i) **Union List** Subjects under this list were controlled by the Central Government. The Union Government also had control over minerals and key industries. Moreover, under Article 356, the Centre had powers to take over a state administration on the recommendation of the Governor.

(ii) **State List** Subjects under the state list were controlled by the State Government.

(iii) **Concurrent List** Subjects covered under this list were controlled by both the Centre and the State, but the highest authority was given to the Centre.

Provision of Fiscal Federalism

- In the case of some taxes such as custom duties and company taxes, all the revenue was kept by the central government.
- For taxes like income tax and excise duties, the revenue was shared between the central government and the states. However, revenue from estate duties was entirely allocated to the states.
- Some taxes such as land and property taxes, sales tax and tax on bottled liquor could be levied and collected by the states on their own.

---

1 Systematic Marginalisation System where groups of people are systematically denied access to opportunities, resources, and rights that are available to the dominant cultural group.

Views of K. Santhanam

- K. Santhanam from Madras, defended the rights of the states. He felt that the Centre would not be able to function properly if it was overburdened. The Centre would be stronger if some of its functions were transferred to the States.
- The fiscal provisions would harm the states since most taxes, except land revenue, had been made to preserve the Centre. Therefore, states could not carry out any development projects due to lack of finances.

The Need of a Strong Centre

- There were several members in the Constituent Assembly who supported a strong Centre as they believed that a strong Centre could stop communal violence[2].
- BR Ambedkar wanted a strong and united Centre, stronger than the Centre under the Government of India Act of 1935.
- **Gopalaswami Ayyangar** and **Balakrishna Sharma** also emphasised the need for a strong centre. They believed that a strong Centre could plan for the well-being of the country, mobilise the available economic resources, establish a proper administration, and defend the country against foreign aggression.
- There were also many leaders who were against the strong centre. They demanded that there should be fewer items in the concurrent and union list.

12.5 The Language of the Nation

Choosing the language of the nation was also an important issue in the Constituent Assembly which was debated over many months.

Language Adopted by the Congress

- By the 1930s, the Congress had accepted **Hindustani** to be the national language which was a mix of Hindi and Urdu. It was popular among many people in India and was a rich language shaped by the interaction of various cultures.
- Hindustani has incorporated words and terms from different sources over the years. Therefore it was understood by people from various regions.
- The Hindustani language started changing from the end of the nineteenth century. As communal conflicts increased, Hindi began to be influenced by Sanskrit, while Urdu was influenced by Persian.

Gandhi's Views Regarding the Language

- Gandhiji felt that everyone should use a language which could be understood easily by all people. Hence, he also wanted to make Hindustani the language of the nation.
- He believed that Hindustani is a **multi-cultural** language. It could unify Hindus and Muslims, and people of the North and the South.

Emphasis on the Need for Hindi

- **R.V. Dhulekar**, a Congressman from the United Provinces, made a strong appeal to make Hindi as the language of Constitution-making.
- He wanted Hindi to be declared as a National Language and not only an Official Language.

2 Communal violence A type of violence that occurs between groups of people based on their ethnicity or communal identity.

Decision of Language Committee

By 1949, the Language Committee of the Constituent Assembly submitted its report and recommended a compromise formula to resolve the deadlock between supporters of Hindi as the national language and its opposers.

- The Committee decided that Hindi in the Devanagari script would be the official language. English would be continued for all official purposes for the first fifteen years.
- Each province was allowed to choose one of the regional languages for official work within the province.

The Fear of Domination

- **Shrimati G. Durgabai** from Madras informed the House that there was a strong opposition of Hindi in the South. She had accepted Hindustani as the language of the people. But she felt that any attempt to take out words from Urdu and other regional languages will certainly create anxiety and fear amongst different language groups.
- **Shri Shankarrao Deo**, a Congress member from Bombay had also accepted Hindustani as a language of the nation but warned that to gain his full support for Hindi, they should not take actions that raises his suspicions or fears.
- **T.A. Ramalingam Chettiar** from Madras emphasised that it is necessary to first address the concerns of the people before pushing Hindi aggressively.

Features of the Constitution

- The Constitution provides the **Right to Vote** to all adult Indians. However, in other democratic countries like the United States and the United Kingdom, the Right to Vote was given gradually, first to only property-owning men. Later to educated men and then to working-class men and eventually to women.
- The Constitution emphasised on **secularism**. This was reflected in the **Fundamental Rights**, including Freedom of Religion (Articles 25-28), Cultural and Educational Rights (Articles 29, 30) and Right to Equality (Articles 14, 16, 17).
- The state treated all religions equally and allowed them to maintain charitable institutions. The State separated itself from religious communities by banning compulsory religious education in state schools. It also made religious discrimination in employment illegal. However, it allowed for social reform within communities to handle the issues like untouchability and changes in personal law.

Conclusion

The Constituent Assembly debates reveal the conflicting voices and demands involved in framing the Constitution. They reflect the ideals and principles the Constitution's makers considered. However, these ideals were often adjusted to suit the context. Over the three years of debates, some members revised their views based on arguments from others, while others changed their positions in response to surrounding events.

Quick Test 3

1. Which taxes can be levied and collected solely by the states?
2. Which members of the Constituent Assembly advocated for a strong and United Centre?
3. Hindustani is a mix of which two languages?
4. How long would English be used for official purposes after the 1949 decision?
5. Which articles of the Indian Constitution contain the Freedom of Religion?

TIMELINE

1945	
26 July	Labour Government comes into power in Britain
December-January	General Elections in India
1946	
16 May	Cabinet Mission announces its Constitutional Scheme
16 June	Muslim League accepts Cabinet Mission's Constitutional Scheme
16 June	Cabinet Mission presents scheme for the formation of an Interim Government at the Centre
16 August	Muslim League announces Direct Action Day
2 September	Congress forms Interim Government with Nehru as the Vice-President
13 October	Muslim League decides to join the Interim Government
3-6 December	British Prime Minister, Attlee, meets some Indian leaders; talks fail
9 December	Constituent Assembly begins its sessions
1947	
29 January	Muslim League demands dissolution of Constituent Assembly
16 July	Last Meeting of the Interim Government
11 August	Jinnah elected President of the Constituent Assembly of Pakistan
14 August	Pakistan Independence; celebrations in Karachi
14-15 August	At midnight India celebrates Independence
1949	
December	Constitution is signed

Mind Map

FRAMING THE CONSTITUTION

1 Constitution of India

The Making of the Constituent Assembly

- India gained freedom on 15th August, 1947 but faced partition.
- Constituent Assembly members were chosen by Provincial Legislatures elections.

The Dominant Voices

- Nehru proposed the Objectives Resolution and India's national flag.
- Ambedkar chaired the Drafting Committee and guided the Constitution.
- Civil servants BN Rau and SN Mukherjee provided crucial legal and advisory support.
- Debates addressed diverse ideas on India's language, values and systems.

2 The Vision of the Constitution

The Will of the People

- Somnath Lahiri criticised British influence over the Assembly's work.
- Nehru emphasized that the Assembly's strength came from people's will.
- The British introduced constitutional reforms through Acts in 1909, 1919 and 1935.

3 Defining Rights

The Problem with Separate Electorates

- B. Pocker Bahadur supported separate electorates to protect minorities.
- Nationalists opposed separate electorates, blaming them for violence and partition.
- NG Ranga saw minorities as poor and downtrodden, who needed rights to live.
- Jaipal Singh highlighted exploitation and neglect of tribal communities.
- Ambedkar stopped demanding separate electorates for depressed castes after the partition violence.

4 The Power of the State

A Strong Government

- Nehru argued for a strong central government.
- Ambedkar wanted a strong united centre to prevent chaos.
- Gopalaswami Ayyangar and Balakrishna Sharma demanded for a strong centre.
- Constitution favoured the union's power over the state's rights.

Centre is Likely to Break

- Constitution divided subjects into Union, State and Concurrent Lists.

Views of Santhanam

- Santhanam argued for re-allocation of powers to strength both levels.
- K. Santhanam believed that the fiscal provisions would weaken states financially.
- He predicted that the proposed power distribution could lead to a revolt by provinces against the centre.

5 The Language of the Nation

Emphasis on the Need for Hindi

- Language issue caused disruption in the Constituent Assembly.
- Dhulekar demanded Hindi as the language of constitution making.
- He wanted Hindi to be declared as the national language.
- Language committee proposed gradual transition to Hindi.

The Fear of Domination

- Durgabai expressed concerns about opposition to Hindi in the South.
- She feared Hindi propaganda was harming provinicial languages.
- Assembly members called for compromise and understanding on the language issue.

NCERT Folder

Intext Questions

1. Look again at Chapter 11. Discuss how the political situation of the time may have shaped the nature of the debates within the Constituent Assembly.

Ans. The political situation during the time may have shaped the nature of the debates and decisions within the Constituent Assembly in the following ways

- **Post-Colonial Background** The Assembly was formed after India gained independence from British rule. There was a strong desire to create a democratic and just society, but this was complicated by the legacy of colonialism, which included widespread inequality and social divisions.
- **Partition and Communal Tensions** The partition of India into Hindu-majority India and Muslim-majority Pakistan increased communal tensions. Debates often represented fears of disunity and violence which led to discussions on the need for protections for minority groups and provisions for communal harmony.
- **Diverse Representation** The Assembly comprised representatives from various political backgrounds, including the Indian National Congress, the Muslim League and other regional parties. This diversity led to intense debates over different issues such as language, representation, and federalism, as each group wanted to ensure its interests were protected.

2. What were the different arguments that Jaipal Singh put forward in demanding protective measures for the tribals?

Ans. Jaipal Singh put forward different arguments in demanding protective measures for the tribals. He spoke passionately about the need to protect tribal communities and improve their living conditions. He argued that tribes, though not a numerical minority, require special protection due to historical injustices. They have lost their lands, forests, and pastures, forcing them to relocate. Society often views them as primitive and has turned away from them. Singh emphasised the importance of connecting with tribal people, stating, 'We are willing to mix with you.' He advocated for reserving legislative seats for tribals, believing it would ensure their voices are heard and help bridge the gap between them and the rest of society.

Answer in 100-150 Words

1. What were the ideals expressed in the Objectives Resolution?

Ans. Jawaharlal Nehru introduced the 'Objectives Resolution' in the Constituent Assembly on 13th December, 1946. The Resolution defined the ideals of the Constitution of Independent India. It provided the framework within which the work of Constitution making was to proceed.

The ideals of the Objectives Resolution were

- It proclaimed India to be an 'Independent Sovereign Republic'.
- It guaranteed its citizens justice, equality and freedom.
- It assured adequate safeguards for minorities, Backward and Tribal Areas and Depressed Other Backwards Classes.

2. How was the term minority defined by different groups?

Ans. The term minority was defined in the following ways

- NG Ranga, a socialist, wanted to interpret the term minorities in economic terms. According to him, the real minorities were the poor and the downtrodden.
- Ranga believed that for a poor there was no meaning of the Fundamental Rights to live, to have full employment or that they could have their meetings, their conferences, their associations and various other civil liberties. There was a need to create conditions where these rights could be effectively enjoyed.
- Jaipal Singh, representative of tribals said the tribals are not numerically minority but they need special protection.

3. What were the arguments in favour of greater power to the provinces?

Ans. The arguments in favour of greater power to the provinces were

- K. Santhanam from Madras, defended the rights of the states. He believed that a reallocation of powers was necessary not only to strengthen the states but also the Centre.
- He felt that Centre would not be able to function properly if it was overburdened. The Centre would be made stronger if some of its functions were transferred to the states.

- Santhanam believed that the proposed allocation of powers would harm the states. The fiscal provisions, would impoverish the states since most taxes, except land revenue, had been made the preserve of the Centre. Thus, it was not possible for states to undertake any project of development without finances.
- On the issue of greater province, AR Mudaliar said that demanding it doesn't mean that person has less national spirit or patriotism.

4. Why did Mahatma Gandhi think Hindustani should be the national language?

Ans. Gandhiji felt that everyone should use a language which could be understood easily by all people. Hence, he wanted to make Hindustani the language of the nation.

Hindustani was a blend of Hindi and Urdu. It was popular among a large section of the people of India and was a composite language enriched by the interaction of diverse cultures. It has incorporated words and terms from different languages over the years.

Gandhiji believed that Hindustani is a multi-cultural language hence would be the ideal language of communication between diverse communities. It could unify Hindus and Muslims, and people of the North and the South.

Write a short Essay (about 250-300 words) on the following

5. What historical forces shaped the vision of the Constitution?

Ans. Historical forces that shaped the vision of the Constitution were

- Basic values were accepted by all national leaders as a result of the Nehru Report and the Fundamental Rights resolution.
- As a result of the 1937 elections, the Congress and other political parties were able to form governments in the provinces. This helped in developing an agreement over institutional design.
- The Indian Constitution adopted many institutional deals and procedures from colonial laws like the Government of India Act of 1935.
- While addressing the meeting of the Constituent Assembly on 13th December, 1946, Jawaharlal Nehru stated the ideals of the new Indian Constitution. He discussed everything in a broad historical perspective.
- He referred to the historic efforts made in the past to achieve the goals of justice, liberty, equality, fraternity and Fundamental Rights.

6. Discuss the different arguments made in favour of protection of the oppressed groups.

Ans. The argument made in favour of protection of the oppressed groups were

- It was felt that the oppressed groups like the tribals and untouchables needed protection and conditions that would bring them up to the level of the general population.
- The tribes were displaced from their land, deprived of their forest and pastures and were forced to settle to a new place. The society did not treat them equally due to their primitiveness and backwardness.
- Some members of the Depressed Castes felt that the problem of the untouchables could not be solved only through protection and safeguards. They believed that social norms and the moral values of caste society were the main reasons of their disabilities.
- They believed that they have been used by the society for services and labour but kept them at a social distance, refused to mix with them or dine with them or allow them entry into temples. The factor lying behind their miseries was to keep them at a margin in society and politics. They had no access to education and no share in the administrations.

7. What connection did some of the members of the Constituent Assembly make between the political situation of the time and the need for a strong centre?

Ans. There were several members in the Constituent Assembly who were in favour of a strong Centre to ensure unity and integrity of the nation. The country was partitioned in 1947, they did not want any such partition in future because of which, except few, all the members supported demand of strong centre.

- BR Ambedkar declared that he wanted a strong and United Centre, stronger than the centre under the Government of India Act of 1935. The supporters argued that a strong Centre could stop communal violence.
- Gopalaswami Ayyangar declared that the centre should be made as strong as possible.
- Balakrishna Sharma, a member from the United Provinces, also emphasised the need for a powerful and strong centre. He believed that a strong centre could plan for the well-being of the country, mobilise the available economic resources, establish a proper administration and defend the country against foreign aggression.

- Leaders like Jawaharlal Nehru also supported this demand as country was going through the phase of transformation. Many areas or regions of the country wanted to establish themselves as a separate entity. Hence, strong centre was the need of the hour. Most of the members of the Constituent Assembly also supported this view.

8. How did the Constituent Assembly seek to resolve the language controversy?

Ans. There were differences in the views between the members of Constituent Assembly over making Hindi as National Language. RV Dhulekar, a Congressman from the United Province aggressively supported Hindi as National Language which was not liked by many others. Many members wanted that Hindustani should be declared as National Language of the country. The members who were from South India were apprehensive of this view. They felt that Hindi language is being imposed on them. They also perceived that Hindi would be a threat to their provincial languages. Sankar Rao from Bombay, TA Ramalingam Chettiar and Shrimati G. Durgabai of Madras protests against the move.

Language Issue Resolution

To resolve the deadlock, a Language Committee was formed to give its recommendation to the Assembly. The Committee decided that Hindi in the Devanagiri script to be the Official Language but the transition to Hindi would be gradual. English was to be continued for all official purposes for the first fifteen years. Each province was to choose one of the regional languages for official work within the province.

9. On a present-day political map of India, indicate the different languages spoken in each state and mark out the one that is designated as the language for official communication. Compare the present map with a map of the early 1950s. What differences do you notice? Do differences say something about the relationship between language and the organisation of the states?

Ans. Students do it yourself

Exam Pattern Questions

Objective Type Questions

Multiple Choice Questions (MCQs)

1. Quit India struggle was started in the year

(a) 1942 (b) 1944
(c) 1945 (d) 1940

2. Whose constitutional status remained ambiguous at the time of Independence?

(a) Minorities
(b) Depressed Classes
(c) Princely States
(d) Tribals

3. Who among the following moved the resolution in the Constituent Assembly that the Indian National Flag be a horizontal tricolour of saffron, white and dark green in equal proportions with a wheel in navy blue in the centre? **CBSE 2024**

(a) Vallabh Bhai Patel
(b) Rajendra Prasad
(c) BR Ambedkar
(d) Jawaharlal Nehru

4. Who among the following was the President of the Constituent Assembly of India? **CBSE 2024 C, CBSE SQP 2022**

(a) Mahatma Gandhi (b) Rajendra Prasad
(c) B.R. Ambedkar (d) Sardar Patel

5. Who joined the Union Cabinet as Law Minister after Independence and also served as Chairman of the Drafting Committee?

(a) Alladi Krishnaswamy Aiyar (b) Rajendra Prasad
(c) Jawaharlal Nehru (d) B.R. Ambedkar

6. Who of the following introduced the 'Objectives Resolution' in the Constituent Assembly? **CBSE 2024 C**

(a) W.C. Bannerjee (b) G.B. Pant
(c) K.M. Munshi (d) Jawaharlal Nehru

7. Who told that the deliberations of Constituent Assembly were under clear influence of British imperialism?

(a) Somnath Lahiri (b) B.R. Ambedkar
(c) Mohammad Ali Jinnah (d) Mahatma Gandhi

8. **Who among the following members of the Constituent Assembly made a strong plea for Hindi to be used as the language of Constitution-making?** CBSE 2024
(a) R.V. Dhulekar
(b) G. Durgabai
(c) Shankarrao Deo
(d) N.G. Ranga

9. **Who among the following demanded justice for women, not reserved seats or separate electorates in the Constituent Assembly?** CBSE 2023
(a) Malati Chowdhury
(b) Hansa Mehta
(c) Begum Aizaas Rasul
(d) Rajkumari Amrit Kaur

10. **How many lists of subject were provided by Draft Constitution?**
(a) Two (b) Three
(c) Four (d) One

11. **Fill in the blank with the appropriate word from the given options** CBSE 2024
The legislature elected under the Government of India Act, 1935 operated within the framework of ....
(a) Indian National Congress
(b) Muslim League
(c) Colonial Rule
(d) Constituent Assembly

12. **Which of the following were the key ideals associated with the social struggles in India since the 19th century?**
(a) Autonomy, hierarchy and traditionalism SQP 2024-25
(b) Democracy, equality and justice
(c) Imperialism, colonialism and bureaucracy
(d) Monarchy, privilege and conservatism

13. **Select the significance of 26th November, 1949 in relation to the Constituent Assembly from the following options** CBSE 2024
(a) Formation of the Drafting Committee
(b) Commencement of the Constituent Assembly
(c) Designing of the National Flag of India
(d) Signing of Constitution by the Constituent Assembly

14. **Identify the primary reason behind the formation of the Constituent Assembly from the following options** CBSE 2024
(a) To establish a legislative body for the governance of provinces
(b) To settle issues of Partition of India through coordination
(c) To negotiate the terms of India's independence with the British
(d) To draft a framework for the governance of independent India

15. **Which one of the following pair is correctly matched?** CBSE 2025

	List-I (Name of Important Committees of Constituent Assembly)		List-II (Name of President)
(a)	Flag Committee	–	H.C. Mookerjee
(b)	Union Power Committee	–	Pandit Jawaharlal Nehru
(c)	Rules of Procedure Committee	–	S. Varadachariar
(d	States Committee	–	J.B. Kripalani

16. **Consider the following statements regarding making of Constituent Assembly.**
(i) The members were elected through direct election.
(ii) Muslim League choose to boycott the Constituent Assembly.
(iii) The assembly also had representatives of the princely states.

Which of the above statement is/are correct?
(a) (i) and (ii) (b) (ii) and (iii)
(c) (i) and (iii) (d) (i), (ii) and (iii)

17. **Consider the following statements regarding Objective Resolution.**
(i) It proclaimed India as Independent Sovereign Republic.
(ii) It guaranteed its citizens justice, equality and freedom.
(iii) It assured adequate safeguards for some section of society.
(iv) It assured nationalisation of all major industries.

Which of the above statements is/are correct?
(a) (i), (ii) and (iii) (b) (ii) and (iii)
(c) (ii), (iii) and (iv) (d) (i), (ii), (iii) and (iv)

18. **Consider the following statements regarding the rights of Depressed Castes.**
(i) BR Ambedkar demanded separate electorate for the Depressed Castes during the national movement.
(ii) Gandhiji supported Ambedkar's view on separate electorate for Depressed Castes.
(iii) J. Nagappa mentioned that Depressed Castes are suffering due to lack of numerical strength.

Which of the above statements is/are correct?
(a) Only (i) (b) (i) and (iii)
(c) (ii) and (iii) (d) (i), (ii) and (iii)

19. **Consider the following statements regarding recommendation of Constituent Assembly with respect to Depressed Castes.**
(i) Untouchability should be abolished.
(ii) Hindu temples to be opened to all castes.
(iii) Reservation for lowest castes in legislature and government offices.

(iv) Reservation only for economically weaker section of Depressed Castes.

Which of the above statements is/are correct?

(a) (i) and (ii)
(b) (ii) and (iii)
(c) (i), (ii) and (iii)
(d) (i), (ii), (iii) and (iv)

20. Which of the following were discussed in the Constituent Assembly for making a strong government at the Centre ? Choose the correct option from the following. CBSE 2024

(i) Planning for the well-being of the country.
(ii). To establish strong administration at the state level.
(iii). To mobilise available economic resources.
(iv). To defend the country against foreign aggression.

Options

(a) (i), (ii) and (iv)
(b) (ii), (iii) and (iv)
(c) (i), (ii) and (iii)
(d) (i), (iii) and (iv)

21. Arrange the following in chronological order and select the correct answer from the option below

(i) Constituent Assembly begins its session
(ii) Congress forms interim government
(iii) Independence of Pakistan
(iv) Constitution was signed

Codes

(a) (i), (ii), (iii), (iv)
(b) (ii), (i), (iii), (iv)
(c) (ii), (i), (iv), (iii)
(d) (iv), (iii), (ii), (i)

22. Identify the name of the person from the following information given below.

- He served as a Chairman of Drafting Committee of the Constitution.
- During the period of British rule, he had been a political opponent of the Congress.
- He had demanded separate electorates for the Depressed Castes.
- He was a lawyer and economist.

Options

(a) Rajendra Prasad
(b) B.N. Rau
(c) B.R. Ambedkar
(d) Sardar Patel

23. Identify the member of the Constituent Assembly with the help of information given below. CBSE 2024

- He was a member of the Drafting Committee of the Constitution.
- He was a lawyer.
- He gave crucial inputs in drafting the Constitution.
- He belonged to Madras (Chennai).

Options

(a) B.N. Rau
(b) K.M. Munshi
(c) Alladi Krishnaswamy Aiyar
(d) S.N. Mukherjee

24. Identify the member of the Constituent Assembly with the help of the following information CBSE 2025

(i) He was the President of the Constituent Assembly.
(ii) He was the first President of the Independent India.

(a) Sarvepalli Radhakrishnan
(b) Zakir Hussain
(c) V.V. Giri
(d) Rajendra Prasad

25. Complete the following with the correct option regarding the civil servants with their respective roles in the Constituent Assembly.

B.N. Rau : Constitutional Advisor :: S.N. Mukherjee : ...

(a) Chief Draughtsman
(b) Calligrapher of the Constitution
(c) Head of Constitution Assembly
(d) Chairman of the Drafting Committee

Assertion-Reason

26. **Assertion** (A) The executive was made entirely responsible to the Provincial Legislature in 1935.

Reason (R) Government of India Act of 1935 was passed.

Codes

(a) Both A and R are true and R is the correct explanation of A
(b) Both A and R are true, but R is not the correct explanation of A
(c) A is true, but R is false
(d) A is false, but R is true

27. **Assertion** (A) By 1949, most Muslim members of the Constituent Assembly were against the idea of separate electorate.

Reason (R) They were of the view that Muslims must take active part in the democratic process to have a decisive voice in the political system.

Codes

(a) Both A and R are true and R is the correct explanation of A
(b) Both A and R are true, but R is not the correct explanation of A
(c) A is true, but R is false
(d) A is false, but R is true

28. Assertion (A) The Congress by the 1930s had accepted Hindustani to be the National Language.

Reason (R) Hindi got developed from Hindustani language only.

Codes

(a) Both A and R are true and R is the correct explanation of A

(b) Both A and R are true, but R is not the correct explanation of A

(c) A is true, but R is false

(d) A is false, but R is true

Match the Following

29.

	List I		List II
A.	Quit India Movement	1.	1942
B.	Royal Indian Navy Mutiny	2.	1946
C.	Government of India Act	3.	1935
D.	Constitution came into effect	4.	1950

Codes

	A	B	C	D		A	B	C	D
(a)	1	2	3	4	(b)	2	1	4	3
(c)	3	4	2	1	(d)	4	3	1	2

30.

	List I		List II
A.	President of Fundamental Rights sub-committee	1.	B.N. Rau
B.	President of Advisory Committee	2.	J.B. Keriplani
C.	Constitutional Advisor to Assembly	3.	Rajendra Prasad
D.	President of Constitution Assembly	4.	Sardar Vallabhbhai Patel

Codes

	A	B	C	D		A	B	C	D
(a)	1	2	3	4	(b)	2	4	1	3
(c)	3	4	2	1	(d)	4	3	1	2

31.

	List I		List II
A.	16th May, 1946	1.	Muslim League announces Direct Action Day
B.	16th August, 1946	2.	Cabinet Mission announces its constitutional schemes
C.	9th December, 1946	3.	Constitution is signed
D.	December, 1946	4.	Constitution Assembly begins its sessions

Codes

	A	B	C	D		A	B	C	D
(a)	1	3	2	4	(b)	2	4	1	3
(c)	3	2	2	4	(d)	2	1	4	3

Picture Based Questions

32. The speech shown in the following picture was delivered on

(a) Eve of Independence in Constitutional Assembly.

(b) the day of commencement of Constitutional Assembly.

(c) First day of meeting of Constitutional Assembly.

(d) Independence Day of India.

33. The picture below shows the discussion on which bill?

(a) Hindu Code Bill (b) Hindu Marriage Act

(c) Uniform Civil Code (d) Citizenship

34. What significant event does the below image depict?

(a) The formation of the Indian National Congress.

(b) The inauguration of the first Lok Sabha Session.

(c) The signing of the Indian Independence Act.

(d) The adoption of the Constitution of India.

Answers

1. (a) 1942
2. (c) Princely States
3. (d) Jawaharlal Nehru
4. (b) Rajendra Prasad
5. (d) B.R. Ambedkar
6. (d) Jawaharlal Nehru
7. (a) Somnath Lahiri
8. (a) R.V. Dhulekar
9. (b) Hansa Mehta
10. (b) Three
11. (c) Colonial Rule
12. (b) Democracy, equality and justice
13. (d) Signing of Constitution by the Constituent Assembly.
14. (d) To draft a framework for the governance of independent India
15. (b)) Union Power Committee - Pandit Jawaharlal Nehru
16. (b) (ii) and (iii)
17. (a) (i), (ii) and (iii)
18. (a) Only (i)
19. (c) (i), (ii) and (iii)
20. (c) (i), (ii) and (iii)
21. (b) (ii), (i), (iii), (iv)
22. (c) B.R. Ambedkar
23. (c) Alladi Krishnaswamy Aiyar
24. (d) Rajendra Prasad
25. (a) Chief Draughtsman
26. (a) Both A and R are true and R is the correct explanation of A
27. (a) Both A and R are true and R is the correct explanation of A
28. (c) A is true, but R is false
29. (a)
30. (b)
31. (d)
32. (b) The day of commencement of Constitutional Assembly.
33. (a) Hindu Code Bill
34. (d) The adoption of the Constitution of India.

Subjective Questions

Short Answer Type Questions

1. What were the immediate events before the making of the Constitution?

Ans. The immediate events before the making of the Constitution are as follows

- India became independent on 15th August, 1947 but was divided.
- Quit India Movement (1942) was launched which was a widespread popular movement against the British, and it was still in the memory.
- Subhas Chandra Bose bid to win freedom through armed struggle and there was an uprising of the Royal Indian Navy in Bombay and other cities in the spring of 1946.
- There were mass protests of workers and peasants in different parts of the country in the late 1940s.

2. 'The discussions within the Constituent Assembly were also influenced by the opinions expressed by the public'. Examine the statement. Competency Based Que

Ans. The public opinions had a considerable effect on the discussions of the Constituent Assembly that were

- There was public debate on all the resolutions.
- The newspapers reported the arguments presented by different members on any issue. Criticisms and counter criticism in the press shaped the nature of the consensus that was ultimately reached on specific issues.
- Suggestions from the public created a sense of collective participation. Many linguistic minorities demanded protection of their mother tongue. Religious minorities asked for special safeguards.
- The low-caste groups or dalits demanded an end to ill-treatment by upper-caste people and reservation of separate seats on the basis of their population in legislatures.

3. Describe the role of Dr BR Ambedkar in the Constituent Assembly. CBSE 2025

Ans. Dr. B.R. Ambedkar played a very important role in the Constituent Assembly of India. He was a lawyer and economist. During the period of British rule, Ambedkar had been a political opponent of the Congress, but on the advice of Mahatma Gandhi, he was asked at Independence to join the Union Cabinet as law minister. In this capacity, he served as Chairman of the Drafting

Committee of the Constitution. He worked with lawyers like K.M. Munshi and Alladi Krishnaswamy Aiyar who gave crucial inputs in the drafting of the Constitution.

Ambedkar himself had the responsibility of guiding the Draft Constitution through the Assembly. He pleaded for the abolition of untouchability and asked for equal rights. He held the key figure due to his interventions and speeches in the assembly.

4. How Objective Resolution played a key role in drafting of the Constitution?

Or **Why was the 'Objective Resolution' introduced in the Constituent Assembly considered as a Momentous Resolution? Explain.** CBSE Term II 2022

Ans. Objective Resolution played a key role in drafting of the Constitution in the following ways

- On 13th December, 1946, Jawaharlal Nehru introduced the 'Objectives Resolution' in the Constituent Assembly. The resolution defined the ideals of the Constitution of Independent India. It provided the framework within which the work of Constitution-making was to proceed.
- The outlines of the Objective Resolution were
  - It proclaimed India to be an Independent, Sovereign and Republic country.
  - It guaranteed its citizens justice, equality and freedom.
  - It assured adequate safeguards for minorities, Backward and Tribal Areas, Depressed and Other Backward Classes.

5. "A communist member, Somnath Lahiri saw the dark hand of British imperialism hanging over the deliberations of the Constituent Assembly." Examine the statement and give your own views in support of your answer. Competency Based Que

Ans. The statement implies that Somnath Lahiri saw the influence of the British imperialism over the deliberations of the Constituent Assembly. As a result, he urged the members to completely free themselves from the influences of imperial rule.

During the winter of 1946-47, when the Assembly was constituted, the British were still in India. An interim administration headed by Jawaharlal Nehru was in place, but it could only operate under the directions of the Viceroy and the British Government in London.

Lahiri asked his colleagues to realise that the Constituent Assembly was made by British and was working according to the British plans and their wish. However, the establishment of Constituent Assembly and subsequent formulation is different in various aspects. Firstly, the assembly was truly Indian unlike previous committees or institutions.

Secondly, the vision it outlined was not of a colonised country but of the Constitution of an Independent Sovereign Republic of India. Hence the statement of Somnath Lahiri was not correct completely.

6. Why the Constitution was regarded a source of expressing the aspirations of freedom fighters?

Ans. Constitution of India has been regarded as a source of expressing the aspiration of the freedom fighters because of the following reasons

- Constitution enshrined all the principle values for which freedom fighters sacrificed their life.
- The ideals of democracy, equality and justice, etc were given preference in the Constitution.
- The nationalist movement was against an oppressive and illegitimate government. In this regard, Constitution established legitimate government which was chosen by people. For this, everyone was granted right to vote.
- Fundamental Rights were also included in the Constitution so that everyone can live with dignity which was not provided during British rule.
- Many provisions were added to provide economic and social justice to the vulnerable sections of the society.

7. "The Constituent Assembly expressed the aspirations of the social reformers of the nineteenth century." Explain the statement. Competency Based Que, CBSE Term II 2022

Ans. The Constituent Assembly expressed the aspirations of the social reformers of the nineteenth century. This statement can be explained by the following points

- When Swami Vivekananda campaigned for a reform of Hinduism, he wanted religions to become more just.
- When Jyotiba Phule in Maharashtra pointed to the suffering of the depressed castes, or Communists and Socialists organised workers and peasants, they were demanding economic and social justice.
- The national movement against a government that was seen as oppressive and illegitimate was inevitably a struggle for democracy and justice, for citizens' rights and equality.
- The Constituent Assembly abolished the practice of untouchability. It also provided various safeguards in the Constitution for depressed castes, minorities, and other backward classes.
- The Constituent Assembly tried to ensure social justice and promoted values like democracy, equality, and justice.

8. What was Govind Ballabh Pant's argument against separate electorates?

Or **Examine the role of Gobind Ballabh Pant or the Unified Nation in the Constituent Assembly.** CBSE Term II 2022

Ans. Govind Ballabh Pant opposed the idea of separate electorates in the Constituent Assembly.

The arguments of Govind Ballabh Pant against separate electorates were

- According to him, the demand of separate electorates was not only harmful for the nation but also for the minorities. He believed that democracy can be judged with the confidence generated by different sections of people.
- For him, every citizen was to be treated in a way that it fulfils not only material wants but spiritual sense of self respect. There was a need for the majority to understand the problems of minorities. But still, Pant opposed the idea of separate electorates.
- He believed that it was a suicidal demand that would permanently isolate the minorities, make them vulnerable, and deprived them of giving any opinion within the government.

9. Why did N.G. Ranga urge to interpret minorities in the economic terms in the Constituent Assembly? Explain.

Ans. N.G. Ranga, a socialist, wanted to interpret the term minorities in economic terms due to the following reasons

- According to him, the real minorities were the poor and the downtrodden.
- He believed that for a poor there was no meaning of the fundamental right to live, to have full employment or that they could have their meetings, their conferences, their associations and various other civil liberties.
- There was a need to create conditions where these rights could be effectively enjoyed for this they needed protection.
- He admitted that the common masses were not able to come up to the Constituent Assembly, thus it was their duty to speak for them.

10. Explain the attributes of a loyal citizen as defined by G.B. Pant. CBSE 2024

Ans. Govind Ballabh Pant, an influential Indian leader and statesman, emphasised the importance of loyalty to the state for the success of democracy. He outlined the following attributes of a loyal citizen

- **Selflessness and Collective Responsibility** Pant argued that loyal citizens must prioritise the welfare of the community and the state over personal or community interests.
- **Self-discipline** For democracy to flourish, citizens must foster self-discipline. This means controlling one's desires, ambitions, and actions in a manner that supports the broader interests of society and the state. Pant believed that only through self-discipline could individuals contribute positively to democratic governance.
- **Unified Loyalty** Pant stressed that there can be no divided loyalty in a democracy. The citizen's loyalty must be singular, directed exclusively towards the state. If individuals or groups create rival loyalties (to caste, religion, or any other entity), it undermines the unity of the state and weakens democracy.
- **Commitment to Democracy** Pant believed that loyalty to democracy required individuals to have faith in the system and to act in a way that nurtures democratic values.

11. Explain the role of G.B. Pant on the united approach of India. CBSE 2025

Ans. G.B. Pant's role in promoting a united approach in India were

- **Opposition to Separate Electorates** Pant argued that separate electorates would permanently isolate minorities and weaken national unity.
- **Integration of All Communities** He emphasised that every citizen should be part of one unified nation rather than being divided by religious or community-based politics.
- **Strengthening Democracy** He believed democracy could only succeed when people prioritised national interest over communal differences.
- **Loyalty to the State** Pant stressed that all citizens should have undivided loyalty to the nation, ensuring collective progress and harmony.

12. "The draft Constitution provided for three lists of subjects on the issue of federalism." Explain the statement with examples. CBSE 2024

Ans. The draft Constitution provided for three lists of subjects on the issue of federalism. These three lists of subjects are union, state and concurrent.

(i) **Union list** This list consists of subjects that come under the domain of the central government. It includes subjects like defence, communication, banking, etc. For example, the central government is responsible for defending the country from any threat.

(ii) **State list** This list consists of subjects that come under the domain of state government. It includes subjects like trade, agriculture, police, etc. For example, police work under the state government to maintain law and order in the state.

(iii) **Concurrent list** This list consists of subjects that come under the domain of both the central government and state government. It includes subjects like forest, education, marriage, etc. For example, providing education to citizens in a state is not just the responsibility of state government but of central government as well.

13. Explain the arguments given in favour of strong centre in the Constituent Assembly. CBSE 2023

Or **Why did some members of Constituent Assembly argue for a strong centre? Explain.** CBSE 2024

Or **"Issues of 'division of power of the government' at the Centre and State level were intensely debated in the Constituent Assembly." Explain the statement with examples.** Competency Based Que, CBSE Term II 2022

Ans. The arguments given in favour of strong centre in the Constituent Assembly were

- B.R. Ambedkar declared that he wanted a strong and united centre, stronger than the centre under the Government of India Act of 1935. The supporters argued that a strong centre could stop communal violence.
- Gopalaswami Ayyangar declared that the centre should be made as strong as possible.
- Balakrishna Sharma, a member from the United Provinces, also emphasised the need for a powerful and strong centre. He believed that a strong centre could plan for the well-being of the country, mobilise the available economic resources, establish a proper administration and defend the country against foreign aggression.
- Leaders like Jawaharlal Nehru also supported the demand of strong centre as country was going through the phase of transformation. Many areas or regions of the country wanted to establish themselves as a separate entity.

14. Describe the views of Gandhiji on the national language of India. CBSE 2025

Ans. Mahatma Gandhi believed that Hindustani is a blend of Hindi and Urdu, should be the national language of India. He felt it was a composite language enriched by diverse cultures and widely understood across regions. Gandhi opposed the Sanskritisation of Hindi and the Persianisation of Urdu, emphasizing that Hindustani should freely include words from regional and foreign languages. He saw it as a unifying force between Hindus and Muslims and across different regions. According to him, restricting the language to Hindi or Urdu alone would harm both intelligence and patriotism.

Long Answer Type Questions

1. How did the Constituent Assembly address the issue of social justice, particularly concerning the rights of the people? Explain. SQP 2024

Ans. The Constituent Assembly of India played a pivotal role in addressing social justice, particularly concerning the rights of individuals and communities. The Assembly approached and resolved these issues in the following ways

- **Diverse Demands** Members of the Constituent Assembly presented a range of demands regarding the rights of individuals and communities. These demands reflected the diverse socio-economic and cultural backgrounds of the representatives and their constituencies. The Assembly had to address issues such as minority rights, social inequalities, and political representation.
- **Debate and Reconciliation** The Constituent Assembly engaged in extensive debates and discussions to address conflicting ideas and opinions. These debates were crucial in reconciling different viewpoints and achieving a consensus. The process ensured that the final decisions on social justice and rights were well-considered and reflective of diverse perspectives.
- **Intense Debates** The issue of social justice, including the representation of minorities and the structure of political representation, was subject to intense debate. Members of the Assembly rigorously discussed how to balance the needs of various groups while ensuring the unity and integrity of the nation.
- **B. Pocker Bahadur's Advocacy** B. Pocker Bahadur made a powerful case for the continuation of minority representation in the political system and governance. He argued for safeguarding the interests of minorities to ensure their participation and protection within the democratic framework, highlighting the importance of inclusive representation.
- **Sardar Patel's Stance** Sardar Patel, a key figure in the Assembly, strongly opposed the idea of separate electorates, describing them as a "poison" to national unity. Patel's stance emphasised his commitment to integrating all communities within a unified political system, reflecting his vision for a cohesive nation.
- **GB Pant's Empathy** GB Pant advocated for understanding and empathising with the aspirations of different groups within the country. His emphasis on empathy underscored the need for the Constitution to address the genuine concerns and aspirations of all citizens, contributing to a more equitable society.

- **Unity of Nation** The overarching argument in the Assembly was the unity of the nation. Members agreed that every individual should be considered a citizen with equal rights and responsibilities, and that various groups needed to be assimilated within the broader framework of national identity.
- **Citizenship and Loyalty** The Constitution was designed to grant citizenship and enshrine rights, while expecting citizens to offer loyalty to the state. This reciprocal relationship was meant to foster national integration and ensure that the rights of individuals were protected within a framework of national unity.

2. Partition of India had made nationalist strongly opposed to the idea of separate electorate. Examine the statement. Competency Based Que

Ans. When Constituent Assembly was constituted, many minority leaders demanded for continuing separate electorates in the country. After partition, the nationalists opposed the idea of separate electorates as they perceived it as poison and upto a large extent it is responsible for the partition of the country. Nationalist leaders were haunted by the fear of continued civil war, riots and violence. Views of nationalist leaders are discussed below

Sardar Patel He declared that separate electorates was a poison that has entered in the political system of the country. Due to it, one community turned against the another and divided the nation. Hence, there was no place of separate electorate in independent India.

Govind Ballabh Pant He believed that it was not only harmful for the nation but also for the minorities. He asserted that it was a suicidal demand. It would permanently isolate the minorities, make them vulnerable and deprive them of effective role in the government.

In order to build political unity and form a nation, every individual had to be moulded into a citizen of the state and each group had to be assimilated within the nation. Moreover, he believed that in order to become loyal citizens, people had to stop focusing on the community and the self. Members of all communities had to act as equal members of one state.

R.V. Dhulekar He believed that in the name of safeguard to minorities, British introduced the idea of separate electorate to fulfill their political objective. As per him, there was no requirement of separate electorate in independent India as governments would function on the basis of the Constitution. There were several provisions for the safeguards of the minorities, hence, separate electorate was not required.

B.R. Ambedkar He was in the favour of separate electorate for the dalits but before independence he gave up his demand. He also opposed members of assembly who were demanding for the separate electorates.

Some nationalist Muslim leaders like Begum Aizaas Rasul felt that separate electorates were self-destructive since they isolate the minorities from the majority. Other Muslim leaders also asserted that separate electorates were against the interest of the minorities. All the minorities need to take active part in democratic process.

3. How did Constituent Assembly of India protected the powers of the Central Government? Explain.

Ans. The Constituent Assembly protected the powers of the Central Government in the following ways

- Constituent Assembly decided to opt for a federation alongwith strong centre. There were arguments in favour of strong provinces which evoked powerful reactions from the leaders who preferred strong centre.
- Dr. B.R. Ambedkar and Jawaharlal Nehru advocated a strong Central Government for India. They stated that only a strong centre can stop the communal disharmony.
- Balakrishna Sharma focussed on size of the nation and stated that only a centre, which was powerful could plan for the well-being of the country.
- Strong centre would help in mobilising available economic resources and proper administration was possible only through strong centre.
- The rights of the states were most impressively defended by K. Santhanam from Madras. Also the decision of the Constituent Assembly to have a strong centre was occasioned by the situations in which it was taken.
- Most of the members felt that strong centre was the need of the hour. It was necessary to ensure peace, prosperity and political stability and hence, Gopalaswami Ayyangar declared to make centre as strong as possible.

4. Explain the distribution of powers between the Centre and the States, as debated in the Constituent Assembly, highlighting differing viewpoints and concerns. CBSE SQP 2024

Ans. The distribution of powers between the Centre and the States, as debated in the Constituent Assembly, highlighting differing viewpoints and concerns.

These are as follows

- **Intense Debate on Division of Powers** The division of powers between the Central and State governments was intensely debated, reflecting concerns about effective governance and national unity. The challenge was to balance authority to ensure both national cohesion and regional autonomy.

- **Three Lists System** The draft Constitution proposed a three-list system for the distribution of powers: the Union List, the State List, and the Concurrent List. The Union List contained subjects on which only the Central Government could legislate, the State List included subjects under the jurisdiction of State Governments, and the Concurrent List allowed both levels of government to legislate on shared areas.
- **Union List Dominance** More items were included in the Union List compared to the State List. This design was intentional to centralise powers on matters of national importance, such as defense, foreign affairs, and atomic energy, ensuring that the Central Government could address issues crucial for national stability and international representation.
- **Central Power Emphasis** The Indian Constitution granted significant powers to the Union Government to maintain peace, security, and coherence across states. This centralisation aimed to provide a unified stance on national and international matters, particularly important for a newly independent nation facing diverse regional challenges.
- **Advocates for Strong Centre** The necessity for a strong Central Government was reinforced by the events of Partition, which highlighted the need for a cohesive national framework. Leaders like Jawaharlal Nehru, B.R. Ambedkar, and Gopalaswami Ayyangar advocated for a robust central authority to manage the diverse and complex issues facing the nation and to maintain national unity.
- **Balancing Authority** The debate ultimately sought to strike a balance between empowering states to address local needs and retaining sufficient central authority to ensure national coherence. The final Constitution reflected this balance, with a strong Central Government designed to manage overarching national issues while allowing states autonomy over local matters.

5. "Within the Constituent Assembly of India the language issue was intensely debated." Examine the views put forward by members of the assembly on the issue. Competency Based Que

Ans. The language issue was intensely debated in the Constituent Assembly. R.V. Dhulekar, Shrimati G. Durgabai, Shri Shankarrao Deo and T.A. Ramalingam Chettiar were prominent members of the Constituent Assembly who gave important views on language.

Their views were as follows

- **R.V. Dhulekar**, a Congressman from the United Provinces, made a strong appeal that Hindi must be used as the language of the Constitution-making. According to him, those people who does not understand Hindustani, they should not participate in the making of the Constitution. Many members of the assembly became agitated and the controversy regarding language continued over the next three years.
- **Shrimati G. Durgabai** from Madras expressed that the controversy regarding language made the non-Hindi speaking people to think that other powerful languages of India would be neglected and it was an obstacle for the composite culture of our nation. She informed the House that the opposition in the South against Hindi was very strong. She accepted Hindustani as the language of the people. But its character was changed as it took out many Urdu words and regional vocabulary. Durgabai believed this composite character of Hindustani if eroded, could create anxieties and fears among different language groups.
- **Shri Shankarrao Deo**, a Congress member from Bombay and a follower of Mahatma Gandhi accepted Hindustani as a language of the Nation but he warned that he supported Hindi only if the House does not do anything which might raise any suspicion and strengthen his fears.
- **T.A. Ramalingam Chettiar** from Madras suggested that there would be fear and bitter feelings among people if Hindi was applied forcefully, although the people might be unjustified. So he believed that to form a United Nation, there should be mutual adjustment and no question of forcing things on people.

In this way, different members of the Constituent Assembly expressed their views regarding the controversy.

6. What were the important features of the Constitution?

Ans. The Constitution of India came into being through a process of intense debate and discussion. Some important features of the Constitution are as follows

- **Right to Vote to Every Adult** There was substantial agreement in the Constitution on the granting of the vote to every adult Indian.
  In other democratic countries like the United States and the United Kingdom, initially men of property were granted the vote, then men with education were granted the right. It was after a long struggle that men of working-class or peasant background were also given the Right to Vote and later women were also granted.
- **Secularism** Another important feature of the Constitution was that it emphasised secularism. This was done through the Fundamental Rights to 'Freedom of Religion' (Articles 25-28), 'Cultural and Educational Rights' (Articles 29,30) and 'Rights to Equality' (Articles 14,16, 17).

All religions were given equal treatment by the state and given the right to maintain charitable institutions. The state also sought to distance itself from religious communities, banning compulsory religious instructions in state-run schools and colleges and declaring religious discrimination in employment to be illegal. A legal space was created for social reform within communities which was used to ban untouchability and introduce changes in personal and family laws.

Source Based Questions

Read the sources given below and answer the following questions.

1. 'We are Not just Going to Copy'

We say that it is our firm and solemn resolve to have an independent sovereign republic. India is bound to be sovereign, it is bound to be independent and it is bound to be a republic....Now, some friends have raised the question : "Why have you not put in the word 'democratic' here.?" Well, I told them that it is conceivable, of course, that a republic may not be democratic but the whole of our past is witness to this fact that we stand for democratic institutions. Obviously, we are aiming at democracy and nothing less than a democracy. What form of democracy, what shape it might take is another matter.

The democracies of the present day, many of them in Europe and elsewhere, have played a great part in the world's progress. Yet it may be doubtful if those democracies may not have to change their shape somewhat before long if they have to remain completely democratic. We are not going just to copy, I hope, a certain democratic procedure or an institution of a so-called democratic country.

We may improve upon it. In any event whatever system of government we may establish here must fit in with the temper of our people and be acceptable to them. We stand for democracy. It will be for this House to determine what shape to be given to that democracy, the fullest democracy, I hope, the House will notice that in this resolution, although we have not used the word 'democratic' because we thought it is obvious that the word 'republic' contains that word and we have done something much more than using the word.

We have given the content of democracy in this resolution and not only the content of democracy but the context, also, if I may say so of economic democracy in this resolution. Others might take objection to this resolution on the grounds that we have not said that it should be a Socialist State. Well, I stand for Socialism and, I hope, India will stand for Socialism and that India will go towards the Constitution of a Socialist State and I do believe that the whole world will have to go that way.

(i) Explain, why Nehru did not mention the word democratic in the resolution?

(ii) Mention the three basic features of the Constitution given in the above passage.

(iii) On what kind of socialism did Nehru give stress to?

Or **(i) Explain the term sovereignty.**

(ii) How has democracy been related with sovereignty in the passage?

(iii) How did the Constitutional framers highlighted the need of economic democracy?

Or **(i) Mention the 'firm and solemn resolve' expressed in the passage.**

(ii) How does the passage emphasise the commitment to democracy ?

(iii) How is democracy explained in the context of republic in the passage ?

Ans. (i) Nehru did not use the word democratic in the resolution. He explains that whole of India's past shows that Indians have always stood for democratic institution.

(ii) Three basic features of the Constitution given in above passage are independent, sovereign and republic.

(iii) Nehru was supporter of socialism and he said that India would stand for socialism, where every citizen would be provided equal opportunities for growth and development. There would be economic democracy and economic justice.

Or (i) Sovereignity means the quality or state of being sovereign, or of having supreme power or authority.

(ii) In the passage, India is going to be a sovereign state which will not be under dominion of another country.

(iii) The framers of the Constitution strived to promote the welfare of the people by securing a social order in which social, economic and political justice should be provided to all. They tried to frame policies through which inequalities to be minimised in income and status.

Or (i) In his speech, Nehru emphasised India's firm resolve to become an independent, sovereign republic. He acknowledged the influence of past revolutions, like the Russian Revolution, and expressed confidence that India would overcome obstacles to achieve its goals. He also supported the idea of India moving towards a Socialist state in the future.

(ii) The passage emphasises India's strong commitment to democracy by referencing historical revolutions, like the American and French revolutions, to highlight the importance of democratic principles. Nehru assures that India is resolutely aiming to be an independent, sovereign republic, with democracy at its core.Thus, the passage reflects India's determination to build a democracy that suits its people's aspirations.

(iii) In the passage, democracy is explained in the context of a republic by highlighting that India is committed to democratic values, even though the word "democratic" is not explicitly used. Nehru stresses that India will create a form of democracy suited to its people, rather than simply copying other countries' models. The focus is on a comprehensive democracy, including economic democracy, that aligns with India's needs and values.

2. "That is Very Good, Sir-Bold Words, Noble Words"

Somnath Lahiri said: Well, Sir, I must congratulate Pandit Nehru for the fine expression he gave to the spirit of the Indian people when he said that no imposition from the British will be accepted by the Indian people. Imposition would be resented and objected to, he said and he added that if need be we will walk to the valley of struggle. That is very good, Sir-bold words, noble words.

But the point is to see when and how are you going to apply that challenge. Well, Sir, the point is that the imposition is here right now. Not only has the British plan made any future Constitution dependent on a treaty satisfactory to the Britisher but it suggests that for every little difference you will have to run to the Federal Court or dance attendance there in England or to call on the British Prime Minister Clement Attlee or someone else. Not only is it a fact that this Constituent Assembly, whatever plans we may be hatching, we are under the shadow of British guns, British Army, their economic and financial stranglehold- which means that the final power is still in the British hands and the question of power has not yet been finally decided which means the future is not yet completely in our hands. Not only that, but the statements made by Attlee and others recently have made it clear that if need be, they will even threaten you with division entirely. This means, Sir, there is no freedom in this country. As Sardar Vallabh Bhai Patel put in some days ago, we have freedom only to fight among ourselves. That is the only freedom we have got...Therefore, our humble suggestion is that it is not a question of getting something by working out this plan but to declare independence here and now and call upon the Interim Government and call upon the people of India, to stop fratricidal warfare and look out against its enemy, which still had the whip in hand of the British imperialism and go together to fight it and then resolve our claim afterward when we will be free.

(i) Why did Somnath Lahiri congratulate Pandit Nehru?

(ii) Explain why Somnath felt that the absence of Constitution will mean dependence on the British.

(iii) Explain the intentions of the British in not framing the Constitution beforehand.

Ans. (i) Somnath Lahiri congratulated Pandit Nehru when he said no imposition from the British would be accepted by India which was his true spirit for India and its free people.

(ii) Somnath felt that in the absence of Constitution, for every basic law and rule, there would be need to refer to British government. British would obviously want control over the governance. He felt that Indians should draft their own Constitution according to their will and will of people, so, it could be truly independent and free.

(iii) The intentions of the British in not framing the Constitution beforehand can be explained in the context of their convenience.

- The interim government could only operate under the direction of the Viceroy and the British government in London.
- The British attached reveral conditions within which assembly had to function to protect their interests.

3. The "British Element is Gone, but they have left the Mischief Behind"

Sardar Vallabh Bhai Patel said: It is no use saying that we ask for separate electorates, because it is good for us. We have heard it long enough. We have heard it for years, and as a result of this agitation we are now a separate nation... Can you show me one free country where there are separate electorates? If so, I shall be prepared to accept it. But in this unfortunate country if this separate electorate is going to be persisted in, even after the division of the country, woe betide the country; it is not worth living in.

Therefore, I say, it is not for my good alone, it is for your own good that I say it, forget the past. One day, we may be united... The British element is gone, but they have left the mischief behind.

We do not want to perpetuate that mischief (hear, hear). When the British introduced this element they had not expected that they have to go so soon. They wanted it for their easy administration. That is all right. But they have left the legacy behind. Are we to get out of it or not?

(i) **Why were separate electorates considered as a mischief?**

(ii) **State the arguments given by Sardar Vallabh Bhai Patel for building political unity and forming the nation.**

(iii) **How did the philosophy of separate electorates result in a separate nation?**

Ans. (i) Separate electorates were considered as a mischief because in the name of giving representation to minorities and making the administration easy, Britishers divided two major communities of India politically. Later, this issue of separate electorates played an important role in partition of the country.

(ii) Following arguments were given by the Vallabh bhai Patel for building political unity and forming the nation

- He asked from supporter of separate electorates that if there was any country in the world which had a provision of separate electorate.
- He tried to explain them that it was not given to minorities for their safeguards but due to political reasons. It will be in the interest of minorities only if they do not demand for separate electorates.

(iii) Philosophy of separate electorates saw Hindus and Muslims as separate political identity.

It believed that interest of Hindus and Muslims were not common, so to represent Muslims there should be a Muslim only, similarly for Hindu, only Hindu should represent. This policy separated the people on the basis of religion and resulted in a separate nation.

4. "I Believe Separate Electorates will be Suicidal to the Minorities"

During the debate on 27th August, 1947, Govind Ballabh Pant said : I believe separate electorates will be suicidal to the minorities and will do them tremendous harm. If they are isolated for ever, they can never convert themselves into a majority and the feeling of frustrations will cripple them even from the very beginning. What is that you desire and what is our ultimate objective? Do the minorities always want to remain as minorities or do they ever expect to form an integral part of a great nation and as such to guide and control its destinies? If they do, can they ever achieve that aspiration and that ideal if they are isolated from the rest of the community? I think it would be extremely dangerous for them if they were segregated from the rest of the community and kept aloof in an air-tight compartment where they would have to rely on others even for the air they breathe. The minorities if they are returned by separate electorates can never have any effective voice.

(i) **What are separate electorates?**

(i) **Why were some Muslims, like Begum Aizaas Rasul against separate electorates?**

(iii) **Why did Govind Ballabh Pant feel separate electorate would be suicidal for the minorities?**

Ans. (i) Separate electorates are that type of elections in which some minorities select their own representative separately, as opposed to joint electorate where representative are selected collectively.

(ii) Begum Aizaas Rasul was against separate electorate as she felt that separate electorates were self-destructive, since they isolated the minorities from the majority.

(iii) Govind Ballabh Pant felt that separate electorates would be suicidal for the minorities because

- It would be difficult for them to become an integral part of a nation.
- If minorities were returned by separate electorates, they could never have an effective voice.

5. "There cannot be any divided loyalty"

Govind Ballabh Pant argued that in order to become loyal citizens people had to stop focusing only on the community and the self

For the success of democracy one must train himself in the art of self-discipline. In democracies, one should care less for himself and more for others. There cannot be any divided loyalty. All loyalties must exclusively be centered round the state. If in a democracy, you create rival loyalties, or you create a system in which any individual or group, instead of suppressing his extravagance, cares nought for larger or other interests, then democracy is doomed. **CBSE Term II 2022**

(i) **Examine the concern of Govind Ballabh Pant for a Unified Nation.**

(ii) **Why was loyalty considered as an important attribute of social pyramid?**

(iii) **Analyse the aspects considered significant for the success of democracy.**

Or (i) **Why did Govind Ballabh Pant lay more stress on the art of self-discipline?**

(ii) **What was considered important for the success of democracy?**

(iii) **'In democracies, one should care less for himself and more for other.' Give your views on this philosophy.**

Ans. (i) Govind Ballabh Pant was concerned for the unity of the nation. According to him, it was important for people to be loyal to the nation and had to stop focusing only on the community and self. For him, in order to have a successful democracy one must train himself in the art of self-discipline. All loyalities in democracy must be centered around the state.

(ii) Loyalty was considered as an important aspect of social pyramid because it served as the foundation for social unity and stability in a society. For example, loyal citizens in a state work for its welfare with the sense of common belonging.

(iii) For the success of democracy one must train himself in the art of self-discipline. In democracies, one should care less for himself and more for others. There cannot be any divided loyalty. All loyalties must exclusively be centred round the state.

Or (i) Govind Ballabh Pant suggested that to make democracy successful, one should be self-disciplined. Individual should care less for personal gain and focus more on collective benefit or for other gain in democracy.

(ii) For success of democracy, loyalty should not be divided, it must be centred round the state, and citizens should care less for themselves and more for fellow citizens.

(iii) This philosophy of democracy suggests that one should be considerate towards other. Nothing should be done for personal gain which can harm the interest of other person or large section of people. This philosophy promotes the feeling of people centric benefits instead of individual centric.

6. "The Real Minorities are the Masses of this Country"

Welcoming the Objectives Resolution introduced by Jawaharlal Nehru, N.G. Ranga said : Sir, there is a lot of talk about minorities. Who are the real minorities? Not the Hindus in the so-called Pakistan provinces, not the Sikhs, not even the Muslims.

No, the real minorities are the masses of this country. These people are so depressed and oppressed and suppressed till now that they are not able to take advantage of the ordinary civil rights. What is the position? You go to the tribal areas. According to law, their own traditional law, their tribal law, their lands, cannot be alienated.

Yet our merchants go there, and in the so-called free market they are able to snatch their lands. Thus, even though the law goes against this snatching away of their lands, still the merchants are able to turn the tribal people into veritable slaves by various kinds of bonds, and make them hereditary bond- slaves. Let us go to the ordinary villagers.

There goes the money-lender with his money and he is able to get the villagers in his pocket. There is the landlord himself, the zamindar and the *malguzar* and there are the various other people who are able to exploit these poor villagers. There is no elementary education even among these people.

These are the real minorities that need protection and assurances of protection. In order to give them the necessary protection, we will need much more than this resolution....

(i) How is the notion of minority defined by N.G. Ranga?

Or **Who are the real minorities according to Shri N.G. Ranga and why?**

(ii) Do you agree with Ranga? If not, mention who are real minorities according to you and why?

(iii) Describe the living condition of the tribals.

Ans. (i) According to Shri N.G. Ranga, the real minorities were the poor and downtrodden, especially the tribals because these people are so depressed, oppressed and suppressed till now that they are not able to take advantage of the ordinary civil rights.

(ii) Yes, I agree with Ranga that masses of this country are real minorities because these people have been depressed, suppressed and oppressed from the very long time.

(iii) According to Professor N.G. Ranga, the living conditions of the tribals can be described as follows

- The tribals were being alienated despite the tribal law according to which they cannot be alienated from their lands.
- When the merchants go to the lands of tribals, they snatch their lands.
- The merchants were able to turn the tribal people into veritable slaves by various kinds of bonds and make them hereditary bond slaves.

SELF ASSESSMENT TEST

Objective Type Questions

1. Which of these was not a member of the Constituent Assembly?
   (a) J.B. Kriplani
   (b) H.C. Mookerjee
   (c) Somnath Lahiri
   (d) Mahatma Gandhi
2. The executive was made partly responsible to the Provincial Legislature through the Act of
   (a) 1909
   (b) 1919
   (c) 1935
   (d) 1892
3. Hindustani language was a mix of
   (a) Hindi and Sanskrit
   (b) Hindi and Sindhi
   (c) Hindi and Urdu
   (d) Hindi and Arabic
4. Match the Following.

	List I		List II
A.	K. Santhanam	1.	Supported Hindi as language for Constitution-making
B.	Hansa Mehta	2.	Argued against the strong centre
C.	R.V. Dhulekar	3.	Rejected the demand for separate electorate
D.	Sardar Vallabh Bhai Patel	4.	Demanded Justice for women

Codes

	A	B	C	D
(a)	1	2	3	4
(b)	2	4	1	3
(c)	3	4	2	1
(d)	4	3	1	2

Short Answer Type Questions

5. What were the views of N.G. Ranga about the problem of minorities and its solution? Discuss.
6. What decisions were taken by the Constituent Assembly to resolve the language controversy?
7. Why did India adopt the path of secularism? Express your opinion with examples.
8. How did members of the Constituent Assembly try to ensure social justice? Explain with examples.

Long Answer Type Questions

9. 'The Constituent Assembly had 300 members. Of these, six members played particularly important roles'. Explain the statement.
10. Examine the challenges posed by separate electorates, focusing particularly on the perspectives of key members of the Constituent Assembly regarding this issue.
11. What were the conflicting views in the Constituent Assembly about the powers of the central government and the states? Why did the Constituent Assembly prefer a strong centre?

PROJECT WORK

Project Work

Meaning of Project

The word project comes from the Latin word 'Projectum' which means 'before an action'. At school level, a project is a research assignment given to a student which generally requires a larger amount of effort and more independent work that is involved in a normal assignment. It requires students to undertake their own fact finding endeavours, either from library, or from the internet or by means of primary data collection. A project report should

- be handwritten
- have diagrammatic presentation
- have topics with suitable headings
- be concise and clear
- have a length of 15 to 20 pages
- end up with conclusion

Utilities of Making a Project

Following points state the uses/utility of project work

(*i*) To provide information about the development and growth of institutions, business products, and government activities.

(*ii*) To provide information to the consumers about the price of commodities, quality and uses, etc of a product as per their interest.

(*iii*) It is helpful in estimating the preference of consumers for petrol car or diesel car, telephone or mobile phone, etc.

(*iv*) Project report is helpful for the shareholders, who may be interested in knowing the earning of an enterprise and possibility of getting dividend.

(*v*) To help in the policy formulation about the economic and social development of any country.

Thus, we can say that project work may help marketers, shareholders, economists, consumers and government in effective and efficient decision-making.

Elements Of Project Report

A good project report should contain the following elements

Title Page

This should include the project title, name of the company on which you are conducting your research and name of the student. You can also list the name of your school, class and subject teacher.

Acknowledgement

It is usual to thank those individuals, who have provided particularly useful assistance, technical or otherwise, during your project.

Content Page

This should list the main sections and sub-sections of your report. Choose self-explanatory titles with their respective pages and use double spacing for clarity.

Introduction

This is one of the most important components of the project report. It should begin with a clear statement of what the project is about, so that the nature and scope of the project can be understood by a reader. It should summarise everything which you set out to achieve and provide a clear summary of the project's background, relevance and main contributions. The introduction should set the context for the project and should provide the reader with a summary of the key things to look out for in, the remainder of the report.

Background

The background section of the report should set the project into action, it specifies the problem of the company, what remedial actions were taken by the company and what are its effects.

Body of Report

The central part of the report usually consists of three or four sections detailing the technical work undertaken during the project. The structure of these sections is highly project dependent.They can reflect the chronological development of the project. It includes the detailed description regarding the matter of the project.

Evaluation

This might involve quantitative and qualitative evaluation such as expressibility, functionality, ease-of-use, etc of a product. At some point, you should also evaluate the strengths and weaknesses of what you have done. It includes certain questionnaires, sampling test which help in evaluating the result on the basis of truths and facts.

Conclusion

The conclusion should list the things, which have been learnt as a result of the work you have done. It shows the ultimate response of the project undertaken by a student. It should be expressive and impressive so that a reader would clearly evaluate the result and rated you on the basis of your presentation.

Bibliography

In this section, you should mention the details of all the secondary sources, *i.e.*, magazines, newspapers, reports, internet links, etc. used for developing the project.

TOPIC : The Architectural Culture of the Vijayanagara Empire

Name : ....

Class : ....

Roll No. : ....

Subject : ....

School : ....

Submitted by ....

Submitted to ....

Acknowledgement

I would like to extend my sincere and heartfelt obligation towards all those who have helped me in making this project. Without their active guidance, help, cooperation and encouragement, I would not have been able to present the project on time.

I am extremely thankful and pay my gratitude to my teacher Mr/Ms .... for his/her valuable guidance and support for completion of this project.

I extend my gratitude to my Principal Mr/Ms .... for the moral support extended during the tenure of the project.

I also acknowledge with a deep sense of reverence, my gratitude towards my parents, other faculty members of the school and friends for their valuable suggestions given to me in completing this project.

Date...........

....

Name of Student

Certificate

This is to Certify that the project work

.... is the bonafide

work of .... (Name of the student) who

carried out the work under my supervision

....

Name and Signature of
Teacher/Supervisor

Contents

S.No.	Particulars
1.	Introduction
2.	Sources of the History of Vijayanagara
3.	Dynasties of Vijayanagara Empire
4.	Architectural Culture of Vijayanagara Empire
5.	Vijayanagara City : Capital City of Vijayanagara Empire
6.	Decline of Vijayanagara Empire
7.	Viva Voce Questions

The Architectural Culture of the Vijayanagara Empire

Introduction

Vijayanagara (city of victory) was founded in the 14th century. Two brothers, **Harihara (Hakka) I** and **Bukka Raya I** of Sangama Dynasty laid the foundations of the Vijayanagara in 1336 CE. Vijayanagara was on the South bank of the River Tungabhadra near the fortress of Anegudi. The writings of medieval European travellers such as Domingo Paes and Nicolo de Conti, and the literature in local languages provide crucial information about its history. Archaeological excavations at Vijayanagara have revealed the empire's power and wealth.

In the first two decades after the founding of the empire, Harihara I gained control over most of the area South of the Tungabhadra river and earned the title of *Purvapaschima Samudradhishavara.*

Sources of the History of Vijayanagara

Colonel Colin Mackenzie, an engineer, antiquarian, surveyor and cartographer had discovered the ruins at Hampi in 1800 CE. He prepared the **first survey map of the Hampi** site. The initial information he collected was based on the memories of priests of the **Virupaksha temple** and the shrine of **Pampadevi.** In 1836 CE, epigraphists (people who study and interpret ancient inscriptions) started collecting many inscriptions found at the temples at Hampi. Later from 1856, photographers started to record the monuments which helped scholars to study them. Historians collected all the information from these sources along with travel accounts of foreign travellers and other literature written in Telugu, Kannada, Tamil and Sanskrit to reconstruct the history of city and the empire.

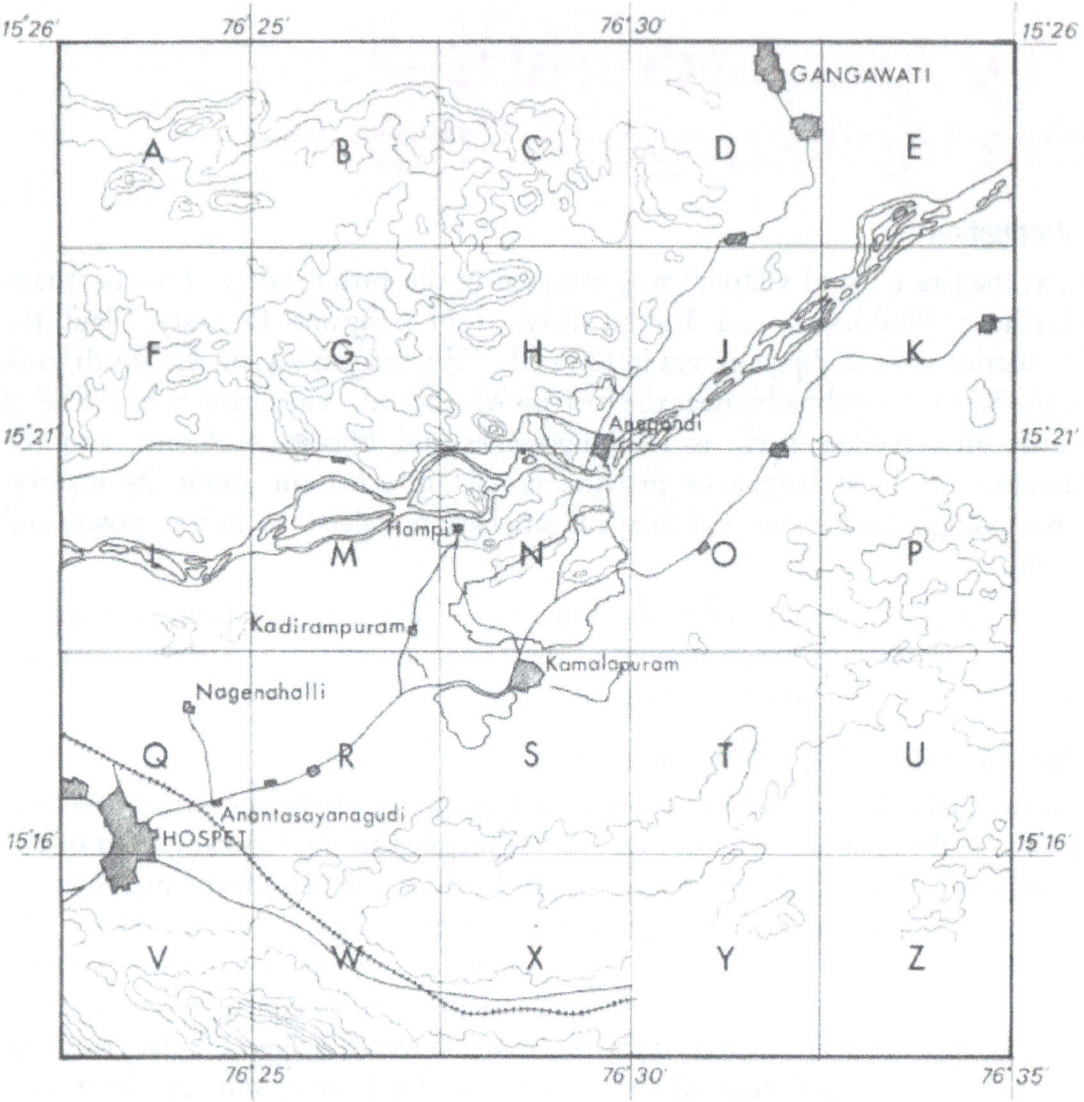

Survey Map of the Hampi Site

Dynasties of Vijayanagara Empire

Sangama Dynasty

The Sangama dynasty was the first dynasty that exercised the control till 1485 CE. Harihar and Bukka were sons of Sangama, feudatories of Kakatiyas of Warangal. Bukka's successor, Harihara II, continued Bukka's campaign through Southern India and managed to take control of coastal Andhra between Nellore and Kalinga and conquer the Addanki and Srisailam areas as well as most of the territory between the peninsula to the South of the Krishna River.

The greatest ruler of Sangama dynasty was Deva Raya II. During his reign, Abdur Razzak, the messenger of Shah Rukh visited the Vijaynagara kingdom. Virupaksha Raya II was the last emperor of the dynasty.

Saluva Dynasty

Saluva Narsimha was the founder of Saluva dynasty. Immadi Narsimha succeeded him. He was a weak ruler and hence the control of State fell into the hands of Narsa Nayaka. Vasco da Gama landed in Calicut during his time in 1498 CE.

Tuluva Dynasty

The son of Narsa Nayaka, Vira Narsimha was the founder of Tuluva dynasty. He was succeeded by his half brother, **Krishnadeva Raya** in 1509 CE. Krishnadeva Raya was the one of the main rulers of Tuluva dynasty.

Krishnadeva Raya's rule was known by expansion and strengthening the empire. During this time, the land between the Tungabhadra and Krishna rivers (the Raichur doab) was acquired in 1512 CE, the rulers of Orissa were brought under the control in 1514 CE and severe defeats were suffered by the Sultan of Bijapur in 1520 CE. Krishnadeva Raya was acknowledged with building some fine temples and adding great looking *gopurams* to many important South Indian temples. **Nagalapuram**, a suburban township named after his mother was founded near Vijayanagara. The most detailed descriptions of Vijayanagara come from his time. Krishnadeva Raya was also known for his literary skills. He himself has written a book named *Amuktamalyada*.

Architectural Culture of Vijayanagara Empire

The architectural culture of Vijayanagara Empire can be explained through the temple and other buildings in Vijayanagara. These are

- Virupaksha Temple is located in Hampi in the Ballari district of Karnataka, India. The temple is dedicated to Lord Virupaksha, a form of Shiva. The main temple consists of a sanctum, three ante chambers, a pillared hall and an open pillared hall. It is decorated with delicately carved pillars. A pillared cloister, entrance gateways, courtyards, smaller shrines and other structures surround the temple.
- The nine-tiered Eastern gateway, which is the largest at 50 meters, is well-proportioned and incorporates some earlier structures. It has a brick superstructure and a stone base. It gives access to the outer court containing many sub-shrines. The smaller Eastern gateway leads to the inner court with its numerous smaller shrines.

- A narrow channel of the Tungabhadra River flows along the temple's terrace and then descends to the temple-kitchen and out through the outer court. One of the most striking features of this temple is the usage of mathematical concepts to build and decorate it. The main shape of the temple is triangular.
- Krishnadeva Raya was a major patron of this temple. The most ornate of all structures in the temple is the central pillared hall. It is recorded that Krishnadeva Raya commissioned this hall in 1510 CE to mark his accession. He also built the Eastern gopuram. The halls in the temple were used for a variety of purposes. Some were spaces in which the images of Gods were placed to witness special programmes of music, dance, drama, etc. Others were used to celebrate the marriages of deities.

Virupaksha Temple (Hampi)

An Aerial View of the Virupaksha Temple

The Kings Palace

Based on the form of the buildings and their functions, different structures were assigned names. The king's palace was the largest of the buildings but there is no strong evidence that it was a royal residence. It had two impressive platforms, called **the audience hall** and **the *mahanavami dibba*.** The entire complex was surrounded by high double walls with a street running between them.

Interior of the Audience Hall at Madurai

Mahanavami Dibba

Mahanavami dibba was located at one of the highest points in the city. It is a massive platform or stage rising from a base of about 11,000 sq ft. to a height of 40 ft. There is evidence that it supported a wooden building. The base of the platform is covered with relief designs or carvings. Rituals associated with the building might have coincided with Mahanavami. It is known as Dusshera in North India, Durga Puja in Bengal and Navaratri or Mahanavami in peninsular India. The Vijayanagara kings showed their prestige, power and control over the empire on this occasion.

Mahanavami Dibba

The Lotus Mahal

The Lotus Mahal, named by British travellers in the nineteenth century was one of the most beautiful buildings in the royal centre. A map drawn by Mackenzie suggested that it might have been a council chamber, a place where the king met his advisers.

The Lotus Mahal is built in Rubble masonry and finely plastered. The structure is laid out symmetrically with equal projections on four sides. The dome gives an illustration of an open lotus bud. The curves of the palace are inspired by the Islamic architecture and protect the palace from harsh weather conditions. It has two storeys, both with arched openings in multiple planes surrounded by elaborate plaster designs. It has total of eight pyramidal towers over the corners and one big tower in the middle of the structure and is supported by 24 pillars. The pyramidal tower is influenced by Indian Architecture. The pillars are decorated with stone carved aquatic animals, plants etc.

An Elevation Drawing of the Lotus Mahal

Hazara Rama Temple

The Hazara Rama temple occupied the Western part of the urban core in the royal centre section of Hampi. This temple was dedicated to Rama of the Ramayana fame, and an avatar of Vishnu. It was the ceremonial temple for the royal family. The temple is dated to the early 15th century. The temple's outer walls portray the Hindu Mahanavami (Dasara) and the spring Holi festival procession and celebrations in parallel bands of artwork. The lowest band shows marching elephants, above it are horses led by horsemen, then soldiers celebrated by the public, then dancers and musicians, with a top layer depicting a boisterous procession of the general public. The depiction mirrors the description of festivals and processions in surviving memoirs of Persians and Portuguese who visited the Vijayanagara capital.

Sculpture from the Hazara Rama Temple

The Vitthala Temple

The Vitthala temple is the most artistically sophisticated Hindu temple in Hampi, and is part of the sacred centre of Vijayanagara. The temple was dedicated to Vitthala, a form of Krishna also called Vithoba. The temple opens to the East, has a square plan and features an entrance gopuram with two side gopurams. The main temple stands in the middle of a paved courtyard and several subsidiary shrines, all aligned to the East.

The temple is a unified structure in a courtyard measuring 500 by 300 feet which is surrounded by a triple row of pillars. It is a low structure of one storey with an average height of 25 feet. The temple has three distinct compartments - a garbhagriha, an ardhamandapa and a mahamandapa (or sabha mandapa).

The Vitthala temple has a Garuda shrine in the form of a stone chariot in the courtyard. In the front of the stone chariot is a large, square, open-pillared, axial sabha mandapa, or community hall. The mandapa has four sections, two of which are aligned with the temple sanctum. The mandapa has 56 carved stone beams of different diameters, shape, length and surface finish that produces musical sounds when struck.

The Vitthala Temple

Vijayanagara City :

Capital City of Vijayanagara Empire

The capital city of Vijayanagara Empire was Vijayanagara. It was like most of the other capitals, known for its distinctive physical layout and building style. A number of inscriptions of the kings of Vijayanagara and their *nayakas* give us information about the city.

Traveller's Views about Vijayanagara City Several travellers such as, an Italian trader named **Nicolo de Conti**, an ambassador named **Abdur Razzaq** sent by ruler of Persia, a merchant named **Afanasy Nikitin** from Russia, **Duarte Barbosa, Domingo Paes** and **Fernao Nuniz** from Portugal visited the city. All these travellers accounts gave information about Vijayanagara. For instance, Domingo Paes's described Vijayanagara that it was very beautiful and large as Rome. He pointed out that the city had many trees, gardens and many water channels and some lakes. The great fortress walls enclosed the city. Abdur Razzaq, an ambassador sent by the ruler of Persia to Calicut in the 15th century, was impressed by the fortifications of Vijayanagara and mentioned about the seven lines of forts.

These fortifications not only surrounded the city but also remote agricultural areas and forests. The hills surrounding the city were linked with the outermost wall. The large construction was slightly reduced in thickness at one end. The mortar or cementing agent were not used in the construction. The stone blocks were wedge (thick at one end and thin at another end) shaped, which held them in place. The inner portion of walls was Earth packed with rubble and square or rectangular fortification was projected outwards.

Decline of Vijayanagara Empire

After the death of Krishnadeva Raya in 1529 CE, conflicts developed within the empire. His successors had faced challenges from *nayakas* or military chiefs. By 1542 CE, control at the centre was shifted to another ruling family of the **Aravidu**, which remained in power till the end of the 17th century.

In 1565 CE, **Rama Raya**, the Chief Minister of Vijayanagara, led the army into battle at **Rakshasi-Tangadi** also known as **Talikota.** Here Rama Raya's forces were decisively defeated by the combined armies of Bijapur, Ahmadnagar and Golconda. The victorious armies looted and destroyed the city of Vijayanagara. Within a few years this city was totally abandoned. Now the focus of the empire shifted to East where the Aravidu dynasty ruled from **Penukonda** and later from **Chandragiri** near Tirupathi.

Viva Voce Questions

1. ***When was Vijayanagra Empire founded?***

Ans. The Vijayanagra Empire was founded in 1336 CE.

2. ***Name the first dynasty of Vijayanagara Empire.***

Ans. Sangama dynasty was the first dynasty of Vijayangara Empire.

3. ***The capital of Vijayanagara Empire was situated on the bank of which river?***

Ans. The Capital of Vijayanagara Empire was situated on the south bank of the river Tungabhadra.

4. ***Name the ruler of Vijayanagara Empire who adopted the title of Purvapaschima Samudradhishvara.***

Ans. The founder of Vijayangara Empire, Harihara after gaining control over the areas of south of the Tungabhadra River adopted the title of Purvapaschima Samudradhishvara

5. ***Who prepared the first survey map of the Hampi site?***

Ans. The first survey map of the Hampi site was prepared by Colonel Colin Mackenzie.

6. ***Under the reign of which ruler, Abdur Razzak visited the Vijayanagra Empire?***

Ans. Under the reign of Krishnadeva Raya, the Persian messenger, Abdur Razzak visited the Vijayanagara Empire.

7. ***The famous ruler of Vijayanagara Empire, Krishnadeva Raya belonged to which dynasty?***

Ans. The famous ruler of Vijaynagara Empire, Krishnadeva Raya belonged to the Tuluva dynasty.

8. ***Name the town founded by Krishnadeva Raya in the memory of his mother.***

Ans. In the memory of his beloved mother, Krishnadeva Raya founded the city of Nagalapuram.

9. ***Who had written the Telugu book on statecraft Amuktamalyada?***

Ans. The Telugu book on Statecraft, Amuktamalyada was written by Krishnadeva Raya.

10. ***The inner wall of shrine of which temple in Vijayanagara Empire, included sculpted scenes from Ramayana?***

Ans. The inner walls of shrine of Hazara Rama Temple in the Vijayanagara Empire included sculpted scenes from Ramayana.

11. ***Name the merchant from the Russia who visited the Vijayanagara Empire.***

Ans. Afanasy Nikitin was the merchant from Russia who visited the Vijayanagara Empire.

12. ***Name the last dynasty of the Vijayanagara Empire.***

Ans. Aravidu dynasty was the last ruling dynasty of the Vijayanagara Empire.

SAMPLE QUESTION PAPER 1

A Highly Simulated Sample Question Paper for CBSE Class XII

(SOLVED)

HISTORY

General Instructions

- Question paper comprises five Section: A, B, C, D and E. There are 34 questions in the question paper. All questions are compulsory.
- Section A: Question numbers 1 to 21 are MCQs of 1 mark each.
- Section B: Question numbers 22 to 27 are Short Answer Type Questions, carrying 3 marks each. Answer to each question should not exceed 60-80 words.
- Section C: Question number 28 to 30 are Long Answer Type Questions, carrying 8 marks each. Answer to each question should not exceed 300-350 words.
- Section D: Question number 31 to 33 are Source Based Questions with three sub questions and are of 4 marks each.
- Section E: Question number 34 is Map based, carrying 5 marks that includes the identification and location of significant test items. Attach the map with the answer book.
- There is no overall choice in the question paper. However, an internal choice has been provided in few questions. Only one of the choices in such questions have to be attempted.
- In addition to this, separate instructions are given with each section and question, wherever necessary.

Section A

(1×21=21)

(Objective Type Questions)

1. Which of the following statements is correct regarding Al-Biruni's Kitab-ul-Hind ? (1)

(a) It is in Persion language.
(b) It is divided into 100 chapters.
(c) It is divided into several subjects like religion, philosophy, festivals, etc.
(d) He used such a language which was not easily understandable by other locals.

2. Vijayanagara city was situated between which of the following rivers? (1)

(a) Krishna in North and Tungabhadra in South
(b) Krishna in the South and Cauvery in North
(c) Tungabhadra in North and Krishna in South
(d) Cauvery in the North and Tungabhadra in South

3. Match the following. (1)

List I		List II
A. 1921	1.	Daya Ram Sahni begins excavation of Harappa
B. 1922	2.	Excavation begins at Mohenjodaro
C. 1955	3.	SR Rao begins excavations at Lothal
D. 1986	4.	American team begins excavations at Harappa

Codes

	A	B	C	D		A	B	C	D
(a)	1	2	3	4	(b)	4	3	2	1
(c)	1	4	3	2	(d)	2	1	4	3

4. Choose the correct option.
The lost Harappan Civilisation was discovered in 1921 by this archaeologist. (1)
(a) RD Banerji (b) Alexander Cunningham
(c) DR Sahni (d) SR Rao

5. Match the List 1 with List II.

List I		List II	
A.	Permanent settlement in Bengal	1.	1818
B.	Santhal rebellion	2.	1793
C.	First revenue settlement in Bombay and deccan	3.	1875
D.	Ryots in Deccan villages rebel	4.	1855-1856

Codes

	A	B	C	D		A	B	C	D
(a)	2	3	4	1	(b)	1	3	2	4
(c)	2	4	1	3	(d)	4	1	3	2

6. Identify the image and write its name. (1)

(a) Lotus Mahal
(b) Mahanavami Dibba
(c) Diwan-e Khas
(d) Palace of Krishnadeva Raya

7. Given below are two statements, one labelled as Assertion (A) and the other labelled as Reason (R). (1)
Assertion (A) The great epic Mahabharata is the work of not one but several authors at different time periods.
Reason (R) Historians suggest, the didactic sections of the epic were probably added later.
Codes
(a) Both A and R are true and R is the correct explanation of A
(b) Both A and R are true, but R is not the correct explanation of A
(c) A is true, but R is false
(d) A is false, but R is true

8. Who travelled through Rajmahal Hills in the 19th century? (1)
(a) Buchanan (b) William
(c) Cleveland (d) Ricardo

9. Which among the following was/were the feature(s) of Harappan Civilisation? (1)
(a) Town planning (b) Citadel or lower town
(c) Drainage system (d) All of these

10. What does the layout of Mohenjodaro reveal about the planning of Harappan cities? Choose the best suitable option from the following. (1)
(a) Cities were randomly built without a structured design.
(b) Settlements included a citadel and lower town with a planned drainage system.
(c) Streets were narrow and unorganised, with no attention to drainage.
(d) Buildings were constructed using unstandardised and irregular bricks.

11. Identify the dynasty who followed the system of endogamy. (1)
(a) Mauryas (b) Pandavas
(c) Pallavas (d) Satavahanas

12. Arrange the following events in chronological order. (1)
(i) Composition of Tripitakas
(ii) Composition of Charak and Sushruta Samhita
(iii) Compilation of Puranas
(iv) Composition of Ramayana
Codes
(a) (i), (iv), (ii), (iii) (b) (iv), (iii), (i), (ii)
(c) (ii), (iv), (iii), (i) (d) (iii), (i), (ii), (iv)

13. Complete the following analogy with the help of given options.
Karaikkal Amaiyyar : Shiva, Andal : ? (1)
(a) Vishnu (b) Bramha
(c) Agni (d) Shakti

14. Consider the following statements regarding revolt of 1857 and choose the correct option. (1)
I. Mughal Emperor Bahadur Shah was declared as the leader of sepoys.
II. There was no participation of common people.
III. Moneylenders and the rich were attacked.
Codes
(a) I and II (b) II and III
(c) I and III (d) I, II and III

15. Identify the incorrectly matched pair. (1)
(a) Halalkhoran - Scavengers
(b) Mallahzadas - Sons of boatmen
(c) Jins-i-Kamil - Peasants
(d) Agricultural labourers - Majur

FULLY SOLVED

16. Identify the famous temple from the description given below.

- While inscriptions suggest that the earliest shrine dated to the 9th-10th centuries, it was substantially enlarged with the establishment of the Vijayanagara Empire.
- The hall in front of the main shrine was built by Krishnadeva Raya to mark his accession. This was decorated with delicately carved pillars.

(a) Gangaikonda Cholapuram Temple
(b) Brihadeshwara Temple
(c) Virupaksha Temple
(d) Vittala Temple

17. Identify the correctly matched pair(s). (1)

(a) Cuthcheries – Court of Zamindars
(b) Amlah – Office of Zaindars
(c) Mandals – Village Headmen
(d) All of the above

18. Who made an aggressive plea that Hindi can be used as the language of Constitution- making? (1)

(a) RV Dhulekar (b) TA Ramalingam Chettiar
(c) Shankarrao Deo (d) Ms G Durgabai

19 Given below are two statements, one labelled as Assertion (A) and the other labelled as Reason (R). (1)

Assertion (A) Cripps Mission failed in its aim.
Reason (R) Congress demanded to appoint an Indian as Defence Member to help British in war.

Codes

(a) Both A and R are true and R is the correct explanation of A
(b) Both A and R are true, but R is not the correct explanation of A
(c) A is true, but R is false
(d) A is false, but R is true

20. Who among the following was active in underground resistence during Quit India Movement? (1)

(a) Jawaharlal Nehru
(b) Jayaprakash Narayan
(c) Subhash Chandra Bose
(d) Dr Rajendra Prasad

21. Compare and contrast the approaches of the Alvars and Nayanars towards caste practices. Choose the best suitable option from the following (1)

(a) Both Alvars and Nayanars upheld the caste system strictly.
(b) Alvars attempted to reform the caste system, while Nayanars ignored it entirely.
(c) Both Alvars and Nayanars included individuals from diverse social backgrounds in their devotional practices.
(d) Alvars were inclusive, but Nayanars focused only on Brahmanas.

Section B

(Short Answer Type Questions) (3×6=18)

22. What are the most important contributions of Mahatma Gandhi in the political sphere of India? (3)

23. Critically examine the Deccan Riots Commission Report. (3)

24. Give a brief description of Megasthenese. What does Megasthenese tell about the administration of Mauryan Empire? (3)

25. Who were Lingayats? Explain their contribution in the social and religious fields. (3)

Or Discuss the role of women devotees in Bhakti Movement with the help of suitable examples.

26. Examine the role of women in agrarian society during 16th and 17th century in Mughal Empire. (3)

27. Discuss the rules of marriage that were prevalent in early societies between 600 BCE to 600 CE. (3)

Or Write a short note on ideal occupations as mentioned in Dharmasutras.

Section C

(Long Answer Type Questions) (8×3=24)

28. Describe the contributions of John Marshall, Director General of the ASI (Archaeological Survey of India) to Indian archaeology. (8)

Or How does the architectural features of Mohenjodaro indicate town planning?

29. Briefly explain the different types of buildings situated in the royal centre. What do you think was the significance of the rituals associated with the mahanavami dibba? (8)

Or The writing of Portuguese travellers has greatly helped in reconstruction of history of Vijayanagara city. In this regard, highlight the aspects observed by the Duarte Barbosa and Domingo Paes on urban core and mahanavami dibba of the Vijayanagara Empire respectively.

30. "Mahatma Gandhi's focus on social reform work after the Non-Cooperation Movement ended and his later re-entry into politics in 1928 played a crucial role in India's struggle for independence." Justify the statement. (8)

Or "Gandhiji told the privileged invitees that there is no salvation for India unless you strip yourself of this jewellery and hold it in trust for your countrymen in India". Justify the statement.

Section D

(Source Based Questions) (4×3=12)

31. Read the following source regarding Quit India carefully and answer the questions that follow.

After the failure of the Cripps Mission, Mahatma Gandhi decided to launch his third major movement against British rule. This was the "Quit India" campaign, which began in August 1942. Although Gandhiji was jailed at once, younger activitsts organised strikes and acts of sabotage all over the country. Particularly active in the underground resistance were socialist members of the Congress, such as Jayaprakash Narayan. In several district, such as Satara in the West and Medinipur in the East, "independent" governments were proclaimed. The British responded with much force, yet it took more than a year to suppress the rebellion.

"Quit India" was genuinely a mass movement, bringing into its ambit hundreds of thousands of ordinary Indians. It especially energised the young who, in very large numbers, left their colleges to go to jail. However, while the Congress leaders languished in jail, Jinnah and his colleagues in the Muslim league worked patiently at expanding their influence. It was in these years that the league began to make a mark in the Punjab and Sind, provinces where it had previously had scarcely any presence.

(i) What was the role of Muslim League in Quit India Movement? (1)

(ii) Discuss the role of youth in Quit India Movement. (1)

(iii) Why was Quit India Movement a genuinely mass movement? (2)

32. Read the following source carefully and answer the questions that follows.

A Demon

This is an excerpt from a poem by Karaikkal Ammaiyar in which she described herself
The female Pey (demoness) with bulging veins, protruding eyes, white teeth and shrunken stomach, red haired and jutting teeth lengthy shins extending till the ankles, shouts and wails while wandering in the forest. This is the forest of Alankatu, which is the home of our father (Shiva) who dances with his matted hair thrown in all eight directions, and with cool limbs.

(i) Who is the author of this excerpt and what is it about? (1)

(ii) How did the author describe herself in the poem? (1)

(iii) What did author try to convey through the poem? (2)

33. Read the following source carefully and answer the questions that follow. (4)

The Importance of Boundaries

The Manusmriti is one of the best-known legal texts of early India, written in Sanskrit and complied between 2nd century BCE and 2nd century CE. This is what the text advises the king to do. Seeing that in the world controversies constantly arise due to the ignorance of boundaries, he should have conceived boundary markers buried-stones, bones, cow's hair, chaff, ashes, potsherds, dried cow dung, bricks, coal, pebbles and with sand. He should also have other similar substances that would not decay in the soil buried as hidden markers at the intersection of boundaries.

(i) Why did the controversies of boundaries arise? (1)

(ii) Suggest the ways to solve the boundary problems. (1)

(iii) Explain with example any such problem being faced by India today. (2)

FULLY SOLVED

Section E

(Map Based Question)

34. A. Locate and label the following places on the map of India. (3)

(i) Thanjavur

(ii) Bijapur

(iii) Place where Salt March was held.

Or

Place from where Quit India Movement started.

B. On given political map of India, two main centres of the 1857 Revolt have been marked 1 and 2. Write their names. (2)

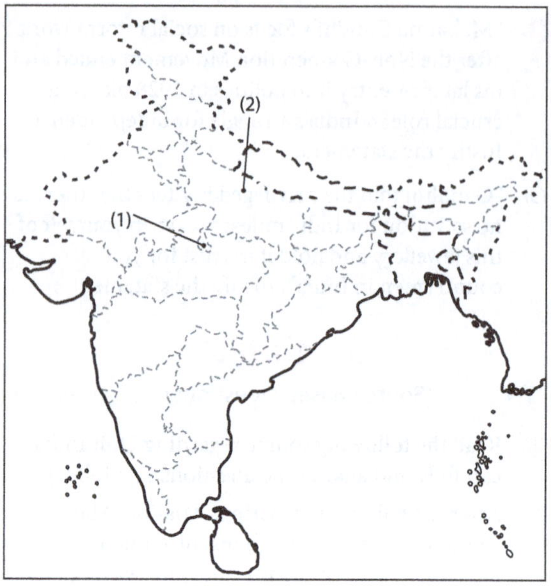

Answers

1. (c) It is divided into several subjects like religion, philosophy, festivals, etc.

2. (a) Krishna in North and Tungabhadra in South

3. (a)

4. (c) DR Sahni

5. (c)

6. (a) Lotus Mahal

7. (a) Both A and R are true and R is the correct explanation of A

8. (a) Buchanan

9. (d) All of these

10. (b) Settlements included a citadel and lower town with a planned drainage system.

11. (d) Satavahanas

12. (a) (i), (iv), (ii), (iii)

13. (a) Vishnu

14. (c) I and III

15. (c) Jins-i-Kamil - Peasants

16. (c) Virupaksha Temple

17. (d) All of the above

18. (a) RV Dhulekar

19. (a) Both A and R are true and R is the correct explanation of A

20. (b) Jayaprakash Narayan

21. (c) Both Alvars and Nayanars included individuals from diverse social backgrounds in their devotional practices.

22. In the political sphere of India, Mahatma Gandhi had rendered invaluable contributions. They are as follows

- He bridged the gap between intelligentisia and masses, it helped in putting a joint struggle against Britishers.
- Mahatma Gandhi through his unique yet effective methods contributed immensly in political awareness of the masses. Techniques such as non-cooperation, civil disobedience, boycott of courts, educational institution, etc created an increased understanding about true nature of British rule.
- Gandhiji also helped in making the nationalist movement a broad based one. His accomodative and decentralised approach led to incorporation of many segments of population such as women, tribals in the political struggle for independence of India.
- The three prominent mass movement of Gandhiji *viz* Non-Cooperation, Civil Disobedience and Quit India forced upon the British, the realisation that their rule would not last forever. Therefore, we can say that Gandhiji through his innovative approach has contributed significantly in political sphere of India.

23. The Deccan Riots Report can be examined through the following points

- Proper enquiries were held in the riot affected districts and the statement of the ryots, *sahukars* and eyewitnesses were recorded. Statistical data on revenue rates, prices and interest rates were compiled in various regions.
- In the Deccan Riots Report, the commission was specifically asked to judge whether the level of the government revenue demand was the cause of the revolt. After presenting all the evidences, the commission reported that the government demand was not the cause of peasants anger. It was the moneylenders who were to blame.

24. Megasthenese was a Greek historian, who came to India in the 4th century BC as an ambassador of Seleucus Nictor. He lived in the court of Chandragupta Maurya for about five years (302-298 BC). He has written an account of India and also that of Chandragupta's reign in his book entitled Indica. Megasthenese had tried to write about everything that he had seen in India like its geographical features, government, religion and society.

Megasthenese has written in detail about Chandragupta Maurya's administration, as well as Indian society in the Mauryan period. Megasthenese mentioned a committee with six sub-committees for military coordination activity. These were

(i) One looked after the navy.
(ii) Second managed transport and provisions.
(iii) Third was responsible for foot-soldiers.
(iv) Fourth for horses.
(v) Fifth for chariots.
(vi) Sixth for elephants.

25. The Lingayats emerged in Karnataka in the 12th century under the leadership of Basavanna, a Brahmana. They worshipped Shiva in his manifestation as a linga.

Some of the beliefs held by the Lingayats contributed to the social and religious order of that time. These beliefs were

- **Shiva as 'Linga'** Lingayats worshipped Shiva in their manifestation as a 'linga'. They usually kept a small 'linga' in a silver case. They hung it over their left shoulder.
- **Salvation** They believed that they would be united with Shiva after their death. After their meeting with Shiva, they would never return to this world.
- **Caste System** Lingayats contributed to the society by rejecting the caste system and promoting harmony.
- **Women Emancipation** They challenged certain practices which was considered deregotary for women and promoted post-puberty marriage and the remarriage of widows.

Or One of the striking feature of Bhakti traditions was the presence of women. For example, the compositions of Andal, a woman Alvar, were widely sung. Andal saw herself as the beloved of Vishnu; her verses express her love for the deity.

Another woman, Karaikkal Ammaiyar, a devotee of Shiva, adopted the path of extreme asceticism in order to attain her goal. Her compositions were preserved within the Nayanar tradition. These women renounced their social obligations, but did not join an alternative order or become nuns.

26. The role of women in the agrarian society during 16th and 17th century was

- Men tilled and ploughed, while women sowed, weeded, threshed and winnowed the harvest.
- Artisanal tasks such as spinning yarn, sifting and kneading clay for pottery, and embroidery were among the many aspects of production dependent on female labour. The more commercialised the product, the greater the demand on women's labour to produce it.
- Women were considered an important resource in agrarian society also because they were child bearers in a society dependent on labour.

27. In the early society, girls had no claims to the resources of the household. At the same time, marrying them into families outside the kin was considered desirable. Exogamy was prevalent which meant that the lives of young girls and women belonging to families that claimed high status were often carefully regulated to ensure that they were married at the 'right' time and to the 'right' person. This gave rise to the belief that kanyadana or the gift of a daughter in marriage was an important religious duty of the father.

Or The Dharmasutras and Dharmashastras contained rules about the ideal 'occupations' of the four categories or varnas. Brahmanas were supposed to study and teach the Vedas, perform sacrifices and get sacrifices performed, and give and receive gifts. Kshatriyas were to engage in warfare, protect people and administer justice, study the Vedas, get sacrificies performed, and make gifts. Vaishyas, were in addition expected to engage in agriculture, pastoralism and trade. Shudras were assigned only one occupation – that of serving the three 'higher' varnas.

28. In 1924, Director General of ASI, John Marshall declared about the discovery of a new civilisation as, 'Indus Valley Civilisation to the World.' It was a landmark discovery. Prior to this discovery, certain progress in this direction was made in starting phase of the Indian archaeology. It helped John Marshall in discovering a new civilisation.

Contributions of John Marshall, Director General of ASI to Indian Archaeology

- **Starting Phase of Indian Archaeology** In the early decades of the 20th century, archaeologist Dayaram Sahni found some seals of Harappa. These seals were definitely much older than early historic levels. Now, their significance began to be realised. Another archaeologist Rakhal Das Banerji found same seals at Mohenjodaro as were found at Harappa. It led to the assumption that both the archaeological sites were the parts of single archaeological culture.
  Based on these findings, in 1924, then the Director General of ASI, John Marshall declared about the discovery of a new civilisation, Indus Valley to the world. SN Roy wrote in the '*Story of Indian Archaeology*' that, "Marshall left India three thousand years older than he had found here."
- **Connection of Harappa to Other Ancient Civilisations** When John Marshall declared about the discovery of Harappa, similar seals were also found in the excavation of archaeological sites of Mesopotamia. By this, not only new civilisation came to limelight, but we also came to know that this civilisation was contemporary to Mesopotamia'n civilisation.
- **Global Experience and Expertise of Marshall** As the Director-General of ASI, Sir John Marshall's term was actually a term of major change in Indian archaeology.
  He was the first professional archaeologist who worked in India. He brought with himself his experience of working in Greece and Crete. Like Cunningham, he was also interested in spectacular findings. But, he was equally interested in looking for patterns of daily life.
- **Loss of Some Valuable Information in the Excavation Technique of Marshall** As John Marshall adopted a technique in which he excavated along regular horizontal units, measured uniformly throughout the mound, ignoring the stratigraphy of the site and this was the biggest drawback in his excavation process. As a result, valuable information about the context of these finds was irretrievably lost.

Or Mohenjodaro was one of the largest cities of the ancient Indus Valley Civilisation. It was the most advanced city of its time with a well civil engineering planning. It indicates town planning due to its features i.e. city, great bath, lower town, drainage system and domestic architecture. These are discussed below

- **The City** The city was divided into two parts:
  (i) Citadel, i.e. smaller but higher settlements.,
  (ii) The lower town i.e. larger but lower settlements. The citadel was the main fortified (protected place from enemy's attack) area of the city. It was walled and it was probably used for special public purposes. These include the warehouse and the great bath.
- **The Great Bath** It was a large rectangular tank in a courtyard surrounded by corridors on all four sides. There were two flights of steps on the North and South to reach the tank. The Great Bath was made watertight by setting brick on edge and using the plaster of gypsum. On three sides of it, there were rooms, in which one has large well. Water from the tank flowed into a huge drain.
- **The Lower Town** It was organised on a grid system which served as foundations. It was also walled as large town with lower settlements in archaeologists believe that, it was probably the city where most of the people lived and worked. Bricks used in settlements were sun-dried or baked, were of standardised ratio, where the length and breadth were four in times larger and twice the height respectively.
- **Drainage System** One of the most distinctive features of Mohenjodaro was the carefully planned drainage system. The streets and roads were laid out in grid pattern, intersecting at right angles. According to archaeologists, it was believed that streets with drain were built first and then the houses were built along with them. For domestic waste, water had to flow into the street drains, then every house was needed to have at least one wall along a street.
- **Domestic Architecture** The lower town at Mohenjodaro provides examples of residential buildings. Many were centered on a courtyard, with rooms on all sides. The courtyard was probably the centre of activities, such as cooking and weaving. There were no windows in the walls along the ground level.

29. The royal centre was located in the South-Western part of the settlement in the Vijayanagara Empire. It had over 60 temples and around thirty building complexes were identified as palaces.

The different types of buildings associated in the royal centre were

- **King's Palace** It was the largest of the buildings but there was no strong evidence that it was a royal residence. It had two impressive platforms, called the audience hall and the mahanavami dibba. The entire complex was surrounded by high double walls with a street running between them.
- **Audience Hall** It was a high platform which had slots for wooden pillars to be placed at close and regular intervals. On these pillars, a staircase was present which went to the second floor.
- **Lotus Mahal** The Lotus Mahal, named by British travellers in the 19th century was one of the most beautiful buildings in the royal centre. Historians are not sure about what the building was used for. A map drawn by Mackenzie suggested that it might have been a council chamber, a place where the king met his advisers.
- **Hazara Rama Temple** It was one of the most spectacular temples. This might have been used only by the king and his family. Though images in the central shrine are missing, but sculpted panels on the walls are still present.
  These included scenes from the Ramayana sculpted on the inner walls of the shrine.

Significance of the Rituals Associated with the Mahanavami Dibba

Mahanavami dibba was located at one of the highest points in the city. It was a massive platform or stage rising from a base of about 11,000 sq ft. to a height of 40 ft. It supported a wooden building and the base of the platform was covered with relief designs or carvings.

Rituals associated with the mahanavami dibba probably coincided with mahanavami i.e. the ninth day of the ten day Hindu festival during the autumn months of September and October. It is known as Dussehra in North India, Durga Puja in Bengal and Navaratri or Mahanavami in peninsular India. The Vijayanagara king showed their prestige, power and control over the empire on this occasion.

Various ceremonies were performed on this occassion like

- Worship of image, worship of the state horse and the sacrifice of buffaloes and other animals.
- Dances, wrestling matches, procession of highly decorated horses, elephants and chariots and soldiers.

Ritual presentations before the king and his guests by the chief nayakas and subordinate kings. Thus, the rituals associated with the mahanavami dibba were significant.

Or The Vijayanagara Empire which ruled from 1336 to 1646 CE in the Deccan Plateau region of the South India had flourishing trade relations with different regions of the world. Their benevolent rulers promoted trade and commerce and laid emphasis on safety and care of foreign travellers. It attracted travellers from many parts of the world. Their travelogue along with archaeological excavation greatly helped in reconstruction of the history of the empire and the city. In 16th century, Duarte Barbosa, Domingo Paes and Fernao Nuniz were the Portuguese travellers and traders who visited the empire.

Duarte Barbosa described the following aspect on the urban core of the Vijayanagara Empire

- The houses have not survived and they had roofs made of straw, palm leaves, etc.
- They were well built and were arranged according to the occupations, in long streets.
- Field surveys show that the entire area was scattered with number of shrines and small temples. This shows that there were present different cults, which might be supported by different communities.
- The surveys also indicate that wells, rainwater tanks, temple tanks were used as sources of water by the ordinary town people.

Domingo Paes had made following observations on the mahanavami dibba of the Vijayanagara Empire

- He called mahanavami dibba along with audience hall as the house of victory.
- These buildings have two platforms one above the other, which were beautifully sculpted.
- On the upper platform in this house of victory, the king had a room made of cloth, where the idol had a shrine. The other in the middle was placed on a dias on which there was the throne of the state and the crown and the royal anklet.

Thus, to reconstruct the history of the empire and architectual marvel of his capital city, Hampi, dozens of scholars from all over the world worked nearly for twenty years. They were greatly helped by the vivid account left by the foreign travellers.

30. Mahatma Gandhi's strategic shift from the Non-Cooperation Movement to social reform work and later re-entry into active politics profoundly shaped India's path to independence. After the Non-Cooperation Movement ended in 1922, Gandhi redirected his efforts towards addressing fundamental social issues affecting Indian society. He was focused on eliminating untouchability, promoting Hindu-Muslim unity, advocating for women's rights, and improving rural sanitation. These initiatives were important in unifying diverse sections of Indian society under a common agenda of social justice and empowerment.

Gandhi's emphasis on social reforms was not merely about addressing immediate social injustices but also about building a strong foundation for a broader freedom struggle. By promoting self-reliance through initiatives like spinning khadi and encouraging village industries, he aimed to reduce economic dependency and empower ordinary Indians. This approach fostered a sense of self-respect and collective dignity among the masses, preparing them for the larger challenges ahead in the fight against British colonial rule.

In 1928, Gandhi decided to get back into politics because the British government sent an all-White Simon Commission to India. They did this to see if India was ready for more changes to its laws. The commission's exclusion of Indian representation triggered widespread protests across the country. Although Gandhi didn't join the protests himself, his encouragement and approval inspired people to oppose British rules even more. This period marked a crucial re-engagement of Gandhi with the political sphere, aligning his leadership with emerging nationalist sentiments. Overall, Gandhiji's social reform work helped create a united, aware, and motivated people to fight for independence. His re-entry into politics and strategic actions, like supporting the anti-Simon Commission protests and organising Independence Day celebrations, were significant. These efforts strengthened the Independence Movement and brought it closer to achieving its goal.

Or

Gandhiji told the privileged invitees that "there is no salvation for India unless you strip yourself of this jewellery and hold it in trust for your countrymen in India". The statement can be justified through the following

- Mahatma Gandhi's speech at the opening of the Banaras Hindu University (BHU) in February 1916 was a strong criticism of the Indian elite's detachment from the struggles of the common people. In his address, Gandhi highlighted the stark contrast between the luxurious lifestyles of the privileged few and the poor conditions of the vast majority of Indians, particularly the peasants and labourers.
- Gandhi's statement, captured his belief that true progress and self-governance for India could not be achieved through the efforts of the elite alone. Instead, it required a deep and genuine commitment to the welfare of the masses. By asking rich and powerful people to give up their fancy things and help poor people instead, Gandhi was advocating for a more inclusive and just form of nationalism.
- Gandhi understood that the struggle for independence was inherently linked to social justice and economic equity. The elite, backed their wealth and status, often failed to understand the hardships faced by the rural poor. Gandhi's emphasis on trusteeship—a concept where the wealthy would hold their excess wealth in trust for the benefit of society—was a radical departure from the prevalent attitudes of the time. It challenged the privileged to re-evaluate their role in the nationalist movement and to align their actions with the needs and aspirations of the wider population.

31. (i) Muslim League worked patiently at expanding its influence during the Quit India Movement. During this period, league began to make a mark in the Punjab and Sind, provinces where it had previously had scarcely any presence.

(ii) During the Quit India Movement, younger activities organised strikes and acts of sabotage all over the country. Young people were energised and in very large numbers, left their colleges to go to jail.

(iii) 'Quit India' was genuinely a mass movement, because it brought into its ambit hundreds of thousands of ordinary Indians.

32. (i) Karaikkal Ammaiyar is the author of this excerpt. In this poem she described herself.

FULLY SOLVED

(ii) Karaikkal Ammaiyar in the poem described herself as a demoness having bulging veins, eyes that were popping out, white teeth, smaller stomach, red hair and teeth coming out, lengthy part of the leg below knee.

(iii) Author is trying to defy the established traditional norms where women are shown beautifully and with feminine characteristics.

33. (i) According to the Manusmriti, controversies regarding the boundaries arises because of ignorance of the king in demarcation of boundaries of their respective kingdoms.

(ii) The boundary problems can be solved by conceiving the boundaries by markers such as stones, bones, cow's hair, chaff, ashes, potsherds, dried cow dung, bricks coal, pebbles and sand can be done. These substance do not decay in the soil and will act as markers at the intersection of boundaries.

(iii) India faces such problems in the villages, where the land records are poorly maintained and various stakeholders try to claim their ownership of the same disputed land. Lands are not properly marked. Controversy regarding the ownership of the agricultural land is very common in India.

34.

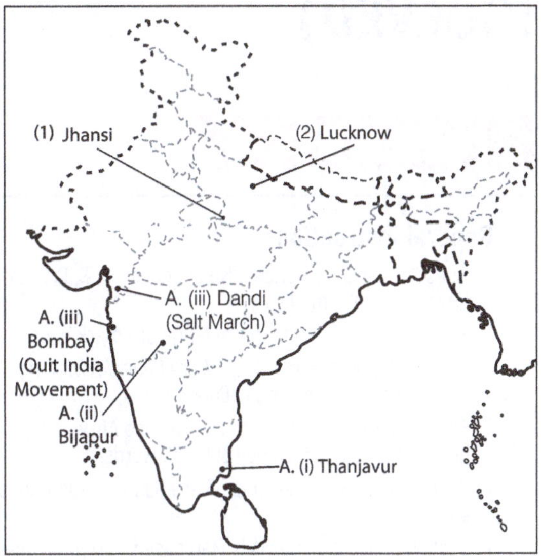

SAMPLE QUESTION PAPER 2

A Highly Simulated Sample Question Paper for CBSE Class XII

(SOLVED)

HISTORY

General Instructions

- Question paper comprises five Sections – A, B, C, D and E. There are 34 questions in the question paper. All questions are compulsory.
- Section A: Question 1 to 21 are MCQs of 1 mark each.
- Section B: Question no. 22 to 27 are Short Answer Type Questions, carrying 3 marks each. Answer to each question should not exceed 60-80 words.
- Section C: Question no 28 to 30 are Long Answer Type Questions, carrying 8 marks each. Answer to each question should not exceed 300-350 words.
- Section D: Question no. 31 to 33 are Source Based Questions with three sub questions and are of 4 marks each.
- Section E: Question no. 34 is Map based, carrying 5 marks that includes the identification and location of significant test items. Attach the map with the answer book.
- There is no overall choice in the question paper. However, an internal choice has been provided in few questions. Only one of the choices in such questions have to be attempted.
- In addition to this, separate instructions are given with each section and question, wherever necessary.

Time : 3 hours **Max. Marks : 80**

Section A (1 × 21 = 21)

(Objective Type Questions)

1. The Non-Cooperation Movement was coincided by which ongoing event by Gandhiji? (1)

(a) Civil Disobedience (b) Dandi March
(c) Champaran Movement (d) Khilafat Movement

2. Why Govind Ballabh Pant cautioned about divided loyalties in a democracy? (1)

(a) It creates group interest which often are in competition with other interest.
(b) It promotes casteism, regionalism and communalism.
(c) It ensures inclusive development of all segments of the society.
(d) Only (a) and (b)

3. Given below are two statements, one labelled as Assertion (A) and the other labelled as Reason (R).

Assertion (A) The Sanchi Stupa is a monument made during ancient period and is still intact.

Reason (R) Shah Jahan Begum and Sultan Jahan Begum provided money for its preservation. (1)

Codes

(a) Both A and R are true and R is the correct explanation of A
(b) Both A and R are true, but R is not the correct explanation of A
(c) A is true, but R is false
(d) A is false, but R is true

4. The given sculpture of Buddhist Goddess Marichi has been retrieved from which region? (1)

(a) Bihar (b) Awadh
(c) Bengal (d) Mathura

5. Given below are two statements, one labelled as Assertion (A) and the other labelled as Reason (R). (1)

Assertion (A) To make democracy a success, people should care less for himself and more for others.

Reason (R) In a democracy, every citizen is considered equal.

Codes

(a) Both A and R are true and R is the correct explanation of A
(b) Both A and R are true, but R is not the correct explanation of A
(c) A is true, but R is false
(d) A is false, but R is true

6. What was the reason for resignation of Congress Ministries in October 1935? (1)

(a) Failure of Cripps Mission.
(b) Appeasement policy of British towards Muslim League.
(c) Participation of India in Second World War without the concurrence of the people.
(d) Undue interference of Governors in day-to-day administration of province.

7. Abu'l Fazl was a court historian of which Mughal emperor? (1)

(a) Humayun (b) Babur
(c) Akbar (d) Jahangir

8. Identify the Hindu God, that Vijayanagara kings claimed that they ruled on behalf of. (1)

(a) Lord Shiva
(b) Shri Virupaksha
(c) Shri Vitthala
(d) Shri Balaji

9. Which of the following pairs is incorrectly matched? (1)

(a) Magadha – Most powerful Mahajanapada between 6th and 4th century BCE
(b) Panchala – A Mahajanapada
(c) Rajgir – Capital city of a Mahajanapada
(d) Vaishali – A Mahajanapada

10. Which of the following category of society of ancient Persia was not recognised by the Al-Biruni ? (1)

(a) Knights and princes
(b) Monks and fire-priests
(c) Peasants and artisans
(d) Children and women

11. Which of the following statements is/are correct?

I. The colonial rule was first established in the Bengal.
II. The earliest attempts were made to reorder rural society.
III. The permanent settlement had come into operation in 1793.
IV. The East India Company had fixed revenue that each Zamindar had to pay. (1)

Codes

(a) Only I (b) Only II
(c) Both I and II (d) All of these

12. Complete the following analogy by choosing the correct option given below.

Shah Mal : Barout, Gonoo : ? (1)

(a) Singhbum (b) Chiraundi
(c) Kanpur (d) Chandausi

13. Arrange the following in chronological order. (1)

(i) Basavanna in Karnataka
(ii) Jnandeva in Maharashtra
(iii) Kabir in Uttar Pradesh

Codes

(a) (i), (ii), (iii) (b) (iii), (ii), (i)
(c) (iii), (i), (ii) (d) (ii), (i), (iii)

14. Identify the personality from the description given below. (1)

- She was a Rajput princess from Merta in Marwar, who was married against her wishes to a prince of the Sisodia clan of Mewar.
- She recognised Krishna, the avatar of Vishnu, as her lover.

(a) Jodha Bai (b) Andal
(c) Mira Bai (d) Rani Padmini

FULLY SOLVED

15. Which of the following pairs is incorrectly matched? **(1)**

(a) Terracotta models of plough – Banawali
(b) Ploughed Field – Gujarat
(c) Canals – Shortughai
(d) Water reservoirs – Gujarat

16. Complete the following analogy by choosing the correct options given below. **(1)**

Great Bath : ?, Ornaments in cemetery : Harappa

(a) Mohenjodaro
(b) Lothal
(c) Kalibangan
(d) Rakhigarhi

17. The Shungas and Kanvas, the immediate successors of the Mauryas, were .... **(1)**

(a) Brahmanas (b) Kshatriyas
(c) of 'low' origin (d) mlechchhas

18. Which of the following statements is incorrect about Ibn Battuta?

(a) Ibn Battuta was a famous Moroccan traveller who visited India during the reign of Muhammad Bin Tughlaq.
(b) He wrote a famous travelogue called Rihla, detailing his journeys across Africa, the Middle East, and Asia.
(c) He served as a judge in the Delhi Sultanate
(d) He travelled only to Islamic countries and never visited regions outside of the Islamic world.

19. How did Govind Ballabh Pant justify his opposition to separate electorates in the Constituent Assembly? Choose the most suitable option from the following

(a) By highlighting that separate electorates would strengthen minority communities politically.
(b) By arguing that separate electorates would isolate minorities and weaken their integration into the nation.
(c) By stating that separate electorates were necessary to ensure cultural preservation for minorities.
(d) By supporting the idea that separate electorates would prevent conflicts between communities.

20. Name the region that was popularly called as the 'nursery of the Bengal Army'. **(1)**

(a) Awadh
(b) Bengal
(c) Madras
(d) Bihar

21. The name Hampi was derived from a local Goddess named .... **(1)**

(a) The Machani Amman
(b) Pampadevi
(c) Durga Devi
(d) Bhavani Devi

Section B

(Short Answer Type Questions) **(3 × 6 = 18)**

22. Citadel has well marked features that separate it from the other section of the Harappan Civilisation. Give a brief description of Citadel in the context of this observation. **(3)**

Or

Write a short note on domestic architecture of Mohenjodaro.

23. How did state help peasants in irrigation sector? How did peasants help themselves by using different technologies? **(3)**

24. Explain, how the Zamindars and merchants were badly affected due to the British rule in India, according to the Azamgarh proclamation of 25th August, 1857. **(3)**

25. What were the provisions of fiscal federalism agreed by the members of Constitutional Assembly? **(3)**

26. Which were the reasons that made Magadha the most powerful Mahajanapada? **(3)**

27. Discuss the contributions of Baba Guru Nanak to the Bhakti Movement in India. **(3)**

Or

Discuss the importance of women devotees during bhakti period.

Section C

(Long Answer Type Questions) **(8×3=24)**

28. What was the relationship between the sufis and the state from 8th to 18th century? Explain. **(8)**

Or

"Kabir's poems and the traditions he drew to describe the ultimate reality were significant." Explain.

29. How did Sutta Pitaka reconstruct the philosophy of Buddhism? Mention about Buddhist Tripitaka. (8)

Or

Write down the significance of Stupa in Buddhism and critically examine why Sanchi Stupa survived while Amaravati did not.

30. "Mahatma Gandhi announced that he would lead a march to break one of the most widely disliked laws in British India." Justify the statement. (8)

Or

"The Salt march was the first nationalist activity in which women participated in large numbers". Justify the statement.

Section D

(Source Based Questions) (4×3=12)

31. Read the following source carefully and answer the questions that follow. (4)

Shankaradev

In the late 15th century, Shankaradeva emerged as one of the leading proponents of Vaishnavism in Assam. His teachings, often known as the Bhagavati Dharma because they were based on the Bhagavad Gita and the Bhagavata Purana, focused on absolute surrender to the supreme deity, in this case of Vishnu.

He emphasised the need for *naam kirtan*, recitation of the names of the lord in *sat sanga* or congregations of pious devotees. He also encouraged the establishment of *satra* or monasteries for the transmission of spiritual knowledge and *naam ghar* or prayer halls. Many of these institutions and practices continue to flourish in the region. His major compositions include the Kirtana-ghosha.

(i) Who was Shankaradeva? (1)

(ii) Why were his teachings referred as Bhagavati Dharma? Mention his one composition. (1)

(iii) Why did he encourage the establishment of Satra and Naam Ghar? (2)

32. Read the following source carefully and answer the questions that follow.

"We want removal of our social disabilities"

Dakshayani Velayudhan from Madras, argued what we want is not all kind of safeguards. It is the moral safeguard which gives protection to the underdogs of this country .... I refer to believe that seventy million Harijans are to be considered as a minority. What we want is the .... immediates removal of our social disabilities.

(i) Why Scheduled Caste of the country were referred as 'Underdog'? (1)

(ii) What are social disabilities suffered by the Harijan of the country? (1)

(iii) How can be the moral safeguard be more effective than constitutional safeguard in protection of underdogs of the country? (2)

33. Read the following source carefully and answer the questions that follow. (4)

Life in a Small Village

The Harshacharita is a biography of Harshavardhana, the ruler of Kannauj, composed in Sanskrit by his court poet, Banabhatta (C seventh century CE). This is an excerpt from the text, an extremely rare representation of life in a settlement on the outskirts of a forest in the Vindhyas. The outskirts being for the most part of forest, many parcels of rice-land, threshing ground and arable land were being apportioned by small farmers.

It was mainly spade culture ... owing to the difficulty of ploughing the sparsely scattered fields covered with grass, with their few clear spaces, their black soil stiff as black iron.

There were people moving along with bundles of bark... countless sacks of plucked flowers, ... loads of flax and hemp bundles, quantities of honey, peacocks' tail feathers, wreaths of wax, logs and grass. Village wives hastened on route for neighbouring villages, all intent on thoughts of sale and bearing on their heads baskets filled with various gathered forest fruit.

(i) Who was the author of Harshacharita? (1)

(ii) Describe the outskirts of a forest in the Vindhyas. (1)

(iii) Describe the activities of the people of that area. Mention two main activities of the farmers of that time. (2)

Section E

(Map Based Question)

34. A. Locate and label the following on the map of India. (3)

(i) Mahajanapada Kuru.

(ii) Mysore *Or* Thanjavur

(iii) Chanhudaro

B. On the given political outline map of India, two centres of Bhakti tradition by Mirabai and Basvanna have been marked as 1 and 2 respectively. Identify and write their name. (2)

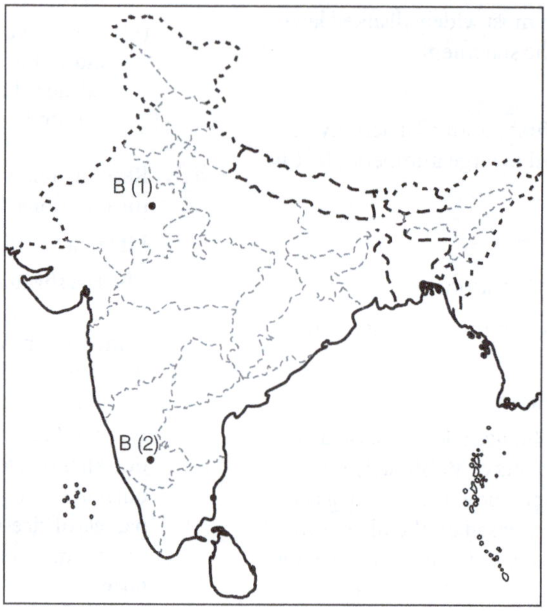

FULLY SOLVED

Answers

1. (d) Khilafat Movement

2. (d) Only (a) and (b)

3. (a) Both A and R are true and R is the correct explanation of A

4. (a) Bihar

5. (b) Both A and R are true, but R is not the correct explanation of A

6. (c) Participation of India in Second World War without the concurrence of the people.

7. (c) Akbar

8. (b) Shri Virupaksha

9. (d) Vaishali – A Mahajanapada

10. (d) Children and women

11. (d) All of these

12. (a) Singhbum

13. (a) (i), (ii), (iii)

14. (c) Mira Bai

15. (b) Ploughed Field – Gujarat

16. (a) Mohenjodaro

17. (a) Brahmanas

18. (d) He travelled only to Islamic countries and never visited regions outside of the Islamic world.

19. (b) By arguing that separate electorates would isolate minorities and weaken their integration into the nation.

20. (a) Awadh

21. (b) Pampadevi

22. The settlement of the Harappan Civilisation is divided into two sections, one smaller but higher and the other much larger but lower.

These two sections are referred to as the Citadel and the Lower Town respectively.

The Citadel was high because buildings were constructed on mud brick platforms. It was separated from the Lower Town by a wall. But, there were also variations in this arrangement in the Harappan settlements.

For example, at sites such as Dholavira and Lothal (Gujarat), the entire settlement was fortified and sections within the town were also separated by walls. The Citadel within Lothal was not walled off, but was built at a height.

The evidence of structures like warehouse and Great Bath are also found in the Citadel. These were probably used for special public purposes on special occasions.

Or

The domestic architecture of Mohenjodaro is discussed below

- The Lower Town at Mohenjodaro provides example of residential buildings. Many were centred on a courtyard, with rooms on all sides.
- The courtyard was probably the centre of activities such as cooking and weaving, particularly during hot and dry weather. There are no windows in the walls along the ground level.
- Every house had its own bathroom paved with bricks, with drains connected through the wall to the street drains. Some houses have remains of staircases to reach a second storey or the roof.

23. The state help peasants in irrigation sector by supporting irrigation projects. In Northern India, state dug new canals (*nahr, nala*) and also repaired old one like the shahnahr in the Punjab during Shah Jahan's rule.

Peasants help themselves by using technologies that often produced cattle energy. For example, using wooden plough, which was light and easily combined with an iron tip or iron blade. This did not make deep furrows which save the moisture better during the very hot months.

A drill, pulled by a pair of giant oxen, was used to plant seeds, but scattering the seeds by hand was the most used method. Hoeing and weeding were done together using a narrow iron blade with a small wooden handle.

24. The Azamgarh proclamation is one of the main source to know about the issues raised by the rebels during the Revolt of 1857. The proclamation raised the issue of the severe British rule and its drastic effect on the various aspects of the society.

According to the proclamation, the adoption of zamindari settlements imposed exorbitant Jumas (revenue demand) and had disgraced and ruined several Zamindars.

Their estates were put for public auction for arrears of rent. Besides this, the Zamindars were annually taxed of subscription for schools, roads, hospitals, etc.

On the other hand, the merchants of India also suffered a lot due to the monopoly of British in all fine and valuable merchandise such as indigo, cloth and other articles of shipping, leaving only the trade of trifles to the merchants.

The profits of Indian traders were taxed with postages, tolls and subscriptions for schools, etc. The merchants were also liable to imprisonment and disgraced at the instance or complaint of worthless men.

25. The members of Constitutional Assembly agreed to the complex system of fiscal federalism in which centre was provided with more power to levy, collect and appropriate taxes in comparison to the state.

The provisions of fiscal federalism were

- In case of some taxes such as custom duties and company taxes, all the proceeds were retained by the centre.
- In the case of other taxes such as income tax and excise, the proceeds were shared by both the centre and the states.
- Income from some other taxes such as estate duties was wholly assigned to the state.
- Some taxes such as land and property taxes, sales tax and tax on bottled liquor could be levied and collected by the states on their own.

26. Magadha became the most powerful kindgom due to the following reasons

- It was a region where agriculture was especially productive.
- Beside, iron mines were accessible and provided resources for tools and weapons.
- Elephants, an important component of the army, were found in forests in the region.
- The Ganga and its tributaries provided a means of cheap and convenient communication in this region.

27. Baba Guru Nanak's message of Bhakti is spelt out in his hymns and teachings. These suggest that he advocated a form of nirguna bhakti. He firmly rejected the external practices of the regions he saw around him. He rejected sacrifices, ritual baths, image worship, austerities and the scriptures of both Hindus and Muslims. For Baba Guru Nanak, the Absolute or 'rab' had no gender or form. He proposed a simple way to connect to the divine by remembering and repeating the divine name.

Or

The importance of women devotees during bhakti period were as follows

- The compositions of Andal, a woman Alvar, were widely sung and even now they are continued to be sung. She saw herself as the beloved of Vishnu and we can see that her verses expressed her love for the deity.
- Karaikkal Ammaiyar (a devotee of Shiva) was another women who adopted the path of extreme self-discipline in order to attain her goal. Her compositions were preserved within the Nayanar tradition.

28. The relationship between the Sufis and the state from the 8th and 18th century was as follows

- There was no absolute isolation from political power. Grants and donations from political elites were accepted by the Sufis.
- Charitable trusts (auqaf) for hospices were set up and tax-free land (inam) were granted by Sultans.
- Donations in cash and kind were accepted by the Chistis and used them on immediate requirements such as food, clothes, living quarters and ritual necessities.
- They became popular among the masses through piety and scholarship and their miraculous powers.
- Kings also required legitimation from Sufis. Thus, when Turks set up Delhi Sultanate they resisted the insistence of the Ulama on imposing shari'a as state law.
- The Sultans sought out the Sufis who were believed to derive their authority directly from God and did not depend on jurists to interpret the *shari'a*.
- It was also believed that the *auliya* could intervene with God in order to improve the material and spiritual conditions of ordinary human beings.
- There were incidences which shows conflict between the Sultans and the Sufis. Both expected certain rituals to be performed such as prostration and kissing of the feet.
- The Sufi Shaikh was addressed with high-sounding titles. For example, the disciples of Nizamuddin Auliya addressed him as Sultan-ul-Mashaikh.
- Other Sufis such as the Suhrawardi under the Delhi Sultans and the Naqshbandi under the Mughals were also associated with the state.

Or

Kabir is one of the most important examples of a poet-saint. He used the range of traditions to describe the Ultimate Reality.

In Islam, he described the Ultimate Reality as Allah, Khuda, Hazrat and Pir. He also used terms from Vedantic traditions, *alakh* (the unseen), *nirakar* (formless), Brahman, Atman, etc.

Other spiritual ideas such as *shabda* (sound) or *shunya* (emptiness) were from yogic traditions.

Diverse and sometimes opposing ideas were expressed in these poems. Some poems took Islamic ideas and used the concepts like belief in one God and the destruction of religious images to attack Hindu's belief in many Gods and idol worship. Some other poems used the Sufi concepts of *zikr* and *ishq* (love) to express the Hindu practice of *nam-simaran* (remembrance of God's name). Kabir's poems have survived in different languages and different forms of languages, and some are composed in the special language of *nirguna* poets, the *sant bhasha*. Other compositions known as *ulatbansi* (upside-down sayings), are written in a form in which everyday meanings are reversed.

These show the difficulties of getting the character of the Ultimate Reality in words and expressions such as 'the lotus which blooms without flower' or the 'fire raging in the ocean' show a sense of Kabir's spiritual experiences.

The rich collection of written texts also signifies that Kabir was a source of inspiration. Kabir's ideas might had formed through discussion and debate with the traditions of Sufis and Yogis in the region of Awadh.

29. After the death of Buddha, his teachings were compiled by his disciples and were known as Tripitaka. Sutta Pitaka was one of the Tripitaka. Buddha's teachings have been reconstructed from stories found mainly in the Sutta Pitaka. Some stories describe his miraculous powers and other stories suggest that the Buddha tried to convince people through reason and persuasion, rather than through displays of supernatural power. Sometimes through stories, the teachings of the Buddha were narrated in the individual effort was expected to transform social relations.

Buddha emphasised individual agency and righteous action as the means to escape from the cycle of rebirth and attain self-realisation and nibbana. By extinguishing ego and desire, individual could end the cycle of his sufferings and renounce the world.

Tripitaka literally means three baskets to hold different types of texts. The main features of it are

- The Vinaya Pitaka included rules and regulations for those who joined the sangha or monastic order.
- The Sutta Pitaka included the teachings of the Buddha.
- The Abhidhamma Pitaka dealt with philosophical matters. Each Pitaka comprised a number of texts.
- According to Buddhist philosophy, the world is transient (anicca) and constantly changing. The world is soulless (anatta), as there is nothing permanent or eternal in it.
- Within this transient world, sorrow (dukkha) is intrinsic to human existence. It is by following the path of moderation between severe penance and self-indulgence, the human beings can rise above these worldly troubles.
- Buddha regarded the social world as the creation of humans rather than of divine origin. Therefore, he advised kings and gahapatis to be humane and ethical.

Or

Stupas are significant as they were those Buddhist monuments where relics of Buddha such as his bodily remains or object related to him are kept. The Stupas were worshipped as an emblem of both the Buddha and Buddhism. By the 2nd century BCE, a number of Stupas like Bharhut, Sanchi and Sarnath has been built.

The Stupa at Amaravati was one of the largest and most significant among the Buddhist Stupas. The Stupa at Sanchi survived while Amaravati did not.

The reasons are

- In 1796, a local raja utilised the stones embedded in ruins of Amaravati Stupa for construction of a temple. Similarly, the reports of Colin Mackenzie who visited the site and discovered several pieces of sculpture were not published.
- The slabs of Amaravati Stupa were taken to different place like Asiatic society of Bengal, India office at Madras, even to London.
- Many British officials posted in that area continued to remove the sculptures from the site on grounds. They were utilised in decoration of homes and garden.
- Amaravati was also discovered before scholars understood the value to the finds and significance of preserving the archaeological remains of the site where they were originally found.
- In case of Sanchi Stupa, which was discovered in the year 1818, the three of its four gateways were still standing, the fourth was lying on the spot and the mound was in good condition. But utter negligence of British authorities and locals led to Amaravati becoming an insignificant little mound and it was totally denuded from its former glory.
- Lastly, the rulers of Bhopal, Shah Jahan Begum and her successor Sultan Jahan Begum, provided money for the preservation of the ancient site. Today, it stands testimony to the successful restoration and preservation of a key archaeological site by the Archaeological Survey of India.

30. "Mahatma Gandhi announced that he would lead a march to break one of the most widely disliked laws in British India". This statement can be justified through the following

- Mahatma Gandhi's decision to lead a march to break the salt laws in British India marked a crucial turning point in India's struggle for independence. The salt laws meant that only the government had the right to make and sell salt. This law was deeply unpopular among Indians because it imposed high prices on an essential commodity and restricted people from making salt for domestic use. By targeting this law, Gandhi sought to unite people from all backgrounds, as salt was a necessity in every Indian household, affecting people across social and economic lines.
- The Salt March was not merely a protest against the salt laws; it was a powerful symbol of resistance and a call to action for the Indian population. Gandhi's decision to break the law

through a peaceful march showed the value of nonviolent resistance as a strong weapon against injustice. This approach was not only morally strong but made sense for reaching their goals, as it gained sympathy and support both domestically and internationally.

- During the Salt march, Gandhi showed how he could inspire lots of people to join together by being a good example and peacefully breaking the rules. His emphasis on non-violence as a means of protest inspired millions of Indians to join the struggle for independence, regardless of their language, religion, or social position.
- The Salt march captured the attention of everyone in the country and also got a lot of notice from people around the world. It made everyone pay attention to the unfairness of British rule. Marching to the sea and producing salt in defiance of the law, showed Gandhi's commitment to telling the truth and not using violence.

Or

"The Salt march was the first nationalist activity in which women participated in large numbers." This statement can be justified through the following

- During this turning moment in India's struggle for independence, women emerged as active participants, breaking free from traditional gender roles to take charge and participate actively in politics. Inspired by Mahatma Gandhi's ideas of peaceful protest and feeling more confident because of leaders like Kamaladevi Chattopadhyay, women from diverse backgrounds joined the march in significant numbers. Their participation marked a break from the usual customs, where women were often limited to supportive roles in political movements.
- Gandhi purposefully including women in the Salt march showed a planned change, aiming to make the nationalist movement more inclusive and involving more people. By inviting women to take part in the protest, Gandhi sought to challenge societal norms and empower women to actively participate in shaping the destiny of their nation. The participation of women was not merely symbolic; it carried profound practical implications, demonstrating the strength and unity of the nationalist cause.
- The involvement of women in the Salt march paved the way for their increased participation in subsequent nationalist activities. The Salt march inspired the inclusion of women in politics and highlighted their significance in India's freedom movement. It broke societal barriers, paving the way for greater female participation in nationalist activities. This shift marked important moment in Indian history, emphasising the importance of women's voices and contributions in the pursuit of national liberation.

31. (i) Shankaradeva was one of the leading proponents of Vaishnavism in Assam during the late 15th century.

(ii) His teachings were referred as Bhagvati Dharma because they were based on Bhagavad Gita and the Bhagavata Purana which focused on absolute surrender to the supreme deity. His major compositions include the Kirtana-ghosa.

(iii) He encouraged the establishment of Satra and the Naam ghar for following purpose
- To emphasise the need of Naam kirtan.
- For the transmission of spiritual knowledge.

32. (i) Scheduled Caste suffers from number of social disabilities in India. They were perceived as weak, mentally inferior and incapable and untrustworthy by many people. That's why they are referred as underdog of the country.

(ii) The social disabilities suffered by the Harijan of the country are
- Untouchability
- Inaccessibility to the religious places
- Caste based violence
- Marginalisation of the community

(iii) With moral safeguard we understand the inculcation of values of equality, fraternity and liberty in the conscience of the masses.

These are more effective than constitutional safeguard as the latter is enforced through state machinery, while for the moral safeguards only people commitment for those values is needed.

33. (i) Banabhatta was the author of Harshacharita.

(ii) The outskirts of a forest consisted of sparsely scattered fields covered with grass and few clear spaces of stiff black soil as black iron. It also consisted of threshing grounds and arable lands.

FULLY SOLVED

(iii) People used to collect bundles of bark, countless sacks of plucked flowers, loads of flax and hemp bundles, quantities of honey, peacock's tail feathers, wax, logs, grass, etc.

Two activities of farmers of that time were farming and animal rearing.

34.

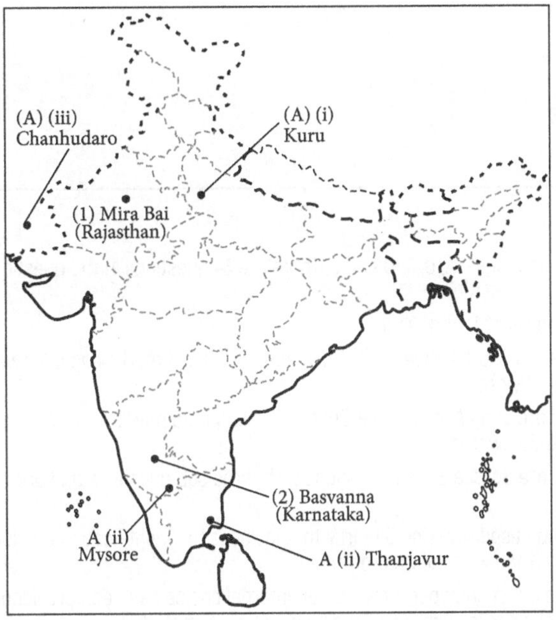

SAMPLE QUESTION PAPER 3

A Highly Simulated Sample Question Paper for CBSE Class XII

(UNSOLVED)

HISTORY

General Instructions

- Question paper comprises five Sections – A, B, C, D and E. There are 34 questions in the question paper. All questions are compulsory.
- Section A: Question 1 to 21 are MCQs of 1 mark each.
- Section B: Question no. 22 to 27 are Short Answer Type Questions, carrying 3 marks each. Answer to each question should not exceed 60-80 words.
- Section C: Question no 28 to 30 are Long Answer Type Questions, carrying 8 marks each. Answer to each question should not exceed 300-350 words.
- Section D: Question no. 31 to 33 are Source Based Questions with three sub questions and are of 4 marks each.
- Section E: Question no. 34 is Map based, carrying 5 marks that includes the identification and location of significant test items. Attach the map with the answer book.
- There is no overall choice in the question paper. However, an internal choice has been provided in few questions. Only one of the choices in such questions have to be attempted.
- In addition to this, separate instructions are given with each section and question, wherever necessary.

Time : 3 hours **Max. Marks : 80**

Section A

(1×21=21)

(Objective Type Questions)

1. Who among the following was the author of the book 'Arthashastra'? (1)

(a) Bimbisara (b) Ajatashataru (c) Chanakya (d) Bindusara

2. Match the following. (1)

List I		List II	
A.	1917	1.	Peasant Movement in Bardoli
B.	1919	2.	Civil Disobedience Movement begins
C.	1928	3.	Rowlatt Satyagraha
D.	1930	4.	Champaran Movement

Codes

	A	B	C	D
(a)	3	4	2	1
(b)	1	2	3	4
(c)	4	3	1	2
(d)	2	1	4	3

3. The characteristic feature of the bricks found in Harappan sites was not among which of these? (1)

(a) Sun dried bricks (b) Baked bricks
(c) Bricks exactly of equal size (d) Standard ratio of bricks

4. Given below are the two statements, one labelled Assertion (A) and the other labelled as Reason (R).

Assertion (A) Santhals felt that it was high time to rebel against the Zamindars. (1)

Reason (R) Zamindars continuously increased their control over the forest areas.

Codes

(a) Both A and R are true and R is the correct explanation of A
(b) Both A and R are true, but R is not the correct explanation of A
(c) A is true, but R is false
(d) A is false, but R is true

5. Compare and contrast the views on separate electorates expressed by B. Pocker Bahadur and Sardar Patel. Choose the best suitable option from the following: (1)

(a) Bahadur argued for separate electorates as a way to ensure that minorities had a voice, while Patel opposed it, fearing that it would lead to further divisions and violence.
(b) Bahadur believed separate electorates would unify communities, while Patel supported it as a means of preserving peace and unity.
(c) Bahadur and Patel both supported separate electorates, but for different communities, to ensure fair representation.
(d) Bahadur wanted separate electorates for all communities, while Patel suggested that they should be implemented only for Muslims.

6. In the case of the Satavahanas, succession to the throne was .... (1)

(a) matrilineal (b) patrilineal
(c) Both (a) and (b) (d) Neither (a) nor (b)

7. Identify the incorrectly matched pair. (1)

(a) Jhansi – Rani Lakshmi Bai
(b) Bareilly – Bakht Khan
(c) Bihar – Kunwar Singh
(d) Kanpur – Nana Saheb

8. The Governor-General in the given picture introduced Subsidiary Alliance. Identify him.

(1)

(a) Lord Wellesley (b) Lord Linlithgow
(c) Lord Dalhousie (d) Lord Cornwallis

9. Complete the following analogy by choosing the correct option given below. (1)

Permanent Settlement : Bengal, Ryotwari Settlement : ?

(a) Bombay Deccan (b) Nagpur
(c) Madras (d) Awadh

10. Consider the following statements and choose the correct option. (1)

I. There was no break between the Early Harappan and the Harappan Civilisation.
II. Mature Harappan culture developed in some of the areas occupied by the Early Harappan cultures.
III Finds of rice are relatively rare in Harappan Civilisation.

Codes

(a) I and II (b) II and III
(c) I and III (d) I, II and III

11. Identify the personality from the description given below. (1)

- He travelled to India at least six times.
- He was particularly fascinated with the trading conditions in India, and compared India to Iran and the Ottoman empire.

(a) Ibn Battuta
(b) Al-Biruni
(c) Tavernier
(d) Abdur Razzaq Samarqandi

12. At which of the following places, Buddha attained enlightenment? (1)

(a) Sarnath
(b) Bodh Gaya
(c) Lumbini
(d) Kushinagar

13. Match the following. (1)

	List I		List II
A.	Shortughai	1.	Pakistan
B.	Khetri	2.	Afghanistan
C.	Banawali	3.	Rajasthan
D.	Kot Diji	4.	Haryana

Codes

	A	B	C	D
(a)	1	2	3	4
(b)	4	1	3	2
(c)	2	3	4	1
(d)	1	3	4	2

UNSOLVED

UNSOLVED

14. On which of the following occasions was/were the ceremony performed at Mahanavami Dibba? (1)
(a) Worship of the state horse
(b) Marriage of the king
(c) Victory over the enemy
(d) All of the above

15. Given below are the two statements, one labelled as Assertion (A) and the other labelled as Reason (R). (1)
Assertion (A) Asoka inscribed his messages to his subjects and officials on stone surfaces.
Reason (R) He wanted to proclaim what religion should be followed by all.
Codes
(a) Both A and R are true and R is the correct explanation of A
(b) Both A and R are true, but R is not the correct explanation of A
(c) A is true, but R is false
(d) A is false, but R is true

16. Given below are the two statements, one labelled as Assertion (A) and the other labelled as Reason (R). (1)
Assertion (A) State dug new canals and also repaired old ones.
Reason (R) The state supported irrigation projects.
Codes
(a) Both A and R are true and R is the correct explanation of A
(b) Both A and R are true, but R is not the correct explanation of A
(c) A is true, but R is false
(d) A is false, but R is true

17. Arrange the following arrivals of foreign travellers in chronological order. (1)
(i) Marco Polo (ii) Ibn Battuta
(iii) Duarte Barbosa
Codes
(a) (i), (ii), (iii) (b) (ii), (iii), (i)
(c) (iii), (ii), (i) (d) (ii), (i), (iii)

18. Tulsidas, a prominent saint of Bhakti Movement belonged to which region? (1)
(a) Uttar Pradesh (b) Bihar
(c) Madras (d) Bengal

19. Identify the Guru whose compositions were included by Guru Gobind Singh in the Guru Granth Sahib. (1)
(a) Guru Tegh Bahadur (b) Baba Guru Nanak
(c) Guru Ram Das (d) Guru Arjan

20. Which of the following statements is incorrect about the royal centre of Vijayanagara? (1)
(a) The royal centre included over 60 temples, showing the importance of temple patronage in legitimising the authority of the rulers.
(b) The royal centre had a distinct layout with large palace structures and many temples, but the secular buildings were made of perishable materials.
(c) The royal centre housed the "mahanavami dibba", a large platform used for rituals, particularly during the Mahanavami festival.
(d) The royal centre was located in the North-Eastern part of the settlement and included only the king's palace.

21. Consider the following statements regarding recommendation of Constituent Assembly with respect to depressed castes. (1)
I. Untouchability should be abolished.
II. Hindu temples to be opened to all castes.
III. Reservation for lowest castes in legislature and government offices.
IV. Reservation only for economically weaker section of depressed castes.

Which of the above statement are correct?
(a) I and II
(b) II and III
(c) I, II and III
(d) All of the above

Section B

(Short Answer Type Questions) (3 × 6 = 18)

22. How did archaeologists made a division between the social and economic life of the Harappan people? (3)

Or

Describe the burial practices prevalent in Harappan Civilisation.

23. Discuss the trade in the sub-continent during 6th century BCE. (3)

24. Explain the salient feature of temple architecture under the Vijayanagara Empire. (3)

25. Write a note on Subsidiary Alliance. (3)

26. Discuss the reasons why Mahatma Gandhi felt that Hindustani should be our national language. (3)

27. Write a short note on Zamindars in Mughal Empire. (3)

Or

Discuss the land revenue system introduced in Bombay Deccan.

Section C

(Long Answer Type Questions (8 × 3 = 24)

28. Discuss the nature of the Revolt of 1857. What values were reflected by Indians during the Revolt of 1857? (8)

Or

Describe how the British celebrated those, who they believed saved the English and repressed the rebels during the Revolt of 1857.

29. Who were the Alvars and the Nayanars? What relations they had with the Southern states? (8)

Or

The wide range of text produced in and around Sufi Khanqahs had helped immensely in reconstruction of history of Sufism. In this regard, explain Malfuzat, Maktubat and Tazkiras as the sources used to reconstruct the history of Sufi traditions.

30. Describe the features of the famous Sanchi Stupa in accordance to the structure and sculpture. (8)

Or

Discuss the development in sculpture and architecture associated with the rise of Vaishnavism and Shaivism.

Section D

(Source Based Questions) (4 × 3 = 12)

31. Read the following source carefully and answer the questions that follow. (4)

Name of Satavahana Kings from Inscriptions

These are the names of several generations of Satavahana rulers, recovered from inscriptions. Note the uniform title Raja. Also note the following word, which ends with the term puta, a Prakrit word meaning 'son'. The term Gotami-puta means 'Son of Gotami'. Names like Gotami and Vasithi are feminine forms of Gotama and Vasistha Vedic seers after whom gotras were named.

Raja Gotami-puta Siri-Satakani
Raja Vasithi-puta (sami-) Siri-Pulumayi
Raja Gotami-puta sami-Siri- Yana-Satakani
Raja Madhari-puta svami-Sakasena
Raja Vasathi-puta Chatarapana-Satakani
Raja Hariti-puta Vinhukada Chutukulanamda-Satakani
Raja Gotami-puta Siri-Vijaya-Satakani

(i) What is the importance of gotra in Brahmanical practice? (1)

(ii) How was Satavahana gotra practice different from the Brahmanical practice? (1)

(iii) What position did women enjoy in the Satavahana society? (2)

32. Read the following source carefully and answer the questions that follow. (4)

"British element is gone, but they have left the mischief behind."

Sardar Vallabhbhai Patel said

It is no use saying that we ask for separate electorates, because it is good for us. We have heard it long enough. We have heard it for years, and as a result of this agitation we are now a separate nation ... Can you show me one free country where there are separate electorates? If so, I shall be prepared to accept it. But in this unfortunate country if this separate electorate is going to be persisted in, even after the division of the country, woe betide the country; it is not worth living in. Therefore, I say, it is not for my good alone, it is for your own good that I say it, forget the past.

One day, we may be united ... The British element is gone, but they have left the mischief behind. We do not want to perpetuate that mischief (hear, hear). When the British introduced this element they had not expected that they have to go so soon.

They wanted it for their easy administration. That is all right. But they have left the legacy bad. Are we to get out of it or not?

(i) Why separate electorate was considered as a mischief? (1)

(ii) Explain Sardar Vallabhbhai Patel's views on the issue of separate electorates system. (1)

(iii) In what ways did Sardar Patel explain that "The British element is gone, but they have left the mischief behind"? (2)

33. Read the following source carefully and answer the questions that follow. (4)

Colin Mackenzie

Born in 1754, Colin Mackenzie became famous as an engineer, surveyor and cartographer. In 1815, he was appointed the first Surveyor General of India, a post he held till his death in 1821. He

UNSOLVED

embarked on collecting local histories and surveying historic sites in order to better understand India's past and make governance of the colony easier. He says that "It struggled long under the miseries of bad management ... before the South came under the benign influence of the British Government."

By studying Vijayanagara, Mackenzie believed that the East India Company could gain "much useful information on many of these institutions, laws and customs whose influence still prevails among the various tribes of natives forming the general mass of the population to this day."

(i) Who was Colin Mackenzie? (1)

(ii) Mention what Mackenzie did to make governance of the colony easier. (1)

(iii) According to him, what benefits would the East India Company gain after studying Vijayanagara? Explain in brief. (2)

Section E

(Map Based Question)

34. A. Locate and label the following on the map of India. (3)

(i) Place of Quit India Resolution.

Or Place of Jallianwala Bagh Massacre.

(ii) One centre of revolt of 1857 in Madhya Pradesh.

(iii) One city of importance in South India.

B. On the given political outline map of India, two places associated with Ashokan Pillar inscriptions are marked as 1 and 2. Write their names. (2)

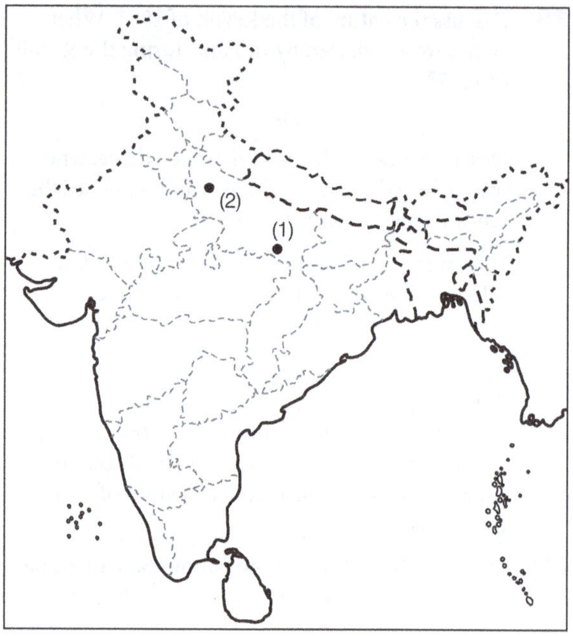

UNSOLVED

Answers

1. (c) Chanakya
2. (c)
3. (c) Bricks exactly of equal size
4. (a) Both A and R are true and R is the correct explanation of A
5. (b) Bahadur believed separate electorates would unify communities, while Patel supported it as a means of preserving peace and unity.
6. (b) patrilineal
7. (b) Bareilly – Bakht Khan
8. (a) Lord Wellesley
9. (a) Bombay Deccan
10. (b) II and III
11. (c) Tavernier
12. (b) Bodh Gaya
13. (c)
14. (a) Worship of the state horse
15. (c) A is true, but R is false
16. (a) Both A and R are true and R is the correct explanation of A
17. (a) (i), (ii), (iii)
18. (a) Uttar Pradesh
19. (a) Guru Tegh Bahadur
20. (d) The royal centre was located in the North-Eastern part of the settlement and included only the king's palace.
21. (c) I, II and III
34.

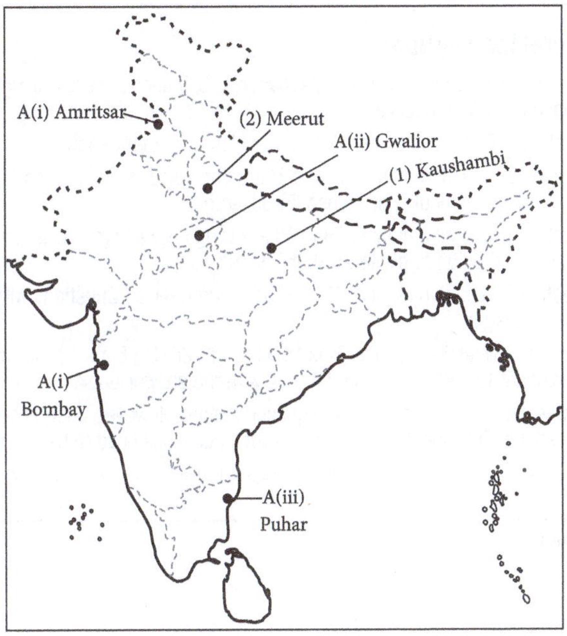

SAMPLE QUESTION PAPER 4

A Highly Simulated Sample Question Paper for CBSE Class XII

(UNSOLVED)

HISTORY

General Instructions

- Question paper comprises five Section: A, B, C, D and E. There are 34 questions in the question paper. All questions are compulsory.
- Section A: Question numbers 1 to 21 are MCQs of 1 mark each.
- Section B: Question numbers 22 to 27 are Short Answer Type Questions, carrying 3 marks each. Answer to each question should not exceed 60-80 words.
- Section C: Question number 28 to 30 are Long Answer Type Questions, carrying 8 marks each. Answer to each question should not exceed 300-350 words.
- Section D: Question number 31 to 33 are Source Based Questions with three sub questions and are of 4 marks each.
- Section E: Question number 34 is Map based, carrying 5 marks that includes the identification and location of significant test items. Attach the map with the answer book.
- There is no overall choice in the question paper. However, an internal choice has been provided in few questions. Only one of the choices in such questions have to be attempted.
- In addition to this, separate instructions are given with each section and question, wherever necessary.

Time : 3 hours **Max. Marks : 80**

Section A (1 × 21 = 21)

(Objective Type Questions)

1. Which of the following represents the correct chronological order of advances in epigraphy. (1)

(i) Decipherment of Asokan Brahmi by James Prinsep

(ii) Founding of the Asiatic Society (Bengal)

(iii) First issue of Epigraphia Carnatica, a journal of south Indian inscriptions

(iv) First issue of Epigraphia Indica.

Options

(a) (ii), (iii), (iv), (i)
(b) (i), (ii), (iii), (iv)
(c) (ii), (i), (iii), (iv)
(d) (iii), (ii), (i), (iv)

2. Given below are the two statements, one labelled as Assertion (A) and the other labelled as Reason (R). (1)

Assertion (A) The Congress by the 1930s had accepted Hindustani to be the national language.

Reason (R) Hindi got developed from Hindustani language only.

Codes

(a) Both A and R are true and R is the correct explanation of A
(b) Both A and R are true, but R is not the correct explanation of A
(c) A is true, but R is false
(d) A is false, but R is true

3. Identify the following image and name the region where this Gopuram is built. (1)

(a) Madurai (b) Konark
(c) Gangaikondacholapuram (d) Thanjavur

4. Consider the following statements. (1)

I. Vijayanagara was noted for its markets dealing in spices, textiles and precious stones.

II. Its most famous ruler Krishnadeva Raya in his work Amuktamalyada advised kings to encourage commerce besides making provisions for safety and security of the foreign travellers.

Choose the correct option.

(a) Both I and II (b) Only II
(c) Only I (d) All of these

5. Arrange the location of the following sites of the Harappan Civilisation in correct sequence from East to West. (1)

(i) Banawali (ii) Dholavira
(iii) Kalibangan (iv) Mohenjodaro

Codes

(a) (i), (ii), (iii), (iv) (b) (i), (iii), (ii), (iv)
(c) (ii), (i), (iii), (iv) (d) (iv), (i), (ii), (iii)

6. Identify the work that is a collection of conversations of Sufi Saint Shaikh Nizamuddin Auliya, compiled by Amir Hasan Sijzi Dehlavi. (1)

(a) Malfuzat (b) Tazkiras
(c) Ziyarat (d) Maktubat

7. What insights do archaeological findings provide about agricultural practices in the Harappan civilisation? Choose the best suitable option from the following. (1)

(a) The use of advanced ploughing machines and highly mechanised tools.
(b) Evidence of ploughed fields, irrigation practices, and domestication of animals.
(c) Complete reliance on hunting and gathering without any agricultural development.
(d) Absence of agricultural technologies, leading to food shortages.

8. Match the following. (1)

	List I		List II
A.	Abdullah Shattari	1.	Punjab
B.	Mir Sayyid Muhammad Gesu Daraz	2.	Gwalior
C.	Bahauddin Zakariya	3.	Gulbarga
D.	Qutbuddin Bakhtiyar Kaki	4.	Delhi

Codes

	A	B	C	D		A	B	C	D
(a)	3	1	4	2	(b)	1	3	4	2
(c)	2	3	1	4	(d)	2	4	1	3

9. Given below are the two statements, one labelled as Assertion (A) and the other labelled as Reason (R). (1)

Assertion (A) In the Objective Resolution, the word democratic was not used for the nature of the state.

Reason (R) The Objective Resolution defined the ideals of the Constitution of independent India.

Codes

(a) Both A and R are true and R is the correct explanation of A
(b) Both A and R are true, but R is not the correct explanation of A
(c) A is true, but R is false
(d) A is false, but R is true

10. How did the representation of Vishnu at Puri differ from other regions? Choose the best suitable option from the following (1)

(a) Vishnu at Puri was depicted as an abstract deity without any anthropomorphic form.
(b) Vishnu at Puri was represented in a wooden form by tribal specialists, unlike other regions where he was depicted in anthropomorphic forms.
(c) Vishnu was visualised in Puri with features identical to other major temples across India.
(d) Vishnu was not worshipped at Puri at all.

11. Identify the term which defines the given below statement and give the correct answer. (1)

"The stupa originated as a sample semi-circular mound of Earth"

(a) Marmika (b) Anda
(c) Amalka (d) Pradakshinapath

12. The Brihadeshwara temple is constructed by ruler from .... (1)

(a) Vijayanagara Empire (b) Chalukyas Dynasty
(c) Chola Empire (d) Hoysalas Dynasty

13. Identify the principalities that was/were annexed by British on a variety of pleas, like mis-government and the refusal to recognise adoption. (1)

(a) Awadh (b) Jhansi (c) Satara (d) All of these

14. Identify the community from the description given below. (1)
- Their life as hunters, shifting cultivators, food gatherers was intimately connected to forests.
- They lived in hutments within tamarind groves and rested in mango shades.

(a) Santhals (b) Kolis (c) Bhils (d) Paharias

15. Which of the following was the primary goal of the Mahabharata's Critical Edition project? (1)
(a) To compare Sanskrit manuscripts and create a unified version
(b) To translate the text into multiple languages
(c) To publish only the regional variations of the Mahabharata
(d) To rewrite the Mahabharata for modern readers

16. To save their property, whom did the Zamindar transferred it to? (1)
(a) Children (b) Servants
(c) Women (d) None of these

17. Choose the correctly matched pair(s). (1)
(a) Zarathrustra - Iran
(b) Aristotle - Greece
(c) Mahavira - India
(d) All of the above

18. Complete the following analogy by choosing the correct option given below. (1)
Chauri Chaura incident : 1922 : : Purna Swaraj : ?
(a) 1929 (b) 1930 (c) 1921 (d) 1925

19. Identify the correctly matched pair(s). (1)
(a) Megasthenese – Indica
(b) Al-Biruni – Kitab-ul-Hind
(c) Ibn Battuta – Rihla
(d) All of the above

20. The act of .... allowed Gandhiji to break the boundaries that prevailed within the traditional caste system, between mental labour and manual labour. (1)
(a) launching movements (b) spinning charkha
(c) organising Satyagraha (d) non-violence

21. Which of the following was not the major centre of revolt? (1)
(a) Lucknow (b) Kanpur
(c) Bareilly (d) Agra

Section B
(Short Answer Type Questions) (3 × 6 = 18)

22. Write a brief note on development of Indian sculptures. (3)

23. Briefly explain the views of Jaipal Singh on Adivasis. (3)

24. Why was the proposals of the Cabinet Mission rejected? (3)

25. Explain the concept of Asoka's Dhamma. (3)

Or

Discuss the administrative system of Magadhan Empire.

26. Analyse the system of irrigation and technology in 16th and 17th century in Mughal Empire. (3)

27. "Amara Nayaka system was a major political innovation of Vijayanagara Empire." Elucidate. (3)

Or Discuss the temple building activity in Vijayanagara Empire.

Section C
(Long Answer Type Questions) (8 × 3 = 24)

28. Explain rules and practices related with kingship in ancient India, especially from 600 BCE to 600 CE. (8)

Or While analysing historical text, historian consider many elements. Explain this with reference to the Mahabharata.

29. "The rulers of Vijayanagara drew on different traditions to create an imperial culture." Explain by giving specific examples. (8)

Or Patronage to both Indian as well as foreign traders was a distinguished feature of Vijayanagara Empire. Elaborate.

30. "Wherever Gandhiji went rumours spread of his miraculous powers." Explain with examples. (8)

Or Gandhiji encouraged the communication of the nationalist message in mother tongue rather than in language of the ruler. Examine how he knitted the Non-Cooperation Movement with his philosophy.

Section D
(Source Based Questions) (4 × 3 = 12)

31. Read the following source carefully and answer the questions that follow. (4)

The Jotedar of Dinajpur

Buchanan described the ways in which Jotedars of Dinajpur in North Bengal resisted being disciplined by the Zamindar and undermined his power: Landlords do not like this class of men, but it is

UNSOLVED

evident that they are absolutely necessary, unless landlords themselves would advance money to their necessitous tenatry. The Jotedars, who cultivate large portions of land are very refractory and know that the Zamindars have no power over them. They pay only few rupees on account of their revenue and then fall in balance almost every kist (instalment), they hold more lands then they are entitled to by their pottahs (deeds of contract). In wake of any action by Zamindar to summon them in cutcherry, they complain at the Fouzdarry Thanna (Police Station) for imprisonment and at the musifff's (a judicial officer at lower court) cutcherry for being dishonoured.

(i) Who was Francis Buchanan? (1)

(ii) What can be inferred from this passage about the relationship between Zamindars and Jotedars? (1)

(iii) What were the functions performed by Jotedars in rural areas of Bengal? (2)

32. Read the following source carefully and answer the questions that follow. (4)

Rules for Monks and Nuns

These are some of the rules laid down in the Vinaya Pitaka:

What a new felt (blanket/rug) has been made by a bhikkhu, it is to be kept for at least six years. If after less than six years he should have another new felt (blanket/rug) made, regardless of whether or not he has disposed of the first, then-unless he has been authorised by the bhikkhus it is to be forfeited and confessed.

In case, a bhikkhu arriving at a family residence is presented with cakes of cooked grain-meal, he may accept two or three bowlfuls if he so desires. If he should accept more than that, it is to be confessed. Having accepted the two or three bowlfuls and having taken them from there, he is to share them among the bhikkhus. This is the proper coures here.

Should any bhikkhu, having set out bedding in a lodging belonging to the Sangha- or having had it set out and then on departing neither put it away nor have it put away, or should he go without taking leave, it is to be confessed.

(i) What is the importance of Vinaya Pitaka? (1)

(ii) Why do you think men and women joined Sangha? Give two reasons. (1)

(iii) What was the Bodh Sanga? (2)

33. Read the following source carefully and answer the questions that follow. (4)

A Sprawling City

This is an excerpt from Domingo Paes's description of Vijayanagara:

The size of this city I do not write here, because it cannot all be seen from any spot, but I climbed a hill hence I could see a great part of it; I could not see it all because it lies between several ranges of hills. What I saw from thence seemed to me as large as Rome and very beautiful to the sight; there are many groves of trees within it, in the gardens of the houses, and many conduits of water which flow into the midst of it, and in places there are lakes; and the king has close to his palace a palm-grove and other rich fruit-bearing trees.

(i) Who is the author of the passage? What is the theme of it? What did king had close to his palace? (1)

(ii) Why could Paes not describe the size of city in the first instance? (1)

(iii) What was the description of the city by Paes later? (2)

Section E

(Map Based Question)

34. A. Locate the following areas under British control in 1857 on the map of India. (3)

(i) Meerut (ii)Calcutta *Or* Kanpur

(iii) Allahabad

B. Identify the early states marked as 1 and 2 on the map. (2)

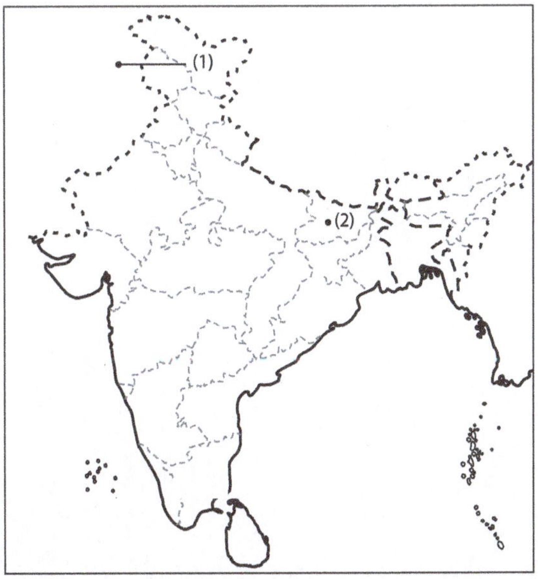

Answers

1. (c) (ii), (i), (iii), (iv)
2. (c) A is true, but R is false
3. (a) Madurai
4. (a) Both I and II
5. (b) (i), (iii), (ii), (iv)
6. (a) Malfuzat
7. (b) Evidence of ploughed fields, irrigation practices, and domestication of animals.
8. (c)
9. (b) Both A and R are true, but R is not the correct explanation of A
10. (b) Vishnu at Puri was represented in a wooden form by tribal specialists, unlike other regions where he was depicted in anthropomorphic forms.
11. (b) Anda
12. (c) Chola Empire
13. (d) All of these
14. (d) Paharias
15. (a) To compare Sanskrit manuscripts and create a unified version
16. (c) Women
17. (d) All of these
18. (a) 1929
19. (d) All of the above
20. (b) spinning charkha
21. (d) Agra
34.

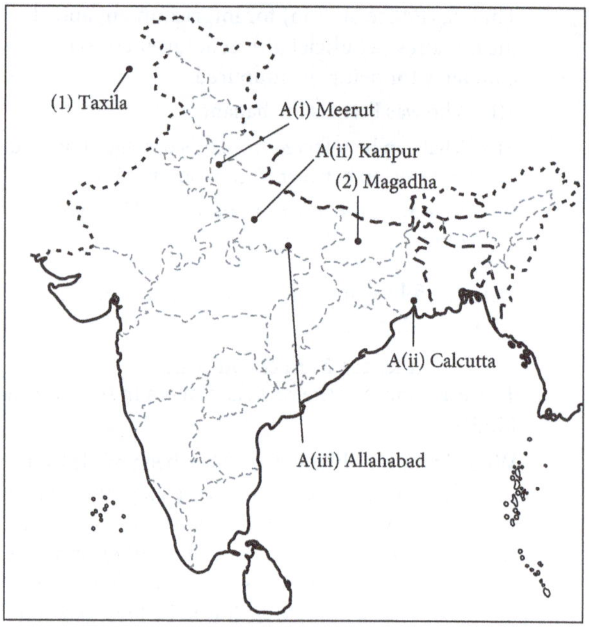

UNSOLVED

SAMPLE QUESTION PAPER 5

A Highly Simulated Sample Question Paper for CBSE Class XII

(UNSOLVED)

HISTORY

General Instructions

- Question paper comprises five Sections – A, B, C, D and E. There are 34 questions in the question paper. All questions are compulsory.
- Section A: Question 1 to 21 are MCQs of 1 mark each.
- Section B: Question no. 22 to 27 are Short Answer Type Questions, carrying 3 marks each. Answer to each question should not exceed 60-80 words.
- Section C: Question no 28 to 30 are Long Answer Type Questions, carrying 8 marks each. Answer to each question should not exceed 300-350 words.
- Section D: Question no. 31 to 33 are Source Based Questions with three sub questions and are of 4 marks each.
- Section E: Question no. 34 is Map based, carrying 5 marks that includes the identification and location of significant test items. Attach the map with the answer book.
- There is no overall choice in the question paper. However, an internal choice has been provided in few questions. Only one of the choices in such questions have to be attempted.
- In addition to this, separate instructions are given with each section and question, wherever necessary.

Time : 3 hours **Max. Marks : 80**

Section A (1×21=21)

(Objective Type Questions)

1. In which of the following states, the Rajmahal hills habitat of Paharia tribes is situated? (1)

(a) Jharkhand (b) Bihar (c) West Bengal (d) Orissa

2. Who among the following was the leader of Santhal rebellion? (1)

(a) Tilka Manjhi (b) Birsa Munda (c) Sidhu Manjhi (d) Shah Mal

3. Consider the following statements regarding 'Resolution of Pakistan'. (1)

I. It was passed on 23rd March, 1940.

II. Resolution did not mention about partition.

III. Unionist party opposes the demand of Pakistan as separate homeland for Muslims.

Which of the above statements are correct?

(a) I and II (b) II and III (c) I and III (d) I, II and III

4. Match the following. (1)

	List I		List II
A.	Gotra	1.	Lineage
B.	Vanik	2.	Common descendants of Vedic seer
C.	Polygyny	3.	Practice of a man having several wives
D.	Vamsha	4.	Merchants

Codes

	A	B	C	D		A	B	C	D
(a)	2	4	3	1	(b)	4	2	1	3
(c)	2	3	1	4	(d)	1	4	2	3

5. Identify the correctly matched pair(s). (1)

(a) Balakot – Shells (b) Khetri – Copper
(c) South India – Gold (d) All of these

6. Who among the following advised 'Mahatma Gandhi' to spent a year travelling around British India in order to better understand about the country and its people? (1)

(a) Gopal Krishna Gokhale (b) SN Banerjee
(c) Bal Gangadhar Tilak (d) Lala Lajpat Rai

7. Which among the following British officers was killed by the rebels at Lucknow in Revolt of 1857? (1)

(a) Thomas Jones Barker (b) Felice Beato
(c) Joseph Noel Paton (d) Henry Lawrence

8. Given below are the two statements, one labelled as Assertion (A) and the other labelled as Reason (R). (1)

Assertion (A) Of the groups of Sufis who migrated to India in the late 12th century, the Chishtis were the most influential.

Reason (R) Akbar visited the famous Chishti Sufi Shrine of Ajmer fourteen times in his lifetime. (1)

Codes

(a) Both A and R are true and R is the correct explanation of A
(b) Both A and R are true, but R is not the correct explanation of A
(c) A is true, but R is false
(d) A is false, but R is true

9. The given image of water carrier woman has been derived from which region? (1)

(a) Mathura (b) Awadh
(c) Hampi (d) Rajgriha

10. Given below are the two statements, one labelled as Assertion (A) and the other labelled as Reason (R). (1)

Assertion (A) Buddha's disciples were very sad and clueless when Buddha was dying.

Reason (R) They wanted to erect a grand stupa so that people can come, place garlands, perfumes and make salutations to Buddha.

Codes

(a) Both A and R are true and R is the correct explanation of A
(b) Both A and R are true, but R is not the correct explanation of A
(c) A is true, but R is false
(d) A is false, but R is true

11. Which of the following statements are correct regarding Krishnadeva Raya?

I. He was famous for his literary skills.
II. He composed Amuktamalyada in Telugu.
III. He was characterised by expansion and consolidation.
IV. He belonged to Saluvas dynasty.

Codes

(a) I, II and IV (b) I and II
(c) I, II and III (d) All of these

12. Who among the following brought the ruins of Hampi to light in 1800 ? (1)

(a) Thomas Hickey (b) Colin Mackenzie
(c) JF Fleet (d) Alexander Greenlaw

13. Which of the following categories of society of ancient Persia was not recognised by the Al-Biruni? (1)

(a) Knights and princes (b) Monks and fire-priests
(c) Peasants and artisans (d) Children and women

14. Identify the incorrectly matched pair. (1)

(a) Ashokan inscriptions – Pali
(b) Inscriptions in North-West – Aramic language
(c) Prakrit inscriptions – Brahmi script
(d) Greek scripts – Afghanistan

15 Imagine you are analysing the religious developments in early medieval India. Which of the following sources would best help you to understand the integration of local deities into Puranic traditions? (1)

(a) Records of the composition and compilation of the Puranic texts.
(b) Temple inscriptions describing the construction of shrines for Vishnu and Shiva
(c) Accounts of royal patronage for Buddhist monasteries and stupas.

UNSOLVED

(d) Manuscripts describing Tantric rituals and their practitioners.

16. Complete the following analogy by choosing the correct option given below. (1)

Garibaldi : Italy, Ho Chi Minh : ?

(a) Vietnam (b) Myanmar
(c) Indonesia (d) Japan

17. Which of the following was/were the main cause(s) behind the Revolt of 1857? (1)

(a) British Land Revenue Settlements
(b) Foreign commerce
(c) Fear of converting population into Christianity.
(d) All of the above

18. What was being auctioned in Burdwan in 1797? (1)

(a) Estates (b) Jewelleries
(c) Paintings (d) Clothes

19. Who represented 'Tribals' in the Constituent Assembly? (1)

(a) Jaipal Singh
(b) Buddhu Bhagat
(c) BR Ambedkar
(d) NG Ranga

20. Identify the personality from the description given below. (1)

- He was the first ruler who inscribed his messages to his subjects and officials on stone surfaces.
- He conquered Kalinga and propagated Dhamma.

(a) Asoka
(b) Chandragupta Maurya
(c) Bindusara
(d) Dhanananda

21. Arrange the following events in chronological order (1)

(i) Establishment of the Delhi Sultanate.
(ii) Ibn Battuta's arrival in India.
(iii) Muhammad Bin Tughlaq's reign.
(iv) The conquest of Delhi by Qutb-ud-Din Aibak.

Options

(a) (i), (iv), (iii), (ii) (b) (iv), (i), (iii), (ii)
(c) (i), (iii), (iv), (ii) (d) (iii), (ii), (iv), (ii)

Section B

(Short Answer Type Questions) (3 × 6 = 18)

22. What was the reason for popularity of Chisti Khanqah? Give four points with examples. (3)

Or Write a note on Tantric form of worship.

23. What were the views of NG Ranga regarding minorities? (3)

24. Discuss the agricultural technologies used in Harappan Civilisation with the help of suitable examples. (3)

25. Describe the concept of gotra and its conditions. (3)

26. Which ceremonies and rituals were performed in Vijayanagara Empire on the occassion of Mahanavmi? (3)

27. What was the aim of British behind introducing permanent settlement in Bengal? (3)

Or Write a short note on Jotedars in Bengal.

Section C

(Long Answer Type Questions) (8 × 3 = 24)

28. Examine the role played by Colin Mackenzie in reconstruction of history of Vijayanagara Empire. How did the writing of foreign travellers aided in reimagining the capital of this empire? (8)

Or Describe the relation between kings of Vijayanagara Empire and their neighbours.

29. "The opening of the BHU was an occasion for celebration, marking as it did the opening of a nationalist university". Justify the statement. (8)

Or "Gandhiji hoped that by coupling Non-Cooperation with Khilafat, India's two major religious communities, Hindus and Muslims, could collectively bring an end to colonial rule". Justify the statement.

30. Commenting on Mahabharata, Maurice Winternitz, a famous historian of Indian literature wrote "It gives us an insight into the most profound depths of the soul of the Indian folk". Discuss. (8)

Or Give detail account of the events related with Ekalavya and Dronacharya from the epic Mahabharata.

Section D

(Source Based Questions) (4×3=12)

31. Read the following source carefully and answer the questions that follow. (4)

A Prayer to Agni

Here are two verses from the *Rigveda* invoking Agni, the God of fire, often identified with the sacrificial fire, into which offerings were made so

UNSOLVED

as to reach the other deities. Bring, O strong one, this sacrifice of ours to the Gods, O wise one, as a liberal giver. Bestow on us, O priest, abundant food. Agni, obtain by sacrificing, mighty wealth for us. Procure, O Agni, for ever to him who prays to you (the gift of) nourishment, the wonderful cow. May a son be ours, offspring that continues our line .... Verses such as these were composed in a special kind of Sanskrit, known as Vedic Sanskrit. They were taught orally to men belonging to priestly families.

(i) Why were offerings made to Agni? Give one reason (1)

(ii) Mention the language in which prayers were made. How it was taught? (1)

(iii) What do you understand by sacrificial fire? What offerings were made in it? (2)

UNSOLVED

32 Read the following source carefully and answer the questions that follows. (4)

The following is how Ibn Battuta described the coconut: These trees are among the most peculiar trees in kind and most astonishing in habit. They look exactly like date-palms, without any difference between them except that the one produces nuts as its fruits and the other produces dates. The nut of a coconut tree resembles a man's head, for in it are what look like two eyes and a mouth, and the inside of it when it is green looks like the brain, and attached to it is a fibre which looks like hair. They make from this cords with which they sew up ships instead of (using) iron nails, and they (also) make from it cables for vessels.

(i) Write the name of two items which held Ibn Battuta's fascination. (1)

(ii) How does he convey a sense that this fruit is unusual? (1)

(iii) What kind of comparison did Ibn Battuta presents to make people understand? Are those comparisons appropriate? (2)

33 Read the following source carefully and answer the questions that follow. (4)

The Rebel of 1857 : Shah Mal

Shah Mal lived in a large village in Pargana, Barout in Uttar Pradesh. He belonged to a clan of Jat cultivators whose kinship ties extended over *chaurasee des* (84 villages). The lands in the region were irrigated and fertile with rich dark loam soil. Many of the villagers were prosperous and saw the British land revenue system as oppressive : the revenue demand was high and its collection inflexible. Consequently, cultivators were losing land to outsiders, to traders and moneylenders who were coming into the area.

Shah Mal mobilised the headmen and cultivators of *chaurasee des*, moving at night from village to village, urging people to rebel against the British. As in many other places, the revolt against the British turned into a general rebellion against all signs of oppression and injustice. Cultivators left their fields and plundered the houses of moneylenders and traders. Displaced proprietors took possession of the lands they had lost. Shah Mal's men attacked government buildings, destroyed the bridge over the river and dug-up metalled roads - partly to prevent government forces from coming into the area and partly because bridges and roads were seen as symbols of British rule.

They sent supplies to the sepoy who had mutinied in Delhi and stopped all official communication between British headquarters and Meerut. Locally acknowledged as the Raja, Shah Mal took over the bungalow of an English officer, turned it into a 'hall of justice', settling disputes and dispensing judgements. He also set-up an amazingly effective network of intelligence. For a period, the people of the area felt that firangi raj was over and their raj had come. Shah Mal was killed in battle in July 1857.

(i) Why the cultivators were losing land to outsiders? (1)

(ii) Who was Shah Mal? How did he urge people to rebel against the British? (2)

(iii) Mention any two steps taken by Shah Mal to support the cause of Revolt of 1857. (2)

Section E

(Map Based Question)

34 A. Locate and label the following places on the map of India. (3)

(i) Kanchipuram

(ii) Kalibangan *Or* Lothal

(iii) A territory under British control.

B. On the given political outline map of India, two major Buddhist sites have been marked as 1 and 2. Identify and write their names on the given lines. (2)

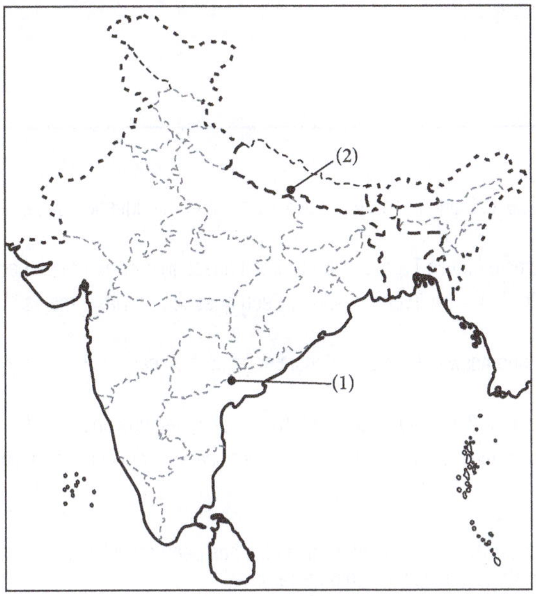

Answers

1. (a) Jharkhand
2. (c) Sidhu Manjhi
3. (d) I, II and III
4. (a)
5. (d) All of these
6. (a) Gopal Krishna Gokhale
7. (d) Henry Lawrence
8. (b) Both A and R are true, but R is not the correct explanation of A
9. (a) Mathura
10. (c) A is true, but R is false
11. (c) I, II and III
12. (b) Colin Mackenzie
13. (d) Children and women
14. (a) Ashokan inscriptions – Pali
15. (a) Records of the composition and compilation of the Puranic texts.
16. (a) Vietnam
17. (d) All of the above
18. (a) Estates
19. (a) Jaipal Singh
20. (a) Asoka
21. (b)
34.

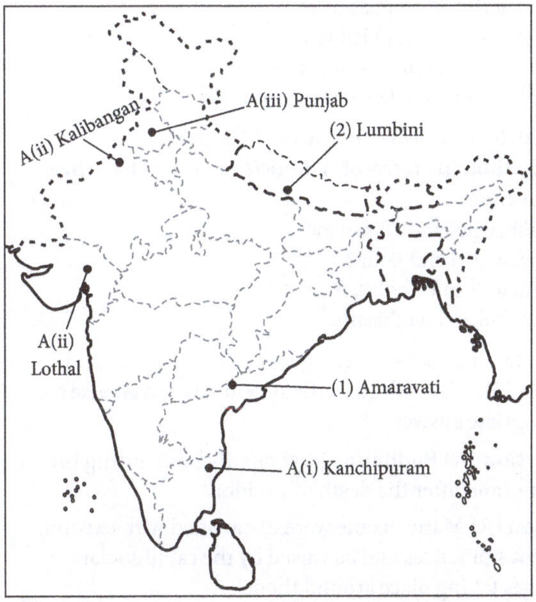

UNSOLVED

CBSE SOLVED PAPER 2025

HISTORY

General Instructions

- Question paper comprises five Sections – A, B, C, D and E. There are 34 questions in the question paper. All questions are compulsory.
- **Section A :** Question number 1 to 21 are Multiple Choice Type Questions. Each question carries 1 mark each.
- **Section B :** Question number 22 to 27 are Short Answer Type Questions. Each question carries 3 marks. Answer to each question should not exceed 60-80 words.
- **Section C :** Question number 28 to 30 are Long Answer Type Questions. Each question carries 8 marks. Answer to each question should not exceed 300-350 words.
- **Section D :** Question number 31 to 33 are Source Based Questions with three sub questions and are of 4 marks each.
- **Section E :** Question number 34 is Map Based Question that includes the identification and location of significant test items. This question carries 5 marks.
- Attach the map with the answer book.
- There is no overall choice in the question paper. However, an internal choice has been provided in few questions. Only one of the choices in such questions have to be attempted.

Time : 3 hours ***Max. Marks : 80***

SET - 1 (61/1/1)

SECTION A

1. Which of the following is correct regarding Harappan script? (1)

(a) This script was alphabetical.
(b) It was written from left to right.
(c) This script has not been deciphered so far.
(d) This script has a few signs or symbols.

2. In which of the following sites of Harappan civilisation, the terracotta models of plough have been discovered? (1)

(a) Kalibangan and Dholavira
(b) Shortughai and Lothal
(c) Banawali and Cholistan
(d) Sanghol and Rakhigarhi

3. Two statements have been given below as Assertion (A) and Reason (R). Read the statements and choose the appropriate answer. (1)

Assertion (A) Buddhism grew rapidly both during the lifetime and after the death of Buddha.

Reason (R) Many people were dissatisfied with existing religious practices and confused by the rapid social changes taking place around them.

Options

(a) Both A and R are true and R is the correct reasoning of A.
(b) Both A and R are true but R is not the correct reasoning of A.
(c) A is true, R is untrue.
(d) A is untrue, R is true.

4. Consider the following statements regarding Jainism and choose the correct option. (1)

I. The cycle of birth and rebirth is shaped through Karma.
II. There is a need to renounce the world.
III. Worldly existence is a necessary condition for attaining salvation.
IV. Principle of Ahimsa is important.

Options

(a) I, II and III
(b) II, III and IV
(c) I, II and IV
(d) I, III and IV

5. Match Column-I with Column-II and choose the correct option from the following.

	Column-I (Ancient Mahajanpadas)		Column-II (Present Region)
A.	Magadh	1.	Qandhar (Eastern Afghanistan)
B.	Avanti	2.	Ayodhya (Uttar Pradesh)
C.	Gandhara	3.	Patna (Bihar)
D.	Koshala	4.	Ujjain (Madhya Pradesh)

Options

	A	B	C	D		A	B	C	D
(a)	3	2	1	4	(b)	3	2	1	3
(c)	3	4	1	2	(d)	2	1	3	4

6. Prabhavati Gupta is best known for which of the following roles? (1)

(a) Wife of Ashoka and promoter of Buddhist Sangha.
(b) Queen of Mauryan Empire and promoter of Buddhism.
(c) Wife of Samudragupta and poet of the Gupta Era.
(d) Daughter of Chandragupta-II and wife of Vakataka King.

7. The following picture shows the structure of a temple carved out of single piece of rock. Identify this temple correctly from the given options. (1)

Options

(a) Deogarh Temple (b) Kailashnatha Temple
(c) Mahabalipuram Temple (d) Brihideshwara Temple

8. Al-Biruni's major work 'Kitab-ul-Hind' is significant for its comprehensive study of India. Which of the following was the primary aim of this work? (1)

(a) Promote Islamic teaching
(b) Map geographical locations
(c) Critique culture and traditions
(d) Document Indian culture

9. Throughout his extensive travels, Ibn Batuta was able to explore unfamiliar cultures and societies. Which of the following competencies did he most likely develop? (1)

(a) Leadership and judicial management
(b) Cultural competencies and skills
(c) Knowledge of administration and army
(d) Scientific and technical expertise

10. Which of the following statements regarding Colonel Colin Mackenzie are correct? Choose the correct option.

I. The ruins of Hampi were brought to light in 1800 by him. (1)
II. He was an official of East India Company.
III. He prepared the first survey maps of the site.
IV. He received information of Vijayanagara empire from the Duarte Barbosa.

Options

(a) I, II and III (b) II, III and IV
(c) I, III and IV (d) I, II and IV

11. Match Column-I with Column-II and choose the correct option from the following. (1)

	Column-I (Foreign Travellers)		Column-II (Countries)
A.	AfanasiNikitin	I.	Persia
B.	Domingo Paes	II.	Russia
C.	Abdur-Razzak	III.	Portugal
D.	Nicolo de Conti	IV.	Italy

Options

	A	B	C	D		A	B	C	D
(a)	3	4	1	2	(b)	2	3	1	4
(c)	1	2	4	3	(d)	2	1	3	4

12. Which of the following is a major source to understand agrarian history of 16th and 17th century India? (1)

(a) Revenue records of Agra & Delhi
(b) Relationship between peasants and zamindars
(c) Important chronicle - the Ain-i-Akbari
(d) Types of agricultural crops grown at that time

13. Which one of the following statements is most appropriate regarding the zamindars of 16th and 17th century India? (1)

(a) The zamindars were the exploitative class for the peasants.
(b) The zamindars collected revenue on behalf of the state.
(c) They always maintained cordial relations with the villagers.
(d) The zamindars had small piece of lands for personal use.

14. In a modern city, a group of friends discusses the relevance of Kabir's 16 teachings in today's society. Some believe these are outdated, while others see their significance in promoting equality and love. Which of the following scenario best reflects Kabir's relevance today? (1)

(a) A debate on Kabir's historical context
(b) A discussion dismissing spirituality irrelevant
(c) Focus on societal norms and traditions only
(d) Seeking simple connection with the divine

15. **Which one of the following was the main cause of the Santhal Rebellion of 1855?** (1)
(a) Imposition of the Summary Settlement
(b) Cultural suppression by the British
(c) Imposition of Western education
(d) Heavy taxes and land annexation

16. **Find the odd one out regarding the Permanent Settlement of 1793.** (1)
(a) The Sunset Law (b) The Burdwan's Auction
(c) The Fifth Report (d) The Deccan Riots Commission

17. **Match the Column-I with Column-II and choose the correct option.** (1)

	Column-I (Leadership of the Revolt of 1857)		Column-II (Regions)
A.	Shah Mal	1.	Lucknow
B.	Kunwar Singh	2.	Kanpur
C.	Birjis Qadr	3.	Baraut
D.	Nana Sahib	4	Arrah

Options

	A	B	C	D		A	B	C	D
(a)	2	3	4	1	(b)	3	4	1	2
(c)	3	2	1	4	(d)	4	2	3	1

18. **Arrange the following historical events in a correct chronological order and choose the correct option.** (1)
I. Making of the Constituent Assembly
II. Jallianwala Bagh Massacre
III. Quit India Movement
IV. Gandhi-Irwin Pact

Options
(a) II, III, I and IV (b) II, IV, III and I
(c) III, II, I and IV (d) IV, III, I and II

19. **Which one of the following was a key feature of the 'Subsidiary Alliance' introduced by Lord Wellesley in 1798?** (1)
(a) Free Trade Policy brought by British
(b) Maintenance of native army by British
(c) Imposition of Western Customs by British
(d) Protection of native territory by British

20. **Which one of the following pair is correctly matched?** (1)

	List-I (Name of Important Committees of Constituent Assembly)	List-II (Name of President)
(a)	Flag Committee	– H.C. Mookerjee
(b)	Union Power Committee	– Pandit Jawaharlal Nehru
(c)	Rules of Procedure Committee	– S. Varadachariar
(d)	States Committee	– J.B. Kripalani

21. **Identify the member of the Constituent Assembly with the help of the following information.** (1)
- He was the President of the Constituent Assembly.
- He was the first President of the Independent India.

(a) Sarvepalli Radhakrishnan
(b) Zakir Hussain
(c) V.V. Giri
(d) Rajendra Prasad

SECTION-B

(Short Answer Type Questions)

22. "Ashokan inscriptions are the most significant sources to understand the administration of Ashoka". Explain the statement. (3)

Or

"The history of Mauryan empire has been constructed on the variety of sources". Explain the statement.

23. "The mid-first millennium BCE is considered as a significant turning point in the course of World History". Justify the statement. (3)

24. Analyse the causes that led to the ruin of Vijayanagara empire. (3)

Or

Analyse why was Amaranayaka system considered as a major political innovation of the Vijayanagara empire.

25. Examine the role of Panchayat in advocating for the rights of common people during the Mughal era. (3)

26. "The rebellion of 1857 was seen as a war in which both Hindus and Muslims had equally to lose or gain". Analyse the statement. (3)

27. Describe the role of Dr. B.R Ambedkar in the Constituent Assembly. (3)

SECTION-C

(Long Answer type Questions)

28. "There were specific features of the familial relationship during the Mahabharata period". Explain the statement with examples. (8)

Or "The political power or kingship was rarely dependent on birth as Kshatriyas but also open to anyone who could muster support and resources". Explain the statement with the examples from sixth century BCE onwards.

29. Explain the main beliefs and teachings of Guru Nanak Dev. (8)

Or Explain the major beliefs and teachings of Chishtis during medieval India.

30. Analyse the impact of national movement in India from 1915 to 1931 on the Indian masses. (8)

Or Analyse the role of Gandhiji after independence of India.

SECTION-D

(Source Based Questions)

31. Read the following source carefully and answer the questions that follow.

The most ancient system yet discovered

About the drains, Mackay noted: "It is certainly the most complete ancient system as yet discovered". Every house was connected to the street drains. The main channels were made of bricks set in mortar and were covered with loose bricks that could be removed for cleaning. In some cases, limestone was used for the covers. House drains first emptied into a sump or cesspit into which solid matter settled while waste water flowed out into the street drains. Very long drainage channels were provided at intervals with sumps for cleaning. It is a wonder of archaeology that "little heaps of material, mostly sand, have frequently been found lying alongside drainage channels, which shows… that the debris was not always carted away when the drain was cleared".

From Ernest Mackay, Early Indus Civilisation, 1948

Drainage systems were not unique to the larger cities, but were found in smaller settlements as well. At Lothal for example, while houses were built of mud bricks, drains were made of burnt bricks.

(i) **Analyse the possible reason behind the uniformity in the drainage systems across the Harappan cities.** (1)

(ii) **Analyse the implications of finding little heaps of material, mostly sand, alongside drainage channels.** (1)

(iii) **Assess the impact of Harappan drainage system.** (2)

32. Read the following source carefully and answer the questions that follow.

A warning for Europe

Bernier warned that if European kings followed the Mughal model: Their kingdoms would be very far from being well-cultivated and Peopled, so well built, so rich, so polite and flourishing as we see them. Our kings are otherwise rich and powerful; and we must avow that they are much better and more royally served. They would soon be kings of deserts and solitudes, of beggars and barbarians, such as those are whom I have been representing. (the Mughals)

We should find the great Cities and the great Burroughs (boroughs) rendered uninhabitable because of ill air, and to fall to ruine (ruin) without anybodies (anybody) taking care of repairing them: the hillocks abandon'd, and the fields overspread with bushes, or fill'd with pestilential marishes (marshes), as hath been already intimated.

(i) **Mention any one prominent contribution of Bernier.** (1)

(ii) **How did Bernier describe the difference between European kingdom and the Mughal territories?** (1)

(iii) **Explain Bernier's views on the socio-economic status of people under Mughal rule.** (2)

33. Read the following source carefully and answer the questions that follow.

On clearance and settled cultivation

Passing through one village in the lower Rajmahal hills, Buchanan wrote:

The view of the country is exceedingly fine, the cultivation, especially the narrow valleys of rice winding in all directions, the cleared lands with scattered trees, and the rocky hills are in perfection; all that is wanted is some appearance of progress in the area and a vastly extended and improved cultivation, of which the country is highly susceptible. Plantations of Asan and Palas, for Tessar (Tassar silk worms) and Lac, should occupy the place of woods to as great an extent as the demand will admit; the remainder might be all cleared, and the greater part cultivated, while what is not fit for the purpose, might rear Plamira (palmyra) and Mowa (mahua).

(i) How did Buchanan describe the view of the lower Rajmahal hills? (1)

(ii) Why did Buchanan believe that the area had high potential for improved cultivation? (1)

(iii) How did Buchanan propose utilising the land for economic benefits? (2)

SECTION - E

(Map Based Question)

34. (i) On the given political outline map of India, locate and label the following with appropriate symbols. (3)

(i) Kalibanga - A mature Harappan site (ii) Amravati - A Buddhist site

(iii) (a) Ambera - A territory under the Mughals

Or

(b) Bijapur - An important town of Medieval India

(ii) On the same outline map, two places have been marked as A and B, as the centres of Revolt of 1857. Identify them and write their names on the lines drawn near them. (2)

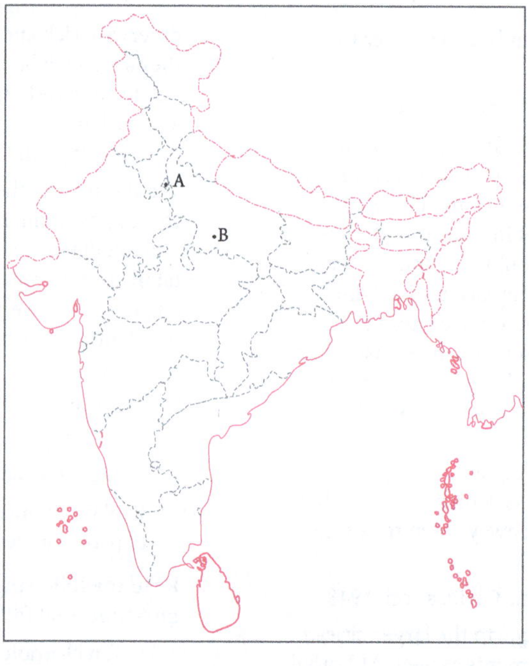

SET-2 (61/1/2)

(Uncommon Questions from Set 1)

23. "Art historians had to acquire familiarity with hagiogrphies of Buddha in order to understand Buddhist sculpture". Explain the statement in context of Sanchi Stupa. (3)

26. Examine how art and literature have helped in keeping the memories of 1857 alive. (3)

27. Describe the views of Gandhiji on the national language of India. (3)

29. Explain the beliefs and teachings of Alvars and Nayanars during the Medieval India. (3)

Or Explain the teachings of Islam.

30. "The salt march was the movement that brought Gandhiji to the world attention". Analyse the statement. (8)

Or "As a consequence of the Non-cooperation Movement, the British Raj was shaken to its foundation, for the first time since the revolt of 1857" Analyse the statement.

SET-3 (61/1/3)

(Uncommon Questions from Set 1 and 2)

23. 'Shahjehan Begum worked extensively for the protection of Sanchi Stupa. Explain the statement. (3)

26. Examine the repressive measures undertaken by the British Government to control the rebellion of 1857. (3)

27. Explain the role of G.B Pant on the united approach of India. (3)

29. Describe the views of Meera Bai on devotionalism (8)

Or

Describe the teachings and beliefs of Virshaiva tradition.

30. Examine the role of Gandhiji in the Civil Disobedience Movement. (8)

Or

Examine the role of Gandhiji in the Non-Cooperation movement.

ANSWERS

Set-1 (61/1/1)

1. (c) This script has not been deciphered so far.

2. (c) Banawali and Cholistan

3. (a) Both A and Rare true and R is the correct reasoning of A

4. (c) I, II and IV

5. (c)

6. (d) Daughter of Chandragupta-II and wife of Vakataka King

7. (b) Kailashnatha Temple

8. (d) Document Indian culture

9. (b) Cultural Competencies and Skills

10. (a) I, II and III

11. (b)

12. (c) Important chronicle - the Ain-i-Akbari

13. (b) The zamindars collected revenue on behalf of the state.

14. (d) Seeking simple connection with the divine

15. (d) Heavy taxes and land annexation

16. (d) The Deccan Riots Commission

17. (b)

18. (b) II, IV, III and I

19. (d) Protection of native territory by British

20. (b) Union Power Committee - Pandit Jawaharlal Nehru

21. (d) Rajendra Prasad

22. Ashokan inscriptions are the most significant sources for understanding Ashoka's administration as they provide direct evidence of his governance, policies and principles. These inscriptions, written in Prakrit, Greek and Aramaic, highlight his commitment to Dhamma, welfare measures, judicial reforms, and efficient communication across the empire.

They also reflect his efforts in spreading Buddhist values and maintaining a just rule. The edicts, placed across the empire, reveal Ashoka's administrative control, moral governance, and the role of officials, making them crucial for historical analysis.

Or

The history of the Mauryan empire has been constructed using a variety of sources, which provide valuable insights into its administration, economy and society. These sources include

- **Literary Sources** Texts like Kautilya's Arthashastra and Megasthenes' Indica describe governance economy and social structure.
- **Epigraphic Sources** Ashokan inscriptions, written on pillars and rocks, reveal the empire's policies and Buddhist influence.
- **Archaeological Evidence** Excavations of stupas, palaces, and pillars provide material proof of Mauryan art and architecture.
- **Numismatic Sources** Coins help in understanding the empire's economy and trade networks.

23. The mid-first millennium BCE is considered a significant turning point in world history as it saw the rise of great thinkers like Zarathustra, Kong Zi, Socrates, Plato, Aristotle, Mahavira and Gautama Buddha. They explored human existence and the cosmic order. Simultaneously, new kingdoms and cities emerged, transforming social and economic life in the Ganga valley. The period also witnessed changes in religious traditions, including Vedic sacrifices performed by priests and rulers.

24. The following were the causes that led to the ruin of the Vijayanagara empire

- **Battle of Talikota (1565)** The decisive defeat by the combined forces of the Deccan Sultanates led to large-scale destruction.
- **Weak Successors** Inefficient rulers after Krishna Deva Raya failed to maintain the empire's stability.
- **Court Intrigues** Internal conflicts and power struggles weakened governance.
- **Continuous Wars** Frequent battles drained resources and military strength.
- **Economic Decline** Loss of trade routes and wealth weakened the empire.

- **Military Exhaustion** Overburdened forces and lack of strong leadership accelerated the empire's downfall.

Or

The Amaranayaka system was considered major political innovation of the Vijayanagara empire because it helped in maintaining administrative control and military strength. The system, influenced by the Delhi Sultanate's Iqta system, involved military commanders (Amaranayakas) who governed assigned territories, collected taxes, and maintained troops for the empire.

They contributed revenue for temple upkeep and irrigation works. This decentralised system ensured efficient governance and a strong fighting force. However, over time, rebellious Nayakas weakened the central authority, leading to the empire's decline.

25. During the Mughal era, the village panchayat played a crucial role in advocating for the rights of common people by acting as a mediator between villagers and state authorities. It addressed grievances related to excessive taxation, forced labour (beggar), and caste-based oppression.

Peasants, especially from lower castes, often approached the panchayat to seek justice against unjust demands by zamindars or officials. The panchayat could suggest compromises or, in extreme cases, support resistance like village desertion, ensuring that customary rights and basic subsistence were upheld.

26. The rebellion of 1857 was seen as a war in which both Hindus and Muslims had equally to lose or gain. The proclamations issued during the rebellion repeatedly appealed to all sections of the population, irrespective of their caste and creed. Even proclamations issued by Muslim princes took care to address the sentiments of Hindus.

The rebels glorified the coexistence of different communities under the Mughal Empire and sought unity in their fight against British rule. Despite British attempts to create religious divisions, such as spending money to incite Hindus against Muslims, these efforts largely failed.

27. Dr. B.R. Ambedkar played a crucial role in the Constituent Assembly as the Chairman of the Drafting Committee. He was responsible for guiding the Draft Constitution through the Assembly, ensuring legal precision and clarity. Despite being a political opponent of the Congress during British rule, he was invited by Mahatma Gandhi to join the Union Cabinet as the Law Minister.

Ambedkar, along with other legal experts, contributed significantly to shaping India's Constitution, incorporating provisions for justice, equality, and Fundamental Rights while addressing the concerns of marginalised communities.

28. The Mahabharata provides valuable insights into the specific features of familial relationships during its time. The epic highlights different aspects of family structures, duties, and conflicts within royal and common households.

- **Patriarchal Family System** The Mahabharata portrays a deeply patriarchal society where lineage was traced through the male line. The Kuru dynasty, for instance, was governed by male rulers such as Shantanu, Bhishma, and later Dhritarashtra and Pandu. Women, though respected, had limited decision-making power in political affairs.
- **Guru-Disciple and Parental Bonds** Education and guidance were crucial in shaping family relationships. The bond between Dronacharya and Arjuna exemplifies the ideal guru-disciple relationship, where Drona, as a teacher, played a significant role in shaping Arjuna's skills and destiny. Similarly, Bhishma, despite being an elder, upheld his vow of celibacy to protect his father's interests, demonstrating duty over personal desires.
- **Polygamy and Polyandry** The Mahabharata reflects the prevalence of both polygamy and polyandry. King Pandu had two wives, Kunti and Madri, while Draupadi was married to five brothers, the Pandavas. This highlights the complex marital customs and the importance of alliances in maintaining political stability.
- **Conflicts in Familial Duties** The rivalry between the Pandavas and Kauravas stemmed from disputes over inheritance and power. Despite being cousins, Duryodhana's jealousy and ambition led to the infamous dice game, exile of the Pandavas, and ultimately the Kurukshetra war. This shows how familial bonds could be strained due to ambition and political motives.
- **Role of Women in Family Decisions** Although men dominated politics, women had significant influence in familial matters. Kunti's guidance shaped the lives of the Pandavas, while Gandhari's curse played a crucial role in determining the fate of the Kauravas.

Or

The statement that political power or kingship was rarely dependent on birth as Kshatriyas but was also open to anyone who could muster support and resources is evident from various ruling lineages from the sixth century BCE onwards. While the Shastras stated that only Kshatriyas could be kings, historical evidence suggests that rulers emerged from different social backgrounds, often challenging this traditional notion.

One of the most debated examples is the Maurya dynasty. While later Buddhist texts suggested that the Mauryas were Kshatriyas, Brahmanical texts described them as being of "low" origin. Despite this, the Mauryas established a vast empire, proving that political power was not strictly limited to Kshatriyas.

The Shungas and Kanvas, who succeeded the Mauryas, were Brahmanas, further demonstrating that kingship was not exclusive to the Kshatriya varna. These rulers gained power based on their resources and political influence rather than hereditary claims.

Another significant example is the Shakas, who came from Central Asia and were considered mlechchhas (barbarians or outsiders) by the Brahmanas. However, their rulers, such as Rudradaman (2nd century CE), played an essential role in governance. An inscription in Sanskrit praises Rudradaman for rebuilding the Sudarshana lake, showing that even non-Kshatriya rulers contributed to public welfare and were familiar with Sanskritic traditions.

Similarly, the Satavahana dynasty presents a complex case. The most well-known ruler, Gotami-puta Siri-Satakani, claimed to be both a unique Brahmana (eka bamhana) and a destroyer of the pride of Kshatriyas. This contradiction highlights that rulers could assert their authority based on their strength and achievements rather than their birth. Additionally, while the Satavahanas claimed to uphold the varna order, they also entered into marriage alliances with non-Kshatriyas, further proving that kingship was not strictly hereditary.

29. Guru Nanak Dev's beliefs and teachings form the core of Sikhism, emphasising nirguna bhakti-devotion to a formless and genderless Divine. He rejected external rituals and promoted a simple, direct connection with God through remembrance and devotion.

Beliefs of Guru Nanak Dev

- **Devotion to a Formless Divine** Guru Nanak emphasised nirguna bhakti, which means devotion to a formless, omnipresent God. He opposed idol worship, ritual sacrifices, and austerities, considering them unnecessary for spiritual enlightenment.
- **Rejection of Rituals and Religious Formalities** He criticised ritual baths, scriptural dogma, and priestly dominance, advocating for personal devotion and ethical living over religious formalities.
- **Singing Hymns (Shabad Kirtan) as Worship** Guru Nanak conveyed his teachings through shabads (hymns), which he sang in different ragas, accompanied by his attendant Mardana on the rabab. This method emphasised music and poetry as a means of spiritual connection.
- **Formation of a Devotional Community** He organised his followers into a spiritual community (Sangat), where people gathered to recite, meditate, and worship collectively. This practice promoted unity, social equality and devotion.

Teachings of Guru Nanak Dev

- **Succession and Preservation of Teachings** Guru Nanak established a lineage of successors, appointing Guru Angad to continue his mission. This tradition ensured the preservation of Sikh teachings for nearly 200 years.
- **Compilation of Hymns in the Adi Granth Sahib** The fifth Guru, Guru Arjan, compiled Guru Nanak's hymns along with those of other saints like Kabir, Ravidas, and Baba Farid into the Adi Granth Sahib, laying a strong scriptural foundation for Sikhism.
- **Formation of the Khalsa and Sikh Identity** In the seventeenth century, Guru Gobind Singh included the hymns of Guru Tegh Bahadur in the Sikh scripture, renaming it the Guru Granth Sahib. He also established the Khalsa Panth and introduced five symbols (uncut hair, a dagger, a pair of shorts, a comb, and a steel bangle), strengthening the distinct identity of Sikhs.

Thus, Guru Nanak Dev's teachings emphasised devotion to a formless divine, rejection of rituals, community worship, and spiritual equality, laying the foundation of Sikhism as a distinct religious tradition.

Or

The Chishti Sufi order played a crucial role in shaping the religious and cultural landscape of medieval India. Their teachings emphasized devotion, humility, universal brotherhood, and service to humanity, blending Islamic principles with local traditions.

Core Beliefs of the Chishtis

- **Universal Brotherhood and Religious** Tolerance The Chishtis preached the idea of universal brotherhood, promoting love and respect for people of all faiths. Their teachings aligned with the Mughal rulers' policies of religious tolerance, as seen in the land grants and tax exemptions given to various religious institutions.
- **Simplicity and Renunciation of Wealth** The Chishti saints followed a life of simplicity and detachment from material wealth, emphasising service to humanity over personal gain. This belief echoed broader Islamic teachings such as zakat (charity) and devotion to spiritual knowledge.
- **Integration of Local Cultural Expressions** The Chishtis embraced local music, poetry, and languages to spread their message. Their practice of devotional singing (Sama) and poetry was similar to the ginans, the devotional songs of the Khojahs, which blended Islamic spiritual themes with indigenous traditions.

Teachings of the Chishtis

- **Love and Compassion for All** The Chishtis emphasised compassion, selfless service, and love for humanity, encouraging their followers to serve people regardless of religion or social status.
- **Spiritual Devotion Through Music and Poetry** The order promoted Sama (devotional music gatherings) as a way to experience divine love and attain spiritual closeness. They believed that music had the power to elevate the soul and deepen devotion.
- **Charity and Helping the Needy** Inspired by Islamic principles of charity, the Chishtis encouraged feeding the poor, caring for the sick, and supporting those in need, making service a central aspect of their spiritual path.

30. The period from 1915 to 1931 was a transformative phase in India's national movement, significantly impacting the Indian masses. During this time, the freedom struggle shifted from being an elite-driven movement to a mass-based struggle, deeply influencing various sections of society.

(i) **Rise of Mass Participation**

- Mahatma Gandhi's arrival in 1915 marked a new era in the Indian national movement. His principles of non-violence and Satyagraha mobilised people from all walks of life.
- The Champaran (1917), Kheda (1918), and Ahmedabad (1918) movements demonstrated the power of non-violent resistance and engaged peasants and workers in the struggle.

(ii) Non-Cooperation Movement (1920-1922)

- The masses boycotted foreign goods, schools, and government jobs, demonstrating their willingness to resist colonial rule.
- Participation of students, women, and traders increased significantly. Khilafat agitation united Hindus and Muslims, creating communal harmony for a brief period.
- However, the movement was withdrawn after the Chauri Chaura incident (1922), leading to disappointment among many followers.

(iii) Peasants and Worker's Involvement

- The 1920s saw growing involvement of peasants through movements like the Bardoli Satyagraha (1928), where Sardar Patel led farmers against increased land revenue.
- Workers organised strikes and protests, as seen in Bombay and Madras, reflecting growing class consciousness against British exploitation.

(iv) Civil Disobedience Movement (1930-1931)

- The Dandi March (1930) symbolised mass resistance, as people across India broke the salt laws.
- Women, students, and rural populations actively participated, broadening the movement's reach.
- British repression through arrests and violence further united the masses in their demand for self-rule.

The period between 1915 and 1931 transformed the Indian masses into active participants in the national struggle. Gandhi's leadership, coupled with movements like Non-Cooperation and Civil Disobedience, awakened a sense of nationalism among diverse sections of society. The impact was irreversible, setting the stage for India's eventual independence.

Or

Mahatma Gandhi played a crucial role even after India gained independence on 15th August, 1947. His efforts were focused on ensuring communal harmony, social upliftment, and guiding the newly independent nation towards peace and stability.

(i) Promoting Communal Harmony

- After independence, India witnessed large-scale communal violence, particularly during the partition. Gandhi undertook fasts and peace marches to restore harmony between Hindus and Muslims.
- His presence in riot-affected areas like Noakhali (in present-day Bangladesh) and Delhi helped in calming tensions.
- He opposed the idea of revenge and insisted on non-violence as the only way forward for a united India.

(ii) Opposition to Partition Violence

- Gandhi was deeply saddened by the partition of India and Pakistan. He worked tirelessly to minimise the impact of violence.
- His fasts in Delhi in January, 1948 were aimed at persuading both Hindus and Muslims to coexist peacefully.

(iii) Ensuring Pakistan Received Its Due Share

- A major controversy arose when India withheld ₹ 55 crore, which was owed to Pakistan as part of the partition agreement.
- Gandhi insisted on the release of the funds, believing it was India's moral responsibility. His stance angered radical elements, ultimately leading to his assassination.

(iv) Focus on Village Development and Social Reforms

- Gandhi continued advocating for self-reliant villages, promoting khadi, rural employment, and removal of untouchability.
- He emphasised 'Sarvodaya' (welfare of all), stressing that independence should benefit the poorest sections of society.

(v) His Last Days and Assassination

- Despite the challenges, Gandhi remained committed to his principles of peace and non-violence.
- On 30th January, 1948, he was assassinated by Nathuram Godse, who blamed him for appeasing Muslims and supporting Pakistan.

31. (i) The uniform drainage systems suggest centralised planning, standardised construction methods, and efficient urban governance across Harappan cities.

(ii) The presence of sand heaps indicates regular drain maintenance but also suggests inefficiency in debris disposal after cleaning.

(iii) The Harappan drainage system showcased advanced urban planning, ensuring efficient waste disposal and sanitation. It minimised waterlogging, reduced health hazards, and improved living conditions. The well-structured drains, cesspits, and sumps highlight their engineering skills and focus on hygiene, setting a precedent for future civilisations in urban infrastructure and public health.

32. (i) François Bernier contributed significantly by documenting his travels in Mughal India, comparing it with Europe, and highlighting political, economic, and social differences, which influenced European perceptions of India.

(ii) Bernier described European kingdoms as well-organised, wealthy, and prosperous, whereas he depicted Mughal territories as poorly maintained, with declining cities, depopulated lands, and ineffective governance, leading to economic and social stagnation.

(iii) Bernier viewed the socio-economic status of people under Mughal rule as deteriorating. He believed excessive state control, lack of private land ownership, and poor infrastructure led to widespread poverty, depopulation, and economic decline, making cities uninhabitable and agriculture inefficient.

33. (i) Buchanan described the lower Rajmahal hills as an exceptionally beautiful landscape with winding rice valleys, scattered trees, and rocky hills but lacked visible progress and extensive agricultural development.

(ii) Buchanan believed the area had high potential for improved cultivation due to its fertile land, suitability for expanding plantations of commercial trees, and the possibility of clearing forests for better agricultural use.

(iii) Buchanan proposed utilising the land for economic benefits by promoting commercial plantations like Asan and Palas for silk and lac production, clearing forests for extensive farming, and cultivating Palmyra and Mahua in non-arable areas.

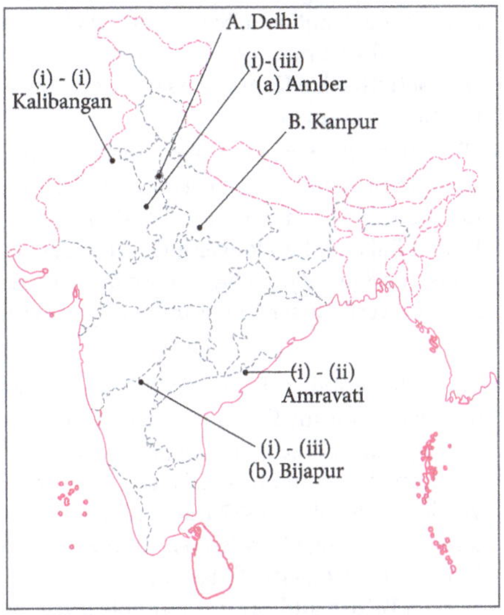

Set-2 (61/1/2)

23. Art historians study hagiographies of the Buddha to understand Buddhist sculptures, including those at Sanchi Stupa. These hagiographies, though not always historically accurate, depict key events like the Buddha's renunciation and enlightenment.

Since early Buddhist art, including Sanchi's carvings, often used symbols (like an empty throne or footprints) instead of direct depictions, familiarity with these texts helps historians interpret the scenes.

The carvings at Sanchi reflect stories from the Buddha's life, and understanding hagiographies allows historians to connect these symbols with Buddhist teachings.

26. Art and literature have played a crucial role in keeping the memories of 1857 alive by portraying the revolt as India's First War of Independence. Nationalist writings depicted leaders like Rani Lakshmi Bai as heroic figures who bravely fought against British rule.

Poems like Subhadra Kumari Chauhan's *Khoob lari mardani* glorified their courage. Paintings and popular prints showed warriors in battle, inspiring future generations.

These artistic and literary works helped sustain the nationalist spirit by preserving stories of sacrifice and resistance against colonial oppression.

27. Mahatma Gandhi believed that Hindustani is a blend of Hindi and Urdu, should be the national language of India. He felt it was a composite language enriched by diverse cultures and widely understood across regions.

Gandhi opposed the Sanskritisation of Hindi and the Persianisation of Urdu, emphasising that Hindustani should freely include words from regional and foreign languages. He saw it as a unifying force between Hindus and Muslims and across different regions.

According to him, restricting the language to Hindi or Urdu alone would harm both intelligence and patriotism.

29. The Alvars and Nayanars were important poet-saints of the bhakti movement in medieval India, particularly in Tamil Nadu. Their beliefs and teachings focused on deep devotion to their chosen deities-Vishnu for the Alvars and Shiva for the Nayanars. These saints played a major role in shaping the religious traditions of South India.

Beliefs of the Alvars and Nayanars

- **Devotion to Vishnu and Shiva** The Alvars worshipped Vishnu and his avatars, such as Rama and Krishna, expressing their love and surrender through Tamil hymns. Their compositions were later compiled into the Nalayira Divyaprabandham, often called the "Tamil Veda". The Nayanars, devoted to Shiva, sang hymns in his praise, which were collected in the Tevaram, forming a key part of Shaiva worship.
- **Rejection of Rituals and Emphasis on Bhakti** Both groups opposed rigid religious rituals and promoted pure devotion (bhakti) as the only path to salvation. They believed in an emotional and personal connection with God rather than relying on priestly intermediaries.
- **Opposition to Caste Discrimination** The Alvars and Nayanars rejected caste-based discrimination and welcomed followers from diverse backgrounds. Saints like Tondaradippodi Alvar and Appar Nayanar openly challenged social hierarchies, emphasising that devotion to God was more important than birth or status.
- **Inclusion of Women in Bhakti** Unlike many religious traditions of their time, the Alvars and Nayanars encouraged women's participation. Andal (Alvar) and Karaikkal Ammaiyar (Nayanar) were among the prominent female saints whose devotional hymns are still revered today.

Teachings of the Alvars and Nayanars

- **Spreading Bhakti Through Hymns** The Alvars and Nayanars composed thousands of Tamil devotional hymns, making religious teachings accessible to common people and popularising bhakti in the local language.
- **Temple Worship and Cultural Impact** Their teachings influenced temple worship, art, and literature, shaping South Indian religious traditions for centuries. Many temples still follow rituals inspired by their devotional practices.

Thus, the Alvars and Nayanars revolutionised spiritual life in medieval South India by breaking social barriers and promoting devotion as a path open to all, regardless of caste or gender.

Or

Islam is a monotheistic religion that teaches the belief in one God, Allah, and considers Prophet Muhammad as last messenger. The teachings of Islam are based on the Qur'an (the holy book) and the hadis (sayings and deeds of the Prophet).

A central aspect of Islamic teachings is the five pillars of Islam, which every follower is expected to follow

(i) **Shahada (Faith)** This is the declaration that "There is no God but Allah, and Muhammad is his messenger". This belief is the foundation of Islam.

(ii) **Salat (Prayer)** Muslims pray five times a day, facing Mecca. These prayers are performed at specific times and are a way to connect with God.

(iii) Zakat (Charity) Islam teaches that helping the poor is important. Every Muslim is required to give a portion of their earnings to help those in need.

(iv) **Sawm (Fasting)** During the month of Ramzan, Muslims fast from sunrise to sunset. This practice teaches self-discipline, patience, and empathy for the less fortunate.

(v) **Hajj (Pilgrimage)** Every Muslim who can afford it must undertake a pilgrimage to Mecca at least once in their lifetime. This journey symbolises unity and devotion to God.

Islam also emphasises justice, kindness, and equality. It teaches that all human beings are equal, regardless of race, wealth, or social status. The concept of ummah (community) is important, as it promotes unity among believers.

While Islam has universal principles, it has also adapted to local traditions. For example, in India, the Khojahs developed ginan (devotional poetry), and Muslim traders in Kerala adopted local customs. This shows that Islamic teachings, while rooted in the Qur'an, also integrate with different cultures.

In summary, Islam teaches faith, worship, charity, and ethical living. It promotes peace and a strong sense of community. Its teachings influenced not only rulers but also common people, shaping societies across regions.

30. The Salt Satyagraha, led by Mahatma Gandhi, marked a turning point in India's freedom struggle. After the suspension of the Non-Cooperation Movement, Gandhiji focused on social reform. However, by 1928, political events such as the opposition to the Simon Commission and the Bardoli Satyagraha reignited his participation in the nationalist movement.

The Congress session in Lahore (December 1929) declared Purna Swaraj (complete independence), leading to the observance of Independence Day on 26th January 1930. This set the stage for Gandhiji's strategic decision to challenge British rule through civil disobedience. He chose the salt tax as his target because salt was essential to every Indian household, and the colonial government's monopoly on it symbolised economic oppression.

On 12th March 1930, Gandhiji, along with his followers, embarked on the historic Dandi March, covering 240 miles to the Arabian Sea. Upon reaching Dandi on 6th April, 1930, he broke the salt law by making salt, inspiring mass protests across the country.

Parallel movements emerged, including breaches of forest laws by peasants, strikes by workers, and boycotts of British institutions by students and lawyers. The government responded with mass arrests, detaining around 60,000 Indians, including Gandhiji himself.

The significance of the Salt March extended beyond India. It gained international attention, with Time magazine initially mocking Gandhiji but later acknowledging his impact as a 'Saint' and 'Statesman'. It also marked a crucial moment for women's participation in the freedom struggle, with activists like Kamaladevi Chattopadhyay encouraging female involvement.

Ultimately, the British were compelled to recognise the strength of Indian resistance. This realization led to the Round Table Conferences in London, highlighting that the British Raj could no longer ignore the demand for self-rule. Thus, the Salt Satyagraha was not just a protest against a tax but a powerful assertion of India's right to independence.

Or

The statement that the British Raj was shaken to its foundation for the first time since the Revolt of 1857 as a consequence of the Non-Cooperation Movement reflects the deep impact of mass resistance against colonial rule. While the Revolt of 1857 was a military uprising that directly challenged British power, the Non-Cooperation Movement (1920-1922) used non-violent methods to weaken British authority at multiple levels, making it one of the most significant turning points in India's struggle for independence.

One of the most remarkable aspects of this movement was its scale and participation. Led by Mahatma Gandhi, it saw widespread boycotts of foreign goods, British schools, government offices, and courts. This directly disrupted the British administrative and economic machinery, making governance increasingly difficult. The movement also mobilised people from all sections of society, including peasants, students, women, and industrial workers, creating unprecedented national unity in the fight against colonial rule.

The movement's impact can be compared to the Revolt of 1857. While the 1857 uprising was largely confined to Northern India and involved sepoys and certain ruling elites, the Non-Cooperation Movement was a mass movement that engaged people across the country. The British had suppressed the 1857 revolt with military force, but in the case of the Non-Cooperation Movement, they had to rely on arrests, censorship, and strict laws to counter civilian resistance, which proved to be an even greater challenge.

A major example of how the movement shook British rule was the widespread resignation of Indian officials from government jobs and the massive decline in the use of British goods. The British faced significant difficulties in running their administration due to the withdrawal of Indian cooperation. Additionally, the unity between Hindus and Muslims in the movement (before the Khilafat issue caused divisions) posed a serious challenge to the British policy of divide and rule.

Although the movement was called off after the Chauri Chaura incident in 1922, its impact was long-lasting. It inspired future movements like the Civil Disobedience Movement (1930) and the Quit India Movement (1942), showing that non-violent resistance could be an effective tool against colonial rule. The British had not faced such a widespread and organised challenge to their authority since 1857, proving that the Non-Cooperation Movement truly shook the foundations of British rule.

Set-3 (61/1/3)

23. Shahjehan Begum played a crucial role in protecting the Sanchi Stupa. She provided funds for its preservation, ensuring the site remained intact.

When European powers wanted to take the Eastern gateway, she helped prevent its removal. She and her successor, Sultan Jehan Begum, supported archaeological efforts, including funding a museum and guesthouse for John Marshall.

Her contributions enabled the site's restoration and survival, protecting it from railway contractors and builders. Her efforts ensured that Sanchi remains a key monument reflecting early Buddhism's rich history.

26. The British government took several repressive measures to control the 1857 rebellion, some of them were

- **Martial Law** Military officers and civilians were given the authority to punish suspected rebels, often sentencing them to death.
- **Recapture of Delhi** The British launched intense battles to regain control of Delhi, the symbolic center of the revolt.
- **Brutal Suppression in Awadh** Entire villages were destroyed, and rebels were executed to crush resistance.
- **Punitive Actions** Rebels were publicly executed, including hangings and being blown from cannons, to instill fear.
- **Divide and Rule Policy** Loyal landowners were rewarded, while rebel supporters were dispossessed to weaken further uprisings.

27. G.B. Pant's role in promoting a united approach in India were

- **Opposition to Separate Electorates** Pant argued that separate electorates would permanently isolate minorities and weaken national unity.
- **Integration of All Communities** He emphasised that every citizen should be part of one unified nation rather than being divided by religious or community-based politics.
- **Strengthening Democracy** He believed democracy could only succeed when people prioritised national interest over communal differences.
- **Loyalty to the State** Pant stressed that all citizens should have undivided loyalty to the nation, ensuring collective progress and harmony.

29. Meera Bai is a prominent Bhakti poet-saint of the 15th-16th centuries, expressed deep devotion to Lord Krishna through her songs and life choices. Her views on devotionalism were centered on total surrender to God, love beyond social norms, and the rejection of material attachments. Unlike traditional religious practices that emphasised rituals and caste-based divisions, Meera's devotion was personal, emotional, and direct.

One of the key aspects of Meera Bai's devotionalism was her unwavering love for Krishna, whom she considered her eternal companion. She rejected the traditional roles expected of her as a Rajput princess and wife, choosing instead to dedicate her life to singing bhajans (devotional songs) and seeking union with God. This reflects the Bhakti movement's emphasis on devotion as a path to liberation, rather than social status or rituals.

Meera's songs, which have been orally transmitted for centuries, express intense emotions of longing, surrender, and divine love. For example, in one of her bhajans, she speaks of preparing her own funeral pyre, showing her willingness to give up everything for Krishna.

Her devotion was so strong that she considered worldly rulers, such as the Rana of Mewar, insignificant compared to God. She sings, "If God is angry, all is lost, but what can the Rana do?" This highlights her belief that only God's will matters, not human power.

Another significant aspect of her devotionalism was her defiance of social norms. She is believed to have been associated with Raidas, a saint from a lower caste, showing her disregard for caste-based hierarchies. She also wore simple robes like a widow or renouncer, emphasising detachment from material wealth. This reflected the Bhakti tradition's inclusive nature, where devotion was open to all, regardless of birth or status.

Meera Bai's legacy continues to inspire people, especially those marginalised in society. Her songs are still sung in Gujarat and Rajasthan, resonating with both men and women. Her devotionalism, based on love, surrender, and defiance of societal constraints, remains a powerful example of Bhakti spirituality.

Or

The Virashaiva tradition, also known as Lingayatism, emerged in twelfth-century Karnataka under the leadership of Basavanna, a minister in the Kalachuri kingdom. This movement played a significant role in shaping social and religious beliefs, focusing on devotion to Shiva and challenging traditional caste-based discrimination.

Beliefs of the Virashaivas

- **Worship of Shiva in the Form of a Linga** The followers of this tradition, called Lingayats, worshipped Shiva as a linga. They wore a small linga in a silver case around their neck or on a loop over the left shoulder, signifying their personal connection with the deity.
- **Rejection of Caste Discrimination** Virashaivas challenged the caste system and opposed the concept of pollution associated with certain groups. This attracted many people from marginalised communities who were previously excluded from the Brahmanical social order.
- **Denial of Rebirth and Karma-Based Hierarchy** Unlike traditional Hindu beliefs, Virashaivas did not accept the concept of rebirth. They believed that after death, a devotee would directly merge with Shiva and would not return to this world.
- **Unique Funeral Practices** As they rejected the idea of rebirth, they also opposed cremation, which was considered

essential in the Dharmashastras. Instead, they followed burial rituals, signifying their distinct approach to death and afterlife.

- **Social Reforms and Gender Equality** The Lingayats introduced progressive social practices, including:
  - Post-puberty marriage, which was not accepted in traditional Hindu customs.
  - Widow remarriage, which was strongly discouraged in Brahmanical traditions.

Teachings of the Virashaivas

- **Devotion Through Vachanas** The Virashaivas expressed their devotion through simple yet powerful sayings called Vachanas. These were written in Kannada and composed by both men and women who joined the movement.
- **Simple and Direct Connection with God** They rejected elaborate rituals and priestly control over religion, emphasising a direct relationship with Shiva through personal devotion.
- **Opposition to Brahmanical Practices** They opposed idol worship and the dominance of Brahmin priests, advocating for a more inclusive religious approach.

30. The Civil Disobedience Movement was a significant phase in India's struggle for independence, and Mahatma Gandhi played a central role in leading it. His leadership, strategy, and commitment to non-violent resistance made the movement a powerful force against British rule.

(i) **Initiation of the Movement** Gandhiji launched the Civil Disobedience Movement in 1930 with the Dandi March. He walked 240 miles from Sabarmati to Dandi with his followers to break the salt law. This symbolic act of making salt from seawater challenged British authority and inspired millions to join the movement.

(ii) **Principles of Non-violent Resistance** Gandhiji emphasised non-violence (Ahimsa) and non-cooperation, encouraging people to break unjust British laws peacefully. He urged Indians to

- Boycott foreign goods
- Refuse to pay taxes (especially salt tax)
- Picket liquor shops and government offices
- Resign from government jobs

These actions aimed to weaken British economic and administrative control over India.

(iii) **Mass Participation Under** Gandhiji's leadership, people from all sections of society participated in the movement. Farmers, women, students, and factory workers actively took part. The movement also witnessed participation from business leaders, who refused to pay taxes and promoted indigenous products.

(iv) **Negotiations with the British** The movement gained international attention, forcing the British government to respond. Gandhiji was invited for discussions, leading to the Gandhi-Irwin Pact (1931). As part of this agreement, the British released political prisoners, and Gandhiji agreed to suspend the movement and attend the Second Round Table Conference. However, when British authorities did not accept India's demand for self-rule, the movement resumed in 1932.

(v) **Impact of the Movement** Though the movement was eventually suppressed, it

- shook British confidence in their control over India.
- strengthened national unity and the demand for independence.
- encouraged future mass movements, leading to the Quit India Movement in 1942.

Or

Mahatma Gandhi played a central role in the Non-Cooperation Movement, which was launched in 1920 as a major step in India's struggle for independence. His leadership transformed the movement into a nationwide mass protest against British rule.

- **Leadership and Ideology** Gandhiji introduced the idea of non-violent resistance (Satyagraha) as the foundation of the movement. He believed that the British were able to rule India because Indians cooperated with them. If Indians refused to cooperate, the British government would collapse.
- **Boycott of British Institutions** Under his guidance, people were encouraged to boycott British goods, services, and institutions such as
  - Government schools and colleges
  - Law courts
  - Legislative councils
  - Foreign clothes and textiles
  - Titles and honorary positions given by the British

  This led to a rise in Swadeshi (indigenous) goods and the promotion of khadi (hand-spun cloth).
- **Mobilising the Masses** Gandhiji traveled across India to spread awareness and involve people from all walks of life, including peasants, workers, students, and women. He made the movement inclusive and non-violent, which attracted millions of followers.
- **Constructive Programs** Apart from protests, Gandhiji promoted constructive activities like
  - Spinning khadi to reduce dependence on British textiles
  - Hindu-Muslim unity
  - Removal of untouchability
  - Promotion of education based on Indian values

These efforts strengthened India's self-reliance.

- **Suspension of the Movement** In 1922, the movement faced a setback when violent clashes occurred at Chauri Chaura in Uttar Pradesh, where a mob set fire to a police station, killing 22 policemen. Gandhiji, being a firm believer in non-violence, immediately called off the movement.